CONGRESS'S OWN

C&C

CAMPAIGNS & COMMANDERS

GREGORY J. W. URWIN, SERIES EDITOR

CONGRESS'S OWN

A Canadian Regiment, the Continental Army, and American Union

HOLLY A. MAYER

UNIVERSITY OF OKLAHOMA PRESS : NORMAN

This book is published with the generous assistance of the McCasland Foundation, Duncan, Oklahoma.

Portions of chapter 1 appeared in an earlier form in "Canada, Congress, and the Continental Army: Strategic Accommodations, 1774–1776," *Journal of Military History* (April 2014).

Library of Congress Cataloging-in-Publication Data

Names: Mayer, Holly A. (Holly Ann), 1956– author.
Title: Congress's Own : a Canadian regiment, the Continental Army, and American union / Holly A. Mayer.
Other titles: Canadian regiment, the Continental Army, and American union
Description: Norman : University of Oklahoma Press, [2021] | Series: Campaigns and commanders | Includes bibliographical references and index. | Summary: "Examines Colonel Moses Hazen's 2nd Canadian Regiment and its contribution to securing American independence"—Provided by publisher.
Identifiers: LCCN 2020040706 | ISBN 978-0-8061-6851-7 (hardcover)
Subjects: LCSH: Hazen, Moses, 1733–1803. | United States. Continental Army. Canadian Regiment, 2nd. | Generals—United States—Biography. | United States—History— Revolution, 1775–1783—Participation, Canadian. | United States—History—Revolution, 1775–1783—Regimental histories.
Classification: LCC E269.C27 M87 2021 | DDC 355.0092 [B]—dc23
LC record available at https://lccn.loc.gov/2020040706

Congress's Own: A Canadian Regiment, the Continental Army, and American Union is Volume 73 in the Campaigns and Commanders series.

The paper in this book meets the guidelines for permanence and durability of the Committee on Production Guidelines for Book Longevity of the Council on Library Resources, Inc. ∞

To my mother, Ruth Mayer, and brother, Jon Mayer

Huzzah!

CONTENTS

Maps

PREFACE

Sergeant Major John H. Hawkins introduced me to Congress's Own Regiment ages ago. In search of soldiers' stories that might reveal a developing consciousness of American identity, I had opened his journal at the Historical Society of Pennsylvania. The brown leather volume held some of the original small memorandum books in which Hawkins had recorded personal and regimental notes. Bound long ago with sections out of order and gaps indicating where Hawkins or time lost his daybooks, the journal revealed an alert observer who wielded a pointed pen and an active regiment that bore arms and axes from Canada to Virginia and back again.

As I transcribed the journal, I compiled questions about the regiment. My search for answers resulted in this study, which looks not only at the regiment's formation and operations but also how it reflected and advanced the enterprise of the Continental Army and construction of the American union that became a nation. Shifting between an examination of the greater organizational relations between Congress, army, and regiment and the collective and personal relationships within it revealed the lived—human—experience of the war along with the institutional conduct of it. Congress's Own Regiment fielded a cast of thousands, and this work introduces some of its members as it illuminates wartime challenges by telling their stories. In sum, this regimental history is a social, institutional, and civil-military analysis of how the members of Congress's Own realized the American Revolution in combat and community.

In a play familiar to many colonists, Juliet, a Capulet, asks Romeo, a Montague, "What's in a Name?" How important is the name to the being? Is it simply a descriptive label, a means of identification? That is the subject of many other studies, but the question applies to my choices and those of the Revolution's participants who touted America's "united states." In 1776, Thomas Paine described the struggle between England and America as the affair "of a Continent" and the "seed-time of Continental union." He continued, with a social, cultural, and political mash-up, by declaring the benefits of identifying as Americans rather than as British subjects. As those supporting the Revolution struggled with who and what they were writ large, political and military officials confronted the task of determining the names of individuals. The adjutant of Congress's Own, Benjamin Mooers, later accounted for problems matching the names of pension applicants with those on regimental rosters by pointing out that different people filled out different rolls at different times, and that names could thus be "Easily altered."[1]

Creative spelling and evolving definitions present a fine puzzle to anyone delving into and drawing conclusions from historical records. There is also the challenge of establishing a common lexicon so that writer and reader can share identifications and understanding. In this case the challenge began with the name Congress's Own. Its members chose it and so I did too, including the use of the extra *s* with the possessive apostrophe, because that was a common presentation during the war and in pensions.

Situational and contemporary usage affected other word choices. Colonists loyal to the British government could and did call themselves Americans, but the term here refers primarily to those from the colonies of New Hampshire to Georgia who rebelled and founded the United States. As "American" was a developing construct that did not comprehend everyone contending for American independence, I follow the lead of the Continental Congress and the Continental Army: the active contenders were Continentals. The term recognizes a liminal, borderland service and state. I also use "rebels" when discussing the commencement of the war in 1775, interchange it with "revolutionaries" through early 1776, and settle on the latter after the Declaration of Independence. As Canadians numbered among the rebels, revolutionaries, and Continentals, I use *"Canadien"* interchangeably with "French Canadian" to refer to the francophone subjects of French descent within Canada, in particular Quebec, while Canadian encompasses both anglophone as well as francophone inhabitants.

Different languages, illiteracy, and penmanship made determining the "correct" spelling of some names quite difficult. If I found examples of the person's signature, I used that version: as in Tarlton Woodson (no *e*) and John Carlile (no *s*). If there were other family or regimental materials presenting a common spelling, I took that lead; William Stuart (not Stewart) is one example. Some recorders anglicized Laurent Olivie to Lawrence Olivier (or Oliver) and François Guilmat to Francis Gilmant (or versions thereof), but both men signed the Society of the Cincinnati institution in May 1783 with the French versions. Otherwise, Francis B. Heitman's *Historical Register* was often my first recourse or fallback resource for officers' names.

In soldiers' cases, if there was an official pension or bounty-land warrant record, then I often used that spelling. Unfortunately, such records also often recorded multiple spellings. Next was Mooers's regimental roster, but as not all names were on it or fully legible, the next step was Hawkins's 1782 list, and then other companies' or veterans' rolls. The French names were particularly challenging because of the various forms of anglicization in different rolls. There is also the problem of the particles *le, la, du,* and the like. Most of the lists run the articles into the family name, and that is what I follow unless the records strongly indicate otherwise. Also, the old *M'* is changed to the modern *Mc* with no differentiation between *Mac* and *Mc.*

When challenged by names spelled every which way with no pattern, it was just a matter of choosing one that seemed clearest. In terms of place-names, except where quoted in the text or particularly descriptive, I usually defaulted to the most common or current spelling, especially in the endnotes (as in Middlebrook rather than Middle Brook).

As with spelling, records sometimes differ over dates, whether about births, deaths, enlistments, commissions, desertions, promotions, or the like. Some enlistment and ending dates were on Mooers's master roster; others I determined from pension applications. Some enlistment years should be considered approximate within a few months, given that some men enlisted at the end of a year or beginning of the next and were not precise. For example, in 1820, the sixty-four-year-old Eben (or Ebenezer) Griswold of Connecticut could not remember if he enlisted in December 1776 or January 1777, but Mooers had noted December.[2] Birth and death years (except those noting war fatalities) were usually taken from pension accounts, with the latter sometimes provided by widows or other heirs. All too few veterans provided birthdays, so I calculated birth years based on veterans' ages in depositions. As there were sometimes discrepancies in ages in different depositions, and given that some depositions were recorded early in a year and others later, birth years are approximations (plus or minus a year or even two).

This book, like its author, has benefited greatly from the interest, labor, patience, and best wishes of numerous people. The University of Oklahoma Press and its splendid editors and associated personnel deserve much applause. Thanks go to Adam Kane, who invited the book proposal and ushered it through the initial vetting process, and to Erin Greb, who was so tolerant with my "oh, wait" additions as she produced masterly maps. Kent Calder and Steven Baker, who shepherded the book through the publishing process, and Stephanie Sykes, who exemplified expertise and consideration in copyediting, were all super. I cannot thank enough, although here I try, the readers who championed publication and offered excellent suggestions—Ricardo Herrera, Mark Lender, and series editor Gregory Urwin.

Yet the book is but the culmination of a long research and drafting process. Many individuals and institutions contributed time, expertise, access, and assistance over the years and miles that I followed Congress's Own Regiment. The journey, which was anything but an expeditious march, took considerably longer than the War for Independence. Like the campaigning diarist Sergeant Major Hawkins, however, I saw and discussed much with many folks along the way, which created an ever-greater appreciation of the myriad communities that are connected by their deep interest in history, in particular that of the American Revolution.

During my journey, Duquesne University and the McAnulty College and Graduate School of Liberal Arts provided a Wimmer Family Foundation Faculty Development Award, a National Endowment for the Humanities Fund Grant, and sabbatical time. I much appreciated that aid, as I did the services of Duquesne's Gumberg Library. I especially applaud the good folks with whom I had the privilege of working, including the students who made teaching a pleasure and the graduate assistants—John Badertscher, Alyson Clover, Tara Ellison, Kerry Jo Green, Meghan Hall, Sarina Johnston, Andrew Spate, and Melissa Johnson Yurochko—who at one time or another checked sources or wended their way through lists of soldiers. I offer fervent thanks to my colleagues in the Department of History (with an extra *merci* to Jotham Parsons for translation help) who supported my various endeavors and continue the essential mission of history and the liberal arts in higher education and the public realm.

I am deeply grateful to the institutions that awarded fellowships; they so enriched my scholarship. Such tribute definitely goes to the David Library of the American Revolution at Washington Crossing, Pennsylvania. Meg McSweeney, Katherine (Kathi) Ludwig, and their associates in and out of the library welcomed me with open arms and resources on many return visits. Among other things, thanks for the memories.

I offer profound thanks to the Library Company of Philadelphia and Historical Society of Pennsylvania for an Andrew W. Mellon Foundation Fellowship. Over the years, during the fellowship and other visits before and after, I benefited from the help of Max Moeller, Sarah Heim, and David Haugaard at the Historical Society, and Connie King and Phil Lapsansky at the Library Company. A Gilder Lehrman Short-Term Residential Fellowship at the John D. Rockefeller, Jr. Library with the Colonial Williamsburg Foundation was greatly rewarding. Marianne Martin, Doug May, Juleigh Clark, and Inge Flester were generous with their attention. So too were Douglas Bradburn, Michael Kane, and Mark Santangelo at the Fred W. Smith National Library for the Study of

George Washington at Mount Vernon. At the Robert H. Smith International Center for Jefferson Studies at Monticello, Andrew O'Shaughnessy, Whitney Pippin, Anna Berkes, and Jack Robertson offered gracious and fruitful support. The Society of the Cincinnati also offered beneficent aid—thank you to Ellen McCallister Clark, Rachel Jirka, Valerie Sallis, and Alexis Jorczyk.

Those scholarships and people contributed mightily to the research and writing, as did the United States Army War College's award of the Harold Keith Johnson Chair of Military History, a visiting position. It was an honor to join the College's Department of National Security and Strategy for 2016–17 and a marvelous adventure to explore the past and present with Seminar Group 13. That sojourn provided valuable perspectives on strategic challenges as well as time to enjoy the resources of the dynamic U.S. Army Heritage and Education Center.

I am also deeply grateful to many other superb institutions for maintaining documents and providing access and assistance. In these places, like those mentioned above, people were wonderfully hospitable as they shared their knowledge and skills. If you are lost, and even if you're not, ask for directions, for archivists and librarians are treasures. The additional institutions and individuals that merit appreciation include the American Philosophical Society; the Bibliothèque et Archives/Library and Archives Canada, in particular Martin Lanthier; the Library of Congress, with bows to Bruce Kirby, Jeff Flannery, and Patrick Kerwin; the Maryland State Archives, New Jersey State Archives, and New York State Archives; and the University of Vermont's Special Collections at the Howe Library, specifically curator of manuscripts Chris Burns. Special accolades go to Debra Kimok and Michael Burgess with Special Collections at the State University of New York at Plattsburgh's Feinberg Library.

Commendations go to those working on the Papers of George Washington, especially the Revolutionary War Series, at the University of Virginia Press. Not only did I dive deeply and often into the published volumes and search for documents in coming editions via Founders Online (another terrific resource), but I also visited the offices and corresponded with some of the editors. Ed Lengel, Bill Ferraro, and Ben Huggins were most gracious with answers and suggestions. Great hospitality also marked my conversations with T. G. Henderson at Putnam Memorial State Park in Connecticut and with Robert W. Cheeseman, the Chazy, New York, town historian.

As a big chunk of chapter 1 is pulled from my article, "Canada, Congress, and the Continental Army: Strategic Accommodations, 1774–1776," in the April 2014 issue of the *Journal of Military History*, I happily acknowledge the support and expertise of its late editor, Bruce Vandervort. Since the publication of that article, I have found more members of the regiment to note, just as I have more people and places to recognize here.

Besides at forums and seminars conducted by the wonderful fellowship-granting hosts noted above, I was able to present my work on Congress's Own before other audiences who graciously listened and provided valuable responses. I thank the following organizations for providing opportunities to hear from such participants: the European Early American Studies Association; the McNeil Center for Early American Studies; the Omohundro Institute of Early American History and Culture; the Organization of American Historians; the Society for Historians of the Early American Republic; the Society for Military History; Fort Ticonderoga; America's History, LLC, Williamsburg conference; the Virginia Military Institute; and Mount Vernon's George Washington Teacher Institutes.

Much appreciation deservedly goes to the friends and colleagues who have listened and read all too much about Congress's Own over the years and have provided valuable comments on varied portions of the manuscript. The good parts owe much to their input, and as to the other parts—well, I didn't always follow their good advice. Mark Anderson, Rick Herrera, Turk McCleskey, J. J. Paterson, and James Scudieri all wrote insightful feedback. (And thank you, Jim and J. J., for that lively Brandywine battle tour.)

Heartfelt kudos go to Judy Van Buskirk, Gail Terry, Janet Coryell, and Jim Smither, who not only reviewed and provided essential input on multiple chapters but have also been valiant and steadfast during the years, zipping much wit and wisdom over wine and wire (well, primarily wireless now). I raise a cup to Jean Hunter, Madeline Archer, and Carmen Stonge, who listened to numerous updates over coffee and pancakes, and look forward to more walks and talks with Christine Devine. I remember with gratitude Caroline Cox, who was a terrific advisor as I began the work; sadly, she is not here to see the conclusion, nor is my father, Jack, who always asked about the sergeant major. To and for friends and family, especially my mother, Ruth, and brother, Jon, I give thanks.

Congress's Own

Placing Congress's Own, 1776–1783. Map by Erin Greb Cartography

INTRODUCTION

Continentals and Borderlands

The soldiers forming Colonel Moses Hazen's regiment fell in at Montreal in February 1776, retreated from Chambly to Albany as the 2nd Canadian Regiment that June, and embraced the nickname Congress's Own by early 1777. The moniker stuck in veterans' minds decades later even though their unit carried the label "Canadian Old Regiment" or just "the Canadian Regiment" when it officially disbanded at West Point in November 1783. The COR insignia on the light infantry caps, whether that designated Congress's Own or later the Canadian Old Regiment, signified troops that included refugees, immigrants, deserters, and citizens of eleven states. In over seven years of service, Hazen's controversial regiment distinguished itself in combat and camp, and by its contributions to Continental dreams, dramas, and diversity in the war of the American Revolution. The Continentals—soldiers, officers, and associates—of Congress's Own battled for national and personal independence in a regimental community that exemplified the military borderland that was the Continental Army and the imagined community of the nation declared to be the United States of America.

Congress's Own Regiment was the Continental Army in microcosm, but with a more contentious commander. By the declaration of the Continental Congress, it was an armed force of peoples from different colonies, countries, classes, ethnicities, and religions united against the authority of Great Britain. Unity within the regiment, as in the army, however, was a challenge for the Continentals as they contested who had what authority among them. Such strife reflected the disputes of colonies becoming states and conflicts among states trying to fashion a union that might forge a nation. Continentals in and out of the army debated the institutions and ideals that were to connect, secure, empower, and identify them even as they pursued interests that sometimes divided them. The debates raged within the Revolution's military, political, and temporal—physical and metaphysical—borderlands where subjects became rebels, soldiers, and citizens. Continental was a borderland identity, but in being a Continental, many took steps toward becoming nationally American.

The regiment and army, like the union, were works in progress throughout the war, and their combined story one of processes: how Continentals in the Congress and the army interacted from 1775 through 1783 and into the postwar era. A look at the processes reveals what they did by design to reflect the ideals of the Revolution and what was ad hoc to serve immediate independence. How they were created and operated reflected the past, in terms of organizational precedents; their present, as they adjusted through necessity; and the future, in the debates and innovations that reflected their political philosophies and plans.

Service and Symbolism

The Continental Congress created the Continental Army on 14 June 1775 as a force to defend American liberties. It adopted troops already in service in Massachusetts and authorized the formation of more. General George Washington, after accepting the Congress's nomination as commander in chief, immediately shouldered the tasks of incorporating the adopted troops into the army of 1775 and creating new, ideally continental regiments for the army of 1776. By that spring, before there were states united, the Continental Army encompassed the Main Army and other units assigned, respectively, to the Canadian, Northern, Eastern, Middle, and Southern Departments, with the Highlands and Western Departments added later. As it strove to fortify the rebellion, army, and Canadian Department, Congress authorized Hazen's regiment on 20 January 1776. With that birthday and its official disbandment in the final discharge of November 1783, the regiment was one of the longest-serving units in the Continental Army.[1]

Length of service alone does not distinguish the regiment, for others served as long or longer. Hazen's regiment, however, offers an example of a developing, contested political identity that intermixed Continental and American senses of self or character.[2] It illustrates the limits of one of Washington's ideals, shared by some others, about a *continental* American army in which distinctions and dissensions between colonies were to "be laid aside; so that one and the same Spirit may animate the whole."[3] "Continental" was to embody a commonality, community, and union for the causes of liberty and independence. That ideal appeared in regimental titles. The Main Army of 1776 had twenty-seven infantry "Continental" regiments on its establishment.[4] Yet, although titled Continental, most of the infantry regiments remained affiliated with a province, which was confirmed when those that continued with the army beyond the 1776 establishment reverted in 1777 to state designations reflecting their personnel and supply bases.

The 2nd Canadian Regiment was similarly authorized when Congress was hoping that the Canadian provinces would join the thirteen rebelling colonies to make resistance to British imperial policies even more continental. The retreat of American forces from Canada in June, however, left the regiment without a home. Although not titled Continental like the infantry regiments in Washington's 1776 Main Army, the 2nd Canadian became de facto Continental with the congressional authorization in October of that year to recruit "in any of the thirteen United States." That November, Congress also gave James Livingston, colonel of the 1st Canadian Regiment, permission to recruit in "any of the United States."[5] Livingston, however, concentrated on New York to fill the 1st Canadian's ranks, whereas Hazen had his officers competing for recruits there as well as scouting farther south and east. The result was a regiment that was indeed continental, with soldiers hailing from Canada to Carolina who belonged to "Congress's Own."

The 2nd Canadian Regiment was unusual, although not unique, in its parentage and its multicultural and multistate makeup. The 1st Canadian Regiment pulled from the same initial pool of inhabitants in Quebec province, but Livingston was in advance of Hazen both in supporting the rebellion and in recruiting others to join him. Indeed, soldiers of the 1st Canadian, like those of the 2nd, may also have occasionally referred to their unit as one of Congress's regiments.[6] Furthermore, a few other Continental regiments—namely, artillery and dragoon units—also heavily enlisted troops from multiple states. Congress's Own may therefore be representative of such units within the Continental line, but the similarities are limited. Its nickname, continuous service, and cultural diversity of troops made it uncommon, especially after 1 January 1781, when, in accordance with congressional orders, Livingston's regiment disbanded and "all non-commissioned officers and privates, being foreigners belonging to any of the reduced regiments and corps," were to be incorporated within Hazen's command, "and all volunteers from foreign states, who are now in the service, or may hereafter join the American army, be annexed to the said regiment."[7]

Such a composition, and status as a confederated rather than a state regiment, created challenges to both civil management and military command. The honorific of Congress's Own did not translate into more money or matériel. It did, however, lead to too much attention in 1777 when the Continental Congress growled about it assuming too great a distinction, and again in 1778 when Congress ordered force reorganization and officer reductions.[8] As it could not be a state regiment given that Canada declined the invitation to join the other colonies in revolt, Hazen had to hound Congress and the states from which he had enlisted soldiers to support the regiment. They, in turn, sometimes questioned the need for the regiment. It, however, survived the reservations as it did battles and hardships, scarred but proud. The commander in chief may have found its colonel troublesome at times, but Washington also found this Continental unit to be useful in various missions.

One mission, though undeclared and generally unrecognized, was symbolic: Congress's Own Regiment represented one of the first nominally "national" units in the American army. It symbolized in actions and composition the revolutionaries' continental aspirations. As long as it operated, it represented an invitation to and threatened invasion of Canada for incorporation into the United States. In both segregating and integrating companies and men from different regions, states, and cultures, it demonstrated pragmatism and flexibility. On the other hand, in the problems it raised or encountered, it also revealed the complications—including factionalism—of managing a multistate (much less national) force.

The 2nd Canadian Regiment, which was commonly called Hazen's regiment by the Continental Congress and others, operated within the Canadian, Northern, Highlands, Middle, and, briefly, the Eastern and Southern Departments during the war. When not specifically attached to a department, it was assigned to the Main Army. Its troops served in Canada, New York, New England, New Jersey, Pennsylvania, Delaware, and Virginia. Some of the men who joined the regiment had earlier fought in the Battle of Quebec, and a few skirmished at Saint-Pierre on 25 March 1776, but after the retreat from Canada and reformation, the regiment as a whole started to earn its reputation at Staten Island in August 1777, followed by actions at Brandywine and Germantown that September and October. It participated in the siege at Yorktown in 1781, and before and after that engaged in such duties as forging roads and guarding prisoners.

Command and Community

This history of the regiment is a story of its members, numbering near 1,900 officers and soldiers (including those who quickly deserted), and hundreds more women and children, by war's end.[9] They were not all with the regiment at the same time or for the same amount of time. Many are named herein, for naming is to remember people just as effacing is a way to forget or dismiss them. One "member," whether it wanted to be or not, was Congress, for by calling the regiment Congress's Own, its personnel claimed that body as their honorary "colonel." Colonel Hazen and Lieutenant Colonel Edward Antill certainly figure prominently as they commanded the unit and communicated with the Continental Congress and General Washington. Some of the company commanders, staff officers, and noncommissioned officers, especially Sergeant

Major John H. Hawkins, figure at times when their acts or records illuminate social and military connections or conflicts as well as the ways orders translated into actions.[10] The privates, corporals, and sergeants are also as essential to the story as they were to bearing arms, blazing roads, and digging necessaries. The story thus moves between congressmen, commanders, soldiers, and followers: from the halls of power to the tents and trenches.

This community study incorporates civil-military and social-cultural relations. It examines not only how the regiment's members battled enemy troops, but also how they fought and accommodated each other as they labored through the Revolution's long war. Was Hazen's regiment as socially or culturally revolutionary in practice as it may first appear by its composition? The invasion of Canada and enlistment of Catholic, francophone Canadians within the American ranks challenged the Continental Army to practice what the Continental Congress proclaimed about civil (and specifically religious) liberties. Yet it was one thing to do that when in Canada, but another when such recruits became refugees in America. How did the regiment accommodate its multiethnic, multilingual, and religiously diverse members? How did those members relate to each other and to the communities through which they marched? In other words, how did they make real the Revolution, or at least aspects of it, and help construct communities both martial and civil that were initially just imagined?

In defining a nation as "an imagined political community," Benedict Anderson premised that "it is *imagined* because the members of even the smallest nation will never know most of their fellow-members, meet them, or even hear of them, yet in the minds of each lives the image of their communion." The image of that communion may exist at the same time through shared experiences, or over time through such events and places as celebrations, museums, and libraries. In this case, in the Continental Army, soldiers did meet more fellow members of the new nation, see more of its territory, and materially construct—not simply imagine or invent in words (though that was done too)—the military community that was to give "the people" the time and space, or places, they needed to form new political communities. Furthermore, Anderson wrote of journeys, indeed pilgrimages, "between times, statuses and places" as meaning-creating experiences that generated a new consciousness of imagined community.[11] Joining and serving with the army was such a pilgrimage. Serving with others and moving through the years and posts together created—or, given some conflicts, compelled—a commonality that mortared the military community and helped construct the national one.

Much was unplanned in these constructions. The 2nd Canadian was an impromptu regiment in early 1776, following in the steps of the impromptu army of 1775; but the revolution of '76 included transitions from impromptu to regular forces.[12] The revolutionaries, uniformed and not, found precedents in other armies and from earlier wars, but they also adopted and adjusted models and standards to manufacture an army of soldiers who were not-so-regular citizens. An examination of Hazen's regiment from its inception through its dissolution, and then of some of its veterans in the postwar but still revolutionary years of the early republic, exemplifies how the army's members served within companies but lived within military communities, which in turn were part of the even-greater emerging community of the developing nation. And as they crafted policies, the revolutionaries directed that emergence in the models that they adopted and the stories they told.[13]

The constructed community that was Congress's Own Regiment operated within and represented the military society and moving borderland that was the Continental Army. The army may be designated a borderland as well as a society because it encompassed both imagined and manifest communities and lands— regiments, encampments, and garrisons—that were scenes of both consistent and contested rules, interactions, and negotiations by different peoples within and without its lines. Sentries guarded passage between the lines, uniforms marked who belonged to the army, and laws differentiated the military from civil domains, and yet the boundaries were not absolute; they overlapped, and civilians and soldiers, civil and military authorities, constantly traversed them.

To analyze the army as a borderland requires defining it not just as an instrument securing borders or asserting control on "internal frontiers," but also as a peripheral province that demonstrated multinational or transnational characteristics, aided hybridization if not assimilation of the peoples and cultures within it, and had institutional means by which to determine who or what may enter or not—namely, who belonged. Multinational and transnational are modern concepts that, as adapted and applied to the eighteenth century, may be more properly termed multi*country* and trans*state*. That said, the military borderland came into existence when members, who originally had little in common except the service itself, came to identify with each other in addition to others of their respective national or regional cultures, and when the characteristics they then shared set their camps or garrisons apart from the country that contained them. The Continental Army, as a borderland within and between states, promoted beliefs and demanded behaviors that challenged and modified its members' original characters as it mapped and occupied spaces in which thousands of the continent's inhabitants blended together as federated soldiers.[14] Migrants and immigrants, officers, soldiers, and followers all thus defined the army's space as a place: a borderland.[15]

What happened at war's end, when the army's members dispersed to other communities—including those on frontiers—is another part of the story. For some of the 2nd Canadian Regiment's initial members, the foremost frontier was between New York and Canada. But the Richelieu River Valley, from which so many of the Canadian recruits came, and the Champlain Valley, where some of the regiment's veterans settled, were not the only borderlands distinguishing the regiment. The regiment itself, like the army, was a borderland created by all of its soldiers and followers, from multiple states and countries, who marched with it.[16] As they marched, camped, and eventually settled, the new peoples of those military borderlands passaged from subjects to soldiers to veterans and citizens. Women and children made similar transitions as they grew old or grew up, lived, and labored in these borderland communities. As revealed in journals, letters, and especially pension records, those narratives of maneuvers, passages, and need, life and service with the regimental community was often the connection between people's identities both before and after the war.[17]

Why, where, and how the 2nd Canadian Regiment formed and fought as it did provide evidence of revolutionary initiatives and limits, emerging American military institutions and ways of war, and the development of military communities that may be defined as borderlands. The officers and soldiers who formed the 2nd Canadian Regiment in 1776 founded a "continental" community that encompassed soldiers and followers from varied states and countries in the borderland that was the Continental Army operating on the territorial and political frontiers of the United States.

Interpretations

This examination of Congress's Own Regiment utilizes ideas and interpretations from various historiographic models—borderlands, social, cultural, and military—to argue that this regiment was a borderland community supporting civil and military missions within frontiers drawn by the American Revolution. Its formation, operations, and disbandment, indeed the very stitches in its uniforms, flags, and tents, delineated cultural borderlands as well as territorial frontiers, or, vice versa, marked territorial borderlands and cultural frontiers. Obverted nouns and adjectives aside, the regiment layered a military culture and identity onto the civilian ones that its soldiers brought with them.

Such an argument may be inferred for the Continental Army as a whole: it was an organization and culture formed at the periphery of colonial, confederating societies that took center stage during the War for Independence. Civil-military relations might have composed a political borderland, but the army was definitely a physical one. It was a borderland with few "permanent" locations, West Point notably becoming one, but many localities. And those localities often served as halfway camps for individuals—refugees—dispossessed by the Revolution and looking to reestablish themselves.

The terms "borderlands" and "frontier" apply both to concepts and places, but exactly how they should be defined and differentiated has been a matter of heated discussion.[18] Are the terms synonymous or do they refer to distinct entities and issues? The difficulty is differentiating cultural, political, and legal issues and distinguishing space from place (encompassing historical process and geography); the terms thus denote the layers excavated—the postholes dug in one generation and uncovered or refilled in others.

Even as some people attempt to brace the conceptual fencing, others show its inherent flexibility. Is it taking the concepts out of context to apply them to the Continental Army? Perhaps, if they are to be applied only to colonial-national-international zones with autonomous peoples. But if borderlands are places where different "entities (usually nations or societies) border each other" and where "distinct societies rub against each other" and there are "spaces of unclear jurisdiction,"[19] then Continental Army encampments qualify. Diverse peoples came together within those camps and different peoples contested camp boundaries or jurisdiction and, by extension, the borders between military and civil law and society.

Defining borderlands is complicated not just by place, but also by time or period.[20] Among the challenges for historians of early America are those of delineating changing colonial, imperial, and Native American regions and boundaries. And like their colleagues studying later eras, they have balked at the term "frontier," weighted as it is by the historiographical baggage of Frederick Jackson Turner's "frontier thesis." Gregory H. Nobles noted a shift from Turner's thesis of the frontier as a "moving line of military and cultural advance and retreat" with its emphasis on conquest, cultural as well as military and territorial, to interpretations along the lines of Bernard Bailyn's frontier as periphery, as a place with connections to the center. Nobles saw two major themes appearing in studies redefining the nature of the frontier in early American history: movements for independence and movements for integration.[21] Such centrifugal and centripetal forces operated in the American Revolution and the Continental Army. Furthermore, as there was no one "common process of contact, struggle, and settlement" to define frontier, Nobles proposed recognizing plural frontiers. Eighteenth-century officials and inhabitants of North America had already done so. According to Patrick Spero, they generally applied the term frontier to zones they perceived as liable to enemy invasion. In those areas, "frontier people" fretted and fought to secure boundaries against their designated enemies rather than act as cohabitants ensuring porous borders for political, cultural, and commercial transactions.[22] As so defined, borderlands could and did become frontiers and vice versa, depending on the changing relations between peoples and nations.

In reinterpreting frontiers or conceptualizing borderlands, early Americanists have utilized the colonial term "backcountry," introduced the "middle ground," and suggested facing east from Indian country as they emphasized Native American agency.[23] In his 2003 summary of the field since Herbert Eugene Bolton's foundational early twentieth-century scholarship on the Spanish borderlands, Daniel H. Usner Jr. noted that "scholars of English North America have begun to use the term 'borderlands' in a more comparative and generic way to explore any region where two or more European empires face[d] each other amidst autonomous Indian societies," but he also called for studies that address other varied factors within and between border regions to ensure that the history of the margins may not be marginalized. Edward Countryman concluded that "no single image explains what we used to call 'the frontier,'" and that neither the notion of a syncretic borderland between Native and European societies nor the analogy of a middle ground works for all times and places in colonial America.[24]

Nor do they apply precisely to all later frontier situations in North America. Yet connotations of the terms "borderland" and "middle ground," or of the analytical processes the words characterize, are useful in understanding the creation of cultures "in cross-social and cross-political contexts."[25] Both explicit and implicit uses have illuminated the fluid conditions and transformative effects of life in so-called peripheral zones that in fact are corridors or centers of imperial, national, and personal challenges that affect the polities, economies, and security of all involved. They are places in which empires, nations, and peoples negotiate opportunities, loyalties, and identities.[26]

Some recent works have focused on imperial or national administrative and diplomatic negotiations for and in these places, while others have highlighted the local actors—original inhabitants and newcomers. Such works often deemphasize the military as a local actor serving the center, while military histories flip the significance. The other focus for much frontier history is a West defined as the trans-Appalachian and trans-Mississippi regions. Yet studies of the "Long War for the West," from the Seven Years' War through the War of 1812, include borderlands and frontiers that were south, east, and north of the Appalachian range. The Richelieu-Champlain-Hudson corridor, a strategic zone throughout that period that was or became home to many of Congress's Own, was one such region.[27]

This study of Congress's Own Regiment adds another facet to the notion of borderlands—or "marchlands," to use an older term suggestive of the defensive purposes of such zones and their peoples—as it analyzes the regiment's civil connections and military operations. Civil and military societies constructed borders so as to contain, command, and control lands and peoples.

When analyzing the borderland of Iroquoia (the territory of the Six Nations), New York, and Upper Canada, Alan Taylor posited that "new nations must define and control their peripheries" in order to empower their core even if local residents resist.[28] Taylor's proposition may be extended to the army as a borderland. Not only did the Continental Congress define and discipline this arm of the new nation through its commands, commissions, and Articles of War, but those acts also established the new nation's political difference to the British government and inaugurated new allegiances and identities among the soldiers that were not always identical to, but were supposedly representative of and symbolic for, those of civilians outside camp lines.

As the American army established its communities and borders, it also framed gates or posts for communication, cooperation, and supplies. Therefore, the borders between military and civilian communities included boundaries erected as good-neighbor fences as well as for security. These were temporary barricades for camps and garrisons during the War for Independence, but the permanent establishment of the United States Army eventually included properties reserved for military purposes. Reflecting extemporaneous measures during the war as well as envisioning possible future needs, the Constitution of the United States (Article I, Section 8) provided for the creation and administration of places later termed military reservations.[29]

When looking at these military borderlands, before or after they were institutionalized, one must consider military versus civilian space and place: spatial limits; territory and natural resources belonging to one or the other; and spaces "in-between" camps and communities (peripheral supply and security zones, and lines of communication for trade and transportation). There was also the issue of military versus civilian jurisdiction in the interactions across borders between authorities and inhabitants. Commanders and governors, informed by civil and military law and in response to the conditions of war, determined who belonged inside and outside their respective boundaries, and such determinations affected identification then and later.

After serving on various fronts throughout the War for Independence, some Congress's Own veterans helped form fronts along the new United States' national borders with Canada and Native American territories. As these soldiers became settlers, they used bounty lands to stake borderlands. When states, particularly New York in the case of Canadian refugees, and the United States tried to establish territorial boundaries and political borders through settlement, not just treaties, they offered lands on their borders to veterans. Such lands were recompense for military service during the war, but they also implicitly provided a way for the veterans to continue to be of service in securing nation and state. That veterans as settlers would be frontier sentinels was not a revolutionary idea, but it was one the new American states found useful.[30] Furthermore, the veterans of Congress's Own who moved into the borderland marked by Canadian, United States, New York, and Vermont boundaries brought their layered civil and military connections with them as they established new communities.

The interpretation of community formation and preservation in and beyond the army not only draws from political community and borderlands studies but also reaches back to the New England town studies and other regional interpretations that deal with demographic analysis, stratification, hierarchy, ethnicity, and social order.[31] This cannot be a study of families over multiple generations in particular locales, as in Philip Greven's analysis of Andover and Kenneth Lockridge's examination of Dedham, but those authors and others asked and answered questions about communities that echo in some borderlands studies and resonate in an inspection of this military society.[32] Robert Gross amplified some of the connections when he showed how the town of Concord for a brief moment moved from the periphery to the center of revolutionary actions. Its residents, who tended to experience the Revolution as a local affair, contended with religious, social, and economic challenges as they faced new political and military demands. A major demand was manpower, and Concord's response was one mirrored elsewhere and confirmed by inspection of military ranks: conscripts and poor men increasingly replaced yeoman volunteers over the years of war.[33]

Demographic data drawn from regimental rosters and federal pension records in conjunction with letters, notes, and journals reveal personal and family connections—kindred groups in and as companies—that sustained the regimental community. The quality and circumstances of the environment— in those previous cases towns, and in this case camps—also shaped lives and attitudes. Furthermore, the promise and assignment of land was important to recruitment and retention. Bounty lands and pensions did not just recognize rank and reward service, but also provided a way to take rank and, in some cases, the ties forged in camp and battle back into civil life.

Related issues as adjusted to this military community include mobility in and out of the regiment, rank related to class, marriage and kinship patterns, and conflict resolution. This study aims to illuminate some—it cannot do all— of the institutional dynamics, interpersonal relations, and living conditions within the Continental Army as manifested in this regiment. In doing so, to echo Lockridge's caveat, there is the risk that detailing a single regiment reveals an untypical rather than the typical example.[34] In so many ways, Congress's

Own Regiment was not a typical regiment, and yet its differences as well as similarities—compared with both historical precedents in the British army and contemporary Continental units—reveal much about the whole army.[35]

The force of authority, of command and control, must be added to the above dynamics. Authority was both centralized (Congress, the Articles of War, and general orders) and localized (regimental orders, detachment command). That led to questions then and since about who had what power over whom and where and when. This regiment's operations, like those of others, offer glimpses of the evolving interactions between a centralizing but not yet constituted civil authority and a regularizing but not yet fully established American army. It provides a case study in civil-military command and control that is distinguished by there being no intervening state between the regiment and Congress.

Like other regiments, Congress's Own had to maintain martial order and inculcate the Revolution's values. Doing so created an inherent tension between coercion and accommodation, between corporate and individual needs. Even as the military imposed discipline, interpersonal relations often confused its uniform application and at times mitigated its severity. Age, ethnicity, gender, religion, culture, kinship, and company all affected the living, working, and command conditions within this regiment and the greater military community. In addressing such topics, this study joins others that have addressed the Continental Army as a community or highlighted aspects and segments of that community.[36] Those works and this examination owe much to the no-longer-new military history that focuses on war and society.

Don Higginbotham wrote of the early American element in the "new" military history over thirty years ago, decades after it first started to appear, outlining some of its themes: war as a means to advance, not just protect, society's interests; civil-military relations; and how military institutions served the needs of nation or peoples, in this case the new Americans. He referenced many significant studies of "war-making in its political, religious, and social dimensions."[37] Among those was Charles Royster's A Revolutionary People at War (1979). Building on an assumption that there was an American national character and that it was revealed during the War for Independence, Royster argued that the army and its soldiers contributed to the Revolution beyond simply winning independence. As service was a trial of character, how Americans won the war was also important. Ways, means, and ends had to correspond. Both the process and product of the mission had to mesh or the American experiment—and the belief in the society's superiority—would be false.[38]

If the ways did not justify the ends, then the Continentals risked winning the war but losing the *revolution*. There would not be true victory. They, therefore, had to establish and respect state powers and individual rights and property even as they mobilized men and matériel to wage war. It helped that they had some military precedents that corresponded to their political philosophies. Actions and relations between colonial provincial soldiers and British regulars in the American theater of the Seven Years' War had particular resonance. As Fred Anderson pointed out in A People's Army (1984), war created or solidified some common attitudes about soldiers as subjects or citizens.[39] Therefore, as much as revolutionaries wanted men to volunteer for ideological reasons, the Continentals accepted that service was also a contract between soldier and state. This story of Congress's Own bears out earlier arguments about how the ideological and pragmatic meshed and clashed in the process and product of the War for Independence while incorporating more recent directions.

Wayne Lee carried Higginbotham's review, incorporating ongoing scholarship, to the twenty-first century in his 2001 article, "Early American Ways of War: A Reconnaissance, 1600–1815." New research into precontact and postcontact Native American warfare has deepened the analysis of clashing cultures in and of war, including how warring state and nonstate actors in borderlands that may be titled "tribal zones" adapted their styles of war. Those studies stand alongside others focusing on how war-makers on both sides of the Atlantic borrowed and adapted practices from each other. The growing body of American military history continues to include traditional institutional studies along with others thickly describing military life and evaluating who fought, why, and how they—and their societies—experienced war. As Lee remarked, there is value in and room for both innovation and tradition in studies of wars and warfare.[40] That belief undergirds this analysis and its sources.

Those sources—archived, academic, and popular—are found in the endnotes and bibliography, and I thank the authors who through the centuries put pen to paper or fingers to keyboards, and those who preserved and published their words so that I and others might use them. Given the regiment marching through this book, I particularly acknowledge Allan S. Everest's Moses Hazen and the Canadian Refugees in the American Revolution (1976). As Everest noted, even as Hazen and the Canadians fought a losing battle for full recognition and recompense for what they lost in Canada, they proved valiant in the field. This work acknowledges their sacrifices and valor with those of the rest of the regiment's members.

Organization of the Book

The first three chapters present the challenges of balancing developing public policies, military exigencies, and cultural biases. Creating an army required looking for comrades in arms just as creating a nation meant looking for allies. The process included a messy mixture of political persuasion and military coercion within and between colonies. That was evident as Americans tried to attract Canadians, both anglo- and francophone, before the siege of Quebec in December 1775, and then incorporate those who remained into the army that retreated in the spring and started to reorganize in the summer of 1776.

The next five chapters address administration and operations, including analysis of command, control, and communications between Congress, Washington, and Hazen, and within the regiment. There is also an inspection of the regiment's community development and esprit de corps as the chapters follow the regiment battling at Brandywine and Germantown, cutting a proposed invasion route in Vermont's Coos Country, surviving bitter times at Morristown, and guarding the Hudson Highlands before marching south to lay siege to the enemy at Yorktown.

The final chapter recounts the challenges the regiment's members faced in the last years of the war and upon the dissolution of the army. As the regiment guarded prisoners of war in Lancaster, Pennsylvania, and then kept watch at Pompton, New Jersey, Congress grappled with complex issues that confounded disbandment. Some of the problems persisted as the regiment's veterans headed back to their old homes or created new ones on the frontiers of the new republic. Short-term settlements and longer-term solutions were the results of much negotiation between veterans, states, and Congress.

In sum, the chapters open a tent flap onto the "Canadian" regiment called Congress's Own. Born in Canada of Moses Hazen's personal ambitions and an invading American force's military mission, it was baptized by a colonial congress with continental political aspirations. Over years of war, civil-military negotiations, and personal challenges, Congress's Own was a borderland of culturally diverse Continentals within an effective but contentious regiment that reflected the Continental Army and the emerging nation it served.

CHAPTER 1

CONTINENTAL ASPIRATIONS

As spring grew into summer 1775, the "Congress of America" preferred peti-tions to preparations for war. Its actions reflected a prayer that war was not inevitable and an awareness that America was in a "delicate situation" after engagements between colonial militia and British regulars in Massachusetts: she was "without ships, without arms, without clothes, without money, without officers, without discipline, without a single fortification." Furthermore, she faced a "considerable faction ready to join her enemies" and was "exposed thro' an immense frontier to the irruptions of savage tribes," and to enslaved persons being "urged by the insidious offer of freedom, to plunge an assassin's dagger in the bosom of domestic security."[1]

That was the Continental Congress's story, constructed during the Ameri-can Revolution's war not only as a narrative of events, causes, and justifications for combat, but also to build a community of states and people "united in this arduous contest upon the principles of common interest, for the defence of common rights and privileges, which union hath been cemented by common calamities and by mutual good offices and affection." Success in the "great cause" required continuing that union, securing independence, and receiving "returning penitents" with mercy.[2] As it had before and after that 1779 obser-vation, Congress encouraged the inhabitants of North America to combine against Britain, by that time declared to be a foreign enemy, instead of allow-ing it to divide them. There were limits to both compassion and inclusiveness, for security sometimes trumped clemency and inhabitant did not equate to citizen, but the point was to have a continental community that superseded colonial communities.

The First Continental Congress of 1774, building on the work of colonial assemblies and committees of correspondence, had tried to create a continen-tal yet still colonial community within the British Empire. Its successor took the next steps to sever that transatlantic tie while twisting strands of political ideas and grievances, regional interests and economics, and social and cultural desires, along with military actions and bloodshed into a chord of union.

Besides traversing the ropewalk of a national narrative, navigating the seas of diplomacy, and building frameworks of government, the Second Continental Congress had to muster military forces. In early 1775 there were already ships, arms, officers, and soldiers in America, and so in that way the story of being "without" took dramatic license. Yet there was also truth to it in that such hodgepodge elements were not of America so much as they belonged to individual colonies. When the Second Continental Congress, also called the American or General Congress, convened on 10 May, colonial militia had already exchanged fire with the "ministerial Army" at Lexington and Concord in Massachusetts. Hearing reports of the events of 18 and 19 April was a priority on 11 May, right after accepting delegates' commissions. Along with those reports was a letter from the provincial congress of Massachusetts saying that the actions of General Thomas Gage's troops made "the Establishment of an Army indispensably necessary." Massachusetts hoped to form a provincial army with New Hampshire, Rhode Island, and Connecticut. The letter's authors wanted support for that action but also suggested more: "a power full Army, on the side of America, hath been consider'd, by this Congress, as the only mean left to stem the rapid Progress of a tyrannical Ministry." Congress did not immediately establish such an army, but after hearing of the taking of Fort Ticonderoga, which was sanctioned by the Massachusetts congress, and of the possibility of invasion from Quebec province, it passed resolutions about defensive actions in New York, what posts to occupy, "and by what number of forces it will be proper they shd. be guarded."[3]

Even with such warning shots and suggestions, Congress focused more on political entreaties. Although it resolved on 26 May that the "colonies be immediately put into a state of defence," the call to arms was tempered by the next resolution to encourage reconciliation. It soon added spiritual petitions to political ones when it recommended that 20 July be set aside for prayer and fasting so that the inhabitants of the English colonies could, "with united hearts and voices," beseech the "merciful Disposer of all events" to instill in their "rightful sovereign, King George," the wisdom to provide for the interests of all of his subjects and thus end "the civil discord between Great Britain and the American colonies, without farther effusion of blood."[4] Such a shared experience was to foster communion among the colonists as they contemplated how to shape the imperial union on their terms.

Prayer and petitions were not enough, however, as the General Congress further considered "the state of America." Thus, on 14 June, the delegates adopted resolutions that companies of riflemen be raised in Pennsylvania, Maryland,

and Virginia and marched to "join the army near Boston." The forces near Boston became the Continental Army, as Congress decided that anyone wishing to serve had to declare: "I have, this day, voluntarily enlisted myself, as a soldier, in the American continental army." Congress also established the base pay for officers and soldiers and created a committee to draft rules and regulations for that army. A day later, it confirmed the establishment of the army when it resolved to appoint a general "to command all the continental forces, raised, or to be raised, for the defence of American liberty," and elected George Washington of Virginia to that command. Upon his acceptance the next day, Congress established other general officer positions for the American army. On 17 June, the delegates, trusting in Washington's "patriotism, valor, conduct, and fidelity," appointed him "General and Commander in chief, of the army of the United Colonies, and of all the forces now raised, or to be raised, by them, and of all others who shall voluntarily offer their service, and join the said Army for the Defence of American liberty, and for repelling every hostile invasion thereof."[5] With the power and authority Congress vested in him, Washington set about incorporating new and adopted troops into the army of 1775 and planning reforms for a genuine continental army in 1776.[6]

Congress's commission notably gave Washington command not only of the army of the United Colonies and the forces being raised by said colonies but also "of all others," a broad phrase that could comprehend individuals as well as forces enlisting to safeguard American liberty and repel hostile invasion. It was truly to be a continental army as well as the army of the United Colonies. The hope was that other North American British colonies, such as Nova Scotia and Canada, would join those already represented in the Congress to protect America from tyranny, and that in so doing, the two names in the colonists' lexicon—Continental and American—would become more nearly synonymous.

The events of those June days saw the Continental Congress—a coordinating body, not yet fully a government—add to and deepen its directive functions as it agreed to raise more troops, select a committee to compose regulations by which to govern those troops (what became the Articles of War), and both appoint and commission general and staff officers for the new army.[7] Moreover, Congress established a "Continental fund, to reimburse the expence" of the army and decided to issue "paper Currency on the Credit of the United Colonies."[8] And yet, even as it labored to establish forces and the finances to support them, and marched closer to being a government, the Congress tried to tread delicately: it said that these actions were for defense and liberty within the British Empire, not offense against it (namely, independence), and that they were done subject to the colonies' concurrence.

In creating an impromptu, ad hoc army by cobbling together militias and levies of New England with new companies and commanders from middle and southern colonies, and in calling for other provinces to join in the defense of American rights, the Continental Congress marched the rebellion closer to civil war. It was not yet officially a war of or for American independence, but it was a war for American liberty—fighting for freedom from a despotic government but not, thus far, from the British Empire. Over the coming year, colonists both leading and following the Continental Congress crossed mental, cultural, and physical frontiers as they imagined and then fought to realize continental unions of regiments and states. In the process, as America's varied peoples tested the conceptions of those unions, the Continental Army became a manifestation of an imagined continental community. Moses Hazen's 2nd Canadian Regiment, Congress's Own, came to figure in the story as it represented both the dream and its limits.

Associates and Compatriots

Liberty within the empire, and then independence from it, required association, but did that in turn prescribe integration into an American continental community? If so, how much? As the rebels, née reformers, expanded the fight over governance and rights in the empire to include Canada, they complicated their civic, ideological, and military enterprises. It was one thing to appeal to fellow "old subjects," the anglophone settlers of the Canadian provinces, but the rebels also debated whether and how they were to appeal to the French Canadians who had become subjects of the king in 1763.[9] The rebels recognized, as did some British officials, that French Canadians might not be inclined "to support an American insurrection in the name of British liberties."[10] Even if they did not fight for Britain, by not fighting against it, the French Canadians, or les Canadiens, could serve to keep British governance in America.[11] These particular Canadians therefore posed a conundrum to the emerging American governments within and between colonies about how to connect and control civil and military affairs in a cultural cauldron that not everyone wanted to be a melting pot.[12]

Continuing the cooperation among the colonies already represented in the Continental Congress was good, but increased support and security was better, so Congress also wanted to expand the colonial union. To do so would help push back and stabilize frontiers against enemies—Indians, officials, and colonists—who threatened American interests as the French and some Indians had in earlier colonial wars.[13] The Second Continental Congress may have initially thought to follow the example of the First by doing that primarily through diplomatic means, but its delegates found that they had to accommodate more militant Americans.

Leading expeditions from Connecticut and Massachusetts, Ethan Allen and Benedict Arnold seized Fort Ticonderoga on Lake Champlain on 10 May 1775. Soon thereafter, in independent actions, both also attacked, but did not hold, Fort Saint-Jean (St. Johns) on the Richelieu River.[14] Some delegates in Congress, such as Edmund Pendleton, approved seizing "the door of Canada" from enemy officials and forces and guarding against their use of Canadians and Indians "to pour Mischief" onto the colonies resisting ministerial maneuvers.[15] But seizing that door—namely, holding Ticonderoga, Crown Point, and Lake Champlain—led to ideas of advancing through it, and not everyone liked that notion. Congress declared on 1 June that it had "nothing more in view" than defense and resolved that "no expedition or incursion ought to be undertaken or made, by any colony, or body of colonists, against or into Canada."[16] Nonetheless, after creating the Continental Army, the Congress gave considerably more thought to invading Canada and inviting Canadians to join the resistance.

One complication was that there was no one "Canada" in 1774, in neither place nor people. Besides the Province of Quebec, the northernmost British possessions included the colonies of Nova Scotia and St. John's (later Prince Edward) Island and the territories of Newfoundland and Rupert's Land. As thousands of their fellow "old subjects" from the original British colonies had moved to Nova Scotia and Quebec province by 1774, the American rebels appear to have thought initially that all they had to do was send copies of their various memorials and invite those old subjects to send delegates to the Continental Congress to have them enlist in the cause.[17] Some of those new "Canadian" provincials, especially if they still had strong family or other ties in New England, were inclined to support the rebellion. Others, echoing the schism in the lower thirteen colonies, declared loyalty to the king or chose neutrality, especially after Sir Guy Carleton, governor of Quebec province, proclaimed martial law there on 9 June 1775 and Governor Francis Legge did the same in Nova Scotia on 30 November.[18]

When discussing Canada, the delegates in Congress usually meant the Province of Quebec. Furthermore, they recognized that they should appeal to all Canadians, the francophone new subjects as well as the anglophone old ones, so as to strengthen colonial and congressional—what they deemed continental—protests by words and arms. Trying to persuade the *Canadiens* of Quebec province to their side induced the rebels to elaborate their definitions of English liberties and natural—what they ultimately called American—rights. Yet words were not enough. When defense of those rights came to depend on the army into which the rebels wanted Canadians to enlist, revolutionary Americans desired that the army practice what they preached. While they could not command an end to discrimination in civil society, they

could attempt it within armed forces. Military implementation of developing and contested cultural, social, and political principles was problematic,
however, and thus the early attempts to recruit the *Canadiens*—not just the
anglophone Canadians who were often transplants from the lower thirteen
colonies—resulted in an imperfect fit between emerging public policy, military exigencies, and older biases.

Commanders followed congressmen in recruiting Canadians for what they
hoped would be a truly continental campaign. Their efforts show both acceptance of and limits on embracing an "other" as a strategy of war and nation or
empire building. War in colonial America, as elsewhere, was generally the result
of a refusal or failure to accommodate, whether by Native peoples, colonists,
or imperial governments. Yet to win at war demanded accommodation in the
forms of alliances and enlistments. The need for allies and soldiers forced governments, societies, and individuals to reconcile with persons and creeds they
formerly rejected. Accommodation did not mean full acceptance or integration
by all involved, but it did encourage toleration in the name of union. Such a
process or goal was not new in either mother country or colonies, all of which
had been growing more heterogeneous in the empire building of the eighteenth
century. But accommodation worked along a spectrum, with some peoples
more acceptable than others depending on time, place, ethnicity, or religion.[19]

French Canadians, somewhat like Native Americans, became people of
intense interest to British authorities and American rebels alike as resistance to
imperial policies became armed revolt. The rebels reached out to the *Canadiens*
as they sought to make opposition into a continental cause. British officials and
loyal subjects did so as a way to maintain empire. Many on both sides hoped
and feared that whither the French Canadians went, so went Canada. Such a
possibility trumped old prejudices, and thus the British and the Americans
chose to court former foes as they themselves became enemies. Officials in
both camps tried to persuade the French Canadians by way of promises and
proclamations, and then, in the case of the rebelling colonists taking a lesson
from the past, by conquest and occupation. As a result, the *Canadiens* faced
the dilemma not only of choosing between former enemies but of expanding
or containing the rebellion as well.

The British and the Americans had their own dilemmas: as they tried to
court and compel the French Canadians to their respective sides, they had to
consider how to incorporate these outsiders. The *Canadiens* were "others" to
both groups due to history, ethnicity, culture, and religion. There had been a
series of wars, culminating in the Seven Years' War—called the French and
Indian War by British colonists in the American theater—due to clashing
imperial ambitions. There were long-standing cultural antagonisms not only

between the rootstock French and English but also between the French Canadians and British colonists. And a burning ember in that hostility was religion: Catholic versus Protestant. Generations of fighting had seemed to prove that the two could not mix and that their inherent differences were intrinsic to what each was. Britons, British colonists, and New Englanders in particular had created their identities in opposition to these others. Revolution and war, however, meant that the old "us versus them" no longer worked, so each of the combatants sought to incorporate the old them into a new us, and that process revealed how cultural divisions could be somewhat subdued by stated political and philosophical commonalities.[20]

The trouble was that the British and British colonists had more in common with each other than with the French Canadians. The *Canadiens* were neither English nor Britons: they were new British subjects acquired by the empire as a subjugated people. They were Britain's colonials, not British colonists, for they were neither Anglo in origin nor part of the colonies originally created under the English flag. Furthermore, while they were not aborigines like the Native Americans, they had become essentially an indigenous people—and British and American attitudes and actions revealed perceptions of them as such.[21] Neither (American iconography aside) was willing to absorb the Native Americans into their developing identities—for the Revolution not only established an American identity but also contributed to the British one—but each found ways to do so with the French Canadians. Integration was equivocal and uncertain—sometimes including physical segregation—as they tried to minimize cultural differences and emphasize shared political and social desires. They negotiated cultural boundaries so as to forge political and military relationships: to create comrades if not compatriots.

Accommodation and Allegiance

When the British won the Seven Years' War and took possession of Canada, the French Canadians had to accept British dominion and legal, social, and religious discrimination. Even so, British officials found that establishing imperial authority in the Province of Quebec was difficult, especially as they tried to balance the rights and needs of both old and new colonists. The new Anglo-American settlers in Canada, who were primarily merchants but included some former military men, tended to promote an assimilation and subjugation policy for the French Canadians and an empowerment one for themselves. Many of the incoming "old subjects" wanted legislation that pushed Protestantism and English law, as well as dominion and rights for colonists of British extraction. The governors, Major General James Murray and then, from late 1766 on, Sir Guy Carleton, however, believed that the Province of Quebec would be more effectively governed—and the empire better served—by attending to the provincial majority. That majority, the French Canadians, desired accommodation in the form of recognition of their language and religion, legal rights, and a share in civil and military offices. Their petitioning of Carleton and his lobbying of Parliament gave impetus to what became the Quebec Act of 1774. With that act, Britain incorporated some of its new French Catholic subjects, who by tens of thousands outnumbered the British ones in Canada, into the governing apparatus of the province.[22]

The British government decided on political and cultural accommodation to solidify imperial control. That decision came out of long study and much debate. Protestant zealots and political radicals in Britain and America saw the concessions to the *Canadiens* as conspiratorial moves against established constitutional rights and order, but ministers and members of Parliament who supported it, whether for expediency or broader philosophical ideas about toleration, proved more powerful. Such officials supported the Quebec Act because it helped resolve governance issues within the newly acquired province and because a few of the more philosophically oriented questioned whether religious faith was essential to national loyalty. Although the decision for accommodation, or conciliation, may not have been a direct response to mounting rebellion in the lower thirteen colonies, it proved to be a key strategic move as resistance to other imperial innovations there and in Canada escalated.[23] On reflection, a British officer said he thought Canadian "affections" may have been wavering at the time of the act, and thus toleration was "politic."[24] Chance may have led to the passage of the Quebec Act in the same period as the Coercive Acts, but the timing of its passage was more than fortuitous.[25] Also, while Parliament may not have meant the act to be coercive, its implementation had that effect. The act thus stoked rebellion among many Anglophones and made choosing sides for the Francophones more problematic.

The fight to determine authority—what in America became a fight about sovereignty—led to a race for the allegiance of the Canadians. Britain surged out of the blocks first, but in passing a baton to the French Canadians, it rattled its subjects who had moved into the province as well as those settled below. The government, however, reached out as it did because it had learned how essential it was for authority and administration to remain connected in order for the empire to remain cohesive.[26] The connection had frayed in the lower thirteen colonies as those colonists vested power in themselves to direct public affairs, but the British government was determined not to let that happen in Canada.

The Quebec Act confirmed British criminal law in the province but nullified some of the other provisions that had been established after France ceded it to Britain in 1763. Parliament also reinstated the "Laws of *Canada*," meaning

French property and civil law, for "His Majesty's *Canadian* Subjects, within the Province of *Quebec*, the religious Orders and communities only excepted." The Catholic clergy, however, could also continue to receive "their accustomed Dues and Rights" from adherents. The act allowed such subjects "the free Exercise of the Religion of the Church of *Rome*, subject to the King's Supremacy." Parliament tried to soften such radical grants by saying that the monarch could make provisions to encourage the Protestant religion and support Protestant ministers in the province. Then, however, it turned around and stated that Catholics in the province did not have to swear the oath established by the Act of Supremacy of 1559 and asserted by later acts, such as the Test Act, which had been designed to keep Roman Catholics (and Protestant nonconformists) from public office. Instead, the Catholic Canadian was to swear to *"be faithful and bear true Allegiance"* to King George and to *"defend to the utmost . . . against all traiterous Conspiracies, and Attempts whatsover"* that may be made against the Crown.[27]

By providing for religious toleration and exempting Catholic Canadians from the Test Act, the British government outraged many Protestant Anglo-Americans in Canada and below. They deemed those provisions and others in the Quebec Act intolerable. Furthermore, not every French Canadian was happy with every provision of the act. Both the British and the Americans, who recognized differences within and between their own communities, stumbled whenever they assumed that they were dealing with a uniform and unified group.[28] In actuality, institutional, social, and cultural tensions weakened solidarity within the *Canadien* community just as they undermined cooperation between the *Canadiens* and either the British or American combatants. The Roman Catholic Church and its clergy appreciated that the British government allowed the church to retain its properties and exercise religious powers. Most seigneurs, those possessing large tracts of land on or within which they could establish mills, tenants, rents, and lumbering and other licenses, were also relieved that they could continue to invoke their privileges. The limited number of bourgeois, merchants, and the like, were torn. Many habitants, the freehold and tenant farmers, however, did not like how the Quebec Act restored the position and power of some of their old overlords. Ironically, therefore, the act may have heightened restiveness among the general French-Canadian population rather than lessened it.

The allegiance of these new northern subjects was then severely tested when the lower thirteen colonies finally openly rebelled against Britain and started recruiting French, not just British, Canadians. Carleton, the provincial governor, was concerned, but he initially believed that French-Canadian gratitude would translate into active support. But as more and more revolutionary propaganda circulated and as word came of militarized resistance in Massa-chusetts, he encountered difficulties in raising local military forces. On one side it was because so much of the English-speaking populace was disgruntled and inclined to support the Americans. On the other side, as Carleton came to realize, the noblesse was generally willing to turn out, but not the common habitants. As Captain Thomas Ainslie of the British militia at Quebec fumed, those "Peasants" demonstrated "a disposition little to be expected from a con-quered people who had been treated with so much lenity by Government."[29]

One reason for that peasant recalcitrance was that Carleton had dealt pri-marily with the French seigneurs and the Catholic clergy, especially the bishop of Quebec, Jean-Olivier Briand, expecting that the elite would ensure compli-ance by the common folk. As vicar general of Quebec, Briand had preached submission to the Crown (and tolerance for Protestants) after the surrender of Canada in 1760 and had worked well with Governor Murray, who recom-mended him for the bishopric in 1764. Although there was resistance in England to the appointment of a Catholic bishop, ultimately Briand was so consecrated in 1766. He then labored to keep Canadian Catholics faithful to the teachings of the church and compliant to the British government.[30] Demonstrating political compromise and conservatism to secure the church's position and ensure that its parishioners could freely practice their religion, most of the Catholic clergy followed the bishop's lead. A few did so to the point that parishioners accused them of having become English and wanting to make them English too. They could have made the former accusation against some seigneurs and merchants who classed themselves with the elite British officials and lumped unruly habi-tants with ill-bred Americans.[31] That suggests that there may have been some habitant uneasiness about a perceived growing Britishness among the elite and what that meant for integration of the whole.[32] Carleton thus found that while the clergy and gentry were useful, both had "lost much of their Influence over the People."[33] Some of those so-called peasants found the idea of emancipation from the English, from church tithes (not necessarily religious ties), from feudal dues (including military duties), and from social deference enticing.

British responses made acting for emancipation more likely. In early June 1775, after mulling Captain Moses Hazen's report about that "Horse Jockey" Arnold raiding Saint-Jean, and after dealing with the "Backwardness" of the "Peasantry," Carleton wrote to Lord Dartmouth, Britain's secretary of state for the colonies, that he was regretting his earlier support for instituting English rights and criminal law. He said that such laws required more public virtue and fidelity than could generally be found among the Canadians. Carleton revealed more bitterness when he remarked that making Canada more advantageous to Britain as it dealt with the emerging rebellion to the south would "require the reintroducing of French Criminal Law, and all the Powers of it's [sic] Government." As stringent French powers could not be reimposed, Carleton tried to suppress resistance, and perhaps the possibility of a French-Canadian revolution, by imposing martial law and establishing defensive forces.[34]

The governor found, at least initially, that recruiting soldiers among the *Canadiens* was as difficult as securing corvée (such habitant public service obligations as repairing roads and hauling goods) to meet his needs, and for some of the same reasons. Those reasons were noted by Carleton's commissioners between May and July 1776 as they interrogated militiamen and others about why so many had refused to bear arms for the British government during the invasion of 1775–76. François Baby and Gabriel-Elzéar Taschereau, elite French-Canadian loyalists, and Jenkin Williams, an Englishman who had settled in the province in 1767, recorded how individuals and parishes demonstrated their resentment of the social, physical, and financial taxes imposed on them by the seigneurs, state, and church. Furthermore, many of the Catholic French Canadians, after weighing the odds in late 1775 between already-present revolutionary troops and promised regular forces, gambled on the Americans. That is what the Plamondons, father and son, did in Vieille-Lorette when they "stirred the *habitants* in favor of the rebels, always assuring them that Quebec would fall, and that the royalists would not receive any reinforcements." In troublesome Pointe-aux-Trembles, Maurice Desdevens, acting as a captain for the rebels, incited habitants to take up arms by having several loyalists imprisoned and declaring that the rebels would take Quebec. A cobbler and roadmender by the name of Pignant praised the rebels and helped them seize rum, while Joseph and Jean Goulet's wives traveled through the parish defaming those who had convinced young men to march with Allan Maclean, the British officer who raised the First Battalion of the Royal Highland Emigrants. Ultimately, all of that parish's inhabitants "helped the rebels with transportation."[35]

Money as well as words fueled the resistance. Most Cap-Santé habitants "did not take up arms," but "willingly delivered provisions to the rebels' camp as long as they were paid in money." In Cap-de-la-Madeleine, residents generally did the same. But the father of the bailiff Michel Dorval showed greater disloyalty, for he disparaged "the King's party . . . [and] even implied that the Bishop of Quebec and the Vicar General of Trois Rivières had been paid to preach submission to the King." At Sainte-Pierre-les-Becquets, "a certain number of *habitants* . . . presented the commander of the Congress's army with a petition . . . against those who disapproved of their zeal for the rebels and against their pastor for refusing them the sacraments. This complaint brought a reprimand and threats to Father Louis, their parish priest, from the rebel commander's aide-de-camp in a December 30 letter." The previous summer, at Saint-Nicolas, even before the American forces made inroads into Canada, Denis Frichet had publicly disparaged his parish priest for "talking like an Englishman" in exhorting obedience to the king, and he questioned the priest's meddling in affairs beyond his purview.[36]

The commissioners, in turn, recommended punishment for those they believed had attempted or encouraged treason. They particularly condemned the actions of Germain Dionne and Clément Gosselin, who "aided and assisted the government's enemies in every way they could. They have stirred the people, enlisted them for the service of Congress, and ridiculed and threatened royalists." Gosselin was a particular "scoundrel," for he had traveled to parishes beyond his own, "preaching rebellion everywhere" and recruiting officers for Congress. The commissioners' regret was almost palpable when they reported to Carleton that Gosselin had not been spotted since the rebel forces retreated.[37] That was because Gosselin had joined one of the Continental Army's Canadian regiments and then went undercover.

When Carleton called up the militia, he actually called up two militias: French-Canadian and British-American. The creation of the two militias shows that British accommodation included segregation, which reflected how condescension affected steps to inclusion. Cultural prejudice was common even among those who supported the *Canadiens*. When Carleton commended the British inhabitants who helped defend Quebec, he noted that "what is still more to their honour (as it was found necessary to mix the guards, British and Canadian), they submitted with the greatest cheerfulness to the command of the Canadian Officers, whom they held cheap, and who were in reality their inferiors, both as to education and fortune."[38]

Ultimately, hundreds of French Canadians did directly serve the British government during the invasion crisis of 1775–76, and even more did so over the course of the war. But hundreds of others, from those in the Chaudière Valley who delivered supplies to Colonel Arnold's expedition as it moved toward Quebec to those who joined the Continental forces retreating from that city, refused to serve with or for the British in general and under their old seigneurs in particular.[39] The Revolution thus contributed to emerging class turmoil if not outright rebellion in French Canada at the same time that it challenged *Canadien* and British cooperation.

Rights and Resistance

Rebels exploited the social and political weaknesses in the accommodation policy by trying to incite subjects in Canada and the mother country into greater protests against the imperial government. These insurgents were also quick to use anti-Catholicism in their initial anti-authoritarian and pro-rights rhetoric. New Englanders used it first, but the First Continental Congress, which convened in September 1774 to consider what could be done against the Coercive and Quebec Acts, adopted it. By 17 September, the delegates had the Suffolk Resolves before them. The delegates, like their countrymen in that Massachusetts county, still declared allegiance to the king, but they agreed with the Suffolk protesters that they had "to maintain, defend and preserve those civil and religious rights and liberties, for which many of our fathers fought, bled and died." The civil and religious connection was specifically laid out in the tenth resolve: "That the late act of parliament for establishing the Roman Catholic religion and the French laws in that extensive country, now called Canada, is dangerous in an extreme degree to the Protestant religion and to the civil rights and liberties of all America; and, therefore, as men and Protestant Christians, we are indispensubly obliged to take all proper measures for our security." Concordantly, the delegates recommended that their brethren continue to persevere, that other colonies send supplies to help Boston, and that its resolutions along with those of Suffolk be published and distributed up and down the Eastern Seaboard and beyond.[40]

Passing along the Suffolk Resolves, however, was not enough. The First Continental Congress continued to debate how to frame its own response to the Quebec Act. The delegates first followed the lead of the New Englanders by setting Catholicism, designated as popery, against Protestantism and British rights. On 14 October, the delegates discussed how the act was "not only unjust to the people in that Province, but dangerous to the interests of the Protestant religion and of these Colonies, and ought to be repealed." Six days later, they listed the Quebec Act among the reasons they were adopting the Continental Association to ban trade between mother country and colonies as an act of economic protest. They charged that in setting up an arbitrary provincial government in Quebec, the ministry discouraged British migration into the newly enlarged province and, "through the influence of civil principles and ancient prejudices," disposed "the inhabitants to act with hostility against the free Protestant colonies, whenever a wicked ministry shall chuse so to direct them."[41]

One day later, on 21 October, the delegates followed the Continental Association with an address specifically directed to their "Friends and fellow subjects" in Great Britain. In the address, the delegates pointed out that Parliament was "not authorized by the constitution to establish a religion, fraught with sanguinary and impious tenets, or, to erect an arbitrary form of government, in any quarter of the globe." They declared that the late war "was succeeded by an inglorious peace" created by a ministry "unfriendly to the protestant cause, and inimical to liberty." They also prophesied that the Quebec Act constructed the dominion, or domain, of Canada so that Canadians would remain separate and "detached from our interests, by civil as well as religious prejudices," and so that with "their numbers daily swelling with Catholic emigrants from Europe, and by their devotion to Administration, so friendly to their religion, they might become formidable to us, and on occasion, be fit instruments in the hands of power, to reduce the ancient free Protestant Colonies to the same state of slavery with themselves." They then warned that those instruments could be turned against the people of England.[42]

That thought soon turned into one about turning those instruments against the imperial government. The combination of old and new *subjects* in common cause might provide for the latter and confirm for the former the rights of British *citizenship*. As some rebels mulled that, they also recognized that while anti-popery may have helped incite and unify New Englanders, it was a less effective instrument for and even an obstacle to unity in the more culturally and religiously pluralistic colonies. There were also pointed jabs from critics, such as Massachusetts Governor Francis Bernard and the English philosopher Samuel Johnson, about whether "liberty of conscience" was a right or an indulgence. Such broadsides and self-interest led some people to reexamine the belief that Protestantism was the major bulwark of civil rights, and to accept broader conceptions of religious freedom and extend, if not embrace, greater toleration.[43]

Exigency sparked enlightenment as it led some Americans to define their rights more inclusively than exclusively. Such pragmatic consideration led the First Continental Congress to do an about-face, although critics just saw it as two-faced. On 26 October, the delegates approved an address "To the Inhabitants of the Province of Quebec." They first recognized the Canadians' "gallant and glorious resistance" in the last war and noted how the British colonists had hoped that "our brave enemies would become our hearty friends" as these new fellow subjects came to enjoy the advantages of the English constitution and government. The delegates deplored how the Quebec Act had deprived the Canadians of the full enjoyment of English rights and privileges. They listed the rights denied the Canadians and then declared that the one right supposedly given them—liberty of religion—was not one to be granted by Crown or Parliament, but one already granted by God. As rebels becoming revolutionaries, they urged the Canadians to consider that if the British ministry treated cruelly those "who are of the same blood," how could it be otherwise for those who were not once they had performed the ministry's drudgery. They asked: "What would your countryman, the immortal *Montesquieu*, have said to such a plan of domination, as has been framed for you?" They flattered as they asked the *Canadiens* to exert "the natural sagacity of Frenchmen" to examine what was before them and consider what he would have advised. The delegates argued that surely Montesquieu, that French philosopher and jurist, would have advised them to join "in our righteous contest, to make common cause with us therein, and take a noble chance for emerging from a humiliating subjection under Governors, Intendants, and Military Tyrants, into the firm rank and condition of English freemen." They added: "We are too well acquainted with the liberality of sentiment distinguishing your nation, to imagine, that difference of religion will prejudice you against a hearty amity with us. You know, that the transcendant [sic] nature of freedom elevates those, who unite in her cause, above all such low-minded infirmities."[44]

The rebels invoked Montesquieu as an intellectual guide for the French Canadians just as they did John Locke for Anglo-Americans. Montesquieu spoke the right language, literally, for the French Canadians and (as the American rebels interpreted his work) philosophically for all. His *The Spirit of the Laws*, published in 1748, had met with great acclaim in Europe, but also vigorous attacks by Catholic (especially Jesuit) critics. Such attacks, in addition to his enlightened conservatism that embraced liberal reform, surely confirmed his attractiveness as a cultural and political bridge to the rebels as they mustered his name for the purpose of enlisting allies. They echoed his warnings against despotism and the politics of fear as they touted some of his lessons about law and republics. Whether their message—their distillation—was received or understood as it was sent is another matter. As Preudhome La Jeunesse of Montreal reported to the Committee of Secret Correspondence over a year later, in February 1776, Congress's addresses to the Canadians "have made little Impression, the common People being generally unable to read, and the Priests and Gentry who read them to others, explain them in such a Manner as best answers their own purpose of prejudicing the People against us [the rebels]."[45] Canadian action, or inaction, was not just a response to what the priests were saying, however, or to Enlightenment ideals. By the time Jeunesse made his report, Canadians were also acting on what the Continental forces and the Second Continental Congress had or had not done.

The Congress had exposed weaknesses in Britain's accommodationist policy for Canada and continued to tout the positive effects of joining the Continental cause. It trumpeted freedom from the old French as well as new British overlords and assured protection of property. It urged the Canadians to establish representative government within Quebec province (the Canadian council, expanded as it was under the Quebec Act, was not representative), and encouraged them to unite with the confederation to ensure all of the above. Also, although its delegates still opposed the establishment of popery—they remained anti-pope and anti-bishop as they became anti-king—the Congress, based on its perception that the fates of the Protestant and Catholic colonies were linked, promised religious liberty. It acknowledged that God gave

Catholics (like Protestants) "liberty of conscience" in religion. In the acknowl-
edgement and promise, the congressional delegates made the rebellion more
revolutionary as well as continental as they co-opted the religious toleration
represented in the despised Quebec Act.[46]

The colonists had been pushed and pulled into toleration before, by the
needs of settlement if nothing else, and thus most of the colonies already
accepted religious pluralism, but that was in terms of Protestant sects.[47] Anti-
Catholicism was still rampant, especially in New England. But seducing Canadians to their side meant accommodating Catholicism. The justification for
rebellion in 1775–76, therefore, came to include greater religious liberty among
the declared civil liberties that revolutionaries started to call American rather
than English. And while the Continental Congress had no power to enforce
religious toleration within the colonies that united and became states, it could
promote it by proclamation and through the commanders—at least some of
them—within its new Continental Army. In effect, the military, an instrument
by which to implement political change, was to advance and showcase a cultural change.

Invasion and Conciliation

Congress and the army continued the campaign of political and ideological
persuasion even as they turned to military coercion by marching troops into
Canada. Major General Philip Schuyler, commander of the New York (or
Northern) Department, issued an address on 5 September 1775 as his troops
prepared to attack Fort Saint-Jean south of Montreal. James Livingston of
Chambly, who was keeping up "a spirit of faction" among the Canadians, sent
copies to various parishes. And when Lieutenant Colonel Ethan Allen arrived
at Chambly on the Richelieu River, he delivered Schuyler's manifesto to the
gentlemen and "captains of the militia" that met him. The Canadians said that
they had withstood Carleton's and the seigneurs' demands for assistance and
were keeping under arms as they watched how the "scale of power" would tilt.
Schuyler, in his address, urged them to help tilt that scale toward the Americans. The Canadians had to be aware, he said, of what "drove the antient
British colonies in America to arms," for the reasons had been presented in
countless letters and in declarations "published by the grand Congress." He
assured them that Congress only ordered an army into Canada so as "to expell
. . . those British troops, which now, acting under the orders of a dispotic Ministry, would wish [to] enslave their countrymen." Congress believed that these
northern neighbors would accept such an action because surely only force
induced the Canadians to submit to the "insult & ignominy" heaped onto
them. Congress and its army wanted "to secure you & ourselves from such

a dreadful bondage; . . . to restore you those rights which every subject of the British Empire, from the highest to the very lowest, or whatever his religious sentiments may be, is intitled."[48]

Major General Washington, as the Continental Army's commander in chief, also penned an address to the Canadians that September. He declared that Congress sent the army commanded by General Schuyler "not to plunder, but to protect you; to animate, and bring forth into action those sentiments of freedom you have disclosed." He added that he was sending Colonel Benedict Arnold into Canada with orders to "act as in the country of his patrons and best friends." And Washington asked these "friends and brethren" to provide Arnold with supplies, while he, in turn, pledged himself, "not only for your safety and security, but for ample compensation. Let no man desert his habitation—let no one flee as before an enemy. The cause of America and of liberty is the cause of every virtuous american citizen; whatever may be his religion or his descent, the united colonies know no distinction but such as slavery, corruption, & arbitrary domination may create."[49] Washington thus offered an expansive, inclusive definition of American and American rights that incorporated the Canadians as fellow Continentals, as compatriots, not just comrades.

Washington, in turn, condemned anti-Catholic actions among the Continental troops encamped at Boston. On 5 November, on what was Guy Fawkes Day in England and generally called Pope's or Pope Day in New England, he scathingly denounced plans to burn an effigy of the pope. He could not believe the lack of propriety and common sense, for the Canadians were brethren in the cause of liberty, and thus "to be insulting their Religion, is so monstrous, as not to be suffered or excused."[50] The general was insistent and consistent as he established precedents for religious toleration in the Continental cause.

Washington had ordered Arnold to behave and respect religious freedom in Canada. Arnold, in turn, dispensed copies of Washington's September address after he crossed into Canada, and General David Wooster also had the letter printed and hundreds of copies distributed when he took command of Montreal at the end of November. That came in addition to the promises that Brigadier General Richard Montgomery made in answer to the articles of capitulation offered by the residents of Montreal on 12 November. After Schuyler fell ill and returned to Ticonderoga, Montgomery had assumed operational command at Saint-Jean and set out to secure territory and adherents. For the latter, he pledged Montreal inhabitants that the Continental Army disdained acts of oppression and had "come for the express purpose of giving liberty and security. The General therefore engages its honor to maintain, in the peaceable enjoyment of their property of every kind, the individuals and religious communities of the city of Montreal. The inhabitants, whether

English, French and others shall be maintained in the free exercise of their religion." He and Arnold then continued to try to "Conciliate the Affections of the Canadians," as instructed by the committee of Congress that had visited Ticonderoga in November. The committee recommended that Schuyler and Montgomery urge the Canadians to act with the rebelling colonies, and in return assure them that Congress would endeavor "to procure for them and their posterity the blessing of free government and the security to their property and persons which is derived from the British Constitution—that they hold sacred the rights of Conscience, and will never disturb them in the free enjoyment of their Religion."[51]

Many commanders and soldiers acted accordingly, whether to honor Congress's promises or because of personal toleration, but not all did. Captain William Goforth, a New York artisan commanding a company of the 1st New York, had the job of facilitating Continental order and activities in Trois-Rivières and apparently had a deft diplomatic touch. General Wooster, on the other hand, may not have paid particular attention to Montgomery's or Congress's messages, which was unlikely, or he may have allowed old prejudices and new pressures to divert him from fully acting on the sentiments of Congress and his commander in chief. He showed a frayed toleration when he clamped down on the Catholic Church and clergy as he tried to stifle protest and rebellion against the occupation of Montreal in December and January. Wooster's decisions, and some unguarded language, resulted in detractors then and later.[52] Although Wooster's actions may simply have been those of a commander trying to juggle civil relations with military necessity and putting the latter first, the actions and reactions provide evidence for how military exigencies, combined with older personal prejudices, continued to challenge or even contradict emerging Continental public policy.

The implementation of that policy of cooperative union faced further challenges as American forces hunkered down after Montgomery failed to take Quebec on 31 December 1775. Yet as union through military means stalled, construction through words continued. Thomas Paine, the political radical newly arrived from England, wrote that independence was "not the affair of a city, a country, a province, or a kingdom, but of a continent." He proclaimed that the present was "the seed time of continental union, faith and honor." Paine began writing *Common Sense* in November 1775 as Continental forces marched into Montreal and camped outside Quebec, and he published the first edition in January 1776, followed by the second in February, as the remnants of those forces suffered from snow, smallpox, and all-too-few supplies. Although Paine wrote expansively of the continent and a continental form of government, he focused on the thirteen colonies already represented in the Continental Congress. Even so, his words echoed and supported Congress's expanding vision: "Europe, and not England, is the parent country of America. This new world hath been the asylum for the persecuted lovers of civil and religious liberty from *every part of Europe*," and "all Europeans meeting in America, or any other quarter of the globe, are *countrymen*." He called for the establishment of a Continental Charter that among other things included "Securing freedom and property to all men, and above all things the free exercise of religion, according to the dictates of conscience." Paine also advocated creating a Continental Charter because such was "a bond of solemn obligation, which the whole enters into, to support the right of every separate part, whether of religion, personal freedom, or property."[53] He specified Canada only in reference to extension of its lands (a nod to the 1774 Quebec Act), but *Common Sense* had a comprehensive resonance at the time it was published. Military advances and reverses challenged expansive geographic and ideological conceptions, and yet the possibility of inclusive rather than exclusive rights encouraged others, including Canadians, to join the rebellion. Furthermore, enlisting in the Revolution—literally, through military service—opened the prospect for more participation in a new political community of citizens.[54]

Ethnicity and religious allegiances continued to play roles in the construction of the proposed continental—what would become national—community and identity, but the foundation was to be shared civic principles and procedures.[55] Membership required supporting the privileges and voluntarily shouldering the obligations of self-government. Yet getting people to volunteer was difficult, so spinning membership as a form of kinship—affinity, not just belonging—helped. Along with promises of economic and political benefits, the storytellers—including Congress, commanders, and commissioners—offered a "sense of self-worth or self-respect" to community members who participated in creating or maintaining "a valuable common identity."[56] In trying to construct a people before and as they constructed a nation, America's countrymen, to borrow Paine's wording, defined and valued citizens over subjects. But who could be a citizen? How did one earn citizenship? That depended in part on the story of the nation and people under construction, the individuals building it, and within what economic, political, and military contexts.[57]

As *Common Sense* circulated, Congress tardily decided to send a delegation to recruit Canadian support through diplomatic means while the army continued to recruit soldiers. This commission, created on 15 February 1776 and including Benjamin Franklin, Samuel Chase, and Charles Carroll (later elected to Congress on 4 July), finally reached Montreal on 29 April. Franklin was an apt choice, for he could volley both ideals and practicalities at Continental officers and Canadian officials alike as the commission tried to draft men and supplies.

In July 1775 he had proposed articles of confederation that included one inviting "any and every Colony from Great Britain," including Quebec, St. Johns, and Nova Scotia among them, to join those already in association and promising "all the Advantages of our Union, mutual Assistance and Commerce" in return. Franklin had also developed an understanding of the difficulties in creating and maintaining military forces through his work on the Pennsylvania Committee of Safety and on committees of the Continental Congress, including a congressional committee that had met with Washington and reviewed the forces at Cambridge in October 1775. His committee work meant that he was in correspondence with domestic and foreign political officials and militia and Continental army officers, as well as spies and other more informal informants.[58]

Congress instructed the commissioners on 20 March to inform and convince the "People of Canada" that helping the Americans establish their rights would help the Canadians establish theirs. Although some Americans wanted to "adopt them into our Union as a Sister Colony," Congress urged the Canadians to set up their own government so as to ensure their own happiness. Congress also stipulated that the commissioners must declare "that we hold sacred the Rights of Conscience," promising "the free and undisturbed Exercise of their Relegion, and to the Clergy the full, perfect, and peaceable Possession and Enjoyment of all their Estates, that the Government of every Thing relating to their Relegion and Clergy shall be left entirely in the Hands of the good People of that Province, . . . provided however that all other Denominations of Christians be equally entituled to hold Offices and enjoy civil Privileges and the free Exercise of their Relegion." The commissioners were also to establish a free press that would publish essays supporting the colonial cause, and to "settle all Disputes between the Canadians and the Continental Troops, and to make such Regulations relating thereto as [they] shall judge proper." Congress furthermore confirmed that civil authority trumped military when it stated that in "establishing and enforcing Regulations for Preservation of Peace and good Order there, and composing Differences between the Troops of the United Colonies and the Canadians, all Officers and Soldiers are required to yield Obedience to you."[59]

The commissioners met with Arnold, now a brigadier general, and other military officers as well as prominent Canadians, but their words could not counter the misery and weakness of the Continental Army. They could not sway Canadians who had grown angry and distrustful of Continentals demanding and sometimes taking supplies without payment (or with paper scrip, which amounted to about the same) and who wanted proof that the Americans could prevail before declaring union with them. Nor had recruiting Charles Carroll's cousin, the Reverend John Carroll, "a popish Priest," so as to confirm

"Friendship and to induce a Coincidence with our Measures," helped.[60] Father Carroll met with a few priests inclined to the American side, but others, in obedience to their bishop's directives, either rebutted his words or refused to receive him. When he averred that Catholics would be more than tolerated, as under British management, but would share the same rights as those of other religions, the Canadians answered that they had nothing to complain of on that score against the British government, and thus allegiance was due it.[61] Carroll, a resourceful manager of the Catholic Church in America and promoter of Catholics as good citizens deserving of all rights and liberties, ultimately became the church's first bishop, then archbishop, in the United States.[62] In 1776, however, his inability to meet with and persuade the Catholic clergy in Quebec province and his refusal to pressure their congregations meant that, despite Congress's hopes, he was no religious trump card.

The result, according to General Wooster, was that the Americans were defeated in Canada not by battles or logistics, but by those others he deemed contrary through personal weakness and clerical error. After lamenting the loss of men at Quebec and bemoaning the defeat's potentially ruinous consequences to the colonies and their frontiers, the general bitterly observed in a letter to Colonel Seth Warner, "You know as well as any Man, the Tempers, Dispositions and Character of the Canadians, they are not Persevering in Adversity, they are not to be depended upon, but like the Savages, are exceeding fond of chusing the strongest Party; add to this our enemies in this Country, of whom there are very many, use every Method to excite the Canadians against us,—the Clergy refuse Absolution, to all who have shewn themselves our Friends, and preach Damnation to those who will not take up Arms against us."[63] The intercepted letter was printed in the *Quebec Gazette*, thus revealing Wooster's biased interpretation of *Canadien* character and actions—one shared by many of his countrymen—to the people of Canada. That, especially when coupled with the Continental forces' inability to sustain both funding and fighting, provided Canadians with ample reason to hesitate to accept the American invitation as they tried to determine what would best serve their interests.

Indeed, all Canadians could rightfully countercharge that the Americans defeated themselves through the weaknesses of Congress, commanders, and soldiers that resulted in the abuse of their persons and property, which was antithetical to what Washington and Congress had promised. Abuse at the command level was due to lack of money and the need for men and matériel. As the commissioners wrote to Congress on 6 May 1776, "the want of money frequently constrains the Commanders to have recourse to violences in providing the army with carriages, and other conveniences, which indispose and irritate the minds of the people. We have reason to conclude that the change of sentiments, which we understand has taken place in this colony, is owing to the above-mentioned cause, and to other arbitrary proceedings." They followed that report two days later with one noting that Canadians "have been provoked by the Violences of our Military in Exacting provisions and Services from them, without Pay." Such "violences" were both institutional and personal, for while spurred by necessity, they were also due, as Captain Goforth put it, to soldiers being out of "humour" with inhabitants "because Some have changed Sides." Goforth understood Canadian concerns about being abandoned to ministerial vengeance, but he also recognized that another problem was the new troops from Pennsylvania and New Jersey who had not wintered with the Canadians but now arrived hungry, arrogant, and under too little authority, both civil and military. The commissioners had also alluded to that in their report of 6 May when they mentioned the difficulties in keeping "soldiers under proper discipline without paying them regularly. This difficulty increases in proportion to the distance, the troops are removed from their own country."[64]

The charges and countercharges mounted in the bitter first months of 1776. Yet before and even during those months, hundreds of Canadians had not only supported but joined the military offensive. Some had enlisted into the invading forces led by Arnold and Montgomery, while others, after evading or rejecting the demands of their old seigneurs to enlist in loyalist French Canadian militias, chose to enlist in partisan militia units or Canadian Continental regiments, with the latter commanded by British-Americans who had been establishing their holdings and power since the last war. Most French Canadians, like their British counterparts, rejected the overtures of Les Bostonnais and Congréganistes to throw off one government for another and thus limited the meaning and scope of "continental" in the Continental Congress;[65] but those who accepted and fought for American independence expanded the meaning of the term in Continental Army. Not all of that army's soldiers may have called themselves Americans, but they were Continentals.

CHAPTER 2

Raising the Regiment

Q uebec's defenders stood victorious after they rebuffed the Canadian invasion of 1775 at the city's walls on the last day of December, but frustrated
American rebels schemed on to enroll their northern neighbors in Continental
resistance. In late January 1776, the Continental Congress announced that
two battalions were to be raised among the Canadians and that the delegates
would rejoice in Canadian "assistance in upholding and fortifying the Fabric
of American Liberty. We flatter ourselves that you will with Chearfulness and
Eagerness seize the Opportunity of co-opperating in so glorious a Work."[1]

There was not much cheerful eagerness among either Americans or Canadians in Quebec province that January, nor indeed through June when Continental forces finally accepted defeat and retreated from Canada. Forecasting other
brutal wartime winters to come, invaders, defenders, and inhabitants faced
miserable days of "cloudy and cold," snow, and "thick weather." They battled
the smallpox spreading among those living "thick, nasty, and lousy," and their
emotions swung high and low as rumors and reports circulated.[2] And through
all the challenges, subjects-turned-rebels continued inventing and reinvent-
ing the revolution as they persisted in recruiting for the war, the Continental
Army, and a new, unusual regiment.

Moses Hazen had not been cheerful or cooperative about the glorious work
of fortifying American liberty in 1775, but in January 1776 he seized the opportunity to establish his position as an officer in the rebellion. It was not enough to
enlist in the cause; he had to command in it. The connection between ambition
and allegiance was not something new to him, nor was his tenacity in negotiating frontiers, whether physical, partisan, public, or personal. Tenaciousness
and perseverance, even pugnaciousness, also later became a marked trait of
other members in his 2nd Canadian Regiment, anecdotally called "infernals."[3]

Hazen was a New England transplant to Canada whose father, Moses Hazen
of Haverhill, Massachusetts, evidently passed on his military and frontier

interests to his son. The father had served as an ensign in a militia detachment in 1725 and then in 1726 was one of the original proprietors, although not a settler, of Penny Cook plantation, later renamed Concord, in New Hampshire. Men claiming that they found it difficult to support themselves and establish their children petitioned the Massachusetts' General Court in 1721 for a land grant farther north on the Merrimack River. A second petition followed in 1725, which the Court granted. The original proprietors included twenty-seven men from Haverhill, among those from Andover and other nearby communities. As family and friends moved together, the new community became a frontier extension of the old ones with room for the next generations to grow.[4] Inheritance (or lack thereof), financial interests, and other inclinations led the next generation of sons in the Hazen family to seek their fortunes to the west and north of Haverhill. Wars both challenged and supported their endeavors.

The younger Moses was born in 1733 at Haverhill as the second son and third of Moses and Abigail White Hazen's six children. He had two brothers: the elder, John (1731–74), served in the French and Indian War and then helped establish Newbury, Vermont, and Haverhill, New Hampshire; the younger, William (1738–1814), also served in that war before moving to Newburyport, Massachusetts, to engage in fishing, fur, and shipping trades that ranged from Nova Scotia to the West Indies. Ultimately, the loyalist William moved to Nova Scotia. One of William's partners, at least short-term, was Robert Peaslee, who was a brother-in-law, for he had married Anna or Anne Hazen (b. 1735). Another sister, Abigail (1728–78) married a Benjamin Mooers in 1749. Both sisters bore sons who later served in Moses Hazen's regiment during the Revolution, along with their cousin Moses White.[5]

Well before the family's revolutionary ventures, the young Moses Hazen may have engaged in the tanner's trade until war against the French and Indians provided him with new opportunities to pursue interests and promotions in military and social ranks. After an enlistment in a colonial unit in 1755 and commission as lieutenant in 1756, Hazen worked at supplying provisions to the British forces until he gained a lieutenancy in one of Major Robert Rogers's ranger companies in 1757 or 1758. A bold fighter, he earned a company command in the rangers and then, with General James Murray's recommendation, bought a lieutenancy in the British army's 44th Regiment of Foot in 1761. That regiment finished out the war at Montreal, where the thirty-year-old Hazen accepted retirement at half pay.[6]

Hazen politicked for land on both sides of the New Hampshire and Quebec province border. He also proposed that a road be blazed from a point on the Missisquoi River, or directly from St. Johns (Saint-Jean) on the Richelieu River, down to the townships at Coos (Cowass, Coös: an Abenaki term for "the pines") in the Upper Connecticut River Valley that he, his brother John, and John's wartime associate Colonel Jacob Bayley wanted to create. He figured that such a route would be "a very usefull Communication to New England" and would increase "the value of land at Cohas, as well as Encourage the Settlement of The Interior part of the province of New Hampshire." By October 1764, Hazen had land at St. Johns but was still awaiting word about his petition for land at Coos. While he waited, he applied for 2,000 acres on the Missisquoi, which Murray, by then governor of Quebec province, ultimately rejected as Indian-designated land.[7]

His interest in the road and land continued for decades, but Hazen meanwhile took advantage of and contributed to transformations in Quebec province. The major change was the establishment of British government. Governor Murray appointed Hazen a justice of the peace in 1765, and Hazen thus played a small role in the institution of British law in the colony. He also bent or broke it: in October 1766, Joseph Kelley, a resident of St. Johns who had moved to the province "to cultivate his majesty's ground," published complaints against Hazen. It was not enough that Hazen had seduced his wife, but after Kelley decided to press charges against the scoundrel, Hazen sent armed soldiers to attack him. Kelley was in jail, possibly on a charge of debt brought by Hazen, asking for justice for himself and against the one "who stiles himself Seignior."[8]

The title "seigneur" reflected another transformation in the province: the redistribution of lands as some of the francophone seigneurs, especially those who had served in the military during the war, sold their lands and sailed to France. As a result, officers and others found bargains in the seigneuries that came on the market after 1764. Many of these new landowners were entrepreneurs as they tried to establish their fortunes not just on the rents of the habitants or *censitaires* (tenants) but also through the exploitation of timber and other resources. In busily establishing their hegemony over the colony's economic as well as political life, they initiated changes that contributed to the eventual shift from a pre-industrial, even somewhat feudal, society to the capitalist, later nineteenth-century one. That, however, was decades in the future as the new Anglo seigneurs inserted themselves into the patron-client relationships that characterized social and political relations in the area.[9]

Moses Hazen acquired two unsettled seigneuries, Sabrevois and Bleury, on the east bank of the Richelieu River in partnership with Lieutenant Colonel Gabriel Christie, deputy quartermaster general for the British forces in North America. They also took joint ownership of various farms, including at Fort Saint-Jean. Christie was often away for long periods because of his military duties, so Hazen took charge. As he actively recruited settlers for Bleury and invested in improvements, Hazen overspent. To cover his mounting debts, he mortgaged some of his property to Christie and then, in 1769, more of it to his brother William and to Leonard Jarvis of Newbury. In 1770 arbitrators appointed by Montreal's Court of Common Pleas divided the Christie-Hazen properties. Hazen received half interest in the leased lands at Saint-Jean and half of the farms there, the La Savanne farm, and the southern part of Bleury where he had focused his settlement efforts.[10]

Hazen, the seigneur of Bleury-Sud, who married thirty-year-old Charlotte de La Saussaye in Montreal in 1770, continued to speculate in lands and settlements elsewhere, including in the Coos region of the Upper Connecticut River Valley, but he concentrated most of his efforts on the rich resources and possibilities of the Richelieu Valley. Hazen was in hot pursuit of prosperity. The empire that he served wanted that and more—namely, security and order. In that desire the British Empire was like the land's former liege lord, France.

Security had been an element in the establishment of seigneuries to support religious institutions and reward civil and military officials. France's original distribution of seigneuries in New France did not do much to grow the colony, but reforms requiring seigneurs to clear the lands and plant settlers—and soldiers if the seigneurs had been military officers—helped somewhat. The seigneurs had responsibilities to the state, which could include ensuring that their habitants performed their king's corvée on such public works as roads and fortifications. Another duty, although not wholly specified in the deeds, was that the seigneurs and their habitants provide military service.[11] The Quebec Act recognized and restored some seigneurial powers, and Governor Guy Carleton tried to tap the implied military ones when he called on seigneurs to compel their habitants to defend the colony. The move backfired: it increased habitant resistance to both the seigneurs and the British government.[12] It also put Hazen in a tough situation as an American colonist, retired British officer, and current seigneur.

Hazen's ties to the British army and to New England and Quebec, especially as he held property in the borderlands—and invasion routes—of both, left him conflicted as the rebellion mounted. First, he performed some services for Governor Carleton, such as carrying dispatches to General Thomas Gage in Boston and then passing to Carleton intelligence on Benedict Arnold's 18 May 1775 raid at Fort Saint-Jean. When Continental forces returned to Saint-Jean that September, Hazen visited their commander, General Philip Schuyler.[13] Hazen crisscrossed boundaries in trying to forestall trespasses on his property, but in the process made himself suspect.

General Schuyler initiated actions against Saint-Jean on 6 September, which was when Hazen informed him that the Canadians were unlikely to join the Continental forces as they wished to remain "neuter." Hazen did, however, add that if the American forces penetrated "into Canada, it would not displease them provided their Persons & Properties were safe and we paid them in Gold & Silver for what we had."[14] Hazen, in turn, supposedly received the general's permission "to Remain at my Dwelling house or to pass and Repass on my law-full Business undisturbed or molested by his Troops." Schuyler, however, was ill and did not remain to confirm Hazen's security. Schuyler passed command to Richard Montgomery, who commenced a siege at Saint-Jean on 17 September. The following morning Hazen went about his business, taking provisions to workers harvesting peas. He did not make it to the field: at about 8 A.M., the partisan Major John Brown took him prisoner. A few hours later, during a skirmish, British regulars grabbed him.[15] That added insult to the injuries Hazen sustained over the course of the siege: the appropriation and destruction of his Saint-Jean property by both ministerial and American forces. For want of provisions, the workers did not pick, and for the want of plucking, the peas were lost—and that was just the beginning. Besides bushels and fields of peas, among the losses that Hazen claimed were "3 large *New-England* cows . . . 6 ditto of half or mixed breed . . . 8 large *French* cows . . . 1 large *New-England* bull . . . 28 gallons *New-England* rum . . . 7 gallons *West-India* rum" and tens of thousands of livres value in other stock, grains, fields, furniture, and buildings.[16]

Unable or unwilling to hold Hazen at Saint-Jean, the British commander, Major Charles Preston, had militia volunteer Claude-Nicolas-Guillaume de Lorimier escort him to Montreal on 23 October. Carleton, who no longer trusted the half-pay officer and seigneur who had not raised troops for the colony's defense, held Hazen there. In the meantime, the rebels captured Forts Chambly (18 October) and Saint-Jean (2 November) before taking Montreal's surrender on 19 November, the day that also marked Hazen's release from imprisonment. Over those autumn weeks, Richelieu Valley residents who had been neutral or quietly aiding the invaders became more open in their support, and some volunteered to accompany and even join the Continental forces.[17] Now the borderland seigneur, who had tried to preserve his property and position by negotiating his own space between the opposing forces, found that he had to choose; and he, like others, had to decide how far to go with that choice.

Hazen was initially more hesitant than some other veteran officers of British regiments, such as Richard Montgomery, Arthur St. Clair, and Horatio Gates, in crossing the line to Continental service. That likely reflected his continuing half-pay status as well as his settlement and ambitions in Canada. Nonetheless, he personifies the officer-settlers on both sides of the border pushed into choosing political and, by extension, territorial sides. Edward Antill exemplifies another kind of adventurer who headed north after the Seven Years' War: one looking primarily for professional or mercantile opportunities rather than just land. He too had to be pushed to make the final, decisive split, but he had been more openly associated with agitators for political and administrative reform in Canada before the invasion of 1775.

Antill was born at Piscataway, New Jersey, in 1742 to Edward and Anne Morris Antill. His father's family was well connected in mercantile and legal circles, and his mother was the daughter of Lewis Morris, the governor of New Jersey from 1738 until his death in 1746. Young Antill's cousin Lewis Morris, carrying the grandfather's name, signed the Declaration of Independence. Edward Antill graduated from King's College (later Columbia), then studied and entered the practice of law in New York. He was in Canada by 1766, where in June he petitioned Governor Murray for and garnered appointments as barrister and attorney at law and a commission as public notary.[18]

To those appointments Antill added that of deputy commissary of the court of the vice admiralty in November 1768. Four years later, he and his associate Thomas Valentine began petitioning for joint grants of land. In 1774, the attorney submitted another for just himself, asking that he be granted "a Tract of Land or Seigniory . . . three Leagues Square upon or Near the River St Francis," so as to provide more for his family and better develop the province. By that time, Antill did have a family. In 1767 the chaplain of the Quebec garrison had married him to Charlotte Riverain. She bore five children in Montreal between 1768 and 1775 and buried three of them before she followed Antill into exile in 1776.[19]

Antill was one of the "Old" or "Antient Subjects" in Canada who associated with the likes of Thomas Walker, a merchant who had moved from Boston to Montreal in 1763, and James Price, who had moved from New England to Montreal in 1764. Both merchants had been great agitators against the Quebec Bill and then for Continental resistance to the act. In November 1773 and January 1774, Antill, along with those activists and others, including later regimental officers Edward Chinn and Joseph Torrey, signed petitions in Montreal directed to Lieutenant Governor Theophilus Cramahé calling for a General Assembly and another on the same topic to the king.[20] It then appears that Antill, the attorney with diverse economic interests and developing political aspirations, offered his services to the rebel forces after Carleton proclaimed on 22 November at Quebec that those townsmen who refused to serve would be treated as rebels and spies after 1 December.[21]

Carleton declaimed against the residents who "contumaciously refused to enroll their Names in the Militia Lists, and to take up Arms in Conjunction with their Fellow-Citizens" so as to preserve the persons, property, and city of Quebec. The governor proclaimed that he was determined "to rid the Town of all useless, disloyal and treacherous persons."[22] Carleton would have counted

Antill among the disloyal as he and other angry inhabitants exited the city, and then placed him among the treacherous because of the steps Antill took to return. Antill volunteered to serve with the invading force, and General Montgomery appointed him "chief engineer."[23] Such a role indicates that he offered knowledge of Quebec's fortifications and probably helped supervise construction of earthworks and batteries to support the siege.

As Montgomery drafted plans of attack, Arnold, Antill, and Price recommended that the main objective be the Lower Town, where they could attack warehouses and thus push merchants to pressure Carleton to treat with the invaders. This tied economic suasion to military tactics; the trouble was that it left Carleton in command of the high ground. Montgomery did not want that, but ultimately, after Quebec's defenders learned of his intentions, the general had to abandon his plan to attack Upper Town and instead try to drive through Lower Town, where he was killed, Arnold wounded, and the assault firmly repelled.[24]

After the attackers fell back, Arnold and Colonel Donald Campbell sent messages to General Wooster at Montreal. Antill served as a courier for Campbell, and probably carried Arnold's report too. He arrived in Montreal on the morning of 3 January, delivered the news, and a few days later headed to Albany, where he arrived on 13 January. Wooster sent him on to Schuyler and Congress because, as James Price put it in the recommendation of his friend, Antill's "extensive knowledge of this country gives him the advantage of any body that can be sent from hence, and will be of infinite service to the Congress, in making them thoroughly acquainted with the minds of the *Canadians* in general, as well as what steps will be necessary for securing this Province and uniting it to the other Colonies. He joined the General on his arrival before *Quebeck*, and continued with him until he fell, rendering every service in his power."[25] As the "express" rider and through his own oral reports, Antill became one of the first interpreters of the events at Quebec. In the process he maligned the actions and courage of Colonel James Livingston's Canadian troops in their failure to reach and destroy the barricades at Saint-Jean Gate and thus divert attention from Montgomery's main attack.[26]

Livingston had just formed his regiment of Canadian Continentals, and over the following years he was competitor and occasional comrade with Hazen over recruitment, recognition, and recompense for their respective regiments. He too was a transplant to Canada. He had been born in New York, probably at Albany, in 1747, but his parents moved the family to the Montreal area after the Seven Years' War. Initially a lawyer, Livingston became a grain merchant in the Richelieu Valley. He married Elizabeth Simpson, and their second child, a boy, was only eight months old when the young father started to send information to and gather supplies for General Schuyler at Ticonderoga in August 1775. Soon words alone were not enough, and Livingston moved to support the invasion by way of the Richelieu River from Lake Champlain. In doing so, he reinforced other Livingston family rebels, including a distant relative by marriage, Richard Montgomery.[27]

After Hazen advised Schuyler on 6 September not to attack Saint-Jean, Livingston urged the reverse, arguing that Hazen had misjudged residents' attitudes. He promised and delivered Canadian help not only for the Saint-Jean siege but also for the taking of Fort Chambly that October.[28] By that month, however, Livingston warned that his Canadian fighters would "drop off by degrees" if not provisioned.[29] Yet because of the partisan success and the coming dissolution of the "Northern Army" (the Continental forces invading Canada) as enlistments ended and soldiers refused to reenlist, on 19 November Montgomery authorized Livingston to recruit a Canadian regiment for the Continental Army. In doing so, the general acted on a recommendation sent from Congress to Schuyler in October and anticipated General Washington's lobbying for Canadian regiments. Washington did so for both military and political reasons: he saw Canadians as "good Troops, & this would be entering of them heartily in the cause."[30] Montgomery also acted in advance of a congressional commission wending its way north.

On 8 November, Congress ordered the committee of Robert R. Livingston, Robert Treat Paine, and John Langdon to consult with Schuyler at Ticonderoga about troop strength for the winter and, if Schuyler had "not yet raised the regiment recommended to him to be raised in Canada, or in case he cannot proceed to Canada, . . . use all the means in your power to perfect the raising of a regiment of Canadians, to join the continental forces."[31] Schuyler was delighted to write to Washington on 28 November, the day the committee arrived at Ticonderoga, that what he had already done accorded with Congress's instructions.[32]

The congressional committee at Ticonderoga was also happy about Schuyler's initiative and Livingston's ability to recruit hundreds of habitants to support the offensive. It also, however, warned Congress that Livingston would probably have trouble completing his regiment quickly because, it opined, most Canadians were farmers "and tho' prompt at a short disultory war, yet have some reluctance to more permanent engagements."[33] Those who did enlist, however, served in severe conditions that winter of 1775 through early 1776.

On 31 December, Livingston took that Canadian regiment into battle at Quebec. Despite Antill's and Schuyler's disparagement of the regiment's performance, Congress lauded the Canadian Continentals in the account it approved on 24 January and then published in the *Pennsylvania Gazette*. It summarized how Montgomery "ordered two feints to be made against the upper town, one by Col. Livingston, at the head of the Canadians against St. John's gate; the other by Captain Brown, at the head of a small detachment against cape Diamond; reserving to himself and Colonel Arnold the two principal attacks against the lower town." Hours later, the troops "being drawn off" elsewhere, including at Montgomery's position due to his death, the wounded Arnold's troops had to withdraw as well. Yet "after this unfortunate repulse," Congress reported, "the remainder of the army retired about three miles from the city, where they have posted themselves advantageously and are continuing the blockade, waiting for reinforcements which are now on their march to join them."[34]

The same day that the delegates approved that official account, they also approved another letter to the inhabitants of Canada reminding them "that your liberty, your honor and your happiness are essentially and necessarily connected with the unhappy contest . . . for the defence of our dearest privileges." The delegates avowed that they would "never abandon" their friends and countrymen, especially after the services they had "already rendered the common cause," and that two battalions were already under orders to march north and that six more were in the process of being raised. Furthermore, "we have directed that measures be immediately taken to embody two regiments in your country. Your assistance in the support and preservation of American liberty affords us the most sensible satisfaction and we flatter ourselves that you will seize with zeal and eagerness the favourable moment to co-operate in the success of so glorious an enterprize." Congress finished its work on 24 January by approving reimbursement and funds to raise a battalion to its newly commissioned colonels, Hazen and Antill.[35]

New Year, New Army

The Continental Congress's decisions in January 1776 reflected not just immediate reactions to the news of Quebec but also months of plans, visits, and correspondence over the reorganization of the American army. The delegates were deeply engaged in supporting General Washington's aspirations for a more unified force while also striving for more unified colonies and colonists. They debated long-term strategies while responding to the pressing advances and reverses on both political and military battlefronts. Their new year's resolutions included instructions to the "friends of American liberty" to treat kindly the "divers honest and well-meaning, but uninformed people" who held "erroneous opinions" about the American cause, and consider their mistakes as due to a "want of information than want of virtue or public spirit." Liberty's friends were to educate the uninformed about "the origin, nature and extent of the present controversy." Congress also advised assemblies and councils "to frustrate the mischievous machinations" of those misrepresenting the American cause and conduct, and it authorized them to call upon available Continental troops to assist in restraining the wicked and unworthy. It recommended that all the United Colonies "aid each other . . . on every emergency, and to cultivate, cherish and increase the present happy and necessary union."[36]

As the delegates instructed their fellow provincials and tried to construct that questionably happy but certainly necessary union for their evolving plans, they engaged in revolution by committee. They assigned letters and problems to small groups, which returned with recommendations on which the greater council that was Congress voted. Each resolve in and for the colonies' defense, if taken separately, might not have meant independence, but when taken together they led to that conclusion. Indeed, delegates broached ideas of both "independency" and a war office on the same day, 24 January, that they provided funds to Hazen and Antill, ordered the account about Quebec published, and approved a new address to the Canadians. As congressional members tried to put out some fires and ignite others in January 1776, they shifted back and forth from issuing sweeping directions to haggling over minutiae. They orchestrated songs of resistance and stories of union as they, among other things, ordered ship movements, commissioned officers, directed funds and supplies, provided for soldiers' pay and postage, and even commanded troop movements (the battalions sent to reinforce those already in Canada were to move out company by company at the distance of a day's march).[37]

While still in blissed ignorance of the repulse at Quebec and in appreciation and anticipation of continued Canadian support, on 8 January the Continental Congress authorized what it and its commanders had earlier sanctioned: it officially commissioned the Canadian Regiment, calling it a battalion, with James Livingston as its colonel. It also called for eight other battalions to be formed and maintained for the defense of Canada through the year. Two were to be created out of troops already serving in Canada, and the others to be marched from below (Pennsylvania, New Jersey, New York, New Hampshire, and Connecticut). Then it set up a committee to figure out how to furnish said battalions. Within ten days, it had to start revising its projections when Antill delivered General Schuyler's letter, substantiated by copies of letters from Wooster, Arnold, and others, reporting the failure to take Quebec.[38]

Antill delivered the news on 17 January after traveling twelve days from Montreal with Hazen.[39] The next day, "Mr. Antill, Son of the late Hon. Mr. Antill of N Jersey . . . was called in and examined for 2 Hours, he gave a very clear Account of every Circumstance, he was with Gen. Montg'y when he fell." Antill recommended that Hazen be given command of a regiment of Canadians, who though "between Hawk and Buzzard" would likely join "our Side" if a strong force was sent immediately. Congress responded to the news by establishing a committee to reflect on the situation in Canada and offer suggestions about what should be done.[40]

Following the committee's advice, on 19 January, Congress resolved that American forces "in Canada be reinforced with all possible despatch, as well for the security and relief of our friends there, as for better securing the rights and liberties not only of that colony, but the other United Colonies." So Congress again prodded the colonies to speed the recruitment of battalions.[41] The next day, it issued directions to Washington, Wooster, and the colonial assemblies and councils, along with orders to the Secret Committee (or Committee of Secrecy) on the distribution of gunpowder and to the treasurers to advance money. Moving at quickstep, Congress also determined, "exclusive of Colonel Livingston and his regiment," that "there be one thousand Canadians more raised, for one year, or during the present disputes," and that the "number shall compose four battalions, and form one regiment."[42]

Congress confirmed the genesis of the 2nd Canadian Regiment on 22 January when it elected Moses Hazen to be its colonel commandant and Edward Antill its lieutenant colonel. Other officers were to be appointed by the Canadian Department's commander on the advice of his general officers, Hazen, Antill, and James Price (whom Congress in March appointed deputy commissary general for the army in Canada). Congress's promise to the haggling Hazen that the United Colonies would indemnify him "for any loss of half pay which he may sustain in consequence of his entering into the service of America" would come back to haunt its successors when Hazen wanted recompense for all that he expended and lost as a result of his service. Long before that problem, however, there arose an immediate wrangle in that someone told the Congress that Hazen was under parole to Carleton not to serve against the king. That meant that he could not honorably take a command, and thus Congress elected Antill to be the regiment's colonel commandant on the 23rd. When a committee checked into the alleged parole, however, it determined that Hazen had been confined within Montreal. Hazen later recorded that he had been in prison for fifty-four days until "set at Liberty by Genl Montgomery." When Montgomery took Montreal, he released Hazen from custody (incarceration nullified the honor-bound restraints of parole). Congress therefore reappointed Hazen as colonel on 25 January.[43] Before Hazen accepted, however, he made a further push for position—to be ranked "first Col. in Canada." Congress refused. Instead of declining service as he had threatened, Hazen accepted the commission anyway, and conferred with a congressional committee of two, Samuel Adams and James Duane, about regimental and Canadian matters before he headed back up, probably once again with Antill, who carried Congress's resolves north.[44]

Who had presented the problem of parole to Congress? It was unlikely to have been Antill, for he had recommended Hazen. It could have been someone who distrusted Hazen or was an advocate for Jeremiah Duggan, another Canadian "Old Subject," who had been a partisan leader and captain with Livingston. While Hazen and Antill were journeying to Philadelphia, newly promoted Brigadier General Arnold began to form another Canadian regiment with Duggan at its head. Congress received Arnold's letter mentioning this on 9 February, and the committee that reviewed it reported on the 17th. Congress resolved that the proposed regiment was to "receive the same pay, and be subject to the same regulations as the other forces employed in Canada, and be accounted part of the number designed to be raised for that service."[45] Weeks later, Congress decided to pay Duggan one hundred dollars for "his services in the Cause of the United Colonies in Canada" and recommended that the commanding officer in Canada "advance him to a post in the army, suitable to his merit and services."[46]

If the colonial ideal was that potential leaders did not openly seek or campaign for office, which would indicate pursuit of personal rather than the public's good, then the contests and conflicts for rank in the Continental Army, as seen with Hazen and Duggan and many others, battered if not buried it.[47] Such jockeying for position and power aside, the symbolism, not just manpower, of establishing Canadian units was important. Besides the invasion, these establishments demonstrated that Congress was committed by action, not just words, to incorporating the inhabitants of that northern province. More particularly, enlisting Canadian regiments into the Continental cause dovetailed with the desires of both Congress and its army not to retreat.

Retreat became less desirable politically even as it became more necessary militarily over the spring of 1776. And the military retreat in the Canadian theater came only after much foot-dragging as Congress and the Continental Army advanced other offenses for, not just defenses of, liberty. Such offenses included Congress's continued attempts to frame the continental community it envisioned as it constructed, in partnership with Washington, the new Continental Army that was to embody as well as defend that community. Both were articulated and authorized through addresses of common rights, common interests, and the commonweal.

The delegates did not want to depend solely on Thomas Paine and other compatriots in the various colonies to carry the rhetorical battle; they also engaged in it. In doing so, they trod closer to the big question of independence. Massachusetts nipped at their heels with the language appointing its delegates for 1776, whom it empowered to determine and direct with the other delegates "such farther measures, as shall to them appear best calculated for the establishment of right and liberty to the American colonies, upon a basis permanent and secure, against the power and arts of the British administration." That February, Congress also heard from the committee that had drafted "an address to the inhabitants of these colonies," which did not, however, include Canada. The address was to render an account of Congress's actions and the principles on which those actions were based. It began with a summary of its political stance: that "the House of Commons neither has nor can have any Power deriv'd from the Inhabitants of these Colonies" not just in taxation but also in "every other Instance." Then it stated how the colonies' rights were violated and how they responded with petitions, remonstrances, and then congresses; for "If common Rights, common Interests, common Dangers and common Sufferings are Principles of Union, what could be more natural than the Union of the Colonies?" When the "ministerial foes" used military force against the colonial "commercial Opposition," the colonies had to oppose "Force by Force" to secure liberty, even if it meant foregoing the peace and safety they desired.[48]

"Our troops," the draft continued, "have fought and bled and conquered in the Discharge of their Duty as good Citizens as well as brave Soldiers. Regardless of the Inclemency of the Seasons, and of the Length and Fatigue of the March, they go, with Cheerfulness, wherever the Cause of Liberty and their Country requires their Service." Congress acknowledged that the troops "have not the Advantages arising from Experience and Discipline," but that would come. The soldiers' "Patriotism will receive no Diminution: The longer those, who have forced us into this War, oblige us to continue it, the more formidable we shall become." And that was not just on land but by sea as well. Congress declared that it raised those land and sea forces, just as it exercised legislative, executive, and judicial powers, with the authority of the people. That authority of the *people*, rather than of the provincial assemblies that sent delegates, was as questionable as the cheerfulness of the troops encamped in Canada, but that was Congress's construction of its force and forces.[49]

In that draft, Congress assured the people that it did not continue the war with the intention "of establishing an independent Empire," but only to defend "the constitutional Rights of the Colonies."[50] Most of the delegates could no longer convince themselves of that, much less others. Perhaps it was also too much or too little in other ways, for they tabled the address. Ultimately, Congress did rely a great deal on Paine's *Common Sense*, other published sermons, songs, and essays, and personal correspondence to frame the continental community rhetorically while most of its delegates concentrated on operational details. They did, however, continue to contribute to that framework in the language of their resolutions. While many of those had limited distribution, they indicate a continued reinforcement of beliefs for both the writers and the readers. Some resolutions were published, including that of New Jersey delegate, later governor, William Livingston for a fast to be observed in May by all the colonies. In consideration of "the warlike preparations of the British Ministry to subvert our invaluable rights and priviledges, and to reduce us by fire and sword, by the savages of the wilderness, and our own domestics, to the most abject and ignominious bondage," Congress agreed that the people should be united in an appeal to God's forgiveness and providence so that the "continental arms" would be crowned by victory and civil rulers would wisely establish "the rights of America on the most honourable and permanent basis." Congress repeated such charges against the king and Parliament in its authorization to fit out armed ships for privateering.[51]

Words required actions, and actions, words. The necessities of the war, whether for independence or not that spring, demanded most of the delegates' attention. One necessity was balancing the quagmire of Quebec against securing persons, property, and troops elsewhere. One part of that balancing act was the committee sent to Canada to parley with American and Canadian civil and military officials. Preudhome La Jeunesse, a Canadian engaged in "American Service," had advised the Committee of Secret Correspondence to send congressional delegates "to explain vivâ voce to the People there the Nature of our Dispute with England, which they do not well understand, and to satisfy the Gentry and Clergy that we have no Intention against their Interests." The committee passed its recommendation to Congress, which appointed envoys Benjamin Franklin, Samuel Chase, and Charles Carroll of Carrollton in mid-February.[52]

Their instructions arrived in March: in addition to intoning the growing political and ideological repertory, the commissioners were to explain how Congress collected "the sense of the people," and how it conducted its affairs "by committees of observation and inspection in the several districts, and by conventions and committees of safety in the several colonies." Besides assuring Canadians of freedom of religious conscience and encouragement of commerce, the commissioners were to "stimulate them by motives of glory, as well as interest," to encourage them to "aspire to a portion of that power, by which they are ruled," and to press them to come into the union. If they joined, Congress promised to "defend and protect the people of Canada against all enemies, in the same manner as we will defend and protect any of the United Colonies."[53] In other words, the commissioners were to put words to tunes already beating throughout colonies and camps—to assemble and to arms.

These civil officials also had military authority. Congress empowered them to reform and enforce regulations to preserve peace between the Canadians

and Continental troops, to "vote as members of councils of war," and to direct
the construction or demolition of fortifications. Among their orders was one
to check into Hazen's request for reparations for property lost or destroyed by
the American invasion (they stayed at Hazen's "wreck" of a house on the way
to Montreal), and another to review issues regarding the deployment of some
New York battalions.[54] In operating as military as well as civil authorities, the
commissioners were to see that the forces in Canada were in compliance with
the new army and directives of 1776. During the highs and increasing lows of
the Canadian campaign, therefore, the commissioners played a role in what
may be called command by council against the bigger roles performed by Congress and the army's commander in chief in the reinvention of the army of the
United Colonies and, upon retreat from Canada, the redeployment of part of it.

Organized on a Different Plan

Among the units symbolizing and serving in that reinvented army was Moses
Hazen's 2nd Canadian Regiment. When Congress reviewed the dispatches
from Canada and mulled over Antill's reports earlier that January, it had
been keen to reinforce, not retire, the ravaged attempt to expand resistance
and intercolonial union. Besides prodding colonies to speed the recruitment
of battalions, it had also determined that "there be one thousand Canadians
more raised, for one year, or during the present disputes, at six dollars and
two thirds of a dollar bounty, and the usual pay." That thousand-man (plus
officers) regiment was to be "organized on a different plan from any other." It
was to have one colonel commandant, one lieutenant colonel, four majors, and
appropriate staff officers. There were to be four battalions with "five companies
of fifty men to each battalion, one captain, one lieutenant, and one ensign, to
each company." The fifty men in those twenty companies were to consist of
"3 Sergeants, 3 Corporals, Fifer, Drummer, and 42 privates." One of the companies in each battalion was to be a rifle or light infantry company.[55] That was to
be the regiment's official complement throughout the war.

While the regiment's men were to draw the "usual" pay, its organization
was unique from the 1776 standard infantry regiment complement that was
to number 728 officers and men, with one colonel, one lieutenant colonel, one
major, and staff, and to be organized into eight companies (one captain, two
lieutenants, and one ensign per company).[56] There was a moment, however,
when it appeared that the 2nd Canadian might have to conform. In September
1776, when Congress agreed to continue Hazen and Antill's commissions—and
by extension their Canadian regiment—in what had become the army of the
United *States*, Congress resolved that they were to "recruit their regiment to the
number of a battalion on the continental establishment." But in late October,

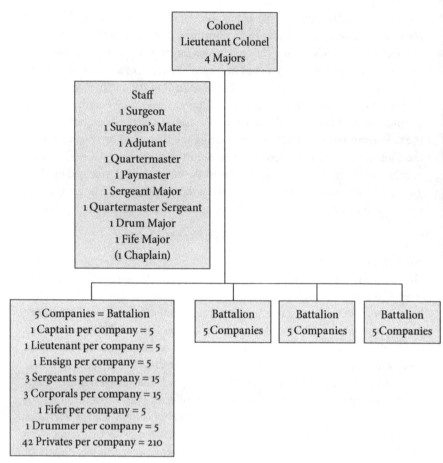

2nd Canadian Regiment, Continental Army—Original Establishment. One thousand soldiers, plus officers and staff.

after a committee reported on Hazen's financial and regimental requests, Congress determined that the regiment would continue on its "original establishment," and furthermore "be recruited to its full complement in any of the thirteen United States." Congress thus accepted Hazen's argument, firstly, that it was on these terms that he had entered into the service, and secondly, that "the said regiment cannot be said to belong to any particular state." Its acquiescence to the third part, however—that the officer-heavy regiment would not "be any additional expence in the mode of officering"—was puzzling.[57]

Hazen's regiment continued to keep its original establishment not only in 1777 but also when the army reorganized yet again in 1778 and the standard new infantry regiment was to have nine companies, one designated light infantry, but fewer than 600 officers and men (from 80 to 56 privates and corporals in a company's rank and file). The lower number more closely reflected the British army's infantry company composition, which suggests that military's continuing influence on the new American force.[58] By comparison, at the outset of the War for Independence, the common, designated strength of a regular or "ordinary" British regiment of foot was 477 men (38 privates, 3 corporals, 1 drummer per company) in an organization of one battalion of ten companies (eight regular, one light infantry, and one grenadier).[59] That model aside, the lowered number in the American regiments was also due to financial and recruiting realities. Even so, few if any regiments—including the 2nd Canadian—ever made their full complement.

The 2nd Canadian may have had the structure (on paper) that it did because it was raised on Hazen's personal promises, and his and other officers' financial investment, rather than provincial or state authorization.[60] It was not the only unit created outside a provincial or state line, although Congress had originally sanctioned the Canadian regiments in the hope that the province would support them and establish a military line. Some other extra-Continental regiments did eventually join state lines, as when the German Battalion became the 8th Maryland. Other extras included the short-lived Ottendorf's Corps (authorized in December 1776 under the command of Major Nicholas Dietrich, Baron de Ottendorf), which was an independent corps modeled on European partisan legions and with primarily foreign officers and German-American soldiers. Colonel Charles Armand-Tuffin, the marquis de la Rouerie, took command of that corps in June 1777, but by 1778 he apparently spent more time and effort constructing the 1st Partisan Corps (Armand's Legion). The former Ottendorf's Corps was disbanded in April 1778 and its elements reassigned. Remnants of two of its "Independent" companies, one commanded by Captain Anthony Selin and the other Captain John Paul Schott, ultimately ended up in Hazen's regiment in 1781.[61] Such units show, despite repeated attempts to regularize or standardize, how the army long included impromptu elements created on an ad hoc basis.

Hazen and Antill likely established the regiment based on British and colonial models of the Seven Years' War rather than the reduced establishments at the beginning of the American Revolution or, as a few have postulated, French models. Early in the Seven Years' War, the British government grew some of its battalions for deployment and asked the colonies to fill in the King's regiments stationed in America. It especially marked the three stationed in Nova Scotia and four in New York for an authorized strength of 1,000 men. Colonies such as New Jersey also raised 1,000-man regiments.[62] Hazen may also have considered the culturally distinct Highlander battalions. A more probable model, however, was that of the oversized Royal American Regiment (first designated the 62nd then 60th Regiment of Foot). That was also ethnically diverse and, unlike the typical British regiment during that war with one, sometimes two battalions, the Royal American fielded four battalions and counted more than 3,800 men at its greatest strength in 1758 (it had under 3,000 in 1757 and again in 1760 and thereafter).[63] Reduced to two battalions after that war, it expanded again to four in 1775.

Hazen was aware of the 60th's history and organization because of its recruiting in the colonies and through his interactions with other British officers in Canada and perhaps in New York. On 28 April 1760, Hazen's company of rangers had served on the left flank at the Battle of Sainte-Foy (Quebec) while the 2nd Battalion Royal Americans served on right. And although his lieutenancy in the 44th came in 1761, fellow officers may have told him of earlier actions, as around Ticonderoga in 1758, in which elements of the 44th and 60th both served. He had also been an associate in the Saint John River Society, a land company founded in Montreal in 1764 to claim and organize lands in New Brunswick. Among the society's members were General Frederick Haldimand and other, more junior members of the 60th. Also, although it is doubtful that they remained friends after dissolving their business ties in 1770, his former seigneury partner, Lieutenant Colonel Gabriel Christie, formerly of the 48th Regiment, was appointed to the 60th in 1773.[64]

Who precisely proposed the organization of the 2nd Canadian remains a question. If not Hazen, it could have been Antill when he reported to Congress and recommended Hazen for command in January 1776. Twenty years earlier, Antill's father, as a New Jersey councilman, had been involved in transportation and provisioning issues for the Royal American.[65] Like Hazen and Antill, many of the delegates in Congress would have been aware of the 60th's colonial service in the previous war when they authorized the 2nd Canadian.

The Royal American Regiment had been born out of Britain's need to bolster its forces in America after Major General Edward Braddock's 1755 defeat in the backwoods of Pennsylvania. The Swiss-born James Prevost, who had held the rank of major in the Dutch service, saw an opportunity for advancement in America. He proposed creating a corps of two battalions with close to two thousand men composed of foreign Protestants and German immigrants within the colonies. The corps, or legion, would serve only in America. Wary of such a foreign military unit, some privy councilors proposed recruiting a thousand Anglo-Americans to add to the mix, and that foreign (transnational) officers would hold no more than half of the command positions. After more negotiations, another thousand was added to the regiment's establishment (based on the precedent of Virginia's Lieutenant Governor Colonel William

Gooch's 43rd Regiment of Foot, which served in the Cartagena expedition in 1740–41 and in which Washington's brother Lawrence had served as a captain).[66] Furthermore, German-speaking immigrant enlistees in the Royal American had to swear allegiance and become naturalized subjects or denizens of Britain.[67] Many of the men were recruited and billeted in Pennsylvania before the battalions served in expeditions and at posts from the West Indies to Quebec and Montreal.[68] Some, like other veterans, then followed their military service by settling in newly available areas. The officers and men, including the Scot Arthur St. Clair, who became a major landowner in Pennsylvania's backcountry and accepted a colonelcy in the Continental Army that had him in Canada in early 1776,[69] extended the empire's frontiers as they served in the multicultural, "borderland" regiment. The Royal American precedent in terms of organization, "foreign" soldiers, and ties between service and naturalization was thus well established in memories and men from Canada to Philadelphia.

That precedent alone would not, however, have justified the creation of Hazen's Regiment. Recruiting Canada and Canadians was the big issue—both symbolically and for the manpower. Canadian units bolstered the congressional contention that invasion was an act of liberation.[70] The units showed that Canadians, both old and new subjects, were accepting the invitation to incorporation. More particularly, enlisting Canadian regiments into the Continental cause dovetailed with the desires of both Congress and its army not to retreat—and then when retreat was necessary, to return. Hazen promoted that return as he promoted his regiment over the following years.

In the meantime, he and Antill had to man the regiment. A different organization did not mean that they had an entirely free hand in commissioning and enlisting its members. First of all, "the appointment of the majors, captains, and subalterns [lieutenants and ensigns] and staff-officers" was "left to the commander in chief in Canada, with the advice of the general officers in that country," as well the recommendations of Hazen, Antill, and Price. That chief was Schuyler, the commander of the New York Department (soon redesignated the Northern Department), who had charge of the army in Canada until the new Canadian Department commander could formally take charge, which Major General John Thomas did when he relieved Wooster on 2 May at Quebec. When Thomas died of smallpox a month later, the duty devolved onto Brigadier General John Sullivan.[71]

The commander of the forces in and for Canada had not only the power of appointment but also of issuing commissions. In theory, and generally in practice, colonial committees or councils made appointments that they sent to Congress, which on its own determination or the recommendations of the Committee on Qualifications then issued commissions. But in reaction to the bad news from Canada, Congress ordered its president, John Hancock, to send blank commissions to General Schuyler for "the field officers, captains, and subalterns, who are to command the battalions ordered to be raised for Canada, in New Hampshire, and Connecticut." Schuyler could fill in the names of those he deemed suitable and who were judged "proper" by New Hampshire's committee of safety and Connecticut's governor and council. Congress warned that such an expedient, however, was not to be made into a precedent for future skirting around Congress's command and control.[72]

When Hancock sent on Congress's resolutions and commission forms, he seemed to broaden the directive—or open a loophole. He did not mention the civil authorities when he wrote to Schuyler to fill in the commissions with those he saw fit, and furthermore, Schuyler was to find "the most accomplished and suitable Men for the Canadian Regiments, and such as have an Influence in that Country and are best attached to our Cause."[73] As there was no Canadian council or committee of safety , Congress and its president both assumed and delegated more authority in saying that the departmental commander, with just the advice of subordinate officers, could not only appoint but even commission officers in and for Canada. Two of those subordinates, Hazen and Antill, reported to Schuyler on 1 February, with the latter carrying the congressional resolves and commissions.[74]

Schuyler, in turn, appears to have delegated the authority to Wooster at Montreal, and then Wooster, being unfamiliar with "the People and Language of the Country, [and] having no one there of his Acquaintance to recommend," entrusted Hazen and Antill with the power.[75] Such discretion did face civil limits. When the congressional commissioners to Canada arrived, they had the power to suspend commissions.[76] Another possible check was when Congress resolved that it would confirm commissions granted by Sullivan if General Horatio Gates and the other general officers in Canada thought them conducive to "public service."[77] After the retreat, the demise of the Canadian Department, and Congress's reauthorization of the regiment, Hazen and Antill usually sent their recommendations directly to Congress.

Commissioning officers was essential to enlisting soldiers. Although Hazen and Antill did enlist soldiers, commonly commanders handed out enlistment papers to junior officers, or would-be officers, who then fanned out to recruit. Yet few men seeking commissions flocked to the new regiment's colonels in those initial icy months. One may have been the James Glenny who supported Hazen's Saint-Jean loss claims, but if so, he did not remain long. Another was a "Mr. Brandimour," namely Jean Ménard *dit* Brindamour, who had led men into Ethan Allen's partisan corps the previous fall and who promised the same to Hazen. Although Hazen advanced the partisan both the benefit of the doubt and the funds to fulfill his promises, he assured the complaining Antill that Brindamour would only "have his Commission as soon as his Company is full." That was Hazen's "rule."[78]

Whether or not they met the rule—generally not—Hazen commissioned other candidates, such as one "Duval" as an ensign, whom he considered promoting and making his clerk in early April.[79] Many of the candidates, like the senior field officers, showed a willingness to cross borders. French-born Philippe Liébert (b. 1733) was a resident of Quebec by 1761, when he married there. A woodcarver who worked primarily for churches, Liébert accepted a captain's commission in February and started raising men for his company primarily at his own expense (which may be among the reasons he later sued Hazen for recompense). Alexandre Ferriole too was likely born in France but was in Montreal by 1761 when he married there. Ferriole was either an ensign or volunteer when he enlisted men into the regiment in February 1776. Pierre Ayotte joined the regiment that month and ably recruited and commanded a company in the months before the retreat. Clément Gosselin had been born at Isle d'Orléans, Quebec, in 1747, and had farmed in Ste. Anne de la Pocatière Parish south of the St. Lawrence before he became a provocateur poking at British governance. His father in law, Germain Dionne, had been born in that parish in 1731. Although both accepted commissions in Hazen's regiment in March, Gosselin as a captain and Dionne as a lieutenant, the two temporarily remained behind when the army retreated, probably gathering information and encouraging dissent. Laurent Olivie, a native of Quebec, joined as a captain in those first months, whereas Murdock McPherson may have been an Anglo transplant to Canada before accepting an ensign's commission that February. And then there was Udny Hay, a Scots-born Quebec timber merchant who cast his lot with the Americans. Hazen dangled a future majority in front of Hay as he made him a captain and asked him to recruit.[80]

Washington had addressed the new army's enlistment procedures in his orders of 12 November 1775, and Congress echoed and added to them in January 1776 when it directed that colonels of its newly authorized battalions order their recruiting officers to go to "where they are best known, and have the greatest probability of success." Washington had also advised against enlisting those "suspected of being unfriendly to the Liberties of America, or any abandon'd vagabond to whom all Causes and Countries are equal and alike indifferent." Furthermore, he forbade enlisting "Negroes, Boys unable to bare Arms, nor old men unfit to endure the fatigues of the campaign," but in January Congress revised that to an admonition to "inlist none but healthy, sound and able bodied men, and not under sixteen years of age."[81] When such a sound man agreed to serve for cause, country, or bounty money, the recruiting officer was to have him swear that he voluntarily enlisted "in the American continental army, for one year, unless sooner discharged: And . . . to conform, in all instances, to such rules and regulations, as are, or shall be, established for the government of the [said] Army."[82]

Hazen and his fellow recruiters administered the oath in French as well as in English, for at least a few volunteers signed or marked that they engaged "pour le service de l'armée du Continent" for "le terme d'une Année, de la date de nôtre Engagement" if not for the possibly shorter or lengthier period inferred by agreeing to serve during the present disorders unless sooner discharged. Notably the written pledge said nothing about obeying rules and regulations. Congress did, however, order the Articles of War translated into French and printed for distribution.[83] Hazen officially started raising the regiment at Montreal on 10 February when he issued a recruiting warrant proclaiming his appointment "par l'honnorable Congres du continent" and his authority "to organize a regiment of four battalions to act in conjunction with the Troops of the United Colonies for the Defence of their just Rights and privileges." He empowered the holder "to enlist by beat of Drum or otherwise all persons fit for service" and volunteering to serve for one year or "until the end of the present troubles."[84]

Antill set out to recruit near Quebec, while Hazen planned to journey in the country around Montreal to fill the ranks there. Hazen wrote to Hancock that he and Antill had "made a good beginning," and he hoped that he would soon report further success and "a friendly Disposition of the Canadians." He, however, also urged Congress to send a committee to meet with the Canadians, warmly assuring that it would be "a Party of pleasure to come to Canada at this season of the year." Then he slapped a reminder that he had agreed to Continental service with the condition that Congress recoup his losses.[85]

Confidence had turned to consternation by early March, when Hazen wrote to Antill that recruiting was slow in his zone and that he hoped Antill was doing better around Quebec. Hazen also spurred Antill to "be very active and diligent in this business. Lay aside the delicate Gentleman and put on the recruiting officer." He suggested that Antill divert some men from Duggan's recruiting officers, implying that Duggan's "elopement" from the area without Wooster's or Arnold's letters (and possibly without their leave) was ample justification.[86] Hazen did not like Duggan, and Duggan and his adherents returned the disfavor. As it turned out, Duggan, perhaps inspired by Hazen and Antill's example, had headed to Philadelphia. At the end of March, after a committee had conferred with Duggan and Colonel Rudolphus Ritzema, Congress ordered 1,000 dollars to Duggan for his services, commissioned him major commandant of a ranger unit, and permitted him to recommend his choices for captains and lieutenants to the commissioners in Canada, who could grant the commissions.[87] Hazen, Antill, and the other recruiters may have netted only 150 men by the end of February.[88] Ferriole claimed to have recruited at least 45 of them. Another February roster listed 61 soldiers, two lieutenants (Antoine Duprie and François Guilmat), and Olivie as captain.[89] During March, while Duggan was away, the colonels may have chivied some of his troops into their regiment, but 123 still were designated as Duggan's at the end of that month. By 1 April, Hazen admitted that he had only about 250 men. He figured that Livingston's Regiment had about 200.[90] Hazen, who at that time also had charge of Montreal, was downhearted but still determined to effect changes—and that meant getting Schuyler and Congress to move.

When Wooster rode off to oversee operations around Quebec, he put Hazen in command of Montreal and the troops there and in the vicinity. Hazen took charge by reporting to Schuyler his "own ideas of the whole country, and affairs in general," and he gave Schuyler permission to pass on his remarks, if he deemed worthwhile, to Congress. If, on the other hand, Hazen had exceeded his authority, he asked Schuyler to excuse it as evidence of his zealous regard for the cause. Hazen did not mince words as he blamed Continentals and the Catholic clergy for the change in the once "friendly disposition of the *Canadians*." Officers and troops had "ill used" inhabitants in demanding, even dragooning, supplies and labor without proper payment. It did not help matters that "neither order nor subordination prevails, and of course shortly no soldiers," for Hazen believed that "neither art, craft, nor money, will prevail on many of them to reinlist to serve in *Canada*." And if Continentals would not reenlist to secure Canada, then why should Canadians join? He again pushed for "able Generals, a respectable Army, a Committee of Congress, a suitable supply of hard cash, a printer, &C." Damn it, sir, he surely sputtered, the Canadians have turned, the Indians may soon fall on the frontiers, and "we have brought about ourselves, by mismanagement, what Governour Carleton himself could never effect."[91]

Schuyler did send the report, and on behalf of Congress Hancock thanked Hazen and wrote that the commanding officer in Canada was to "punish severely every Violation" of military discipline and the politically incorrect "Acts of Insinuation & Address."[92] Hazen had not waited for Congress's approbation, or for the committee it had already dispatched. He was already trying to counter growing disintegration and hostilities by calling for meetings with Native nations and by parrying priestly orders. Whereas Governor Carleton worried that Bishop Briand and the Catholic clergy did not have enough influence on their parishioners' political ideas and military activities, Hazen and other Continental commanders—and congressmen—worried about the reverse. John Adams approved of the Reverend John Carroll accompanying the commission to Canada, thinking that among other things, he could baptize the children and "bestow Absolution upon Such as have been refused it by the toryfied Priests."[93] Hazen acted on a similar sentiment before Carroll arrived, aided in part by the Jesuit priest Pierre-René Floquet, who gave his troops "Absolution when every other Priest in the Country refused." Colonel Livingston also managed to hold on to some of his troops, possibly due to the assistance of his regiment's chaplain, the Abbé Louis de Lotbinière, although this "priest of Canada and chaplain of the united States" who had agitated against Briand and the British was under interdict and not supposed to perform the sacraments.[94] By having priests affiliated with their units, Hazen and Livingston accommodated their Catholic soldiers and retaliated against the interdiction and excommunication that Bishop Briand threatened—an ironic act given historical relations—to all who did not remain loyal to the British government and, by extension, to the Roman Catholic Church.

The Canadians' faith—both religious and revolutionary—and perseverance were further tested when the siege of Quebec failed and the army retreated south. Neither Floquet nor Lotbinière stayed with the regiments, nor did other Catholic chaplains replace them. Religious concerns, property and family issues, and disenchantment with Congress's promises weighed on the Canadian Continentals as they decided whether to remain in Canada or with the army. They were taking a chance either way, for they could only pray for pardon if they remained or for succor and eventual success if they went. Eventual was the key word, for success was anything but immediate.

Retreat

Whatever remaining optimism there had been about a Canada in arms for the Continental cause was quenched by the reports of the commissioners who arrived at Montreal at the end of April and saw the beginning of the retreat at the end of May. The commissioners confirmed what others had already reported. Officers commandeering property and the lack of money to pay for services and goods had led the people there "to consider the Congress as bankrupt and their cause as desperate." Furthermore, the officials concluded, unless and until funds arrived, "it seems improper to propose the federal union of this Province with the others, as the few friends we have here, will scarce venture to exert themselves in promoting it, till they see our credit recoverd, & a sufficient army arrived to secure the possession of the Country." The commissioners warned Congress, "Our Enemies take the advantage of this Distress, to make Us look contemptible in the Eyes of the Canadians." British pressure and American misconduct had changed "their good Dispositions toward Us into Enmity." They pointedly reminded Congress, if "the powerful British Nation cannot keep an Army in a Country where the Inhabitants are become Enemies," then surely the delegates understood the analogous necessity "to make this People our Friends." The commissioners heard that the common people were still inclined to side with the revolutionaries, but they had to conclude that "no assistance can be expected from them, unless they find themselves supported by an army able to cope with the English forces."[95]

Changes and disputes among the expedition's leaders in addition to the plagues of pox and logistics failures weakened the American forces in the face of increasing British strength. In mid-April, shortly after Wooster took command at Quebec, Arnold rode off for Montreal, where he relieved Hazen of command and soon welcomed Congress's commissioners. Before Arnold had arrived, and on hearing of his old Saint-Jean escort Lorimier's escapades recruiting Indian allies, Hazen sent Colonel Timothy Bedel with a detachment to establish a fort at Les Cèdres (The Cedars) to guard approaches there. Hazen, in turn, had Wooster's orders to march to Quebec with his regiment, which was probably, given detachments to other places and duties, but a "handful of men." Hazen worried that he would lose more soldiers on the march as Brindamour had a few weeks earlier, when nine of his twenty-two had deserted on the way to Quebec.[96]

Hazen soon lost men, but in action and on retreat, not on a march to Quebec. Arnold, with the concurrence of the commissioners (who may not have realized Arnold was countermanding Wooster), had Hazen replace Lieutenant Colonel Nathaniel Buel in command at Saint-Jean and Chambly, where he was to build defenses and possibly establish provision magazines. The reason was Hazen's command of the French language and influence over the people in that region.[97] Hazen did not have much time to exert influence, for British reinforcements were sailing up the St. Lawrence. They landed at Quebec on 6 May, sortied out against the Americans, who were already evacuating their sick, and pushed them into retreat by the 7th. General Thomas, who had taken command from Wooster, conferred with his subordinate commanders, including Antill (who wanted to take a stand at Quebec), and aimed to reorganize at the mouth of the Sorel (one of the names then for the Richelieu River) to hold the line there.[98] They held for about a month, but then the Continentals crossed the line and kept moving. Spurring them all the more were British and Indian actions at Les Cèdres.

On 12 May, Captain George Forster set out from Oswegatchie with light infantry soldiers of the British 8th Regiment of Foot. Two days later, at St. Regis, Lorimier joined them with Indian warriors. Others followed, so that by 18 May Forster's force included over two hundred Native Americans. By that point, Bedel had transferred command to Major Isaac Butterfield and was off to warn Montreal. Arnold sent reinforcements with Major Henry Sherburne, but Butterfield did not stand fast; he surrendered before Sherburne could arrive. That allowed Forster to send Lorimier with some warriors and Canadian volunteers to intercept Sherburne's force on the 20th. Between that successful ambush and the short siege at Les Cèdres, the Continental forces suffered casualties, and had over 480 men taken prisoner by the British forces and their Native American allies, with the latter denounced for mistreating the prisoners and killing some of the wounded.[99]

Arnold issued out to meet the foes, and Forster advanced to the challenge. They skirmished, but various factors, including the arrival of the 1st Pennsylvania Battalion at the scene on 25 May, made Forster decide that disengagement was the better part of valor. Arnold, however, continued to press until Forster's forces repulsed his attempt to land troops near Quinze Chiens (Vaudreuil). Then, at a council of war on the 26th, some of Arnold's officers argued against attacking into the night just as Forster, worried about his allies attacking the prisoners, proposed an exchange. The greater part of the prisoner exchange occurred on 27 May, with most of the remainder on 30 May after Arnold was back in Montreal and Forster in Oswegatchie.[100] It was not a happy ending, however. Arnold was angry at Hazen for arguing so forcefully against continuing the operation; Congress in turn angrily repudiated Arnold's agreement to exchange and threatened to treat enemy prisoners the way the British had allowed the Indians to treat those at The Cedars; and Hazen was furious that the Canadians from his regiment were not included in the exchange.[101]

The colonel still flamed fury when he provided a history of Congress's promises and the regiment's service in his 1778 case for the regiment's continuance. Hazen fumed that many of the officers and men believed themselves "Ill-used by a partial Agreement in the Exchange of Prisoners taken at the Cedars; at which a Subaltern Officer and sixteen Men . . . who had the Misfortune to be made Prisoners with the other Troops, in the same Service, and excluded in the Agreement for the Exchange" were left "a Sacrifice to the Vengence of a cruel Enemy."[102] Major Butterfield had testified in 1776 that the Canadians taken included nine soldiers put in irons and one lieutenant put under guard. He said that Forster refused to exchange them because they could "be treated as deserters from the King's troops by their taking up arms against their own military laws and Government."[103]

Hazen did not name the officer or soldiers taken at Les Cèdres. Was the officer Brindamour? Possibly, but he had been angling for a captain's commission and a subaltern ranked below captain. Nonetheless, he disappeared from Hazen's correspondence after April and never appeared on the unit's rolls. David Dill Fellows had been captured and mistreated by the Native Americans at The Cedars, but at that time he was an ensign in Colonel Charles Burrall's Connecticut State Regiment; he accepted a commission in the 2nd Canadian later that year in November.[104] Perhaps it was the Ensign or Lieutenant Duval, whom Hazen said he commissioned earlier, but like Brindamour, his name does not appear on the regiment's rolls. Did Hazen mean Antoine Duprie (Dupuir) or Pierre du Calvet? On 10 August, Congress's committee on "sundry Canadian petitioners" recommended that the latter be awarded eight months' ensign's pay and be brevetted a lieutenant, but it did not say why. That same committee recommended that John Hamtramck be paid for his work as a deputy commissary from 15 September 1775 to 5 February 1776 and then as a captain from 5 February to that day. In his petition for restitution, Hamtramck protested against how Hazen had commandeered him and the soldiers he had been raising to join Duggan's troops. Furthermore, Hazen made him a lieutenant rather than a captain, as Duggan had offered, so Hazen was probably referring to Hamtramck and his men.[105] The regiment's records for this period are as dismembered as Hazen said the unit was that spring.

Hazen declared that the regiment's officers, "chiefly" at their own expense, had "inlisted, armed, accoutered, and clothed" 477 men in those early months of 1776, and that those men had served at "the Siege or Blockade of Quebec, Garrisons of Montreal, Chamblie[,] St. Johns and the Cedars; as also a Detachment, sent down the River sixty Leagues below Quebec [possibly referring to Antill surveying Deschambault] on public Service."[106] The regiment was thus in a dismembered state with detachments assigned to various posts as the retreat began. Furthermore, its commanding officers were riding out and writing on various additional duties and disputes.

Congress's commissioners appointed Antill to the additional duty of adjutant general for the forces in Canada by 27 May after Brigadier General William Thompson and Colonel Arthur St. Clair complained about General Thomas's appointee and Arnold provided a recommendation. The commissioners admitted that they were not "proper judges of [Antill's] abilities and fitness for that station," but they understood that "it requires a gentleman of great activity and abilities."[107] Arnold, in turn, soon had Antill counting troops at St. Johns and Chambly. By 13 June, Antill reported to Sullivan that he had done his "utmost," but was "not yet finished, owing to the scattered situation of our men, for twenty miles in length." He tallied about 1,500 at St. Johns and more than 1,200 at Chambly, but few were "fit for duty." Antill also bemoaned the loss of Deschambault, which he said signaled the loss of Quebec province, and conceded that "prudent retreat" was the only option until the Continental forces could better face the British on Lake Champlain.[108]

While Hazen was with Arnold chasing Forster, General Thomas ordered Colonel Elisha Porter to take command at Chambly on 25 May. Three days later, Porter delivered the command to the Baron Frederick William de Woedtke, whom Congress had commissioned a brigadier general. On the 29th, Wooster, Arnold, and several other officers, Hazen included, arrived back at Chambly, as did the remaining commissioners. After General Thompson appeared the next day, Wooster presided over a council of war. The commissioners, generals, and field officers reviewed "present circumstances" and discussed what was "practicable." That meant making provisions for "an orderly retreat" while resolving to hold "the country between the St. Lawrence and Sorel," but only "if possible."[109]

The possible became the impossible. On 2 June at Chambly, General Thomas died and General Sullivan took command of a disintegrating army. Initially, Sullivan thought that he could turn things around, especially as he said Canadians were "flocking" to serve and supply.[110] Unfortunately such support rapidly disappeared, as did troop strength. When Captain James Wilkinson, whom Arnold had just made an aide-de-camp, rode into Chambly to report the enemy's movements and request cover for Arnold's retreating troops, he found troops "overwhelmed with fatigue . . . scattered in disorder over the plain, and buried in sleep, without a single sentinel" on watch. In turn, Sullivan and Colonels William Maxwell, St. Clair, and Hazen were "astonished" at his report of the enemy's proximity to Montreal. They decided to send Wilkinson to Woedtke, who was commanding the rear. Likely cursing Hazen's directions after going astray in the darkness, Wilkinson found Colonel Anthony Wayne who, dismissing Woedtke as drunk, assembled and marched the reinforcements. But Arnold had effected the escape of his troops to St. Johns, where the rest of the troops soon joined him by 17 June—that is, all of the troops except those under General Thompson who had been killed or taken prisoner at the 8 June Battle of Trois-Rivières, which served as another vigorous boot to the Americans' behind.[111]

On the morning of 18 June, generals and field officers in a council of war resolved to "retire to Crown Point." The troops burned Saint-Jean, as they had Chambly, boarded overloaded bateaux, and pushed off to the Isle Aux Noix on the Richelieu River.[112] Sullivan lamented, "By a strange reverse of fortune we are driven to the sad necessity of abandoning Canada." He mourned a dispirited army almost "lifeless" from "small-pox, famine and disorder." After Les Cèdres, there had been panic among officers and soldiers with, he believed, no fewer than forty officers begging "to resign their commissions upon the most trivial pretences, and this even extended to Field Officers." He said that there had been almost unanimity in the council's decision to quit the ground. Arnold had not been at the council, but he delivered Sullivan's report along with his own and letters from Hazen and Antill when he reported to Schuyler at Albany on 25 June.[113]

Eleven miles south of Saint-Jean, the Isle Aux Noix was a filthy, miserable rest stop for the defeated and dying as they awaited more transports to continue a dozen miles down the Richelieu River and cross the border into New York and Lake Champlain.[114] Among those Continentals were hundreds of Canadians, but certainly not the number that Sullivan had imagined or Hazen had reported earlier, nor were they all troops; they included refugees, not only men but also women and children.

As Hazen later told Congress, because the regiment was raised solely for the defense of Canada, and its members "seeing themselves neglected in Point of pay; and Ill-used by a General Officer while on their own Ground, some of the Officers and Men had not Fortitude enough to abandon their Country, forsake their Wives, Children, Relations, Friends, and Estates, consequently resolved to throw themselves at the Feet and implore the Mercy of a humane Governor." Hazen particularly blamed Arnold for the antagonism to his regiment that led "several Officers, and a considerable Part of the Men he had inlisted, in Canada, leaving their Colonel and the Regiment in a Day of Distress."[115] The retreat was marked by an escalating feud between the two touchy, combative officers, a fight that led to a court martial on the other side of the border. In the meantime, however, Hazen and his remaining officers had to oversee the retreat of whatever troops continued on with them on 18 June, and evacuate families and other refugees.

Having lost their homes, Hazen's wife and Antill's family either joined the initial evacuation or removed over alternate routes as did other refugees during the coming months.[116] Among the immediate evacuees was Theotist Paulint, her son, and daughters. Her family was living in St. Denis Parish, Madame Paulint remembered decades later, "when the war began between the Colonies & Canada & the American army entered Canada." That fall, her husband had joined the American forces "and went to Quebec and remained there through the winter & did not return till the next spring after, when he returned home he remained but a few days and then took his family me his wife & four children and abandoning his Land & house & buildings & all his property he could not carry, went to St John where we embarked in a [bateaux] and went first to Crown Point and then to Albany." Nine years earlier, in January 1767, Theotist at seventeen had married Antoine, then thirty or thirty-three, at St. Antoine Parish on the River Richelieu in the district of Montreal.[117] Born in France,

Antoine Paulint had arrived in Canada while serving in the French army during the Seven Years' War. He stayed after the war, but apparently never quite settled under the new British regime. He gambled family, property, and livelihood by supporting the rebellion and becoming a captain of an independent company of Canadian volunteers in November 1775. His company may have been attached to Hazen's regiment by February 1776, but Paulint's regimental commission as captain came later.[118]

Antoine Paulint's commission, like so much else, awaited confirmation that the regiment, army, and revolution continued. Congress, states, and generals soon confirmed the latter. Meanwhile, Paulint and the other remaining officers, soldiers, and refugees with Hazen's regiment faced boundaries both physical and mental to rebuild the ruins of the regiment into the new 2nd Canadian of the Army of the United States—but first Hazen had to deal with Arnold and Congress.

CHAPTER 3

CANADIAN TO CONTINENTAL

The first of the Continental Army's retreating companies reached Crown Point on 1 July 1776.[1] Over the following days commanders, soldiers, and refugees buried their dead as Congress birthed a new nation. As Thomas Jefferson and his fellow delegates midwifed the Declaration of Independence, they knew things were dire in Canada, but they still hoped that they could reinforce the army there. A week after the commanders in Canada resolved to abandon Saint-Jean and retire to Crown Point—and on the same day, 25 June, that Benedict Arnold delivered John Sullivan's report to Philip Schuyler at Albany—John Hancock, speaking for Congress, was still trying to prod colonies to deliver more support. "Remember," he said, "your own Safety, & the Security of Canada, are exactly one & the same Thing. If our Enemies are not opposed at a Distance, we must engage them in our Borders."[2]

The latter proved to be the case. Loss in and of Canada interrupted provincial traffic and reconfirmed a northern boundary between antagonistic peoples and governments. As much as some Americans had wanted—and continued to want—a softer border, the priority became guarding and securing it. In retreating, as it had in invading, the Continental Army pushed and pulled at what territory was Britain's and what the Americans could claim. Trails, sails, settlements, and encampments designated those borderlands—regions and regiments encompassing communities imagined and manifest, civilian and military—that had become part of a wartime frontier. And soldiers as sentries patrolled the borders between countries and camps.

Those sentries included hundreds who had to dissolve ties and abandon property in Canada. They did so unhappily and often incompletely: although some brought family with them, many left relations behind. Most, if not all, still hoped that they would eventually recross and erase the border that they were now to defend and define. Meanwhile, they had to survive the separation. Not all did in the immediate or longer terms. Sergeant James Robinson, also called Robinet, of Philippe Liébert's company, died that July, leaving his French-Canadian wife a widow with daughters Polly and Mary Therese (Sally). Decades later, Polly remembered that she "was about thirteen years old when I was brought out of Canada with my fathers family in the year 1776." She believed that her father had been "a Sergeant major in Hazen's regiment, & he died at Crown Point on the retreat from Canada." Her sister Sally had been seven or eight at the time. The forlorn followers did not return to Canada as the mother eventually married François Guilmat (an ensign and later lieutenant in Laurent Olivie's company), and by war's end the two girls had married other refugees, Peter and John Chartier, respectively, who had volunteered with General Montgomery's troops, retreated with the American forces, and finally enlisted in Hazen's regiment at Albany.[3]

Separation from Canada did not equate to immediate independency for the refugees. In fact, if they did not want to return to Canada and beg pardon from Governor Carleton, they were even more dependent on the army—and congressional action—than other soldiers for sustenance, shelter, and fellowship in return for service. Such Canadians and the volunteers who joined them later had to be Continentals, whether or not Americans, championing Congress's declarations. Their retreat was migration, and soldiering a form of settling, at least in the near term. The Continental Army sustained them as they served in it, and if the revolution were ultimately successful, not only national independence but also individual independency might follow. First, however, there was the matter of resuscitating the remaining northern forces encamped along Lake Champlain. Second, those forces, like the entire army, had to be reconstituted. The attempt to add to and strengthen the United Colonies had failed, but now the army's mission was to secure the United States. That mission required that the army keep and attract officers who would accept the challenge of raising troops in the midst of adversity. Moses Hazen, for his part, defined those national and army objectives in regimental and individual terms.

Disorder

Colonels Hazen and Antill contemplated personal ruin as they counted the remains of their regiment at Crown Point. They, like Arnold's aide James Wilkinson, saw diseased, enervated, yet troublesome combatants. A disgusted Colonel Elisha Porter recorded a mutiny in a Captain Bernard Romane's (Romans's) Pennsylvania artillery company on 3 July. The physician Lewis Beebe, already exasperated about cursing in the corpse tent, did not call it a mutiny, but huffed about soldiers releasing confined troublemaking compatriots by pulling down the guardhouse. The next day, 4 July 1776, Beebe criticized the generals—who could only have been Sullivan and Woedtke that day—"prancing their Gay horses" around camp while the field officers attended courts-martial, the captains and subalterns visited grog shops, and the soldiers slept, swam, fished, or rendered duties with profanities. Some of those soldiers ended up before Porter, one of the field officers who endured a court that tried thirty-three prisoners. On the rainy evening of the 5th, Brigadier General Arnold, and Major Generals Schuyler and Horatio Gates arrived. Gates later wrote to Governor Jonathan Trumbull Sr. of Connecticut that when he first joined "the troops (or rather the Hospital) at *Crown Point*, all was in the utmost disorder—the pestilence raging, not a cannon mounted the vessels lumbered with stores, the men dispirited with defeat and fatigue, and, in short, the whole a scene variegated with every distress and disappointment that could conspire to ruin an army."⁴

General Gates had ridden north after Congress appointed him commander of the army in Canada. By the time he had reached Albany, that army was in bateaux steering south, but Gates then interpreted the orders to mean he had command of those forces in New York. That assumption, however, undermined General Schuyler's command of the Northern Department. Schuyler wrote to Washington that if Congress wanted Gates to "command the Northern Army wherever it might be," then it should have informed the departmental commander. Schuyler wanted the commander in chief to present his letter to Congress and have the matter clarified.⁵ He sent his protest through the chain of command in hopes that Washington would help him solidify his authority, and perhaps as a way to remind Congress to use that chain in turn. Congress actually had used it when it directed Washington to send Gates into Canada, but events had moved faster than communication. Once Congress received Schuyler's protest, it confirmed him as the superior commander, but its members sincerely hoped that the two generals would work together to ameliorate rather than add to the current misfortunes.⁶ The commanders needed to strengthen the forces of the Northern Department and confirm possession of the region.

Establishing commands—who had control where and over what—was essential for military cohesion and the civil-military coordination necessary to secure the frontier: in other words, to close the gate against the ministerial troops and their Native American allies after Continental forces retreated through it. The problem was determining the location of that gate. Schuyler assured Washington that both he and Gates were in agreement on the priority "to prevent the Enemy from penetrating into these Colonies."⁷ The other vital concern was assisting, if not fully protecting, the frontier inhabitants. When he led the retreat, General Sullivan tried to help some colonists move out of the danger zone and protect others by posting a guard at the Onion River (the Winooski flows into Lake Champlain on the Vermont side south of Valcour Island;

see map 1).[8] That, however, was not a defensive line. Many officers wanted to draw it at Crown Point, but the generals preferred to put it farther south.

The dispute added another layer to the wreckage of the Northern Army. On 7 July, Schuyler, Gates, Sullivan, Arnold, and Woedtke determined to move the sick to Fort George and the healthy to Ticonderoga and reinforce both sides of the lake there.[9] Most of the field officers protested, for they wanted to hold what had once been the French Fort St. Frederic as a means to secure Lake Champlain and its borderlands. In a remonstrance reminiscent of colonial petitions to imperial authorities, Colonel John Stark and other field officers informed Schuyler that they had participated in previous councils of war and complied with the orders coming out of them: from trying to hold on in Canada to retreating from it to Crown Point, where, they resolved, they would "make a stand against the Ministerial Army." Given, as General Schuyler told them, that Congress directed the force to maintain possession of the lakes, they questioned the order to remove to Ticonderoga. Just as colonists had declared allegiance to the Crown while resisting regulations, the officers assured Schuyler that they would neither disobey nor dictate what orders the generals should issue, but that they thought Crown Point was the most appropriate spot from which to control the northern lakes. If the army quit the post, the enemy would take it; if the enemy held the point, it would destroy lines of communication and make it easier for ministerial troops to invade New England and the "frontiers of *New York*," and for Indians to attack settlements. Retreating to Ticonderoga would spur "hundreds of families" to quit their farms and "drive them upon other towns," where they would have to subsist the refugees instead of supporting soldiers in public service. Finally, they added that Ticonderoga was "unhealthy" ground. Twenty-one of the general's "most obedient humble servants" signed that remonstrance on 8 May, but neither Hazen nor Antill were among them.[10]

That did not mean that they agreed with the generals. Hazen did not hesitate to warn Congress later that year that Indian incursions might "depopulate" the frontiers. And if the Continentals manned only Ticonderoga, "that *American grave*," then British troops would move down, fortify Crown Point, control the lake, and have easy access to the countryside. In turn, disaffected inhabitants would have easy access to the enemy.[11]

Hazen and Antill, however, did join twenty-five other officers (of whom nineteen had also signed the protest) in an address to Brigadier General Sullivan thanking him for his service. Disturbed that Gates, recently promoted above him, had received command of the forces in—now out of—Canada, Sullivan was determined to ride to Congress and tender his resignation.[12] Ultimately, after he survived an examination about the defeat in Canada, Congress promoted him to major general. The field officers' address showed that they thought he deserved praise rather than criticism, command rather than replacement. He had "comforted, supported, and protected the shattered remains of a debilitated army, and with unwearied care . . . landed the publick stores . . . without almost the least diminution, safe at this place." They thanked him for preserving property and persons and praised his humanity and impartiality.[13] In commending Sullivan, they implied reservations about Gates. In Hazen's case, it was no implication if he knew that his foe Arnold was happy about Gates's appointment.[14] The observing Dr. Beebe did not care for most of the generals—their conduct that of "Villany, treason, & murder"—and he despised giving up the post as cruel abandonment of the inhabitants.[15]

The officers were right: removal did mean that the borderlands north of Ticonderoga, on both sides of the lake, were more vulnerable to penetration. That alarmed the provincials and authorities who feared what would happen if the army that had failed at offense failed at defense too and allowed the enemy to pass over the lake and deeper into the country. Inhabitants to the east of Lake Champlain sent Colonel Seth Warner and others to Schuyler to detail the threat and propose a solution. They asked Schuyler to authorize their raising a force, on Continental pay, for self-defense against the Indians. Schuyler, answering them and probably the officers' remonstrance, authorized six companies, contingent on Congress's approval, to prevent the locals from fleeing and "creating terror in the more southern inhabitants."[16]

Governor Trumbull of Connecticut outlined a cascade of problems if the borderlands were not secured as a buffer zone for the more settled colonies. There was the likelihood of Indian raids on the northern frontiers of New York and New Hampshire. Settlements in the Onion River area were already breaking up as their people left, for the people there could not defend themselves. Trumbull therefore asked Washington to recommend that Congress order a battalion be raised for defense there. In his view, supporting such a battalion not only would help secure the frontier but would be less of an expense on the affected colonies than that of supporting the refugees' families. Trumbull apologized for pressing Washington, but said that "the Anxiety of the Friends and Relations of many, if not most of those Settlers, who emigrated from this Colony, and the Importance of the matter" were weighing on him.[17] He followed that 4 July request two days later with a letter saying that he could not comply with Congress's directive to divert to the Northern Department the two Connecticut battalions already raised, and reiterated that it would be best to raise another battalion, preferably one with men who had already had smallpox.[18]

Washington was not happy with the decision to remove to Ticonderoga. He agreed with Trumbull that the retreat from Canada would alarm the frontier inhabitants and embolden enemies, but he answered with a tentative hope that incursions would be prevented or repelled. Washington could send only hope, for he could not send troops: he needed them to defend the approaches to New York City. Washington did not, however, minimize his concerns to Gates. He viewed the situation the same way the field officers did: that retreat to Ticonderoga equated to relinquishment of the northern lakes. The enemy could then also press further into New England. What prevented him from countermanding the evacuation order was his "fear of creating dissensions and encouraging a spirit of remonstrating against the conduct of superior officers by inferiors."[19] Washington disagreed with the resolution of the northern generals, but he was not going to belabor the point while he had the enemy before him.

In the meantime, the Northern Army continued to deal with enemies within its borders as it prepared to face those behind and around it. Officers continued to jab at each other as they tried to avoid being trampled by the horsemen of the apocalypse: conquest, war, famine, and death. They redirected their fears and frustrations into anger and blame against each other.

Brigadier General Woedtke, the young former Prussian officer depicted by Father John Carroll as laughably awkward when the general accompanied the commissioners north, had come to dislike and distrust Antill. In early July, Woedtke described the lieutenant colonel with a poisonous pen. Granted, Woedtke complained about much more too, but it is notable that he took the time and trouble to single out Antill. One possibility is that Sullivan had taken Antill's advice over his own. (Antill was acting as adjutant general, not aide-de-camp as Woedtke wrote.) Another, given that he also condemned Colonel John Philip de Haas as the greatest Tory in the army, suggests that Woedtke may have been taking sides in the Arnold-Hazen split and inferring that Antill was a Tory too. Woedtke whined to Benjamin Franklin that Antill meddled in engineering matters though he lacked both appropriate knowledge and experience, but also insinuated that Antill had influence because the general—apparently Sullivan, although Woedtke did not name him—was a close friend of Antill's wife. The slurs never became formal charges as Woedtke succumbed to illness by the end of July.[20] As Dr. Beebe observed, "dysentery, Jaundice, Putrid, intermitting, & Billious fevers, were the principal diseases that attended the troops, which proved fatal in a variety of instances."[21] Any of those could have carried off Woedtke.

Hazen surely wished that one of them had felled Arnold, and Arnold probably returned the sentiment. Woedtke's condemnation of Antill was small stuff compared with the fight between Arnold and Hazen. The opening rounds had been at Fort Anne after the Quinze Chiens argument and at Chambly over goods confiscated by Arnold that Hazen deemed plunder and refused to accept or protect. After the general criticized the colonel and commanded him to gather what was left of the goods as they prepared for the retreat, Hazen complied but wrote Sullivan demanding a court of inquiry or court-martial to defend his actions.[22] Arnold made the next move after the other generals left Crown Point and he was in charge of its evacuation. On 9 July, he had Hazen, along with Colonel de Haas and some captains, arrested. Beebe did not know the charges, but this ally of the Allen family (including Ethan) in Vermont figured Arnold was the problem and thought someone should "make the sun shine" through Arnold's head with an "ounce ball."[23]

Colonel Enoch Poor convened the court judging the charges between the two combative officers on 31 July at Ticonderoga. Before it met, Hazen, who while under arrest could not superintend his regiment's remnants at Albany, complained about the court's composition as he continued to disparage Arnold. His target, in turn, focused more on creating a fleet for operations on the lake.[24] The acrimony between the combatants enveloped the court by the next day when it first questioned and then refused to accept evidence from a key witness for Arnold, saying that this Major Scott had a personal stake in the trial. Hazen added insult to injury by using the trial to denigrate Arnold further. Arnold then insulted the court as he scorned the proceedings. The court in turn found him in contempt, and then cleared Hazen and wrote Gates of its desire to obtain satisfaction by arresting and trying Arnold.[25]

General Gates took a middle course by accepting the court's verdict on Hazen's actions but dissolving it before it could proceed against Arnold. That did not end the matter, however, for both Arnold and the court's members appealed.[26] Gates then defended his actions and made recommendations to Congress, while Hazen later filed his own charges against Arnold. As Gates wrote to Hancock on 2 September, "I am convinced if there was a fault on one side, there was too much acrimony on the other."[27] Both descriptions fit all three of the actors—Arnold, Hazen, and court. Congress thought the court's resolution to uphold its standing and honor in the face of Arnold's ill behavior understandable, but it approved of how Gates ended the contest.[28]

Hazen was not finished battling Arnold, however. He charged that Arnold had cast aspersions on his character over actions in Canada, and by the end of the year, a court of inquiry agreed with him but took the issue no further. And yet perhaps Hazen did taste revenge, for the battles with him and other "artists of calumny" had a toll on Arnold professionally.[29] Arnold was often his own worst enemy, but others pricked and prodded at his weaknesses for their own ends.

It was little wonder that Arnold and Hazen clashed, for Hazen also was excessively combative in his personal and professional ambitions. Hazen too never achieved the rank, recognition, or financial rewards that he thought he deserved.[30] That was due in part to controversial actions—not just against Arnold but also others—that affected his reputation. When he asked for compensation for his lost property, the first congressional committee looking into it found that he overrated much of his losses. He charged Congress for what was destroyed by ministerial troops as well as by American forces and asked for reimbursement on what was conjectural—what his mills might have made in the year—not just direct loss. The result was that the congressional commissioners that spring, as if they did not have enough to do, had to appoint persons to examine Hazen's property against his claims.[31] And Jeremiah Duggan continued to fume about how Hazen had undercut his reputation and aspirations, while other refugees complained about his harsh interference as they tried to move their property in the retreat. Hazen's actions led William Haywood from Montreal to intimate that he was actually "unfriendly" to the cause. Although their own behavior on the retreat may have been questionable, refugee accusations did lead Congress, just a day before the Ticonderoga trial commenced, to ask that Schuyler check whether Hazen had mistreated some Canadians at Chambly in the midst of the evacuation.[32]

In reporting on the Ticonderoga trial's disputants and contentions, Gates said that he had not received word of the other charge against Hazen until after he had sent him on to Albany, but that he figured Schuyler would see to the issue.[33] Schuyler wrote that there would be an inquiry, but there is no evidence of a formal hearing.[34] Silence may have reflected doubt as to whether Hazen still had a regiment and would thereby retain his position. As Woedtke had observed before he expired, the 2nd Canadian Regiment barely existed in July 1776.[35]

As the remains of the Northern Army removed from Crown Point to Ticonderoga and Albany, Washington's Main Army at Manhattan and Long Island kept watch against British forces on Staten Island, and Major General Charles Lee's troops countered "the mercernary Instruments of the British Tyrant" at Sullivan's Island in South Carolina. Connecting the forces and actions besides their own dispatches and chain of command was Congress, but Lee, among other commanders, did not have a great regard for that body's military astuteness. Congress had censured his proposal to augment the cavalry to secure the southern provinces "on the principle that a Military Servant shoud not take the liberty to propose any thing." Lee accepted that principle if government was close and the enemy distant, but when it was the reverse, he thought it a general's duty to not only propose but also adopt measures necessary for the public's safety. He was therefore relieved (mistakenly) that Washington was at Philadelphia (he was actually in New York), for he thought that Congress's "Councils sometimes lack a little military elictricity."[36]

Lee's comments and actions, like those of his northern brethren in arms and political assemblies, show how peripheries—provinces and departments—were linked directly and indirectly "through a common center of power" and a common rhetoric not just of rights but also of threats and needs.[37] Congress confirmed its centrality through its orders, resolutions, and the Declaration of Independence, while the Continental Army's brigades and regiments substantiated its reach into the marchlands of the new United States and the territories they prized. Another center of power was obviously the commander in chief, who acted as the nexus between Congress and peripheries.

Refugees and Reformation

The Continental Congress quickened the Revolution as it declared independence, advised new domestic states, addressed old foreign ones, and with General Washington made plans for the Continental Army as the Army of the United States, complete with revised oaths, organizations, and Articles of War. The armed forces took note of the declared independence of the states and their full powers to levy war, conclude peace, and "do all other Acts and Things which Independent States may of right do" as they received word from Congress. Brigades posted in the vicinity of New York City huzzaed the Declaration on Tuesday, 9 July. The news hit Albany around the 12th, Crown Point on the 16th, and Ticonderoga likely close to the same time, but the latter did not officially celebrate until Sunday, 28 July, when after a worship service Colonel St. Clair read the declaration to the troops.[38] Then, after the cannonades, cheers, and quaffs, officers and soldiers went back to work reconstructing the forces needed to win the war for American independence and confirm the nation just declared.

As Schuyler concentrated on meeting with Native Americans among other departmental matters, Gates set to reconstituting the Northern Army. Both continued to hear from inhabitants "well attached to the *American* cause" who wanted protection,[39] but Gates focused on the probability of a British incursion rather than the certainty of Indian raids. One of his first actions was to reform the regiments at Ticonderoga into four brigades, with Arnold in command of the first. Yet brigade administration was not Arnold's first duty: constructing and deploying a fleet on Lake Champlain was. As Gates instructed Arnold on 7 August: "preventing the enemy's invasion of our country is the ultimate end." Gates, however, limited what Arnold could do in this "defensive war." Furthermore, Arnold was not to tell anyone of those restrictions. Gates hoped "that words occasionally dropped from you . . . may, together with all your motions, induce our own people to conclude it is our real intention to invade the enemy, which, after all, may happen."[40] Perhaps he believed that a little misdirection might raise spirits and a sense of security among soldiers, settlers, and possibly politicians.

Gates and Schuyler were still smarting from criticism not just from their subordinates but also from military officers and government officials elsewhere about the removal to Ticonderoga. Congress's critique of the "miscarriages" in Canada stung them further—especially Schuyler. Defending the new nation's northern borderland was tied, therefore, to defending their reputations. But should they concentrate on invasion routes down from St. John's or across by way of Fort Stanwix (renamed Fort Schuyler)? Schuyler was not sure, so he dispersed troops north and west and tried to build roads to better move men and supplies.[41]

Residual members of the Canadian regiments played minor roles in Schuyler's attempts to determine enemy plans and prepare defenses, and they do not appear to have done much for Gates. Neither of the Canadian regiments appeared in the Ticonderoga brigades, nor it seems did they send men into the Battle of Valcour Island with Arnold.[42] After initially remaining behind at the retreat, a few officers from Colonel Livingston's regiment made their way down through the American lines and provided reports to local officials at Prattsburgh (now Swanton), Vermont, and to Gates at Ticonderoga before being sent on to Albany. Besides reporting on numbers of troops and vessels, they reported on how officers who had served with or in Congress's forces—whether they were commissioned in the Canadian militia or held commissions from Congress—were forced to burn their commissions down to their fingertips.[43] British authorities also threatened imprisonment and confiscation of property, which the Canadian Continentals must have expected.

Humiliation and threats aside, the reality was that Governor Carleton offered clemency to the majority of the inhabitants who had assisted the Americans, especially if they could prove that they had been compelled to do so by the invaders or their collaborators. Accommodation and reconciliation fostered compliance if not fealty. American weakness and defeat, along with property, family, and faith, also led some wavering Canadians to choose compliance. Yet not all did. One reason was that Carleton was not so lenient with those who had openly acted in and for the rebellion by leading others into it—to wit, officers and provocateurs.[44] Most such rebels knew that they had gone too far to go back. Others chose not to equate retreat with total defeat.

Choice or no choice, the retreat presented the prospect that the territorial and military borderlands—namely the Richelieu/Champlain region and the Northern Army—threatened to become no man's lands for the Canadian Continentals; they had lost their homes in one and faced losing their place in the other. As not all members of the Canadian regiments had followed the army across the border, the members that remained in the gutted units grappled with the possibility of losing the military communities that were their refuge. More soldiers than officers peeled off from Hazen's regiment in the retreat, but a few officers did remain behind in Canada. After Antill appointed him a captain in February, Pierre Ayotte had raised a company that in early May was at Point Levi, across the St. Lawrence from Quebec. Only four of his soldiers joined the retreat, while the rest and their captain returned to their homes. Ayotte tried to conceal his presence, but the authorities found and imprisoned him for the rest of that year.[45] Captain Clément Gosselin and his father-in-law, Lieutenant Germain Dionne, also went into hiding as they continued to act for the rebellion covertly. They were eventually caught in late 1777 and imprisoned into 1778, after which they and Clément's brother Louis made their way south and joined the regiment at White Plains.[46]

Hazen and Antill had to leave with the Continental Army. As Antill later recounted, his strenuous support of the peoples' causes and complaints had made him "obnoxious" to the governor of Canada, leading to "ill Treatment and Imprisonments" even before he joined Montgomery and served as a volunteer at Quebec. During that "severe winters Campaign" he had "servd as Chief Engineer and till the August following as adjutant General to that Army," while also accepting appointment as lieutenant colonel of the regiment. He added, with perhaps a jab at Hazen or Duggan, that he had declined the command "from a diffidence of his own military Abilities having in View the service of his Country rather than the Agrandisement of his Rank and Emoluments." As Congress had established the regiment "to Encourage the Canadians to Enter into the service and attach them more firmly to the Cause of these States" and had promised them support and protection, he had exerted himself "to further the Common good." Unfortunately, the army was forced "to retire, and those in the Country who had been most Zealous and Active in the Cause" had then to abandon "all their Hopes, their possessions, Friends and Connections; and submit to their Fate." He and his family were "among the Unfortunate number."[47]

Other officers among that unfortunate number included Major Udny Hay, whom Hazen said he promoted at Crown Point, and Captains Philippe Liébert (who left his family in Canada) and Laurent Olivie. There were Lieutenants Antoine Duprie (Dupuir), Alexandre Ferriole, François Guilmat, and Ensign Murdock McPherson. Among the refugees who were already or soon affiliated with the 2nd Canadian Regiment were Antoine Paulint, Joseph Torrey, Francis Martin (François Martin-Pelland), Felix Victor (possibly Félix-Victoire Caseveuve), and Edward Chinn. Perhaps a hundred soldiers remained with those officers and other refugees that summer—fewer than half of those reported by Hazen in April, and not even a quarter of those he later claimed that he had enlisted that spring. Among them were Noel Belanger, Rene Gil-brand (Galbrun, Guilbrand), Thomas Lapierre, Lewis Lavoix (or Louis Lavois), and Claud Monty; recruited by Ferriole back in February, they all continued with the regiment into 1783.[48]

The Canadians had removed to Ticonderoga with the rest of the retreating forces, but they did not long remain there. By mid-July, some were at Albany or other posts such as Fort George. The ailing Woedtke had advised Gates to recall them to Ticonderoga, but on 21 July Gates instead ordered, "the Regiment of *Canadians*, with all the *Canadian* families, now at *Ticonderoga*, to march tomorrow morning, under the command of Lieutenant-Colonel *Antil*, for *Albany*."[49] Antill may have briefly accompanied those troops, but on 3 August, he was with his colonel as he sent Captain Olivie and the detachment at Fort George on to Albany.[50] Any number of factors might have influenced Gates's decision to shift the Canadians: the general may have wanted more space between Antill and Woedtke, or to separate Hazen's soldiers from their commander and his fight with Arnold. Maybe it was to remove people he saw as possible security threats, or to rid his post of the necessity of sustaining not only the Canadian troops but also their followers.

On 18 August, Schuyler wrote to Hancock that "part of *Livingston's*, *Hazen's*, and *Duggan's* corps of *Canadians*" were in Albany and in need. He ordered a month's pay for them and planned to "employ them in repairing the road to *Fort George*, which is exceedingly worn," until Congress directed "what to do with them, and whether they are to be paid up and discharged, or what." He added that the Canadians had "several women and children with them, who draw provisions, having not the means of subsistence without that aid." Furthermore, other Canadian refugees, "not belonging to the above corps," were also in Albany "naked and destitute of every necessary." Schuyler figured that he had to provide for them "as their misfortunes are occasioned by their attachment to our cause," but he wanted congressional directives on this refugee crisis.[51] Albany, like the Northern Department overall, had become a "landscape of refugees" and recruits, of displaced persons needing to be placed.[52]

Congress, busy drafting articles of confederation, model treaties, and seductive promises to foreign officers, did not provide quite the direction Schuyler desired. Although it promised foreign officers who left the "armies of his Britannic majesty in America" and became citizens hundreds of acres in unappropriated lands, it was less immediately attentive and forthcoming with those men foreign, domestic, or something in between already aboard.[53] The refugee conundrum continued into the postwar era, at which time Congress was still considering how far it had to go in making good the losses the Canadians sustained. It acknowledged that many of them, "induced by the recommendation of Congress, and actuated by a love of Liberty," embraced the American cause and then "when the Americans were unsuccessful in Canada, those generous friends followed our fortunes and retired with our army, which has occasioned the loss of the greatest part of their property and reduced many of them to the utmost distress." Yet both during and after the war, some thought that as the Canadians had been invited, not commanded, and as they had chosen to join, they had voluntarily risked loss, so the nation did not owe recompense. On the other hand, gratitude and humanity impelled compensation.[54]

A congress and army still reeling from defeat and trying to apportion blame were not as inclined to show appreciation. Furthermore, both had other priorities in the summer of 1776. More concerned about Native Americans than refugees, Congress paid slightly more attention to the first part of Schuyler's 18 August letter. It referred the letter to the committee on Indian affairs, which likely ignored the second part about the Canadians.[55] Congress, however, had presciently answered Schuyler's concern in its 10 August agreement with the committee on Canadian petitioners, about which the general may not yet have been aware. At that time, Congress continued the Reverend Louis Lotbinière, the refugee Catholic priest, as "a chaplain in the pay of the United States." More comprehensively, Congress instructed "that all persons who have acted as volunteers in Canada, and retreated with the army, be referred to General Schuyler; and that he be directed to enquire into their services and characters, and to order them such rewards and wages as shall appear to have been merited."[56] But was the term volunteer to be applied to the soldiers and officers of the Canadian regiments? For general ad hoc purposes, it appears so, even though Congress did have a committee or committees dealing with the individual petitions and claims of Canadians.[57]

Even as Congress dumped the refugee problem back into Schuyler's lap, the Canadian regiments' commanders reasserted the value of their units and petitioned that they be reauthorized and continued. Livingston was quicker in his request, probably because other matters had diverted Hazen. Once again, the 1st Canadian was first, when on 15 August Congress acted on the Board of War's report and resolved that Livingston retain a colonel's commission and be given "orders to inlist as many companies of Canadians as are willing to engage in the service." Schuyler was to make recommendations to Congress about appropriate subordinate officers.[58] It was a renewed commission for a regiment of refugees and other Canadian volunteers in the army of the United States to replace the old charge recognizing Canadians as fellow colonials.

Livingston's reauthorized commission and then Hazen's in September also reflected a continuing, albeit battered, strand of hope that Canadians might yet rise in rebellion. Reports of oppressed Canadians hoping to see the Americans again were salve to the wound. In September, a British deserter deposed that the Canadians were "obliged to work without being paid for it" and wishing that Americans "were in possession of the Country again."[59] The following June, Francis Monty, his son, and "an Englishman who spoke French" stole into Bellville (Beloiel), between St. Charles and Chambly, where they learned other American spies had been at St. Denis shortly before them. Besides reporting on British troop numbers and movements, Monty said that British officials were trying "to excite the Canadians to take up Arms" by inducements of regimentals and money on one hand and threats of imprisonment and being "sent to England as Rebels" on the other. He also mentioned that the Canadians generally favored America and wished "to see the Bostonians once more."[60]

The movement of deserters, spies, and refugees showed how porous and malleable the border was. The armies sought to draw a firm line to secure their frontiers, but instead the line (if indeed there was one) swayed according to the sentiments, strength, and position of people as well as forces. Agents scuffed that line when they crossed to serve as military and political brokers.[61] Among the many that crisscrossed the borderlands to gather information and instigate action were Francis Monty and his son. They were also among numerous Monties who had supported the American invasion and ended up in Livingston and Hazen's regiments.

On 24 September, after committee vetting, Congress took up a petition by Hazen. It resolved that Hazen and Antill "be continued in their offices, in the army of the United States." Besides authorizing recruitment to Continental battalion strength, which it soon increased to the regiment's original establishment, Congress provided that Hazen be paid 1,095 dollars, which together with the 533 1/3 dollars already dispersed, was to account "for his neat cattle, sheep, swine, poultry, hay and other articles alledged to have been taken and used for the benefit of the continental army, near St. John's." It said that damages to his buildings by American or enemy troops were not to be paid unless similar compensation was provided to others also hurt, which was a subject that might be worth considering after the war. Congress also discharged the committee looking into Arnold's conduct as it had directed Washington to open an investigation into officers' conduct in Canada. It created a committee to figure out how to provide for the Northern Army more effectively, and then resumed discussion on formulating a treaty with France. Deep into such diplomatic, political, and other military matters, on 30 September, when yet another Hazen petition appeared, Congress simply sent it to the Canada committee.[62]

Congress was trying mightily to regularize military organization and operations. It was forming the new nation's military establishment at the same time that it was formulating a national governing establishment. The Declaration of Independence announced and accompanied those actions; it did not initiate them. After a committee, created in January, reported on the need and duties for a "war office," Congress established a Board of War and Ordnance on 12 June, the same day it established the memberships of the committees that were to draft a plan of confederation and to prepare a plan for treaties with foreign powers.[63] Then, after the Declaration, the delegates, like soldiers and statesmen elsewhere, increased their labors to institute independence. Having a Board of War to provide continuity and standardization in policies and process in addition to ad hoc committees was an essential step. As John Adams wrote to General William Heath in August,

> We have now a nation to protect and defend; and . . . the prosperity of a State depends upon the discipline of its Army. . . . If there is not wisdom and vigour enough in the civil Government to support the military officers in introducing and establishing such a discipline, it must be owing to the advantages of soil and climate and our extreme distance from our enemies, not to our own strength, virtue, or wisdom, if we do not fail.
>
> The Army must be well officered, armed, disciplined, fed, clothed, covered, and paid;. . . Time, I hope, will assist us; and every officer of the Army would do well to suggest to his friends and correspondents in Congress and in the Legislatures of the several States every defect and every improvement in those particulars which occurs to him.[64]

Hazen had not waited for such an overture, and he certainly continued to make such suggestions throughout the war. He, like Washington and other commanders, agreed with Adams that the United States would not fare well until they had a regular army with greater discipline, and that would not happen until there were longer enlistments, more generous inducements for recruitment and retention, and the right officers to implement the changes.

Commissions

When Congress reauthorized Hazen's regiment in September 1776, it did so within a blizzard of resolutions to recruit, arm, and train a Continental Army that was also a nationalizing force—as signaled, among other things, by gunpowder casks marked "U.S.A."[65] Then it was time to redraw and regulate that new army. After directing Washington to order all officers to conduct training every day, Congress approved revised Articles of War, which included the new enlistment oath that added national allegiance and congressional compliance to military obedience. A recruit was to swear or affirm "to be true to the United States of America, and to serve them honestly and faithfully against all their enemies or opposers whatsoever; and to observe and obey the orders of the

Continental Congress, and the orders of the generals and officers set over me by them." At the end of the Articles, Congress tacked on the provision that "all persons, not members of, nor owing allegiance to, any of the United States of America, [but residing or visiting within them and deriving protection from their laws], who shall be found lurking as spies in or about the fortifications or encampments of the armies of the United States . . . shall suffer death, according to the law and usage of nations, by sentence of a court martial, or such other punishment as such court martial shall direct."[66] They tied allegiance to the country, not just the cause, and applied both to security, which surely added to the Canadian refugees' anxieties about their own status in or near the American military.

The movement of peoples not owing allegiance concerned both military and civil authorities in the borderlands. As ministerial forces held Canada, occupied New York City, and moved into Newport, Rhode Island, in late 1776, the earlier worries of officers, officials, and inhabitants seemed prescient. As they had failed to establish boundaries against their enemies, they had to secure camps and operations within claimed regions, and that ensnared the Antill family. In December under flag of truce, the ship *Hope* appeared at Verplanck's Point carrying the Reverend Charles Inglis, John Moore, Philip J. Livingston, and letters from other active loyalists. They asked General Heath and the convention, or committee, of the state there for permission to escort their families and property through the lines. When Inglis learned that the families might not be allowed to exit because authorities feared they would carry information, Inglis suggested that his family be administered a secrecy oath, which he would ensure was kept. To support his case, he mentioned that Mrs. Antill was allowed to move from Brunswick, New Jersey, to New York upon taking such an oath. Yet he also depreciated such precautions: "there is much better intelligence conveyed to both armies in this unhappy contest than could be given or communicated by women."[67] Inglis may have hoped that naming Mrs. Antill would remind the committee that families crossed lines. In this case it was Lieutenant Colonel Antill's sister-in-law (his brother was the loyalist John Antill). Inglis also certainly hoped the New York committee would follow the New Jersey example. It did not.

The committee and Heath rejected the petitions because the members thought it perilous to permit the men to pass; furthermore, allowing their families and property to go would furnish "a dangerous channel of intelligence, prove an incentive to rebellion, and be an act of direct aid and comfort to the enemies of the freedom and independence of the *United States of North America.*" While the committee allowed that the widow Jane Knox could not "do mischief to the *American* cause," and thus could have her property sent down once it was inspected, it adjudged that Lady Johnson, "a lady of great art and political intrigue," could neither remain in Albany where communication with her husband, Sir John Johnson, was "dangerous to the publick safety," nor could she return to her home. It recommended she be removed to a state in New England "under such circumstances as may be consistent with her rank and her sex."[68] Refugees, both men and women, posed risks.

Besides reconstituting military and martial law, which commanders and committees as above applied, Congress reconsidered the structure of the force. Upon the Board of War's recommendations, it resolved on 16 September that the army was to have eighty-eight battalions apportioned among the states by available manpower. Furthermore, the states were to induce noncommissioned officers and soldiers to serve for the duration of the war by offering not just an immediate twenty-dollar bounty but also a future land grant of 100 acres to a soldier and 150 to a noncommissioned officer; Congress promised more land to officers allocated by rank. The states would bear the expense of procuring the lands promised by the United States just as they were to "provide arms, cloathing, and every necessary" for their respective quotas of troops. The states, as they did when colonies, were to appoint all company and field officers, who in turn were to be commissioned by Congress.[69]

Congress made exceptions on an individual basis, as in the Livingston and Hazen reauthorizations, and then opened a way for more trans-state or non-state-line units. On 27 December, after "mature" reflection, though impelled by fear as well as Washington's recommendations, Congress greatly augmented the general's powers as commander in chief. In response to recruitment concerns and another retreat, this time of the Main Army through New Jersey, it increased his war powers as a temporary measure to arrest the current American crisis. Rumors of the action at Trenton may have supported the decision. Among the many provisions, Congress gave Washington permission to raise and officer sixteen additional infantry battalions beyond those already authorized, and also to "raise, officer, and equip three thousand light horse; three regiments of artillery, and a corps of engineers." The horse, artillery, and engineer units aside, eighty-eight plus sixteen plus the "Six to be raisd out of the Continent at large" amounted to 110 battalions or regiments. The 2nd Canadian counted among the six, although a veteran later mistakenly put it among the sixteen. Washington could also "displace and appoint all officers under the rank of brigadier general, and to fill up all vacancies in every other department in the American armies."[70] This extreme ad hoc measure—which Congress quickly had to justify to the states—further legitimized the reauthorization of the Canadian regiments within the Continental line, but in seeming to bypass state associations the measure further complicated supply and command.[71]

Congress said that these extraordinary units could be raised and collected together "from any or all" of the states, which could be interpreted as recruitment between states, not just within them, and thus appeared to implement one of Washington's ideals for a more continental American army. The commander in chief had wanted the regiments of '76 to accept within them men from different colonies serving together in a shared cause for one country. It was an unpopular idea that was considered impractical, and also perhaps impolitic, by most other commanding officers, but it was an ideal shared by General Schuyler, who collected and, after the Canadian Department dissolved in July 1776, reconstructed forces in the Northern Department as Washington was reorganizing the Main Army.[72]

The Main Army of 1776 had had twenty-seven infantry "continental regiments," plus Colonel Henry Knox's Continental Artillery Regiment and a few other companies.[73] Yet although they carried the title of "Continental," ultimately, in response to provincial preferences, the infantry regiments remained colony- and then state-affiliated, which was confirmed when those that continued beyond 1776 reverted in the 1777 establishment to state designations. Their designations reflected their personnel, financial, and supply bases—which were the states, not the Continental Congress. They included the 1st Pennsylvania Regiment (William Thompson's Rifle Battalion) becoming the 1st Continental Regiment on 1 January 1776 (1st because of its colonel's seniority) and then reverting back to the 1st Pennsylvania on 1 January 1777. The 3rd New Hampshire, which became the 2nd Continental, was again the 3rd New Hampshire in 1777. Except for the 1st, all of those "continental" troops were New England units, and all were assigned to the Main Army in the Eastern and Middle Departments. Units serving in other departments kept their provincial designations.

Congress initially authorized Hazen's 2nd Canadian thinking that not only would it help tie Canada to the union but that Canada, in turn, would support it. The retreat of American forces from Canada, however, left both Hazen's and Livingston's regiments without a home. How could they remain Canadian if there was no state of Canada to supply them with men and matériel? That, in turn, substantiated the problem that they did not have enough men. It was one thing to reauthorize the regiments, and another to encourage recruitment among the refugees on one side of the border and the disaffected on the other, but ultimately the regiments had to have permission to range farther afield to fill their ranks. As Washington remarked months later about a request from some French officers to form a regiment of Canadian exiles, "I have no conception that there are Canadians enough to be found . . . neither Colo. Livingston nor Colo. Hazen could ever compleat their Canadian Regiments when they had [Canada] open to them."[74]

On 23 October, after reviewing a report on Hazen's petition (possibly the one referred to the Canada committee on 30 September) and responding to his personal lobbying in Philadelphia, Congress approved yet more reimbursement to Hazen, this time for tools and equipment appropriated by Montgomery's forces. More significantly, it resolved that Hazen's regiment was not only to keep its original establishment but also "be recruited to its full complement in any of the thirteen United States, as it was upon these terms [Hazen] entered into the service, and the said regiment cannot be said to belong to any particular state."[75] It may be, therefore, that this approval was a precedent for the new regiments authorized in December.

It surely was for Livingston's regiment. Either he or someone else with an eye to equity must have mentioned the 1st Canadian, for on 11 November, Congress gave Livingston "leave to recruit his regiment in any of the United States." That, however, followed more specific congressional directions to Schuyler to complete Livingston's regiment with available officers "who have served in Canada, according to their ranks and merits."[76] Yet the Canadian connection was not complete nor the process smooth, as Lieutenant Colonel Pierre Regnier de Roussi's complaint to Congress indicated; Roussi had lost his position in the 1st Canadian as Livingston reorganized the regiment in late 1776.[77]

Given Congress's orders to Schuyler, its earlier August authorization, and Livingston's connections, the 1st Canadian probably had an edge among Canadians and New Yorkers. Nonetheless, Hazen offered vigorous competition as both he and Livingston scouted the New York encampments for officers and soldiers. By early November, Schuyler counted 13,397 officers and soldiers, "about half of whom were fit for Duty." There were also eight officer-heavy regiments of militia.[78] As the British withdrew from Crown Point, Schuyler sent some battalions to assist Washington and discharged militia and state forces whose service was expiring. Officers and soldiers were once again "betwixt hawk & Buzzard" as their orders kept changing and they filled and emptied posts as the weather worsened.[79] Schuyler figured that he would have enough winter quarters for the following: approximately 2,500 troops at Ticonderoga and Mount Independence; 1,000 at Saratoga; 500 at Schenectady and Albany; 400 at Fort George and Fort Schuyler; and 100 at Skenesborough, Fort Ann, Johnstown, and Fort Dayton.[80] It made sense for recruiters to trawl those pools before discharged soldiers and militiamen marched home.

The obvious first targets were those in their own dwindling ranks. In mid-November, some of Livingston's troops were with Roussi manning bateaux down in the Hudson Highlands between King's Ferry, Fort Constitution, and Fishkill.[81] Others apparently sat at Albany along with Hazen's troops and the refugees. Some of the Canadian troops had probably worked on the road to Fort

George as Schuyler had planned in August, but they were likely back. By the end of September, Gates was begging for men to finish a road near Ticonderoga: "Could not a number of the Canadians, now at Albany, be employed in this business? They are excellent fellows at labour." A frustrated Schuyler responded, "the *Canadians* will not do any duty of any kind."[82] That exaggeration discounted those who did work, and Schuyler could have ordered those still in service to go, but the refugees were another matter. The French Canadians had not liked corvée at home and were obviously not volunteering for similar duty at Albany. That likely contributed to Schuyler's question in early November, echoing that of August: "What is to be done with the Remainder of Livingston's, Hazen's and Duggan's Canadian Corps, and with the Canadian Refugees now in Albany?"[83]

Congress sent an answer before it got the question: expand the recruitment pool. Resolution to the issue was also in the actions of the respective commanders and the officers they set to recruiting duty. Livingston and Hazen were successful. (Duggan was not, and his tiny corps disappeared.[84]) In the process, these units became "continental" in ways that the 1st through 27th infantry regiments in Washington's 1776 Main Army never were and most others never could be. The "Canadian" regiments epitomized the distinction by their origins and their responses to the congressional authorization to recruit in any of the United States. State-affiliated units did not have such permission.

Hazen and Livingston's regiments were called Canadian—by reference to their creation and original officers and recruits—but they could not remain purely Canadian. That was particularly the case with the 2nd Canadian. Livingston's regiment remained small and primarily populated by refugees and New Yorkers, but hundreds of Americans soon enveloped the Canadian core of Hazen's. That core, however, was essential, for without it Hazen would have had nothing and no one upon which to rebuild the regiment. Once Hazen had permission to appoint officers as he had in Canada and to recruit men from all of the states, he and Antill rode out to roust a new coterie of Continentals. Hazen took the high road, namely New York and the "Eastern" states, and Antill the low, New Jersey through Virginia.[85]

Although illness temporarily waylaid Hazen at Albany, which may have affected commissioning decisions and recruitment numbers, he had the advantage of being in the vicinity of discharged Northern Department officers and soldiers. He could also reappoint the Canadian officers who had accompanied the retreat and set them to work among the refugees. Indeed, the first order of business for both colonels was to appoint more officers. One challenge, as Washington had seen from the army's commencement, was to find gentlemen deserving of commissions.[86] Another was beating other regiments to the men they were to recruit.

Finding someone who had already had a commission or acted well in the capacity of an officer while a volunteer was a prize. Hazen lost a few and engaged some. Although he later said that Major Udny Hay did not leave the regiment until January 1777, when Congress brevetted him a lieutenant colonel in the Quartermaster Department, in reality Hay had already been coopted as an assistant deputy quartermaster-general since July. Captain Gosselin and Lieutenant Dionne were still in Canada, but Hazen had Captains Liébert and Olivie at hand. Lieutenant Ferriole and Ensigns Guilmat and McPherson also remained. Joseph Torrey, a New England native who had settled in Canada after the previous war, accepted a captain's appointment that November; the same month, Antoine Paulint, who had captained an independent company in Canada, was confirmed in his rank but found his company attached to Hazen's regiment. Antoine Duprie and François Martin-Pelland (Francis Martin) accepted second lieutenant commissions in November and December, respectively. Pierre du Calvet (or Calvert), whom Congress had recognized with ensign's pay and a brevet lieutenancy in August, realized the promotion in December. Refugee Edward Chinn joined later, as paymaster, in June 1777. C. H. Delagard, who was likely among the Canadians, took the post of adjutant. Of those, Calvet was taken prisoner in August 1777, Delagard was gone by October 1777, and Martin-Pelland died in 1778, the year that Duprie resigned. Two or three accepted early release in 1782 as the regiment downsized, while Liébert transferred to the Invalids Corps.[87] Yet in time, a few more Canadians became officers, and Clément Gosselin and Germain Dionne eventually rejoined the regiment, thereby helping maintain the continuing Canadian core of the corps.

Hazen and Antill, however, swamped that core as they successfully grew their borderland regiment by crossing state lines. By June 1777, the colonels and Congress had appointed and commissioned more than fifty other officers to the regiment, close to sixty if counting surgeon's mates and other staff. These officers hailed from Virginia, Maryland, Delaware, Pennsylvania, New Jersey, New York, Connecticut, Rhode Island, and Massachusetts. Hazen's "Canadian" Regiment thus came to embody what Washington had to abandon in the 1776 reorganization: the notion of infantry regiments with officers mixed from different states (see the appendix). Washington had proposed the idea not just to "continentalize" the regiments but also to advance men of military ability over those of regional or political attachment. The war would test whether ability and stability marched with such diversity in the regiment.

In the immediate term, Hazen and Antill made a bumpy but strong start on rebuilding from the ruins of 1776, although they did not—and never could—enroll and keep the numbers of officers and men necessary to complete the organizational plan of 1,000 men distributed between four battalions with five companies each. The plan called for four majors, twenty captains, twenty lieutenants, and twenty ensigns. By January 1777, after only two months of recruiting, the regiment nominally had one major (two if still counting Hay), sixteen captains, one captain-lieutenant, twenty-five lieutenants, and about eight ensigns. Perhaps the *rage militaire* was not yet dead at the end of 1776—at least not in the northern borderland and among young men wishing to officer.[88]

More continued to volunteer for the remaining positions in 1777, and about half of the officers who joined Hazen's regiment between November 1776 and the following June had served before, either with Hazen or in another unit. Seven switched from Colonel Samuel Elmore's regiment. They were Palmer Cady, Lyman Hitchcock, Mark Mazuzen, William Munson, Jeremiah Parmelee, William Satterlee, and Alexander Sloan. Back in August, soon after he had sent off some of the remaining Canadian troops to repair the road to Fort George, Schuyler had ordered Elmore's and Colonel John Nicholson's regiments, which did "not exceed five hundred effectives," west to Tryon County. Elmore's unit moved on to Fort Schuyler in October. Both of those regiments, Elmore's of Connecticut and Nicholson's of New York, had formed after Congress's January 1776 request for new regiments to serve in Canada. They served, they retreated, and then Congress and Schuyler had to decide what to do with them under the new plan. Congress punted that to Schuyler. The end result included Nicholson's regiment disbanding in December and some of its officers joining Livingston's regiment. As many of Elmore's men had enlistments running to April, that regiment did not officially disband until then, but some of the officers, looking for retention and promotion in the reorganizing army, transferred earlier.[89] As they had served in Canada, through the retreat, and with the other diverse units in the Northern Department, accepting a commission with Hazen's regiment rather than trying for a state-affiliated one was opportune.

While Hazen dangled opportunities at the northern posts, Antill looked for available officers and gentlemen within the Main Army and in states south of New York. Among them were Lieutenant James Duncan and possibly Chaplain James Francis Armstrong, who may have known each other (and Captain James Randolph Reid) previously as students at the College of New Jersey. At least three officers from Colonel Samuel Miles's Pennsylvania Rifle Regiment (Robert Burns, Robert Campbell, and John Thompson) and two from William Thompson's 1st Continental Regiment of Foot (Benjamin Chambers and Matthew McConnell) joined.[90] These officers, like those from Elmore's and other units from Connecticut to Virginia, brought their connections from their old units to the new one. Those connections contributed to and challenged those forming in Hazen's regiment, as did the accompanying assimilation of the singletons—those individuals new to both regiment and army.

Captain-Lieutenant Robert Buchanan and Lieutenants Samuel Alexander, Alexander Sloan, and John Gibson left by June. Charles Markle, who may or may not have had an appointment to the regiment, also disappeared.[91] Newcomers such as James Anderson remained and were joined by others over the year, including Major Tarlton Woodson. Hazen made adjustments in the midst of these exits and entrances, promoting from within as well as from without. Ambrose Walden enlisted as a sergeant in February 1777, but then acted upon a promise of promotion made by Major John Taylor, who appears to have been a family friend. Walden earned an ensign's commission in May by recruiting seven men, likely all Virginians, and delivering them to the regiment.[92] Robert Burns, Michael Gilbert, and Thomas Pry could all sport captains' sashes by spring; in fact, Hazen seems to have promoted Gilbert and Pry before Congress got around to confirming their commissions as first lieutenants.

States were to appoint and Congress commission, but as the 2nd Canadian had no home state, Hazen and Antill sent their recommendations directly to Congress. They did not, however, wait for that body to act before sending their designated captains out to recruit companies. It was a risk. Although it took prodding by Antill, Congress was relatively speedy in commissioning John Taylor as a major on 24 January 1777, backdating his rank to 13 November, but it took until 8 April 1777 to confirm the commissions of some of the men appointed at the end of 1776, along with later nominees.[93]

Congress may have clogged the system at times, but problems in synchronization between the two colonels trying to scoop up likely candidates also created jams, as did Washington when he exercised one of the powers Congress granted him on 27 December: that of filling vacancies in the various departments of the army. The problem was not just systemic; it was personal. Hazen wanted to maintain tight control of appointments. He gave Antill permission to appoint just one major, which Antill did with John Taylor. Hazen became unhappy, however, when, as he inferred, Antill and Washington colluded on another major.[94] Frustrated by Schuyler and Gates, Hazen had requested to serve under Washington's "immediate command," but this appointment dispute with the commander in chief may have had him reconsider that desire.[95]

Antill had been communicating with Congress and Washington as he sought officers. That contact showed a careful deference, for Antill was looking for seasoned candidates within the Main Army and Virginia regiments even though he also accepted inexperienced applicants.[96] Perhaps he was being too much the gentleman while recruiting—something against which Hazen had warned almost a year earlier in Canada—but it was one thing to invite officer candidates and check with their current commanders about availability, quite another to poach. In January, after Antill asked for his approval on the offer to Taylor and to three officers then in the 1st Virginia, or any other three he might recommend, Washington gave blanket permission: "As you and Colo. Hazen had the Nomination of your own Officers by Virtue of your Commissions, I shall have no objection to any Gentlemen of good Character that you may think fit to appoint."[97] The three gentlemen that Antill had in mind for captaincies did not join the regiment. But months later, Washington exercised his congressional commission in appointing Christian de Colerus a major in the regiment.

Colerus was one of many volunteers, foreign and domestic, who sought position and promotion in the American army. Some of these volunteers followed the army, becoming what the Articles of War termed retainers to the camp, as they waited for a commission rather than enlisting as a soldier.[98] American volunteers had to await placement in regiments belonging to their states or be willing to leave home affiliations for trans-state units. Foreign volunteers had primarily the latter option. Further limiting their placement, as they tended to arrive with previous service, they desired—even demanded—command rank. These men and their actions reflected a broader, transatlantic, shared military society. The military culture in which they participated—another kind of borderland between countries—could help operations between both allies and enemies as it provided common customs by which to relate to each other. But it was also a society in which some officers and soldiers, whether termed adventurers or mercenaries, put ideals or national allegiance second to the profession of arms. That allegiance to arms rather than political ideals disturbed many Americans, but not as much as the demands for preferment.[99]

The assignments of foreign officers rankled American ones. Rumblings threatened revolt in at least one case: The French artillery officer Philippe du Coudray arrived in America in May 1777 with an appointment as major general of the artillery and ordnance from Silas Deane. Deane, who was in France contracting for arms and making other connections to serve American interests, issued a number of appointments to foreign volunteers. Some—such as the marquis Marie-Joseph Paul Yves Gilbert du Motier de La Fayette (Americanized then as General Lafayette) and the baron Johann de Kalb (DeKalb), who arrived together in June 1777—proved politically as well as militarily adept. Perhaps they learned from the Coudray crisis. Generals Sullivan, Nathanael Greene, and Henry Knox protested and threatened to resign if Congress honored Coudray with a commission. Congress, in turn, found their letters imprudent and deplored how they tried to influence its decisions; the generals were to acknowledge that danger or they were free to resign and retire. Ultimately, Washington made Coudray an inspector general of ordnance, who in turn also accepted the regular rank of captain, all of which served to acknowledge Congress's authority and preserve the generals' positions. The coda to the crisis was that Coudray, who apparently performed well at the Battle of Brandywine, drowned after his horse bolted during a crossing of the Schuylkill River in September 1777.[100]

Officers chafed at foreign volunteers superseding them in rank. Congress confronted their dissent and worried how the American people, who did not like standing armies to begin with, would accept such a "monarchical production" with "Foreigners placed in the highest trusts." Soldiers, in turn, did not much like serving under officers they did not understand. If a foreign officer, such as the purported baron Friedrich Wilhelm von Steuben and Polish nobleman Casimir Pulaski, embraced America and Americans, that was another matter.[101]

Colerus did neither, although he promised—or pushed—enough that Congress brevetted him a major in September 1776 and sent him on to Washington, who in turn allowed him to serve as a volunteer until his command of English improved enough for command in the army. Washington probably also wanted proof of his martial abilities. Colerus's performance in fall and winter engagements plus continued importuning led Washington to offer him one of the vacant majorities in Hazen's regiment in May 1777. Washington knew of the opening because of his correspondence with Antill, who was then commanding the regiment at Princeton, New Jersey, in Hazen's absence. The commander in chief did not like how Colerus whined about others being promoted over him and reminded him of the conditions for appointment. Washington condemned "the over sanguine, unjust, ambitious expectations of those, who think every thing should be made to yeild [sic] to gratify their views." Nevertheless, there was now an open position, and Colerus could take it or leave it and the army.[102]

Colerus tried to take it, but the regiment did not take to him. The officers, most of whom had only been in the regiment a few months, treated the foreign newcomer "with indifference & disrespect" despite the fact that Congress had commissioned him and the commander in chief had appointed him to the position. Washington sent a biting letter to Hazen: he understood that Hazen was not at Princeton when his officers rejected Colerus's assumption of the post, but he did not want to hear of objections, just compliance. Yet it was one thing to order obedience, another to create acceptance, which apparently did not happen on either side, for Colerus soon left the regiment.[103]

Years later, Hazen criticized Antill and, indirectly, Washington, for some of the problems that attended filling the majorities of the regiment in 1777. The criticism marked Hazen's rebuttal to James Reid, who accused Hazen, among other things, of falsifying the date of his promotion to major. Reid said that he had replaced Colerus, but Hazen disputed that with a summary of how then-Lieutenant Reid of Anthony Wayne's regiment, "who had disagreed with his Colonel," arrived at Albany with a recommendation from Major Hay for a company command. Hazen referred him to Antill, who set him to recruiting. In the meantime, Antill had offered Taylor a majority and Hazen promoted Joseph Torrey, "the oldest Captain in the Regiment, a Refugee from Canada, and who had inlisted more than a Hundred Men," to replace Udny Hay. Torrey was not, according to existent records, the longest-serving captain, but he may have enlisted the most men.[104] He was also Anglo rather than French Canadian. Taylor's and Torrey's appointments gave the regiment two of its four majors.

Then Hazen bitterly noted that Antill, "without my knowledge, and contrary to the System we had laid down, applied to your Excellency to fill up one of the other two Majorities," upon which Washington appointed Colerus. He did so just as Hazen, with the general's approbation, appointed Tarlton Woodson. The regiment therefore had a full complement of field officers by taking in the "Brevet French Officer" along with the others, even though it had only eighteen of its authorized twenty companies and its battalions were not complete. Hazen implied that was the reason he did not support Colerus when the foreign officer, "miffed" at not being accepted as senior to Major Taylor, left the regiment. The colonel then determined "not to fill up that Vacancy, as we still had a large Proportion of Field Officers for the Men in the Field; [and] as Mr Collerus had not been commissioned in the Regiment, was not considered as an Officer of it." Hazen may not have been at Princeton when the other officers (in what may have been a bonding moment) rejected Colerus, but he obviously had agreed with them, and he blamed Antill and Washington for the problem—which lingered when he responded to Reid's charges years later. Hazen asserted that he had jumped over more senior captains to appoint Reid a major in October, backdated to 1 September, only after Antill and Woodson were taken prisoner at Staten Island in August and Torrey became ill after the Battle of Brandywine in September.[105]

The new officers, commissioned by Congress's authorization to recruit in all of the states, advanced the regiment's metamorphosis into a continental arm of the new American army. Its internal continentalism started with its senior officers. Besides its colonels Hazen and Antill, at various times the unit's majors included John Taylor and Tarlton Woodson from Virginia, Udny Hay and Joseph Torrey of Canada, and James Reid from Pennsylvania. Their subordinate officers came from Canada and all of the states, except the Carolinas and Georgia, with the majority from Canada, Pennsylvania, New York, and Connecticut. Yet despite the regiment's origins and authorizations, those officers quickly hardened the borders between who was acceptable in what role and who was not. A regiment first created to attract new subjects—the French Canadians still deemed foreign by many—and then allowed to recruit Continentals from all the states, closed ranks against more foreign officers. Foreign soldiers, any soldiers, were another matter.

CHAPTER 4

CONGRESS'S OWN

It was one thing to declare a "new army" for 1777, but another to recruit, assemble, and fight it. After authorizing reconfigured battalions, congressional delegates exhorted inhabitants to fill them. Their 10 December 1776 address summarized Britain's offenses and heralded the "universal desire of the people" and "approbation of every Province" when Congress had declared the independence of the United States. It trumpeted how present resistance showed the "spirit and resolution becoming a free people." But the enemy was nigh. Its advances were not due "to any capital defeat, or a want of valour in the Army . . . but to a sudden diminution of its numbers from the expiration of those short inlistments" that had been adopted "to ease the people." A passing reference to lengthening enlistments was followed by a call "on all the friends of liberty to exert themselves without delay." Thomas Paine said it much better when he chided the "summer soldier" and "sunshine patriot."[1] Congress never forgot that it had to unite and excite the will of the people and the states, but more often it was for others—writers such as Paine, state officials, and military officers—to encourage recruitment while Congress and the states tried to systematize it. None were fully successful.

Although Governor Jonathan Trumbull Sr. of Connecticut wrote in January that the new army surely "will soon be filled under the great Encouragements that are given,"[2] such optimism dwindled over the following months. At the beginning of April, General Washington was groaning, "Our Troops come in exeedingly [sic] slow—whether owing to an unwillingness in the Men to Inlist, or to the Idleness and dissipation of the Officers, and their reluctance to leave their friends & acquaintance, I shall not undertake to say; but it looks to me as if we should never get an army assembled." Weeks later, he was still lamenting the "present unassembled State of the Army."[3]

It was an unpromising start to the heralded new army for which Congress had had the "Continental" infantry units of 1776 revert to state designations and requisitioned the states to field the planned eighty-eight infantry regiments proportionally by their populations. Additional infantry, artillery, and dragoon regiments were not, initially, to count toward the required numbers of units and men. Titles and quotas reflected continuing negotiations between Continental—Congress and Army—and state authorities. They were trying to find a middle ground in and with the military forces that acknowledged both the unified and unique interests and identities of the states and their inhabitants.

Commentaries then and since suggested that the sluggish assembly of this new army was due in part to too few veterans answering the beat of the recruiting drum. Only a thousand or so soldiers of the previous year's forces were believed to have reenlisted, offering but a small veteran core around which to build a strong formation. Furthermore, most of the new recruits stepped forward from ever-poorer and less powerful social ranks. Enlistment was an act of desperation for many.[4] Does Hazen's regiment, which recruited Continentals for "Congress's Own," fit those interpretations of the "new" Continental Army?

Hazen's remade and relabeled regiment partly confirms but also challenges the generalizations. Congress's Own had, for example, a substantial number of reengaged veterans to offset new-made soldiers. Besides the Canadian refugees, such veterans included James Wakeland, who in May 1775 had enlisted in Colonel David Waterbury's Connecticut regiment and had participated in the siege of Saint-Jean. After his discharge, he mustered in Colonel Samuel Elmore's regiment. Wakeland then enlisted in Hazen's regiment in December 1776, joined it in April 1777, and served in Captain William Satterlee's company, eventually rising to corporal.[5] Enlistment may have been an act of desperation for some, but it was also a choice, and in choosing to enlist, and then whether to stay or to desert, would-be and enrolled soldiers exercised some power. They were not just pushed or pulled by chance, circumstance, and recruiters. Each person decided whether enlistment was an act of allegiance, a possible escape from poverty, or an opportunity for advancement and adventure.

Motivation was and remains difficult to parse. Complicating the efforts both to assemble the army then and to analyze it now is that enlistment was but one step, actually joining or mustering another, and finally marching together yet another. The actions of Wakeland and others in joining the new army may not have been the volunteering of the *rage militaire*, but still they chose to enlist. And even though there may have been fewer volunteers from America's middling social ranks and more from the poorer ones, those men could still choose between British, loyalist, militia, or Continental forces, and decide whether they would serve on land or at sea. In joining, the recruits met others in similar circumstances, and their numbers and the knowledge that they were needed empowered them in negotiating enlistment terms and navigating military service.

Hundreds of soldiers enlisted with the officers of Hazen's regiment by mid-1777.[6] As some soldiers died, deserted, or departed when their contracts expired, others continued to join. Over the course of the war, more than 1,800 recruits enlisted in the regiment originally called the 2nd Canadian. That count includes men transferred into the regiment and in-and-out deserters. Most, like the approximately ninety officers, came not just from Canada but also from all of the states except South Carolina and Georgia. Others were recent immigrants, including deserters from British and German forces. The refugees and immigrants belonged to no individual state, just the United States.[7] Such belonging—and not—created recruiting issues, supply problems, and an identity crisis. The regiment proclaimed that it was "Congress's Own," but Congress asserted that it was not. Decades later, veterans finally decided the issue.

The controversy began within the derangement of reassignment and recruitment. Colonel Hazen's regiment was transferred from General Schuyler's Northern Army to the Highlands Department under Major General William Heath's command on 12 November 1776. Eight days into 1777, Hazen got his wish to serve more directly under Washington's command when the regiment was assigned to the Main Army. Meanwhile, he and Lieutenant Colonel Antill appointed officers they hoped would be active, able recruiters.[8] Ability, however, had to be paired with resources and incentives to be effective. Officers and soldiers required currency and a common cause that was both inclusive and exclusive—namely, bounties, belonging, and distinction. Congress offered the first two, the men forged the latter two, and they wrangled over all three for years. In the meantime, Congress and Continentals had to battle internal and external enmities and enemies.

Recruit and Enlist

The new army of 1777 arose from the army of '76 as veteran and novice officers sought to enlist both old and new soldiers. The competition to meet quotas and fill the authorized battalions began as soon as word of Congress's 16 September resolution arrived. In Hazen's case, that competition began as soon as Congress reauthorized the 2nd Canadian Regiment on the 24th and increased a month later when he had its permission to recruit in any of the thirteen states. He and Antill reconfirmed the commissions of fellow refugee officers who wished to continue; enrolled new officers, whose appointments they sent to Congress; and then with their junior officers set to recruiting their "new" regiment. They immediately faced challenges inside and outside the army.

Difficulties included determining who would do the recruiting, how, with what, and where. Congress claimed the power of commissioning officers but accepted that states had the power to appoint them, which meant that it waited for the states to determine the officers who could then recruit. William Hooper, a delegate from North Carolina, complained, "What is everybodys is nobodys business." Congress undermined its own power and the "common cause" by allowing states to appoint most officers. Hooper believed politics rather than ability would determine appointments, asserting, "Our Troops will no longer look to the Continental Congress as the power which is to direct their movements, they will consider themselves as the Creatures of the respective Assemblies."[9] Hooper's use of the term "our" was telling: the troops of the United States, not of the independent states, were to be Congress's. Yet while that was the case for some individual commands—such as Hazen's—it was not for those in the state-designated regiments. Recruiting policies and practices confirmed that.

Hooper fretted that the "Enlistment of 9/10ths of our Army will expire before the last day of December," if not earlier. As a result, Continental troops at "the beginning of January will not be above 2000, a handful to conflict with 25000 British troops." Despite that, he was appalled to note, "no measures have yet taken place for recruiting in Camp."[10] Hooper echoed many of his fellow delegates, and thus Congress acted by resolving on 4 November that Washington, after consulting with available generals, was "to grant warrants" to men he believed deserved commissions but whose state appointing officers had not yet arrived in camps. Those warranted officers were to hustle with recruiting their regiments to full strength.[11] Within days, Congress sent blank commissions to General Schuyler so that he could appoint and rearrange officers to better secure the army on the northern borderlands.[12]

In tackling top-down administration in matters of recruitment, Congress was dealing with a relatively easier problem than the bottom-up challenge of enlistment—personal choice. Mid-level administration was also made easier within the army by how many officers wished to remain in the service: approximately half of those authorized in 1776.[13] Some officers had to be reappointed among the reorganized regiments, but even so, they provided a veteran core for command in the new army. Hazen's success in appointing so many officers by December reflected that fact. Not counting its colonels, the regiment was authorized sixty-nine officers; at least forty of them were officially enrolled in November (many on the 3rd alone), and approximately half came from other units. That January, counting the officers who had already served with Hazen, over half of the officers in Congress's Own were veterans (see the appendix).

Congress was not immediately aware of Hazen's success, nor did it perceive a favorable foundation elsewhere. Thus, by the end of November, the fidgety Congress sent blank commissions to Washington and empowered him to fill in the names of those he thought fit, with the caveat that he could not revoke appointments made by state commissioners. It also charged Washington, commissioners, and officers "to recruit, by all the means in their power, the regiments now or lately in the camp." Congress also created a committee to meet with and assist Washington, which included checking into any grievances held by soldiers.[14] These resolves were the immediate responses to the recruitment crisis that Congress further addressed in December when it gave greater powers to Washington, including that of displacing as well as appointing officers.[15] Those extra powers were intended to be temporary, lasting only until the new army was well established.

During the coming months, as the officers appointed by generals, states, and Congress fanned out across their respective territories, problems arose over how they recruited and the money they expended. On the basis of financial requisitions from the states, Congress distributed funds directly to some commanders, such as Hazen, as well as to state officials for the purpose of recruiting.[16] Those officers and officials were to be accountable for their use, but bookkeeping was often irregular, and costs and demands catapulted.

Congress established committees to research the discrepancies between the money expended and men gained and to propose solutions. On the basis of one committee's report, in April 1777 Congress recommended that each of the states evaluate the conduct of their respective recruiters and remove those guilty of abuse. It also asked that all of the states procure and send exact rolls of companies. Those companies unable to muster to their authorized strength were to be dissolved, as were the commissions of their officers, and the men transferred to other companies. It further recommended that if a state could not enlist its quota for the service, then it should draft men from its militia. Finally, again trying to balance command and control of the regiments between Congress, commander in chief, and states, Congress authorized the states to order officers from their battalions and companies to remain in state to aid in the enlistment and collection of recruits.[17]

In response to another committee's recommendations, and probably after too many direct demands, that July Congress issued instructions to the paymaster general and departmental deputies about regulating bounty and other advances to recruiting officers. It reconfirmed that the paymasters general were to advance the funds, not Congress directly. Furthermore, they were to advance only enough to cover ten levies (inductees). Once a recruiter had ten, and provided vouchers and certificates attesting to enlistment, the paymasters general could advance more funds to the recruiter. These officials would then transmit accounts to the regimental paymasters for accounting.[18]

In the midst of trying to recruit the new army, Congress was constantly fiddling with the process, as were the states. At the same time, the commander in chief wanted officers recalled from recruiting and back leading troops. Ultimately, on 31 July 1777, Congress tried to hand recruiting over to the states. That did not fully work, and thus recruiting remained a hybrid operation that undermined accountability at all levels, including to the soldiers who put their marks to the enlistment papers.[19]

The army did not wait for Congress and the states to smooth the kinks in the recruiting systems between the fall of 1776 and the summer of 1777. It got what orders and monies that it could and commenced rebuilding the force. Appointments as line officers came with warrants to fill the units they were to command. A captain needed not only a commission but also a company, and at this stage in the war, it was usually not simply a matter of getting a company but of raising one. Lieutenants shared this duty. An additional incentive for energetic recruiting was that an officer could earn a bonus of one and one-third dollars per each enlistee. Congress initially tried to limit that to new enlistments, but after protests, especially by Schuyler, the bonus continued to apply to reenlistments too.[20] That provided extra encouragement to reenlist experienced soldiers as well as to troll for new recruits.

Captain Philippe Liébert and Lieutenant Alexandre Ferriole of Hazen's regiment certainly requested the "usual perquisite" or bonus when they submitted returns of the men they quickly enlisted. Ferriole recorded twenty-three enlistments in Albany as of mid-November 1776, with most if not all of them Canadians, including his teenaged son, Alexander Ferriole (later anglicized to Ferriol). Most of the elder Ferriole's enlistees officially joined the regiment as of 1 December. Ferriole also recorded the delivery of enlistment bounties to each, whereas Liébert recorded not bounty but subsistence costs for his twenty-two Canadians who had enlisted between November 1776 and March 1777 but joined in April.[21]

Officers required, and Congress allowed, funds to cover recruiting expenses—including subsistence costs for food, lodging, drink, and sometimes clothing—for themselves and for enlistees who needed to be sustained for a period of time before they could join their regiments.[22] Lieutenant James Stedman enlisted twelve men for the term "During War" between 7 April and 19 May. Nine of those joined the regiment on 17 June and three on 7 July. Stedman submitted a return not only for the recruits' subsistence costs in the period between enlistment and joining but also for his own, for hiring and subsisting a drum and fife, buying twelve cockades, and for other "extraordinary" expenses.[23] Captain William Satterlee delivered a return for enlisting sixty-five men for "During War" at Fort Schuyler, Johnstown, Albany, and Mohawk River between the end of December 1776 and April 1777. Except for the five who deserted in April and the two who mustered on 16 June, the majority joined the regiment on 2 June. All, including the deserters, received the promised bounty of twenty dollars. Satterlee, however, recorded subsistence for only eight of the recruits, likely new enlistees or returnees with a gap between their old and new indentures. He added a subsistence claim for himself from 1 April to 31 June, and for Lieutenants Alexander Sloan and Thomas Bell from mid-December to 30 June. The account also included the dollar and a third bonus for each man enlisted, and cash paid for sixty-five cockades ("half Dollar each"). Satterlee's total was 1,649.75 dollars out of the 2,350 that Hazen had advanced him, with the balance due to the United States.[24] Recruiting was expensive.

Congress advanced funds to Hazen and Antill, who in turn distributed them to their recruiting officers. The thousands of dollars were never enough. A committee for Continental business reported in January 1777 that it had advanced a thousand dollars to Antill for recruiting. But Antill wanted more. He echoed others, such as the New Jersey recruiters who agreed "that Men enlist very fast and we hope there will soon be a Respectable Army, but we must have more Money."[25] In early February, Antill complained to Hancock that he had sent Congress recruiting returns and a list of needs; there had been no answer, and the unhappy Antill on his arrival at Wilmington had found the gathered recruits "Naked & many of them sick for want of blankets & cloathing." It was also necessary to advance them part of their promised "pay and subsistence to keep them Quiet & enable them to procure a few Necessary's." Antill had thus drawn two thousand dollars on Congress's account, which he hoped would be honored and, of course, charged to the regiment.[26] He used those dollars, thousands more, and even his own funds for caps and coffins, gaiters and gaolers, drum cords and regimental books, and other expresses and sundries related to the "recruiting Service in the Different States." All of the officers were to be accountable for the funds: Hazen and Antill to Congress and their recruiters, in turn, to them. They were still settling those accounts after the war.[27]

Money was also a prime concern for the recruiters' targets. Congress had acknowledged that in September 1776, when, in authorizing the new army, it supported "for the duration" enlistment with the promise of an immediate bounty of twenty dollars and future land grants.[28] In October, it offered extra inducements for the indefinite enlistments: an annual clothing issue "to consist, for the present year, of two linen hunting shirts, two pair of overalls, a leathern or woolen waistcoat with sleeves, one pair of breeches, a hat or leathern cap, two shirts, two pair of hose, and two pair of shoes, amounting, in the whole, to the value of twenty dollars, or that sum to be paid to each soldier, who shall procure those articles for himself." It wanted the states to raise their required numbers by 10 November and ensure that "each man be well clothed, armed, accoutered, and furnished with a blanket."[29] The states were not forthcoming on all of those counts, but commanders and recruiters did spread the word. At Ticonderoga they announced the promises and indicated that the clothing was in addition to the twenty-dollar bounty. That aside, the bounty and land promised were "such an Ample and Generous Gratuity from the United States," surely "no American will hesitate to enroll himself to defend his Country and Posterity from every Attempt of Tyranny to enslave it."[30]

The Canadians who enrolled may not have called themselves Americans, but country and posterity figured into their decisions too. Facing hardship as refugees was a spur, but as some exiles over the years enlisted for the term "until the conquest of Canada," liberating their country from Britain may also have remained a motivation.[31] In the meantime, survival and future opportunities were tied to service. The Canadian Continentals also qualified for bounty money and lands but, like pay and supplies, Congress still had to work out the how and where for these soldiers (and later ones) who belonged to no one state but were listed on the regimental roll as "US." As it turned out later, the appropriation and confirmation of borderlands offered a solution.

State financing and concessions to state control in the hybrid recruiting system challenged Hazen's regiment. State-affiliated recruiters did not seek to enlist soldiers for units outside their lines. Congress partially addressed that issue in 1779 when it authorized the states to count toward their own quotas residents enlisted in such independent commands as Pulaski's and Armand's corps and others not apportioned to a particular state.[32] The independent commands, including Hazen's, were to record the recruits' states and send to those states the recruits' names. The first step was to ask for or assign state affiliations. As the veteran John Ryan remembered decades later, "when this deponant and a number of others joined [Hazen's] regt. it war told them thay mite choos what line thay wold be and this deponant made choice of Jersey line but that it may be that he was kept in york line."[33] Former private Jeremiah Parmelee said the regiment was in the Connecticut line on the Continental establishment, whereas fellow soldiers Henry Young and John Carter remembered the regiment being in the Pennsylvania line.[34] The states received quota credit, but then they were also supposed to contribute toward their soldiers' pay and supply—which worked as well as recruiting did. A complication in 1777, however, was Washington's belief that "Each State is bound . . . to furnish their proportion of the additional Battalions, as much as they are of the Eighty Eight." So initially, the states were to man not only their designated regiments of foot but also additional units such as "the Regt calld Hazen's or the Congress's own."[35]

What was more problematic for recruiting was that some states topped Congress's established bounty as they attempted to fill not just their quotas in general but their regiments in particular. In November, Schuyler lamented that Massachusetts's promise of extra pay to reenlisting soldiers was "doubtless meant to promote the service," but had the opposite effect by undermining "recruiting on the Continental allowance."[36] Men in the camps could comparison shop.

An unhappy Hazen complained to Congress that on his arrival in Albany, "a Barrier [was] thrown in the way of my recruiting in the eastern states by their giving an additional encouragement to Soldiers over and above what I was authorized by Congress to offer." The frustrated colonel recommended that Congress move "to put the army of the united States on an equal footing—which will not only leave me an opportunity of raising the Regiment from the different States agreable to the resolve of Congress but will prevent in your army the greatest Discontent." He was still fighting for such regularity years later, but in the meantime, with Schuyler's approval, Hazen rode to Ticonderoga hoping that the appointment of officers "then on the ground," likely from the Pennsylvania and New Jersey troops, might give him "an equal chance to recruit out of the Southern Regiments at that place." He was again disappointed, however, as the regimental commanders there "would not consent to their soldiers Inlisting into any other corps until regularly Discharged."[37]

Elias Dayton must have complained about poachers, for Schuyler passed word that "No Officer of any Corps whatsoever is to recruit from the Regt. command'd by Col: Dayton."[38] Yet Hazen did sign on Lieutenant Richard Lloyd in November 1776, and later the soldiers John Ryan and Stephen Collins, and probably others, joined from that regiment.[39] Colonel Anthony Wayne, one of the commanders at Ticonderoga, also likely did not appreciate Hazen's competition as soldiers such as Jacob Doddridge switched regiments.[40] Even before Hazen arrived, Wayne was trying to sweeten enlistment offers. On 30 October, he had promised soldiers who agreed to reenlist that they would get not only their bounty money but also "a Dram together with a full Assurance of Returning to Pennsylvania as soon as the Enemy are Defeated, which the Col: hopes will be in a few Days, perhaps in a few Howers."[41] Perhaps Wayne had had a dram himself when he offered such a rosy assurance so soon after General Arnold's defeat at the Battle of Valcour Island. On the other hand, reinforcements had arrived at Ticonderoga, so he showed confidence about meeting the British assumed to be on the way. The soldiers did not get to go home in a few days, but the fact that after taking Crown Point the British reversed course to winter back in Canada may be one reason why in December Schuyler offered one-month furloughs to noncommissioned officers who reenlisted and whose garrisons were relieved.[42]

Another reason was that Schuyler and the other officers had to make a concession to soldiers. At a November council of war, Schuyler, Gates, Arnold, and militia Brigadier General James Brickett all agreed that "few of the soldiers now in service will reengage ... unless they are permitted first to return to the different States" from which they joined. They thought it prudent to allow furloughs to those not necessary for garrison duty, but they also tried to make it advantageous by giving them orders to recruit. The hope was that the soldiers and noncommissioned officers would not only return but bring new soldiers too. Schuyler accepted the necessity, but he grumbled to Governor Trumbull that he had hoped "experience would have taught us not to depend on the patriotism of our common men"—they had left at critical times during the previous year as their enlistments expired—yet his advice about preventing "the periodical *American* distemper" had been ignored. And so, yet again, "as soon as the first cold is felt, we are seized with the home-sickness, and it increases with the severity of the weather."[43]

In the meantime, Schuyler had to deal with Hazen, his recruiting officers, and those of other regiments. Out of the numerous officers that Hazen had appointed on 3 November, four—Captains Jeremiah Parmelee and William Satterlee and Lieutenants Mark Mazuzen and William Munson—were from Elmore's regiment, which was slated to be disbanded. Fellow member Lieutenant Alexander Sloan joined Hazen's regiment in December, and two more followed a few months later. These officers turned to the soldiers who had already been serving with them in Elmore's regiment to fill their new companies. Schuyler tried to curb the practice in late December. He believed that most of the men in Elmore's regiment would reenlist, and some had already done so, but he prohibited "recruiting officers of other corps to inlist any more of the men, as they are still to serve to the middle of *April*, and Congress may perhaps order that regiment to be kept up, that there may not be so many officers unprovided for."[44] Congress did not order the regiment's continuance, and thus many of its soldiers chose from among its officers offering alternative enlistments.

Although many soldiers still had time to serve in Elmore's regiment, more than seventy of them reengaged for the service in Hazen's regiment, and more than sixty of those, including James Wakeland, with Captain Satterlee, most but not all having been in his former company.[45] Amos Ames had entered Satterlee's company of Elmore's regiment in the spring of 1776, served out that enlistment, and then, as he put it, reenlisted "for the war in the same company" as attached to Hazen's regiment, "called the Congress regiment."[46] Date discrepancies among rolls suggest that Satterlee and his lieutenants started reengaging the soldiers by late December, but then made the new commitment official as of April after the earlier enlistments ended. It also appears that Satterlee did not subsist them as he did new recruits, except for a few, such as the fifer Abijah Stowe, whose previous service may have expired earlier.

Schuyler was not the only commander hearing complaints about how and who was recruiting when and where. General William Heath at Peekskill wrote to Washington that he thought recruiting was going well but wanted to know "if the men belonging to one State are to inlist under officers belonging to another, as there is a diversity of opinions on the matter." He believed they should not. Washington assured him that officers of one state were not to be allowed to enlist soldiers of another.[47] The commander in chief, however, amended that in February 1777: after forbidding recruiting officers to offer bounties greater than Congress's, he also forbade them to enlist men from their own states to serve in units of another state, "unless they are of the Additional Battalions, the Congress's own Regt, or the Train of Artillery."[48] Washington's command and the state affiliations of the regiment's officers helped when they trolled for their countrymen in camps and communities. Captains Robert Burns and William Chambers recruited fellow Pennsylvanians such as Henry Hilger and John Gregory,[49] but they also had soldiers from other states in their companies. Although companies showed regional ties, the regiment was not state-affiliated, which was one of the reasons its recruiters faced pushback. Another was that some of them were as aggressive as their commanding officer in manning their companies.

New York's civil officials assured Washington that they were not trying to encroach on his authority when they complained about how some of his commanders were interfering with the recruitment of the state's regiments. If New York had only to raise its quota of five battalions, it would have met it, but Colonels Hazen, James Livingston, and Seth Warner and some of their officers were siphoning recruits within the state.[50] New York wanted its inhabitants in its own regiments if and when they chose to enlist.

Officials in other states surely grumbled like their New York brethren as Lieutenant Colonel Antill rode southward and appointed officers who competed with state-line recruiters in camps and communities from New Jersey, Pennsylvania, and beyond. Colin McLachlan joined fellow New Jersey inhabitant Captain James Heron's company in Princeton. John Barr, who like Henry Young was from Pennsylvania and had served six months in the Flying Camp (a mobile reserve force in 1776), enlisted with fellow Pennsylvanian Captain Burns. So too did James Dixon, who had marched to Quebec in Colonel John Philip de Haas's 1st Pennsylvania and then probably returned with it from New York before making the switch. William Liggins enlisted in York County,

Pennsylvania, while Hugh McCleland did so in Lancaster, both in Pennsylvanian Captain John Thompson's company. Angus O'Near, Edward Quigley, and William Sharp signed up for Captain William Popham's company from Delaware. The latter two had served in Colonel John Haslet's Delaware Regiment, as had Popham, its former lieutenant. John Battin enlisted with fellow Marylander Captain John Carlile, but Charles Badger of the same state enlisted under Captain Thomas Pry, a Pennsylvanian.[51] Badger was not alone in crossing state lines within the regiment. On the promise of a commission from fellow Caroline County Virginian Major John Taylor, Sergeant Ambrose Walden recruited his fourteen-year-old brother John and six other privates in February 1777. After marching to Philadelphia, where they underwent smallpox inoculation and quarantine, they were assigned to Pennsylvanian Captain Matthew McConnell's company at Princeton and Walden was promoted to ensign.[52] Such mixing increased later after some captains resigned and their companies were reassigned. But initially, the regiment more closely mirrored the army in that it was continental in conception but regional in its companies.[53]

In the scramble to secure troops, Congress, states, commanders, and soldiers also contended over the length of service. Washington and other commanders wanted service for the duration of the war. Congress initially complied when it set enlistment terms for the new army. Yet, although states and people readily accepted most of the new provisions, many fretted that requiring enlistment for the war's duration would retard recruitment. Congress compromised: On 12 November it offered two tiers of service and recompense. Men could choose to serve for the duration or for the term of "three years, unless sooner discharged by Congress." All would have the same bounties and pay, but only the former would receive land. Initially, Congress charged the recruiters to keep two rolls, but within weeks it said that states could have their recruiters "inlist their men either for the war or three years, upon the respective bounties offered by Congress, without presenting inlisting rolls for both terms . . . keeping it always in view that . . . the public service will be best promoted by inlistments for the war, if the recruiting business is not retarded thereby."[54] That short-term solution, along with enlistment papers that combined "three years or the duration," created problems later, but in the winter of 1776–77, the priority was to fill the regiments. Hazen's recruiters accepted both three-year and duration enlistments, but it appears there were more of the latter.

Men sought commissions and signed enlistments for ideological, social, professional, financial, and, occasionally, no good reasons. Sometimes enlistment may just have been a matter of where and in what condition someone was at a particular time. Most of those reasons appear to have spurred William Calder. As an asthmatic veteran in his sixties, he deposed that he had been a laborer when on 19 April 1775, he joined Captain Jonathan Allen's company "at the alarm at Boston." He then stormed Quebec under Arnold, before enlisting in Captain Parmelee's company of Elmore's regiment for a year, and then, in June 1777, reengaging with Parmelee in Hazen's regiment. He later made sergeant in Captain James Duncan's company. After serving at the Battles of Brandywine and Germantown and the siege at Yorktown, he was discharged at Pompton. Calder truly embodied "one of the 'During the War men' as they were called."[55]

Duty, honor, need, and rewards in different measures spurred men to enlist and reenlist. Belonging—a sense of community, fellowship, and even family—often was part of or added to all of those elements. The original soldiers of the 2nd Canadian Regiment who reengaged, whether for three years, the war, or the conquest of Canada, provided a veteran foundation, but so too did the soldiers from Elmore's regiment who reenlisted with their former officers. Other new-made or old soldiers joined for similar reasons. But something more may have attracted them to Hazen's regiment.

Names and Numbers

The fierce competition for recruits likely spurred the creation of the title "Congress's Own." It was one thing for Lieutenant Ferriole to recruit fellow refugees for Hazen's "Regiment of Canadians" at Albany in November 1776, but would recruits from the states—whether fresh or veteran—join a regiment named for a province that did not choose to join the revolutionary union? Unlikely. That dilemma plus the fact that Congress, not a state, had authorized the regiment, sanctioned its recruiting in all the states, and provided money for that recruitment induced its members to adopt this distinction associating it with Congress.

The desire to foster professionalism and esprit de corps was a contributing factor. Material interests and rewards, such as bounties, attracted men to the army, but they alone did not keep them in it. Distinction, discipline, and belonging helped forge the mettle to stay. The Valley Forge encampment in the winter of 1777–78 impressed a professionalism that contributed to a greater group identity, increased solidarity, pride, and improved performance.[56] That experience was critically important to the army in adding uniformity to the growing unity of the corps. However, it was but part of the process, not the beginning nor end of it. Hazen's regiment, which merely passed by or through Valley Forge, started developing its own political-military character well before that. Its officers already perceived what another remarked: "The usefulness of a Regiment depends on Regimental Spirit or Pride, without this it will never have that emulation, which is the life and Soul of a Corps."[57]

The name "Congress's Own" harked to the creation of the Canadian regiments. In February 1776, Arnold had believed that the Americans would hold

Canada, because "we shall have the Intrest of the Country in general to which the raiseing Two Regiments of Canadians (which Congress have Ordered) will Not a little Conduce."[58] He was soon proved wrong about holding the country, but by the end of 1776, "Congress's Own" probably seemed an apt designation to the regiment's *congréganistes* or *congressistes,* as French Canadians may have called their countrymen who had served with the occupying American rebels.[59] Supporters of all or some of the aims promulgated by Congress—liberty, self-determination, and perhaps annexation, among others—had thus already provided something of a history for the name and the regimental community it was to denote.[60]

The title must also have seemed desirable to the officers who used it as they recruited in the winter of 1776–77, when the moniker appeared. It signified that the regiment served by and at the will of Congress, for Congress's—to wit, the Continental—cause. It was, in modern parlance, a good "brand" for enticing recruits who were not Canadian.

An officer likely coined the name, and since Hazen was more of a pugilist and Antill a politician, it may have been the latter. Antill signed a return of cash paid for carriages sometime between December 1776 and early January 1777 as "Lt Col of the Congress's Own Regt."[61] He had not used the designation in his December 1776 petition, in which he asked Congress to confirm the appointment of ten captains whom he had already sent out on recruiting forays and to authorize him to draw bills upon recommended suppliers for arms, equipment, and uniforms.[62] He did, however, use it in a 2 January 1777 letter recounting the origin and state of "the Congress's Own Regiment." Riding from Baltimore to Lancaster and Wilmington to check on the officers' recruiting efforts, Antill wanted Washington's approbation as he made more appointments.[63]

Other clues to the tie between the name and recruitment appear in veterans' pension accounts. Francis Lester, a seventy-six-year-old Massachusetts laborer, testified in 1818 that he had served with the Massachusetts militia at Ticonderoga in 1776, and then that December at Albany he had enlisted with Captain Joseph Torrey of Massachusetts (Torrey had been a transplant to Canada). Lester deposed that the "Regiment to which I belonged was said to have been raised for the Congress Guard and was known in the army by the name of the Congress Regiment."[64] The Canadian Peter Chartier deposed in 1820 that he had retreated with General Montgomery's troops, and then on his arrival in Albany he had enlisted in Hazen's "Congress regiment." His compatriot, Charles Tessie (Tellie/r), said much the same thing, just elaborating that it was called "Congress' own Regiment." Abijah Stowe asserted that when he enlisted as a musician in Satterlee's company in the spring of 1777, the regiment was "then called the Congress regiment."[65] Other regimental veterans applying for pensions remembered being in Congress's or Congress's Own Regiment, but did not specify what it was called when they enlisted.

The title's invention served recruiting as it helped reconstitute the regiment with an imagined elite and encompassing identity. Joining the army was choosing, with varying degrees of ardor or coercion, to serve a cause, whether one's own or the nation's. Enlisting in a specific regiment generally reflected common interests, identities, and ties. A soldier could combine both civic allegiance and principles with other cultural, territorial, or particular concerns when enrolling in the military. Bounties were important, but recruiters also had to get men to see that choosing their particular regiment would serve their needs and values in the company of others like them.[66] The latter was a marked challenge for Hazen's regiment.

Hazen's officers met that challenge by touting a political identity for the regiment even as they used former service and regional ties to fill their companies. Their regiment belonged to and defended the nation represented in Congress. They laid an enlistment form before recruits in early 1777 that specified: "I . . . do voluntarily enlist myself into Captain . . . 's Company of Foot, belonging to the CONGRES's OWN Regiment, in the Service of the United States of America, to continue during the War, and to be subject to such Rules and Articles as are or shall be established by Congress." The form also had a section to record receipt of "the Bounty ordered by Congress," and another by which to "swear (or affirm) to be true to the United States of America, and to serve them honestly and faithfully against all their Enemies or Opposers whatsoever and to observe and obey the Orders of the Continental Congress, and the Orders of the Generals and Officers set over me by them." The key refrain, spoken and written, was Congress.[67]

Being in the right place at the right time was important to recruiting, but there was also power in the name. Despite state objections and competition, Hazen's recruiters added hundreds of men to Congress's Own by the spring of 1777. The regiment included its colonels, one major, two staff (quartermaster and paymaster), and eleven companies in a return of 461 men as of 1 March. The 1 April return ignored the field officers and staff and recorded three volunteers and 454 men among fourteen companies. (By comparison, Colonel Livingston reported that his officers had recruited 210 men for the 1st Canadian by early April.)[68] Hazen's regimental returns, however, reveal that some companies were not counted, namely those of Captains Gilbert, White, Parmelee, and Satterlee. The latter two were still assembling the men they had recruited out of Elmore's disbanding regiment. And Hazen appears not to have included Paulint's attached independent company.

Similar reasons may account for the smaller numbers at Princeton in May. There, Hazen's regiment was recorded as having 354 men on 3 May and then 385 on the 10th. Those tallies did not count the colonel or other officers who were likely absent, but the second suggests that another captain and his subaltern had marched in that week with their company. A different record put the regiment's strength in New Jersey at 460 in May 1777; and Washington apparently eliminated the officers and sick from that count to put the regiment's strength at 393. Even though a 1 June return gave a total of 413, Hazen claimed that 720 men "were carried into the Field in June 1777."[69]

Miscounts were connected to funding woes, and together they showed that administering the army was just as big a problem as fielding and fighting it. Congress and the commander in chief wanted better accounting. A dissatisfied Washington vented to General Alexander McDougall in March that "extraordinary" returns of enlistments and desertions suggested possible recruiting fraud, so he was demanding "accurate returns of the troops raising in every state."[70] Hazen's regiment tried to comply, but staffing woes complicated the effort. The regiment had an adjutant, a C. H. Delagard (possibly Joseph C. Delazenne), to register orders and maintain records, but there are no papers preserving his work, and he resigned in October. Thomas Pry then assumed the duties for a few months. Robert Dill joined as paymaster in January but left in July. Edward Chinn had the post of paymaster as of 1 June, but may have been diverted by (or perhaps even a prisoner of) the British after the Battle of Short Hills at Scotch Plains, New Jersey.[71] The full regiment did not participate in the 26 June battle, but a detachment apparently did. Detachments, vacancies in the staff, and lost papers (then and since) played havoc with record keeping.

The regiment's records indicate that between 820 and possibly over 970 men enlisted or reenlisted between 1 October 1776 (after the regiment was reauthorized in September) and 30 May 1777. Among the youngest were thirteen-year-olds Edward Wall (Maryland), and fifers Abijah Stowe (Massachusetts) and Alexander Ferriol (Canada). Among the oldest was Henry Young (not a pun) of Pennsylvania at forty-four. During that period, around 156 to 188 new-made and reengaged soldiers deserted, and likely 26 to 40 died. The greater numbers account for probable members not listed on a combined roll of two rosters compiled in 1782–83.[72] For example, although the majority of the men listed on Ferriole's recruiting return showed up on the principal roll, including Jean (John) Dennis, who died at Albany in 1776, some did not: Joseph Nichola drowned in January 1777, and two others died in Philadelphia (Joseph Lorgel or Loigel in December, and one with an obscured name "before muster"). There were also other deaths in 1777, but those months were not recorded, so it is not known when those soldiers joined the "Congregation of the dead" due to accidents, camp diseases, or battle.[73] Deleting the departed from the enlistees of late 1776 through May 1777 (not including those for whom no month is recorded) suggests 642 to 750 solders—not all fit, effective, or encamped in the same place—in the regiment by May's end.

Desertions as well as enlistments showed the regiment's distinctive conception and diverse composition even as they modified its numbers. Although desertions diminished the regiment's strength, alerts for the fugitives' return trumpeted the regiment's distinctive name and revealed increasing diversity. A notice posted by Captain McConnell on 25 January 1777 described two recent deserters from his company in "Congress's own regiment": William Cockran from Ireland was about 32, five feet, ten inches tall, with fair hair. He was supposed headed to Reading. Patrick Ferrel, believed headed to Bucks County, was about 22 and five feet four with black hair. The captain offered a ten-dollar reward for each of them.[74] Cockran disappeared but he may have joined another regiment, as there were other William Cockrans or Cochrans in the army. Ferrel appears to have returned—by capture or choice, perhaps in response to a later general pardon—for he mustered with the regiment in March 1782 and deserted again that August.[75] Captain Benjamin Chambers also emphasized "the *Congress's Own Regiment*" when he offered a reward of five dollars each in March 1777 for Isaac Baker, John Grimes, and James Reed, all in their mid-twenties and between five feet five and six, who had deserted at Reading. Isaac Baker died that April in Philadelphia, while Grimes (or Grahams) and Reed, who both enlisted on 11 February, dropped from the roll.[76]

The desertions of 1777 and other years disclosed conflicting views about where, when, and how autonomy and authority were exercised. Of particular note in 1777, especially because of sensitivity over new bounties, was the matter of men enlisting and then disappearing before mustering, between attaching the cockade and donning the uniform. Congress's Own suffered that sting. Captain Heron noted that Israel Spice and John Taylor had enlisted on 9 and 10 March, respectively, and both deserted on the 10th. Taylor was not the only man to enlist and desert on the same day, but he did appear on the regiment's master roll, unlike Joseph McCurree and Joseph Michael.[77] Did such men act within a psychological and legal liminal zone? Did they believe they were free to change their minds and depart? What did military and civil officials contend? Was that desertion in the same manner as that of a soldier who quitted the ranks? Antill thought so, for he advertised on 29 March that "ALL RECRUITS belonging to the CONGRESS's OWN REGIMENT . . . whose furlows are out, are required to repair to the barracks in Philadelphia, on or before the twenty-third day of April next. Those who neglect this notice, will be deemed deserters, and treated accordingly."[78] If recruits accepted bounty money but refused to serve (in a later war called bounty jumpers), they engaged in fraud, and that was certainly the case if they enlisted many times for multiple bounties, even if they did eventually muster with one of the units.

Congress deplored desertions but debated how to handle deserters, and the debates, like those about other military issues, revealed the delegates negotiating the liminal space that was the Revolution—in particular the balancing of autonomy and authority at different levels. Congress had criticized states that undermined its bounty resolutions, including Maryland for its decision to pay ten dollars in lieu of the congressionally promised bounty land, a practice that Congress believed would lead other soldiers to demand the same option. Furthermore, showing how growing "federal" thought related to administering the Continental Army, Congress said that what it promised "must be obligatory upon their constituents; that no one state can, by its own act, be released therefrom." That was far from the last word. When in February Congress passed a resolution empowering constables and others to take up deserters and deliver them to justices of the peace, Irish-born Thomas Burke of North Carolina protested that such direct congressional authority bypassed the states and endangered individual liberty. Debate ensued over congressional—or Continental—authority and whether or not by deputizing justices of the peace essentially as officers "of the army" to deal with such fugitives, Congress was creating a power within the states that would act independently of them. The delegates also debated whether soldiers and officers were subject only to Congress and the Articles of War or had recourse to the laws of the states. Were the Continentals solely Congress's own, or were they still freemen with rights? Burke insisted that the states had a duty to interpose in desertion cases when there was a question of whether or not the accused was a soldier, so as to ensure that a citizen was not subject to martial law without consent or without appeal to civil authority.[79]

Aside from such civil-military issues, the delegates agreed that military officials had to prevent and punish bounty fraud and desertion. Washington, in turn, advised Congress about what it might do to help; disciplined officers; and warned, punished, and pardoned soldiers. As he and other civil and military officials knew, sometimes civilians encouraged recruits to desert and engage in bounty fraud. Furthermore, the enemy offered a greater bounty to those who enlisted in its forces, especially if carrying arms. The commander in chief thus recommended better bounties to reverse the course of desertions, and also appointing auditors to ensure that officers both disbursed and accounted for pay and recruiting funds. He also pardoned deserters who voluntarily returned, and selectively executed the worst offenders. As Washington averred that May, "I would recommend the execution of only the most notorious, and such, whose punishment would strike Terror into their accomplices and adherents who are not yet apprehended. By making Executions too common, they lose their intended force and rather bear the appearance of cruelty than justice."[80]

Hazen's regiment saw the gamut of punishments meted out to its own, other soldiers, and even civilians. Not all accused faced courts-martial. Perhaps Antill thought that jail time had been enough punishment for Charles Dougherty (Daugherty), who had deserted on 9 April, and Richard Brooker (Brooks) and James Johnston (Johnson), who were also likely taken as deserters. Gaoler Michael Jmeel provided a receipt in August 1777 to Antill "in the Congresses own Ragement" for the costs of his services as a turnkey, for providing wood and bread to the prisoners, and for putting on and off the irons.[81]

Hugh Wallace, who had enlisted in Burns's company in December, faced court-martial for deserting to the Maryland regiment into which he had previously enlisted. The court sentenced him to refund the money received from Hazen's recruiter, but after a review found the sentence too lenient; he remained a prisoner pending further investigation. He was "taken by prior enlistment" on 28 April, which could mean he was arrested or returned to his former regiment on that date. On the other hand, Sergeant Richard Burrows, also of Burns's company, was shot for desertion at Princeton on 6 June. His execution might have been ordered to make an example of someone of his rank, or because he had been encouraging others to desert.[82]

Notwithstanding the concerns of Thomas Burke and others about who was subject to martial law, civilians sometimes found themselves before courts-martial if they degraded military operations or abetted the enemy. Major John Taylor of Hazen's regiment confined Richard Ennes on suspicion of having incited desertion. On 31 July, a Newark court-martial convicted him of the offense based largely on a camp follower's deposition. Alice Wood (or Ward), whose husband Jeams (Games or James Ward) had been absent at that morning's muster, recounted how she and her husband had visited Ennes's house, where her husband and two other soldiers (one was John Pendergrass) of Hazen's regiment had complained of being stinted in provisions and pay. Ennes promised them that they would have plenty of both if they deserted—extra if they brought their arms. He said that they did not have to join the British army but could have passage to Ireland or work for good wages in New York if they preferred. While drinking the tea that Ennes and his wife had offered, Ward asked his wife if she would go with him; she answered that she preferred to head to Philadelphia and home to her child. Before she could do that, she reported on the actions of her husband and Pendergrass, and a private from the 4th Maryland substantiated her account. Brigadier General Philippe Hubert Preudhomme de Borre, who was later reprimanded by Washington for such treatment of a civilian, sentenced Ennes to hang. Privates Ward and

Pendergrass were already gone.[83] Others continued to desert that summer, including James McMullen of Captain Henry O'Hara's company, who instead of getting to Ireland was sentenced to a hundred lashes on his bare back and to serve the remainder of his enlistment on a Continental frigate.[84]

Hundreds more, however, stood fast in the regiment. Congress's Own had recruited over 80 (possibly 90) percent of its authorized strength of 1,000 soldiers in the eight months since reauthorization in late September 1776. The substantial desertion rate plus deaths had it mustering near two-thirds in May. Yet, especially if the approximately sixty officers at the time are counted with the remaining soldiers, the number corroborates Hazen's purported 720 entering the 1777 campaign season in June. Although the regiment did not hit its authorized strength, and soon tumbled from the recruited high, it embodied a sizable force that spring, especially in comparison with other regiments of foot, all of which fell far short of the 1776–77 model of 728 officers and men.[85]

Adversities

By late spring 1777, Congress's Own was not just a name; it was a large, confederated regiment with a growing story. Part of that story was the retreat from Canada and the sacrifices of the "Volunteers for the United States" who had "no Parent State to reward their meritorious Services." Another part was the officers' "Activity, Alacrity and Spirit in the public Service." A third was about companies "immediately sent on actual hard Service." When Hazen later recounted the regiment's story, he touted the service of Captain William Chambers, who enlisted fifty-four men in the waning days of 1776 and marched them to Philadelphia in twenty-one days. Chambers's detachment "joined the Army at a most alarming Period, at or near Trenton." Annexed to Colonel Charles Scott's regiment, the company served with it through the following months until Chambers rejoined Hazen's regiment in May with only nine men left, for "forty-five had been expended in the Course of the Winter in the Service."[86] Although general accounts of Trenton, Princeton, and Scott's 5th Virginia do not mention that an element of Congress's Own participated, a few old veterans recalled in their pension applications that they had been at the Battle of Trenton. They likely meant the Second Battle of Trenton or the Battle of Assunpink Creek on 2 January. As none of them said they had enlisted in Chambers's company, and records indicate that they joined after the battles, maybe they had served with another unit, maybe they misremembered, or maybe they exaggerated to bolster their pension applications. On the other hand, Zephaniah Henderson (Hendrickson), Thomas Rose, and John White of Chambers's company were killed on 2 January, and John Hicks and William Dunevan (Donnavan) died on the 10th and 12th, respectively;[87] it is thus possible that some of Congress's Own's soldiers fought and died near Trenton and in the forage war that followed.

Chambers might have pulled some of the most energetic recruits into what amounted to a light infantry company to support the regiments, in particular Colonel Scott's, that were harassing the enemy's foraging parties. The company took hits in the process, but maybe not quite so dramatically as Hazen put it. The company's March and April rolls both noted one captain, two lieutenants, and three corporals, but it dropped a drummer, and went from three sergeants to two and from fifty-six privates to twenty-one over those months. The losses from January onward were due not just to deaths, however, but also to desertions and being taken prisoner, as John Ryley may have been on 2 January.[88]

As Chambers and his company marched into action and others may have responded to a Board of War directive to join Washington's army and curb further enemy actions in New Jersey, another part of the regiment was on duty in Lancaster, Pennsylvania.[89] The regimental members there were gathering and stowing Continental stores in what proved to be a volatile area. Lancaster, a major inland farming and trading center, was also a storage depot not just for goods but for prisoners of war. The initial set appeared after the 1775 invasion of Canada. Then German prisoners arrived after the battle at Trenton. Most of the residents were staunch revolutionaries who did not see a problem with employing the prisoners while some of their own men served in the war. On the other hand, the influx made people wary, and when other newcomers arrived bearing arms and behaving badly, civil-military disputes ensued.[90]

According to Lancaster County officials, on 17 March, St. Patrick's Day, soldiers from Hazen's regiment "armed with Clubs & Blugeons ... marched through Town in a hostile Way, using the most insolent and opprobrious Terms, and threatening Expressions." Antill hustled out and "ordered the Rioters to their Barracks," where he reinforced the guard on the advice of the ranking officer, Colonel Edward Hand. To augment the guard under Captain Thompson, Antill kept Adjutant Edmund Minyier—a gentleman and disciplinarian "lately from France"—and his soldiers on duty beyond their shift. Antill told various officials to call the guard should there be another fracas, and commanded Minyier to take up "riuotous Disorderly People and Confine them, and to obey the orders of any Civil or Military officer," but gave him no orders to fire on anyone.[91]

Late that afternoon, "public Tranquility" was again broken, "civil and military Power were set in Opposition," and "natural Prejudices were inflamed." It started around twilight, when "some Boys in Queen Street had an Affray with a young Lad belonging to the Regt." But while "the Affairs of Children are soon over," this escalated when officers of the regiment appeared with their swords drawn, crying "Where are they?" The guard led by Adjutant Minyier followed.[92] The events, which echo some of those in the fatal Boston brawl of March 1770, were confusing in action and deposition, and they ultimately left one man dead and another charged with murder.

Edmund Minyier declared that he had been shot at, with the ball passing "between his Chin & Neck Cloth," when he marched out the guard to deal with the disturbance. When he arrived on the scene, a uniformed gentleman handed over Jacob Gross, but then Gross ran and three or four of the soldiers pursued him. Witnesses charged that Minyier slashed down his sword and commanded the guard to fire. Minyier, in turn, said he believed that the soldiers in pursuit might have fired at Gross, who was shot in the hip at some point in the brawl. Minyier, however, also noted that when he caught up with his men there were others fighting with "Guns Bayonets Knives and Clubs." Men were "pulling each other by the Hair" and rolling on the ground.[93]

Other deponents said there was no such fighting, and no one with a gun, bayonet, knife, or club "except Gross who had a Chunk of Wood about two feet long in his hand." But Jacob Kuhn admitted he was armed. He said that he was defending some young men when he turned to face some officers, and asked "why they drew their swords, one of the soldiers seeing a Club in the Deponants hands asked him why he Carried it, He said for the same reason you have one now and your People have Carried them the Preceeding part of the Day." About then, "the officer of the Guard (in Boots and a large Hat)" appeared and cried out something or other. Other officers cried "Fire." Myer Solomon swore that two of the guard aimed their bayonets at his brother Levy, who was with John Jordan, and muttered something in French before returning to their ranks. Levy Solomon said he had told the person who advanced on him to "keep your Ranks you son of a Bitch," but then said that he saw "No quarrelling in the street Nor observed the Guard in any names insulted or misused." And yet "orders were given by the French officers to Fire."[94]

Inhabitants armed themselves to attack the guard but were eventually "pacified by Col. Antill & some of their Fellow Citizens." The Lancaster committee that met that night and the next morning disputed reports that some inhabitants had snapped their guns at Antill, but by the morning it had a bigger problem: Jacob Gross had died. The committee added punishing murder to preserving peace among its duties as it examined witnesses and invited Antill to help Minyier, who knew little English, cross-examine them. Antill refused because he did not think that the committee had the right to try and sentence Minyier. The committee argued that it was not judging Minyier, just charging him and demanding that he be jailed pending trial. The next day, Antill proposed to deliver Minyier to authorities in Philadelphia, for he believed that his "raw Recruits" might try to rescue Minyier if he was confined in the local jail. The committee was appalled that men recruited to defend the people would subvert the state's constitution and defy law and justice.[95]

Ultimately, Antill and the committee compromised: he would deliver Minyier to them and they would deliver the accused to the President and Council of Pennsylvania. But then the committee wrote its summation and asked the Pennsylvania delegates in Congress to ensure that Minyier was returned to Lancaster for trial. Besides condemning the idea of a military officer having the power "to command a Guard to fire upon the Inhabitants," the members averred, "The People will dam themselves miserable indeed, when the Military shall rise superior to the Civil Power, and prevent Offenders from being brought to Justice."[96]

On 29 March, Congress resolved that as an inquisition performed before the Lancaster county coroner had charged "Edmund Minyer, adjutant of the regiment commanded by Colonel Moses Hazen . . . with the murder of Jacob Gross . . . That the said Edmund Minyer be delivered to the civil authority of Pensylvania, that he may receive his trial according to law." Two days later, Hancock directed Antill "to Deliver up to the Civil Authority of this State the person mention'd in the said Resolve."[97]

Antill wrote to Congress, perhaps both before and after its review, to protest the committee's version of the events and offer a defense for Minyier. According to Antill (echoing Minyier), inhabitants had been armed, and Jacob Gross, apprehended as a rioter, had tried to escape. The mob had yelled fire, not the adjutant, but even if Minyier had called fire, he was doing his duty. Minyier could not get a fair trial among the prejudiced people of Lancaster. Furthermore, he could not defend himself in English nor call defense witnesses, for most of those witnesses, members of "the Congresses own Regiment," had since marched from Lancaster for New Jersey.[98]

The Minyier affair brought the regiment to Congress's notice at a bad time and in a negative way. Congress did not acknowledge the title that Antill employed in his address in its decision, nor on 7 April when it read Antill's appeal for Minyier, nor on the 8th, when it authorized more of the regiment's officer commissions in between advancing funds, delaying a report on proposed articles of confederation, approving memorials, and establishing the Medical Department.[99] Upset at units adopting special designations, on 15 April Congress ordered Washington to see the practice discontinued. It specifically denounced the "appellations, 'Congress's own regiment,' 'General Washington's life guards,' &c." The etcetera might have referred to some of the sixteen additional regiments recruiting as "guards," in particular as "Washington's

Guards." Or perhaps it was a way to avoid disrespecting Martha Washington by implicitly censuring the nickname "Lady Washington's Horse" for the newly forming Baylor's Horse, the 3rd Continental Light Dragoon Regiment. Congress declared that all of the Continental battalions were on the same "footing" with equal privileges and "liable to the same kind of services."[100]

Washington responded that he had not consented to the names and that he had charged the units to end the distinctions. He echoed Congress in responding that "all the Battalions were on the same footing and all under the General name of Continental." Yet in his general orders of 1 February, he had specifically referred to "Congress's own Regt" in allowing its officers to enlist men not of their own state, and he had named it so again in a letter to General Knox.[101] Washington may not have referred to Hazen's regiment as Congress's Own after that, but he himself did keep what was called the Commander-in-Chief's Guard.

Why was the Continental Congress so upset by special unit designations? There were well-established European precedents in giving regiments honorifics. The British army, the primary model for the American army, had named regiments in honor of members of the royal family. Furthermore, if the precedent for the organization of Hazen's regiment was the Royal American Regiment, then there was another logic in naming it Congress's Own. But, of course, the revolutionaries were not to resurrect monarchical or royal trappings. Also, perhaps, members worried about comparisons with loyalist units such as the short-lived Queen's Own Loyal Virginia Regiment or the Queen's American Rangers raised by Robert Rogers.[102] As Congress had noted—and Washington concurred—there was to be equality among the Continental regiments.

Congress balked because distinguishing regiments, especially unusual ones external to state lines, seemed contrary to the expectations of the revolutionaries and the governments they were creating. They wanted an army that was part of—not distinct from—the "united" states, but that also belonged to the "Independent States of America."[103] They accepted the need for a regular army, but that army was to represent the republic as it served the Revolution. Congress and states thus implicitly and explicitly incorporated checks and balances so as not to empower a standing army that would be a threat to liberty.

The 1777 reorganization, recruitment, and composition of the Continental Army had it more closely resembling European counterparts. As it became a regular army, was it also to become a standing one? Revolutionaries who knew some history believed that standing armies—forces that continued in peacetime—could be offensive instruments of tyranny. They had the examples not just of monarchs, but also of Oliver Cromwell, the seventeenth-century English revolutionary turned Lord Protector. Then in the Glorious Revolution of 1688, Parliament had asserted its authority over the army, but that was not enough for America's radical Whigs. They preferred militias that upheld liberty by being local, defensive instruments.[104] Yet they were also made realists by their war's lessons. A solution was to expand civil power as they expanded military force.[105] One way to do this was to impose time limits on certain powers of the commander in chief, such as the six months allowed Washington to raise and collect additional battalions beyond the eighty-eight already authorized.[106] Another was to put time limits on the army, which, echoing most of the enlistments, was to be only for the duration of the war. A third way was to accept and maintain state lines and state control that not only reflected past provincial army precedents and logistical realities but also signaled regional authorities.

Even though Congress had put a temporal limit on some of Washington's extra powers, some members remained unhappy about those powers, and how Washington applied his authority. One cause was Washington's proclamation of 25 January 1777, which required people who had sworn loyalty to the Crown to obtain protection when the British army marched through New Jersey to now swear allegiance to the United States or withdraw to the enemy's lines. Washington's critics in Congress were not the only unhappy ones—some people feared that Congress had made him "dictator."[107] Congress was sensitive to the perceptions as well as realities not only of Washington's authority but also of its own. As its members deliberated the "Articles of Confederacy," they debated the powers of future congresses. Despite dissension, most accepted "that all sovereign Power was in the States separately, and that particular acts of it, which should be expressly enumerated, would be exercised in conjunction, and not otherwise." North Carolina delegate Thomas Burke defined it in the strictest terms: "the Congress should have power enough to call out and apply the common strength for the common defence: but not for the partial purposes of ambition."[108]

Congress may have balked at authorizing the regimental designation Congress's Own because Americans might have found it suspect—dangerous even—for Congress to have its "own" regiment, one outside of a state's control. Congress had authorized Hazen to raise and command the regiment, thus within the traditions of the time, it carried his name. But by assuming the title Congress's Own, the regiment declared Congress to be its honorary, symbolic colonel. Yet what if, in turn, the regiment did not reflect well on the honor of Congress? That aside, the honorific likely served as a reminder of proprietorship. Reauthorizing the regiment when there was no state to support it indicated that Congress owned it, and owning the regiment meant caring for it.[109] Hazen, who remained colonel-commandant, the regiment's operational commander, applied to Congress for the regiment's pay and provisions. Congress then had to figure out how to do that. It did so by asserting power while making concessions—in this case by telling the states that citizens of their states who enlisted in the additional regiments would be counted toward their quotas.

The fact that Congress's Own had so many "foreigners" or strangers in its ranks could also have been a factor in the name game. People might have asked whether the regiment was to defend Congress or defend America. They might also have wondered whether it was properly American like the state regiments. Yet Hazen's regiment simply could not belong to any particular state, for its people came from all over. It was called Hazen's and Canadian, reflecting its origins and echoing the designations of regiments by states, but it was more truly Congress's and continental. That was especially the case by 1781, after yet another army reorganization, when it incorporated more foreign noncommissioned officers and soldiers, the remains of Livingston's 1st Canadian, and other "flotsam and jetsam" of the American army.[110] At that time, it also became known as the Canadian—more specifically the Canadian Old Regiment—which was a fine finger wave to the establishment as the regiment kept the initials COR.

Despite Congress's orders not to use the title Congress's Own, the nickname continued to identify the regiment throughout the war and afterwards. There are signs that the regiment's officers did not fully comply with Congress's demands. In the June and July 1778 payrolls for his "Compy in a Regiment of foot in the service of the United States of America Commanded by Moses Hazen Esqr. Col. Commandant," Captain Thomas Pry penned a small "COR" under his signature. In a payroll titled similarly to Pry's but encompassing March, April, and May 1779, Captain John Carlile added "C.O.R." after his signature.[111] The headings heeded Congress's directive, but the endings did not. Antill had appointed both officers (Pry initially as a lieutenant) during the big recruitment drive in November 1776 (though Congress did not confirm their commissions until April 1777, the same month it ordered a halt to the nickname). Other extant payrolls by these officers and others, which regrettably do not cover all years, do not appear to have this refractory jab, but the quartermaster general did certify a receipt to Antill of the "C.O. Regt." in 1782.[112] And decades later, regimental veterans continued to proclaim what the Continental Congress had tried to prohibit earlier; their federal pension applications show that the name stuck.

The name tied the regiment to the civil center of the Revolution. "Congress's Own" obscured the outsider Canadian and Catholic connections to proclaim the regiment's civic allegiance: it belonged to Congress. The name promoted a positive regimental identity, but numbers, organization, and actions created a divided reputation: the officers and soldiers of Hazen's regiment fought well but quarreled much. The regiment, like the army and Congress, could never completely eradicate colonial distinctions or ameliorate individual rivalries. It, like the army, never entirely filled its ranks, but hundreds of men did attach its cockades that spring and summer of 1777. In joining Congress's Own Regiment within the borderland that was the Continental Army, many came to identify with each other as Continentals in addition to their respective national or regional cultures. And as those recruits drilled, they started to become soldiers. Then came battle.

CHAPTER 5

INFERNALS?

As Pennsylvania Congressman Robert Morris remarked in February 1777, "the Men must be cloathed, Armed, embodied & in some degree disciplined before they can be formidable."[1] They were not yet formidable when they went into action that summer. The regiments, Hazen's included, had not met enlistment goals and the states had not fulfilled their requisitions. The army's commanders, however, continued to collect whom and what they could to embody their regiments and endeavored to build the esprit de corps that incarnated the sentiments of the Revolution. To the discipline of drill and courtsmartial they added republican rhetoric and, on occasion, divine services.

Sermons worked in combination with speeches and songs, salutes and standards, arms, accouterments, and uniforms, and ultimately battles to imprint all of those belonging to the army. Together, they were not quite the tattoo that Washington inadvertently inferred to General Alexander McDougall when he reported that Congress resolved, "All belonging to the public, with their Accountrements, shall be stamped with the words United States & that they shall be seizable wheresoever they are afterwards found." Washington quickly clarified that all Continental arms were to be so marked.[2] Although such a stamp might have helped identify deserters wherever they were found, other signs marked a soldier.

Those signs were sometimes as threadbare as the unity within the army and Congress's Own Regiment. Tensions within the regiment and some suspicions regarding it and its "infernals" characterized the period from the expedition to Staten Island in August through the battles at Brandywine and Germantown in September 1777. Both the regiment and the army were still trying to coalesce, and those battles tested the process of formation against the backdrop of the continuing struggle to balance the Revolution's military and civilian goals.

Out of Many, One

"Fellow-soldier" Chaplain John Hurt reminded assembled troops in the spring of 1777 that "the name of Patriot . . . carries in it the idea of a public blessing; it implies a power of doing good, exerted and extended to whole communities; and resembles, within its sphere, that universal providence which protects and supports the world." He touted the family bonds of mother America's children, but especially the cultural and institutional connections that showed "the reasonableness of an affectionate attachment to the community." He emphasized those connections as he argued that everyone in that community was obliged to carry "on the great work of social happiness." It was not enough to support and applaud those who executed and managed the "glorious cause." Love of country—of its peoples' freedom and security—required "giv[ing] up every inclination which is incompatible with it . . . All the train of darling vices must therefore be . . . offered up as victims on the altars of liberty." The Reverend Hurt encouraged moral conduct for the common weal, and that included sharing the burdens, not just the benefits, of society.[3]

The denominational parts of sermons surely challenged the religiously orthodox, whether Catholic, Protestant, or Jew, but the services encouraged both churched and unchurched soldiers to heed a civil calling. By ordering attendance at "divine worship," as he did at Morristown in April and Middlebrook in June, Washington sought not to promote a particular religion but virtue generally, which included avoiding the "scandalous practice of *profane Swearing*" and acknowledging a common desire for divine favor.[4] While some regiments had a chaplain and a shared religious identity, many did not. Too few chaplains and too little money, or a desire for more consolidation and oversight, led Congress to determine that there would be brigade rather than regimental chaplains, and that it would appoint them upon the recommendations of the generals commanding those brigades.[5]

The resolution caused controversy within the army, as Washington revealed when he reviewed responses and recommended that the old regimental allocation of chaplains remain. Officers did not want to "introduce religious disputes into the Army" by dismissing some chaplains and choosing just one for a brigade. They worried that such an establishment of religion "would compel men to a mode of Worship, which they do not profess." They believed that the old regimental apportionments showed greater toleration.[6] But their responses did not solve the problem of too few chaplains, nor acknowledge diversity within regiments. The quiet compromise was that those regiments with chaplains retained them until they resigned or until a brigade chaplain was appointed.[7] Some brigades apparently put off the decision, and Washington did not push it. As he later reflected, "our Religious Liberties were as essential as our Civil," and so he tried "to encourage and promote the one, while . . . contending for the other."[8]

Contending for independence to secure civil liberties was a priority shared by Washington and Congress's Own, which had such a diversity of religions in its ranks that attempting uniformity, like acquiring enough uniforms, was impossible. There was also no Catholic chaplain to serve them. Father Floquet had not accompanied the 2nd Canadian Regiment on its retreat from Canada in 1776, and sixty-one-year-old Monsieur Lotbinière of the 1st Canadian preferred to stay near Congress while he regularly solicited it for pay and rations.[9] Perhaps Catholic Continentals could have petitioned for a special chaplain, as some "German officers" did in 1778,[10] but instead the French Canadians, like other Catholics in the ranks, awaited the visits of missionary priests for the sacraments and attended interreligious services that promoted virtuous conduct, martial community, and civil duty. Fledgling Presbyterian minister James Francis Armstrong appears to have been slated to serve as the regiment's chaplain in 1777, but whether he actually ministered to it before resigning in February 1778 is a question. Armstrong served as a volunteer aide-de-camp to Brigadier General William Smallwood at the Battle of Staten Island in August 1777, and then the following July, perhaps complying with Congress's directive, became chaplain to the 2nd Maryland Brigade.[11]

There is little evidence of the soldiers in Hazen's regiment attending religious services and how they responded to them. The rare mentions tend to corroborate that attendance was by command and that such services were to confirm the providential nature of the army's mission or to strengthen lessons about allegiance and duty. An example of the former was the first anniversary celebration of General John Burgoyne's Saratoga defeat, during which soldiers appeared more interested in food and firing their muskets along with the artillery and "Sky Rockets" than the Reverend Dr. Israel Evans's oration. Months later, in February 1779, Evans, chaplain to Brigadier General Enoch Poor's brigade (to which Hazen's regiment was attached), "made a long discourse, well adapted to the Occasion" of the executions of Danbury inhabitant Edward Jones and soldier John Smith of the 1st Connecticut. A general court-martial had found Jones guilty of guiding and spying for the enemy and Smith of desertion and trying to go to the enemy (and declaring he would try again). The soldiers, "under arms," of Poor's, Parsons's, and Huntingdon's brigades attended the hanging of Jones and shooting of Smith as did "a vast Concourse of Country People."[12]

While sermons (and on occasion punishments) sought to impress a common purpose, uniforms conveyed a common identity. Uniforms distinguished soldiers, though sometimes the distinction was the lack thereof. Washington wanted to clothe his troops uniformly, but "discretionary changes" and supply deficiencies undermined that objective throughout the war. In March 1779, Congress authorized the commander in chief to "fix and prescribe the uniform," which Washington did that October.[13] Money and manufacturing bedeviled the supply chains, but as logistics improved the delivery of uniform items over the course of the war, there continued to be alterations, by choice and necessity, that differentiated regiments.

Regimental markers—uniforms, emblazoned drums, and standards—heralded unit pride on one level, but more importantly they helped distinguish identity and location on the battlefield. Coats were primarily blue or brown, although some riflemen and dragoons donned green. Coat facings and cuffs alternated between red, white, buff, blue, and occasionally green. The facings were, in turn, to determine the "Colours" each regiment was to bear along with the standard of the United States.[14] While some units had distinctive buttons and some plain, by the end of the war many had buttons inscribed "USA." The common headgear was a black three-cornered cocked hat with a black cockade, except when Washington recommended cockade colors to indicate rank, or when the army added white to indicate the alliance with France. Soldiers also wore wool caps in winter, small round hats, fantail hats, and hats cut down and altered into caps with the brim trimmed and turned up into a frontispiece that made them resemble the light infantry cap or helmet, which was often made of leather.[15] The light infantry cap's front plate distinguished who belonged with what regiment. The uniforms thus represented the nature of the union: one army out of many regiments.

Most of the men in Hazen's regiment probably wore black cocked hats or the cut-down, remodeled caps. Members in the light infantry companies (with James Heron and William Chambers in 1777 and Thomas Pry afterwards) donned leather caps when available. The painted letters "COR" in a "cypher" or calligraphic script adorned the flat front.[16] The decoration probably posed a bit of a problem after Congress prohibited the title "Congress's Own" in mid-April. But the soldiers likely continued to display the "COR" until the caps disappeared or disintegrated, which did not take long. By June 1778, the regiment reported that it needed five hundred hats or caps. It also needed hundreds of pairs of breeches and shoes, shirts, hose, rifle shirts, overalls, black stocks, and blankets (which could also serve as clothing).[17] It did not ask for coats on that June return, but they too remained a major concern.

Hazen's was a brown-coat regiment. That was due more to allocation than choice. Although Hazen may have originally wanted white coats with green facings, approval and resources were never forthcoming. As Washington recommended in November 1780, when refashioning soldiers' uniforms, officers were to stick to the "Facings, Linings, And buttons already Assigned to the states to which they belong."[18] Hazen's partiality aside, many officers and soldiers preferred the blue coat, which Washington and Congress recognized when establishing uniform regulations in 1779. Limited supplies, however, meant that thousands of men, including in Congress's Own, continued to don brown. Initially, the brown coats for Hazen's regiment were faced in white, but in 1779 the facings were changed to red. The silver-toned buttons were probably pewter and plain but could perhaps have had "USA" on them like those of some other regiments. Although Captain Henry O'Hara sported silver buttons with "COR" inscribed on them, his was probably a discretionary change that he, and perhaps a few other officers, could afford.[19] Waistcoats and breeches were to be white, but again that depended on availability—and laundry soap. Even if soldiers had the designated uniform, they did not wear it all the time. Sometimes they may have packed up their regimentals and worn hunting shirts and overalls, which is what Hazen preferred, but did not always get, for summer campaigns.[20] With clothing in short supply, soldiers had to "make their old Clothing go as far as Possible." That included laying aside coats when on fatigue duty and regimental tailors cutting up old coats and reworking them into jackets. Such alterations also affected uniformity even when meant to maintain it.[21]

The uniform, or bits and pieces of it, visually connected the religiously, regionally, and ethnically diverse members of the regiment. That diversity grew over the course of the war as continuing recruitment added immigrants and prisoners of war and then other personnel transferred in the army's 1781 reorganization. Among the Catholics and Protestants, French Canadians and "this country born," were also Germans, French, English, Irish and Scots-Irish. A January 1779 desertion notice included seven Germans, two English, one French, and one Irish among the thirteen runaways. But, as Hazen noted, "They all had new Regimentals, being brown Coats faced with red, and white Waistcoats and Breeches."[22] Other desertion notices that year again noted the uniform coats of brown faced with red, but also mentioned hunting shirts and "overhalls," red coats "formerly belonging to the British," and in the case of drummers John McColgain (born in Ireland) and John Wright (from England), "white coats faced with pale blue."[23]

Among those donning the regiment's brown coat were at least a few members of African descent. One was John Saratoga of Canada. Saratoga enlisted on 10 December 1776 with Captain Moses White, but may have been on command with Paymaster Edward Chinn when the latter was at the Battle of Short Hills and possibly made prisoner. Saratoga was listed in the companies of Captains Robert Campbell and then John Hughes through 1779, and probably continued with the regiment until the end of the war, although the master roll did not record a discharge in 1783. The reason appeared in 1786 when Chinn acknowledged receipt of five certificates issued to "John Saratoga, my slave for life . . . being in full for his services as a soldier in General Hazens Regement including his pay cloathing and gratuity."[24] Major John Taylor had the enslaved Michael Hailstock mustered as a drummer.[25] Prince Pettibone (Prime Petty Bone) enlisted in Captain James Duncan's company in June 1778, but he deserted one month later; he was likely the free person of color listed in the 1830 census records as living with three female family members in Whitehall, New York. Another possible Black member was Cato Mumford, who enlisted in Campbell's company in May or June 1778 and deserted that December. He may have been the "other free person" Cats Mumford residing in Providence, Rhode Island, in 1800.[26] As the officers did not record race on their rolls, assigning racial identity based on naming patterns is conjectural.[27] It is speculation too that Mumford, Hailstock, and Saratoga may have been among the twenty-seven "Negroes in the Army" counted for Poor's brigade, which included Hazen's regiment in August 1778.[28] That roll did not break out the regimental numbers.

While ethnicity, along with language abilities, size, scars, hair color, and clothing were vital in notices asking people to grab deserters, state affiliation was more important for those who stayed. Belonging to a state while serving in the regiment meant that the state was to fund and supply the soldier, and yet the regiment's consolidated roll did not record a place for Mumford, Pettibone, or hundreds of others. At the end of the war, the regimental adjutant recorded just one soldier each for North Carolina, Virginia, and Rhode Island; from five to fifteen for Delaware, New Jersey, New York, Massachusetts, and New Hampshire; about twenty-five for Connecticut; more than thirty for Maryland; more than eighty for Pennsylvania; and more than two hundred as "US." Two-thirds of the men on the adjutant's roster, more if including the officers, had no affiliation listed. In some cases the omission was a recording oversight, as the sergeant major's 1782 list and some state records show.[29] But the major reason appears to have been that the adjutant's register was compiled after many members had come and gone and left no record of affiliation through depreciation certificates or discharge papers; indeed, the adjutant missed some members altogether.

One of those who wore the regiment's uniform to the end of the war and yet whose state affiliation was not listed on the adjutant's master roll was Sergeant Major John H. Hawkins. John Harper Hawkins is distinguished from the thousands of the Continentals who came from nowhere to appear on the rolls before disappearing again because he kept notebooks. Cobbled together, their ragged, incomplete remains create a journal that hints at his background and illuminates his and his regiment's war.

Hawkins was a self-conscious writer who edited what he recorded: he crossed out words and sentences, attempted erasures, and made numerous insertions. His attention to the written word may have come from training as a printer in Philadelphia and a desire to pursue that trade. In March 1778, someone stole a packet from his coat pocket that among other things included "an old American Magazine," a copy of "The American Vine" (a sermon by the Reverend Jacob Duché while chaplain to Congress), no. 19 of the *New-Jersey Gazette*, and a copy of a letter that he had drafted "to the Committee in the City of Albany respecting a Printing-Office laying useless in their Possession." When the regiment marched through Dresden, New Hampshire, in April 1779, Hawkins commented that he was "greatly surprised tho' as much pleased to find a Printing-Office established in this Part of the World. This Vehicle of Learning, this Liberty of Liberties is in the South-End of [Dartmouth] College." He checked out what the printers were doing and noted proposals to print a newspaper there. On 6 May, he had a chance to read the first issue of the *Dresden Mercury*.[30]

In the summer of 1781, as the regiment passed by Philadelphia, Hawkins visited friends and "procured a Number of News-Papers, &c. from my Typographical Brethren." Earlier that year, he had been in town during the Quaker Half Yearly Meeting of Friends, which allowed him to meet with relatives and acquaintances from Philadelphia and Chester counties. At that time, he sorted through books and burnt papers "which contained some Disputes I had from Time to Time with ~~Stenson, Jarvis, W. Hawkins, Sellers and Shoemaker with~~ several Men who had wronged me, as I chuse however injured I have been by them that those old Disputes or Animosities should be buried in Oblivion, . . . I have ~~now~~ excluded them from appearing hereafter in the History of my Life." (Nevertheless, here they are.) There was also an undated memo about going to Baltimore to pay William Douglass and wife, or their family, thirty pounds and visit "Wm. Stinson, and procure from him some Family Papers of mine which fell into his Hands at Chester ~~about~~ in the Year 1772 or 1773." Hawkins also wanted to settle affairs with a Mr. Kerlin "at the White Horse Tavern on the Lancaster [Road] . . . [and get from him some] Books, and papers left at his House" and, finally, settle with the estate of the late Mr. Chandler.[31]

Hawkins never mentioned a wife or immediate family, nor did he indicate that he had been a Quaker, but personal reflections and memos indicate that he came from the Philadelphia area and had relatives associated with the Society of Friends. There was more than one John Hawkins in Philadelphia during the mid to late eighteenth century, but the one who served in Hazen's regiment may have been the son of Hannah Harper who was read out of meeting for marrying non-Quaker James Hawkins in 1742. If so, then John's mother was likely the daughter of Jane Breintnall Faucit (Fawcett) Harper and his father possibly the son of Jane Hawkins and stepson ("son-in-law") to the glover Oliver Williams. If this was the case, then John had a brother William and a sister Jane. Jane died in 1776 and left her worldly goods to her brothers, cousins, and friends. Her cousin Jacob Shoemaker was named executor of the will.[32] Was this the Shoemaker who wronged Hawkins? Did his brother wrong him? Was the Sellers who wronged him William Sellers the printer?

In the *Pennsylvania Gazette* of 18 February 1768, William Sellers posted a runaway notice for an "Apprentice Lad, named JOHN HAWKINS, by Trade a Printer, between 19 and 20 Years of Age, about 5 Feet high, of a dark Complexion, with short black Hair, or may probably cut it off, and wear a Wig." Hawkins had run away on the 7th taking with him "Everlasting Breeches," shoes with "Pinchbeck Buckles," and a "new Beaver Hat." Sellers offered a three- pound reward for the return of the runaway. Someone may have collected the money or Hawkins may have turned himself in, or there may have been some other resolution. Whatever the case, it appears that Hawkins tried to follow the example of the famous runaway printer's apprentice Benjamin Franklin, who had made the *Pennsylvania Gazette* the premier paper of its day before turning it over to his partner David Hall and pursuing other interests. William Sellers, who had been David Hall's journeyman, became his partner in the printing house in 1766 after Hall's partnership with Franklin dissolved.[33]

Hawkins probably completed his apprenticeship and then competed with other journeymen contending for positions in Philadelphia or neighboring towns and cities. After the war began, he may have been the Corporal John Hawkins who served in Captain Joseph Hubley's company, 3rd Pennsylvania Regiment, to 7 January 1777. On 8 January, John Harper Hawkins enlisted in Congress's Own Regiment, made corporal in Chambers's company on the 16th and then sergeant in Burns's company, possibly on that very day. According to his calculations about what was due him in 1780 for depreciation of wages, he was a sergeant on 16 January 1777 and a sergeant major as of 20 September 1778. The latter is a puzzle, because he scribbled in his journal that he was promoted to sergeant major on 17 October 1777, and he is noted with that rank in Duncan's company in June and then William Satterlee's in July 1778. It may be that the promotion was not confirmed until the spring of 1778, for an order that February essentially nullified promotions of sergeants or corporals for procedural reasons until there was new approval.[34] A likelier reason for the delay is that Hawkins assumed the duties of sergeant major while his predecessor remained a prisoner of war, and then, upon Lawrence Manning's return and promotion to ensign in September 1778, Hawkins was confirmed in the rank.[35] As he performed the duties of sergeant and then sergeant major, with perhaps an eye on an officer's promotion like Manning before him, Hawkins had first to survive the war before he could pursue the possibility of opening his own printing shop.

Battles and Belonging: Staten Island

In belonging to the United States rather than one state, Hazen's regiment was often divided into detachments, and those detached elements, like the regiment itself, were frequently transferred between brigades. Pulling out a company supported operations but affected regimental cohesion, just as moving in and out of brigades affected affiliation between regiments. In late May 1777, the regiment, which had been in Major General Israel Putnam's division, was supposed to fall in line with Brigadier General John Peter Gabriel Muhlenberg's brigade of Virginia regiments, which was part of Major General Nathanael Greene's division. When Major General John Sullivan, who replaced Putnam at Princeton, requested that Hazen's regiment remain under his command in lieu of Colonel Henry Leonard d'Arendt's German Regiment, Greene readily agreed.[36] Sullivan, in turn, placed the regiment within Brigadier General Preudhomme de Borre's 2nd Maryland Brigade. As Borre, a volunteer from France, tried to solidify his command, he appointed Captain Matthew McConnell of Hazen's regiment to act as brigade major (a staff position).[37] His choice of a Pennsylvanian from the attached unit may have added to his unpopularity with the Marylanders.

During that period of transition in New Jersey, Hazen's regiment welcomed back a detachment from Peekskill.[38] Yet even as it added those members, it also lost a few in the days before and during the Battle of Short Hills (Scotch Plains) on 26 June. American detachments, including from Hazen's regiment, nipped at General Sir William Howe's heels as he withdrew his forces from northern New Jersey. Colin McLachlan remembered "surprising the enemy at Hanover in 1777 where severals of them were either killed or wounded by only two small companies under the command of Captains Heron and Chambers, without the loss of any on our side."[39] Then Howe turned to tease and trap some of the American forces. Major General William ("Lord Stirling") Alexander's command fought Howe's forces as Washington led a withdrawal in which the soldiers of Hazen's detachments that had been part of the earlier harassing actions may have participated. The tough but short William Deacons (his mates laughed at his five feet, one-and-a-half inches), thin from ague, and about thirty-seven when he enlisted in March, was in one skirmish at the Short Hills and two on Staten Island, before being wounded by a ball in the left shoulder at Brandywine. The English-born Marylander continued to serve to Yorktown.[40] Sergeant Thomas Smith died on 20 June, the day that John Brooks was taken prisoner. Brooks returned in June 1778 only to desert the following June. Paymaster Chinn might have been a prisoner by the 27th, but if so, he appears to have soon rejoined the regiment.[41]

Through July and into August, as Hazen and other commanders continued to embody their troops, General Washington dealt with congressional examinations of the army, reviewed intelligence of the enemy's movements, and tried to position his forces most effectively. Were the British going to attack fortifications up the Hudson, or would they move against Philadelphia? He ordered and counter-ordered troop movements. In the process of what amounted to a shakedown march up and down New Jersey, there were problems with wagons, women, and plundering. Sullivan's almost shoeless division, undoubtedly trying to rectify that lack and others, engendered numerous complaints from the Quartermaster Department and residents, which led to a reprimand from the commander in chief: the troops were not to disgrace the cause or disaffect the inhabitants.[42] As Washington demanded that the troops shape up, he also complained that the shoe was sometimes on the other foot and that it was the civilians who disaffected the soldiers.[43] The army therefore had to maneuver around civilians as it moved to obstruct the enemy. Everyone expected an engagement; it was just a matter of who would hit whom and where. At that point, in mid-August, Sullivan's division of about 2,000 men, including Hazen's regiment, was not with the main body of Washington's forces near Coryell's Ferry but near Morristown.

With Howe's forces absent from New York, Sullivan decided to strike the loyalist battalions encamped on Staten Island. As drums beat the march, about half of Sullivan's division set off from Hanover Township in the afternoon of 21 August. After marching about twenty-two miles, the weary and hungry soldiers reached Halstead's Point near Elizabethtown, New Jersey. They started the trip across the sound at 3:00 A.M. and were on the other side by sunrise. Sullivan had divided the force into two brigades: Smallwood commanded the 1st Maryland and Borre the 2nd. Colonel Matthias Ogden—in command of his own 1st New Jersey plus much of Elias Dayton's 3rd New Jersey and some militia—joined the attack, making it a three-pronged endeavor to hit foes at the Old and New Blazing Star and Decker's ferries. Initial success, for they did take the enemy by surprise, soon became something else.[44] The operation suffered from an overly complicated plan, a lack of sufficient coordination, and a deterioration in discipline.

Hazen's regiment contributed to the early success despite weaknesses and contentions in its arrangements. Those weaknesses, however, and some

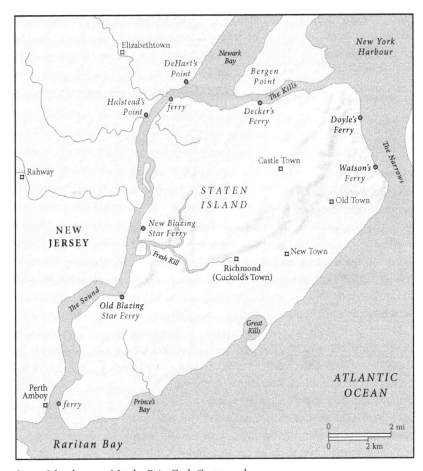

Staten Island, 1770s. Map by Erin Greb Cartography

individuals' misbehavior that was mirrored in other units, contributed to the operation's ultimate failure. There were leadership issues. Hazen was not with the regiment at Staten Island; he was likely in or near Philadelphia, where he was lobbying Congress about his finances.[45] Antill had command, but he disappeared at some point during the expedition and was barely mentioned in the reports that immediately followed it. With Antill gone, the senior major present, John Taylor, had charge of the retreating regiment at the end of the engagement, and afterwards he was hot to explain to his colonel and others what had happened to his men.

Major Taylor blamed Major General Sullivan for the "numerous & ruinous" misfortunes that befell the expedition.[46] A court of inquiry, convened primarily in response to Taylor's and the 4th Maryland's Lieutenant Colonel

Samuel Smith's accusations, met to review Sullivan's plans and execution, which Sullivan deflected in part to the actions of Smallwood and Borre. They, along with Sullivan, also urged the court to look at their subordinates' negligence and imprudence. The actions, charges, and countercharges revealed tribulations that continued to dog the new army. Battles within, often over authority, undermined unified operations.

Major Taylor initiated the post-battle dispute by stating that Hazen's regiment had marched through the August heat with little rest and provision, rowed across the sound, and grabbed prisoners and supplies by 9:00 on the morning of the 22nd. If they had then ferried back, Taylor would likely have no more than grumbled about the tough march, but successive "unfortunate" actions led to disorder and loss.[47]

Taylor decried how the march had fatigued the men before the attack. Yet even so, Captain James Reid was leading soldiers at the front of General de Borre's brigade when they came upon some of loyalist Lieutenant Colonel Joseph Barton's 5th New Jersey Volunteers on the way to the New Blazing Star Ferry. Barton's soldiers quickly fell back. Sullivan ordered Reid to pursue, which he did until confronting more enemy troops, then he prudently waited for the brigade. As it, with Taylor commanding the advance guard, passed him in pursuit of the loyalists, the "much fatigued" Reid, who was still recovering from an ague, caught a saddled horse and inventoried the stores the enemy left behind. When finished, Reid rejoined the soldiers, who returned from their pursuit with horses, plunder, and prisoners. The brigade then started marching back, but on the way met with Smallwood's brigade, and together they marched south to where Ogden was operating near the Old Blazing Star Ferry instead of returning to their initial, closer crossing point.[48]

While Reid and others from Borre's brigade pursued Barton's troops, Smallwood's brigade had moved toward Decker's Ferry behind the two light infantry companies detached from Hazen's regiment and commanded by Captains Benjamin Chambers and James Heron. These companies initially had the mission to find and, if possible, capture the infamous Brigadier General Cortland Skinner, the former attorney general of New Jersey who had been very successful at gathering men and intelligence for British service. Upon learning that Skinner had moved his headquarters out of their reach, the companies were tasked to be Smallwood's advance guard as the brigade headed toward a British regiment. When the enemy's guard moved toward the companies, they backed beyond a bridge, where Smallwood ordered them to return to the brigade, leaving other troops to watch the enemy. Upon arriving back at the brigade, Chambers found the soldiers scattered about, collecting "Clothes & Water out of the neighbouring Houses." His troops did not have much time to do likewise, for after a quarter-hour pause they were back on the road, but without Heron's company. Then they heard arms fire to the rear, and Chambers halted his men near the fork in the road leading to the New Blazing Star. Sullivan ordered him to stay there and collect stragglers to deliver to the rear guard. After an hour or so of such collection and delivery, Chambers led his company to rejoin its regiment, which was embarking at the Old Blazing Star.[49]

As Chambers was moving down, Reid was coming up. Reid gave the "much fatigued" General de Borre his horse. But back on foot, Reid's own strength waned, and he fell toward the rear of the brigade, where he "saw our people in a scattered disorderly and dangerous situation." He tried to "stop the greedy grasp of our Soldiery, but found they had such a propensity to plunder" that he failed and left them to it. Reid proceeded to Cuckolds Town, where he heard that Heron had been killed or made prisoner, so he and Captain Edward Old-ham found horses to ride back up the road. They crossed paths with Chambers, who mentioned that there were still some people to the rear. Reid continued on with Oldham, halting briefly to pass back word to the light company to skir-mish with some skulkers in the woods. Before Chambers had to turn around, Reid found the prowlers "to be our own people [and] sent them forward telling them their danger." Reid and Oldham continued and met more soldiers sitting along the road complaining that they could go no further because they were so tired and hungry. The officers got them to their feet and shepherded them forward to Cuckolds Town, after which they rode past the soldiers trudging toward the Old Blazing Star. Upon reaching the ferry, Reid rejoined the regi-ment for the crossing. Once in New Jersey, he looked back wishing that they had emplaced some artillery there so that they could have fired the timid loyal-ist "Green Coats" away from the remaining troops still needing to embark.[50] Instead, those troops had to turn to face the enemy.

Taylor explained to Hazen that "before we had got all our Men over, the Enemy came up & attack'd our rear of about 150 who were on that [Staten Island] side, our people behaved bravely, several times drove the Enemy from the Charge, but all their Ammunition being gone, they dispers'd; some swam the river and the rest were taken."[51] Ensign Andrew Lee and Captain John Car-lile were part of the picket of about one hundred men commanded by Major Edward Tillard of the 6th Maryland trying to embark the remaining men, but some were so fatigued that they never made it to the ferry point. Others did not make it because they had been taken in earlier skirmishes or were delayed by the search for plunder or a hideaway. Lee heard that "Maj. Powell, . . . Capt. Herrin, Lieut. Campbell, Lieut. Anderson, Ensign Hall, and Mr. Hall, a sergeant major, being in a house, were surprised by the enemy and made prisoners, except Powell, who was slain. Lieut. Campbell [was] wounded and lost his arm."[52] Heron, Campbell, and Anderson were among the eight or nine officers in Hazen's regiment who saw sunset as prisoners of war. Major Tarlton Woodson, who had been superintending the re-embarkation, and Carlile and Lee who were supporting it, also did not make it back. Surgeon's Mate Timothy Duffy was among those taken, and possibly Lieutenant Pierre du Calvet.[53] Finally, there was Antill.

When Taylor reported to Hazen that Heron, Campbell, Anderson, and Lee were not mentioned in a flag exchange about prisoners, and thus he expected they were killed, he added that the liaison had averred that Antill was not on the list because he did not wish to return. Sullivan reported that Antill "went over to the Enemy," and that "his Brother officers Say they have Long Since Suspected his Intentions from the whole Tenor of his Conduct."[54] Who were those brother officers? Was the mistrust specific to Antill, or reflective of an insecurity that led some people to question motives whenever someone was taken?[55] Was Sullivan deflecting criticism by setting up Antill and others to be scapegoats?

Sullivan fed some congressmen's anxieties in reporting that papers seized in the raid indicated that Quakers had been passing information to the enemy. That may have spurred a look for other treachery. But Antill had been active in recruiting and administering the regiment, so how was his conduct suspicious? On the other hand, he was second in command of a different, difficult regiment. Sullivan had been furious with Antill just before the expedition. Antill had dared to question and contravene Sullivan's authority over the possible transfer of a soldier.[56] Furthermore, there had been Antill's defense of the foreign adjutant Minyier in the earlier civil-military brawl at Lancaster. A few officers may also have remembered General Woedtke's criticisms of Antill during the retreat and retrenchment of 1776. Finally, Antill had been back in New Jersey, where his relations leaned loyalist. His brother John was a major in the 2nd New Jersey Volunteers. Perhaps they had met on Staten Island and John had tried to persuade Edward to turn his coat? If so, it did not work. The brotherly connection might have helped the colonel get parole, but given how soon the other officers were paroled, that does not appear to have been significant.

As Andrew Lee remembered captivity, from 22 to 28 August "our usage was rather cruel than otherwise," for the prisoners ate only "four times in seven days," and spent "two nights in the open field without blankets or the least kind of shelter from the weather." After a day or two under German guards, whose officers were polite to the prisoners, they were moved by ship to New York, where on Monday the 25th they were "conducted to the city hall through a multitude of insulting spectators." Three days later, they were paroled to the liberty of Frankfort Street, all two hundred yards of it. They lived on a two-thirds allowance there until 4 November, when they were allowed to move to the Long Island flatlands on the condition that they would pay board. They were settling in when an alarm over American army movements led to their shipboard incarceration by the end of November. Lee said that about 255 of them were put on two transports. The provisions were scant and badly cooked, "there being but one fire and one kettle to a ship," but when not attempting to cook they played whist, walked, or even danced on the decks, and sang after blowing out the lights and turning into their berths. Even so, the provisions were so bad, they would surely have sickened (except for the three officers who escaped) were it not for the fact that the general ultimately allowed the prisoners to return to Long Island.[57]

Lee did not specify other officers from Hazen's regiment on the prison ship, though they, including Antill, could have shared the experience. In November, Charlotte Antill asked Congress to permit her and her children to join her prisoner husband in New York. She also fired a shot at his detractors by asserting "that the zeal with which he hath always served the United States of America and the Sacrifice which he & I have made in their cause ought to scatter all Suspicion injurious to his honor, and that his Fidelity will merit for me this Favor."[58] Congress sent her note to the Board of War without comment on his or her sacrifices. She did join Antill on Long Island. From there, in May 1778, he, with Major Woodson and other paroled field officers, petitioned Congress for relief.[59] Antill continued to participate in similar petitions about prisoner conditions and exchanges. An August 1778 request located prisoners, including those specified from Congress's Own, at various places on Long Island. That fall, Antill wrote to Major General Lord Stirling about the sending of flags for more aid and exchanges, but in that case the enemy pilfered the post for propaganda. In October, James Rivington's *Royal Gazette* published a "Copy of a Letter from Mr. Edward Antill, Colonel of the Congress's OWN Regiment, now a Prisoner on his Parole on Long-Island."[60] Foes used the title, condemned by Congress in 1777, to prick Congress's pride over a year later.

"Having some Leasure, in Consequence of my very Unhappy Situation, as a Prisoner of War," Antill continued to try to "be of some Service, to my Country: at present struggling under all the Hardships, of an Unjust, & Cruel War." Antill was on a limited parole: although not imprisoned, he was restricted within British lines. Within those confines, he busied himself by transcribing scientific tracts, offering advice on exchanges, and serving as a liaison between the British authorities and other prisoners of war.[61] Antill was finally exchanged and returned to duty in 1780. In 1788, he was still trying to obtain reimbursement for "rations due while a prisoner" from 22 August 1777 to 25 October 1780 to the tune of 1,159 days at five rations per day. He and others were supposed to have continued to receive their pay while on parole, but if they did, it did not cover their needs.[62]

Anderson, Campbell, Carlile, Duffy, Heron, Lee, and Woodson rejoined the regiment at various times between 1778 and 1780, with some controversy about whether Lee had broken parole when he appeared in August 1779. Anderson, Carlile, and probably Lee continued with the regiment to war's end. If Calvet had been taken prisoner and released, he never returned.[63]

The numbers of men taken or killed are difficult to confirm. Hazen lumped those killed with those taken prisoner to say that the regiment lost eight officers and forty men on Staten Island. Taylor estimated that the regiment "lost a very few men except the prisoners." Lee provided a total for the division of about 260 taken, of whom twenty-two were officers, whereas Sullivan proclaimed that not more than 150 men were lost.[64] The rolls of Congress's Own indicate that William Mercer died in August 1777 and possibly Samuel Patterson, but Patterson may have either deserted or been taken prisoner and then died in April 1778. The rolls name at least thirty-three, including Sergeant Major Manning, lost on Staten Island.[65] The soldiers taken prisoner had it worse than the officers because they were imprisoned on land and ships with no parole. Deemed to lack a gentleman's honor, they could not be trusted to abide by a parole's limits on freedom. Therefore, they had to endure foul, sickly walls and hulks until exchanged in the intermittent cartels of the war.[66] Thirteen, perhaps more, rejoined the regiment between 1778 and 1779. Among them was Manning, whose treatment was ameliorated by his rank and actions as a senior noncommissioned officer, and by Antill's advocacy. When Antill heard that Colonel Elias Boudinot, commissary-general of prisoners, was arranging an exchange in May 1778 that would include Surgeon's Mate Duffy, Antill asked that "my Serjeant Major a Young Fellow of Great Merit and who Deserves Promotion" be "Thrown into the Bargain."[67]

In the meantime, as the regiment tried to recoup from Staten Island and later hits at Brandywine and Germantown, Taylor maintained his charges of faulty leadership against Sullivan. Sullivan, in turn, trumpeted how his expedition had not only routed the enemy, but also took, killed, or wounded hundreds, destroyed stores, took many arms, blankets, cattle, and horses, and "marched victorious through the Island." In addressing the complaint that horses got priority over men on the re-embarkation, Sullivan's aides swore that the general had ordered that no horses and cattle were to be crossed until after all soldiers. His adherents supported Sullivan's contention that losses were due to the "Imprudence" of some officers and soldiers and by "Accidents which no human Foresight Could have prevented."[68] Ultimately, the board of inquiry that met in mid-October dismissed Taylor's charges as "not founded in the best Information," and maintained that the orders were appropriate and that the expedition could have succeeded but for accidents. It advised that Sullivan be acquitted of the charge "unsoldierlike conduct," which Washington and Congress accepted.[69] That decision, however, was not the end of the controversy. Sullivan contended that Samuel Smith and John Taylor had traduced him in retaliation for some disciplinary measures he had taken at Hanover before the expedition to Staten Island. Furthermore, Sullivan maintained that Borre—by inference both stupid and a coward—had spurred them on. To supplement his countercharge, Sullivan asked for letters of support. A few officers in Hazen's regiment acquiesced, which Sullivan puffed to mean that many supported him. One, Lieutenant John Erskine, asserted that he wished they could be as happy with the regiment's field officers as they were with Sullivan's conduct. Erskine's comments may have reflected a grievance, not ameliorated by acquittal, against Borre for accusing him of striking a wagoner. Lieutenants Lyman Hitchcock and William Munson and Ensign Palmer Cady (all formerly of Colonel Elmore's regiment) responded to Sullivan's "orders" by saying that without reservation they "had no Reason to dislike your Conduct in Commanding the Division," and hoped to have the continued honor and satisfaction of being commanded by someone who "has so nobly distinguished himself in the Cause of his Country."[70] Hitchcock continued to serve in Hazen's regiment until 14 October, when he became brigade major to the 2nd Maryland (replacing the absent McConnell). Erskine sent a letter of resignation on 7 October, but apparently did not leave until March 1778, whereas Cady stayed until 1780 and Munson to the end of the war.[71]

Taking sides and taking leave that summer and fall of 1777 revealed continuing fault lines in the regiment; and they were not all about general and field officers. Captain O'Hara griped against Paymaster Chinn, who, he said, refused reimbursement without receipts for all the advances O'Hara had made to his men. O'Hara may or may not have gotten some of his money back by the time he resigned after Brandywine (but he would have appreciated knowing that the government dunned Chinn about accounts after the war).[72]

The officers were still adjusting to those brown coats that supposedly marked a uniform regimental identity. The external attacks on Hazen's regiment, including the suspicion of Antill that might have reflected suspicions about the regiment as a whole, probably drew some officers and soldiers together to defend and distinguish themselves. But such attacks also reflected and engendered schisms within a regiment—and an army—still trying to coalesce.

Brandywine and Germantown

Succeeding engagements in the fall of 1777 further tested the process of formation as well as operational proficiency. Each contributed to the other. Congress knew by 26 August that General Howe's forces had landed at Head of Elk,

Maryland, and were heading north. As its members digested that news and the losses of Fort Ticonderoga and Mount Independence, they heard of the Sullivan expedition results. Congress wanted answers—and eventually got some through courts of inquiry—but the immediate concern was confronting competent enemies rather than examining possibly incompetent commanders, although the two were connected.

During late August and early September, Congress urged Pennsylvania, Delaware, Maryland, and Virginia to call out their militias to help repel the enemy coming up the Chesapeake. These auxiliary forces were to be in the Continent's pay through November unless Congress or the commander in chief dismissed them earlier. Yet even though Congress assured Washington that it did not intend "to supersede or circumscribe" his command "of all the continental land forces within the United States," it also debated sending orders to Sullivan about how to move down his troops to join the forces around Philadelphia.[73] So Congress still had trouble disengaging operational issues from its role in strategic planning.

Congressmen as armchair generals wobbled between assurances that the American forces were strong and spirited enough to counter "pitifull" Howe and despair over the "Insipidity" of the Continental Army. John Adams was "sick of Fabian Systems" and officers who "drink [to] a long and moderate War," for his toast was for "a short and violent War."[74] Yet while he and others chaffed at Washington's strategy of attrition and critiqued military leadership, they had to turn their attention to other threats, such as the possibility that some Quakers harbored "a Disposition inimical to the Cause of America." When Sullivan reported that papers found in the Staten Island raid showed that Quakers were passing information to undermine the Continental cause, he was not only defending his actions but also feeding Congress's suspicions. With the British army moving toward Philadelphia, Congress and the Executive Council of Pennsylvania would not accept a professed Quaker neutrality, especially if individuals acted otherwise. Thomas Paine had hammered the point in April when he affirmed religious liberty but made independence the priority. The purported Quaker threat created an ideological crisis. On the advice of Congress, the Council "caused divers persons chiefly of the people called Quakers to be seized & their Papers inspected." And it proposed to send those most unfriendly either to Winchester or Staunton in Virginia. Congress concurred.[75]

As politicians debated, soldiers marched, and "old Women and young Children [went] to the Jersey shore to make Salt," insecurity warred with optimism along the Delaware. While the former led to persecution and prayers, the latter meant that Adams and others hoped that even if it "be the Will of Heaven that our Army should be defeated, our Artillery lost, our best Generals kill'd, and Philadelphia fall into Mr. Howes Hands, still America is not conquered."[76] But Washington, Sullivan, Hazen, and the other commanders of the American forces preferred not to place the unconquered spirit in such extremis, and deployed accordingly.

After the retreat from Staten Island, Sullivan marched his division from Springfield, New Jersey, to join Washington's army near Wilmington, Delaware. By 29 August, it was with the Main Army confronting General Howe's forces on Red Clay Creek. There, the American brigades and regiments, including Hazen's, received Washington's successive general orders against plundering ("Why did we assemble in Arms, was it not to defend the property of our Countrymen?"); for bold actions ("to free the Land from Rapine, Devastations & burnings"); and that those who "skulk from Danger . . . are to be instantly Shot."[77] As the generals laid plans, the two armies scouted and skirmished.

When Howe slipped his forces around to the north of the assembled Continentals and militia, Washington quickly repositioned his troops between the enemy and Philadelphia in the dark hours of 8–9 September. By the 10th, the contending armies were established on opposite sides of the Brandywine River. Washington had a force of approximately 12,000 Continentals and 3,000 militia, while Howe's army numbered about 18,000.[78] The American front stretched for miles on either side of Chadds Ford. Sullivan's division—which still consisted of Smallwood's 1st Maryland Brigade (temporarily without its general) and Borre's 2nd with their attachments—was posted to the northeast, about a mile upstream at Brinton's Ford. Sullivan, in turn, detached the Delaware regiment from Smallwood's brigade to guard Jones's (or Painter's) Ford, about a mile north of Brinton's. He also sent Hazen's regiment to cover Wistar's Ford, a mile and a half north of Jones's, and Buffington's Ford, yet another mile or so beyond Jones's, essentially at the forks of the Brandywine.[79]

The unpopular Borre later complained that in detaching "the Congress regiment," Sullivan removed "the greatest half part" of his brigade. Furthermore, Borre claimed that he had wanted to move up with the detachment, but Sullivan insisted that he remain with the 2nd, 4th, and 6th Maryland regiments, which comprised about 350 men. Given enlistments, desertions, and deaths since June and the prisoners taken at Staten Island, Congress's Own probably comprised over five hundred soldiers and about fifty officers in early September, but a few may have been detached to a light infantry corps, and some were likely unfit and not present at the battle.[80] Privates Samuel Johnson, John Pool, Ambrose Willson, and James Willden were absent because they had been killed or taken in a skirmish on the 4th.[81] Those present and fit were divided between the two northernmost posts on the right flank.

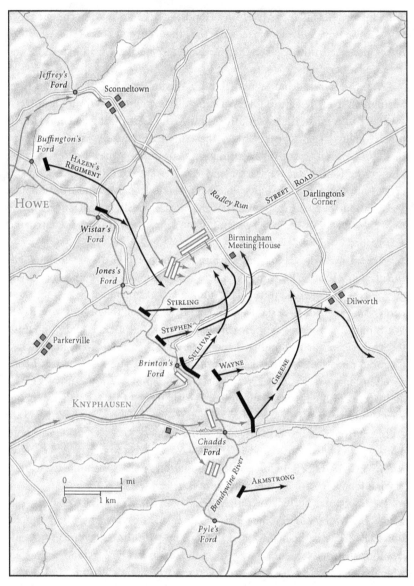

Brandywine Battle, 11 September 1777. Map by Erin Greb Cartography

Hazen may have ridden between the posts, but he was at Jones's Ford early on the 11th when he sent a report to Sullivan. Ensign David Fellows had returned from a reconnaissance mission late the previous night herding seventeen head of cattle and twenty-eight sheep. Captains Patterson and Chambers of the 12th Pennsylvania Regiment had grabbed the livestock from the enemy about a mile from Welch's Tavern and six miles from Jones's Ford and then delivered their take to Ensign Fellows. Hazen asked what Sullivan wanted done with the animals, though he wished to "detain a Milch Cow, for a few days." Besides such activities, Hazen reported all was quiet in that sector.[82] He wrote too soon.

Before the fog rose, Howe's army was on the move. Lieutenant General Baron Wilhelm von Knyphausen led one column toward Chadds Ford, where it hit hard. Knyphausen's maneuver was a diversion that enabled Howe and the second column led by Major General Lord Charles Cornwallis to head north and then northeast across the west branch of the Brandywine. The column moved east above Buffington's Ford and then crossed the east branch of the Brandywine as it turned southeast to attack the Americans' rear. Washington and his subordinate commanders had not sent out enough scouts, and they had concentrated them to the west and southwest rather than north.[83] In other words, they did not concentrate on finding the enemy's flank or securing their own. In thinking that the enemy would attack his front, Washington did not fully credit initial, admittedly partial, reports suggesting something different. He did not ignore them, but he gave priority to reports that confirmed what he believed Howe would do. That meant that neither Washington nor Sullivan gave enough weight to Hazen's later midmorning report, which left the men at the northern fords highly vulnerable.

As Hazen's troops at Wistar's and Buffington's Fords heard the guns at Brinton's and Chadds, their colonel received a disquieting report about movement beyond the forks, which he passed to Sullivan. Sullivan sent that information to Washington, but soon discounted it with a report from militia Major Joseph Spear, who had heard nothing of the enemy in that sector. Sullivan later claimed that Spear's information did not alter his belief that a flanking action made sense, but he also tried to divert possible blame for misleading Washington by saying that he had to pass on all intelligence, even when it did not "coincide with [his] own opinion," especially if, as was still possible then, the major action was to the front. Yet Sullivan also said that he "never made a comment or gave my opinion on the matter," even though on the morning of the battle he had scribbled "Colo Hazens Information must be wrong" on the report he forwarded from Spear.[84]

Sullivan had received Spear's report just as he was preparing to lead the bulk of his division across the Brandywine to attack Knyphausen's left. That activity distracted Sullivan from the conflicting reports over northern movements. Washington, in turn, who had ordered the attack across the river while Howe's forces were split, started to worry that perhaps Cornwallis had engaged in a feint and would soon join his column to Knyphausen's. Washington called back his moving forces to await more information. It came in a few hours. Colonel Theodorick Bland (of the Light Dragoons), who observed the enemy's advance parties near and on Osborne Hill around 1:00 P.M., passed the alarm to Sullivan, who forwarded it to Washington at 2:00. The commander in chief passed orders to reposition divisions, and their generals put their brigades in motion.[85] Colonel Hazen had not waited for orders. According to Sergeant Hawkins, their regiment also saw the enemy advancing at 1:00.[86] Hazen then withdrew the troops at Buffington's, Wistar's, and Jones's Fords before they could be cut off.

At half past two, Sullivan received Washington's orders and began marching his division north to join with those of Stirling and Major General Adam Stephens coming from the southeast. Sullivan was to command the right wing along a ridge near Birmingham Meeting House against Cornwallis's column. Before that, however, he had to gather the detached regiments, find the other divisions, and determine the nature and direction of the enemy. The first and third were quickly resolved, for Sullivan had barely moved a mile before he met the regiments being led down by Hazen. Hazen warned him that "the principal part of the British army" was right behind him. Before Sullivan could cavil at the possible size, he saw the enemy advancing. The general ordered Hazen's regiment to file to the right and cover the artillery as it passed, with other troops following. Hazen's troops thus provided cover as the rest of the division formed on Birmingham Hill, in line with but slightly to the front of the other divisions and separated from them by about half a mile. Sullivan left Borre in charge of the division as he rode over to consult with Stirling and Stephens. The conversation and view led Sullivan to order his division to fall back closer to the other divisions, which adjusted to the right. Shortly after 4:00 P.M., as the 1st Maryland Brigade circled around to the new position with the 2nd following, the enemy attacked.[87]

When the oncoming forces fired, the troops following with Borre fell back about "50 steps" to reform. The enemy fired again. General de Borre's "half brigade" returned fire and then broke before a bayonet charge; Borre found it impossible to rally the men and ended up riding after them into a messy mix-up between the 1st and 2nd brigades. The brigadier, who resigned in disgrace days later, blamed Sullivan—the "very bad general who hate me since his shameful marche in Staten island," for not ordering "the Congress regiment" to solidify his brigade before the battle began—and American troops, who "run away at the first shot of the enemy."[88]

As Borre disgraced himself, Sullivan and four aides rode in to try to reform the retreating soldiers. Sullivan soon gave that up to concentrate on holding the hill where the artillery was emplaced. He used the guns to "give the Broken Troops time to Rally & form in the Rear" of the artillery, and also to support Stirling's and Stephens's divisions and the regiments that "Stood firm on our Left." Those included the resolute Congress's Own and Dayton's and Ogden's New Jersey regiments in Stirling's division. Hawkins claimed that Congress's

Own was the first regiment attacked, which may have been the case if it was still at the rear covering the artillery when the enemy commenced firing. Hazen retained control of his regiment and likely anchored it to the New Jersey units at the left flank and near water, which was a boon on a hot day of combat. When Stirling's division finally gave way, Hazen's and the New Jersey regiments, with their veterans of Staten Island, continued to fight as they retreated. Hawkins declared that Hazen's was among the last to leave the field.[89]

These regiments and the remaining divisions gave way after extended "Close & heavy" fire. Sullivan later declared that "five times did the Enemy drive our Troops from the Hill & as often was it Regained." The soldiers did not abandon the hill until they "had almost Covered the Ground between that & Breming-ham meeting House with The Dead Bodies of the Enemy." Sullivan probably exaggerated, but Sergeant Hawkins confirmed the heavy fire of artillery and musketry that continued without intermission as the remains of the Continental Army's right wing fought an enemy superior in numbers.[90] Finally, however, as Cornwallis's division overran the American northern rightwing positions and Knyphausen's crossed the Brandywine to hit the center, the entire Continental Army began its retreat: pell-mell in some places and more deliberate in others.

As he retreated, Hawkins moved fast but almost not fast enough. His cumbersome, swinging knapsack nearly strangled him as he climbed the fences between capture and freedom. He finally shucked it to avoid being "gripped . . . by one of the ill-looking Highlanders" firing and advancing quickly on the rear of the regiment. The Highlanders gaining on them may have been a company of grenadiers from the 42nd Regiment of Foot, who were among the troops who "pursued the fugitives thro' the woods & over fences for about 3 miles." Hawkins managed to recover his hat in the exertion, but regretted the loss of all the things he had stuffed in his sack: besides papers, ink, books, soap, and a cup, he lost a pair of stockings and knee buckles, a ribbon, a shirt, and a brown uniform coat faced with white.[91]

Sergeant Hawkins not only lost part of his regimental uniform, he temporarily lost the regiment. In the smoky dusk, many soldiers lost sight of the regiment but kept moving. In Hawkins's case, it appears that after lightening his load he ran past his regiment. At dark, Hawkins fell in with North Carolina troops that had been part of the reserve. They arrived at Chester about 2:00 A.M. on the 12th in time to see the wagons rolling out to Philadelphia. Hawkins searched among the regiments resting by fires, but he found only one officer and a few soldiers from Hazen's regiment. The rest of the regiment had halted a few miles back and arrived about 8:00 A.M., just in time to join all the troops marching toward Darby. After a two-hour rest near there, they marched on until they halted at the edge of some woods near "Gardner's old Place" on the Lancaster Road. The next day, they marched to the Middle Ferry on the Schuylkill River, passed the floating bridge and the Northern Liberties of Philadelphia, and pitched their tents near Germantown. They struck those tents the next morning and sent them with the baggage to Bethlehem. The troops waded up to their waists in water at Swede's Ford and marched past the Merion Meeting House and up the Lancaster Road before halting at the eleventh milestone. That night, the 14th, Hawkins recorded, "several of our Men came up with us whom we thought had been lost taken."[92]

At some point over those days, Hazen affirmed "that no Troops behaved better on that Day, nor any that came off the Field in greater Order." The colonel may have been commending the movement at the first attack or the later retreat; probably both. Hazen and Hawkins also counted losses: "Four Officers and Seventy-three Non commission[ed] Officers and rank and file of the Regiment were killed, wound[ed] and taken Prisoners in that General Engagement."[93] Lieutenant Mark Mazuzen and Captain Matthew McConnell, who had suffered a broken leg, were taken prisoner. Captain Jeremiah Parmelee and Lieutenant Alexander Teas were wounded. Teas died on 15 September of those wounds. Mazuzen drowned on 30 November while trying to escape from a prison ship. McConnell spent most of the following years on parole in Philadelphia, which was more generous than that accorded Antill and other officers held within British lines in New York. McConnell engaged in trade during his parole, including supplying rum to the Continental Army, before being exchanged at the end of 1780 and transferring to the Invalids Corps the following February. The rolls are not as forthcoming about the seventy-three soldiers and noncommissioned officers lost, which might have included some deserters. Besides those taken or killed in the 4 September skirmish, which Hazen likely included in his figures, over twenty taken prisoner can be named. Among them were many who returned after being exchanged, but Samuel Furguson (Ferguson) said he escaped from imprisonment in either Wilmington or Maryland. Sergeant Alexander Thompson, on the other hand, never left the field where he fell.[94]

As some straggling soldiers returned to the regiment, others ended up at a hospital. They surely included the wiry William Deacons, recovering from a shot to the shoulder. After combat, marches, and "great Rains" (which ended the "Battle of the Clouds" on the 16th), Hawkins battled a pounding headache on 24 September and was "much indisposed in my whole Frame with severe Pains of the Rheumatism." He and others were sent to the hospital in Reading, where the sick joined the wounded and dying. Hawkins was not among the latter, and as he recovered he said he was determined to rejoin the regiment, figuring his service would soon be required again.[95] The news certainly indicated that it would be, for there was no doubt that the British would move on Philadelphia, and that Washington would again try to interpose his forces between them and the city. In the meantime, he moved the troops around and rallied them with rum and congratulations for their actions and those of the Northern Army at Freeman's Farm on the 19th. There were speeches, sermons, and essays to spur continued resolution. One loss did not mean defeat. As Thomas Paine reminded patriots in and out of the army, fortitude was key in the crisis: "Those who expect to reap the blessings of freedom, must . . . undergo the fatigues of supporting it."[96]

Samuel Adams believed that the troops showed much fortitude, for they were in "high spirits & eager for action." To reassure himself and others, he also claimed that American "Affairs were never in a better Scituation" given the Saratoga victory, divided enemy forces, and a country both "populous & fertile." If the Americans did not soon beat the enemy, "will not the faithful Historian record it as our own Fault"? He reiterated, "We shall be free if we deserve it."[97] He, like Washington and many others, believed that ways and ends had to correspond even as they acknowledged the difficulties and some-times failed to resolve them. Congress was determined to do its part, but to do so, it also had to move. It packed up its papers, ordered the removal of printing presses so essential to communication, and evacuated Philadelphia on 18 Sep-tember. It was in session at Lancaster on the 27th, but then deemed York more secure. By the 30th it resumed operations at York, where, among other things, it continued deliberations on another major ends, ways, and means challenge: drafting articles of confederation so as to have a duly constituted union.[98]

As Congress moved to secure its work, membership, and legitimacy, it also stipulated a civil-military borderland by temporarily providing the com-mander in chief with more executive powers. Before leaving Philadelphia, given the immediate threat of internal and external "enemies to the liberties of America," Congress authorized Washington "to suspend all officers who shall misbehave, and to fill up all vacancies in the American army, under the rank of brigadiers," until it could deliver decisions. The commander in chief was also allowed to take "all such provisions and other articles" necessary to sustain his army providing the owners were paid or given vouchers for them. Such powers could be exercised within seventy miles of headquarters for sixty days unless Congress revoked them sooner. Two weeks later at York, Congress authorized Washington to court-martial and sentence to death any person convicted of delivering supplies or intelligence or acting as a guide to the enemy in or near Philadelphia, providing the person was taken within thirty miles of enemy-held towns in Pennsylvania, New Jersey, or Delaware.[99]

Washington used restraint in exercising the expanded powers, especially on civilians, but with the enemy at his heels, he wanted supplies and information to flow his way. Respecting patriot property was important but containing if not defeating Howe's army was the immediate imperative.[100] British forces, however, were more than ready to prick that priority, as Major General Charles Grey's detachment did to Brigadier General Anthony Wayne's troops at Paoli, Pennsylvania, on 20 September. The well-executed attack gored Wayne's forces, but made the survivors and their compatriots angrily determined to strike back.[101]

The opportunity came on 4 October and Hawkins missed it (and a court's acquittal of Lieutenant Robert Craig for disobedience of orders on the 28th). On the 6th, while on the road from Reading to rejoin the regiment, he "received a Letter from a Friend in Camp" informing him that the regiment had "participated [in] the Honours" at the Battle of Germantown. It had been "a part of the Troops who were rewarded with his Excellency's the Commander in Chief's Thanks for their Behaviour" in the fighting.[102] Or, as John Adams reflected after hearing of the battle: "One Thing is now becoming more and more certain every day. That is that our People will and do fight, and altho they make a clumsy Hand of it, yet they do better and better."[103]

While Hawkins had been recuperating, the Crown's troops marched into Philadelphia on 26 September. Howe then distributed his forces between that city, Wilmington, and Germantown. The disposition and numbers at Germantown—around 8,000—made a tempting target for Washington with his 11,000 to 12,000 troops, of which approximately 3,000 were militia. Washington's strategy was for two columns of Continentals to roll over the enemy's northern sentries and attack down the center while the militia served on the flanks and another small detachment provided a diversion closer to Philadelphia. After the commander in chief urged his troops not to be outdone by their northern compatriots, nor let wounds go "unrevenged" in the righteous fight, the soldiers stepped out between 6:00 and 9:00 P.M. on 3 October and marched all night. General Greene had the left wing. General Sullivan, although still facing charges for Staten Island and under suspicion for Brandywine, commanded the right wing, which Washington accompanied. Brigadier General Thomas Conway's troops led off the march on the right, followed by Sullivan's Maryland division and then Wayne's division of Pennsylvanians. Dragoons completed the wing.[104] Hazen's regiment continued with the Maryland division, but as Smallwood had charge of militia for the flanks and Borre was gone, Colonel John Hoskins Stone commanded the 1st Maryland Brigade and, it appears, Hazen took the 2nd. If Hazen commanded the brigade, then Taylor, the senior major and vociferous Sullivan critic, likely led the regiment during the battle. Sullivan did not commend, condemn, or name the regiment in his summary of the actions.[105]

The 2nd Maryland Brigade, composed of the 2nd, 4th, and 6th Maryland regiments plus Congress's Own, was at the left of Sullivan's wing in the battle

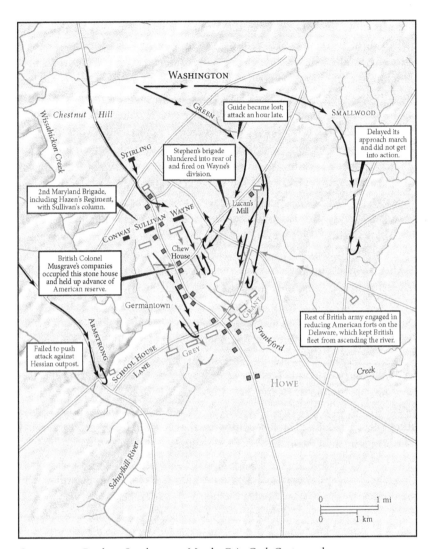

Germantown Battle, 4 October 1777. Map by Erin Greb Cartography

through the town. The soldiers advanced through fields until, as dawn broke and fog spread, they engaged with British light infantry in an orchard a few hundred yards to the right of William Allen's Mount Airy at the north end of town. After twenty or so minutes of sharp action, the British fell back. The 4th Maryland had several wounded and killed in the encounter, and this is probably where Hazen's lost some of its people, but the regiments left the wounded and dead where they lay and continued south to the right of Germantown Road. They passed Benjamin Chew's lovely—and solid—stone mansion, Cliveden. A few shots whizzed from its upper windows, but the troops moved on at the rear of some other stone houses until coming to another orchard. Hazen halted them there, probably on orders from Sullivan. The brigade, if not the entire division, had at least fifteen or twenty minutes to rest and take stock of its remaining ammunition before the soldiers had to move again. They could hear the attacks on and around Cliveden. But as Major John Eager Howard of the 4nd Maryland Regiment recalled, "Whilst we were halted, the British Army were formed in the School-house lane, directly in our front, six or seven hundred yards from us; but owing to the denseness of the fog, which had greatly increased after the commencement of the action, we could not see them." In the fog and clamor of battle, the respite became retreat.[106] It was another tough lesson in combat, but as Adams remarked, the Americans were learning.

Reports suggested that Washington had about twice the number of officers and soldiers killed—30 and 122, respectively—as the foe. He may also have had considerably more officers wounded. There was a closer match in wounded soldiers, with slightly over 400 on the American side and 395 for the British.[107] The estimated 673 wounded and dead does not include the missing or captured Continentals. Both Hazen and Hawkins recorded that "three Officers and Nineteen Men of the Regiment were killed and wounded" at Germantown.[108] The Congress's Own officers were among the wounded, for none were named as killed. Captain John Thompson resigned on 30 October and Surgeon's Mate William Garnet died in February 1778, possibly due to the lingering effects of wounds. Soldiers John Harris and Alexander McClure died in October, the latter on the 25th, and Reuben Bass followed on 1 November. William Jordan might have been killed at Fort Mifflin on the Delaware River soon thereafter. But the regimental records do not specify the nineteen men.[109]

Sergeant Hawkins rejoined the regiment near Perkiomen Creek on 8 October, and the next day marched with it toward "Towamensing" (Towamencin). Before the troops marched out, Brigadier General Francis Nash was interred with military honors. On the 10th, the honors were given Sullivan's volunteer aide-de-camp, Major John White. That same day, however, dishonor hanged John Farndon, and sixty men from each brigade were ordered to stand witness. Hawkins noted that the body hung on the gallows from noon until sunset to serve as "an Example to deter others from the like or similar Crimes." Word was that Farndon had deserted from the American army to the enemy, "and piloted some of the bloody Highlanders in the Night to Genl. Waine's Brigade, whereby they were bayonetted in a most shocking Manner."[110]

While the army buried its honored and dishonored dead and marched from campsite to campsite, its commanders discussed what was next. They evaluated reports on enemy plans and actions, rode among the threadbare Continentals and diminishing militia, and contended over officer appointments.

They decided that there would not be another big push against Howe's army before winter.[111] There were to be attempts to prevent it from controlling the Delaware, however. Washington reinforced Fort Mifflin on Mud Island, and its neighbor Fort Mercer in New Jersey. Lieutenant Colonel Samuel Smith of the 4th Maryland had been parrying an escalating siege at Mifflin with a detachment of approximately two hundred men, including members of the "Congress Regiment." Washington sent news on 18 October of a change of command and another two hundred soldiers on the way, but within days, Smith was back in charge of keeping the enemy at bay, while Major François-Louis de Fleury fortified the defenses. Washington sent even more reinforcements, but days and nights of intense bombardment ultimately led to the evacuation of Mud Island during the dark early morning hours of 16 November. Yet officers and soldiers from different regiments in united action had disrupted British logistics for weeks and helped distract the enemy.[112]

Besides trying to control lines of communication and supplies, Congress and commanders turned once again to the state of the Continental Army. The year 1777 had started with a reorganization and major recruiting drive. Although thousands had enlisted, the army had not completed its regiments, and the Philadelphia campaign had taken a toll in soldiers dead, disabled, and deserted. Despite immediate accolades for fighting prowess, post-Germantown reflections tarnished the optimism of September. Washington lamented the "general defective state of the Regiments," and warned Congress that a review of the returns showed that they "do not amount to near half of their just complement."[113] The states needed to pay more attention to filling their battalions and rounding up deserters. The deserters, in turn, needed to rectify their offense by returning voluntarily; if they did so, Washington promised a free pardon instead of the full punishment merited under the Articles of War.[114]

Not only did the states need to increase recruiting and the return of deserters, they had to roll in more supplies. The army was in desperate need, but Washington did not want to have the army seize supplies; he thought that such seizures would not only be inadequate but would also "imbitter the minds of the People, and excite a hurtful jealousy against the Army." He counseled Congress to advise the states to appoint agents to buy and take supplies.[115] His reasoning may have been to legitimize the taking of supplies, but he also probably wanted to divert inhabitants' resentment away from the army. The states started to comply that November—Pennsylvania and New Jersey promptly—and Washington then called in the officers on collection duty in those regions.[116]

It was a short respite, for Congress lobbed the hot coal back to him in December. A committee considered the state of the counties bordering the enemy and neighboring Washington's army as it evaluated how best to subsist the army and distress the enemy. Upon receiving its report, Congress concluded that Washington's "forbearance in exercising the powers vested in him by Congress" earlier could only be attributed "to a delicacy in exerting military authority on the citizens of these states; a delicacy, which though highly laudable in general, may, on critical exigencies prove destructive to the army and prejudicial to the general liberties of America." It ordered him to supply the army as much as possible from the areas nearby, and especially from those quarters most liable to enemy depredations.[117] The people in the borderland between the two forces were doubly damned by each army's need for provisions and the desire to prevent the enemy from getting the same. Officers continued to lead foraging parties.

The officers also had other things to do. As junior officers concentrated on camp conditions and troop drill, field and general officers again turned their attention to remodeling the army. They barraged Washington and visiting congressmen. A congressional committee that inquired whether the army could carry on a "Winter's Campaign with vigor and success" was again advised no— primarily because of the army's condition but also due to its officers' discontent and uneasiness.[118] Generals Sullivan, Wayne, and William Maxwell, recalling the charges of the past campaign and reflecting their own and others' concerns about a too-democratic army, complained to Washington that "the Encouragement given to Inferior Officers to arraign the Conduct of their Superiors, has already gone but too far in destroying the small distinction which those Gentlemen have been pleased to make in their own minds, between themselves and Officers of the first Rank in the Service." They granted that general officers had to be answerable for unbecoming conduct, but if they were to continue serving with honor, they also wanted to call false accusers to account. They and others followed with a direct protest to Congress about irregular promotions.[119] Some field officers, in turn, although also concerned about promotion issues, raised questions and offered suggestions about how to reduce supernumeraries (officers over the number needed for the reduced regiments of 1778); about whether to reward them with land and half pay; and about how to redistribute positions and commands among the officers that remained. Washington worried that such adjustments would promote discontent among the soldiers and disgust among the citizens, and would sink the states under yet more debt. And as to the redistribution of positions, he remarked, "To abolish Colonial distinctions, however desirable it may be, is next to impossible. Great pains in the early part of this war was used, in vain, to do this; but even in the New England States, where the Sentiments, and customs of the People have an exact similarity, it was found impracticable."[120]

Hazen's regiment, designated Congress's Own by its members but sometimes "infernal" by others, both proved and challenged Washington's assertion about abolishing distinctions. One storyline is that the "infernal" nickname acknowledged the regiment's fierce fighting in battle, perhaps at Brandywine. But it could have been a criticism of its officers' contentiousness, or a disparagement of its regionally, religiously, and ethnically diverse ranks.[121] If so, a few members might have adopted the label, commonly an invective, to flip a response to critics. Whatever the case, it probably appeared a suitable label to those in and out of the regiment who had to contend with the conflicts and complications that attended the maintenance and command of a nascent national regiment. Congress had authorized it but struggled to resource it: it had to push the states to supply its members and those of other additional regiments, but they prioritized their state units. Most of the other additional regiments disappeared into state lines, but Hazen successfully fought every attempt to do away with his regiment. He was successful in part because Congress still had its eye on Canada, and because the infernal but intrepid regiment was easily transferred and divided as needed to reinforce various divisions and departments.

Congress's Own Regiment stayed with the 2nd Maryland Brigade in December 1777 as Washington determined where to encamp the Main Army for the winter. After months of almost constant movement, the army was to halt, repair, and prepare for the next campaign. On 12–13 December, the troops filed over the Schuylkill River on a bridge made of wagons and encamped at Gulph Mills. There they "remained without tents or blankets in the midst of a severe snow storm."[122] After the soldiers dug out and the officers reconnoitered the chosen site, Washington thanked them on the 17th for their fortitude over the campaign and asked them to demonstrate it again through the winter. Although they had failed in some engagements, "yet upon the whole Heaven hath smiled on our Arms . . . and we may upon the best ground conclude, that by a spirited continuance of the measures necessary for our defence we shall finally obtain the end of our Warfare[:] Independence, Liberty and Peace."[123] On the 18th, the army observed the day of public thanksgiving declared by Congress, and on the 19th, the Main Army marched from the Gulph to Valley Forge. Hazen's regiment could only nod in that direction, for a day later, before dawn, the soldiers of Congress's Own left the Gulph with the two Maryland brigades. They marched up the Lancaster Road "as far as the White Horse Tavern; then turned to the Left Hand Road and steered for Wilmington."[124]

CHAPTER 6

CANADA AGAIN?

When Hazen's troops marched into winter quarters at Wilmington, Delaware, in December 1777, they also moved into a new era, one defined by martial developments at Valley Forge and by a more formal compact between the states. Accommodating diverse interests had complicated drafting the "permanent union," and the war had diverted and delayed revisions of the articles that were to bind the confederation. Finally, however, with the British ensconced in Philadelphia, on 15 November the congressional delegates at York voted to adopt the Articles of Confederation. Two days later, Congress sent out copies and urged speedy ratification because it was absolutely necessary to unite "all our councils and all our strength, to maintain and defend our common liberties."[1] The Articles could not officially be constituted until all of the states ratified them.

Instead of approving the Articles by 10 March 1778, as Congress had asked, the states requested clarifications. Congressional delegates responded on 25 June by rejecting proposed amendments and ordering a new printing of the Articles with the ratification statement attached.[2] Ten states signed by the end of July, but others delayed. Delegates from Maryland, the last of the thirteen states to ratify, did not sign until 1 March 1781. Meanwhile, Congress—and by extension the army—operated ipso facto under the Articles.

The Articles constituted a confederacy born not only of political ideas but also in and of war. Five of the thirteen articles mentioned powers and requirements related to defense, security, or armed forces. The delegates wrote their experiences and hopes into the Articles, including number XI, which promised Canada full admission as a state if it accepted the confederation and joined in the "measures" of the United States. Within two weeks of provisionally adopting the Articles in late 1777, the delegates had tasked a committee to have the Articles translated into French and to make new plans to coax the Canadians into the union. On 2 December, the committee—William Duer, James Lovell, and Francis Lightfoot Lee—recommended more fortifications on Lake Champlain and the establishment of a "French Legion." Its soldiers, who would be entitled to the same pay and bounties as other Continentals, were to be "such Canadians as are now Prisoners, and are willing to enlist, and such other Canadians or French as may be engaged for the Service of these States." Leading this legion would be "the best French officers," primarily meaning reputable Canadians, and its commander would be allowed to appoint as chaplain "any Canadian Priest, Minister or Deacon of Good Character who shall assist him in completing the said Battalion, and in promoting the Accession of Canada to the Union of these States." The commander was to help "conciliate the Minds of the Canadians toward these States, and to prepare them for Effecting a Revolution."[3]

Congress postponed discussion on the Canadian resolution several times as other matters intervened—from its president Henry Laurens's attack of gout to debates over the terms of General John Burgoyne's surrender in the Saratoga Convention—which essentially tabled the measure.[4] General Lafayette may have tried to resurrect an alternative version when he proposed putting some troublesome French Continentals under the command of a French officer.[5] Ultimately, however, other regiments could serve as a foreign legion. Six months later—on the same day, 25 June 1778, that it had dismissed proposed amendments to the Articles—Congress authorized Colonel Armand, who had been commanding the Independent Corps (previously Ottendorf's), to complete the renamed "Free and Independent Chasseurs" with "Deserters from the Enemy's foreign Troops, French Men, and others not owning Allegiance to the King of Great Britain."[6] But well before these developments, another regiment had already qualified as such a legion, and its commander was eager to move north, cross borders, and recruit not just more Canadians but also other Americans to the Revolutionary cause.

Hazen's regiment tramped through the northern borderlands over the next three years as Washington, foiled in his desire to assault the enemy occupying New York City, deployed forces to attack and defend elsewhere. As the states continued work on the nature of their union, Washington reframed strategies and maneuvered against challenges both to his command and within the army's administration. Hazen, in turn, found his desire to invade Canada frustrated time and again as national necessities trumped personal interests.

An Irruption

While the soldiers at Valley Forge staked out huts and cut down trees, Hazen's regiment with General Smallwood's Maryland Brigade was to stand between the enemy and Wilmington and its nearby flourmills. Hazen's troops patrolled this Philadelphia perimeter only briefly, however, for Washington soon reassigned them to the Northern Department. He did so because, as in 1775, simply inviting Canadians to join the new union was not enough for some revolutionaries. Canada remained a temptation, a threat, and a distraction. And the rumored alliance with France emboldened some congressmen and commanders to make new plans.

These men initially planned around Washington. When it reorganized the Board of War that winter, Congress made the victor of Saratoga and former adjutant general, Major General Gates, the board's president, and added Major General Thomas Mifflin, formerly quartermaster general, and Colonel Timothy Pickering, a former adjutant general. The latter two were open critics of Washington, and Gates probably believed he was the superior general, given his success and Washington's losses the previous fall. Gates and Washington clashed in early 1778 over comments by Thomas Conway, whom Congress had made inspector general and promoted to major general. Irish-born and holding a French commission, Conway was another of the foreign officers who garnered rank and animosity in the American army. Conway denigrated Washington while lauding Gates, and his comments coupled with those of other Gates adherents in Congress led Washington and his supporters to perceive a conspiracy. Calling the maneuvers against Washington's authority a conspiracy or cabal engendered much debate then and since. The Board of War's actions, however—especially as allowed by Congress—substantiate that there was organized opposition to Washington as commander in chief. Besides appointing Conway as inspector general and trying to reorganize quartermaster operations without Washington's input and approval, the board initiated the "irruption" into Canada.[7]

On 20 January 1778, Lafayette told Washington that Gates and Mifflin were assigning Conway a leading role in a proposed Canadian incursion. Lafayette protested at an Irishman getting such a command, suggesting that a ranking French officer would better inspire the Frenchmen of Canada.[8] Congress deplored partisan wrangling in the army; therefore, balancing affirmation and alienation of Washington in its actions, it pushed Conway aside for Lafayette. That did not conciliate Washington, who did not like the idea of another invasion of Canada, but Gates carefully pointed out that it was Congress's plan. He intimated the same about his orders to Lafayette, which he asked Washington to deliver along with releasing the young general for the new assignment. He also queried if Washington could "spare Hazen's Regiment or even that Part of it, which is composed of Canadians." Washington responded that he could little spare it, but that as it appeared needed for "some particular purpose," he would order the regiment to march from Wilmington to Albany.[9]

In the meantime, Major John Taylor, who was commanding Hazen's troops at Wilmington in his colonel's absence, sent Washington a letter from Hazen stating that he wanted the regiment on the Canadian expedition. Taylor added his own assurances that the regiment really wanted to go: "The greater part of our men are Canadians & New England-men, to whom this step would give new life, and who would act with redoubled vigor, besides their presence in [C]anada might be productive of many good consequences." Taylor added that heading north might result in more members.[10] Battle losses and desertions had taken a toll. Although there were relatively few desertions between December and February, lower numbers reflected men away on command as wagoners, a few in jail, hospital, or on furlough, and, in the case of Joseph Linton, "working at the Shoemaking Business in or near Bethlehem."[11]

Washington authorized the transfer of Hazen's regiment on 28 January and ordered Taylor to march immediately "with all that are fit for duty." The regiment was to move in "two divisions one or two days apart" with minimal baggage through Bethlehem and across the Schuylkill River at or near Valley Forge. Taylor was also to leave behind some officers to see to the invalids not yet able to make the trek.[12] The regiment's elements with Washington's army drew 21,501 rations out of 24,883 due them that February. If the regiment drew most of February's rations at the end of January to sustain the march, the differential implies that hundreds of soldiers (or soldiers and followers who received partial rations) were elsewhere or initially remained behind.[13]

Taylor's troops may not have moved as lightly as Washington had directed. At least ten men with sleighs carried baggage part of the way to Albany. Yet that appears close to the guidelines issued a year earlier of ten carriages, carrying a ton each, for a regiment's baggage.[14] While they trekked north, Hazen communicated with Coos Country ally Colonel Timothy Bedel and the Vermont Committee of Safety about raising troops and provisions for the Canadian expedition. He also visited Boston, where he obtained supplies and asked General William Heath to send some men from the Kennebec River settlements to the French ones on the Chaudière River "to spread a report of a large body of Troops coming that way." Heath sharpened the disinformation by ordering the scouts to spread the news "that they are sent forward to mark a road, and that a large Body of Troops are to follow." He also wanted the scouts "to enquire if provisions can be purchased for the Army, at what rate &c. and indeed to hold up every colouring of deception."[15] Diversion was to be followed by deployment.

Hazen reunited with the initial part of the regiment in Albany, where on 24 February, he commended the shivering, ill-clad men on how quickly they had made the march. One reward was new clothing and milled (felt) caps. The next day, after cleaning up, powdering their hair, and donning the new clothes, they paraded before Lafayette, who appeared pleased. Others, however, were not so happy, for Hazen's troops had taken most of the items in the hands of the local clothier general.[16]

As the 316 noncommissioned officers and soldiers in Albany donned new clothes, some companies gained new captains as the colonel reorganized his regiment. Hazen, with the two majors and one quartermaster present, redistributed the troops among the seven or more captains and nineteen lieutenants there.[17] Captain Gilbert, who had been in command of Major James Reid's company, was likely one of the captains, for he was to take the "Canadians lately recruited, and those Men inlisted by Capt. Giles." Michael Gilbert and Edward Giles were both from Maryland. Gilbert had joined the regiment in November 1776 after service with the Maryland Flying Camp; he stayed until 1781. Giles appeared in 1778, but transferred within a year, returning to Maryland and a regiment there. He later served as an aide-de-camp to General Daniel Morgan at Cowpens in 1781, for which he was brevetted a major.[18]

The other captains with companies of Canadians were also probably among the number at Albany. They included Philippe Liébert, Laurent Olivie, and William Munson of Connecticut, who had assumed Major Joseph Torrey's company. As Antoine Paulint's company was still nominally an independent, although attached, command, he was probably there but not counted among the seven.

Hazen ordered Reid's company to be incorporated within Captain John Carlile's, with Lieutenant James Duncan taking temporary command. Carlile, taken at Staten Island the previous August, was still a prisoner, but remnants of his company remained on the books with Ensign Samuel Sanford in charge. Captains Heron (Staten Island) and McConnell (Brandywine) also remained prisoners, so Lieutenants Joseph Lewis and John Erskine were to step in for each, respectively, but Erskine was gone by March. Hazen confirmed the command of Richard Lloyd, who had been a lieutenant in Henry O'Hara's company, but who was promoted and acting as commander since O'Hara's resignation. The newly promoted Captain Reuben Taylor of Virginia took over John Thompson's company (the Pennsylvanian had resigned in October). Thomas Pry took Benjamin Chambers's company, perhaps combined with the remnants of his brother William's company. The Chambers brothers resigned before or as Major Taylor marched the troops north, possibly to oversee the affairs of their infirm father, Colonel Benjamin Chambers of Chambersburg, Pennsylvania.[19]

Besides Captains Gilbert, Liébert, Olivie, Munson, Lloyd, Taylor, and Pry, the early Albany element may also have included the newly promoted Robert Campbell or Robert Burns. When Sergeant John H. Hawkins had recorded what was stolen out of his coat pocket on 9 March, the contents included "A little Book which contained the State of Capt. Burns's Company; and some Memorandums, by way of a Journal, which commenced the Day I left Wilmington, in the Delaware State, and ended on my Arrival in Albany." It must have been a capacious coat pocket, for the bundle also included a little book with guard details and a roster, an old *American Magazine* (old indeed, if it was the magazine published in 1741), a sermon by the Reverend Jacob Duché when chaplain to Congress, an edition of the *New-Jersey Gazette*, a letter he had drafted about an unused printing office in Albany, a note of hand, twenty-six dollars, and a pen.[20] The former printer's apprentice obviously carried his trade and interests with him as he followed the officers.

Other captains were Jeremiah Parmelee, William Popham, William Satterlee, and Moses White. Parmelee, ill or perhaps still weak from wounds received at Brandywine, died on 24 March. The others had gathered the regiment's remaining members for the journey to Albany, where the newly promoted Captain Duncan took command of Parmelee's company.[21] The reunited regiment was transferred to the Highlands Department in April and encamped at Fishkill, where it numbered at least 494 (which may not have included Paulint's attached independent company).[22] The staggered movements and readjusted companies then, as before and later, constantly challenged the regiment's command and count.

Reservations about the mission also challenged the regiment's commander. From the first, Washington had believed another Canadian invasion to be "the child of folly." But because it was "the first fruit of our new board of War," he did not publicly protest.[23] He did not promote it either. He had permitted Hazen's regiment to go, but that was more politic than encouragement.

Hazen did not need encouragement. As difficulties mounted in mid-February, whenever generals talked about delaying or halting the operation, he resisted by recounting his acquisitions as deputy quartermaster general for the expedition. Conway commended such zeal but ordered Hazen to gather more transport sleighs, and wrote to Gates that Hazen had fallen far short in impressing sleighs and supplies. Conway added that news from Canada was not good, and that there was unrest among the troops, but he assured Gates that he had told the men at Albany that Congress had promised them their pay and they would soon receive it.[24]

Lafayette was dismayed by what he saw at Albany. He acknowledged Hazen's efforts, but asked him for a full accounting of what was in hand to cover provisions, equipment, arms, artillery, and ammunition "for an Army of three Thousand Men" over sixty days. Hazen defensively replied that New York had empowered him to impress five hundred carriages and drivers for twenty-four days' service, and that he would be able to collect other items, including forage.

He had already put in stores at some magazines and was ordering others to be established. Furthermore, cattle were coming—beef on the hoof—so fewer sleighs would be needed to transport provisions. Hazen thought that the only problem might be manpower, but he had already tried to counter that with his earlier requests and advice.[25]

Generals Schuyler, Arnold, and Benjamin Lincoln all counseled cancelation, and other officers agreed—except for Hazen, who had been, according to Lafayette, "with great impropriety appointed to a place which interfers in the province" of those generals. Lafayette suspected that Hazen's fervor arose out of "other motives than a mere love of the american Cause." Yet even Hazen admitted that the troops were not yet strong enough to head north. Lafayette groused, "the troops they are disgusted, and (if you except some hazen's canadians) afraid to the utmost degree to begin a winter incursion in a so cold country." Lafayette also believed that the Board of War had deceived him, and that Gates and Conway were conspiring to shove him out and put Conway in command. Furthermore, he worried that "the want of money the dissatisfaction among the soldiers, the disinclination of every one (except the canadians who mean to stay at home) on this expedition" would make him a laughingstock.[26]

"Hurt" by the thoughts of abandoning the expedition, Hazen wrote to Gates that the "principle Officers" in Albany had dissuaded Lafayette and laid the blame on the quartermaster general's department—namely, Hazen—for failing to provide the carriages and forage necessary to invade Canada. Hazen countered that New York and Massachusetts had authorized him to impress transports, and that he had provisions ready at Bennington, but that Conway's order to gather supplies and sleighs at Albany before the troops were ready to move would undermine his ability to transport provisions economically. Hazen had planned to move some of the supplies with the troops and then have the rest follow. Thinking Conway's plan unwise and too expensive, Hazen had complained to Lafayette, who then countermanded Conway's order. Hazen believed, as he informed Gates, that Conway had good intentions but bad advice. Another problem was that Hazen's old nemesis, Benedict Arnold, had taken command at Albany and both countermanded Hazen's orders and required "the Cloathier Genl to Issue Cloathing I procured at Boston by his orders only." Still, Hazen assured Gates, the expedition would not fail if there were enough men for it. He stated that his 366 effective men and officers (more than the 345 on the official roll) were "so warm for the expedition that they would consent to go almost Naked into Canada." He inferred that that might happen if Arnold would not have leggings issued to his regiment. But how long and how many of his men might remain was a question: many of his men deserved furloughs, and the soldiers enlisted by Major Torrey had done so under the terms of serving for the reduction of Canada only. Hazen hoped to enlist more Canadians, but in the meantime, he would train and equip his regiment so that it could take the field in the spring.[27]

As they awaited instructions in March, Lafayette and the expedition's second-in-command, Major General Baron Johann DeKalb, reviewed and disciplined troops and made arrangements for the upcoming campaign season. That included certifying officers' oaths of allegiance to the United States,[28] and Lafayette attending a conference with representatives of the Six Nations at Johnstown. Ultimately, given weak support, Congress determined "that the irruption ordered to be made into Canada should be suspended." Washington, his authority confirmed, ordered Lafayette and DeKalb to rejoin the Main Army. Conway was to remain in command at Albany and cooperate with New York Governor George Clinton and General Israel Putnam in fortifying the North River.[29] Hazen's regiment also remained in the North to secure the borderlands, first as part of the Highlands Department and then with the New Hampshire Brigade.

New Plans

The regiment had to wait a year for another chance at Canada. That chance ultimately came as a result of Hazen's dogged advocacy, and because of French actions, congressional ideas, and Washington's strategic sense. In September 1778, Hazen petitioned Congress to support his troops, pointing out that "if a Reduction of Canada, and a Union of that Country to the Independent States of America should be thought an Object worthy public Notice," then Congress should be thinking about how his regiment could serve that end. Furthermore, Hazen noted, upon the confederation of Canada, "this Regiment would most undoubtedly be taken up and considered as a Regiment belonging to that State, supported and provided for accordingly, which would be perfectly agreeable to the whole Regiment without Exception."[30] Hazen exaggerated, but although Canada had rejected Congress's earlier invitations to join the rebellion, the Canadians fighting for American independence still believed that their countrymen would join if American troops and French forces could get up there.

Others agreed with the Canadian Continentals. Jacob Bayley, who in 1776 became a brigadier general of militias in New York counties that became part of Vermont, and Colonel Bedel, whose original New Hampshire regiment had been disbanded, also dreamed of marching into Canada. In the spring of 1776, Bayley had had men cutting a route through the forests north of the Wells River. He had been forced to stop that June when the American forces retreated from Canada and Washington warned against finishing a route that could be used by the enemy.[31]

Bayley and Bedel were both delighted at word of a possible expedition in early 1778. When Bedel received orders from Hazen in January to rendezvous for a march north, he immediately mustered men, only to have that order retarded, first by Conway in February. Then, in March, Lafayette informed Bayley and Bedel that the expedition was off. Nonetheless, Lafayette wanted Bedel to assure frontier inhabitants that "Congress means to use every step in their power for their security, and expects in return that they themselves will exert every Nerve in favour of our common cause."[32]

Bayley, Bedel, and Hazen continued to press for an invasion of Canada by land, which would secure the area for their territorial and political plans.[33] Hazen visited the two men in July to discuss plans for a route north; they, in turn, wrote to Gates supporting the plans and outlining the steps they had taken to scout the enemy and lay in supplies for an expedition. By the end of the month, however, a frustrated Hazen mourned yet another postponement, for "the arrival of the french fleet and the effectual measures which they have taken to block up Lord Howes fleet both at New York and Rhode Island, Commands the attention of our Generals to this Quarter, in hopes of Burgoining [trapping] Clintons Army." All the three officers could do was to continue scouting, guarding the frontier, and petitioning Congress.[34]

Washington responded to the pressure by asking Gates, Bayley, and Hazen to review and advise "upon the best ways, and means, for the Invasion, & possession of Canada." Meeting at White Plains on 10 September, they began their report with a summary of political ends: incorporating Canada would serve peace and trade with the Indians, secure frontiers, and contain an expansion of Canada; occupying part of Canada "would give the Canadian(s) an Opportunity to unite, join the American Arms, and assist in expelling the British Tyrants from that Country." As the enemy controlled Lakes Champlain and Ontario, the officers also recommended land routes from "Newbury at Co'os" angling northward to St. Johns and other settlements. They figured "five Hundred good men" could clear the way in one month "at a proper season of the Year," but acknowledged that the number depended on the enemy's strength in Canada. Gathering intelligence was a critical first step. If they found that the enemy had not been reinforced, then a winter expedition (January) was feasible. If the enemy was larger than currently known, then a summer expedition was prudent. In either case, beef would "carry itself," and oxen and horses could transport the other necessary provisions.[35]

After reading the report, Washington ordered Bayley to send agents into Canada to gather intelligence about force numbers and locations, the dispositions of Canadians and Indians, the strength of the authorities, and the state of provisions. If Bayley received credible favorable accounts, he had permission to set part of Bedel's new regiment, "if it be continued," or other men to work "Cutting a Road from your House into Canada." Washington also copied the officers' report to Congress with the caveat that this was a conditional invasion plan "in case our future prospects and circumstances should justify the entreprise." He reiterated that the expedition was only advisable if the enemy withdrew from the United States—the first priority was to secure them—and did not reinforce Canada. There had to be an enemy weakness to exploit. Also, because of the "peculiar nature of the interprise"—the political as well as military ramifications of an invasion—Washington wanted the concurrence of Congress. He had Hazen deliver the letter so as to be available to answer questions.[36]

Hazen did more than deliver Washington's orders and reservations—he sent scouts across the border. By the summer of 1778, Clément Gosselin, who had kept watch in Quebec province after the 1776 retreat, had rejoined the regiment, along with his brother Louis and father-in-law, Germain Dionne. In October, Gosselin led a small party back into Canada. He and his brother went to Lotbinière near Quebec, while Captain Traversie of Bedel's Regiment and Lieutenant Enoch Hall (of the Vermont rangers, formerly of Bedel's) headed to St. Francis. They reported back to General Bayley at the end of November with positive assurances as to troop numbers and Canadian support. If Gosselin's note to his wife is any indication, he not only gathered information but also spread word of Admiral Charles-Hector comte d'Estaing and plans for the French fleets to sail into Canada in the spring as troops entered by land.[37]

Gosselin had jumped the gun, for those plans were soon quashed. Congress had asked Lafayette and, through him, d'Estaing about the possibility of a joint invasion to the north. While tweaking the terms of the French alliance and ensuring that it materially and militarily benefited American ends, Congress drafted plans substantially more ambitious than those of Gates, Bayley, and Hazen. It contemplated a multipronged attack against ministerial forces in Canada—moving against Detroit and Niagara to the west and up the St. Francis River to between Trois-Rivières and Sorel to the east, with both expeditions destroying enemy aborigine settlements in between. In the meantime, French forces would sail up the St. Lawrence, take Quebec, and then join with the Americans to move against Montreal. Congress was, however, willing to rework the plans "if the reduction of Halifax and Quebec are objects of the highest importance to the allies."[38]

D'Estaing responded diplomatically and prepared an appeal to the French Canadians in October 1778, which he passed to Congress that December. The admiral addressed his king's former subjects, the "American Frenchmen," and asked them not "to raise parricidal hands" against their mother country. Lafayette in turn wrote a letter to the Indians in Canada that December in an attempt to entice them to the French and American side. He also consistently pressed both the French ministry and the American Congress to invade Canada.[39]

Washington also responded diplomatically, though forcefully, in the negative. He considered "the emancipation of Canada, as an Object very interesting to the future prosperity and tranquility of these States," but found the plan unsuitable in vision and details, largely due to what he saw as America's strategic weaknesses. Because he wanted those weaknesses to remain confidential between Congress and commander in chief, he refused to send his comments to Lafayette, arguing that it was "impolitic to enter into engagements with the Court of France for carrying on a combined operation of any kind, without a moral certainty of being able to fulfill our part."[40] Washington did not know how Congress would respond, so he continued to explore invasion options. If ordered to proceed, his preference was to move via Oswego while diverting the enemy's attention to Lake Champlain and the Coos Country with "false appearances."[41]

On 5 December, Congress acknowledged that Washington's reservations about the proposed invasion were "well founded" and that the plan could be "simplified to Advantage." Furthermore, an invasion should await confirmation of cooperation from France. On 1 January, after considering the report of the committee that had met with Washington and that listed all the foreign and domestic hazards, Congress confirmed that the plan was impracticable. But it still wanted to facilitate "the freedom and independence of Canada and her union with these states; . . . which Congress, from motives of policy . . . as well as of affection to their Canadian brethren, have greatly at heart."[42]

Congress kept its options open for a possible later invasion by sending Admiral d'Estaing's declaration into Canada. In early spring, Clément Gosselin was tasked to deliver to other couriers in Canada that proclamation and Lafayette's letter to the Indians. General Frederick Haldimand, who had succeeded Carleton as governor in Canada in 1778, learned of the invitations and proposed invasion. He controverted the French and American rhetoric with warnings and promises of his own, as well as a liberal supply of presents to the Native Americans. Haldimand also deployed his regular and militia forces to detect and capture scouts and spies and to keep watch on the frontiers.[43] He prepared to counter whatever steps his enemies might take into Canada in 1779.

Haldimand received and sent reports that indicated rising Canadian unrest and alarm over the possibility of invasion from 1778 through the early months of 1780. What he could not realize was that Washington had essentially ensured that Congress's indefinite postponement of the proposed Franco-American invasion was definite. Washington did not inform Hazen of that fact. Washington opposed a Franco-American invasion because he feared that a result would be the reestablishment of French Canada, which could eventually threaten American interests. The French government, in turn, ultimately preferred that Canada remain in the hands of the English. It did not want to raise the suspicions of its American allies, but it did want to contain the United States. Although the Continental Congress expressed its continued desire that Canada join the United States in the Articles of Confederation, by January 1779, the Continental Army no longer had the mission of compelling that unification.[44]

The army, however, did still have the mission to secure the borderlands. Washington began 1779 mulling over various strategic options: "the question does not turn upon military principles only—The state of European politics and our own prospects of Finance and supplies of every kind are essential to a right determination." Should American forces take the offensive against British forces at New York and in Rhode Island while retaining a defensive posture elsewhere? Should they move against Niagara to secure the northern frontier and push against Canada? Or was it best to remain on the defensive against British regular forces while commencing "smaller" operations against the Indians "to divert their depredations from us"? Washington ultimately chose the third option.[45]

As he explained to John Jay, then president of Congress, Washington made his decisions in part to answer Gates's charges that he had been wrong to consider invasion via routes from Albany. Gates had argued that the only possible route was through the Coos Country, and that even that would only work if the French navy sailed down the St. Lawrence in a coordinated attack. Washington maintained that Gates was in error. First of all, Washington said and later repeated, he had only thought about planning operations against Canada if the British evacuated that area. With that as a condition, he agreed with Gates that the Coos route was the most direct and practicable one, and thus in September 1778, he had written to Congress asking whether it would be advisable to build magazines and open a road in that area. He had also believed that if circumstances ultimately prevented an incursion, the work there could serve operations elsewhere.[46]

The commander in chief reminded Jay that Congress had approved his proposal even as it communicated with Lafayette about getting France to cooperate in an expedition against Canada. Washington had opposed its elaborate plan because, as he had explained in November, "we ought not to enter in any contract with a foreign power, unless we were sure we should be able to fulfil our engagements." He also believed it "uncertain whether the enemy would quit the states or not, and, in case they did not, it would be impracticable to furnish the aids which we had stipulated." Furthermore, it was "better to remain at liberty to act as future conjectures should point out." Nevertheless, as the enemy might leave, he had recommended making preparations to take advantage of such an exit so as to take possession "of Niagara and other posts in that quarter for the security of our frontiers and to carry our views still further, with respect to a conquest of Canada, if we should find ourselves able to prosecute such an enterprise."[47] The general had called a halt to invasion plans because there were too many "ifs."

Washington chose as he did for political and military reasons, including the British occupation of areas of New York and Rhode Island, naval raids along the Connecticut coast, and loyalist and Native raids and skirmishes inland. He thus ordered Generals John Sullivan and James Clinton to march into "Indian Country," engage the enemy's warriors, and burn the fields and homes of enemy tribes so as to harry them north out of the region. While that was the major offensive that punctuated Washington's defensive posture, he also initiated another movement that intimated possible future offensive actions along the northern border and into Canada. For Washington, defense included discouraging enemy actions (including incursions from Canada), diverting domestic "factious and discontented Spirits" (General Gates among them), and reassuring civilians.[48] Related to those plans was Washington's even quieter, more closely held objective of keeping the French allies from possibly using a joint invasion of Canada for French rather than American aims.[49] All of these elements informed his decision to reassign Hazen's regiment from the New Hampshire Brigade back to the Northern Department, and order the regiment into the Coos Country, which included the Upper Connecticut River Valley, New Hampshire, and Vermont borderland.[50]

The Coos Campaign

On 6 March 1779, Washington ordered Hazen's regiment into the Coos Country to scout the area, build a road, and engage the populace. He asked Hazen to find out whether the inhabitants would support an expedition to Canada "if they could have a well grounded hope of a French fleet & Army appearing in the St Lawrence to co-operate with them." Washington did not say that the French would actually be there; he just asked how people might react to the possibility. A week later, Washington directed that Hazen maintain communications with contacts in Canada with the hope "that our enemies will find so much employment in other quarters, that it will afford us an opportunity of turning part of our force to the northward."[51] Washington's orders suggested that he was still keeping an invasion option open, but it was actually part of his overall campaign of disinformation and diversion directed against the enemy in Canada. It was also a "bone" thrown to advocates—Hazen included—of a campaign across the border. Hazen chomped on the bone as he entered "upon a

Service I have So much at Heart" and happily embraced the reference to French forces along the St. Lawrence.[52]

Hazen was sure that the French alliance, d'Estaing's proclamation, and the "Success of the american arms in a four years war will prove to [Canadians] our Strength, and will Contribute to Inlighten the Ignorent in the Justice of our Cause," and that even the clergy there would become friends. Trotting out old arguments, Hazen maintained that if Continental forces entered Canada, the Canadians "would receive us with open Arms, feed, assist, and if required fight with us—The Canadians are a war like hardy people Inured to armes hardships and fatigue," and "uniting our friends in Canada with us in this Glorious Contest" would counter their current neutrality. Hazen also warned that if the Americans did not get there, the Canadians might join "the british flag in Canada[,] that arsenal for all the Savages on our frontiers."[53]

Washington, however, had moved on, and what he wanted from Hazen was intelligence from Canada to prove that his planned distraction was working: that the enemy perceived Hazen's expedition as another jab to pull Canada into the United States. Hazen's expedition was a feint to help other operations secure the northern theater. It also provided another chance to explore an alternate strategic objective, expand the areas that the enemy had to cover, and contribute to American nation building by showing the flag—namely American forces—to the peoples of the region. As it chopped through the Coos Country, the regiment not only opened a road but also embodied Congress and the army for the inhabitants. It invited not just Canadians but also Americans to support the union and join the regiment composed of members from different regions and cultures.

Upon receipt of its orders, Hazen's regiment prepared to leave "Putnam's Folly" (or, appropriate for "infernals," the "Devil's Den"), the winter encampment near Danbury and Redding that was temporarily perhaps the largest, although not grandest, "town" outside of Hartford in Connecticut. Leaving its comforts, including the soap house, bake oven, and convenient springs just outside or even inside the corners of their log huts,[54] the soldiers bundled up all the blankets, shoes, and other supplies and equipment they could gather, and trudged north.

The first objective was Springfield, Massachusetts. To facilitate movement and lodging while underway and comply with Washington's directives, the regiment of slightly over three hundred men fit and present for duty divided into three divisions. After a snow delay, the first division (six companies commanded by Captain Satterlee) set out on 25 March. The second division (Captain Pry with five companies) set off in the tracks of the first at 6:00 the next morning, with the last division (Captain Liébert with six companies) following

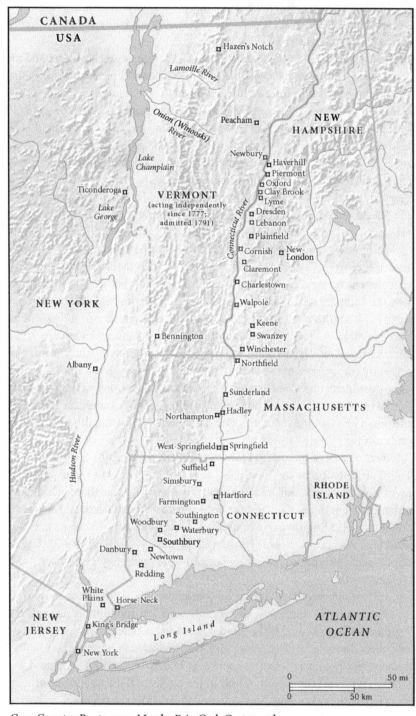

Coos Country Route, 1779. Map by Erin Greb Cartography

at half past. A shortage of wagons and teams prevented the baggage from moving immediately and together. Eventually the wheels turned, but apparently
only after Hazen stabled horses and quartered troops upon a magistrate until
the official impressed the teams. On the 30th, Colonel Hazen rode out with
Major Reid, Captain Heron ("lately returned from Captivity"), and a number
of other officers and soldiers coming off furlough or out of hospitals. Bringing
up the rear was a small guard with the colonel's baggage and one small artillery
piece with its keepers—twelve men under the command of Lieutenant Flor-
ence Crowley, detached from Captain Henry Burbeck's company of the 3rd
Continental Artillery. All traveled on roads that were wet and dirty from the
melting snow.[55]

Conditions improved over the next few days, but problems with wagons,
teams, authorities, and stony roads marked the start of the expedition.[56] By
3 April, however, Sergeant Major Hawkins was able to record better conditions.
After passing along dry and level roads, he found the second and third divisions billeted in houses throughout the village of Farmington. The first division
had left the previous morning. On the 4th, the two divisions with their baggage
trundled through light rain to Simsbury, "a pleasant though scattered Village."
The next day dawned clear, and the troops marched on to "handsome" Suffield,
where the second and third divisions remained billeted until the 9th. Hawkins
hated leaving Suffield, where "the Inhabitants were all extremely kind to the
Soldiery," especially Squire Leavitt's "genteel" family with whom he had lodged.
But the two divisions had to trudge on to West Springfield to be near the first.[57]

From Springfield, Hazen wrote to Bedel that the regiment was marching
for Coos, but, trying to maintain operational security, he asked Bedel to reveal
that the regiment was heading only to "No. 4" (Charlestown, New Hampshire).
He also hoped that the reports of Indians and Canadians gathered at Coos
were true and that they would still be there when he arrived. Bedel had told
him in February of Natives waiting for support. He had also mentioned that
he had scouts travel through Hazen's patent lands on their return from the St.
Francis area. In other words, Bedel was keeping his eyes open for prime land to
purchase for Hazen, and he stood ready to join Hazen in a trading partnership,
possibly with Robert Peaslee, who was acting as a courier for them.[58] Robert
Peaslee was likely Hazen's brother-in-law, who had once been a partner with
Hazen's brother William, and the father of Zacheus Peaslee from Dover, New
Hampshire, who enlisted in the regiment in May (and was promoted to ensign
in 1782).[59] The plans and connections confirm why securing the territory was
such a personal mission for Hazen.

At daybreak on 14 April, all three divisions marched out, followed by the
baggage train. Hawkins recorded eight wagons and twenty-one teams, all well

loaded with spades, shovels, axes, and picks; carbines, horsemen's swords, pistols, and other military stores; carpenters' and armorers' tools; and provisions. The regiment had also acquired a traveling forge that was to follow under Ensign William Torrey's charge. Although the march had started in somewhat hilly territory, the troops wended their way along essentially level roads through a "beautiful Pine Tree Country," where the trees shaded the road on a hot day. When they left the woods, they saw "fine Houses and Farms" and entered Northampton, "a handsome and large Village, tho' much scattered. The Court of Justice is a small, tho' a very elegant House; the Inside Work is very grand. An elegant Meeting House they likewise have in this Town." Part of the regiment stayed there and part in the nearby village of Hadley, where Hawkins spent an agreeable evening on the 15th.[60]

After a rainy 16 April, the weather cleared enough for the regiment to march off to "tolerable large" Sunderland on the 17th. Snow and melt overnight had left sopping roads for the troops proceeding through "monstrous high Mountains" to Northfield on the 18th. Hawkins thought that "The Weather this Day deserves particular Notice: It was, by Interval cold and warm. One Quarter of an Hour it was very cold; the Wind was so bleak it almost skinn'd ones Face—the next Quarter of an Hour it was very warm; so moderate that it made one faintish. This Kind of Weather sometimes stood for Half an Hour at a Time, and [contained its Constrasts] the whole Day. The whole Night it was excessive cold."[61] The weather-worn regiment, enduring what is now called "mud season," remained in Northfield through the 21st until the weather finally turned more agreeable.

The soldiers passed through Winchester, New Hampshire, and "despicable" Swanzey before arriving at Keene before sunset on 22 April. Some of the baggage arrived about an hour after dark. The rest arrived around midnight, except for two wagons that could not get up the "monstrous bad" roads. The wagoners barely had time to rest before the regiment and part of the baggage left Keene at about 6 A.M.. Most arrived at Walpole in the late afternoon. Hawkins arrived there after dark "and found the Troops much scattered; some in Dwelling-Houses and others in Barns; the poor mean despicable wretched Town could not afford one Regiment Room in their Dwelling-Houses for one Night. This is the first Night that our Men has been under the Necessity of laying in Barns on this march." Hawkins was happy to leave miserable Walpole on the 24th and arrive in Charlestown, "a handsome tho' small Village," which he thought resembled Princeton. He also noted that "on the other Side of Connecticut River, is what, is called the State of *Vermont*," to which both New York and New Hampshire laid claim.[62]

The regiment had just marched into another borderland conflict: the fight over sovereignty in the New Hampshire Grants, or, as Hazen and others put it, "the pretended State of Vermount." Bayley and Bedel were deeply engaged in the dispute, and the former's actions in particular raised mistrust. Hazen's relations with them and his Coos Country property also drew him into the fight over who had what authority where along the Connecticut River and its adjacent territories.[63]

Governor Benning Wentworth of New Hampshire had started granting land west of the Connecticut River in 1749, claiming that the colony's border was about twenty miles east of the Hudson River, along the same line as Massachusetts. The governor of New York had replied that his colony's eastern border was at the Connecticut River.[64] The "Royal Determination" of 1764 backed New York, but the battle over grants and governments continued into the Revolution, when another faction gained power—the Allens (Ethan and his brothers) and their adherents, who supported the creation of an independent Republic of Vermont. Others continued to support either New York's or New Hampshire's authority.

Bayley, who deplored the Allens, first favored New Hampshire, and then New York, before supporting Vermont independence in 1777. He later appeared open to reunion with New Hampshire or a separate Connecticut River state. Bedel entered the fray when he and others, upset at New Hampshire policies, supported the towns (including Dresden/Hanover and Haverhill) on the east side of the Connecticut River that applied for annexation to Vermont in 1778.[65] New Hampshire protested to the Continental Congress, which wrestled with the Vermont problem—its fluctuating borders and loyalties—for the rest of the war.

In April 1779, however, Hazen was more concerned about security than secession or sovereignty. He announced in Charlestown on the 22nd that his soldiers were marching to Coos "for the protection of this frontier Country." He asked the selectmen and surveyors to smooth the way by repairing roads and bridges, so that his regiment could continue on the next day (although not all the soldiers were there yet). As neither the townsmen nor his troops were as ready as he was, Hazen was still in town on the 25th, when he asked Major Childs for flour. If he did not get it, he threatened that he would "be under the Disagreeable necessity of Quartering my Troops on the inhabitants for their daly subsistence." He promised that the commissary general would soon resupply both the regiment and the townsfolk.[66] Hazen also took the additional time to inform Washington that the troops had halted sixteen days on the 191 miles to Charlestown due to bad roads and problems obtaining carriages and flour. He noted how he had diverted people from the expedition's "real Design," which he interpreted as "to take post and build a fort on the Boundry line Betwen New Hampshire and Canada." Before closing, he provided his estimates on what troops—militia and Continentals—and routes would "reduce" Canada.[67]

At Charlestown, Hazen also dealt with some miscreants in the ranks. He had Hawkins deliver five handcuffed "notorious" thieves to the town's gaoler. The "Villains" had been confined in the regiment's quarter guard the past summer and fall, and then with the provost guard at Redding over the winter. Neither confinement, the march, nor leniency (one had been "reprieved under the Gallows at Hartford" the past November) had reformed them. Hawkins believed that they would be sent to the navy or imprisoned for the war. He noted that Colonel Hazen had tried everything "to find out the few bad Men in his Reg[t] being fully determined that no such after being found out shall ever carry Arms again in his Regiment, or wear the a Continental Coat."[68]

On 26 April, those still worthy to wear the Continental uniform pulled out of Charlestown, but some of the baggage had to be left behind to await more teams. Hawkins stayed until enough oxen were found to pull three wagons and traveled with them for the next few days. They arrived at "handsome" Dresden (Hanover) on the 28th, where he found the regiment dispersed among different houses. Hawkins, the former printer's apprentice, delighted in Dresden, noting that it had "that Seminary of Learning called Dartmouth College." More importantly, at the college's south end was "This Vehicle of Learning, this Liberty of Liberties"—a printing office. Posted on its wall was a proclamation by Vermont's governor ordering a day of fasting (for reflection), and the printers were setting the "Laws and Fees of Officers in the Civil Department of the State of Vermont."[69]

As Hawkins recorded his observations of woodlands, working landscapes, and signs of learning and liberties, he was examining what was different, similar, and common among the various regions and peoples. He was practicing what John Adams had proposed to do in 1777 after Congress fled to Baltimore to avoid British forces. So long as Congress continued in its "rolling Humour," Adams was going to observe and describe Americans and their "cities." Adams, with reference to Ulysses (Odysseus), planned to "inquire into their Religion, their Laws, their Customs, their Manners, their Descent and Education, their Learning, their Schools and Colledges and their Morals."[70] As Congress's Own rolled along on its own odyssey, Hawkins remarked on peoples, places, and, by extension, the nature of the union. Although there were some unfavorable comparisons, he often was positive, especially when the local folks quartered the troops and shared their Revolutionary sentiments. Like his commanding officer, he was also eyeing locations for future opportunities.

Hazen did not give Hawkins much time to smell the ink in Dresden, for the regiment moved out early on 29 April. Part of the baggage was loaded on eleven bateaux and sent up the Connecticut River, but Hawkins traveled with the other baggage. The stony, mountainous road took its toll when a wagon turned over and another broke an axletree and tongue that took time to fix. The next day, after exchanging the teams, his group ran into hard rain. But the dripping men then came across Colonel Hazen at Major Child's place, where they stored the baggage in the major's barn and dried themselves around a "comfortable large Fire."[71]

On 2 May, most of the regiment reunited at Haverhill, "a long straggling Village," before marching another five miles the next day to the Haverhill courthouse. The soldiers converted the lower part of the courthouse into a commissary's store and the upper part into a hospital, while pitching their tents near this "Oxbaugh" of the Connecticut River. There, across the river from Newbury and in an area the indigenous peoples called "*Little* or *Lower Coos*, as a number of Miles above is called Big or Upper Coos," soldiers and locals mingled.[72]

Within a day, inhabitants, including Native Americans, visited the busy Continentals, who were laboring through rain and snow—"March Weather in the month of May," as the sergeant major from Pennsylvania put it. By the milder 8th, the regiment had "daily Fatigues at Work, who have cleared and levelled round the Camp—dug a Celler on the Side of a rising Ground, near the River for to place Barrels of Beef, &c. [and] built two neat Ovens and a large Log House over it. . . . The Carpenters, Armourers, Shoemakers and Bakers of the Regt. are likewise at work." Such work supported one part of the regiment's "Business," which was "to Guard the Stores here"; another part was to prevent Native incursions "on these Frontiers."[73] Securing the area included helping the provincials. Hazen had offered the selectmen from nearby Piermont the labor of part of two companies to assist in repairing the local roads. On the 10th, one company headed out to Peacham to protect residents and "to prevent Spies from the Enemy, or Intelligence being carried to them by disaffected People from these States." Hawkins recorded that the company was also to help residents repair "the Roads and Bridges from *Ryegate* to *Peacham*."[74] A few weeks later, Hazen assigned some soldiers to help build Bedel's barn.[75]

Collecting intelligence and denying it to the enemy was a vital element of Hazen's mission, and he sent eight details into Canada while based at Haverhill. Another element was protecting the inhabitants—both the original and newer ones—by assessing, assisting, and recruiting them. Resident Native Americans and more recent settlers had to be protected from and engaged in the repulsion of British, loyalist, and Indian raiders.

The American Indian dynamic was a tricky one given interests on both sides. The western Abenakis, who claimed the Green Mountain range and the Coos Country as their homeland, had welcomed traders but long pushed back against intruders in their territory. That resistance had included allying with the French and battling Rogers' Rangers during the Seven Years' War. When their allies lost, the Abenakis could not contain the incursion of English colonists. Therefore, some who had moved north to join others at Missisquoi Bay and St. Francis during that war stayed there, but others returned to their former homes, including at "Cowass," the oxbow on the Connecticut River. They continued to live there as colonists moved in and established the towns of Newbury and Haverhill in the early 1760s.[76]

When war erupted between colonists and British authorities, most Abenakis tried to remain neutral, but some chose or moved between sides. Both the British and the Americans were suspicious of them, but also wanted them as allies. The Americans hoped that the western Abenakis would help protect the upper Connecticut settlements, or at least refuse British recruitment. Colonel Bedel supported such objectives by cultivating connections, moving more Abenaki families near the new communities and trying to supply them with food. In January 1779, he reported that there were approximately thirty Indian families near Haverhill; they were willing to provide service but needed some provisions.[77] Hazen supported Bedel's efforts, which by fall included a recommendation to confirm an officer's commission for Joseph Louis Gill, a chief of the St. Francis tribe, whom he commended for his support over the summer. Washington seconded the recommendation to Congress, adding that Gill should be allowed to engage and command those of his people willing to enlist in Continental service. Congress agreed, though as it turned out, Gill ultimately preferred British and Abenaki connections.[78]

Hawkins was not complementary about the seven Indians who visited on 4 May, and whose apparel, he thought, "was remarkable dirty." Yet he chatted with them and learned that about seventy Native Americans "lived not far from here, on the other Side the River[.]" These neighbors continued to be frequent visitors, and Hawkins expected more as others returned from hunting, paid calls, and received food and rum.[79]

Hawkins showed a markedly different tone when commenting on visits from Euro-American residents. On 16 May, the Reverend Peter Powers preached near the encampment at Hazen's request. Inhabitants came from miles around, and Hawkins was pleasantly surprised at such "a large Circle . . . of the fair Sex in this Part of the World among the Number." He found some to be "handsome and genteel" and all to be lively. Perhaps among them was the twenty-three-year-old Lydia Sanborn, who had just given birth to her fourth child on 4 April. The Reverend Mr. Powers had officiated at her wedding in Haverhill in 1772. When the war began, her husband, Ebenezer, had marched out of town as a sergeant with Bedel's New Hampshire troops in the Canada campaign. He made it home again, but reenlisted in Bedel's regiment in April 1778 for one year's service, which was extended until the arrival of Hazen's regiment. Mistress Sanborn then saw her husband trade service in the ranks to service as a commissary of hides for the rest of the war.[80]

Lydia Sanborn's deposition about her husband's service revealed nothing about her feelings at the appearance of Hazen's regiment, but its sergeant major was happy to note that when it paraded on 16 May, it "made a handsome Appearance; the Men were clean and neat, and . . . marched in Platoons to and from the Place w[h]ere Divine Service was performed." He believed that the curious inhabitants, young and old, male and female, who had come from miles around found pleasure in what was surely a "strange Sight to them." Hawkins also noted that one of the sergeants, who had been successful in enlisting several young men during the march, managed to hook another "fine young Lad who came to hear the preaching."[81]

The regiment was thus firmly engaged in introducing American forces— and, by extension, Congressional authority—to the peoples of the region, as well as in building a vital line of communication. In advancing through the Coos Country, Hazen's regiment engaged in a trade of sorts: as it recruited men, supplies, and information, it in return and in spades helped open and fortify the northern frontier for inhabitants and speculators betting on the backcountry's development. The mission thus incorporated civilian—both private and public—and military interests, as well as immediate and long-term goals.

As Hawkins noted, Hazen's force met with success in enlisting men and support. Ezra Gates, who may have been between twenty to twenty-six years old in 1779, had enlisted in Bedel's regiment in March 1776, only to be taken prisoner in Canada shortly thereafter. The sick soldier was exchanged and sent home, but he enlisted again for a short term in 1777. Then, at Haverhill in May 1779, he enlisted in Hazen's regiment. After the war, he moved to Newbury, where the disabled veteran struggled to support his family by farming.[82]

John Shepherd (or Sheppard), age fifteen, also enlisted that May, apparently the day before Reverend Powers preached. He, like Gates, served to the end of the war and then moved to northern New York, where he labored as a carpenter until, as he deposed when he was ninety-one, infirmities prevented that.[83] Thomas Hazeltine (Hazleton) joined the regiment then "called the Congress Regiment & afterwards known by the name of Canadian, ol[d] Regiment" at Newbury in June. He earned a promotion to corporal and served to the war's end before returning to Vermont and supporting his large family on a small farm.[84] A local lad by the name of Josiah Pratt also joined the regiment at Haverhill. After serving until the end of the war, he returned to the area, eventually wedding Mary Pratt in 1785 at Newbury.[85] Another Pratt, by the name of Jonathan, was so young when he joined the unit in New Hampshire that his mother tried to intercede. He served as a fifer.[86] Michael Salter, who enlisted on 3 May, served as a drummer, while Joel Ried (Reid) had enlisted as a private on 29 April.[87]

Fourteen-year-old Stephen Burrows tried and tried again to enlist. Lieutenant Crowley first signed him into the artillery detachment, from which his father "with some difficulty" had him released. Then young Stephen, "his mind inflamed, by many fair promises and airy encouragements, with unappeasable desires to join the service," escaped his father and enlisted with Captain Lloyd as the regiment left Coos. By December, he was back home. Disappointed with the service, Burrows had deserted, and his father was making apologies to Washington and asking that his son be discharged.[88]

These new recruits joined Zacheus Peaslee and other New Hampshire men in the ranks. William Gledin (or Gleedon) had enlisted into Hazen's regiment in June 1778, a year before it marched up into the Coos Country. Gledin served as a private for five years until the war ended.[89] Benjamin Heath, in his mid to late twenties when Hazen's regiment marched into Haverhill, had first served "agants the Common Enimy on the continental establishment" for eighteen months in a company attached to Bedel's regiment in 1775. He then enlisted into the "Congress regiment" and served about eight years total.[90] Musician Merifield Victor was around sixteen in 1779. Decades later, he said that he had enlisted in the regiment at Charlestown, New Hampshire, in 1778 (other records indicate September 1779), and that during the three-year enlistment he served in numerous skirmishes before reenlisting. The regimental roster notes that he deserted in 1779, returned to the unit in 1781, and served to 1783.[91]

As the unit built up its ranks, it gathered intelligence and sowed disinformation. In early May, Washington relayed news from General Schuyler to Congress that the Cayugas were possibly interested in establishing peace with the Americans. Washington interpreted this as perhaps a result of his use of "artifice . . . to excite jealousies of an invasion of Canada, and induce the Enemy there to keep their force at home."[92] In other words, the Indians foresaw no support from the British forces hunkered down in Canada.

That was exactly what Washington wanted, and because he did not need more, he denied Hazen's requests for more support and more action. The general informed the colonel, "Oeconomy in the state of our affairs is a principal consideration. To hide a real intention from the enemy another; or should this be discovered, to perplex as to the moment, as well as the points of operation." Washington ordered Hazen to continue pushing "enquiries into Canada" and to carry "on the clearing of the roads."[93]

Hazen continued, and on 28 May, Hawkins recorded that "four Men, Natives of Canada, properly equipped and furnished with Necessaries by Col Hazen, went from here, bound to some Part of Canada." Before they could report back, Hazen received news from other informants. Clément and Louis Gosselin, with two or three soldiers, had entered Haverhill on 7 June, just as Hazen was preparing to leave it. They had been spying in Canada and "appeared like Indians by their Dress and being painted."[94] With them were four men who had escaped confinement in Quebec. Hazen passed on their news to Washington, which appeared to corroborate information from other sources. As the general explained to Governor Clinton of New York on 28 June, "By some intelligence from Canada received through Col. Hazen concurring with what Col. Van Schaick communicated some time since, it is said that 1500 Men were sent early in the spring to the posts on the Lakes." Washington did not believe everything in Hazen's account, but he thought that "as it may be true," he should reinforce Sullivan's expedition "to avoid an accident."[95] Washington continued to compare intelligence reports on the enemy's possible plans and movements in Canada throughout the summer to ensure that Sullivan's expedition had the greatest chance for success—and to prevent its being taken by surprise by British troops swooping down from Canada.[96]

Washington wrote to Hazen in July that he appreciated the transmitted intelligence and wished he could credit all of it, but that he believed that the persons in touch with Captain Paulint and communicating with Major Benjamin Whitcomb (New Hampshire rangers) had slender grounds for their reports. After that caution, Washington stressed that he did not want Hazen to "put the public to any expence" in his operations, but did not object to Hazen's "building Block Houses and Stores, if it can be done entirely by your own people." Washington reminded Hazen that his "command was to answer a particular Object, intimately connected with or at least intended to promote . . . a plan which I had in view." Hazen's mission was to facilitate Washington's greater strategy, even if he was not fully aware of all of its details and what role his regiment played in it. He was not to raise expectations or expenses among the civil authorities that the commander in chief did not want to meet.[97]

Hazen, however, had been building expectations along with blockhouses as his troops cut a road toward Canada. On 1 June, Sergeant Major Hawkins noted that a detachment of four captains, four subalterns, eight sergeants, eight corporals, one drummer and fifer, and one hundred men took their tents and headed to Peacham. Five days later, another much smaller detachment with one captain and lieutenant, two sergeants, two corporals, and twenty-seven privates followed the route of the first, taking flour, beef, and rum instead of tents with them.[98]

On 7 June, Colonel Hazen's baggage wagon moved out "escorted by Part of two French Companies" of the regiment. After hearing from the just-returned Gosselins and meeting with "A Number of Indians (several of whom attends daily for Provisions & Rum)," the colonel left around noon, following in the tracks of his troops. As Hazen set off, Major Joseph Torrey arrived from Boston, but he too was to go on forward. That left Major Reid in command in Haverhill and later, possibly, Captain Duncan.[99]

Perhaps it was Reid or Duncan who wrote the letter quoted in the *Virginia Gazette* and other newspapers a few months later. The "letter from an officer on the northern expedition, dated at Co'os, June 28, 1779" revealed that much of Hazen's regiment had "advanced as far as the river la Moile [Lamoille] . . . making a road and building block-houses." Furthermore, it added, "intelligence received from Canada . . . is greatly in our favour, the inhabitants of that country are almost determined to a man to join us the moment we enter their territories." The writer thus echoed what Hazen had told Washington back in March, also noting the number of men guarding St. Johns, Chambly, Trois-Rivières, and Montreal before claiming that the enemy had destroyed or removed its fleet on Lake Champlain. All this, he concluded, "you may rely on."[100]

Those who remained in Haverhill labored on the starting stretch of the road from Newbury, relayed supplies, and supported the local populace. That support included medical assistance from Theodore DeKelley (or DeCalla). Naomi DeKelley had a mighty fight trying to get a widow's pension fifty years later, but depositions, including by Lydia Sanborn, Edward Clark (another local lad who enlisted on 1 May 1779), and Moody Bedel (Timothy Bedel's son), confirmed DeKelley's presence and aid. Moody Bedel recalled that he met Dr. DeKelley when his mother's physician was sick and could not attend her. They turned to the doctors of the regiment, apparently including DeKelley acting as surgeon's mate, for Nicholas Schuyler was the regiment's official surgeon. Bedel remembered DeKelley as a German speaking broken English. He also declared that the other doctors paid particular heed to his advice, which had helped his mother recover. Although DeKelley then "left this Frontier for the south" in the fall, he returned "in a Year or Two after the Revolutionary War was over . . . & Called at my House then in Haverhill . . . & he told me that he had taken a likeing to this Country when here with Hazens Regiment, & said that he had now come with the Intent of staying in it, & Practising as a Doctor or a Surgeon & Physition." He not only did that but also married "Naomy George a Person with whom I was well acquainted with from her Infancy."[101]

As some members of Hazen's regiment forged ties in Haverhill, other members worked in the detachments blazing the road northward. As they did so, they tended to keep to the highlands, the ridgelines of the hilly terrain, and avoid lower wetlands. When they could not avoid the boggy spots, they laid down logs, sides touching and covered in earth, to create corduroy roadways.[102] They built blockhouses to facilitate the movement of soldiers and supplies along the route. One blockhouse was at Peacham, another near what became Cabot, and yet others at what were later named Walden and Greensboro (all in Vermont). The men trudged up and down the hills, axing through the trees, until they encamped near the spots that became Lowell Village and Westfield. They were there on 24 August, a Tuesday, when Hazen wrote to Bedel from the "Camp at the End of the Road," fifty miles from Haverhill, to let him know his plans. Hazen expected to finish blazing the road to the nearby mountain notch by the following Saturday, the 28th, and had ordered Major Reid to bring up provisions with three captains, two subalterns, and eighty-five men. Hazen figured that his detachment would return to Haverhill after finishing the provisions. Worried that they could come under attack, Hazen confided that he would be happy to see Bedel and his soldiers "If Mrs. Bedel's health will admit of your leaving home."[103]

The attack did not come, but other orders did. The very Saturday that Hazen hoped to have his road reach the notch in view, Washington dispatched orders "to put your regiment under marching orders, and proceed without delay by the best and shortest route to rejoin this army." Washington had learned that the enemy had received its expected reinforcements at New York, and thus he had to "draw together as much of our force as possible on the occasion." The regiment was to rejoin the Main Army.[104]

Hazen had not yet received the orders on 31 August, when he wrote to Bedel from his camp on "Hazens Rout" requesting resupplies, offering sympathy about his wife, and noting that Boileau and Mooers had arrived with information from Canada. Ensign Benjamin Mooers, likely Ensign Pierre Amable Boileau, and nine others had scouted St. Trois. But by 8 September, Hazen was back at Haverhill offering condolences to Bedel on the loss of his wife (which challenges Moody Bedel's memory of his mother's recovery) and perturbed that no flour was available for his regiment, which was expected the next day.[105]

Washington recalled the regiment as he was rerouting troops and supplies while reevaluating possible options in the fall of 1779. In early September, he instructed Jeremiah Wadsworth, the commissary general of purchases, to form magazines necessary for future operations and place them "according to the present prospects of the war"—at Albany as the principal deposit, and others to the southward as far as the Susquehanna. There were to be magazines along the Connecticut River "from Coos downward as far as Hartford" because, Washington said, he was still considering "an expedition into Canada by way of Coos." Yet he acknowledged that was "a precarious event," and thus he was "unwilling to let it have more influence than will be perfectly consistent with public oeconomy." Wadsworth was not to incur any unnecessary expenses as he acted on Washington's plans, and he was to keep the possibility of a Canadian expedition "a secret to others."[106]

Washington's conference with the French minister, Anne-César, Chevalier de La Luzerne, on 16 September was also confidential. They discussed naval support, New York, and the Floridas as they danced around who would or could do what in possible combined operations. The chevalier mentioned that several gentlemen in Boston, some who were members of Congress, had talked with him "on the subject of an expedition against Canada and Nova Scotia." His king, he said, was interested in having "those two provinces annexed to the American Confederacy and would be disposed to promote a plan for this purpose; but . . . would undertake nothing of the kind unless the plan was previously approved and digested by The General." It was a shrewd assurance, given that Washington had deemed a proposed joint invasion unfeasible just one year earlier. Luzerne said that whenever Washington thought conditions were favorable for such an expedition, the chevalier would be happy to recommend his plans to the French court. Washington responded that as long as large numbers of effective enemy forces remained in the states, the problems he previously noted still existed, but should that enemy force be routed, "it would be a leading object with the government to wrest the two forementioned provinces from the power of Britain." Washington also noted that naval cooperation would be necessary in such an event.[107] The commander in chief was engaged in an intricate diplomatic, political, and military minuet: as much as the Americans wanted French help, many also feared that France might try to retake its old territory, even though the 1778 treaty of alliance included a provision that France was not to retake Canada or acquire other areas in America. Could Congress and Washington trust their ally? On the other side, France refused to conquer Canada for the Americans.

As the Washington-Luzerne exchange confirmed, the Franco-American alliance had spurred Americans to consider again the possibility of invading and acquiring Canada. After the aborted irruption in 1778, Washington had "walked forward," in the parlance of the dance, in the spring and summer of 1779, but that fall he walked back: he ordered Hazen to return, but initially desired him to "move slowly." If Hazen was concerned that the magazine at Coos would be left too vulnerable after his troops' withdrawal, then he was to move it to a safer location on the Connecticut River; but if it was "safe where it is, there will be an advantage in letting it remain."[108] Shortly thereafter,

Washington advised Commissary General Wadsworth to form his magazines "low down the river" to avoid the danger of an enemy incursion.[109] In early October, Washington brought the dance to a close when he ordered Hazen to "march as expeditiously as possible with your Regiment, by the way of Litchfield, and join the division under the command of Major General Howe," who was at or near Bedford, New York.[110] Hazen obeyed orders and retraced his steps out of the Coos Country, but he still wanted the region secured, especially since the new road could now serve as an invasion route for the enemy. Besides recommending that Joseph Louis Gill and other Abenakis whom Gill might recruit be taken into Continental service, Hazen continued to push for another expedition north and encouraged Bedel to do the same.[111]

Coos Country inhabitants were not the only ones who felt insecure. The Massachusetts Council also expressed concerns about an exposed frontier and asked Congress whether Hazen's or another force might continue in the region. As Washington explained to Samuel Huntington, the recently elected president of Congress, in November 1779: "I cannot send any Troops for the defence of the Frontiers of New Hampshire and Massachusetts bay. As to public stores being deposited there, . . . There are none there that I know of, nor will there be any Magazines of forage or provisions laid up so high or to such a considerable amount on Connecticut River toward the Coos Country, as to be an Object for a body of the Enemy." He had already taken care of that issue. Washington also reminded Congress that when Hazen was detached to open a road, "it was for the purpose of exciting jealousies at Quebec—and at the Enemy's posts on the St Lawrence &c.—and of making a diversion in favor of the late expedition under General Sullivan, by preventing Reinforcements being sent into the Upper Country to oppose him. This very happily succeeded—and it was always my intention to recall [Hazen], when ever the Object of his command was accomplished." Washington hoped "that the cutting of a Road towards Canada, which appeared to me essential to make the feint complete, will not have the least tendency to expose the Country to incursions."[112]

Washington wanted Hazen's troops available for other operations. The commander in chief had drafted plans for another invasion into Canada, but then put them aside for both long-term and more immediate political and military reasons. The time spent figuring out how to mount such an offensive was not wasted, for he used elements of the plans to respond to invasion advocates and to support actions elsewhere. As one of those advocates, Hazen—who was as energetic in pushing the Coos route as perhaps Washington had been for Braddock's Road in another war decades earlier—got part of what he wanted: he was able to advance some smaller personal objectives, even if he did not secure the larger one. Some soldiers and Coos inhabitants, in turn, were introduced to other peoples, places, and forces that were constituents to the forming union.

Hazen's "Canadian" regiment did not make it back to Canada in 1778 or 1779, but it did mature as a Continental regiment and community over those years. As its commanding officer advanced the regiment, he reorganized and further established it. And while its operations provide evidence of Washington's growing strategic sense and sensibility, they also reveal some of the logistical and civil-military complexities, constraints, and opportunities faced by the Continental Army.

An Imperfect Corps

O n 29 January 1778, just one day after he had authorized the transfer of Hazen's regiment to the Northern Department in support of that year's Canadian plan, General Washington puzzled: "I am at a loss what to propose, concerning the German battalion, Hazen's Regiment and the sixteen addition-als. Appertaining to no particular state or states, they will have no chance of being filled by drafts, and as little by any other means. They must either remain weak and imperfect corps, be adopted by the states or incorporated into each other and then, if possible, recruited."[1] Over the next few years, Hazen's regiment contended with the label, diagnosis, and remedies Washing-ton identified, which also applied to the army and the confederation. As the regiment tramped through borderlands and highlands between 1778 and early 1781, its members battled personnel and personal issues as they reorganized and recruited companies, made camps and community, and engaged enemies foreign and domestic.

The imperfect corps reflected an imperfect union, both military and civil. In 1775, Washington had desired a continental American army in which provin-cial distinctions were shelved "so that one and the same Spirit may animate the whole."[2] By 1778, he was fretting not only about dissension in the army but also growing discrimination against it. Congress's diffidence in further regulariz-ing the army subverted the shared spirit necessary to shared action. In essence, some of the reasons why Congress may have earlier kicked at the regiment's calling itself Congress's Own now informed distrust of the army. "The *jealousy* which Congress unhappily entertain of the Army," Washington despaired, was "unjustly founded." He acknowledged that the jealousy arose from a common understanding "that Standing Armies are dangerous to a state." But, he argued, other countries only deplored them in peace, and generally because members of such armies did not have any of the ties—the concerns or interests of Citizens or any other dependence, than what flowed from their military employ—in short from their being mercenaries—hirelings. It is our policy to be prejudiced against them in time of *War*—and tho they are Citizens, having all the ties—& interests of Citizens, and in most cases property totally unconnected with the military line. If we would pursue a right system of policy, in my opinion, there should be none of these distinctions—we should all be considered, Congress—Army &c., as one people, embarked in one cause—in one interest; acting on the same principle, and to the same end.

The distrust was "impolitic in the extreme," for the jealousy that some politicians entertained "of the army in order to [ensure] a due subordination to the supreme, civil authority, is a likely mean to produce a contrary effect. . . . It is unjust, because no order of Men in the thirteen States have paid a more sanctimonious regard to their proceedings than the Army."[3] In his frustration, Washington disregarded that not all Continentals were citizens as he pressed civil and military authorities to work with him to realize a united continental force.

Washington also needed civil authorities to work with each other. Civil administration of the army was disjointed because state officials were as determined to keep Congress, not just the army, subordinate to their authority. It could request, not command. The escalating problems in coordination and cooperation led to such measures as the system of state-specific supply in 1780, which in turn further undermined unity in the Continental Army.[4] Congress's Own Regiment revealed some of the calamitous results in its own and the army's crises of 1780 to 1781.

Hazen both fought and fueled dissension as he made some distinctions within his regiment while protesting those made against it. He accommodated the regiment's multiethnic, multilingual, and religiously diverse service members and followers through both segregation and integration. The result was a regimental community of relationships and interests bound by joint orders, shared experiences, and common goals within a borderland of contested and negotiated opportunities, loyalties, and identities. This borderland community contended with the governance of military versus civilian members and the intersection of institutional and interpersonal dynamics.

From March 1778 through early 1781, the regiment moved between Albany, West Point, and White Plains in New York, to Putnam's Folly near Redding and Danbury in Connecticut, through the Coos Country of New Hampshire and Vermont, down to Morristown, New Jersey, and then back to the New York encampments. Over that period, the army moved Congress's Own from the Northern to the Highlands Department (April to July 1778), the New Hampshire Brigade (July 1778 to March 1779), and back to the Northern Department

(March to August 1779). It then assigned it to the Main Army (from August 1779), which included shifting it to General Edward Hand's brigade (late November 1779 to August 1780) and on to the New Hampshire Brigade, before reassignment to the Highlands Department on 1 January 1781.[5] The regiment moved, as did others, in accordance with strategic plans, theater operations, departmental numbers, command relationships, and the dictates of logistics.

In the midst of the moves, the regiment reorganized, tried to manage and support its followers, and witnessed personal and professional battles that subverted unity. The 1778 reorganization was primarily internally driven, whereas the 1781 model owed more to external factors, but during both the regiment responded to administrative disorder, army reforms, and decreasing soldiers. Reorganization, whether internally or externally driven, affected not only officers and soldiers: it included family members trailing service members who tried to find space and sustenance for their followers. The followers also shaped and supported the regimental community. Wrangles among members, disputes with authorities, and battles against enemies challenged and confirmed community cohesion and regimental discipline.

Congress's Own to Canadian (Old) Regiment

The Continental Army's reconstruction between 1778 and 1779 addressed the realities of a continuing war marked by wasted flesh and flagging spirits. The army could not recruit, sustain, and retain enough soldiers, and some officers increasingly complained of their unrecognized sacrifices "for the common benefit of the rest of the Society." Many of those officers were not happy with one of the solutions, which was "new modeling the Army" to consolidate the soldiers into fewer regiments that needed fewer officers.[6] The drive for greater administrative efficiency and economy adversely affected morale and combat efficiency, but it also showed that Americans were still determined to mesh martial needs, material constraints, and political ideologies. The Continental Army was becoming a regular army, but American style, which the 1781 reorganization's focus on consolidation and efficiencies further confirmed.

Research and debate were the first steps in 1778. While Hazen's regiment was marching north to Albany, a congressional committee met with Washington and other officers between 28 January and 12 March. The civil and military officials discussed the number of regiments, the number of companies and men in them, staff positions, and half-pay pensions for officers. By the time Congress could revise and approve the proposals, it was too late to implement all of them before Washington's troops left Valley Forge and chased Lieutenant General Sir Henry Clinton's army into New Jersey that June. The organizational changes came over the year following the Battle of Monmouth. The officers and soldiers, in turn, had to continue their sacrifices to the end of the war to collect on the promises of '78: seven years' half pay for officers and a payout of eighty dollars to soldiers.[7]

In the meantime, Congress asked the states to fill up what battalions they had with men drafted from their militias. Those drafted, in contrast to those who enlisted, were to serve for nine months—just long enough to maintain the army's strength over the coming campaign and reorganization. Congress also asked the states "to provide shoes, stockings and shirts, sufficient for their respective Quotas of Troops in the Continental Army."[8]

Looking to the states for provisions was a major problem for Hazen, nor he did have the draft option to fill the ranks that they did, so he continued to barrage Congress and Washington for support. Hazen also championed his regiment's interests within the various departments and divisions to which it was assigned. And, like other commanders, he shifted around officers and soldiers for more effective command and control within his regiment. His actions did not endear him to some superiors or subordinates.

Through February and March 1778, as Hazen busied himself in Albany rearranging his companies and pushing like Sisyphus for an irruption into Canada, Washington was considering how to strengthen superintendence of the various works on the North (Hudson) River. General Parsons was directing the troops at West Point in General Putnam's absence and complaining about the perplexities of the command to both Washington and Governor Clinton. He wanted his authority clarified, more supplies, and five hundred to a thousand more troops to help erect fortifications. Despite that plea for manpower, Parsons begged Clinton not to command Lafayette to release "the 'Congress' Own' regiment of infernals to make part of the number."[9]

Parsons obviously believed that Hazen's troops were troublesome, which may have reflected Lafayette's criticisms of Hazen's interference in command decisions about that year's proposed Canadian expedition.[10] It may also have reflected ethnic and regional tensions, or been due to Parsons's desire not to have disputes in the Canadian regiments embroil his command. He had enough problems with "refractory" artificers.[11] There was some unrest in Albany, but there was more in James Livingston's regiment at Johnstown, which did ultimately involve Hazen. Colonel Livingston had refused to reappoint Captain John Baptist Allen (Jean Baptiste Allin) at the end of 1776 when he was reestablishing the 1st Canadian Regiment. Livingston alleged that Allen had been drinking with soldiers and been drunk on duty, but General Schuyler reinstated him by late 1777 after Allen undertook a spying expedition to Canada. Other officers in Livingston's regiment protested to the extent that an observer supposed there was a scheme "to rid the Regt of the Canadian

Officers, by causing them to put one another under arrest." At least two were under arrest by the end of January 1778, but troop movements delayed resolution until a court-martial on 14 June at the Continental Village, with Hazen presiding, acquitted Captain James Robichaux of trying to foment a mutiny and Captain Allen of drunkenness "while on Piquet Guard." The court also acquitted John Brooks, a soldier in Captain Thomas Pry's company in Hazen's regiment, of desertion.[12]

The controversy over Allen's position, not behavior, somewhat echoed that of Lieutenant Colonel Pierre Regnier de Roussi. Roussi had also lost his position in Livingston's Canadian regiment at the end of 1776, but was then commissioned in Colonel Henry Beekman Livingston's 4th New York. At Valley Forge in early 1778, Roussi was disputing the date of his rank because he was angry that New York officers who had been junior to him in 1776 were now senior. Roussi tied his case to regional and state prejudices: "Am I, likewise . . . to have no Rights of Promotion, and to all purposes, [be] like a Bastard who has never any Rights in his father's state &c[?]" If so, he figured that " no stranger Should serve in this army, nor any one from one province to another," unless assured otherwise.[13] With reorganization came more arguments over who qualified and who did not for decreasing positions. Hazen was not involved in the Roussi case, but he was an instigator or participant in many others as he fought to ensure that neither he nor his regiment were disqualified from rights in and to the national estate. His actions, plus the eagerness of the Canadian troops to move north rather than stay to secure the Highlands, may have led to Parsons's aspersion.

Washington shared Parsons's concerns about reinforcing the Hudson Highlands, and so sent Major General Alexander McDougall to take command of the forts and informed Congress that he agreed with Governor Clinton about pulling troops down to "carry on the Works."[14] Scarce troops limited options, so Washington chose to leave the borderlands north of Albany open and concentrate forces around West Point; but instead of immediately shifting Hazen's "weak" regiment, he ordered Colonel Goose Van Schaick's fresh one to go. Then, at the end of March, Washington ordered both the 1st and 2nd Canadian Regiments to Fishkill, and to place themselves under McDougall's command.[15]

McDougall barely had a chance to review his new command before Washington asked whether it was practical to attack the British in New York City with the combined force of Parsons's and John Nixon's brigades, the regiments of Van Schaik, Hazen, and Livingston, plus militia from New York and Connecticut. McDougall regretfully reported that the debilitated state of his command contravened such action. Instead, he returned Van Schaick's regiment and focused on securing West Point.[16] After leaving Valley Forge and battling Sir Henry Clinton's forces at Monmouth in June, Washington moved his army to White Plains in order to defend the Hudson River lines of communication and to be in position to coordinate operations with the French should an attack on New York City become viable. But as British forces might attack Rhode Island (indeed, the Battle of Newport began 5 August), he put General Sullivan there. Ultimately, British naval reinforcements, weather woes, and other issues squashed hopes for a vigorous campaign in the Northern and Highlands Departments through the rest of the year.

Hazen's regiment supported defensive and foraging operations from its arrival in April 1778 at Fishkill, through its move to Peekskill, and, by August, to White Plains near Dobbs Ferry.[17] Hazen also continued the company restructuring he had begun in February. In mid-August, acting Sergeant Major Hawkins listed seventeen companies and their designated captains: Satterlee, McConnell, Popham, Heron, Burns, Olivie, Liébert, Carlile, White, Munson, Gilbert, Lloyd, Pry, Campbell, Taylor, Duncan, and Paulint (the latter's as an attached independent company).[18] Robert Campbell was either still on parole or had just rejoined the regiment (transferring to the Corps of Invalids in September), while John Carlile was back after a prisoner exchange that summer.[19] Matthew McConnell and James Heron were not yet exchanged. Hawkins, who had been certifying company payrolls that summer, did some arithmetic on 3 September. After deducting seven officers as prisoners, he noted that the regiment had 561 members (present and absent), and that of those, 125 officers, noncommissioned officers, and soldiers were in the "French" companies (adding that several in those companies were not Frenchmen) commanded by Olivie, Liébert, Gilbert, and Paulint. The 125 also included one possible Frenchman or Francophone in each of Satterlee's and Munson's companies.[20]

As Hawkins made those distinctions, he penned, "I am unacquainted with the People or Language of the Country, as well as their Mode of Relgion, and should chuse ever to be so." Was he reflecting his own or others' provincialism? Hawkins crossed out the statement and he does not disparage the "French" in the rest of his journal. Nor did he denigrate the other ethnic groups increasingly represented in the regiment over the years. He was jotting notes for or from Hazen's memorial to Congress, for the statement mirrored what Hazen said was General Wooster's reason for authorizing Hazen and Antill to commission officers in early 1776. In his 3 September 1778 memorial, Hazen laid out why the regiment, and especially its Canadians, "have real Claim to Favours," and why "reducing the Regiment to the present intended Establishment of the Army" not only would hurt him but would also be a "particular Hardship on many brave worthy Gentlemen, and good Officers." He argued that "such a Reduction would eventually ruin one of the best Regiments in the Service of these United States," which was unnecessary, because the regiment would be provided for by a state upon Canada's incorporation. Hazen's numbers did not quite match those recorded by Hawkins, as Hazen included himself, Antill (although acknowledging he was still a prisoner of war), Major Torrey, four captains, seven subalterns, and "near" 150 noncommissioned officers and soldiers among the Canadians then present in a regiment of sixteen companies and thirty-three officers (some doing duty outside the regiment and excluding field officers).[21] Hazen likely downplayed the officer count and maximized soldier numbers to push back on the army's reorganization plans, counter slurs against the regiment, and put in another plug for an invasion of Canada.

After conferring with Generals Gates and Bayley at White Plains about the best ways to invade Canada, Hazen traveled to Philadelphia, where on 20 September he submitted another petition in support of the regiment. He counted 522 noncommissioned officers and soldiers and sixteen companies, plus one attached independent company of Canadians (Paulint's). He reminded the delegates that the regiment was first raised in Canada to serve there, adding that both officers and men wanted to march into "that Country, and that in case of its uniting with these states, [t]o become the state Troops of Canada." Given that and the favors due them, he continued, the Canadian officers "cannot be Dismiss'd the service," and dismissing the others would not be right either, for that would mean "Dismissing some of the best officers of their Rank in the Army." He assured the delegates that the proportion and expense of officers to men would be no more than that for other regiments on the new establishment, and that he would "be answerable for the good behavior of the Regiment."[22]

Hazen was still answering slurs and defending the regiment's honor in April 1779 as he assured Washington that, a few desertions aside, his troops were behaving superbly as they moved into the Coos Country. He declared that "the undeserved bad Charactor, ungenerously Indeavoured to be established on this Regiment, is Totally eradicated at least through that part of the Country where we have marched by ourselves."[23]

In November 1779, while addressing supply issues, Hazen again championed the regiment's character— in particular that of the Canadians. After acknowledging Congress's previous orders confirming the regiment's establishment but halting new officers' appointments and promotions, and the orders of 15 March 1779 about crediting members to states' manpower quotas, he pointed out a major problem: while the states were counting the men, they were not providing for them as they did those in their state units. Hazen reported that of the 471 noncommissioned officers and soldiers on the November 1779 rolls, 460 were enlisted for the war and had only received Congress's twenty-dollar bounty; they were serving without additional state bounties or supplies. Furthermore, there was no provision for the sixteen officers and 111 noncommissioned officers and soldiers from Canada. Hazen was adamant: "The Canadian Soldiers are not inferior to any in the Regiment, in Point of Morality, Bravery, or Attachment to the Cause and Service." He pointed out that only one Canadian had deserted the regiment since the 1776 retreat from Canada. They had stayed during the previous summer's Coos expedition, despite being so close to home and families in Canada. Despite hardships and "notwithstanding the different States, Countrys and Nations from which this Regiment has been raised, yet a perfect Harmony and a general Unanimity has always subsisted amongst the Officers, as well as a most passive-Obedience cultivated amongst the Soldiers." Hazen had "the Honour to command as good a Corps as any in the American Army."[24]

Hazen then advised Washington about how he might solve the problem. He also enclosed a letter that twenty-three officers had sent him in which they pointed out their "misfortune (though five hundred Combatants) to be too inconsiderable a body to divert the *people* in *power* from the grand and more weighty concerns of the nation and attract their attention as a Regiment." Another misfortune was their being from different states and far from their provinces, and thus cut off from resources even as they served alongside other well-supplied troops. Their conundrum, in essence, was leaving with nothing or serving with little. They declared, "It is not enough for us barely to serve our Country, we wish to serve it with reputation."[25]

Resources, rank, and reputation continued to bedevil members of the regiment, and especially its colonel, for the rest of the war. Notwithstanding Hazen's assertion of harmony and unanimity in the regiment, there were battles between members even when they combined to pressure Congress and the army to recognize and meet the requirements of their distinctive regiment. The distinction and requirements grew with each reorganization.

Confirming the regiment in November 1778 had played into planning for a possible expedition into Canada. Yet there was still the need to address Washington's concern about it being one of the army's imperfect corps. Besides character and composition, numbers figured in the judgment, yet the regiment was not as weak as it appeared against the 1,000 men called for in its original establishment. Although it did drop below the 50 percent mark, it still maintained a strength comparable to or greater than most other regiments. While Hawkins counted the regiment at 561 in September 1778, other records indicate 536 that August at White Plains and around 507 at Danbury that September. A year later, in September 1779, it was about 490, and then in fall 1780, it hovered around 400.[26] The numbers went up and down depending on detachments, deaths, desertions, transfers, and enlistments. What helped maintain a baseline strength was that most of the soldiers in Hazen's regiment had enlisted for the war, not just for three years, and thus were not due to depart in 1780.

Table 1. Congress's Own Regimental Strengths, 1778–83

January	1778	1779	1780	1781	1782	1783
Colonel	001	001	001	001	001	001
Lieutenant Colonel	001	001	001	001	001	001
Majors	004	004	003	003	003	002
Captains	017	018	017	017	012	012
Lieutenants	013	008	008	011	000*	013
Ensigns	008	012	011	005	004	000*
Men	592	491	446	443	443	470
Total	624	544	487	481	464	499

Source: "Strength of General Hazens Regimt. at different Periods, 1786," PCC, roll 52, item 41, vol. 9, pp. 395–401.

*Other records indicate ~10 lieutenants in 1782; ~1 ensign in 1783.

January	*December 1777	1779	1780	1781	1782	1783
Total	479	485	322	415	426	621

Source: Lesser, Sinews of Independence, 54, 85, 148, 194, 212, 242.

Note: Incomplete data, including missing reports, affected strength returns during the war and continued to challenge summations thereafter. The approximate numbers should be interpreted as time- and place-dependent.

When it reauthorized Hazen's regiment in late 1778, Congress had stated that there were to be "no new appointments or promotions of officers" in it until Congress issued new orders.[27] In the midst of laying down rules for deciding disputes over rank and downsizing the number of officers, Congress evidently did not want Hazen to use the regiment's original establishment as a loophole. That did not immediately concern Hazen, perhaps because he had already made three or four new appointments and promoted about twelve officers that year before the prohibition.

The new officers in 1778 were Captain Edward Giles (Maryland), Ensign Benjamin Mooers (Massachusetts/New York), and surgeon Nicholas Schuyler (New York). Pierre Amable Boileau (Canada) may have been appointed in 1778, but more likely in 1777. The twenty-year-old Mooers was Hazen's nephew and had been a lieutenant in the New York militia. Mooers later said that he had been with the militia at Ticonderoga when the Declaration of Independence was proclaimed there in 1776, and in 1777 arrived at Saratoga two days before

General Burgoyne surrendered there. Appointed ensign in Hazen's regiment on 20 March 1778, Mooers joined it at Peekskill around 1 June. During the Coos Campaign in August 1779, he led a scouting expedition into Canada near St. Johns and St. Trois. Hazen promoted him to lieutenant in March 1780, and then appointed him adjutant.[28] Mooers's record-keeping as adjutant later proved critical in his postwar activities and those of his fellow officers and soldiers.

In addition to those new officers, the regiment welcomed the return of others from "long and tedious" captivity between 1778 and 1780. Captains Campbell, Carlile, and possibly Heron may have returned by August 1778. Sergeant Major Manning was back by September and was promoted to ensign on the 19th, clearing the way for Hawkins's permanent promotion to sergeant major on the 20th. Prisoner exchanges in 1780 saw the return of Lieutenant James Anderson that August or November, Major Woodson and Lieutenant Colonel Antill in October and November, and Captain McConnell in December.[29]

When Hazen heard rumors by fall 1780 that there would be another army reorganization, he again mounted what he admitted was his "Hobby Horse" and pressed anew for the regiment's retention on its original establishment and for possible service in Canada. He added that he had been "almost Silent on the point of promotion." That was not true, for when he had been riding his hobby horse the previous February while seeking the inspector general's "Patronage" for the regiment, he had insisted on his right to promotion. Hazen had also, it appears, suggested combining the two Canadian corps into one. Major General Friedrich Wilhelm von Steuben had been reviewing all corps at the time so as to propose reforms in the army. The following month, both Steuben and Lord Stirling proposed incorporating Livingston's members into Hazen's regiment.[30]

A congressional committee considered both finances and Washington's desires in planning another reorganization, which Congress finally approved with a few amendments on 21 October. The reorganization, effective 1 January 1781, reduced (that is, disbanded) the remaining sixteen additional regiments that had not already been annexed to state lines. It also reduced separate light corps and the German battalion, but even before Hazen had asked, Congress kept his regiment with the other forty-nine regiments of infantry. Noncommissioned officers and privates in the reduced units were to be moved into the regiments of their states. Soldiers who did not belong to a state were to be transferred as Washington directed. Congress added, however, that all foreign noncommissioned officers and soldiers in the reduced units were to be incorporated into Hazen's regiment; that included the remaining members of Livingston's 1st Canadian. Congress thus made Hazen's the only Canadian regiment—soon dubbed the Canadian Old Regiment by its members.

Congress also specified that "volunteers from foreign states, who are now in the service, or may hereafter join the American army, be annexed to the said regiment." That could apply to new recruits, for whom it may be assumed that recruiting officers would receive the two-dollar payment (increased from 1777) for enlisting able-bodied men. Yet Congress and the army were also still looking to reduce officers, not just regiments. The new arrangement made many officers into supernumeraries (that is, in excess of the number allocated to each unit). Congress offered reduced officers "half pay for seven years" and grants of land after the war (as promised in a September 1776 resolution). It then added that if not enough officers volunteered for reduction, the decision would be determined by seniority, which also opened a backdoor to retaining a few supernumeraries. The companies in an infantry regiment only needed eighteen subalterns under the new establishment, but regiments were allowed twenty-two, with the four supernumeraries to do the staff duties of recruiter, paymaster, quartermaster, and adjutant. Continued supernumeraries, like other officers who were not reduced, were entitled to half pay for life.[31]

These developments affected Hazen's regiment through the incorporation of new members, the combination of companies, and the retention and promotion of officers. Despite Hazen's efforts to turn wishes into reality—which continued into 1782 when he drafted another detailed plan on how the army should march into Canada—his regiment was not going to become the state troops of Canada. The regiment, however, kept the Canadians that it did have, for "the wife has not endeavoured to persuade her Husband to leave our Service, nor has the parent the Son; or the Sister or Brother the Near Relation."[32] The issue was retaining and recruiting other members. The army's consolidation of 1781 did not immediately build the regiment's roll numbers. In fact, Hazen reduced the number of his companies for the coming campaign.[33] The reasons included the small number of transferred men, who replaced those who died, deserted, or legitimately left that year, and the fact that not all the newcomers appeared on the regiment's roll unless or until they reenlisted (and sometimes not even then) in the regiment.

In November 1780, Livingston's regiment counted two remaining officers besides its colonel among a total of perhaps 118 members. By January 1781, the officers had lost their positions and the men had dispersed to relevant state units (primarily New York's) or to Hazen's. Captain Robichaux and Lieutenant Francis Monty asked to continue as officers or be accepted as volunteers with the regiment. Among the seventeen soldiers who transferred to Hazen's regiment were volunteers from the Monty family—Amable Enfant (or Enfont), and Jacques, as either a volunteer or private—and soldiers Jean Dubé, Joseph Labé, and Francis Turcout. Furthermore, Captain Paulint's attached independent company was incorporated into the regiment.[34]

Other reductions and transfers followed. Captains John Paul Schott, "brought up a soldier in the Prusian Army," and Anthony Selin, a Swiss, had command of independent companies originally attached to Ottendorf's Corps. Schott had been taken prisoner at the Battle of Short Hills in June 1777. When he returned fifteen months later, Washington allotted him an independent infantry corps. In March 1779, Schott reported one sergeant and eleven rank and file in the company under his direct command. That same month, Selin had one lieutenant, one quartermaster sergeant, two sergeants, one drummer/ fifer, and fourteen rank and file, with another absent in confinement. Supposedly Selin was within Schott's corps, but in 1780, he refused to acknowledge the senior captain's command. What men remained in both companies at the beginning of 1781—many had enlisted in 1777 on three-year terms and had left—were incorporated into Hazen' regiment by April, but only Selin retained a position after the transfer. Schott became a supernumerary in financial straits like so many others.[35]

Hazen was happy to add soldiers from the reduced units and pleased about the provision for incorporating foreign "volunteers," but he appeared keen to use this sign of congressional favor to push for promotions. His officers pushed too. Antill voiced their concerns in November 1781, when he observed that Hazen's brevet to brigadier that spring was the only promotion "that has taken place with Us in the Course of three Years hard service." He was not counting noncommissioned officer promotions: just that January, when Hazen transferred two sergeants (including one of "Late Livingstones Regiment") between companies, he had promoted three corporals to sergeant and three privates to corporal. Antill asked, in support of harmony and justice, that he and Hazen be permitted to promote, as previously allowed by Congress, or to get Washington's approval for some promotions. Hazen immediately forwarded the request to Washington confirming their previous (in 1776) appointment power, "which altho' suspended by Congress for a time Yet by subsequent resolutions, has as I conceive been recontinued, the Regt being still on its original Establishment." He emphasized that they had always acted "with the greatest precaution, dellicacy and Oeconomy." Yet contradicting Antill's contention that there had been no officer promotions over the previous three years, Hazen had quietly made some.[36] Perhaps they were contingent appointments and Hazen had assumed congressional agreement given the original establishment. From July 1779 through 1782, he made about a dozen such promotions and appointments, which contravened the contractions in other infantry regiments. The ensuing controversies no doubt added to his regiment's "infernal" reputation: a later review of the regiment's strength "at different periods" led to the conclusion that "there was too many Officers for the Men at all times in the Regiment and no promotion or New Appointments in Equity ought to have taken place."[37]

As the reorganizations, appeals, and reviews proceeded over the years, the members of Hazen's regiment continued to perform missions, make camps, and build relationships. They constructed a community of shared hardships and connections both martial and familial. Yet provincialism also continued to affect administration and personal relations. Accommodation often took the form of segregation: maintaining separate "French" companies alongside the other, more diverse ones.[38] It was a matter of choice and discrimination on both sides. The ethnic smorgasbord of names on rosters suggests that there was some assimilation of others within the French companies and of French-named individuals within the other units. Later pension applications that revealed marriage patterns and family connections also indicate some cross-cultural connections as well as a continued insularity among Hazen's Continentals.

Congress's Own Community

The Continental Congress contributed to the concept of a national community as it declared the rights of "the People," formulated a confederation of states, and created an American army. The construction of that purported national community, like that of a national government, rested on the contributions of communities distinguished by geography, demography, ideology, economy, ethnicity, and history. Community, like borderland, is a relational concept—a community is defined or understood in relation to place, power, and other communities.[39] It is also distinguished by relationships within the community: as people live and work together, they invent a community, as it in turn identifies them.

Congress's Own Regiment constructed its own community of combatants and followers within the greater one established by the Continental Army, and both operated within geographical borderlands among, between, and beyond the states. These greater and smaller communities also operated as borderlands when they incorporated different peoples from varied places and traditions and forged a hybrid society through military means—a continental community. That greater military society included not just regimental but also campaign and garrison communities as determined by who (belonging to a unit), what (reconstituting, preparing, or moving to action), and where (in the field, in camp, or in barracks or town). As John Lynn defined them, garrison communities formed when troops lived for long periods in a town, as standing armies did in peacetime, or field armies did when in winter quarters, whereas campaign communities were the armies of combatants and noncombatants in the field.[40]

The Congress's Own community was part of the army's garrison and campaign communities—often both at the same time, depending on what detachments were doing and where, and whether the regiment left some of its members behind when it went on campaign, as it did in August 1781 when it marched to Virginia. By that time, the community connecting the refugees of 1776 with the enlistees and followers of 1777 and beyond was well established. Among the noncombatants at various times and places were sutlers and contractors supplying the regiment,[41] but the majority were the attached women and children.

The colonels' wives were among the first of the followers. Charlotte de La Saussaye Hazen lost her "mansion" when it was "plundered by the American troops [in fall 1775], and afterwards burnt by order of . . . Gen. Sullivan, upon the retreat from that country" in June 1776. According to her nephew-by-marriage, Moses White, she then "followed the fortunes of her husband into the United States, and through the war." Charlotte Riverain Antill also lost her home during the Canadian campaign. While in command at Montreal in March 1776, Moses Hazen provided her with room and board at headquarters, the Château Ramezay, until "better" provisions could be made. Comfortable provisions were not quickly forthcoming, and they were never permanent throughout the war. In the meantime, the paymaster of the Northern Department provided funds or reimbursement to Mrs. Hazen that April, to Mrs. Antill in May, and then to soldier or volunteer François (Francis) Monty's wife in July.[42] These women and others carried financial as well as familial burdens as they followed the regiment.

Mesdames Hazen and Antill were refugee followers as well as colonels' wives and lived the experiences and expectations of both. Senior officers' wives, if and when they could, visited camps and garrisons in winter and then departed when active campaigning began. Their place in camps, like those of other women with the army, reflected social rank. Visiting versus following for other officers' wives generally depended on who and what could maintain them, their children, and their property at home.[43] The sacrifice of their family properties in Canada, however, left the two Charlottes without homes. It does not appear, however, that they were campaign followers: they were part of garrison or camp communities. Within those communities, both women acted in accordance with their own and their husbands' ranks. They exchanged social pleasantries, expected certain services, and defended their husbands' honor and interests when necessary.

Charlotte Hazen may have visited her husband's relations or his Haverhill, New Hampshire, property when Moses was on campaign, but it appears she spent more time in or near encampments. In November 1779, Colonel Udny Hay asked General Nathanael Greene about housing for Mrs. Hazen, his "old Colonele's Lady," who was "on the road to the Jerseys." That trip and others included rough traveling, such as by sleigh when she moved in February 1782 from near Peekskill, New York, to join her husband at Lancaster, Pennsylvania. It was not just a matter of joining her husband, but also of being able to associate with other military couples: in 1780, Greene mentioned the possibility of his wife and Mmes. Knox and Hazen spending the winter in camp together. Charlotte Hazen battled sickness through the years—including "Ague" in October 1780 and "Cholic and other Disorders" in early 1783—but remained attentive to the social niceties. As her husband saw to her care during the war, she saw to his in the postwar years, including deputizing for his property claims after he suffered a stroke.[44]

Charlotte Antill was a young mother who had buried two daughters and a son in Canada before she and two other daughters followed Edward into New York in 1776. She bore another daughter in Lancaster in May 1777, about six weeks after the riot and Minyier case there. When her husband was captured at Staten Island in August 1777 and controversy erupted over whether he had changed sides, Mrs. Antill defended his dedication and honor and asked to join him on Long Island during his captivity. Life on parole was a family affair, which provided comfort but also financial pressure. In March 1780, Edward Antill wrote to Washington asking for a "Reasonable provision" within American lines for his "affectionate & delicate wife" and family—which then included four children after the birth of a son the previous December—for he did not feel able to continue supporting them within British lines. He, in turn, gave assurance that the "Same Love of my Country, that dro[ve] my Sword, will Support me with a Manly fortitude" should "England, Hallifax or Prison Ships, be [his and his fellow prisoners'] Doom." That was not his destiny. On 18 November 1780, General Heath reported to Washington that Antill, his wife, "and three or four children" (actually five, for Charlotte had birthed another daughter in September) had just arrived at West Point, and that Antill had asked for temporary "Relief" for his family. Heath ordered "one Ration of provision to be issued to his wife and one Ration to the children collectively, making with his own four Rations to be charged to his account." Heath also passed on Antill's information about how hundreds of Convention (Saratoga) prisoners had made their way from Albemarle, Virginia, to New York assisted by loyalists. As Edward resumed his regimental duties—and was exonerated by the court of inquiry that he had requested to examine his actions at capture— Charlotte continued to face family challenges. Her twenty-two-month-old son died around the time her husband was besieging Yorktown. She had another wartime daughter in December 1782 who barely made it into the new year, and then a last daughter in May 1785 as the husband and father struggled to establish his family in peacetime Long Island.[45]

While on parole on Long Island, Major Tarlton Woodson corresponded with his family in Virginia about taking care of his interests there and his need for money in New York. Woodson found the restrictions of parole tiresome, but apparently flexible enough for courtship: he married Anne Der Veer in December 1779. After his exchange late the following October, Woodson was on furlough through that December if not longer, which he likely used to move his wife to his family in Virginia, where the British invaded and Anne gave birth to a son in 1781.[46] The other majors—James Reid, John Taylor, and Joseph Torrey—were not married through the war years.

Most of the junior officers were unmarried young men. Many if not most of the married members' wives stayed home. Captain William Satterlee's wife probably stayed with family in Connecticut or Massachusetts. Captain William Munson's family, including a young son he uniformed and "mustered," was in New Haven, Connecticut. Captain Thomas Pry wed Elisabeth Weithaed in August 1782 while the regiment was stationed at Lancaster. That same month, Surgeon Nicholas Schuyler married Shinah Simon, whose father was a leading Jewish businessman in Lancaster. The two new wives did not have long to follow the army, if they did, before the war ended.[47]

The wives of Captains Philippe Liébert and Clément Gosselin, and Lieutenants Louis Gosselin and Germain Dionne (whose daughter Marie-Beuve was Clément's first wife) appeared to have stayed in Canada as their husbands moved across the border (with return visits when reconnoitering). Lieutenant Alexandre Ferriole's wife Marie-Appoline Mailhot had at least eight children; one was born in 1780, but whether that was because she was with Alexandre in camp or because he visited her while on a scouting expedition from the Coos Country in 1779 is unclear. As their barely teenaged son Alexander did follow his father in 1776, it is possible that she did too. Captain Laurent Olivie's wife Marie-Joseph Guibord followed the regiment in retreat, as did a few other refugee officers' wives. Geneviéve Boucher Martin, wife of Lieutenant Francis Martin (François Martin-Pellend), not only followed her husband but then stayed close to the community after he died in October 1778, marrying former Ensign Felix Victor at Fishkill in spring 1782. These women generally moved only between garrisons and winter encampments rather than following on campaign. Theotist Cotard Paulint, who packed up her children and followed her husband Antoine on the retreat in 1776, described the common practice for not only officers' wives but many of the soldiers' wives too: she "continued near her husband through the war, [and] she generally laid with him in the Barracks in the winter," including "some time at West point barracks. [And] in the summers when her husband was in active service she lived with her children generally away from her husband."[48]

Theotist Blow, the daughter of Theotist and Antoine Paulint, recalled that near the end of the war, her father's family and other Canadian families resided at Fishkill. Her family had lived near Lieutenant François Guilmat's, whose wife had two daughters from her first marriage to Sergeant James Robinson, who had died on the retreat from Canada. The young Theotist and Sally Robinson had spent most of their childhoods with the army, for Blow said she had been about twelve years old at war's end and that Sally was a few years older.[49] In support of Sally's application for a widow's pension in 1837, former follower Blow and others offered snippets about camp marriages, family connections, and both cultural continuities and Americanization.

Blow deposed that Sally was living with Private John Chartier as his wife before the Canadian refugee families moved from Fishkill to West Point.[50] After a camp courtship, the French-Canadian Chartier had married the teen-aged daughter, about half his age, of a regimental couple, whose sister Polly was married to his brother Peter. The family and community connections were durable, extending into the late 1830s as the sister-widows, their witnesses, and children corroborated each other's pension applications. They showed how the military retreat from Canada in 1776 was also a family exodus, and revealed how French-Canadian Catholics—and, by implication, others—legitimized marriages, both civilly and religiously, in the borderland communities that were military camps and garrisons.

Alexander Ferriol, former private and son of Lieutenant Ferriole, remembered retreating from Canada with John Chartier and serving with him during the war. He met "Sally Robinet or Robinson in 1776 when she was about seven or eight years old, her Father was also a Reffugee, having married a French woman in Canada & was a sergant in . . . Hazens Regiment." Another veteran, Basil Nadeau, who had served in Olivie's company, claimed to have been "well acquainted" with Private Chartier of Paulint's company and had known the family of "Sergeant Robinet (so called in french) or Robinson in English" before the retreat from Canada.[51]

Polly Chartier recalled being about thirteen years old at the retreat from Canada, and that she had been married to Peter at about twenty by a "Mr. Deferm," a priest, near Fishkill. That reputed age at marriage did not compute with her earlier claim that she may have married Peter in November 1779 or, probably, 1780. She explained discrepancies and her lack of documents by saying that she was "a woman of no learning & cannot read nor write & have been many years infirm in health."[52]

Alexander Ferriol not only confirmed the marriage of Polly and Peter but also indicated what may have been the reason for the age-date discrepancy: they had a common-law marriage and a religious wedding. He remembered being present in the spring of 1780 when Peter Chartier and Polly Robinson, at or near Fishkill, "agreed before a witness to live together as man and wife until they should be able to find some Roman Catholic Prist to solemnize their marriage." Then, supposedly in spring 1782, about three miles from the Fishkill barracks, Ferriol was again in attendance "when the marriage between [them] was solemnized by a Mr Ferm or Farm a Roman Catholic Priest who came from Philadelphia to visit the Canadian Roman Catholics of the Regiment." Sally, on the other hand, thought that the wedding conducted by the "aged" Father Defarm was in 1779 or 1780, but figured there were no confirmatory records.[53]

Sally [Mary Therese] Chartier said her 13 May 1783 marriage to John was performed "by the Revd father Francis Vall[ ]y a Catholic Priest at a place called the Highlands in the State of Newyork, the troops then being stationed at Pompton." Ferriol corroborated that "a Roman priest of the name of Valley" had married the couple at Fishkill in the spring of 1783. Nadeau added that when the regiment was at Pompton, he and others "obtained leave to go to Fish Kill . . . to see a Roman catholic Prest, who had come to visit the Canadian families or the families of the Officers & soldiers—who then resided at Fish Kill." Nadeau remembered the marriage of fifteen- or sixteen-year-old Sally to John taking place about a mile out from the Fishkill barracks at a farmer's house where the priest was staying.[54]

Enoch Woodbridge, a justice of the peace in Addison County, Vermont, who had known the Chartiers for decades, supported their declarations. He believed that the priests who married them were "traveling ministers attending on Hazen's Regt. most of whom [the soldiers] were Refugees."[55] Woodbridge was partially right: there was a missionary who ministered to the Catholics in camp. Father Defarm was Father Farmer, as the Jesuit missionary Ferdinand Steinmeyer was called. Father Farmer began his missionary efforts among the German settlers of Lancaster in 1752, moved to St. Joseph Catholic Church in Philadelphia in 1758, and then for decades until his death in 1786 made, a regular circuit through New Jersey, which during the war years expanded to the Hudson Highlands.[56] Father "Valley" could have been a reference to one of the chaplains of the French army, but it was probably to Father Peter Huet de La Valinière. Deported from Canada to England in 1779 for his support of the American revolutionaries, Valinière eventually made his way back across the Atlantic, and likely visited Newburgh and Fishkill in the fall of 1785. He also established a short-lived church in northern New York in the 1790s.[57] Perhaps in Sally Chartier's case, as in Polly's, deponents conflated memories of civil and religious weddings.

Another memory issue appeared in 1849, when two of Polly Chartier's children, the "very poor" Peter and James, applied for pensions. Their mother said that after she married Peter, she gave birth to her son Peter at West Point on 5 July 1778, and then James at Fishkill on 13 May 1781. Polly's statement presents another discrepancy over when she wed and raises the possibility that she bore Peter before marriage. Yet legitimate or not, her sons' births while their parents were with the army did not merit a pension. Their mother, however, argued that "after the birth of my said sons, they were both enrolled or enlisted by their Father & attached to the service of the United States . . . in the said Captain Oliviere's Company, and I distinctly recollect that after their enrollment or enlistment as aforesaid, they, or their father for them, regularly drew their rations as soldiers until the close of the war, which I now believe was somewhere about two years." She had heard that other boys so enrolled had received recompense, so she thought her sons were also entitled.[58] They were not.

Hawkins listed a "Peter Chartier, Junior" as a volunteer in 1781, but did that refer to a three-year-old boy? Maybe, if such enrollment was for rations alone. Peter, James, and their mother Polly may have been thinking about the Monty clan, with members in both Canadian regiments, in making their argument. Like "Peter Junior," there was a Jachin (Jachem) Monty noted as a volunteer in 1781, but more significantly, there were Joseph and John. Both deposed that they had enlisted at Fishkill in 1780, which according to their ages in 1820, would have made Joseph thirteen and John nine. It may have been their enlistments that Lieutenant Monty protested, as they occurred while he was away scouting. Their father's argument may have worked for John, for only Joseph was on the regiment's master roll, but both had sufficient evidence of service for later pensions. The Chartiers may also have been thinking of Alexander Ferriol, who was about twelve at enlistment. But those boy soldiers were old enough or big enough for labor. The boys, like their mothers and sisters, also showed how family ties served the regiment.[59]

The grandchildren of another regimental couple tried to obtain the arrears that they said had been due their grandmother, Charlotte Constantine, before she died in 1845. They had the support of octogenarian Alexander Ferriol in 1846, who deposed that he had attended the marriage of Charlotte and Nicholas Constantine in "the common barrack room" at Schenectady in the winter of 1779; his father, Lieutenant Ferriole of Satterlee's company, had married the couple. Also providing a witness account was the eighty-five-year-old pensioned soldier's widow Mary Louisa, "Lozelle," La Fond of Point Au Meule, Canada East, whose maiden name was Chartier. She said that her sister's marriage took place in November or December of 1778, and that Lieutenant Ferriole had performed the ceremony at the Schenectady barracks because "both parties were Roman Catholics; and there was no priest of that persuasion there at that time." Those accounts reinforced the 1841 depositions of Charlotte

Constantine and Mary Cayeaux. Mrs. Cayeaux said that she had retreated from Canada with Charlotte Chartier in 1775, and then in the winter of 1779 saw her married to Nicholas Constantine by "Captain Ferniall." Cayeaux claimed that Ferriole had married several of the Canadian refugees that winter, among them herself, to her late husband Joseph Cayeaux.[60]

Former Private Ferriol vividly described the community when he supported the Constantine claim in 1841: "the Canadian families that lay at the Schenactada Barracks in the winter of 1779- [ha]d no other language than the French, n[o]r could they understand any other—that they were composed of old & young people of both sexes, most of them retreated from Canada together, the young Men principally as soldiers, some became soldiers after they came out.—some of the Girls were too young to be married when they first came out—some were married before they came out." He added that when "his Father performed the rites of matrimony for Nicholas Constantine & Charlote Chartier, there was no Chaplain to the French troops." Although "there might have been English & Dutch Clergymen in the City at the time," he never saw them at the barracks, and "besides the French Canadians were all Catholicks." Ferriol avowed that he could name many of the people present when the Constantines, "as well as Madam Cayeaux & Madam Defoe were married, but they are all dead." Ferriol also noted that it had been "customary, during the War, for the officers among the French Canadians, to perform the rites of Matrimony." He reported that he had a sister married at West Point by an officer, and recalled that Captain Paulint had presided at the marriage of a soldier at Fishkill.[61]

Not all *Canadien* Continentals married French-Canadian followers. Timing, location, and availability all played a part in camp courtship. At the end of the war, Peter (Piere) Blanchard was in Rhode Island, where, as former adjutant Benjamin Mooers testified in 1818, he was serving as "a waiter with some of the French officers."[62] While there, he courted an American, Martha, who declared in 1836 that the minister Joseph Snow had married the couple in June 1782 at Providence. Basil Nadeau said he had served as "bridesman" at the marriage. The widow recalled living in a small house at the northern end of the town while the troops occupied the college. She stated that her husband left the army shortly after her first child, William, was born at Coventry, Rhode Island, in May 1783.[63] The family ultimately settled in Clinton County, New York, near other veterans of the regiment.

In some of the French-Canadian pension cases, authorities questioned the lack of documentation. Yet to suggest, as a few officials did, that certain social or economic groups were not particular in such things, was superficial: unsettled churches and ministers in addition to the disruptions of revolution and war confounded record keeping. In 1836, the "poor & unlettered" but

"much respected" widow Elizabeth Heaton and her advocate Henry Muhlenberg explained the lack of a church record documenting her 1776 Reading,
Pennsylvania, marriage to James as a matter of having been wed by an itin-
erant minister of the German Reformed Church. Although a witness stated
that "Elizabeth lived with James Heaton aforesaid in the Early begining of the
Revolutionary War as Man & Wife until his decease," unfortunately neither he
nor she specified whether she did so with the regiment.[64]

Other veterans' widows applied for pensions, but they, too, generally did not
explain where they were or what they did during the war years, which suggests
that they stayed home—they did not "marry" the army the way followers did.
That both eased and challenged their soldier spouses as they tried to fulfill both
marital and martial obligations to support and defend family and country.

When she applied for a pension in the 1840s, Mary Heirely Dick said that
she had married Jacob Dick in November 1782 at the Bethlehem Church in York
County, Pennsylvania. There was no record, but she recalled that the banns
were read in open church. At least one of her eleven children may have been
born before or just after the wedding. A supporting witness said that he recalled
the marriage because Jacob Dick had told him at the time that he had "returned
from his revolutionary service . . . expressely to get married." Dick then "left
his wife and returned to his service."[65] This suggests that he married Mary in
acknowledgment of paternity. As Jacob Dick had enlisted from Pennsylvania,
he may have come from York County and had courted Mary before leaving, or
they might have met when the regiment garrisoned at Lancaster (with detachments at York and elsewhere) to guard prisoners of war through most of 1782
before marching to northern New Jersey and New York that November.

Abigail Stanley Roberts declared in 1838 that she had married William
Roberts at the Congregational Church in Coventry, Connecticut, in October
1772. She may have followed William, who enlisted on 10 December 1776, but
that was not recorded. Two of her children, however, were born during their
father's service as a fifer—Seth in September 1778 and Isaac in January 1781,
who died that March.[66] Although an extramarital liaison was a possibility, it
is more likely that William took either approved or unapproved leaves to visit
home, or that his wife visited or lived with him in camp.

The number of soldiers with wives, whether at home or in camp, was limited
by ages, finances, and itinerancy. Yet although military service made getting
married and maintaining family life a challenge, it obviously was not impossible. Availability and flexibility played key roles in the formation of families
and the military community. Were prospective partners who shared cultural
beliefs and practices available? Were others willing to cross cultural divisions
to wed? In their marriages, members of Hazen's regiment answered yes to both

questions. And it appears that the regiment's members did what other soldiers and civilians did, regardless of religious background, when without a minister: they established common-law marriages followed by religious weddings, if possible. Marriage, in turn, legitimized requests and allocations of support—of rations, housing, and later, pensions.

Followers challenged the army's ability to house and feed them. Those who were Canadian refugees and stayed in northern garrisons, such as Albany, might have had some congressionally mandated subsistence, but that was limited.[67] There were thousands of women and children with the army over the course of the war, but as the regiments did not keep regular records, it is impossible to be precise. Furthermore, the circumstances of each regiment—timing, places, and recruiting pools—affected the number of dependents in each. A well-researched study estimates that the number of women with the army averaged about 3 percent, or one woman to thirty men. The army tried to keep the number low, especially when provisions were scarce (such as at the 1780 Morristown winter encampment), but around 1782, perhaps bowing to the reality of more followers, Congress considered subsisting more (perhaps 5 to 6 percent), which Washington confirmed in December 1782 with approval to ration one woman for every fifteen men. When Congress in 1783, however, considered the "military peace establishment of the United States," it specified that regiments could ration and pay no more than four women who served as nurses.[68] Congress clearly tied rations to work, and it authorized an entire ration for a working woman.

The women with detachments from the Canadian Old Regiment while stationed at Lancaster in 1782 received rations. They were undoubtedly carrying supplies and doing chores for the men who generally marched out for four days of patrols and other duties. The detachment that left on 1 June included two officers, four sergeants, two drum and fifers, fifty-six rank and file, and one woman, in addition to a quartermaster and another woman from the York County militia. The detachment for 5–8 June was likely a continuation of the preceding one, for the numbers were the same—with the clarification that it was the quartermaster and wife from the militia unit. Other provision returns reveal up to four women with the detachments in July.[69] The women with those detachments mirrored what women with the regiment on campaign did: they packed up, moved with, and worked for the officers and soldiers.

Hazen's regiment likely had more family followers than most other regiments. The refugees certainly added to its numbers, but it was not the only regiment with members displaced by war. Furthermore, the majority of soldiers in Hazen's regiment were not from Canada, and that affected the number of women and children with it—numbers that fluctuated with each year and campaign. Whatever the number, not all of the women carried packs for detachments or followed on campaigns.

Throughout the war, commanders reviewed where followers were to go, how they were to get there, and what they were to do when accompanying the army. Regimental, brigade, division, and army orders regarding women generally demanded that camp women labor, such as laundering and nursing as required, and obey regulations and commands so as not to hinder operations, undermine troop health and welfare, or clog camps and garrisons. Women were not to ride in the wagons, or even "walk in the Ranks," unless given permission. If they tried to follow anyway, especially if "embarrassed with Young Children," they were ordered back to camp. Those who remained in a camp, along with the sick and "useless Baggage," could find themselves supervised by an officer tasked with that duty. Followers, like soldiers, were not to overcharge for their goods or services, such as for the milk produced from the cows they pastured in camp, nor were they to peddle in camp or barracks without permission, for that was deemed prejudicial to "good order morality and military Discipline."[70]

Sexually transmitted diseases were also prejudicial to good order. Men were not dismissed for this, but women were: West Point's remedy against increasing "Venerial Complaints" in May 1781 was an order that "all unmarried women Above the Age of 14 Years" and "all others of ill fame" were to "Leave the Garrison or Regiment ... on or before Wednesday next" to avoid being drummed out (publicly shamed and banished). If a soldier consulted a surgeon for treatment, he had to reveal the person from whom he got it (although the surgeon's letter about Charles McCormick's condition in September 1782 did not include that information).[71] Such proscriptions, in addition to the need for a place and provisions in camp, may have been another reason for early marriage among some followers.

Not all followers obeyed orders all the time, and a few behaved badly enough to end up before courts-martial. Imperfect behavior reflected on the regiment's character and affected community relations. As Sergeant Major Hawkins described the winter encampment near Redding, Connecticut, in February 1779, with its "Upper Town" for officers and public huts for artisans and suppliers, and "Lower Town" for the noncommissioned officers and soldiers "with their Wives and Concubines," he mused that the inhabitants "are like those to be found in other Towns." They were "rich and poor, black and white," and as they were "good and bad," the camp also had "Courts of Justice, which is opened almost daily."[72]

One such regimental court, on 6 July 1780 at the Preakness encampment, reviewed the complaint of Sergeant Colin McLachlan (McLaughlin) against

"Margaret Batten [Battin], a Follower of the Army." It judged her guilty of the charges (not recorded) and banished her. If she returned, she would receive "25 Lashes and be drummed out of the Regiment."[73] The proceedings of another case a few days later indicate that her offenses and those of the other parties before the new court included disruptive behavior that escalated into assault and battery. The new court reviewed charges against McLachlan, Mrs. McLachlan, Mrs. McLane (possibly McClain), and John Battin for actions during and after a fight that erupted a few days before the regiment left Ramapough.[74]

When Captain Carlile had pushed through a noisy crowd at Ramapough, he discovered McLachlan and his wife fighting with a soldier. Carlile grabbed the woman's stick and with it struck aside both her and the soldier. McLachlan snarled at Carlile that because he hit his wife, he would shoot Margaret Battin for starting the fight. Did she? Major Reid said that before the brawl, Mrs. McLane had been muttering threats against Mrs. Battin, whom she believed had "abused" her. She must have found her target or expressed her fury to Private Battin, for there was a "Fray," which escalated when Mrs. McLachlan waded into it. Sergeant McLachlan may have intervened to stop the fight, but when he saw Private Battin hit his wife, he hit Battin, who struck back. Quartermaster-Sergeant John Jones said that he separated Battin and McLachlan, after which McLachlan ordered his wife away and the brawl ended. Reid said Carlile and other officers ended the fight.[75]

Yet the fight had not quite ended, because McLachlan made a formal complaint against Margaret Battin, which resulted in her court-martial and banishment; Captain Carlile charged McLachlan with escalating a dispute between two women, hitting a soldier instead of simply confining him, and then for being insolent when Carlile intervened. McLachlan admitted striking the soldier. The court found McLachlan not guilty for the most part and acquitted him for striking Battin, which it saw as justified. It then acquitted Battin of threatening McLachlan after the sergeant had read the previous court's verdict against his wife. It also acquitted Mrs. McLachlan and Mrs. McLane for lack of evidence. The court released all of the prisoners from confinement and ordered them back to work.[76] That was probably not the first and certainly not the last time that women were at the center of regimental discord.

Women appeared at courts-martial as the accused, as victims, and as witnesses. In June 1781, "on board the sloop Liberty," as the regiment transferred from Fishkill to Albany and then Caughnawaga (now Fonda) to patrol there, James Hopkins of Carlile's company faced a court martial for "insulting a woman—stealing her Bonet & selling it." Jacob Holland of Olivie's company had been walking with the woman on the evening of 4 June when Hopkins and his buddies stopped them. Hopkins tried to persuade the woman to go with him, and when she refused, he grabbed her hat before leaving. Mrs. McClellen testified that she did not know of Hopkins insulting a woman or stealing her bonnet, but that he did come "to her Barrack and proffered a Bonet for Sale." She bought it only to have a woman claim it the next day. When McClellen asked Hopkins to return her money, he confessed. Hopkins also confessed to the court that he had been very drunk. Because of Hopkins's youth and former good conduct, the court excused him from a whipping but ordered him to do double duty for three weeks.[77] The victim was never named, only noted as belonging to Major Kees's house, but the case shows socializing outside regimental lines, and a woman—Mrs. McClellen—living in the barracks.

The McLachlans, wife and husband, challenged good order again a year after their actions at Ramapough, but only the husband was censured. On 7 July 1781, aboard the transport *Tryon* to West Point after the short-lived Caughnawaga expedition, Sergeant Sharp (likely Thomas Sharp) faced a court charged with "abusive Language to and threatning Sergeant McLoughlin." The court decided in favor of Sharp because McLachlan had interfered in a dispute that was not in "the immediate line of his duty"—a heated dispute between Sharp and McLachlan's wife, who had offered considerable provocation.[78]

Personal and professional provocations resulted in numerous disputes and courts-martial within Hazen's regiment, as they did outside it. Sometimes the immediate or most pressing enemy was not the British army, but internal dissension within the continental community. Minor crimes and resistance to authority and good order were generally handled in-house through regimental courts-martial. Senior officer complaints and major violations threatening the army, nation, and public welfare required general courts-martial at the brigade or army level. Military law, often imperfectly understood and applied, defined the community and adjudicated the relationships and actions within it.

Duty, Discipline, and Disaffection

The combination of discontent and dedication within Hazen's regiment echoed that within the army in 1780 through early 1781. Ragged Continentals increasingly decried institutional weaknesses that resulted in enlistment and provisioning discrimination between and within regiments. In Hazen's regiment, as the officers disciplined restive soldiers and followers, they also engaged in their own personal and professional contests. Yet even as both officers and soldiers challenged command and community, they also continued to perform their duties to deploy an effective force against wartime foes. They soldiered on for common ends—national and personal independence—but argued over conduct and costs.

During the frigid months at Morristown with Hand's brigade, Hazen warmed himself with Staten Island raids and court-martial charges. The frozen Sound between New Jersey and Staten Island offered a route by which troops could march on the enemy there. The regiment had taken a beating on the island in August 1777, so some members may have seen Lord Stirling's raid—with Hazen in command of a detachment of about a thousand men on the left—as payback. Hazen was so eager for action that he moved his troops into position more quickly than envisioned by the planners, who then worried that the enemy was forewarned. Despite that, on 15 January 1780, Stirling sent his three thousand troops against the smaller number of British and loyalist troops. Mooers laconically remembered being "ordered to join and lay on the heights, a very cold night, and many were frost-bitten. The enemy from New York came over, on the ice, with cannon. After some skirmishing, we returned without much effect." John Battin, who was wounded there, may have questioned that.[79] Because of enemy dispositions, New Jersey militia troops too enthusiastically plundering (thus alienating) the inhabitants, and Jack Frost gnawing at the soldiers, Stirling retreated.

Within days, after billeting his troops and posting guards from Elizabethtown, DeHart's, and Halstead's Points, and down across from the Blazing Star Ferries, Hazen proposed a return engagement, possibly for the night of the 27th. Washington was amenable to the possibility, for headquarters issued an order that a detachment of 990 privates, along with drummers, fifers, and noncommissioned officers, was to parade on the 25th with two-days cooked provisions. Hazen's regiment was to provide one captain, two sergeants, two corporals, one fifer, and thirty-four privates. But then British and loyalist troops not only reinforced Staten Island but precluded a second American raid with their own attacks at Elizabethtown and Newark on the 26th.[80]

Hazen was humiliated by the attack at Elizabethtown that got through his pickets. He offered a partial justification by saying that he had pointed out the need for more men to cover such a large area. He wanted to retaliate, and Washington considered it. Washington sent Major General Arthur St. Clair to review the situation and work on options. The result was a plan to attack Lieutenant Colonel Abraham Van Buskirk's New Jersey Volunteers (the Elizabethtown raiders) on 2 February. Then, as the conditions were not ideal, St. Clair canceled the expedition.[81]

In addition to his critique of defenses and support for a possible counter-raid, Hazen arrested Lieutenant Colonel John Eager Howard, who had been commanding the 2nd Maryland troops with Hazen's temporary detachment. Hazen charged Howard with disobeying orders about emplacing his battalion on 17, 18, and 24 January and for not having his troops ready for action per the orders of the 30th. Hazen also charged him with neglecting his reports and for "unjustifiable orders or returns," including extra rum for his officers. A general court-martial on 16 February found Howard guilty of disobedience for not parading his troops and not having them "fit for action" on 30 January. The court also found problems with his reports and provision orders and sentenced him "to be reprimanded in general orders." Washington rapped both the court's and Howard's knuckles in his review that March. Howard's failure to parade his men and have them ready was due not to his neglect but to the dispersal of the troops and severe weather. Howard, on the other hand, should have complied with Hazen's order about provisions, and his returns and reports were not "entirely satisfactory."[82] Hazen likely found that an acceptable resolution, and the court-martial did not hurt Howard's military or political career, as he ultimately served as a governor of Maryland and in Congress.

Hazen had also been fuming about Isaac Tichenor, deputy purchasing commissary, since the previous summer's Coos expedition. In February, Hazen brought eight charges against Tichenor that in sum accused him of disobeying orders, misrepresenting provisioning situations, neglect in storing provisions, a "want of a proper exertion" in procuring supplies, misapplication of public money, and interfering in the operations of his own assistant Mr. Child, who was trying to fulfill obligations. Washington broadened the inquiry to include Hazen's Coos Country compatriots, Jacob Bayley and Timothy Bedel. The court assessing Hazen's charges against Tichenor met at Springfield in April, but Hazen and his Coos allies had to wait until October for its conclusions and Washington's review to be published. Hazen was undoubtedly not happy that the court dismissed six of the eight charges and that Washington disagreed on the other two; instead of a reprimand, Washington released Tichenor from arrest.[83] Although Tichenor faced financial difficulties due to his wartime duties, he, like Howard, continued in public service, ultimately as a senator and governor of Vermont. Hazen, in turn, had to face his own critics.

While challenging others' actions on one hand, Hazen sought to defend his own actions and advance his interests on the other. In a memorial to Washington and Congress that February, Hazen recounted how he had ameliorated the hardships his regiment had faced in 1779 due to Tichenor's neglect. That initiative mirrored others. Furthermore, he was "now the fifth Colonel in the Continental Army," and thus due for promotion on the basis of seniority without regard—as he did not belong to a state—to the proportion and positions of general officers in the state lines.[84] He did not immediately receive the answer he wanted, and so he continued his campaign for greater recognition and reward into the following year.

Hazen also juggled business interests with regimental affairs. He flipped back and forth discussing private and public property when he wrote to Colonel Bedel about horses, oxen, wheat, and potatoes. But it was definitely personal when he detailed buying tracts of land and establishing deeds. He also provided advice related to Vermont's statehood and state line with New Hampshire, and another possible Canadian campaign.[85] Hazen, like so many other citizen-soldiers and officers in the fifth year of the war, was already considering postwar challenges while addressing immediate needs and problems.

Long-term considerations and short-term needs led some of the officers in the regiment to go around Hazen, and sometimes to challenge him directly. In December 1779, the Pennsylvania officers composed a letter to Joseph Reed, president of Pennsylvania's Supreme Executive Council (i.e., governor). They addressed points that Hazen had made in his 20 November memorial: first, that in March 1779, Congress had resolved that regimental returns would note members' state affiliations so that the states could credit them toward their quotas, but also, in return, supply and reward those men; second, that the officers and soldiers had not been supplied and rewarded (the Canadians could not be); and third, that there needed to be equity in provisioning the soldiers from different regions. Major Reid, Captains Heron, Pry, and Duncan, Lieutenant William Stuart, and Ensigns Andrew Lee and Lawrence Manning stated that when they took commissions in the regiment, they believed that they "could render as much service there as in any other Corps, and by no means expected to be considered as aliens, or excluded any benefit common to the officers of the same State." Were citizens serving outside of state lines to be deemed foreigners? They had "cheerfully" gone to war "not only to protect the rights of mankind, but our own individual Liberty." But "now when the war is apparently drawing to a conclusion," they will "leave the work unfinished" if no provision was made for them. Reid followed up with a visit to Philadelphia to make the case and told Hazen. Hazen then whipped off a rebuttal, arguing that "Partial provision" would be "prejudicial to the service generally and injurious to his regiment in particular."[86]

The Pennsylvania council asked for Washington's advice. Washington acknowledged the force of Hazen's argument and said he wished that supplies "were perfectly equal to the officers & men respectively, throughout the army." He did not know, however, how this was to be accomplished given the system of outsourcing to the states. Congress had recommended to the states that they provision their officers and soldiers in additional regiments the same way they took care of those in their state lines, so Washington supported the partial provision of the Pennsylvanians: "It can only be considered that they are more fortunate than the rest belonging to their regiment. Nor is this discrimination peculiar to Colo. Hazens Corps."[87]

Hazen countered, "If Congress cannot provide for their own Regiment; or such volunteers as have Joined their Cause from foreign Countrys, . . . they had better in that case give us an Honourable Dismission." He was blunt in opposing the partiality of state distributions while advocating that his regiment be on equal standing with state regiments.[88] Hazen's argument for equity was a critique of the Congress's cobbled arrangement and an early statement for a federal military system. Although he wrote of taking quota moneys and supplies and putting them in a common regimental pot for a uniform distribution, the point about a common fund for standard distribution had broader applicability. The argument had merit and was appropriate for maintaining a regular army, but the reality was that the Continental Army was composed primarily of states' regiments. Furthermore, Hazen's position, essentially that of "if not all get it, then none get it," alienated some regimental members even as others appreciated his championship. In pulling for equal provisions and recompense, he pushed factionalism. There was anything but the "perfect Harmony and a general Unaminity" he had earlier proclaimed.[89]

Hazen was a dynamic combat commander but flawed manager. The colonel tended to act like a contentious seigneur in his attempts to help the Canadian minority and control the effects of uneven provisioning by the states on his regiment. Washington had similar problems at the army level but was more politically astute in dealing with them. Hazen first irritated the regiment's members from Connecticut when he—with, he claimed, the concurrence of his Connecticut officers—had the regiment's paymaster hold four months' pay from that state in 1779. Then came the Pennsylvanians' petition, and in September 1780, the officers from Maryland petitioned Washington for permission and funding to appeal to the state's governor for their allowances in person. Washington permitted one to go with a horse, if available, supplied by General Greene.[90]

These debates, compounded by a regimental reorganization in July that temporarily combined eighteen companies into eight (two primarily Canadian), laid the groundwork for even greater disputes in the regiment.[91] Major Reid led a faction disheartened by weak congressional oversight and distrustful of Hazen's personnel and fiscal management. Reid, Carlile, and ten other officers presented their grievances and recommendations to Washington on 20 September. They mourned their prospects for promotion, pay, and provisions. "Richly Clothed and Comfortably supplied with Resolutions," they had neither the uniforms nor supplies needed. Should such arrive, "we should not be in Uniform but the Regiment as a body would be patched with the Uniforms of every state line." They asked, therefore, that the regiment either be reduced to an establishment similar to other regiments and attached to a state line or be dissolved, with the officers and men returned to their state lines. Although they did not specify the Canadians, they acknowledged them by recommending that something be done for the resulting supernumeraries: "some of those who have made the greatest sacrifices . . . would make much better [pensioners] than able officers and as the original establishment of the Regiment exists upon their account the *Public* will have a happy opportunity of convincing the World that *they* have a disposition to reward the virtuous according to their merits."[92]

Their recommendation for regimental reduction or dissolution was buried by the reorganization of 1781, and seven of the memorialists ultimately continued with the regiment until it was disbanded in 1783. The fight about Hazen's leadership was not over, however, and factionalism continued. Although the factions may have appeared anglophone versus francophone, they were really rooted in disputes over pay, power, and patronage.[93] Reid's charges against Hazen in November 1780 brought more of those disputes to light. On a personal level, Reid accused Hazen of wrongfully dating his majority (affecting seniority for promotion). Reid said he had been made major in June 1777, whereas Hazen rebutted that he had promoted him that October, backdated to 1 September. Hazen said he had not promoted Reid to replace Christian de Colerus that June, but when the regiment needed another field officer after losing Antill and Woodson at Staten Island and Torrey ("sick with a Disorder in his head") after the Battle of Brandywine.[94] This accusation fueled Hazen's fury at Reid's other charges.

Hazen and Reid faced off against each other at a general court-martial conducted in Mason's Hall at West Point. Brigadier General John Stark presided, and Deputy Judge Advocate John Strang served as a prosecutor, although Reid essentially led the prosecution himself. The trial began on 9 November with the charges: one, for fraud "in drawing Money for the Regiment (or Part of the Regiment) and appropriating it to other Purposes without their consent, and by detaining it from them a considerable Time"; two, for "making false Musters and false Returns," and having junior officers do the same; and three, for "ungentleman and unofficer-like Conduct in exacting advanced Prices from the Regiment" for private and publicly supplied articles. In short, Reid accused Hazen of "cheating the soldiers" and the army.[95]

The prosecution's case, which concluded on 17 November, involved questioning and interpreting a series of actions and accounting entries that occurred between March 1778 at Albany through the Coos Campaign in 1779 and Morristown in 1780. It included a review of Moses White's competence when acting as paymaster. Richard Varick, the deputy commissary-general of musters, deposed about irregularities, such as improper counting of absent men, that he had found in the Albany, Peekskill, and White Plains musters of 1778. He mentioned that Hazen had contended that there was no harm to the public if money due to absentees remained in the paymaster's hands as a regimental fund for incidentals. Varick said that there was no such thing in the army. He also commented that Edward Chinn serving as the regiment's paymaster at the same time he was commissioner of accounts for the Northern Army was against a congressional directive about holding two positions. Other witnesses brought up discrepancies between when someone left the regiment and when the person was removed from the rolls, whereas still others questioned the mustering and payment of servants or slaves and young sons (namely Captain Munson's) as soldiers. There were accounts of soldiers distressed by delays in pay as well as unfair stoppages, or deductions, for food (in particular for rum on the Coos expedition) and clothing, especially shoes. Among the witnesses, willing or unwilling, were noncommissioned officers such as Hawkins, McLachlan, and John McNamara, junior officers, and Reid himself.[96]

After being granted time to prepare, Hazen began his defense on 28 November by stating that the prosecution had not proved its case—and "without establishing the first Part of this Charge, viz. the intention of Fraud and the actual drawing the Money, the latter part cannot be a Question with the Court"—before moving into more pointed refutations. He questioned witnesses' veracity, as he did with Sergeants McNamara and James Wand, whom he described as British deserters. He said McNamara must have been mistaken about false musters in Munson's company, "or otherwise have paid as little Regard to his Oath, in this Case, as he had once before done at another Time." Hazen punched holes in the reputations of many of his critics as he rebutted their statements. He questioned how some of the officers, including Reid, who had been away from the regiment for long periods (whether on furlough, sick, or detached duty), could know what actually happened. He used the flip side of that argument to excuse himself: he said that he had not superintended a muster or signed a muster roll since October 1779 (implying that if there were errors, they were not his).

Hazen admitted to diverting some funds on the Coos expedition but blamed that on Tichenor, the deputy purchasing commissary. For want of "an Axe, a Hammer, a Nail," and other supplies and provisions, the expedition would have failed, had Hazen not bought tools and hired artisans to make more—in other words, he did Tichenor's job as well as his own. He admitted delaying some pay and authorizing stoppages but argued that it was for the good of the regiment. If the Connecticut troops had received all of their pay during the

Coos expedition, Hazen feared he might have lost the Canadian members who were within a few days march of their old homes. If he allowed some troops all of their state provisions, they might have trafficked their excess, while others would have had none; so, in the case of shoes, he ordered that if a soldier wanted more pairs above his allotment, the soldier would have to pay for them. He said that General Putnam had approved of the plan as had some officers in the regiment. Hazen finished his defense on the 29th by summarizing his military career and financial contributions: "In short my Purse and Credit has always been open to the Services of this Country, and to the Officers and Soldiers of my Regiment."[97]

After hearing that the court had acquitted Hazen, the dismayed Reid wrote to Washington for help. Reid contended that the court believed the charges but dismissed the case for lack of evidence. He criticized the judge advocate's deficient abilities and mourned his own against Hazen's performance. He wished that he had had the chance to give more evidence and argue more about how Chinn's double appointment and "Hazen's happy connection with his Nephew Capt. White" undermined accountability. Reid added that Hazen's stoppages from the beginning of 1779 to June 1780 had resulted in the loss of 126 soldiers by desertion. He wanted justice for the "injured Regiment" and for himself, for after the court's decision, Hazen arrested Reid and confined him to quarters. Reid asked for release from confinement and a trial as soon as possible.[98] Washington was thus saddled with ending the regiment's internal rebellion and mitigating the schisms in its command structure in early 1781, at the same time he was dealing with the mutinies of the Pennsylvania and New Jersey lines.

Hazen, meanwhile, was likely crowing as he had after another court-martial in October, which capped other controversies. Through the summer and fall of 1780, as the regiment moved northward, Hazen fought challenges not just from below but also above. One was about his and his regiment's rank in comparison with Livingston's: in June, a court established that Livingston had seniority to Hazen, but that Hazen's regiment ranked Livingston's. Another developed over the brigade orders of 6 July, when General Hand expressed his mortification at seeing the soldiers paraded without provisions. He was therefore "under the disagreeable Necessity of calling on the Officers commanding Regiments, to be more attentive in future, to have their Men supplied with as many Days Provisions as can be kept sweet, as otherwise it will be impossible to comply with the Orders for Detachments, or any Emergencies."[99] The affronted Hazen said that he had properly dealt with the provision returns, so "if his "Quarter-Master, Adjutant, or other Officers of the Regiment, have neglected their Duty let them be responsible for it." He and Colonel Adam Hubley argued with Hand to rescind the censure. After Hand refused, Hazen asked for a court to review his actions and redeem his character. Hand instead put the commissary on trial. That was not enough: the disputatious colonel wanted public reparation. If Hand did not provide it, Hazen said he would complain to Stirling and, if he did not help, to Washington. Hand said to go ahead. When Stirling then refused his demand, Hazen wrote to Washington.[100]

Washington replied that as Hand was "accountable for his Brigade, . . . he properly addressed himself" to the regimental commanders to see that their men were supplied. He did not believe "that the order applied personally to [Hazen] or particularly" to his regiment, and so it could not be seen as disrespectful. There was a lesson about professional accountability in Washington's reply, but Hazen refused to see Hand's actions as other than a personal injury that attacked his honor and thereby undermined his authority. He said Hand's order was a declaration to the soldiers "that their Want of Provisions has been owing to my Neglect, and thereby not only let down that Confidence which ought to be preserved, but sapped the very Dignity necessary to be supported by the Commanding Officer of a Regiment."[101] That was a valid concern: repute, especially for integrity, affected authority within the army just as it affected transactions outside of it. Honor, and where, when, and with whom honor did not apply, then contracts established the credit and confidence necessary for future actions.

Washington did not continue the argument with Hazen, but in the general orders of 1 August, he transferred Hazen's regiment. By the end of the month, Hazen was temporarily commanding Poor's brigade in that general's absence. On 23 August, as the army was marching from Tappan to Liberty Pole (Englewood) in New Jersey, General Steuben arrested Hazen for undermining good order and security on the march. A court-martial conducted between 28 and 29 August reviewed the charges: disobedience and "unmilitary" conduct "in halting the brigade under his Command without any orders therefore from the General commanding the division and thereby occasioning a vacancy of near half a mile in the Centre of the Left Column." To that was added a charge of unprofessional and ungentlemanly behavior in "falsely asserting" that he had had permission from General Stark. The court agreed that Hazen had created a hole in the line of march, but as he appeared to have had orders to halt, it acquitted him of disobedience and the follow-up charge of lying. Washington accepted the decision but added that it was "highly improper" for a brigade commander to order halts except when absolutely necessary, and then he should immediately inform the division or column commander so that proper adjustments could be made.[102]

Hazen had written his Coos allies, Bedel and Bayley, of the arrest and about being a "good hand in making a Retreat [in such matters, and so] shall not suffer death by the Censure of the Genl Court martial this time." Furthermore, he countercharged Steuben about the manner in which he had criticized Hazen. Steuben declared that if his ignorance of English led him into improper expressions, he "shall always be happy in giving that satisfaction for them which is due from one Gentleman to another." Hazen crowed about not only being acquitted with honor on all charges, but also about gaining "a most Compleat victory—I managed the matter in such a manner as not only to acquit myself of the Charges, but in the course of the Trial to Impeach my accuser of all the Charges on which I was Tried, and after the Publication of the Centence brought him the Baron to a Court of Honr to ask pardon &c. &c. &c: on the whole I have not lost but gained Honr by the Trial."[103]

Hazen was deeply sensitive about his own and his regiment's reputations, but his methods to maintain them did not always result in the ends he imagined. He and other regimental members usually acted honorably in the field, but they also provided fodder for an imperfect, even infernal, reputation in camp. Officers, soldiers, and followers of the regiment disputed complaints in and out of courts-martial for both personal and professional reasons. Officers battled over their integrity as gentlemen and for changes or reforms in policies and practices. If they did not win or could not accept institutional realities, they could—and some did—resign. Soldiers sniped and pummeled at each other while complaining about commanders and command decisions. They could not just resign, so some deserted while others petitioned for relief or submitted grievances for redress. In July 1780, the regiment established a court of inquiry to "examine into the Pretensions of the Non-commissioned officers and Privates of the Regiment" who were claiming that their enlistments had expired and that they should be officially discharged. There were at least thirty complainants. The board of officers determined that fifteen had enlisted for the duration of the war, thirteen without papers had likely enlisted for the duration, and one enlisted for three years or the duration. Only one, Morris Casey, was to have his discharge, and Hazen promised it "as soon as he may be clothed in a decent Manner, and paid up all Arrears of Pay."[104] That was a telling caveat about conditions in the regiment that paralleled the imperfect circumstances that led to even greater acts of disaffection in the wider army.

CHAPTER 8

GREAT OBJECTS, GREAT EVENTS

The internal frustrations that roiled Hazen's regiment echoed those in the army even as enemy actions recalled officers and soldiers to the great object of securing the nation. On 26 September 1780, while encamped at Tappan, New York, the regiment learned about "Treason, of the blackest dye." Benedict Arnold had handed the plans of West Point to Major John André, deputy adjutant general of Sir Henry Clinton's army. André had then been captured by partisans operating between the lines, but Arnold fled before he could be arrested. At Tappan on the 29th, André faced fourteen general officers at a board of inquiry. While the board met, the regiment buried one of its own: Corporal Avery, who "although he was unfortunate to die out of the field he has Left behind him the memory of an honest man and a Good soldier." Regimental orders reminded members to show "how much they Respect such a Character."[1]

Respectful conduct that would reflect well on the honor of the army was also expected when members stood witness to the hanging of Major André at noon on 2 October with "a Battalion of Eighty files from each wing" in attendance. One eyewitness remembered:

> [T]he place of execution was near the centre of the encampment of the American Grand Army, and in full view of many of its regiments. The lofty gibbet was surrounded by an exterior guard of nearly five hundred Infantry, with an inner guard of a captain's command. None were admitted within the square but the officers on duty and the Assistants of the Provost Marshal. The spectators outside the square were very numerous. Proceeding to the place of execution, under the above guard, Andre was accompanied by two of the officers of the inner guard, which he at first, as I larned, thought had been detailed as his executioners.

Benjamin Mooers recollected that Captain John Hughes had command of the guard and that "the prisoner walked between the Captain and Lieutenant, arm in arm, to the place of execution. One hundred of our Regiment, as also myself, as Adjutant, on horse-back, . . . [saw] the execution of the prisoner, a most affecting scene." In the 1890s, another person remarked hearing that William Torrey had been in command of the detachment that executed André. As Torrey had been a lieutenant, he may have been part of, but not commanding, the guard.[2]

André's guard and other observers would have preferred to see the traitor rather than the spy hanged, for frustration did not justify Arnold's treason any more than it did mutiny. Nor did discontent justify Sergeant Louis Marney's "Insolent and Abusive Language" to Lieutenant Germain Dionne about the recent rum distribution or, as they marched and encamped to the northward, "Insult and violence" against inhabitants and depredations against their property. The army was supposed to be a model sentinel and neighbor to the beleaguered inhabitants in the borderland between Continental and British lines. Courts-martial and orders to maintain discipline gave Hazen's troops much to mull over as they built huts between the North Redoubt and Soldiers Fortune across the Hudson from West Point and the fort renamed for General James Clinton to expunge that of "Arnold the traitor." But frustration surely colored language again when they were ordered to Fishkill and to leave their handiwork to another regiment.[3]

In the early months of 1781, the Canadian Old Regiment stood guard at Fishkill as a reserve unit unannexed to any brigade in the Highlands Department. To counter "unjust aspersions" against the regiment, and perhaps as an effect of his November court-martial, Hazen instituted more accountability measures.[4] During the same time, some congressional delegates in Philadelphia, bemoaning weaknesses, celebrated the great event that was ratification of the Articles of Confederation by trying to increase congressional powers. Officials and inhabitants of Virginia, in turn, debated executive actions and asked for assistance as they suffered invasion.

Weary military and political warriors wanted to believe that they would meet with ultimate success by year's end, but their best wishes initially faltered against the chronic debilitating disorder and disconnections between army, Congress, and states. The previous September, Delegate Ezekiel Cornell from Rhode Island had lamented how some officers cursed Congress for inattention or even "a wicked disposition to distress them," when "perhaps the real cause was a train of disappointments that no humane prudence could foresee." Congress had faced daily complaints from the army and creditors without the "means of Satisfying them on one Side," because state executives on the other side answered congressional appeals by submitting "the exhausted state of their several Treasurys and the inability of their constituents to pay the Quotas of Taxes assessed upon them."[5] That did not change over the following months, for Oliver Wolcott, a Connecticut militia general and congressional delegate, echoed Cornell's lament in December: "Congress have many Things to do, but Want Materials to Effect any Thing Very Material. They must be supplied with money from the States and until that is done, the States must in their individual Condition Support the War. This is conducting it under great Disadvantages."[6]

An implication was that if the states would not fund Congress so that it could in turn allocate resources to support the military for common defense, then the states would have to provide for their own troops to secure their own territories without reinforcements from sister states. Was political localism to subvert a united, secure America? Wolcott sputtered, "It would be a Most Scandalous Story to tell, that a Country was undone, because it did not know how to make Use of it's Wealth for it's Necessary Defences."[7]

Virginia's congressional delegates certainly worried about their state coming "undone" as word came of thousands of British troops embarking from New York. Speculation was that they were headed south, but no word followed as to how to "counteract those vigorous operations." The delegates reported to Governor Thomas Jefferson that they had little information on the status of the "new" army, or of supplying it, or of redeeming the old currency with specie so as to be able to finance everything. They admitted on New Year's Day, "This is a crisis at which we conceive a most assiduous application to these great objects to be necessary, and (next to the completion of the Confoederacy which is perhaps the Basis of the whole) of the first importance to America," for, they averred, "the measures of so large a state as ours cannot but have considerable effects on the other states in the Union."[8]

Jefferson did not ponder the effects on other states so much as those in Virginia. By the time the delegates' letter reached the governor, there was no speculation as to where the British were going; they had arrived. That "Traytor," the "detestable," now British brigadier was sailing a combined army-navy force up the James River and delivering destruction along the way. The Virginians' initial response was underwhelming, and their delegates informed Congress that Arnold's harassment would distract Virginia from supporting the Southern Army operating in the Carolinas. They were most concerned about their "Country," and its need for an organized militia, gunboats and galleys, and fortifications on the rivers.[9] Virginia was not in a condition to defend herself, so delegates and governor looked to the Continental Congress and army for assistance, arguing that defending Virginia secured the nation.

The new year thus began with the old year's crises. Delegates, legislators, governors, and commanders continued their vigorous debates over what powers, and who or what had them, were necessary to strengthen and secure the union and the states within it.[10] Officers and soldiers in the Continental Army, in turn, continued to contend for position, power, and pay as they prepared for a campaign that ultimately marched them into Virginia. In the midst of those civil and military disputes, Congress brevetted Hazen a brigadier, which the commander in chief validated by providing him with a brigade. Not everyone was happy with that. Although Washington diplomatically described Hazen as "a sensible—spirited and attentive Officer," some officers preferred to be "under the command of any other service officers in the line of army." That was Colonel Alexander Scammell's opinion when his light infantry regiment was later attached to Hazen's brigade for the Yorktown siege. He, however, was willing to postpone his request for transfer that September until "the present affair with Cornwallis is terminated."[11] Scammell was honor-bound to protest and honor-bound to serve at that critical juncture. Other officers and soldiers acted on the same sentiments not only through the 1781 campaign but to the end of the war.

Governing Powers and Imperatives

"The Want of a fixed Confediration frustrates almost every Measure, and the dull, inergetic Mode of Proceedure . . . render our Efforts too feeble and dilatory to effect the greatest Objects," deplored General and Delegate James Varnum of Rhode Island.[12] Frustration and feeble efforts over pay and other issues propelled a mutiny in the Pennsylvania line on New Year's Day. The army responded to contain the rebellion while Congress and Pennsylvania sent committees to negotiate. Pessimists bemoaned signs of dissolving union, but optimists relievedly noted how the mutineers spurned Sir Henry Clinton's offer of money and protection if they would lay down their arms and go home. On the evening of 10 January, Congress's Committee on the Pennsylvania Mutiny wrote to Washington of successful negotiations in which "no Concession has been granted them that the critical Situation of our affairs did not Warrant and Justice dictate." The committee members believed, the first "Tumult" aside, that the soldiers acted "with a consistency, firmness and a degree of Policy mixd with candor that must astonish every theorist on the nature of the American Soldiery."[13]

Washington had ordered General Heath at West Point to organize a detachment to act against the Pennsylvania mutineers, but the successful civil-military negotiation meant that Heath could put the five battalions on hold. In the meantime, as Colonel Rufus Putnam and a woman from Colonel John Greaton's regiment reported, the waiting soldiers expressed their unease about the possibility of fighting their brothers in arms and echoed some of the mutineers' grievances. Such reactions raised concerns about the protests widening, so when some discontented soldiers of the New Jersey line mutinied at Pompton, Washington did not wait for negotiated results; he ordered out the readied detachment, which was to include about two hundred soldiers from Hazen's regiment attached to Scammell's New Hampshire regiment. Major General Robert Howe commanded the detachment as it made a rapid, hard slog through snow to Pompton, where its elements set guards and restored order by 28 January. Washington commended Howe and his troops for performing their duty despite their reluctance to act against "fellow Soldiers." They had shown proper "attachment to the service, sense of subordination and abhorrence of the principles which actuated the Mutineers in so daring and atrocious a departure from what they owed to their Country, to their Officers to their Oaths and to themselves."[14] Washington was not going to be civil about outright rebellion in the face of the enemy.

Congressional and state actions and inactions, not just military administration, had spurred the January mutinies, which again prodded officials to consider political and financial reforms. Derided for "inergetic" procedures, Congress began "seriously, & *industriously*" working on proposals to establish "a permanent fund" on which "to build a future credit." It asked the states to grant the United States in Congress the power to establish a duty on foreign imports for the purpose of paying debts and supporting the war effort. Given the history of debates over duties for revenue versus the regulation of trade, it was not surprising that this was a sensitive issue.[15] So too were others about the respective powers and properties of the independent states and those shared between them in the Confederation. Those sensitivities had delayed ratification of the Articles of Confederation, but on 2 March, Congress's President Samuel Huntington sent a letter to the states congratulating "our Constituents on this important Event [ratification], desired by our Friends but dreaded by our Enemies."[16]

Within days of the ratification, more debates ensued over interpreting and applying the powers of the Articles. Delegate Thomas Rodney from Delaware was "Sorry to See Such a keen Struggle to increase the power of Congress beyond What the States Intended." Rodney supported strict construction, but James Varnum wanted even more than a loose application. He believed that "There are two Obsticles to that Energy and Vigor wch. are absolutely necessary in the United States." One was vesting Congress "with the Power of calling out effectually the Resources of each State." The other was the "Jealousey" of many delegates against creating a more effective system. If the government was too weak to "support Armies, fight Battles and obtain compleat Victory," then he proposed there be a convention "not composed of Members of Congress" to reframe the Articles.[17] That suggestion, and others echoing it, ultimately had to await the Continental Army's survival under the Articles and success against the British forces. In the meantime, Virginia was demanding assistance.

Virginia, unlike her northern sisters, had not had a constant strong Continental Army presence over the years, so it had not had that physical reminder of the continental union to encourage confederative cooperation. Virginia had certainly been sending soldiers and supplies to the army, but it tended to expend more effort against loyalist and Native American neighbors. The state's government was also suspicious of command authority, which affected military operations. Virginia had limited executive power in its constitution, and a governor who was constitutionally disinclined to exert executive power beyond the stated limits. Not only was Jefferson ideologically constrained in exerting authority, he lacked the military experience that might have aided command decisions. His successor, Thomas Nelson Jr., had military as well as political experience, having commanded the state's militia and served in its General Assembly, and as a delegate to the Continental Congress. He also had fewer constraints and qualms about exerting executive power in support of military forces. Both labored to defend the state in 1781, but the first prioritized political ideals whereas the latter prioritized securing the country.

The governors' priorities affected their actions, and Virginia's assembly sharply criticized both by the end of their respective terms, Jefferson's in early June and Nelson's in November, although it ultimately papered over censure with appreciation in December 1781. By then, the relieved state was free of British forces, and its assemblymen could reflect on how military exigencies had challenged constitutional precepts and administrative conduct. It rescinded assertions of incompetence against Jefferson on the 12th, and charges of exceeding authority against Nelson about two weeks later. The General Assembly commended the first "for his impartial, upright, and attentive administration of the powers of the Executive, whilst in office," and legitimized the actions of the latter as necessary for the common good.[18]

That common defense became the primary definition of the common good was part of Virginia's crisis of 1781. Jefferson recognized the importance of security and strove to strengthen the state's defenses, but ranking protection over individual rights was another matter. He believed that the means and ends of the Revolution should correspond. Therefore, he acted as far as his understanding of the powers of governor allowed, but no further. If the people wanted their government, especially the executive, to act more forcefully when the state faced armed threats, then they should constitute that authority. Ideally, they were to approve it after collective reflection and debate, and vote for a reformed or new constitution. He did not want to undermine popular sovereignty, nor for the people to undermine their own authority, by accepting the exercise of expanded executive prerogatives due to exigency. Jefferson knew that an invasion was "no time for deliberating on forms of government," for he admitted that when "an enemy is within our bowels, the first object is to expel him." But he wanted the mode of defense to be constitutional. He argued that as the current state compact had not been properly ratified as a transcendent constitution, providing for immediate necessary powers was a matter of passing new legislation. After the crisis was over, he wanted Virginians to convene and create a suitable constitution.[19]

Jefferson approached the military crisis as an intellectual with a legislative inclination, asking for more information and waiting for it to make a decision. Jefferson, like another leading Virginian, George Washington, operated on a strong foundation in political ethics. Both contended for independence and a republic, but Jefferson found it more difficult to move from the theoretical or the ideal to the real. He adjusted but resisted all the way. A result was that the blows of war bruised General Washington as he moved with them, whereas they battered Governor Jefferson as he tried to stand against them.

Jefferson did make and execute severe decisions, especially as they related to loyalist threats within the state and securing the western borderlands.[20] They were executive decisions that the assembly supported, but were they "command" decisions? The governor tried to exert control, but he did not so much want to command it as to receive it. When the enemy moved down from New York and up from the Carolinas, there was not always time for the assembly's review and recommendations.

Benedict Arnold sailed up the James River in early January 1781, stopping along the way to exercise his forces, invite residents to show allegiance to Great Britain, and insist on southern hospitality. He was not always a gracious guest. A resident who feared that he and his neighbors would have to play host decried how "General Arnold obliged the inhabitants of Richmond to turn out all their rum, sugar, &c. into the street, and then destroyed the whole." After leaving the state's capitol, Arnold's troops moved back down the river, burning structures and carrying off enslaved persons along the way. Furthermore, the Virginians believed the enemy would quarter in Portsmouth. The state was in turmoil, but its citizens tried to reassure themselves by passing word that Major General von Steuben, with Brigadier Generals George Weedon, Peter Muhlenberg, and Thomas Nelson, were gathering troops to resist.[21]

The reassurance was as feeble as initially were the ranks of militia. General John Sullivan, now one of New Hampshire's delegates to Congress, was appalled: "the Traytor Arnold has Landed in Virginia. Burnt all the publick Buildings and Destroyed what publick Stores were to be found there & altho he had but 1500 men not a Shot was fired at him. . . . It . . . Does the Virginians no

Honor." The word was that Arnold was "Incamped opposite Williamsburgh & Baron Stuben & General Nelson are opposed to him with only Fifteen hundred men but that more were Collecting."[22]

The generals and governor in Virginia did start mounting a defense with the soldiers who turned out promptly. What they also confronted, however, were slow, half-hearted responses by the remainder. The contending British and Continental forces were advancing into an ongoing conflict, even nascent civil war, over mobilization that had pitted the marginal and middling ranks of Virginians against the elite. Continental commanders thus had to navigate local disaffection as they prepared to meet the enemy.[23] They had to operate on two fronts—civil and military—and they were not always deft in the doing.

Adding to the difficulties were disputes over who had what for whom. Steuben had arrived in the state at the end of 1780 to manage a supply chain of men and matériel for General Greene's Southern Army in the Carolinas. As Virginia confronted incursions, however, it wanted not only to keep its own men and matériel in state but also for Steuben to divert supplies meant for the Southern Army to Virginia's militia.[24] That and Steuben's taking command of Continental and militia forces to counter the invasion spurred an increasingly tense relationship between Steuben and Jefferson (and his fellow Virginians). Steuben wanted more support than Jefferson could or would provide, and he was not as adept in dealing with civil authorities as either Washington or Greene. The governor's and general's frustrations over ways and means reflected the problems inherent to civil-military borderlands—places of unclear jurisdiction—in a war zone. The erosion in civil-military relations was partially reversed upon General Lafayette's arrival with more troops and assumption of command.

Lafayette arrived at the head of a light infantry corps. After ordering the formation of a light infantry company in each regiment, Washington had drawn some of them into a corps of three battalions commanded by Lieutenant Colonels Elijah Vose, Jean-Joseph Gimat, and Francis Barber. Major Reid had charge of three companies in Barber's battalion, two from New Hampshire and one from Hazen's regiment, the latter captained by Thomas Pry.[25] Washington gave the corps command to Lafayette on 20 February for use against the enemy in Virginia. As Lafayette headed south, he had to deal not only with logistics and transportation complications but also with lingering resentments from the mutinies, as well as a storm of officers and soldiers against Major William Galvan in Vose's battalion of Massachusetts companies. Officers protested the appointment of the foreign officer in lieu of one of their own, and soldiers protested his treatment of them. Galvan responded with how he had exhausted his health "in preventing Drunkenness, Suppressing riots and quarrels which had taken place between our [Massachusetts] Soldiers and those of the jersey line." Barber, in turn, deplored the "turbulent" behavior of the Jersey troops. Personnel disputes were obviously not specific to Hazen's regiment, but in this case, Major Reid was not a provocateur. Lafayette was not pleased with Galvan, but he found Reid to be an excellent officer who was happy to remain with the corps. Lafayette was also perturbed by the desertions of soldiers who, "Amazingly averse to the people and climate" of the South, found the idea of remaining there for a campaign "Intolerable."[26] There was a distinct fraying of Continental fellowship as the corps marched south.

Similar strains appeared in Virginia, as the general was dismayed to observe in August that "The Pennsylvanians and Virginians Have Never Agreed But at the Present time, it is worse than Ever." Virginia's governor, by then General Nelson, and Council of State complained about General Anthony Wayne and his troops, who had marched down to augment Lafayette's corps and Virginia's militia, whereas Wayne complained of abuse by the state. Lafayette perceived "the Seeds of a future Dispute Between States—and Every Day the troops Remain Here adds to the Danger."[27] In the meantime, he and Greene also expressed consternation and exasperation with Virginia's organization and operations.

Jefferson had clued Lafayette to the situation when welcoming him to the command in March. He wrote that the state executive—governor and council—fully supported the military commander in operations against the enemy. But he also warned that "Mild Laws, a People not used to war and prompt obedience, a want of the Provisions of War and means of procuring them render our orders often ineffectual, oblige us to temporize and when we cannot accomplish an object in one way to attempt it in another." He asked for forbearance and cooperation. Lafayette assured him of the respect he had for civil authority, but also indicated that his operations required "Great Expences and Great Means of transportation," and thus he would impress, but with "delicacy," as needed. Jefferson understood, for "In a Country whose means of payment are neither prompt nor of the most desirable Kind, impressing property for the public use has been found indispensible."[28]

The impressment of horses, however, escalated tensions between people and army, which Jefferson had tried to tamp by saying that the army did not have to return all horses when he asked General Greene to rectify "unreasonable and imprudent impresses." Greene agreed that it was lamentable that officers had not been more prudent in their sweeps, but the assembly's sweeping resolution demanding returns was equally unfortunate. Horses were needed for the dragoons serving state and nation, but "The Assembly of your State appear to have taken up the matter from a principle tho' acknowledged to be virtuous, yet from its tendency must be allowed to be impolitic. The rights of Individuals are as dear to me as to any Man, but the safety of a community I have ever considered as an object more valuable."[29]

Similar heated but courteous exchanges occurred between Continental and state authorities over the numbers and deployment of the militia, which accompanied related exchanges in state between the governor and county and militia officers. As Jefferson wrote to Colonel Abraham Penn in May, "We have called on eleven Counties to furnish a reinforcement to General Greene [in the Carolinas] and hope it will be the last Time we shall have occasion to require our Militia to go out of their own Country, as we think it most adviseable to put that distant disagreeable service on our Regulars, and to send them forward as fast as raised, and to employ our Militia on Service in our own Country." The trouble was that seven counties wanted to be excused from such disagreeable service, so Jefferson and the council had to requisition the needed reinforcement. Jefferson figured that if his fellow Virginians did not support Greene "out of their own Country" until more aid arrived, then they "would have the whole War on us."[30] His accurate forecast revealed biases: such disagreeable duties were meant for regulars, and state identity impeded confederation community.

As General Cornwallis's forces moved into Virginia, and as Virginians resisted drafts of men and regulations affecting property, Jefferson, in his final days as governor, advised the House of Delegates that something had to be done "to enforce the calls of the Executive for militia to attend in the field," and to address "the total want of authority of the military power over citizens within the vicinities of his and of the enemy's encampments." Jefferson then retired, believing, as he later reflected, that "the public would have more confidence in a Military chief, and that the Military commander, being invested with the Civil power also, both might be wielded with more energy promptitude and effect for the defence of the state."[31]

Virginia responded to the escalating exigencies with a volley of acts, and among the delegates driving the action was a former Congress's Own major, John Taylor of Caroline County. Besides mobilization and monetary acts, there was one to apply martial law within twenty miles of military—American or British—camps. Virginia's house and senate also agreed to an expansion of executive powers, and to General Nelson's appointment as governor.[32]

Nelson then acted beyond even those expanded powers in trying to sustain Virginia's militia and the American and French armies. He buttressed relations between Continental and state forces as he became in practice a governor-general. He was willing not only to command but compel Virginia's citizens to their duty as long as Continental commanders ensured that their officers respected civilian limits. "As first magistrate of the State and Guardian of the Rights of the People," Nelson requested that Lafayette, as "Commander in chief of the American Forces in the State of Virginia," regulate "the Conduct of all subordinate Officers," with specific reference to General Wayne, who had seized state stores, and his Pennsylvania troops who had arrogated private property. While Nelson put limits on Continental-sanctioned impressments, he broadened his own. He did not want to hear about inhabitants refusing to provide resources when "Salvation" of persons and property depended on the very troops they refused to support.[33] In effect, civilians faced a similar paradox to that of soldiers: preserving property depended on sacrificing it, just as soldiers had to surrender some of their civil rights during service in order to preserve them. Nelson ultimately faced censure for exerting blunt force at the time, but he believed that the means were contingent on immediate needs as long as valid ends remained in sight.

The crises of 1781 raised constitutional questions in Virginia as they did for Congress. They also brought home that Virginia could not stand apart from the Confederation. The responses of Virginians, their legislators, and governors echoed those of their counterparts in other parts of the nation that had faced enemy invasion and then Continental imposition. They worried about securing their "country," which most defined as state, but they had to have the help of other states, Congress, and the Continental Army. In the process of requesting and providing assistance, they all acknowledged fellow citizens, even when they were not quite ready to embrace them as fellow countrymen. Their mixed reactions were reciprocated by the Continentals, who were also still debating the definition of compatriot for those outside of the army as well as in it.

Regimental Advances

As Virginia confronted new challenges inherent in maintaining civil order and military operations in the same place at the same time, and as the army reorganized and reordered its troops, the Canadian Old Regiment mended rips in its uniforms, if not its community. Comradery and community had taken a beating, but the regiment's reason for being remained. It continued to face trials by courts, at Congress, and in spirit, but it steadfastly fulfilled its duties in support of the army's mission.

The regiment had entered the new year awaiting a conclusion to Major Reid's court-martial. After being acquitted of the offenses charged by Reid, Hazen had arrested the major on charges including "Disobedience of Orders and unmilitary conduct"; "Defrauding the United States, or the regiment . . . and embezzling or misapplying public property"; and "Unofficer and ungentlemanlike conduct." The charges echoed those that Reid had delivered against Hazen, but in this case, the emphasis was on disobedience and conduct unbefitting an officer and gentleman. The court convened on 21 December, but because of intervening adjournments did not conclude until 8 January. It then sent its decisions and recommendations to Washington for review and sentencing.[34] In the meantime, Reid remained under arrest and confined to quarters.

The review was not a top priority for Washington as he dealt with mutinies, approved strikes against the enemy, and established the light infantry corps. The latter, however, prompted a decision. On 18 February, Washington publicly accepted the court's determination that Reid was guilty of disobedience in disregarding regulations by having sergeants perform as "Officers of Police," and of unsuitable conduct in his "Inflammatory Expressions" and other instances of disrespect against his commanding officer. In his reprimand to Reid, Washington lessoned others: subordinate officers were not to try to make their commanders "odious" to their corps, and he regretted that "it is too common for Officers on trial to indulge themselves in a vein of invective and abuse as inconsistent with decency as with the respect they owe to themselves and to others." Reprimanded and relieved from arrest, Reid quickly followed Pry's company to detached duty with the corps of light infantry."[35]

Reid's censure and absence from the regiment proved to be a pause—not an end—to the feud. Other officers in the regiment, including most of the Canadians, had been insulted by Reid's "Indecent reflections, Illiberal Sentiments, and pointed Impeachments" during his trial. Believing themselves incriminated, they wanted Washington, Heath, Hazen, and Reid to know that they declined to do "any kind of Military Duty" with Reid unless he publicly supported his assertions, which would allow them to respond openly.[36] Reprisal and resolution had to wait, however, on the war's progress and the regiment's duties.

Reid's court-martial aside, Hazen had begun 1781 at Fishkill saluting the regiment for its part in "the Glorious Struggle for Liberty and Independence," warning members against actions that undermined the regiment's reputation, and ordering inspections of personnel and property. That led to a command on 5 January "to make their old Clothing go as far as Possible." Tailors were to cut up "old Coats and Convert them into Comfortable Jackets" according to a pattern provided by Antill. Five days later, there was some new clothing, but "Great Care must be taken of the Coats that may be Issued, they are not to be worn on any kind of Work or Fatigue" unless so ordered. Soldiers were not to alter the new coats or sleep in them. To disobey meant "two days hard Fatigue for the first Offense" and a court-martial for the second.[37]

There were other measures for uniformity and order as well. Once new barracks were ready, Antill was to assign officers their quarters in them. Passes for noncommissioned officers and soldiers were to be signed by the appropriate company commander and officer of the day, and all were to follow the same format showing name, rank, company in the "Canadian Old Regiment," and time requested.[38] The orders thus recognized the new regimental title, and showed that Hazen and Antill were resolved to rehabilitate the regiment: its members were to look good and be good.

Hazen's resolutions, along with his sensitivity about unequal provisioning, immediately caused problems with Quartermaster General Timothy Pickering and his officials at Fishkill. Hazen had demanded reports on the distribution of rum, forage, quarters, and the like so as to fix distribution. Pickering complained that Hazen's "overbearing disposition aimed at the absolute control of every transaction at that post" interfered with his department's operations, and so he had ordered his officials not to obey Hazen. Heath and Pickering both turned to Washington with arguments about civil (staff) and military authority. Heath had not only delegated supervisory powers to Hazen, he believed that if the commander in chief had "command of the Q.M.G. & his Department, the Commanding Officer at every Post, has command of those Officers of the Staff Department, stationed at the Post." Pickering countered that that was "confounding a civil with a military post." Fishkill was more than a simple military garrison, it was a "magazine for stores of every kind" for the public service. Washington agreed with Heath about the subordination of the Quartermaster Department, but he also did not want to "unhinge" the department in New York. He confirmed Heath's authority but wanted the broad delegation of powers checked to prevent putting the ordering of "provision, forage, and fuel" into the "hands of too many persons."[39] Hazen's actions had spurred a quarrel over civil-military jurisdiction that showed how such strife was not just between Congress and states, and states and army, but within the Continental borderlands that were military posts as well.

Hazen was undoubtedly happy to put management wrangles aside for more active service. He was the type of officer who heard the guns, drums, and fife and quick-marched toward them. While the regiment awaited orders about Pompton, General Samuel Parsons had plans for deploying it elsewhere. His initial idea was to have it relieve the garrison at Wyoming, Pennsylvania. As Connecticut and Pennsylvania were still contending claims to the area, he proposed the regiment as a neutral choice because, forgetting or ignoring the multistate nature of the regiment, he figured that Hazen's soldiers were not residents of either. He also noted that "twenty men of Schott's Corps" were already at Wyoming and were to be annexed to the regiment.[40] Washington, however, prioritized operations against British and loyalist raiders in the borderland that was Westchester County.

Washington put Parsons in command of an attack on the enemy at Morrisania. On 21–22 January, Lieutenant Colonel William Hull's 3rd Massachusetts battalion conducted raids while detachments under Hazen, Scammell of the

1st New Hampshire, and Lieutenant Colonel Isaac Sherman of the 5th Connecticut provided support. Hull's troops hit hard, fast, and successfully, but the enemy moved quickly to block retreat. Hazen, however, had concealed his hundred men behind a stone fence on the escape route, who then, as Hull's men safely passed them, opened fire, scattering and dispersing the following enemy. British troops approaching by other routes paused in the face of Scammell's and Sherman's forces. With the mission accomplished, the enemy too close, the men fatigued, and the weather worsening, Parsons marched his troops to Horseneck with plans for them to recover for a few days at Bedford before returning to their winter quarters. But then came word of Howe's detachment heading to Pompton, and so there was to be no rest for those who had also been detailed to the counter-mutiny mission. When Hazen marched out with Parsons, he may have left those designated for Howe behind, and thus they may have already been on their way down. However, if some were engaged in the Morrisania enterprise, they may have marched with Scammell, who did not arrive at Pompton until 29 January, the day Howe left it to return north.[41]

Hazen's "infernals" surely savored the accolades that came their way after Morrisania as much as their colonel did. Parsons sent his commendations, including for Hazen and his troops, to Heath, who passed them on to Washington. The commander in chief then passed his approbation down the line so that Hazen could offer that and his own to the regiment on 28 January. Hazen thanked the detachment "(a few Individuals excepted) for their decent, orderly and soldierlike Behaviour on the late Command." Their "pointed Attention to duty and the spirited Conduct of the Officers and Soldiers when the Detachment of one hundred men of the Regiment only were ordered to Cover the retreat of upwards of Eight Hundred men who had fought the Enemy bravely on a Retreat for more than an hour with a Considerable Loss, would do honour to the best troops in the Universe." Hazen regretted that "it was totally out of his power to indulge himself or the party in taking such Advantages of the Enemy as he might otherwise have done," but he was consoled that "he not only Answered every Purpose that was by the General Expected from the Detachment, but to the Generals Surprise brought [off] the party, in a retreat of more than a mile, in the face of the Enemy without the loss of a man, on which Col. Hazen had the Honor to receive the Generals Public thanks." There was more public approbation in the general orders of 30 January, and then when newspapers published Parsons's letter to Heath in mid-February.[42]

Basking in the honors, Hazen resumed his campaigns for personal and regimental advancement and recompense. Before leaving Fishkill, however, he hosted a dinner for Washington, his aides Lieutenant Colonels Alexander Hamilton and Tench Tilghmann, and the Baron Ludwig von Closen of the Royal

Deux-Ponts on 2 March. He also reviewed court-martial sentences, addressed supply issues, and reorganized companies, combining them to make nine. He made the newly transferred Captain Anthony Selin the captain of the ninth, which other officers were still complaining about when encamped at Yorktown. On 15 March, leaving Antill in charge, and accompanied by Hawkins who had obtained leave, Hazen headed to Philadelphia to place his arguments directly before Congress.[43]

Hazen and Hawkins traveled the same route to Trenton before Hazen chose to continue by land and send Hawkins by water. The sergeant major arrived in Philadelphia at sunrise on the 22nd, and soon met up with many friends and relations who were in town for the Quaker Half Yearly Meeting. As he attended to his own affairs, Hawkins also apparently (judging by the handwriting) helped Hazen prepare his petitions to Congress.[44]

Hazen submitted his first petition on 2 April. Congress referred it the next day to the Board of Treasury, which reported back on the 24th. Hazen had asked for repayment of the personal money and commodities he had expended for army. Congress ultimately decided to credit him with over 13,386 dollars specie bearing 6 percent annual interest.[45] Congress also had another committee consider Hazen's appeal for depreciation for the officers and men in his regiment not belonging to any of the states. On the 20th, it approved the disbursement of loan office certificates and arrears of pay, which it sent back to the Board of Treasury. That board sent the resolutions to the Board of Claims, which delayed settlement until authentic papers substantiating claims were presented. Hazen responded with another petition to Congress on 31 May, which then on 7 July, again after committee review, clarified what proof was necessary. Hazen was still in town on 18 July waiting for the issue of 182 certificates.[46] After doggedly navigating the bureaucracy, he was determined not to return to Fishkill without the certificates.

His tenacious lobbying also resulted in a partial victory for promotion. When Congress approved arrears and depreciation on 20 April, it decided that Washington was to determine whether Hazen's recommended officer promotions were warranted. That day, Congress also proposed that Hazen be brevetted a brigadier general and ordered further consideration of a promotion with full pay and powers. On the 30th, Hazen wrote to John Sullivan of the committee reviewing the request. He touted how Congress not only kept the regiment on its original establishment but determined to augment it with foreign volunteers. He argued that such resolves meant that Congress intended him to have "an honourable Command, superior to any Colonel in the Army." Unfortunately, being driven from Canada and lack of money meant the numbers in his command had dwindled, which was also a result of the army's drawing of men for artificers, wagoners, sappers, miners, and light infantry detachments. Nonetheless, Hazen wanted Sullivan and his committee to remember his exertions in raising the regiment and his commendable conduct in battle. He also argued that although there were two colonels senior to him, his promotion should not await theirs, which were tied to their state lines, because he commanded a separate corps. He closed by also urging the promotions of Captains Olivie and Satterlee and commissions for a few volunteers and sergeants. Despite Hazen's efforts and merits, Congress answered on 29 June that "the particular circumstances of the Army" only allowed it to brevet him at that time. Hazen gracefully (but temporarily) accepted it on 3 July, even before the new president of Congress, Thomas McKean, forwarded him the official appointment on the 12th.[47]

As Hazen and Hawkins addressed regimental and personal agendas in Philadelphia, Antill directed Congress's Canadian Old Regiment and Washington pondered campaign options in the Hudson Highlands while trying to secure men, supplies, and the New York-Vermont frontier. Washington was fielding demands from Generals Schuyler and Stark, as well as civil officials such as Vermont Governor Thomas Chittenden and New York's George Clinton about defense against British incursions from Canada. On 18 May, Schuyler and General James Clinton warned of a threatened invasion from Canada, "unfavourable prospects from Vermont," and the destruction of Fort Schuyler (Stanwix). On the 25th, their letters tolled the possibility of the enemy landing at Crown Point and moving down the Mohawk and Hudson Rivers. In response, Washington alerted Colonel Van Schaick's companies at West Point to be ready to move. Then on 1 June, with the generals warning that the enemy had intercepted reports from Albany detailing troop strength and disaffection among some settlements, Washington directed the quartermaster general to provide boats so that Hazen's regiment and companies from Van Schaick's could "proceed immediately to Albany & put themselves under General Clintons orders." They got to Albany, and then Clinton wrote, in effect, "oops": on 20 June, Clinton sent word to Washington that questioning of prisoners taken at Crown Point, especially in conjunction with Washington's other intelligence, indicated that no troops had landed there, only some enemy shipping. Washington responded by ordering Continental troops up north to be prepared "to join the army on the shortest notice," and writing Clinton that new state levies and nine-months men would be sent to relieve him.[48]

Clinton recalled Antill from Caughnawaga, where he had posted the regiment (with a supply company at Schenectady) to patrol that area on the Mohawk. The general had not been pleased by the regiment's attachment to his command. Perhaps he had heard of Ensign Murdock McPherson's 2 May court-martial for neglect of duty, which allowed prisoners to escape his guard. That aside, Clinton believed that the regiment was disposed to mutiny, which made its members susceptible to "the numerous disaffected Tribes" at Albany. Their minds "inflamed," Clinton averred, the newcomers became "almost ungovernable." Some said they would not march without money. When Clinton had two of the leaders confined, one being John Burk of Satterlee's company, their "Fellows" forced their release and "disorderly Conduct ensued." The leaders were retaken and a court-martial followed, after which Clinton reported on the 18th that "Hazens Regt marched in good order for their Station." Nine days later, Clinton commended Antill for the "situation of your Camp, the disposition of your Scouts, & the Measures you have adopted for the Security of the Frontier." He also alerted Antill to be ready to move on short notice. As it turned out, the regiment was back at West Point by 10 July.[49]

Freed from concern of an immediate attack from Canada, Washington moved to consolidate Continental forces for other purposes. That put the onus of frontier defense on local militia and, if New York could entice them, longer-term levies. As the Continental Army, Congress, and state governments seemed unable or unwilling to defend their persons and property, some of the borderland residents contemplated secession and joining the proposed independent republic of Vermont, which in turn had leaders negotiating with Governor Haldimand in Canada to ensure their security.[50] It was an explosive situation by June 1781, and it was left up to New York and Vermont to negotiate it, for Washington had other plans.

Washington had made those plans in a 22 May meeting at Wethersfield, Connecticut, with the commander of the French army in America, Lieutenant General Jean-Baptiste Donatien de Vimeur, comte de Rochambeau. The French troops were to join American forces at the North (Hudson) River and begin operations against the British forces garrisoned in and around New York City. Washington gathered intelligence and had his officers estimate the respective needs of their departments or commands.[51] By 18 June, he had rearranged the army, and then between 21 and 24 June had it march in three divisions to new encampments. Washington moved his headquarters down to Peekskill to join the army there, and on the 25th saw off his wife, talked with New York officials about the rearrangements of Continental and state troops, ordered General Stark to go to Saratoga to command "the Troops on the Northern & western frontier," and alerted General Clinton to have his Continentals "in the most perfect readiness to join the Army."[52]

Washington had received word that the French admiral, François Joseph Paul, comte de Grasse, would move his fleet into position to support operations in mid-summer. He also knew that Rochambeau would soon set his troops on the road from Newport, Rhode Island, to join the American forces. He was so eager to begin that he did not wait for the allies. On 28 June, he ordered General Lincoln, with troops that included Colonel Scammell's new light infantry detachment, to make a surprise attack on British-held outposts near King's Bridge. Other American units and the Duke de Lauzun's legion were to provide support. The surprise failed on 2 July, as Lauzun's troops were too late and the outposts had reinforcements. Washington then shifted his forces "a little to the left of Dobbes ferry," and set a camp location for the French, who encamped there on the sixth.[53]

At that point, Sir Henry Clinton was on his guard in New York, and Washington needed more information before he could truly initiate the campaign. He continued to evaluate reports, confer with civil and military officers, and move troops. In compliance with his directives, the Canadian and 1st New York regiments moved down to West Point by the 10th, though not before some of the New Yorkers had mutinied about pay and deserted—a reminder that general disaffection continued.[54]

As Rochambeau awaited Washington's final plans, Washington waited for information on Admiral de Grasse's movements, and for the states to supply the requested men and matériel. All they could do, he answered his ally, was "prepare, first, for the enterprize against New York as agreed to at Weathersfield and secondly for the relief of the Southern States," if ultimately, he had neither the men nor means to take New York. By 1 August, Washington was more seriously considering the latter.[55]

As their commander in chief practiced patience, brevetted Brigadier General Hazen and Sergeant Major Hawkins headed north from Philadelphia to rejoin their regiment. They generally traveled on parallel paths as Hazen visited acquaintances. Hawkins enjoyed his trek as he remarked on people balancing personal pursuits, such as "going huckleberry," against wartime demands. The sociable Hawkins hitched rides on wagons, helped unload them, and listened to people's stories. Folks, in turn, shared provisions and, as a family "friendly to the States" did when he was trekking alone north of Tarrytown, invited him to rest overnight with them. After a six-and-a-half-day journey, on 3 August, Hawkins entered West Point, where he "was almost torn to Pieces for Joy by the Men of the Regt. who was much pleased at my return." Then, as he resumed his duties, he checked out his neighbors: the troops at West Point under the command of General McDougall included Hazen's regiment, part of the New York brigade, detachments from various other regiments from the eastern states, and invalids transferred from Philadelphia.[56]

Hawkins rejoined his military community on a day when garrison orders clarified what women could charge for washing if they received food, "house room or wood from the Garrison," and when a regimental court-martial tried Corporal Dennis Norget of Olivie's company for overstaying his pass with the intention to desert. Norget said that desertion was not his intention but that, yes, he had overstayed his pass. Major Torrey asserted that he had provided a three-day pass so that Norget could leave his wife in the country, and that the prisoner had overstayed the permission by one day. Captain Olivie, in turn, deposed that he had given Norget "liberty to take his wife home to her fathers and return immediately as he had done staying only one day more than he Expected which he forgave him." The court threw out the desertion charge and recommended that his captain reprimand Norget for overstaying his pass.[57]

The court resumed on 4 August, as Sergeant Timothy Dady of Satterlee's company stood charged with disturbing the camp at an "unusual" hour (between 1:00 and 2:00 A.M.) the previous night. Corporal John Gregory, who had been in charge of the quarter guard sent by the adjutant to check out the ruckus, "found the prisoner with a number of others drinking and singing" on the parade ground. He told them to be quiet or face confinement. When they continued to be noisy, he took "a file of men and confined them." Returning from grand rounds, Major Woodson passed the quarter guard, where the men asked for release, saying that they had been wrongfully confined. Woodson refused. He returned to the quarter guard in the morning at Satterlee's assertion that they were men of "unexceptionable Character as Soldiers." The adjutant offered to withdraw the charges if the men admitted their error, but Dady "refused to acknowledge he was in the wrong any further than going out of his Tent in the night." He also defended his fellows' exasperation at "being Confined as they suffered wrongfully." The court found him guilty and sentenced him to be reduced to a private. Torrey approved the sentence, but due to the prisoner's "former good character and the solicitations of the Officers in his favour," restored Dady to his former rank. Hawkins was thus welcomed back to drama as well as duties.[58]

On the 6th, the light infantry component of Colonel Philip Van Cortlandt's 2nd New York Regiment marched out to join the Main Army. Hawkins noted that the "well-sized" men made a martial appearance dressed all in the same uniform.[59] That he specifically noted their presentation indicated that not all units could provide such a fine martial image six years into the war; as foreign officers observed, some men did not have shoes, much less uniforms.[60] Although the soldiers and noncommissioned officers in the Canadian Old Regiment had received some newer items since December, the newer coats must have made a stark comparison to the weathered brown and blue ones of the others in the ranks when they paraded in the New York garrisons that spring and at Yorktown later that fall.

Washington took the 2nd New York's light infantry company along with that from the 1st New York and joined them with two companies of New York levies, forming a battalion commanded by Lieutenant Colonel Hamilton and Major Nicholas Fish and "placed under the orders of Colo. Scammell as part of the light Troops of the Army." Washington then sent orders that Hazen's Regiment and the 1st New York were to march immediately from West Point to join the Main Army. Newly arrived soldiers from the Corps of Invalids and militia from Connecticut and Massachusetts would, in combination with the remaining companies of Cortlandt's regiment, take their places to ensure "perfect security to the Posts."[61]

When Cortlandt's light infantry detachment had marched out on 6 August, the remaining soldiers continued their duties and other activities, which included looting fruit from nearby orchards. There appeared to have been no sense of urgency, for Hawkins got permission to visit friends in Fishkill on the 10th. When he returned the next day, however, he learned that the regiment had marching orders. That day, or the next morning, in the midst of all the activity to gather gear and assemble, a soldier from Colonel Van Schaick's 1st New York was to have been executed, possibly for mutiny, but the gallows went unused. Instead, between 9:00 and 11:00 A.M. on 12 August, Hazen's and Van Schaick's regiments embarked in over thirty bateaux. Weather, wind, and tide were against them. Van Schaick's troops made it only to Peekskill, but Hazen's regiment made it safely to King's Ferry before dark and encamped near Verplanck's Point just as the rain fell harder.[62]

After an uncomfortable night of heavy rain, wind, and waves making a "hideous Noise," the troops struck their wet tents at 9:00 A.M., packed them into the bateaux, and again headed down river. When the tide was in their favor, the weather and wind were not, and when the wind finally shifted, the tide turned. They were, however, able to put up a sail and arrive at the east side of Dobbs Ferry by 2:00 P.M. About an hour later the sun came out, which helped account for the "fine appearance" of the more than twenty bateaux carrying Van Schaick's regiment, which arrived at 6:00.[63]

They awoke on the 14th to sunshine and breezes by which to dry their wet tents and baggage. Situated about a mile above Colonel Elisha Sheldon's dragoons, they saw that there were assorted guards and fortifications on both sides of the Hudson. Before the soldiers could get too comfortable, however, ox or horse teams with wagons arrived around 11:00 A.M. The two regiments then loaded their tents and followed the teams, with Van Schaick's going one way and Hazen's regiment going about two miles to the back of the "Main or Post Road" and encamping in an orchard. The regiment shifted again on the 15th, moving to a small rise "from whence we have a clear Prospect of the two Rivers;

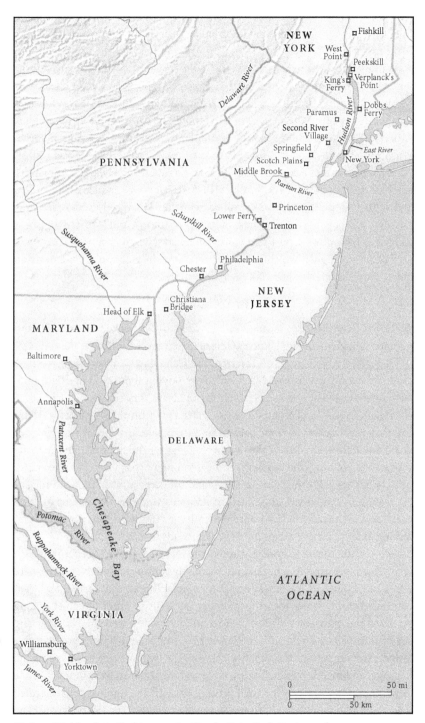

Hudson Highlands to Yorktown, 1781. Map by Erin Greb Cartography

the East River and Part of Long Island to be seen in our Front, and the North River in our Rear."[64]

While those regiments parked themselves near the Main Army, Washington and Rochambeau evaluated intelligence reports in conjunction with Lafayette's reports from Virginia and de Grasse's missive that he was heading for the Chesapeake. They spent the 14th contemplating and debating options. Although Rochambeau vigorously championed an immediate march south, Washington mulled over the available men, matériel, and money as well as what Clinton might have planned for New York. Ultimately, the commander in chief decided to aim south. Once that decision was made, commanders and staffs had to plan the armies' movements to be as speedy and as secret as possible. As they discussed routes, the order of troops, and assorted logistical concerns, Lafayette's report that Cornwallis had gone to ground at Yorktown arrived on 16 August, which not only confirmed the rightness of the decision but also quickened the tempo of the preparations.[65]

To Yorktown

At Dobbs Ferry, as they awaited orders, the troops checked equipment, and perhaps talked about the French soldier hanged on the 17th and the one shot the day after. About noon on the 18th, the Canadian Old Regiment received orders to march at 4:00 P.M., but it ended up moving about 6:00 in a light rain. At 7:00, it arrived at Dobbs Ferry, joining the New York troops that had come with them from West Point days earlier. Hazen's regiment crossed before those troops, with Hawkins ferrying over around 11:00, thankful for the starlight that illuminated the trip. Most of the regimental baggage did not make the opposite shore until 1:00 A.M. the next day, and the riding horses, teams, and oxen not until hours after daybreak. The animals and soldiers marched on, with the latter resting in the houses and barns of Paramus that night so as not to pitch their tents in the rain that had started to fall; wet tents would have meant either halting to let them dry out or much heavier loads to carry.[66]

Shortly after daybreak on 20 August, the regiment moved deeper into New Jersey, passing Paramus Church and eventually coming to Totowa, where there was a one-hour halt for breakfast. They marched to Wesen, rested, and then continued through the sometimes breezy, sometimes sultry day to the "long scattered tho' pleasant Village called Second River" (the Belleville area), where they encamped in a field with the Jersey Line two miles below them. They followed a similar pattern the next day: striking the tents at daybreak, loading the baggage, and marching out. Taking an hour for breakfast, this time at Orange Town in Essex County, they then proceeded until encamping in an elevated field about two miles from Springfield. Once again, the Jersey Line bivouacked about two miles from them.[67] There, on 21 August and until the American and French armies joined them, the regiments carried out their mission of misdirection.

Washington had ordered the advance regiments "to take Post on the heights between Spring field & Chatham & Cover a french Battery at the latter place to veil our real movement & create apprehensions for Staten Island." In the meantime, after a delay over horses, the other forces started to move out on 19 August. The American units crossed first at King's Ferry on the 20th and 21st. Besides the Canadian and New Jersey regiments that were already over, the American forces included Scammell's light infantry, two light companies each from the New York and Connecticut lines, two New York regiments, a Rhode Island regiment, Colonel John Lamb's artillery regiment (2nd Battalion, Continental Artillery), and companies of sappers and miners. The French took until 25 August to complete the crossing. Then the forces split into three columns, with the French taking a route on the right, Lincoln's column taking the Paramus to Springfield route, and the artillery and baggage moving by way of Pompton. They arrived and bivouacked at their assigned juncture points on the 28th and 29th.[68]

As the Main Army entered the Canadian Regiment's neighborhood near Springfield, Hawkins recorded that the "illustrious General, the Commander in Chief paid us a Visit, but his Stay was short." Washington's visit was followed by orders on the 28th to be ready to march by 4:00 the next morning. That wrecked Hawkins's plans to visit the printing office in Chatham; he had been too busy to leave camp, and the orders ensured continued labors.[69]

Washington hoped to keep the enemy guessing for at least one more day about the possibility that he was aiming for Sandy Hook or Staten Island, so he again had the forces move out in three columns. Hazen's regiment was in the middle one with Lamb's artillery, the sappers and miners, and the baggage.[70] Reveille beat at half past two on 29 August, followed by drumming the general for striking tents and loading baggage between three and four, after which the troops marched out. The regiment then waited at the burnt remains of a church at Springfield for the other troops to get under way before falling in at the rear. After a short while, some troops went one way while Hazen's regiment and the artillery took another, passing through Scotch Mains and arriving at Quibble-Town (New Market) about noon. They rested three hours before proceeding, passing through Bound Brook before arriving at and encamping at a field near Middlebrook before dark. At this time, Hawkins, like others, not just the enemy, was wondering about the reason for all of the movement: "Our Destination is kept so secret that our Officers are at a Loss to know where they are going. There are various Conjectures or Opinions, but none that can be relied on; the

Major Part I think seem to be on Opinion that we are bound for the Southern States—but Time will best determine. I wish that all our travelling Manoeuvres had been kept as secret; it would have been much better for America at this Day—as the Enemy would not have known any of our Preparations until they were put in Execution."[71]

Still in the dark, the Canadian Regiment and the artillery roused at half past two again on the 30th, loaded tents and baggage, and before daylight were back on the road for a return to Bound Brook. They took the right-hand road over a bridge and marched up the east side of the Raritan River. Hawkins wondered whether the countermarch was supposed to be a feint or due to ignorance, but then—with a soldier's fortitude—figured it did not matter, for they all marched it anyway. They followed a roundabout route through Somerset and Millstone. There was a three-hour halt for refreshment before moving on to Rocky-Hill, another halt, and then through Princeton as darkness fell before finally coming to a rest a mile and a half down the road to Trenton.[72]

The general beat at daybreak on the 31st, and Hazen's and Lamb's regiments marched through Trenton toward the Lower Ferry, where they halted. Shortly thereafter, Scammell's light corps, Rhode Island and New Jersey troops, part of New York's line, and the sappers and miners passed them to encamp at their front nearer the river. The French forces were behind them toward Trenton. That evening at 6:00, part of the army, including the Canadian Old Regiment, embarked on shallops with artillery and baggage while the wagons and horses continued by land.[73] The 2nd New York got to travel to Christiana Bridge by bateaux, but as there were not enough vessels for the entire army, most of the troops marched to Head of Elk, Maryland. Those on foot participated in the festive parading of American and French troops through Philadelphia on 2 through 4 September. As sailing was quicker, however, Congress's Own missed the festivities.[74]

Hazen's regiment was among the first to embark on the 31st, but the boats did not set sail until daybreak, passing Bordentown, Bristol, and Burlington before approaching Philadelphia at noon on 1 September. A few of the regiment went ashore, Hawkins among them. He delighted in visiting friends and acquaintances again and getting some newspapers "&c. from my Typographical Brethren." Then, with Antill's approval in hand, he tried to get his depreciation note. He called on John Nicholson, a businessman who was one of the auditors handling payments for those belonging to Pennsylvania, including in Hazen's regiment. Nicholson was out, so Hawkins tried the other auditor, the inebriated James Stevenson. Stevenson apologized "with much ado" and much repetition that he could not help for he had not the books. After that wasted effort, Hawkins visited his "old friend" Captain McConnell, who advised him to try

Governor Reed; and so, the sergeant major waited on the governor, who said much the same (but not in the same manner) that Stevenson did. With daylight fading, Hawkins returned to the shallop.[75]

The shallop set sail about three the next morning, dropping anchor about a half hour later two miles from Chester so that a few of the officers and Hawkins, with a soldier or waiter to cook, could step onshore. They were back on board in three hours when the vessel set sail again, this time with the tide, though against the wind. They tacked past Chester and Marcus Hook, the Christiana Creek at sunset, past Wilmington and Newport, finally arriving at Christiana Bridge around midnight. On 3 September, shortly after daybreak, the regiment disembarked, unloaded the shallops, and took the baggage about a mile into the woods, where the regiment encamped with Lamb's artillery on its left.[76]

By the 5th, the first of the marching troops had joined them. The next day, they moved to Head of Elk, where the French arrived on the 8th. The advance parties remained there for transport, but the bulk of the armies marched on to Baltimore or Annapolis to be picked up by various American and French vessels.[77] During the trek south, Antill served as commandant of the Canadian Regiment. Washington and Lincoln had detached Hazen for other duties, including overseeing the transshipment of ordnance and supplies between Christiana Bridge and Head of Elk. While still at the latter on 10 September, Hazen wrote to Washington asking for a brigade command either in the light infantry corps, should it expand to two brigades, or in one that he would form of his and the Rhode Island regiments. If he were to retain just a regimental command, he asked that his light infantry company with Lafayette's corps be returned. Hazen was "anxious to shew in the Honor of this Campaign."[78]

Lincoln had intended to embark with the remaining regiments and stores on the 12th, but Captain Duncan remembered Hazen's regiment pushing off on the 15th. He also recounted the hazards of sailing their assigned flat-bottomed boats down the bay. When they were crossing the mouth of the Rappahannock, "furious wind" and rough seas wrecked masts and sails, but the regiment made it to Williamsburg by 26 September.[79] There, the troops found the American and French forces reforming as their commanders evaluated what they knew of the enemy and the situation around Yorktown.

They were not going to confront Arnold, who was back in New York. The foe was Cornwallis, an able commander who had delivered major blows in the Carolinas against Lincoln and Greene, and had spiked Lafayette's advance forces at the Battle of Green Spring on 6 July. Now the allies had run him to ground at Yorktown. Following instructions from Clinton, Cornwallis had looked for the best spot from which to protect British naval operations and anchorage in the Chesapeake. Portsmouth was too unhealthy and Old Point

Comfort too difficult to fortify, so Cornwallis had decided on Yorktown, where there was housing, hospital, and storage facilities available for the land forces and wharves and warehouses for the navy. The small town was also easier to encompass defensively as it rose from the York River and stood above surrounding land and streams. Cornwallis's engineers used those features in designing the fortifications of ditches, ramparts, and batteries.[80]

Cornwallis did not initially think of a land siege when he occupied Yorktown: he was looking to support the navy and move troops by water. Within Yorktown and Gloucester across the river, Cornwallis had over 8,000 men (excluding sailors) in his combined British, German, and loyalist forces. Disease—especially smallpox—and other factors reduced the number fit to fight, or to build fortifications. Effective strength could have been as low as around 5,000 by 1 October.[81] By that date, Cornwallis was preparing his defenses against the oncoming enemy but hoping that his troops might yet be either evacuated or reinforced.

Washington and Rochambeau were intent on denying him either. When they arrived at Williamsburg on 14 September, Lafayette's forces were already there with their commander despairing about feeding not only the Continentals but also the French troops delivered by Admiral de Grasse from the West Indies. Lieutenant General Claude Anne, marquis de St. Simon had landed his division at Jamestown on 2 September and joined the American troops at Williamsburg on the 8th. Three days later, the "distressed in the extreme" Lafayette wrote to Governor Nelson that he could not sleep because there was "not one grain of flour in camp either for the American or French army." He had just written General Weedon requesting his help in getting some vessels in the Rappahannock loaded with flour and sent down, and he now asked whether Nelson could "issue an order to have it seized, and instantly brought round by water." He reminded the governor how, when it had been close to "disbanding for want of provisions," the army had seized private property in the winter of 1780. Lafayette knew that impressing supplies was unpopular, especially for an army that needed state government and popular support, but the army had to be ready to fight, and to fight it needed to be fed. This pressing request came on top of earlier ones throughout the summer for the loan of levies and militia, Black pioneers and wagoners, horses and sundry other items so that the "poor continentals" would not fall off "for want of spirits and flour."[82]

The poor Continentals did not fall off, for they were reinforced by supplies, more Continentals, as well as militia and French land forces. The combined total was approximately 18,000 men, not counting the thousands of French sailors providing support at sea (and victory at the Battle of the Capes on 5 September). Rochambeau's troops started ashore south of Williamsburg on the 18th, the Americans on the 20th, and more provisions along with artillery shortly thereafter. Not everyone marched to Williamsburg: Some French troops joined the militia under General Weedon near Gloucester to keep watch on the British there.[83] And Congress kept watch in Philadelphia, calling on militia from Delaware, Pennsylvania, and New Jersey to help secure that area in case Clinton took advantage of the Main Army's absence. Its delegates reassured themselves that "Nothing less than a Miracle can save Lord Cornwallis and his Army. So great a Victory will give a finishing Turn to our political Manoeuveres and compel Great Britain to acknowledge our Independence. . . . Great Events will mark the present Year."[84]

There was much to be done, much of it mundane, to ensure a great outcome. Lieutenant William Feltman of the 1st Pennsylvania, who arrived in Williamsburg on 4 September, had to make sure that his soldiers not only performed reconnaissance but also did laundry. He also took time to tour the town, go crabbing, and socialize with other American and French officers, which included being introduced to General Washington on the 14th and to Rochambeau on the 23rd, before all of the "Northern troops" had assembled.[85] Among those northern troops was the regiment still sometimes called Congress's Own, whose members had only a few days to acclimate and wonder with whom they were to serve.

Washington organized his army, which was the right wing of the allied forces, into three divisions on the 24th. Brigadier Generals Wayne and Mordecai Gist commanded the brigades in Steuben's 3rd Division. Brigadier General James Clinton and Colonel Elias Dayton led the brigades in Lincoln's 2nd Division. And Brigadier Generals Muhlenberg and Hazen had the brigades in Lafayette's 1st, or light division. Washington had thus answered both Hazen's wish for a brigade assignment and Lafayette's desire to keep his light infantry corps that had "gone through the fatigues and dangers of the Virginia Campaign."[86] Muhlenberg, who had served with Lafayette during that campaign, received Vose's, Gimat's, and Barber's battalions. That meant that the light infantry detachment with Reid and Pry stayed with Barber instead of returning to the Canadian Old Regiment under Lieutenant-Colonel Commandant Antill in Hazen's brigade.

Washington also assigned Scammell and Hamilton to Hazen's brigade. Scammell protested the assignment, but also acknowledged that it was not the time to transfer him. He did not, unfortunately, have to endure Hazen's command long, for while he was performing reconnaissance on the 30th, the enemy shot him, and he died on 6 October. Washington then divided his regiment into two battalions, one commanded by Lieutenant Colonel Ebenezer Huntington of Connecticut and the other by Lieutenant Colonel John Laurens of South

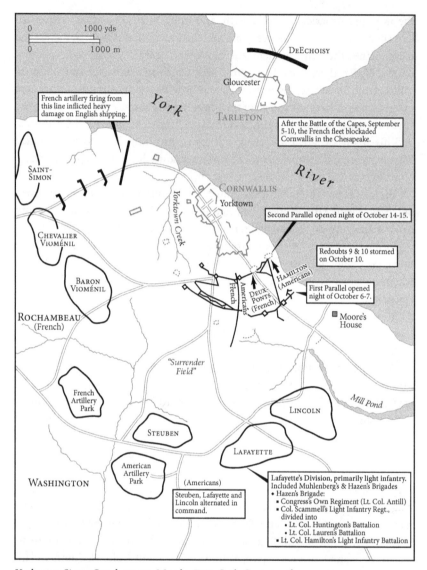

| 0 | 1000 yds |
| 0 | 1000 m |

DeEchoisy

Gloucester

York

French artillery firing from
this line inflicted heavy
damage on English shipping.

TARLETON

After the Battle of the Capes, September
5-10, the French fleet blockaded
Cornwallis in the Chesapeake.

SAINT-
SIMON

River

CORNWALLIS

Yorktown

Yorktown Creek

Second Parallel opened night of October 14-15.

CHEVALIER
VIOMÉNIL

Redoubts 9 & 10 stormed
on October 10.

BARON
VIOMÉNIL

French

Americans

DEUX-
PONTS
(French)

HAMILTON
(Americans)

First Parallel opened
night of October 6-7.

ROCHAMBEAU
(French)

Moore's
House

"Surrender
Field"

French
Artillery
Park

Mill Pond

LINCOLN

STEUBEN

LAFAYETTE

American
Artillery
Park

WASHINGTON

(Americans)

Steuben, Lafayette and
Lincoln alternated in
command.

Lafayette's Division, primarily light infantry.
Included Muhlenberg's & Hazen's Brigades
• Hazen's Brigade:
  • Congress's Own Regiment (Lt. Col. Antill)
  • Col. Scammell's Light Infantry Regt.,
    divided into
    • Lt. Col. Huntington's Battalion
    • Lt. Col. Lauren's Battalion
  • Lt. Col. Hamilton's Light Infantry Battalion

Yorktown Siege, October 1781. Map by Erin Greb Cartography

Carolina. Both Laurens and Hamilton had been Washington's aides-de-camp, knew French, and had strong ties to Lafayette, so one may wonder how much influence the brigade commander had with them—Hazen appears not to have figured in the correspondence of either of those battalion commanders.

Lafayette's division was passing before the enemy's works at Yorktown on 30 September when Hazen's brigade halted, and Muhlenberg's moved forward and sent a picket out to reconnoiter. Major Reid, Hazen's old antagonist, led that picket up close to the enemy's works until a few well-aimed shots obliged the scouts to return.[87] Reconnaissance continued and the making of gabions and fascines for earthworks commenced. As the enemy had abandoned its outer works, the allies moved in with shovels, spades, and pickaxes to start digging trenches and building protective parapets so as to move forward as the engineers laid out the first siege line or parallel.

The backbreaking labor of a siege continued day and night under almost constant cannon fire. A shot ended a too-curious drummer's observations on 2 October, while another took out four of the Canadian Old Regiment's men in a "covering party" on the 3rd. One was Private Robert Smith, whom Captain Duncan mourned as "one of the finest men in the army." Initially, however, Duncan or others often recorded that the enemy's shots were without effect; that is, they did no harm, though they certainly encouraged most people to move through—not over—the trenches and to keep their heads down.[88]

Digging and manning the trenches required maintaining the health and discipline of the forces. Besides keeping the men properly provisioned, Washington ordered the troops to avoid contact with people and items coming out of smallpox-ridden Yorktown. Putrid bodies, dead horses, "offal and other offensive matter" also lay in and around the stinking camp. The adjutant general had to supply parties to bury the decomposing bodies and other matter. As Captain Carlile became an assistant to the adjutant general on 2 October, he may have helped organize such public health measures. Misconduct and insubordination were also offensive and dangerous. Any would-be deserter found within enemy lines was promised an instant hanging. Other offenses meant facing courts-martial. John Dubee (Duba) of Gosselin's company—likely Jean Dubé, who had just transferred from Livingston's regiment—discovered that preparing for a siege did not halt the courts. On 13 October, a court found him guilty of hitting Lieutenant William Torrey and sentenced him to death. Washington approved the sentence.[89]

Although Washington did take the time to attend to such matters, his first priority was enveloping Yorktown. He borrowed from his French allies to establish the regulations by which the divisions would construct the fortified trenches (saps) and put the men on rotations between work in the trenches, guarding the trenches, and constructing the gabions and fascines that fortified the trenches. The trenches were to be relieved every twenty-four hours, and every soldier entering them on duty was to deliver a fascine.[90] That was the lowly routine of the great event, though there were moments of high excitement and drama.

Lafayette's light infantry division had the honor of ceremonially opening the American side of the first parallel on 7 October. After Lafayette inspected

Muhlenberg's and Hazen's brigades, they marched with drums beating and colors flying through the Wormley Creek ravine to their posts within the parallel. They planted their standards on the parapet with at least one of those flags waving *Manus Haec inimica tyrannis* (this hand an enemy to tyrants) at the foe. That was not enough for Hamilton, who ordered his men up top to perform the ordering and grounding of arms. Duncan figured that the only thing that kept the enemy from firing was sheer astonishment.[91]

Such astonishment did not last long. As the allies trundled their artillery pieces into the first parallel and then began the second on the 12th, the barrage of howitzer and cannon shells and shots escalated, with the French and Americans returning the salutes. Lafayette's division took some hits when on duty in the second parallel between noon on the 13th to noon on the 14th. On the first day, a horizontal shell blasted through and killed Captain William White and a private of a Massachusetts's light infantry company. It also hit Private George Lamb, fifty-one, of Pry's company, severely wounding him in the leg. During the night, as they tried to rest at the rear of a battery—a prime target— Duncan's company and others of the Canadian Old Regiment had numerous narrow escapes. Around midnight, one shell hit the center of the trench just two feet from Duncan. He flung himself "on the banques among some arms, and although the explosion was very sudden and the trench as full of men as it could possibly contain, yet not a single man was killed and only two of my own company slightly wounded."[92]

Pry's company suffered five killed and wounded out of the ten casualties in Barber's battalion through that night and the continuing fatigue duties of the morning. Thomas Davis of Carlile's company may have been mortally wounded by a bursting shell then, or possibly when another shell wounded two men on the return to the encampment after the division was relieved. That may have been the incident that Lieutenant Mooers remembered, but he added a fatality: "after reaching camp, found on my pantaloons, scattered entirely over them, the blood and brains of the soldier killed."[93]

Duncan and his friends Captain Hughes and Dr. Anderson all counted their survival of the midnight shelling a "miraculous escape." That might have impelled Hughes to give more thought to leaving the regiment, though he did not fear shells so much as he despised Hazen. Hughes, from Maryland, had been one of the officers who signed a grievance against Hazen in September 1780. Then the following March, after Hazen combined his company with Satterlee's, Hughes complained about Hazen to General Smallwood, said he planned to resign, and inquired if he could serve Smallwood as a volunteer aide. Smallwood asked Washington in August about indulging the "Young Gentleman of Family and Merit." Washington replied that Hughes did not have sufficient reason to resign, even less since Hazen had been promoted and was "not immediately connected" with the regiment.[94] So Hughes was bombarded with the regiment at Yorktown.

Hughes was probably at the back of Lafayette's division with most of the Canadian Old Regiment on the evening of the 14th. The regiment, like the rest of the division, had not had much time to eat and rest before being ordered back to the trenches. The allies needed to take redoubts 9 and 10 so as to complete the second parallel and bear down on the enemy. At 7:00 A.M., the French attacked redoubt 9 and Hamilton led the American attack on 10. The vanguard from Lieutenant Colonel Gimat's battalion of Muhlenberg's brigade and Hamilton's battalion (under Major Nicholas Fish) of Hazen's brigade had the right, while those from Laurens's battalion took the left so as to go around the redoubt and attack from its rear. Barber's battalion, which still included the light infantry detachment from Hazen's regiment, was at the front of the supporting column and arrived at the redoubt as the first troops went over the works and pushed after them. The remainder of Muhlenberg's and then Hazen's brigades followed in reserve.[95]

Lafayette enthusiastically seconded Hamilton's praise of the vanguard's swift assault, adding that "the remainder of the Column under Generals Muhlenberg and Hazen advanced with admirable firmness and discipline." He commended the troops "that under the fire of the enemy" acted "with perfect silence and order." The assault may have begun with stealth, but the enemy beyond the redoubts soon responded with "a fire of cannon, grape shot, shell and musketry."[96] The Continentals lost men but continued to move forward.

About sixty veterans from Congress's Own mentioned being at Yorktown in later pension accounts. Five of the applications—for William Calder, Isaac Chace, James Heaton, Jonathan Pratt (a rejected widow's petition), and Adam Sybert—specified attacking or assisting in the storming of a redoubt. Heaton, likely of Pry's company, was wounded in the leg during the assault. Sybert, wounded in both legs by two musket balls, applied for a disability pension. Merifield Victor did not specify the redoubt assault when he deposed that he was wounded in the arm and shoulder "from the sword of the enemy, which occasioned a partial disability." Nor did Edward Clark of Pry's company specify when a shell wounded him in the leg. Both Colin McLachlan and Zachariah Sherwood said that they had been wounded at Yorktown, but neither mentioned exactly how.[97] Nor does a return of the killed and wounded mention exactly when and how Captain Gosselin was wounded sometime between the opening of the second parallel on 11 October and the 14th.[98]

Even as the direct assaults ended, barrages and labors continued. Although Lafayette's division had just finished trench duty before the assault, some of his troops joined those in Steuben's division who immediately set to work on a trench linking redoubts 9 and 10 and another to serve as a communicating trench between the two parallels. By the next day, the allied forces were moving artillery platforms from the first to the second parallel and firing on the enemy from there. Lafayette's division was back in the trenches when, shortly after 10:00 A.M. on the 16th, Cornwallis sent a flag of truce. Negotiations led to a cease-fire, and by the 18th, the troops were using the parapets more as viewing stands than protective earthworks.[99]

On the 19th, visitors and camp followers were on the parapets, while the troops were in formation on the borderland between allied and enemy camps that had become the surrender field. The next day, Hazen's brigade paraded again at its own encampment before assuming post-siege duties. The assignments included guard and fatigue parties in Yorktown and, after all the labor in erecting them, leveling the earthworks. Some of the men also undoubtedly were assigned to the continuing burial of the dead, human and animal. Perhaps Private Dubé had that duty upon his return to the regiment? Washington, in congratulating the army on the 20th and desiring "to diffuse the general Joy" of victory, had pardoned soldiers in confinement and ordered them back to their corps. Washington was not so forgiving of the deserters found bearing arms with the enemy, who were sentenced to be hanged by the neck until dead.[100]

As the divisions cleared the grounds, Washington started planning for operations elsewhere, which included dissolving divisions and disbanding brigades. As Major James McHenry, an aide-de-camp to Lafayette, wrote to Governor Thomas Sim Lee of Maryland, "The capture of Lord Cornwallis has finished our war in Virginia. The army is folding up its tents." Lafayette bid his division farewell at the end of October before heading to Philadelphia and then on to France to encourage more aid.[101]

In late November, General Lincoln, commanding a temporary division of troops heading northward, gave Hazen a transitory brigade of Jeremiah Olney's Rhode Island battalion and the Canadian and two New Jersey regiments to lead to their respective assignments. Lincoln, as he mulled his appointment as secretary at war, also redistributed the light companies that had been part of Lafayette's corps. Some, including the light company from Hazen's regiment, were to wait at Head of Elk until their corps arrived so that they could join them on the trek to their posts. Pry's light company was slightly delayed. Smallpox had killed the pilot of the schooner transporting it up the Chesapeake and resulted in a landing at the nearest harbor on the Eastern Shore. Then the company, with Lieutenant Stuart in charge, marched for Dover. As some of the men were lame and others ill-clothed for winter, Stuart found a vessel to take the men and baggage to Philadelphia. Unfortunately, an enemy cruiser pulled them over and plundered the baggage, including Pry's portmanteau. Pry's list of losses showed how much better clothed he had been than the soldiers: he lost both worn and new stockings, shirts (ruffled), stocks, jackets, breeches, and handkerchiefs, along with cloth to make new items. He also lost a regimental coat, a silver epaulet, bedding, and camp furniture.[102]

Hazen's regiment, once reassembled, was initially directed to return to New York. General Heath wanted Hazen to take command of the northern district in lieu of the ailing General Stark, but then Washington diverted Hazen to Pennsylvania. The regiment was to guard prisoners at Lancaster.[103]

It had been a year of great events, but the war was not over, nor the challenges to the Canadian Old Regiment. As the light infantry detachment reunited with the regiment, Major Reid applied to Washington for a leave of absence. As Hazen and Antill had put in their requests first—and there had to be enough field officers to superintend at Lancaster—Washington would grant only a short leave that would have Reid return before the colonels left on theirs. The officers had had to put aside their issues during the campaign, but the schism remained. Captain Hughes, however, did not stay; he resigned. Private Dubé did not have that option, and he continued with the regiment until discharged in 1783.[104] Although some members left the regimental community during 1782, others joined it as the army kept watch and Congress debated domestic and diplomatic dilemmas.

CONTINENTALS TO VETERANS

The Continental Army and Congress's Own Regiment were defined as much or more by their members and what happened before, between, and after battles as by those battles. The Continentals distinguished both army and regiment with their tales of camp life and strife, scars of combat, and marks of valor. Many found, however, that although they had helped ensure American independence, establishing personal independency was another prolonged battle. Transitioning from martial to civilian communities, from military service to self-sufficiency, was often as difficult as constructing siege works, and with no guarantee of even an extra ration of rum, much less success. The Continentals foresaw the challenges in the final years of their service and tried to forestall them by pushing for state and national recognition and recompense before they left the disbanding army in 1783, but their campaigns for personal independency moved in fits and starts over decades.

The War for Independence did not conclude at Yorktown in October 1781, for British forces still occupied American territory, the French navy remained in action, and numerous raids and skirmishes, often by militia, continued on land. The independence of the nation had yet to be confirmed by treaty with Britain, and persons and property still had to be secured. In that period between active war, confirmation of peace, and the discharge of the Continentals in late 1783, the army remained a contested space, and compensation for its members a contested proposition. The Continental Army had become a "regular" army but not a standing one: it was not to continue as a fully manned and operational force in peacetime. Trying to stand it down, however, launched new debates over the ad hoc measures that had been passed to retain and regularize the force. Congress and the states would have much preferred to have discharged the army as they did militias, but they had made some promises that had connected welfare to warfare in recognition of service; not keeping them would hurt the character and credit of the nation.[1] As Congress debated the nation's commitments, the Continentals remained on guard.

When Hazen's Canadian Old Regiment, Congress's Own, marched from Yorktown, Virginia, to Lancaster, Pennsylvania, in late 1781, its members moved from the intensity of a siege and the exhilaration of victory to the routine duties of guarding prisoners and sentry patrols. Old and new challenges, however, disturbed the wait-and-watch period. Although enlistments and training kept the regiment manned and ready for possible new operations, many of the newcomers reinforced its alien and stateless status. Recruitment among prisoners and reprisal against one—Captain Charles Asgill—also placed the regiment in the midst of controversy. Against the broader issues of retaliation debated in that case were some personal ones within Congress's Own, as lingering resentments dogged the regiment into its final encampments. Yet even as some members continued to crack the community that they had constructed in the first years of the war, others continued to value the connections. Even as members negotiated loyalties, the regiment as a whole persevered in its duties until dismissed, showing the worthy "tenor of behavior" that General Washington declared had distinguished the army and its detachments.[2]

Internal and external challenges had partially dismembered the community, and contestations over the regiment's identity had marred its sense of union. Congress's initial attempt to disown the regiment by denying it its name had not helped. Identifying it as Canadian gratified some members but alienated others. Finally, it carried the name of a contentious commander who estranged still others. Yet living, not just fighting, the war had twined connecting threads. As factions formed and split, they were not the identical constituencies that had initially joined the regiment. There were similarities, yes, but there had been movement in and out of the companies and, by extension, the original groups that had formed them. Group alterations went hand-in-hand with adaptations by persons. Naturalization, if not full accommodation and toleration, also marked this regiment's contested borderland identity, which continued as the founding, core constituency marched almost full circle to settle near where its members began the war. The veterans there and elsewhere had a shared history, and they all remained connected by their regimental experiences and with Congress through its recurrent establishment of the regiment and then later veterans' legislation. The regiment disbanded and its members dispersed, but the veterans showed in accounts decades later that they were still Congress's Own Continentals.

Constabulary Duties

Commissioned, enlisted, and attached members of Congress's Own attended to their cracked community and personal interests as they performed constabulary duties at Lancaster. Paradoxically perhaps, given their own fights and insecurities, their task was to police prisoners and support local security and stability while delegates and diplomats worked out the international ramifications of independence. The regiment's duties straddled warfighting and peacekeeping, for as they managed the latter, they still had to "perfect" their "Discipline & Exercise" and be ready to march.[3]

Washington drafted plans for another campaign but had to defer them pending the availability of the French navy and actions on the political front. Hazen, however, did not want to defer yet again what he desired and contended that most Canadians would welcome. He did not want the war to end without Congress and the army achieving one of the initial goals: the incorporation of Canada. In his long rationale for invasion that March, Hazen argued that a force of light troops, which he volunteered to lead, moving rapidly by way of Coos, could contain the enemy in their posts and provide the Canadians with the time they needed to form their own government and prepare to support the follow-up American forces in securing the region. He advocated sending some French troops to convince any Canadians "Ignorant" of the Franco-American alliance and said that no navy aid was necessary beyond transporting some artillery. He averred, "It is a Plan that I am willing to live or Die by," and should his or any other plan be adopted for Canada, he wished "the most Difficult and Dangerous part may fall" to him. Washington deftly delayed: he asked for more information. Within two weeks, Hazen answered his commander's questions, addressed his reservations, and added that annexing Canada would eliminate the expense of guarding the border.[4]

Washington tabled the invasion proposal, but assured Hazen that there was no intention of keeping the regiment on its present guard duty beyond the opening of a campaign. As that did not occur, the regiment remained in Lancaster through October, doing the "Disagreable Duty of guarding Disarmed men." There were about 1,400 prisoners at Lancaster and hundreds more at York, and not all were confined to barracks; many, primarily the Germans, had permission to work in the surrounding area. The movement of prisoners, some laboring and others escaping, required numerous patrols. State and local authorities could not handle the demands and secure the prisoners, so Hazen's regiment remained in place.[5]

As local farmers hired or indentured some prisoners, Hazen's regiment recruited others. At least one was a repeater. Jacob Horn had probably marched from Yorktown to Lancaster as a prisoner of war with a lump of déjà vu and dread in his stomach, for he was also a deserter who had seen what had happened to others after the siege. Horn may have escaped discovery at Yorktown by being German. Taken prisoner at Bennington in August 1777, Horn had enlisted in "the Congress regiment" in June 1778, only to "leave" that service after nine months to return to the British army. Immediately upon his arrival at Lancaster, he heard that Washington had issued a general pardon (what his comrade Jesse Blakeslee recalled as "Lady Washington's proclamation") to deserters in the enemy's service who returned to their regiments and duty. Horn accepted and continued with the regiment until discharged in 1783, as did two other Horns, Christian and Frederick, who enlisted in the fall of 1782. There was no indication that they were related. Christian likely was recruited from among the prisoners, and Frederick definitely was—he had been taken prisoner at Saratoga in October 1777, transported to Virginia with the Convention Army, and then moved north to Pennsylvania. It is possible that he met his future wife, Anna Maria (Mary), while laboring as a prisoner in Berks County, which might also have been an incentive to enlist.[6]

Hazen was not able to find servants from among the German prisoners for General Henry Knox as requested, but his officers successfully found soldiers. Although recruiting among prisoners was controversial—raising questions of ethics and trust—the practice and results reflected the Board of War's observations as well as financial and political pressures. In November 1781, the board had recommended strict confinement for "British troops whose attachments to service are not to be conquered," or at least hutting them under guard in safe parts of the country. But the board thought that German and "Scotch" prisoners were less inclined to "desert" and that the Germans could safely "be let out to work," and thereby pay for their upkeep. The latter became more pressing with the increased number of prisoners after Yorktown.[7] The year 1782 was the regiment's third most fruitful in recruiting, after 1777 and 1776. The prime months were September (with 84–86 enlistees) and October (with 69–74), with the year's total between 270 and the mid-280s. Over a third of the new soldiers carried German names, but given misspellings and anglicization, there were likely more. A few were transfers from Captain Selin's independent company; others were probably drawn from the local, heavily German region. Under 20 percent of the new recruits with Germanic names deserted, whereas more than a quarter of the others did. Nonetheless, the regiment entered 1783 at a greater strength than it had been in years, and even more ethnically diverse.[8]

Hazen was lenient with paroled officers, issuing passes for them to go to New York with multiple soldier-servants (until Washington and Secretary at War Lincoln ordered a halt in early October), but resolute about apprehending his own and other deserters and prisoners escaping into the countryside and, especially, trying to reach British lines.[9] The task was made more difficult by a network of sympathizers who aided the fugitives. Congress tried to counter the increasing number of escapees by offering rewards; it promised eight dollars and reimbursement for expenses to anyone seizing a "prisoner of war belonging to the British army" who had escaped from confinement. It also asked the states to exempt those who apprehended escapees from "a tour of militia duty." Those rewards were not enough, however, so the regiment continued to collect and confine prisoners. Hazen did more than send out patrols—he had men infiltrate the fugitive network so as to nab collaborators as well as escapees. Ironically, others on the lookout for fugitives arrested Captain Lee, "who, in disguise with three British soldiers, began their route from Martin Myers's [Lancaster area], and continued it from stage to stage, undiscovered, until they reached Bucks county," where a justice of the peace had them seized and "carried in irons to Philadelphia." Lincoln, who knew about the operation, released Lee. The writer from Lancaster regretted the mission's ending, for he was appalled that people (he blamed Mennonites) had been helping convey the fugitives to New York for over two years. Hazen's reward was compliments and thanks for reducing escapes and establishing more order.[10] It was a nice reversal from the hard feelings over the street fights and the Minyier affair in 1777.

As commandant of prisoners at Lancaster, Hazen ended up in the middle of a particularly sensitive case that tested both the Continental Army's and Congress's ethics. On 12 April 1782, the Associated Loyalists in New Jersey hanged militia and privateer captain Joshua "Jack" Huddy in revenge for the killing of one of their own. Outraged New Jersey militiamen and others demanded that the army take action or they would. Local partisan fighting thereby embroiled the American and British armies, for Washington asked British generals Henry Clinton, then Guy Carleton, to hand over loyalist Captain Richard Lippincott, who conducted the hanging, or see that he was brought to justice. A British court-martial acquitted Lippincott of murder in June. In the meantime, angry about actions contrary to the conventions of war, Washington authorized an act of reprisal, which Congress supported: he ordered Hazen to choose by lottery a British captain or lieutenant "who is an unconditional Prisoner" (that is, not under a surrender agreement's conditions) to be executed.[11]

Over the following months, officers and delegates debated the ethics of retaliation, especially given the prospects of the war ending. They worried that they would be accused of vengeance, rather than legal retaliation. The former was to inflict unacceptable injury even if declared to be punishment for harm done, whereas the latter could be a legitimate response to deliberate provocation if the intent was to prevent or deter other such offenses. But even if the latter, was this the right act at the right time? Was this a good way to conclude the war, which, according to James Duane in Congress, had been conducted by Americans "with the Humanity which a benevolent Religion, civilized manners, and true military Hounour inspire." Alexander Hamilton and Henry Knox also worried about the timing and circumstances and how retaliation would reflect on the character of the nation and the commander in chief.[12] Washington shared those sentiments; while he had to act, he was also willing to delay and accept alternatives.

An initial alternative, which Washington was not happy about, was having to choose among officers who were not "unconditional." When it appeared that the army had no appropriate prisoners, he ordered Hazen to proceed with the captains "who are prisoners either under Capitulation [Yorktown] or Convention [Saratoga]." Captain Asgill was the unfortunate one chosen by a lottery on 27 May. Only after the lottery did Hazen learn that there were two possible "unconditional" choices: one was an ensign of the South Carolina Rangers at Winchester, Virginia, and another was Lieutenant Thompkins Hilgrove Turner of the 3rd Foot Guards at York. At that news, Washington wanted Asgill put on hold and Turner sent to Philadelphia.[13]

The alternatives were not viable, so there was no switch and the debates over executing Asgill continued. By the end of October, one faction in Congress was arguing that new events had rendered retaliation unnecessary and unwise— namely, promises by General Carleton to abolish the Associated Loyalists board that had authorized Huddy's execution, and the ongoing diplomatic negotiations. Another faction, however, argued that should Washington and Congress not follow through on their resolves, it would stain their character, and furthermore, that showing weakness would not protect others. But word of the preliminary articles of peace, a plea from Asgill's mother for her son's life, and a recommendation from the French foreign minister changed the situation dramatically. On 7 November, Congress authorized Washington to free Asgill, though the next day it drafted a declaration that the commander in chief and the commander of the Southern Army were authorized to demand satisfaction should the enemy commit acts of "cruelty or violence contrary to the laws or usage of war," and then effect "suitable retaliation" if no satisfaction was forthcoming.[14]

People critiqued the case then and later in accounts that touched on the honor of those involved. Washington, dismayed to hear in 1786 that Asgill, among others, had criticized his conduct, countered calumnies with his own remembrances. Asgill combatted explanations of Washington's "*humane procrastination*" with one of Carleton's "*judicious conduct.*" Hazen did not figure much in Asgill's chronicle, but apparently did in other narratives. When

Benjamin Mooers decades later read an English journal article about the Asgill affair, he felt that he had to correct inaccuracies about Hazen's part in it, starting with the point that the general's name was Hazen, not Hogan. Mooers averred that Hazen "was too honorable a soldier to transcend his duty, and too much a gentleman and man of feeling to use unnecessary severity, even in language, to those whom fortune of war had placed in his power." Besides objecting to some of the statements that the article's author attributed to Hazen, he rebutted the contention that Hazen had immediately sent off Asgill after the lottery. That dramatic license ignored the intervening overnight hours. Mooers said that not only had Hazen granted the captain time to get his affairs in order, he concluded that Hazen was a "highly meritorious officer and patriot—one who served his country with fidelity and courage, and who was as humane as he was brave."[15]

Major James Reid might have raised objections to that description as he did to some of Hazen's and other officers' actions during the war. They returned the disfavor. On the very day that Hazen conducted the lottery that resulted in Asgill's selection, he arrested Reid. Hazen had received word confirming Major Tarlton Woodson's resignation, which meant that the regiment was down to two majors, Reid and Joseph Torrey. He wrote to Washington that keeping Reid was not going to work because twenty-four officers would not do duty with him; he demanded that Reid be court-martialed, recounting how the current grievances were founded on old ones that had been put aside during the Yorktown campaign. The dispute had remained in hiatus while Reid was on furlough and then "sick present," thus not on duty. Hazen said that Reid then asked him for help in restoring "Harmony, and promoting Unanimity amongst the Officers." The complainants, however, insisted on a public hearing to clear their characters of the "Epithets of Thieves, Robbers and every Thing that is infamous and dishonourable" that Reid had publicly intimated when defending himself in his 1780–81 court-martial. Reid's answer was so be it: he was not going to answer them as they wished, so arrest him and let there be a trial. It took a while to establish the general court that the grievants wanted, but in the meantime, Hazen supported the others in their complaints and advocated promoting Olivie and Satterlee to major.[16] Reid protested to Washington about being tried at the request of Hazen's "party" and how Hazen wanted him to resign. In December, he added that when Hazen gave him a furlough in November, Hazen did not tell him about the regiment's move from Lancaster to Pompton, New Jersey, and thus he had to hurry on his own to get there and find quarters. He asked for a trial as soon as possible.[17] Between arrest and furloughs, Reid had not performed duty for a year.

A general court-martial at New Windsor on 30 December addressed the charges of "disobedience of Orders, unmilitary Conduct and behaving unbecoming the Character of an officer and Gentleman." Although the feud was purportedly about character assassination, the accusations ran the gamut from disobedience to making false musters and returns and embezzlement or misapplying funds. The court acquitted Reid of all charges except misattribution on a regimental account, and that one they thought so "trifling and that it so strongly marks the nature of the whole prosecution against him, that they think it proper to pass no censure on him." Washington confirmed the court's opinion and released Reid from arrest on 21 February 1783.[18]

Reid responded that it would be hard to leave the army that had "effected a glorious revolution" before war's end, but an earlier retirement appeared prudent. He acknowledged that he "unhappily got into a current of ill fortune, and have been twice in arrest and as often embroiled in difficulties which is generally the characteristic of a bad man," but Reid was happy that Washington was fully aware of the circumstances and that he had the friendship of other officers "of distinguished merit." Reid asked for and eventually received a furlough to put some of his affairs in order.[19]

Neither the acquittal nor furlough were acceptable to what Reid called "the artful and very powerfull combination long since formed against me." Hazen wrote to Washington on 31 March that all of the regiment's officers at Pompton, with the exception of Captain Pry, "still continue firm in thinking themselves much injured, and particularly unfortunate." They requested a "Public Investigation of their Conduct" upon the charges that Reid had made, and they wanted Reid back for that. Washington authorized a court of inquiry, which met in May, to determine whether to proceed with another court-martial. Reid objected to the legality of the inquiry and continued to refuse to charge any of the officers with the offenses to which he had earlier alluded at his court martial in January 1781, thus denying them the opportunity to defend themselves before a court.[20]

The officers claimed that they did not desire to "persecute" Reid, as he and others in the army declared. They wanted a public apology that would put them "on the Ground we stood before he made the vile Attempt to injure us." Washington regretted that the previous measures had failed to give Hazen and "the complaining Officers" satisfaction, but nonetheless indicated that the inquiry was at end. They, however, returned on 6 June with a new set of complaints against Reid, including charges of infamous conduct at Germantown on 4 October 1777 and Yorktown on 14 October 1781, as well as improper behavior in his prejudicial statements that dishonored the "Corps of Officers to which he belongs" and the American army. They added breaking arrest after Hazen ordered him confined to quarters on the basis of the new charges. Reid explained that he had Washington's permission to go home and, furthermore, based on Congress's 26 May resolution, he had a furlough, "which makes me eventually a citizen [civilian]."[21]

Washington confirmed that Reid had obtained his permission to go home because of the congressional resolution, but also said that he would deliberate on the officers' request for another review. He then provided questions to a board of general officers that met at Newburgh, New York, on 24 June. The board answered that all proper measures had been pursued in the case of Hazen et al. versus Reid; that Reid should not be prosecuted for alleged infamous conduct at Germantown and Yorktown because of the time elapsed; that he should not be arrested for the prejudicial statements because the charges were too broad; and finally, that he should not be charged for breaking arrest because of the "particular circumstances." Washington informed Hazen that "altho' the new subjects of complaint . . . appeared to me to arise rather from a spirit of persecution, than a desire to promote Service," he had sanctioned a review. He provided the results and stated his "sincere hope, that you will consider this as finishing an affair that has given so much trouble to the Army."[22] That was not just a hope; that was an order. Washington was dealing with other unrest in the army, initiating its dispersal, and keeping a wary eye on enemy forces in New York. He had no more time or patience to reconcile Hazen's regiment.

Regimental members were going to break camp without the matters fully resolved but with significant issues substantially revealed. One was that they had shared a desire to belong to a distinguished regiment, but disagreed—sometimes passionately—about what that would look like and how it was to be achieved. Another was that the officers who wanted to belong within this regimental community had tried to resolve their problems within the army's still-developing judicial system. Those who did not or could not, left (an option more for officers than soldiers). What had begun as groups striving for support had become factions fighting against each other. Frustration against congressional actions or inactions and army directives had been redirected into aggression against groups within the regiment. By war's end, there were two parties distinguished by regional, cultural, or personal ties, and other persons—Edward Antill, Anthony Selin, Thomas Thompson, and Zacheus Peaslee among them—trying to remain neutral.[23]

Hazen had informed Washington in May 1782 that two dozen officers refused to do duty with Reid. In May 1783, seventeen officers, including Hazen, signed a memorial against Reid, and nineteen did so in a follow-up that June. They included Hazen's young relations, Mooers and Moses White, but not Peaslee, and all of the remaining Connecticut and Canadian officers except Antill. Antill had requested retirement in 1782, which Secretary Lincoln had supported, yet Antill appears to have had temporary command of the regiment in April through May 1783, while Hazen was away on other matters. At that time, Antill reported that the regiment had sixteen other officers at Pompton—one major, four captains, seven lieutenants, two ensigns, and one surgeon. Surgeon Nicholas Schuyler did not sign the grievances against Reid, nor did Lieutenant William Stuart, who was trying to fend off a civil suit in New Jersey. In addition to Stuart, most of the remaining officers who had signed the September 1780 petition with Reid about reforming the regiment did not sign the grievances. They were the mid-Atlantic contingent. Many of those had transferred or retired, so that group, which included John Carlile, Thomas Pry, and James Duncan, was small. In Duncan's case, he was probably also still angry about his assignment to the dilapidated blockhouse at Sidman's Clove over the winter, and his loss of a company command when Hazen had reduced and redistributed companies (giving a francophone one to Gosselin and one with many German speakers to Selin). Richard Lloyd of New Jersey, however, did switch sides to sign the grievance against Reid.[24]

Professional and group concerns had become personal grudges as arguments over issues devolved into ad hominem attacks. Those attacks revealed the sensitivities of each side. Whereas Reid and his adherents averred persecution by Hazen as he favored his partisans, members of the other side had had enough of the prejudices and abuse they believed they had faced. They did not like the "infernal" label unless it complimented their fighting prowess. And they did not appreciate being deemed inconvenient. That became more evident as they shifted from the Reid fight to struggles with congressional and state authorities for recognition and recompense for their service and sacrifice.

The many layers to the lengthy dispute between Hazen and Reid, and the associated factions, showed how faults or shortcomings in the regimental community had widened into substantial cracks since the 1779 Coos Country expedition and the disputes in New Jersey in 1780. Personal dynamics account for some of the slippage, but another factor was that the cultural and social exchange initiated at the establishment of this military borderland had not had enough support—and perhaps not enough time—to create a fully integrated community. The result was a fractured community and yet still disciplined regiment when Congress authorized furloughs as a step to disbanding the army. By various accommodations, Congress's Own had recruited a regiment and forged a "continental" community through 1779, but the pressures of the continuing war, including insufficient and inequitable provisioning by the states in and out of Congress, had stressed some budding social bonds to breaking. The weak national union had undermined regimental unity, and thus the factious regimental community reflected the still-developing national one.

Transitional Transactions

On 19 April 1783, eight years after the war began at Lexington and Concord, Thomas Paine exulted that "'the times that tried men's souls' are over." Yet, he amended, "to pass from the extremes of danger to safety—from the tumult of war to the tranquillity of peace . . . requires a gradual composure of the senses to receive it." In his last "American Crisis" essay, he urged the revolutionaries to recall their fortitude and resolve against mounting difficulties and to see that the nation's strength was in union, not numbers. Paine proclaimed, "citizenship in the United States is our national character," whereas citizenship in a state is but a "local distinction."[25] In peace as in war, however, the Continentals had to contend with the distinctions, even discrimination, as they endeavored to settle into civilian life as American veterans while federal and state governments continued to figure out the attendant costs of armed forces.

Similar to the Canadians within the army, all of the veterans sometimes felt like they were treated as aliens within the nation. Washington acknowledged as much to his civilian and military audiences in his farewell to the army in November 1783. He asked who would exclude those who had given so much to ensure the nation's independence "from the rights of Citizens and the fruits of their labours"? In turn, in order "to remove the prejudices" that some of the "good People of the States" may hold, he recommended that the troops carry "strong attachments to the Union" and "conciliating dispositions" as they returned to civil society. He asked that they prove no "less virtuous and usefull as Citizens, than they have been persevering and victorious as Soldiers."[26]

The transition from shared struggles in the military to sharing challenges within networks of veterans started well before the war ended. It began with negotiations for postwar financial settlements, persisted against uproars over pensions by states and Congress, and continued spasmodically through both retreats and advances in implementing remuneration. A shared concern of Continentals during and after the war was how to translate national independence into personal independency, but they faced "popular ferment" over bonuses, and even "public rage" over inequities in those bonuses and the possibility of pensions. Opponents suspected that pensions, along with officers creating the Society of the Cincinnati, were steps to establishing oligarchic despotism, whereas the officers contended that they simply wanted recompense and "to perpetuate the memory of the revolution, the friendship of the officers, and the union of the states."[27]

Washington had warned Secretary at War Lincoln in October 1782 about widespread "discontents" in the army, including those of officers still complaining about promotion stoppages and lack of pay. That was certainly true of

Hazen. He had submitted yet another lengthy petition in June 1783 delineating why he should be a brigadier not just by brevet but of the line, with appropriate compensation. Although Massachusetts-born, he presented himself as a foreigner who had hazarded—and lost—everything to support the United States. As he made his case, he also tried to hasten promotions for Joseph Torrey to lieutenant colonel and Laurent Olivie and William Satterlee to major, which Adjutant General Edward Hand questioned and Washington suspended.[28]

Hazen and his regiment's members exemplify the officers and soldiers that Washington said were "goaded by a thousand stings of reflexion on the past, & of anticipation on the future, about to be turned into the World, soured by penury & what they call the ingratitude of the Public." Washington believed there would be no "Acts of Outrage" by servicemembers when the army was in the field, but worried about possible eruptions in winter quarters.[29] The Continentals wanted what was due them, and they required the funds not just as recognition of service but also to cover immediate expenses once the army was no longer paying and rationing them and, if any remained, as seed money for their futures.

The need for recompense led some officers at Newburgh in March 1783 to threaten action against Congress. Washington quashed their protest with appeals for forbearance, recognition of their patriotism and honor, and his pledge to serve them in the matter. He kept that pledge by openly arguing that the public character of the United States would suffer if it was "faithless" to "those who have lent their money, given their personal Services, and spilt their Blood; and who are now returning home poor and pennyless." He also authorized publication of some of his papers to document "the justice, oeconomy, and even the necessity" that Congress had been under to promise half-pay pensions earlier, and now to substitute a lump-sum payment so as to serve immediate personal and public interests.[30]

Congress's 1776 promise had been half pay for officers and enlisted men disabled by their service, with such pay to last only so long as the disability prevented them from earning a living. As amended in 1778, the promise became seven years' half pay to the officers and eighty dollars to the soldiers who served to war's end. Congress amended the promise again in October 1780 when it resolved to provide officers half pay for life, but in March 1783, juggling some states' opposition and officers' petitions, it ordered the pension to be commuted to five years' full pay. The certificates for that payment were to bear 6 percent annual interest.[31]

On 22 March, after hearing Washington's report on the Newburgh crisis, Congress approved the commutation. In turn, on 4 July, it authorized the paymaster general to settle "all accounts whatsoever between the United States and the officers and soldiers of the American Army," and deliver certificates guaranteeing payment of what was due. There was, however, to be a delay on reimbursements until the paymaster had returns of all payments and advances by the states or public departments, for the settlements were to cover only that which remained unpaid by war's end.[32]

Starting that July, and with most delivered by September 1785, John Pierce, paymaster general and commissioner of army accounts, eventually delivered "over 93,000 certificates showing the indebtedness of the Government to each person." Some veterans received more than one certificate, as each covered a different category of debt: for arrears in monthly pay, to account for currency depreciation, and for the commutation payouts on Congress's earlier promises.[33]

The officers welcomed having five years' pay—or its promise—in hand, but some later rethought the trade's value. Moses White returned his commutation certificates in 1787 so as to qualify for a half-pay invalid's pension in accordance with a 1785 resolution.[34] A few of his brother officers applied for other pensions decades later. William Torrey requested one in 1818, when Congress granted them to officers and soldiers if they had served in the Continental Army, Navy, or Marines for at least nine months or until the end of the war. William Irving of the Department of Interior's Pension Office vouched that Torrey's "life has been a tissue of misfortunes and he never could be called rich and very rarely well off." Yet when too many veterans applied, Congress amended the act to provide only for those who demonstrated destitution. Torrey applied again in 1828, after Congress allowed pensions for those who had been eligible for benefits under the old 1778 resolution. Mooers, who did not have the need that Torrey did, also applied, as did Noah Lee. Following the application procedure, they all acknowledged that they had received their commutation certificates, but pointed out that the sum had been in lieu of the half pay for life to which they had been entitled under the October 1780 resolution.[35] The implication was that this was a way by which Congress was honoring the earlier promise. But all of that was yet to come, for as it worked out long-term financial issues against the immediate ones of continuing to pay and ration the army while awaiting the peace treaty, Congress decided to furlough the troops enlisted for the war while keeping the three-year enlistees on watch in the Hudson Highlands.

Washington made the furlough-to-discharge announcement on 2 June 1783. Regimental commanders were to make their final returns, divide their commands into those who were to go and those who were to stay, and ensure enough officers to supervise marches home or remaining duties. Responses mixed eagerness and hesitation. As Hazen informed Washington, those men who did not belong to a state, and who had no connections or place to return to, preferred to stay in service until provisions were made for them. Indeed, although most of the regiment wanted to leave, not one "amongst the whole" wanted to go "on Furlough or otherwise until he is paid up as far as the other Parts of the Army." Lincoln had figured that the Canadians would be distressed by the furloughs, "as they have no Homes to which they can retire." New Yorkers awaiting British evacuation of the city had a similar problem. Lincoln thus believed that it would not be much of an additional expense to allow these soldiers "to take the places of the three Years men." Washington was ahead of them both, for he had already permitted such substitutions.[36]

The officers and soldiers of Hazen's regiment breaking camp in early July 1783 numbered possibly as many as 580 men (22–29 officers, 1–4 staff, 50–52 noncommissioned officers, and 497–502 rank and file). Of the approximately 1,900 members enlisted or commissioned into the regiment during the war, over 160 had died before it ended, including at least 22 killed and some who may have succumbed to wounds. Other members had left after serving their specified terms, or by desertion or resignation. Yet close to 250 of the over 450 soldiers that Mooers listed as officially discharged at war's end had served over six years, including most of the Canadian Continentals. If counting Antill (despite a supposed 1782 resignation), so too had 18 of the officers. The regiment's 3 July return indicated that the remaining noncommissioned officers (from the sergeant major to the drums and fifes) were absent with leave and that all of the rank and file were on furlough. It was no wonder that Adjutant General Hand questioned it. Besides noting promotions that had not yet been confirmed by Congress, the return did not indicate which of the noncommissioned officers and men were in the two companies that Washington wanted Hazen to send to Newburgh. It is possible that the detachment Satterlee accounted for on 29 June—with one major, four captains, four lieutenants, twelve sergeants, six drums and fifes, and eighty-nine rank and file—was what remained of the active-duty regiment until the formal discharge of 3 November 1783.[37] Throughout the war and after, incomplete data and fuzzy math affected the regimental returns.

Names, not just numbers, became ever more important as the army, Congress, and the states tried to settle accounts with the Continentals. That was likely an impetus for Sergeant Major Hawkins to list the regiment's members in 1782, and for Lieutenant Mooers as adjutant to start compiling a roll of all who had served in Congress's Own. Completed in 1783, that roll named in full or part 77 officers and 1,425 soldiers. Mooers missed 27 of the 495 soldiers on Hawkins's roll. The total of 1,452 soldiers from the two rolls was still incomplete, for Mooers overlooked many of the Canadians who had enlisted in early 1776 but did not remain with the regiment upon the retreat from Canada, and he missed a dozen officers and hundreds of soldiers who came and went before he set to work on the list.[38] The gaps and spelling issues created some problems in later pension applications, but less so for the initial certificates issued for service to the close of the war.

Starting in the summer of 1783 and through the following year, Richard Lloyd, one of the captains brevetted a major by Hazen, acted as the settlement agent for the regiment. He received the certificates covering balances of pay and other previous deficiencies in March and June 1784, and then had the task of distributing them to the scattered men or their designees. Lloyd had hoped for suitable compensation for the onerous duty. Instead, Congress resolved in September 1786 that agents not connected to a state-affiliated unit would receive a 1 percent credit on the sum of the certificates they issued, and that this recompense would be issued as yet another certificate bearing interest. Lloyd could not wait for the certificate to attain full value. He sold it for but an "eighth of its value." He petitioned Congress in 1790 that he be granted an additional percentage in specie. Congress asked Secretary of War Henry Knox, who agreed that Lloyd's labors had been great and that valuing the certificate in specie would have been "moderate compensation," but he did not like establishing a precedent by which others who had sold their undervalued certificates would make similar demands. The newly formed House of Representatives tabled the issue until Lloyd's follow-up petition in 1792, at which time a House committee moved against it.[39]

Lloyd's complaint about the worth of his compensation was valid, and it was echoed loudly by other veterans whose "certificates were valued at no more than two shillings sixpence on the pound."[40] Like Lloyd, many other officers and soldiers could not wait for them to increase in value but sold them to speculators. The certificates were just another promise on top of earlier ones that did not make up for the financial sacrifices of service. States had not only been late in paying their troops, but during the delays, the pay depreciated. States then issued treasury or commodity certificates that promised later reimbursement with interest. In the case of Massachusetts, home to Mooers and Moses White, it promised 6 percent interest and pegged the money against the value of certain commodities such as corn and beef.[41] The problem was getting the states to pay out on their promises.

White wrote to his cousin "Ben" in February 1783 of his adventures with the treasurer of Massachusetts. First, the treasurer was not going to pay on all the notes together, but in order of disbursement. Second, "As to the interest on the due Bill—if you want to be laughed at—come & ask for it." White was also bitter about the state's response to his petition asking that Massachusetts men in the Canadian Old Regiment be granted the state's bounty. The General Court was "so exceeding *reasonable* as to resolve that I might be permitted to withdraw my petition."[42]

White pressed on about what was due on the certificates, and by December reported that the Treasurer "was near six months in arrears." Later that month, White gave Mooers the bad news about "Mr. Morris's Notes" that Mooers had sent to Boston for reimbursement. Robert Morris, Congress's superintendent of finance, had issued notes backed by his own wealth to pay soldiers and buy supplies to make up for what the states did not cover. White said that if Mooers had left the notes with him when he had visited Boston earlier, he could have negotiated reimbursement at par, but the value of the notes had dropped. Mooers did not get the full ninety dollars promised in the notes.[43] Even so, he and his fellow officers who had the time, energy, and connections to press the authorities were fortunate to retrieve at least part of what was due them.

As some members of Hazen's regiment worked through their states, others petitioned for immediate assistance from Congress. These were the members who counted themselves not just as Continentals but also among the Canadian and Nova Scotian refugees. They needed food and housing as they awaited loan office certificates for depreciation, commutation certificates, and the allocation of bounty lands promised by Congress. While Lloyd was the regiment's agent for certificates, and Mooers would assume a major role in the disposition of bounty lands in the Lake Champlain area, Hazen continued to act not just as the regiment's commander but also somewhat in his previous persona as a seigneur, trying to accumulate lands, finance new enterprises, and manage the former habitants who had served as Canadian Continentals and now faced the task of transforming into American settlers.

At least some of the Canadian officers who had been discharged earlier as supernumeraries had been drawing rations for themselves and their families as refugees at Albany. Other Canadian Continentals asked for the same as they faced furloughs in 1783. The topic of provisions came up in April as Congress reviewed Hazen's memorial on behalf of himself, fellow officers, and refugees. It denied Hazen's request that land be set aside for them adjacent to Lakes Huron and Erie because some states had claims there, but when it could grant lands, it would reward the Canadians' "virtuous sufferings in the cause of Liberty." It referred questions about interest on certificates to the superintendent of finance and put provisioning on hold. Congress returned to the issue in August as it considered the petitions of Captain Clément Gosselin and other refugees then living at Fishkill. The petitioners reminded Congress that they had left their country, homes, and friends to support "the Liberties and rights of America," and had been assured of protection and "a prospect of Liberty." They had persevered in the American War for Independence, but they remained exiles without any stipulation in the peace treaty supporting a return to or recompense for their homes. Congress answered with a recommendation that New York accept such officers and men "as citizens of the said State. And to grant them such lands and aids as the legislature of the said State may . . . think fit." It also resolved that the officers of Hazen's regiment who had been inhabitants of Canada when the war commenced would continue to receive provisions "until the further order of Congress: and that each of the men, women and children, referred to in the petition of the said officers, shall respectively receive a ration per day for their subsistence, until such further order."[44]

Congress approved the welfare measure as a temporary one that was to serve only until the refugee veterans received the remainder of their certificates and bounty-land warrants. The precedent for subsisting refugees and army dependents at Albany and Fishkill had been set earlier in the war, but so too had the precedent for cutting them off. Rationing had been irregular due to changing instructions from Congress, supply and money problems, and the diligence or negligence of officers in charge of disbursement.[45] The veterans could expect the pattern to continue. Hazen and a few of his officers, however, tried to facilitate operations.

While some of the refugees—Congress's own dependents as it were—remained in or moved to Albany to be near the commissary there, others made their way farther north. In both cases, regimental connections supported the rationing: first in demonstrating a legitimate claim and then in the actual distribution. In the process, Lieutenant Murdock McPherson became another officer connecting the civil and military lives of the regiment's members.

Hazen wrote to McPherson in August 1784 that Congress had sanctioned provisioning for the Canadian refugees. After mentioning that a commissary remained at Albany for that purpose, he asked McPherson to assist "those poor unfortunate people (who for the want of Language are unable to transact their own business) in drawing their provisions." Just days before Hazen issued that endorsement, thirty-three of the refugees had empowered Hazen, as witnessed by Mooers and McPherson, to draw their rations and any other allowances that might be due them. These seem to be other than the thirty-two men on a previous return submitted to Bethuel Washburn, the issuing commissary. By 21 August, when Hazen added his authorization, the listed refugees had "gone to settle on Lake Champlain." Hazen noted that the witnesses (primarily McPherson) were to take "due bills" from the commissary "for full Rations of Provisions as they are now supplied at my Expence."[46]

Twenty-three of the thirty-three men authorizing Hazen as their agent were on a 1782 roster of refugee servicemen compiled for the Land Office of New York by Hazen and his fellow Canadian commander, James Livingston. Of those twenty-three, sixteen had been affiliated just with Hazen's regiment, whereas the others had either left the army when Livingston's was disbanded in January 1781 or transferred to Hazen's. The remaining ten may have served with the military at some point, or just sought refuge in the Albany area as they awaited the possibility of returning to their former homes. As that possibility waned, these men, some with families, ventured to New York's northern borderlands to try settlement there. John Bateman, who had been an adjutant in Livingston's regiment, and Private Louis Lisote of Hazen's took their wives. Wives and children accompanied at least eight others: Privates Noel Belanger, Pierre (Peter) Boileau, Nicholas Constantine, Jacque Laframboise, and Francis Monty Jr., Sergeant Louis Marney, and Lieutenants Amable Boileau and Francis Monty.[47] In sum, approximately fifty-nine persons, including ten women and sixteen children, set out that August, and all were to be provisioned by order of Congress.

A little over a year later, Hazen wrote to McPherson "to Continue to superintend the Drawing Provisions for the Canadian Refugees—for which I shall endeavor to obtain from them a suitable recompense." McPherson continued the task into 1786. He and Hazen, like Lloyd, expected remuneration, yet found little profit but plenty of problems, due primarily to lax accounting and tardy payments.[48]

Compensation was likely in the form of the difference between the price of the rations and the cost of what Hazen actually supplied the refugees in goods, services, credit, or money. Instead of trying to ship rations to the designated refugees on Lake Champlain or demanding that they pick them up, Commissary Washburn retained—that is, did not issue—the rations for those not in Albany. He then notified Hazen, usually via McPherson, of the cost of the retained rations. Hazen, in turn, was "to draw the money from the contracter (viz) William Duer in lieu of the Provisions & to Account to them for the same."[49] Accounting from commissary through contractor to refugees was supposed to check profiteering.

On 10 December 1784, Duer scribbled receipt of a due bill for 2,490 rations from Hazen. If that had been for the month of November, it represented the equivalent of eighty-three rations per day for the refugees (one daily ration for each enrolled man, woman, and child) on the northern borderland. Another due bill from Washburn, which Hazen received on 13 July 1785, was for 2,175 rations. That same month, Hazen wrote to McPherson that Congress had announced that the provisioning would end as of 1 June 1786, and so he asked McPherson to warn the refugees that they had to start looking out for themselves.[50] That push out of dependency applied to those still at Albany as well as those to the north.

As it turned out, however, some of the refugees, under certain conditions, could continue to receive rations to mid-1788. Congress offered the extension on 30 June 1786 in the midst of discussions about organizing "the Indian department, for the purpose of extending to the frontiers regular and certain security against the future designs of the Indians." Congress resolved that treasury commissioners were to "take the necessary measures for removing immediately, and placing on the lands given by the state of New York, such Canadian inhabitants as are now residing in the said state, and who have accepted donations of lands from the same, and who will settle thereon." Furthermore, they were to assure fifteen months' rations to "the said Canadians who shall be removed as aforesaid," commencing that June.[51]

Canadian "removal" to the northeast corner of the state reinforced the personal and community connections forged in war. It was there that Mooers, operating as a nexus between past service and present needs, conducted numerous land deals with the veterans and established employer-employee, seigneur-habitant, or landlord-renter relationships with some of them.

Such personal civil-military connections began as Mooers the adjutant became Hazen's land agent. Hazen had shown interest in New York property as early as 1761, when he and associates—following his old commander, the ranger Robert Rogers—had petitioned to purchase land in Albany County. Although his primary interests shifted to Canada after the French and Indian War, the loss of his lands there due to his service in the War for Independence had Hazen again looking at New York. The Continental Congress had promised lands to officers and soldiers who served to the close of the war or were otherwise properly discharged, but in March 1783, New York offered more generous provisions for those in its line. Although neither the state nor Congress initially specified Canadian refugees (among whom Hazen counted himself), Hazen lobbied to have both national and New York lands designated for the émigrés. In the meantime, Hazen initiated settlement south of Point au Fer on Lake Champlain on what was unoccupied but not unclaimed land. He gambled on New York granting lands in that area to the Canadian and Nova Scotian refugees, only later making a deal with the landowner, William Beekman, after the state constituted the refugee tract in 1784.[52] The tract was just south of Hazen's and the other refugees' former properties in the Richelieu Valley.

In execution of Hazen's plan, Mooers left Newburgh on 25 July 1783 and traveled to Poughkeepsie, where he took command of a bateau and ten men—including his cousin Zacheus Peaslee, Lieutenant Francis Monty, Sergeant John Tessie (Tessier), and seven soldiers who were also Canadian refugees. After adjustments at Albany and Fort George, the party moved up Lakes George and Champlain, arriving at Point au Roche on 10 August. The men began cutting timber the next day. Despite little help from Francis Monty Jr., who was often "sick, no work," the pioneers made progress erecting a house in which Mooers was able to sleep on the 21st.[53] He did not, however, stay there long.

Mooers, Peaslee, and their uncle, who had visited to check the progress, with a few others headed down for Crown Point on 12 October. The three related officers struck out across Lake Champlain three days later and trekked east. Hazen stopped at Bennington, Peaslee eventually turned off to ride for Dover, while Mooers continued to "old Haverhill," his family's home in Massachusetts, where he arrived on the 30th. Just days later, the new veteran was back on the road to Boston to mix business with the pleasure of meeting friends and family, including the ailing and worried Moses White.[54]

Translating past service into future success concerned them all. Although Lloyd enjoyed some "good sleighing" while wrapping up regimental accounts in January 1784, he was also laboring to ensure the "health happiness and prosperity" that he likewise wished for Mooers. He was pleased that the lieutenant had finally reached his "former dwelling in safety after a long & dangerous war," but he also remarked Mooers's "rambling" situation. There was a subtext of unease. How were the officers to ensure independent, comfortable lives? To that end, Lloyd advised Mooers to take a wife so that when he moved "into the Bush at Coos," she might occasionally "take your pack from your shoulders whilst you rest yourself from the fatigues of your Journey many of which you must take, and very lengthy ones too." (Mooers waited until 1791 to follow Lloyd's advice: he married Hannah Platt, the daughter of Nathaniel Platt, one of the brothers who founded Plattsburgh.) Lloyd had confused Mooers's enterprise in upstate New York for a venture in the northern Vermont-New Hampshire region, but perhaps Mooers had once talked of emulating his uncles' examples there as he followed the family tradition of military service and land speculation. Other officers and soldiers rambled as they too explored their options. Lloyd mentioned that "[William] Stuart is going to turn [land jobber] and some to one thing, some to another to make an honest living whilst in this transitory world. I wish them all well and happy." Moses White in Boston, who saw "Bill Torrey daily," noted that "Dick Lloyd" had been chasing clothing accounts in Philadelphia in February 1784, where he saw Pry and Stuart, the latter planning to go "trading up in the Indian Country." Actually, Stuart ended up visiting Europe, studying law, and then serving in various New York counties as a district attorney and ultimately a judge.[55]

Many veterans returned to their former homes and occupations, but others ranged near and far for new opportunities. If they had resources and connections, as Mooers did, opportunity could be a matter of turning land jobber— buying land on speculation or buying and selling it for others—or landowner and yeoman farmer. Presumably, service connected the veteran Continentals to their state and national governments, which in turn provided the resources, such as bounty lands, to help them become or remain American yeomen and citizens.

Offers of property were not only to recompense refugees and veterans, but also to tie them to the land and, by extension, the state and nation guaranteeing it. Whereas commutation certificates represented a one-time payout for past deeds, bounty lands and pensions recognized the past but served the present and future by expanding individual and collective commitments to the nation and states through the disbursal of economic means. Access to such resources required allegiance; and loyalty, in turn, entailed service.[56] The state was to stand as security for soldier-settlers while they were to stand as security for the state.

The hope and implication that veterans as homesteaders would be frontier sentinels was not new, for in 1764, Colonel Henry Bouquet and General Thomas Gage had proposed similar ideas for the Ohio Country after continuing battles with Native Americans.[57] Close to twenty years later, General Washington suggested to Congress that if it could not find the funds to subsist the Canadian Continentals and compensate them for their losses, it could surely make them a grant from unallocated lands "in the interior parts of our Territory and some means advanced, to place them on such a Tract; this perhaps might prove satisfactory, and would enable them to form a Settlement which may be beneficial to themselves and useful to the United States." Congress, as noted, offered temporary subsistence, even as it urged New York to accept the refugee officers and soldiers as citizens and grant them lands.[58]

Besides fostering mutual reliance and benefits, Congress and New York wanted to convey veterans, in this case, particularly the Canadian refugees, from dependency into independency. The governments did not want to continue funding refugees or veterans, but it did want citizens who could pay taxes on their properties. The veterans, in turn, desired the purported independency of property (even with taxes), but government plans did not always meet individual needs, abilities, and resources. Mooers, from his 1783 ramblings to his 1830s affidavits supporting veterans' pension and other applications, showed that both the desires and disconnections continued for decades.

Mooers's acts continued those of his uncle, who had reminded Congress many times to take care of its "own" stateless soldiers. In 1780, Hazen had counted sixteen officers and 111 men from Canada who did not belong "to any of the united states—some of them old Infirm and even unfit for service . . . [who] have sacrificed their Interest Country and friends; their all in this service—They are now to be considered as Pensioners on Congress Rather than able officers."[59] After the 1st Canadian Regiment disbanded in January 1781, some of its members swelled the 2nd. Over a year later, Hazen listed men he considered to be Canadian refugees and who were with his regiment or had been with Livingston's. Including himself, Colonel Livingston, and some other officers, he counted about 177 such men.[60] That stands in comparison with the 496 noncommissioned officers and soldiers in an August 1782 return, of which 279 were classed as belonging to the United States rather than any one state. There were also fifteen United States volunteers.[61] The numbers included recent immigrants and recruited deserters or prisoners, not just the Anglo and French Canadians. While not exact, the numbers indicate that at the end of the war, over half of the Canadian Old Regiment's members had no proper state affiliation, but perhaps near 30 percent had Canadian ties.

Those ties kept many of them within the Lake Champlain borderlands on New York's northeastern frontier while the rest of the regiment's soldiers dispersed to their old communities or made new homes on the republic's other frontiers from Maine to Kentucky.[62] New York's frontiers were not part of the Northwest Ordinance and thus, although appropriations and disbursement of lands may have had similarities to federal acts in the old Northwest Territory, they were not exactly alike. In this case, a state government claimed the lands that it then awarded to veterans and others it wanted to reward—and who, it hoped, would defend its territory.[63] As in the Northwest Territory, however, the combination of needy veterans and opportunistic speculators undermined the hopes for such security and the plans for an equitable distribution of lands.

New York was more organized and quicker to distribute grants than Congress.[64] Even so, distribution plans were challenged by Vermont residents determined to create their own state with lands claimed by New York (resolved in 1791 when Vermont became the fourteenth state); Massachusetts claiming territory to the east of what is now Geneva, New York; and the Haudenosaunee, who also disputed New York's land claims. Most members of the Mohawk, Cayuga, Onondaga, and Seneca tribes had sided with the British during the war, and so found that the new United States, and particularly New York, deemed their lands forfeit. Yet the Oneida and Tuscarora, who had sided with the Americans, also found their territories constrained.[65] The Iroquois peoples who stayed were pressed onto much reduced tracts of land, while those who moved to Canada received land on the Grand River in Upper Canada (Ontario), where they could be, as it were, "doorkeepers" against the Americans.

On the other side, New York wanted sentinels against the Native Americans and British subjects of Canada. The state promised bounty lands to soldiers in 1781 and then sought where it could best put them. In 1784, the New York legislature created the "Old Military Tract" in the northern part of the state. The land there was not a great draw. Then, in 1789, the legislature established the "New Military Tract" in central New York, using lands appropriated from the Iroquois and secured from Massachusetts. Many of the veterans who earned grants to land in that area ultimately sold them rather than move there. It appears, however, that at least a few of Hazen's New York, not Canadian, recruits settled in that tract. When filing pension claims, Samuel Johnson reported from Genesee County, John Shepherd from Ontario County, while David Murray and Patrick McGee filed in Oneida and Onondaga counties.[66]

The "Canadian and Nova Scotian Refugee Tract" in the Champlain area originated in May 1784, when New York's senate and assembly incorporated two previous acts for veterans' bounties into a new one with a provision "for the further defence of the frontiers of this state." The 1784 act tied reward to defense, explicitly in terms of service rendered and implicitly for service to be performed. Upon receipt of returns by Hazen and Livingston designating the Canadian refugees, and by Colonel Jeremiah Throop listing those from Nova Scotia, the surveyor-general was to lay out "townships of unappropriated and unoccupied lands for the Canadian and Nova-Scotia refugees," and do so "at such place in the northern part of this state as they shall think proper, not exceeding one thousand acres to each of the commissioned officers, and five hundred acres to each other person or persons, refugees as aforesaid."[67]

There was a notable difference between the acreage awarded refugee officers and that offered citizen officers. On 27 March 1783, New York had declared itself ready not only to honor the Continental Congress's 1776 resolution to reward veterans, but also to show how highly it regarded "the patriotism and virtue of the troops of this state, serving in the army of the United States." New York offered its citizens who had served in the state's regiments, or in special units such as Colonel John Lamb's 2nd Continental Artillery Regiment and the companies of sappers and miners, generous grants of five hundred acres to privates and noncommissioned officers, a thousand to subalterns (ensigns and lieutenants), and increasing amounts up the ranks.[68]

Citizens in the ranks of captain and above were thus promised more than their Canadian refugee brothers-in-arms. Yet both New York acts offered more than what the Continental Congress did in its 16 September 1776 resolution to provide land grants to officers and soldiers who served "to the close of the war, or until discharged by Congress, and to the representatives of such officers and soldiers as shall be slain by the enemy." The lands were to be provided by the nation with the expenses for procuring them borne by the states "in the same proportion as the other expenses of the war." Congress's initial recommended allocations ran from one hundred acres for a private to five hundred

Table 2. Congress and New York State Bounty-Land Allocations

	Sergeants, Corporals, Privates	Ensigns	Subalterns	Lieutenants	Captains	Majors	Lieutenant Colonels	Colonels	Brigadier Generals	Major Generals
Congress	100	150	—	200	300	400	450	500	850	1,100
NY	500	—	1,000	—	1,500	2,000	2,250	2,500	4,250	5,500
NY Refugees	≤500		≤1,000		≤1,000	≤1,000	≤1,000	≤1,000	≤1,000	

Sources: 16 September 1776, JCC, 5:763; 12 August 1780, JCC, 17:726–27; *The Balloting Book*, 5–6.

for a colonel.[69] That was in 1776, however, and depreciating enlistment in the war may account for the inflation of the state's bounty offers by the 1780s.

Although many veterans sold their bounty certificates to speculators, some did move to the state's frontiers. The American army's Canadian regiments had served on various fronts during the war, and then afterwards, some of their veterans helped form "fronts" along the United States' national borders with Canada and Native American territories. On these porous fronts—for some Continentals moved back and forth across the borders—veterans established borderland communities founded on their experiences as refugees, their connections as soldiers, and their economic and cultural struggles afterwards.[70]

Veteran settlement along Lake Champlain and the Canadian border provides a glimpse of a northern borderland served by waterways that were lines of communication and marked by personal, military, and state obligations and interconnections. These Continentals settled on what had been Mohawk lands as well as territory once claimed by France as part of its new world empire. France relinquished its claim to Britain upon its defeat in the Seven Years' War. Although Continentals tried to solidify American claims to the territory through military actions during the War for Independence, British troops defended Britain's title to it by defeating the rebels at Valcour Island in October 1776, and later by taking Crown Point and Ticonderoga. Although the British army did not hold the territory throughout the war, neither did the Americans; it was an unsecure, contested area. Such a history informed American decisions after the 1783 Treaty of Paris designated the 45th degree north latitude as part of the border between Canada and the United States (from the Connecticut River headwaters across to the St. Lawrence waterway and along its middle to the Cataraqui River and into Lake Ontario). As the United States and state of New York tried to establish territorial and political borders through settlement, not just treaties, they offered lands on that border to their veterans.

Some Canadian Continentals, refugees like their civilian counterparts, returned to Canada just as some loyalists decided to reestablish themselves in the new republic.[71] Most of the Canadian revolutionaries, however, like the United Empire Loyalists who settled primarily in Ontario and Nova Scotia, decided to start fresh in a part of North America that was more politically comfortable and offered financial incentives. Some settled in Vermont, while others stayed west of Lake Champlain in New York. But even as these Canadian Continentals began anew, they also tried to hold onto some pieces of their past. Just as they had taken their domestic associations—family, friends, and neighbors—to war, they took their war associations with them to their new homes on the front that was so close to the prewar homes that, for many of them, had been just south of Montreal.

The veterans who settled in what was called Washington County in 1784, and specifically in the part that became Clinton County after 1788, were in the northeast corner of New York, bordered by Lake Champlain to the east, Canada to the north. Depending on whether they settled near Rouses Point, Champlain, Mooers, or Chazy, the Canadian refugees were fewer than fifty-five miles to Chambly and less than thirty-five to Saint-Jean in Quebec province. They settled north of the 33,000-acre tract (previously claimed by a loyalist) bought by Colonel Zephaniah Platt (of the New York militia) and other investors who applied to form the township of Plattsburgh in 1785.[72]

After writing to Mooers in March 1786 that it was probable that "the Canadian Refugees will have some of their Lands on Lake Champlain," Hazen acknowledged that he could not afford to pay him properly and that it was unreasonable "to wish you to give up your time without." Nevertheless, he continued to task Mooers in settling the Point au Roche claims and preparing for patents in the designated refugee tract. Less than a month later, Hazen wrote to Mooers that the "Canadian Lands" would soon be surveyed and "settlements pushed on there the Insuing Sumer. It is necessary that William Torry should be on the spott to Look after his share[.] I have wrote to him accordingly . . . I wish to see you there if you think it will answer your own Purpose—In which case the sooner you set out the better as I hope to be on the spot my self by the 10th." Within a week, Hazen urged Mooers again: "If therefore you wish to be an adventurer in wild lands in this state you have not Time to loose."[73] Mooers did not lose time and was in those "wild lands" by August, when Moses White wrote, "I hope . . . that you will make your fortune—there . . . [and] happiness with it." White also asked him to "Take care to let my farme be laid out adjoining yours & Wm's [Torrey] so as to live all in a neighborhood together &c, &c, &c"[74]

As requested, Mooers not only saw to Hazen's affairs, but also to those of the regiment's other veterans with interests in the area. Between January 1790 and February 1793, Mooers appeared as the assignee for federal bounty-land warrants awarded to at least forty-three of the regiment's soldiers and four officers, including himself.[75] He was also likely the assignee for other soldiers settling along that northern borderland. Like other veterans elsewhere, they chose to sign over the warrants in favor of "bounty land Mony" rather than waiting for promised acres of unknown value.[76]

Federal land warrants confirmed their eligibility for veterans' bounty lands, but most of the Canadian Continentals took the patents, with the guarantee of more acreage, as balloted to them as refugees by New York. Over 220 Canadian and Nova Scotian refugees were entitled to 500 or more acres from the state as distributed in 420-acre and 80-acre lots in late 1786 and thereafter. Approximately 140 of those refugees, if not more, had been soldiers or officers with

Hazen and Livingston. Because some of the land was not suitable for cultivation, or they wanted to fund endeavors elsewhere, many of the veterans and refugees cashed in their state lands. Others traded some of the land so as to pay the bills on the other part. Those bills included the cost of surveying, in which Mooers was heavily involved by 1789 and through the mid-1790s.[77]

Few of the veterans showed up on a list of assessed properties in 1798. Mooers was the principal assessor of the district that included northern New York, and his notes reveal about fifteen regimental veterans with enough property for assessment. Among them were Edward Chinn (former paymaster), Alexander Ferriole (probably the father Alexandre rather than his son, the private), Francis Monty (likely senior rather than junior), Louis Gosselin, Laurent Olivie, and Antoine Paulint, as well as Mooers, McPherson, and Torrey. Others appear to be Louis Lisote, Louis Marney Jr., Amable Paulint, and Michael Toyen. Although a James Morey occupied an old log house owned by Hazen, the general did not show up as a major landowner in the area, probably because he had lost lands due to suits for debts.[78]

That 1798 assessment revealed that the former lieutenant from Massachusetts, who did not qualify as a refugee for New York bounty lands, had 36,840 acres within the Canadian and Nova Scotian Refugee Tract. Additionally, he had 130 acres in Monty's Bay, adjoining the properties of Francis Monty and Louis Lisote, including one log house. This land jobber accumulated thousands more acres until he found it difficult to pay the taxes and lost some. Mooers bought or acquired by other means the bounty land deeds from other veterans and refugees, including his uncle. Among them was Claud Monty, who deeded over his lands to Mooers, "Gentleman," for fifteen pounds on 16 September 1786. Noel Belanger made over lands at Point au Roche to Mooers for thirty-one dollars and one shilling in November 1788. Clément Gosselin, acting with power of attorney (provided at Three Rivers, Quebec, in 1787) for Corporal Ferman Lorillon, transferred the soldier's refugee property claims for five hundred acres "on or near Lake Champlain" to Mooers on 14 November 1788.[79]

Mooers may have received some of the lands in trade or as payment of an obligation, for he had funded or helped some of the veterans before they received their grants. Indeed, other officers may have done the same and then traded the deeds among themselves, as McPherson did when he signed a promissory note in 1789 to convey Joseph Chartier's deed to Mooers whenever Mooers should demand it.[80]

Before, during, and after his land deals, Mooers established employer-employee, landlord-renter, or more descriptively seigneur-habitant and patron-client relationships with some of the veterans. The northeast New York borderland was a cultural middle ground, a "Creole corridor," as its people used military connections to forge new social and economic relationships in an area that entrepreneurs such as Mooers believed would be a farming, trading, and communications nexus between New York City, Albany, and Montreal.[81] The evolution from officer-soldier to patron-client relationships began when the former adjutant employed some of the soldiers on that first ramble up to the area in 1783, and continued during those uneasy years of waiting for the tracts to be surveyed and the bounty lands distributed. When Mooers recorded expenses for his travels "on the west side of Lake Champlain" in September 1785, he noted paying both Francis Monty Sr. and Jr., Barbau (possibly John Barber), Peter Boilou (Pierre Boileau), Basil Nadau (Nadeau), and Ferman Lorillon, among others.[82]

Like their fellows elsewhere, these veterans did not keep all of their bounty lands, but many settled in the area nonetheless, and gave proof that they were still there decades later when they applied for pensions. In March 1818, the United States Congress finally passed a service-pension act for Revolutionary War resident veterans needing assistance that did not require proof of disability. When the federal government faced financial straits because so many veterans applied, Congress tightened property and income provisions in 1820. That reduced the number of pensioners temporarily, but in 1828 and 1832, as the veterans continued to disappear—and after General Lafayette's 1824–25 visit to the United States commemorated their service—Congress abolished the requirement to demonstrate need and liberalized the time-of-service eligibility for benefits. In the 1830s and after, Congress also extended pensions to their widows.[83]

Congress's Own Veterans

Most of the Continentals born on the American continent became Americans, as the revolutionaries defined that identity, as they lived the transition from colonial to citizen. They, and the foreign-born Continentals who joined them, were part of the founding if not first "born" generation of Americans. They had served not only in physical borderlands but also in a temporal one. Furthermore, securing the new nation militarily had required not only conjoined actions in reimagined places and institutions over eight years but also sacrifices. Those sacrifices reinforced one of the ideals of the developing American culture and character: the pursuit of happiness defined as the personal independence of financial sufficiency. With such independence came not just rights but privileges, as in political participation and positions. But the time and tolls of service had undermined self-sufficiency, much less prosperity, for many Continentals. Moreover, as the aging Continentals tried to reestablish themselves in civil society, they had to compete for opportunities not just with members of their own generation who had stayed home but the rising ones as well. Only later, as those rising generations reflected on the meaning of the American Revolution, did they fully ponder the financial and cultural debts due the veterans.[84]

Many, perhaps most, of the nation's first veterans attained personal independence in the new republic, and some achieved prosperity and power, but many others were still struggling for competency decades later. Quite a number of veterans also contended with broken bodies that affected their ability to work. The effects of service, positive and negative, from community and connections to financial and bodily wounds, were felt immediately and long into the future by the veterans of Congress's Own.

There was, however, no future for Benjamin Davidson, Thomas Donaldson, and Joseph Torrey, who had all served over six years. Private Davidson died on 17 June 1783 just before Hazen's troops were furloughed (which became a discharge with the official end of the war and dissolution of the army that fall). Donaldson, who appears to have been busted from sergeant to private at Yorktown in 1781, died in July, shortly after receiving his furlough-cum-discharge on 30 June. Torrey, recently brevetted to lieutenant colonel, died in September. At Torrey's funeral on the 22nd at Boston, "Major Davis's corps of artillery marched in funeral order, then proceeded the officers of the Boston regiment, after them the officers of the continental army, the band playing a funeral dirge. When the body was deposited, three vollies were discharged by the corps of artillery.—In honour to so brave an officer, the flag on Oliver's dock was hoisted, half staff high, and 47 minute guns were discharged by those heroes who live in that vicinity."[85] There was no mention as to whether his nephew William was there to represent family and regiment, but his funeral honors were noted in Philadelphia as well as Massachusetts as a salute not only to him but to other Continentals too.

Donaldson and Torrey were the first Congress's Own veterans to die. John Shepherd (b. 1764), who died on 14 October 1857, was one of if not the last. Shepherd had enlisted at Haverhill, New Hampshire, in 1779, was discharged at Pompton on 19 June 1783, and then lived, married (apparently twice), and worked as a carpenter in Ontario County, New York. Initially granted a pension in 1818, he reapplied in 1820 to keep it, noting his "reduced circumstances" due to "bodily infirmities" that affected his ability to labor and support his wife (who had lost her hands) and two children.[86] He did not appear to be destitute or desperate, just a common man with a common story of hard work and either personal disabilities or family distress that subverted independence. Although the regiment's officers had additional resources and connections, which helped many of them achieve success, some shared a version of Shepherd's story.

Moses Hazen never gave up but never fulfilled all of his aspirations. He trekked between Canada, the Lake Champlain settlement, and his Vermont property, investing in new ventures and petitioning about old ones. Then the man of action "was taken with a Violent fit of the Appoplexy" in April 1786. He credited extensive bloodletting with saving his life, but the stroke left him partially paralyzed. Although his wife, in asking for help settling some claims, wrote to Washington in 1795 that Hazen had "been Confined to his bed, without the Ability of ever turning himself therein for upwards of Nine Years," he actually did manage some travel, but he also escalated his demands on Mooers, Torrey, and then Moses White as they acted as his agents. Charlotte Hazen remarked that it could not be surprising "that this truly distressing situation should have greatly Affected the Natural Mildness of his disposition." Knox had been blunter a few years earlier: "The unfortunate Hazen," he observed, had been marked by nature "with as obstinate a temper as ever afflicted humanity." Hazen failed to get his Canadian lands returned or be fully reimbursed for his losses. He also lost most of his American acquisitions as he was dunned (including by Philippe Liébert and Laurent Olivie) and arrested for debts multiple times. But as he pushed for his own interests, he generally continued to advocate for the other "foreign" officers of his "late Regiment." Hazen died in 1803, leaving his wife and White—who had his own health problems (from lung damage in 1782) and money woes—still trying to settle his financial morass.[87]

Edward Antill, who had been one of the eager first advocates of independence and American union in Canada, reentered civilian life asking for provisions for his "five Canadian Refugees." He moved his wife and four children to New Jersey in September 1783, and then established himself as an attorney in Manhattan by March 1784. In December 1785, he applied for a position as a translator of French in the office of the secretary of foreign affairs, writing to John Jay that "the small Practice that falls to my Lot, the late sickness in my Family, the daily expence of it, and the Loss on my paper securities: has reduced me to the Necessity of Looking out for other resourses." The sickness was the death of his wife and perhaps his own depression. Without that position or enough business and still suffering, Antill left his youngest daughter, Frances, with the family of a fellow member of the Society of the Cincinnati, Alexander Hamilton, and in 1787 moved back to Canada, where he died at St. John in 1789.[88]

As Hazen and Antill struggled, by 1785 James Reid "had beaten his sword into a plough-share" and was growing "a thousand bushels of wheat a year" on his farm across the Susquehanna about five miles west of Harrisburg, Pennsylvania. He also served in the last term of the Confederation Congress. Following that, he had hoped for a position as a revenue collector, but became ill and died in January 1789. Another contentious major, John Taylor—who had charged

General Sullivan with incompetence after Staten Island in 1777, and who had resigned in 1779 after becoming increasingly disenchanted with army service—returned to Virginia, practiced law, engaged in politics (including serving as a United States senator), and became an eminent political philosopher of agrarian (Jeffersonian) democracy.[89]

The French-Canadian officer Philippe Liébert returned to the Montreal region of Canada, where he resumed work as an accomplished sculptor of tabernacles and altars. His francophone compatriots Laurent Olivie, Antoine Paulint, and Louis Gosselin settled their families around Champlain, New York, within that region's refugee community. Alexandre Ferriole also settled in the borderland, as did his son, but the father had either moved again or was visiting in Canada when he died in 1800. Clément Gosselin also moved back and forth across the border.[90] These officers, like their fellow Canadian Continentals, continued to show how nations may draw boundaries but people traverse them.

Among the more junior set of officers, James Duncan and William Munson, unlike Antill, did find government positions. Duncan, who had first been a storekeeper, served as prothonotary of Adams County, Pennsylvania, between 1801 and 1821. The moderate Republican won election to Congress in 1820, but resigned before it met in 1821 and moved to Mercer County, where he had bounty lands. Munson, who helped distribute settlement certificates in Connecticut in 1784, first applied for a federal appointment in 1789 by writing to Washington of his loyalty, service, and sacrifices "to the Cause of my Country." He averred that he "cheerfully Shared with my Brother officers and Soldiers in all the fatigues and Dangers" and believed that he had always acted "to the Satisfaction of my Superiors." He described how the British had plundered his home when they raided New Haven in 1779, and his subsequent financial straits. He was not successful in that bid, but was with another in 1792: he received a federal appointment as a surveyor and inspector at New Haven in February 1793.[91]

Munson had mentioned being brevetted a major when he applied for an appointment. He was not the only one to note promotion. William Popham did the same, but in his case, he and an advocate argued that after being detached from Hazen's regiment and appointed aide-de-camp and brigade major to General James Clinton, he was promoted to major. Yet brigade major was a staff position to which captains could be and were appointed, not promoted. Popham followed his service in the regiment and army with the practice of law, first in Albany and then New York City, where he also acted as clerk to the exchequer in the city. He also served as the Society of the Cincinnati's seventh president general between 1844 to 1847.[92]

Popham prospered, but Captain by brevet (with a certificate to prove it) William Torrey did not. He apparently made a comfortable but not rich living as a merchant and magistrate in New York City up to 1810 or 1811, but by 1818 was describing himself as a pauper and applying for a pension. When he applied, he mentioned his "messmate" Benjamin Mooers as someone who could vouch for his service.[93] While most of Congress's Own's officers did not suffer the reverses that Torrey did, few did as well as Mooers.

Mooers manifested—appropriately given that he actively constructed and pulled the strings—the personal, military, and state entanglements that created the borderland that was Clinton County, New York, at the end of the eighteenth century and into the next. Besides acting as adjutant, agent, and advocate for former members of Congress's Own, he also acted for New York and the United States to secure the border by political and military means, not just by physical settlement. In 1788, Mooers became county sheriff. That was a first step to other offices and powers, including serving as an elector in the presidential election of 1808. As the principal assessor of properties in his district in 1798, as a member of the New York State Assembly (1803 to 1805, 1815 to 1817), and as a state senator from 1819 to 1822, he labored to integrate that borderland and its people into the state. He also served to secure the border as an officer in the state militia. Major General Mooers commanded a militia division in coordination with Brigadier General Alexander Macomb's regular troops to rebuff Lieutenant General Sir George Prevost's advance from Chambly to take control of Lake Champlain in the War of 1812.[94] The Americans may have lost at Valcour Island and Crown Point back in 1776, leaving the Champlain Valley unsecure during their War for Independence, but they won at the Battle of Plattsburgh on 11 September 1814.

Mooers long experienced the health, happiness, and prosperity that Lloyd had wished for him in January 1784, but late in life he lost an arm to a "fungous tumor." What was likely cancer reappeared and he died in February 1838, lauded as a "devoted patriot" and "beloved citizen."[95] Mooers had had the means, connections, and time to engage in land speculation and development. Interpreted positively, his success was due to his entrepreneurial nature and ability to negotiate opportunities. Interpreted negatively, it rested in part on the exploitation of his fellow veterans' short-term financial needs. The grants of bounty lands in the refugee tract, as in other tracts, therefore had mixed effects: while some of the veterans could and did use their lands to become self-sufficient yeoman farmers, a few became landlords, and others, renters. The results appear in federal pension applications.

Charles Amlin, who following a French-Canadian family tradition often went by the name Baptiste, had to account for the different names in order to qualify for the 1818 federal pension. Amlin applied, as did thousands of veterans, because "by reason of his reduced circumstances in life is in need of assistance from his country for support." The country had depended on him, and now he depended on his country. In March 1818 and again in June 1819, Mooers swore before a common pleas court that as the former adjutant of Hazen's regiment, he knew that the impoverished shoemaker Amlin applying for the pension was the same Amlin who had served in the regiment. Another veteran of the regiment, Alexander Ferriol, supported Agathe Amlin's application for widow's benefits in 1838. The former private stated that after the war, Baptiste Amlin settled on a farm in what was then called Champlain, now Chazy, and had lived there until he died in July 1829. Ferriol had settled in the same area, within a mile and a half of Amlin, in 1795, and continued to live on the same farm.[96] Mooers also supported Claud Monty's applications. In 1819, Mooers noted that Monty "has lived near him a great part of the time and he has for some part of the time lived with [Mooers] as a labourer." Mooers made a similar deposition for John (Jean Baptiste) Vinet in 1819: "he laboured for this Deponent after the war for some time & this Deponent has seen him from time to time ever since."[97]

Mooers had been the assignee for Amlin and Vinet's bounty land warrants in 1790, and so too for Louis Marney's. In October 1820, Marney deposed that "I own Forty acres of land lying on the lake shore in the town of Champlain, about twenty five acres of which is improved land on said land is a log house with two rooms & a small log buttery—on said land Benjamin Mooers holds a Mortgage on which is due about one hundred & seventy five dollars the above land is worth about five dollars an acre which after deducting the Mortgage will leave . . . $25.00." He owned a horse, a cow, two hogs, an axe, a hoe, some "old" chairs, six knives and forks, plus a few pails, all worth less than ninety dollars; and he owed over six hundred dollars to nine men, including Mooers. This infirm farmer, "troubled with the rheumatism," supported a feeble wife, a teenaged son and daughter who had physical problems, and a toddler. Marney was in need, but he appeared better off than many others who applied. Mooers did not offer a deposition in Marney's case, but a copy of the mortgage agreement probably served.[98]

Mooers and Ferriol were the most frequent witnesses for Congress's Own applicants in Clinton County, which may be why their advocacy came under scrutiny in the evaluation of John Gauley's application in 1828. Ferriol's truthfulness was questioned because he had once been convicted of "an infamous offence," but as he had been pardoned by the governor, his testimony was allowed. C. K. Averill, a justice of the peace, questioned the veracity of Mooers's roll and recollections, to which D. B. McNiel, collector of customs for the Champlain district, huffed a defense of the distinguished patriot's integrity. Record-keeping and recompense once again, decades after the war, embroiled regimental members in controversy, though in this case they were caught in a feud between Averill and McNiel.[99]

Besides former officers and messmates, siblings, in-laws, and children (usually for their widowed mothers) supported the applications. Family ties knotted and tightened by war and settlement appeared often among the Canadian veterans. They were not as prevalent in the applications of the regiment's veterans elsewhere, but those applicants also benefited from the support of their former officers and fellow soldiers. James Hole of New York City deposed in 1820 that he had enlisted in Henry O'Hara's (later Richard Lloyd's) company and had served through many battles but was wounded (three ribs and the little finger of his right hand broken) by a soldier named Shields in a Captain Mercer's company. A laborer, single and suffering from rheumatism, with possessions worth less than eight dollars, he earned his nightly lodging by sweeping the street in front of William Pye's house. Previously assisted by his friends and charity, he now asked for the "aid of the General Government." Abraham (Abram) Lufberry, a former sergeant in Lloyd's company, swore to Hole's service, as did the officers William Popham and William Torrey. Torrey recounted that Hole had acted as his servant for a time while in the regiment and affirmed his present indigency.[100]

The 1820 pension legislation required a statement of resident-citizen status and a schedule of property, occupations, and family members who were dependent on or who might assist the veteran. Congress dropped the residency and need requirements in 1828, and thus many later applications were less revealing of the veterans' situations. Yet not everyone who applied under the 1820 act clearly stated their work status—some simply stated they were disabled or destitute—but most did, like the thrice-married, rheumatism and "stone" afflicted baker Abraham Lufberry whose third wife, Jennett, supported him and two children by taking in washing. Lufberry and Hole aside, among eighty-six other former soldiers and noncommissioned officers of Congress's Own who specified their current or, usually, former occupations, twenty-seven listed laborer and twenty-five specified farmer, to which could be added a planter, gardener, and three husbandmen. One veteran said that he was a cartman, one was a well-digger and salt-borer, and another rang an academy and meeting house bell as well as dug graves. Three men worked with metal, one as an iron refiner and two as blacksmiths, while another four hewed stone as masons. Five worked with wood: two carpenters, one joiner, one chairmaker, and one cooper. One veteran distinguished himself as a cordwainer in comparison to another four shoemakers. The clothworkers included three weavers, a fuller and dyer, and two tailors. Of the three veterans who noted that they had been schoolteachers, William Woodward, a sergeant in 1781, had tried a number of occupations. He declared in 1820 that as he had entered service in 1776 at age fifteen, he had not been "brought up to any particular trade or occupation," so after the war he tried various means "to obtain a comfortable subsistence." Besides having "formerly taught School. (Some,) I have been a County trader, in merchandize, and failed; I have been a toll Gatherer, at a turnpike Gate And I had taken up the Cobler trade. But owing to the loss of my Eye sight, and the infirmities incident to old age Being afflicted Considerable with Rhumatism, I am, *now* unable to precure a subsistance by manual labour." His family included only his fifty-eight-year-old wife, "a poor, feeble woman."[101]

Disability was a dirge through most of the early pension applications. Veterans commonly noted not just what they called the infirmities of old age, which included rheumatism and failing eyesight, but also breeches or ruptures (hernias) and war wounds that had damaged or destroyed livelihoods. "In Consequence of my age and of having my feet frozen during the revolutionary war," Francis Turcoat declared that he was crippled and thus could not work. Jacob Doddridge was unable to practice his trade as tailor because he had been wounded in his left hand and arm and subsequently lost the use of them. Another kind of wound may have festered unmarked until a veteran committed suicide. Although cause and effect cannot be certain, Joseph Martin in 1834 shot himself at Rouse's Point. The connection was clearer with Corporal Alexander Picard. Around sixty years old in 1788, Picard had "been an invalid since the year 1780," and for the past year had lived as a domestic with Colonel Jeremiah Wadsworth of Hartford, Connecticut. He worked "with great faithfulness and integrity, and never having shewn any signs of uneasiness or discontent, after dining heartily [on 6 June], retired to his chamber, undressed, covered himself up on his bed, and with a razor cut his throat."[102]

While some veterans, generally officers, provided success stories that could be celebrated as individual examples of national progress, many others suffered and suffered greatly. Their disadvantages and distresses fill the pension applications of the 1820s. Many others, however, sustained themselves and their families, and thus could not apply until the pensions recognized just service, not need. Countless others, however, just disappeared. Some may have been like Abraham Shelley, who left home in search of other opportunities and never returned. He left his wife and at least one son in Connecticut between 1795 and 1799, contacted her once or twice about coming to get her, and then nothing.[103] Others left no family, property, tax, or census records. Or they are in those records, but name changes and spelling issues hide them; or the records were lost to flood, fire, and cleared attics. Quite a few of the Continentals who served in Congress's Own disappeared, including Sergeant Major John H. Hawkins.

Hawkins had reflected that "an Inferior in our Army sets out with many disadvantages, which are not so much his Demerits as the common Consequences of his Situation." Quartered in November 1782 with Hazen's military family in

Arent Schuyler's house at Pompton, he was surely comparing his future options with those of the officers around him. He could not think them through then, however, because of a distracting bustle: "For tho' there is none but our General's Family in [the] House, yet some are passing the Evening [hours?] talking Dutch—some French—some in singing—and dancing, which . . . suits this part of the Country, it being the chief Things done here in the Winter Evenings, both among whites and Blacks." Hawkins appreciated the comradery, but it was hard to draft a letter while someone was laying the cloth for supper "on the very Table that supports my Elbows and my Paper (which the Cook every Moment officiously displaces) while brandished Knives & Forks puts me in bodily Fear." What was going to be his future, beyond that table, outside the regiment? He did not finish his thoughts but did scribble that he tried to apply his friend's precept, "'Be humble, and be happy.'"[104]

Did that maxim apply after the war? During his tour of duty, Hawkins occasionally jotted reflections about what he wanted to do next. Yet although he had kept his eyes open for opportunities, it does not appear that he opened his own print shop. Instead, he may have pursued mercantile endeavors similar, but more modest, to those of Zacheus Peaslee and Matthew McConnell. The former ensign had a general store in Burlington, Vermont, while Hawkins's "old friend," Captain McConnell, became a dry goods (textiles) merchant and opened an exchange office providing cash for securities and certificates. Through his business enterprises and connections, including in the Society of the Cincinnati, the Hibernian Society of Philadelphia, and the Third Troop of Light Horse of Philadelphia, McConnell was one of the city's financial leaders by the 1790s. Although he lost his country house—a major symbol of elite status—in settlement of a debt, McConnell recovered as a stockbroker, becoming the first president of the Philadelphia Stock Exchange in 1800.[105] Hawkins, in turn, if he returned to Philadelphia, may have become a grocer or cordwainer.

The 1785 *Philadelphia Directory* notes a John Hawkins, grocer, on Third Street between Union and Spruce. Later directories do not have that grocer but do list a John Hawkins, cordwainer—indeed, sometimes two cordwainers so named. Setting up as a grocer sounds reasonable for the sergeant major's talents, but if his grandfather had been a glove-maker, he might have had some leather-working experience for shoemaking. A John Harper Hopkins married Elizabeth Gay, whose last name may have been Gatgen, Gagen, or Gageri, in August 1784 at Christ Church in Philadelphia. If the minister was not quite sure of the bride's name, was he of the husband's? What is known is that Hawkins signed over the 250 acres that Pennsylvania allotted him in the Donation District of Westmoreland County to Francis Murray of Bucks County for "Twenty

Pounds Pennsylvania Currency" on 10 February 1787. Then, in July 1790, he signed receipt of the survey warrant for one hundred acres of bounty lands in Ohio.[106] Those aside, his postwar life is left to the imagination, as are the lives of most of the Continental Army's veterans.

Hawkins and his fellow Continentals did not have to imagine the emerging community of the forming nation; they had trekked through its borderlands, fought on its battlefields, and labored in its encampments. They had endured a long, hard war with the army, but they had also created and experienced the connections of a greater community that was often messy, muddy, and miserable, though also spirited—including, at times, dancing and singing in multiple languages. In 1783, when he bid them farewell, General Washington proclaimed,

> Every American Officer and Soldier must now console himself for any unpleasant circumstances which may have occurred, by a recollection of the uncommon scenes in which he has been called to act, no inglorious part; and the astonishing Events of which he has been a witness ... Who, that was not a witness could imagine, that the most violent local prejudices would cease so soon, and that Men who came from the different parts of the Continent, strongly disposed by the habits of education, to despise and quarrel with each other, would instantly become but one patriotic band of Brothers?"[107]

The members of Congress's Own Regiment might not have disputed that publicly, but they knew that creating and maintaining that band—the bonds of community—had been much more than the work of a moment and a sentiment. Washington certainly did too, but a glorious cause required a glorified story. Congress's Own members and actions delivered a grittier story of how the Continentals lived and fought within the Revolution's military and political borderlands, where subjects became rebels, soldiers, and citizens.

Appendix

Congress's Own Officers

Name	Place	Previous Service[a]	Ensign	2nd /1st Lt.[b]	Captain	Other Rank/Info.	End	Death
Antill, Edward	Canada	Vol. at Quebec				Lt. Col. 1776	1782-1783	1789
Ayotte, Pierre	Canada				Feb. 1776		Jun. 1776	
Boileau, Pierre Amable	Canada		1777?	Sep. 1778		Trans. Invalid	Jan. 1782	1805
Calvet (Calvert), Pierre du	Canada		Feb. 1776	Aug. 1776			Aug. 1777	
Chinn, Edward	Canada			May 1782		PM Jun. 1777	Jun. 1783	1802
Dionne, Germain	Canada			Mar. 1776			Jun. 1783	1788
Duprie (Dupuir), Antoine	Canada		Feb. 1776	Nov. 1776			Apr. 1778	
Ferriole, Alexandre	Canada		Feb. 1776	Aug. 1780			Jan. 1782	1800
Gosselin, Clément	Canada				Mar. 1776	Ens./Lt.? 1776-79	Jun. 1783	1816
Gosselin, Louis	Canada		1779				Jun. 1783	1823
Guilmat (Gilmat), Francois	Canada		Feb. 1776	Aug. 1780			May 1782	
Hay, Udny	Canada				Feb. 1776	Maj. 1776	Jul. 1776	
Hazen, Moses	Canada					Col. Bvt. Brig.	Nov. 1783	1803
Liébert, Philippe	Canada				Feb. 1776	Trans. Invalid	Apr. 1783	1804
Martin-Pelland, François (Francis)	Canada	Paulint's company?		Dec. 1776			Oct. 1778	1778
McPherson, Murdock	Canada		Feb. 1776	Apr. 1782		Trans. Invalid	Jun. 1783	1799
Miffit (Miffert), Francis A.	Canada		Sep. 1777	May 1778			May 1779	
Olivie, Laurent	Canada		Feb. 1776		Apr. 1777	Bvt. Maj. 1783	Jun. 1783	

Name	Place	Previous Service[a]	Ensign	2nd/1st Lt.[b]	Captain	Other Rank/Info.	End	Death
Paulint, Antoine	Canada	Ind. company			*Nov. 1776*		Jul. 1782	1813/16
Torrey, Joseph	Canada				Nov. 1776	Maj. 1777	**Jun. 1783**	1783
Victor (*Caseveuve*), Felix	Canada	*Livingston's 1st*	Nov. 1777				Feb. 1781	1820
Minyier (Minger), Edmund	*Canada?*					Adj. Feb. 1777	Apr. 1777	
Delagard, C. H.	*Canada?*					*Adj.? Nov. 1776*	Oct. 1777	
Cady, Palmer	Conn.	Elmore's	Feb. 1777	Mar. 1778			Jun. 1780	
Fellows, David	Conn.	Burrall's	Nov. 1776				Dec. 1779	**1779**
Hitchcock, Lyman (or Simon)	Conn.	Elmore's		May 1777		Trans.	Oct. 1777	
Mazuzen, Mark	Conn.	Elmore's		Nov. 1776			Nov. 1777	**1777**
Munson, William	Conn.	Elmore's		Nov. 1776	Jan. 1778		**Jun. 1783**	
Parmelee, Jeremiah	Conn.	Elmore's			Nov. 1776		Mar. 1778	**1778**
Robinson, Samuel	Conn.	*Pvt./Cpl.*				QM 1777	Apr. 1782	
Satterlee, William	Conn.	Elmore's			Nov. 1776	Bvt. Maj. 1783	**Jun. 1783**	1798
Sloan, Alexander	Conn.	Elmore's		Dec. 1776			Jun. 1777	
Thompson, James	Conn.	4th Conn.				QM 1777	Jan. 1778	1804
Lee, Noah	Conn./Vt.	Green Mt. Boys	Nov. 1776		Jun. 1778		**Jun. 1783**	1840

(continued)

Congress's Own Officers (*continued*)

Name	Place	Previous Service[a]	Ensign	2nd /1st Lt.[b]	Captain	Other Rank/Info.	End	Death
Popham, William	Del.	Del. Regiment			Nov. 1776	Bde. Maj./ADC/Trans.	Jun. 1778	1847
Torrey, William	Mass.		Jan. 1778	Oct. 1780		Bvt. Cpt. 1783	**Jun. 1783**	1831
White, Moses	Mass.			Nov. 1776	Nov. 1776	ADC 1781	**Nov. 1783**	1833
Carlile, John	Md.				Nov. 1776		**Jul. 1783**	
Gilbert, Michael	Md.	2nd Md. FC		Nov. 1776	Apr. 1777		Apr. 1781	
Giles, Edward	Md.				1778	Trans.	1779	
Hoops, Adam	Md.			Dec. 1776	Oct. 1779	Trans.	Nov. 1779	
Hughes, John	Md.			Nov. 1776	Sep. 1778		Dec. 1781	
Lewis, Joseph	Md.	Md. Battalion FC		Nov. 1776			Nov. 1780	
Teas, Alexander	Md.			Nov. 1776			Sep. 1777	**1777**
Peaslee, Zacheus	N.H./Mass.	Pvt./Vol. 1779	Jan. 1782			*Bvt. Lt. 1783?*	**Jun. 1783**	1810
Anderson, James	N.J.	2nd N.J.		Nov. 1776			**Jun. 1783**	1825
Armstrong, James Francis	N.J.	N.J. militia				*Chaplain. Trans.*	*Feb. 1778*	*1801/16*
Heron, James	N.J.			Jul. 1776	Nov. 1776		Jul. 1780	

Name	Place	Previous Service[a]	Ensign	2nd /1st Lt.[b]	Captain	Other Rank/Info.	End	Death
Lloyd, Richard	N.J.	3rd N.J.		Nov. 1776	Sep. 1777	Bvt. Maj. 1783	**Jun. 1783**	1792
Alexander, Samuel	N.Y.			Nov. 1776		QM	Jun. 1777	
Bell, Thomas	N.Y.		Jan. 1777	Sep. 1777			Jun. 1779	
Buchan[n]an, Robert (Wm.)	N.Y.				Nov. 1776		May 1777	
Church, Samuel	N.Y.					Surg. mate Apr. 1777	Nov. 1777	
Dill, Robert	N.Y.					PM Jan. 1777	Jul. 1777	
Duffy (Duffee), Timothy	N.Y.	Sgt.				Surg. mate Apr. 1777	Oct. 1778	
Erskine, John	N.Y.			Nov. 1776			Mar. 1778	
Erskine, William	N.Y.			*Apr. 1777*		*(Heitman record only)*	*Nov. 1777*	
Garnet, William	N.Y.					Surg. mate 1777	Feb. 1778	**1778**
Gibson, John	N.Y.			Mar. 1777			Jun. 1777	
Mooers, Benjamin	N.Y.	N.Y. militia	Mar. 1778	Mar. 1780		Adj. Aug. 1780	**Jun. 1783**	1838
Russell, John	N.Y.		Dec. 1776	Jan. 1777			Dec. 1777	
Schuyler, Nicholas	N.Y.	North. Gen. Hosp.				Surg. 1778	**Jun. 1783**	1824
Stedman, James	N.Y.			Nov. 1776			Jan. 1778	
Tillotson, William	N.Y.					Surg. 1777	Dec. 1777	

(continued)

Congress's Own Officers (*continued*)

Name	Place	Previous Service[a]	Ensign	2nd /1st Lt.[b]	Captain	Other Rank/Info.	End	Death
Wilson, Alexander	N.Y.			Nov. 1776			Apr. 1780	**1780**
Burns, Robert	Pa.	Miles's Pa.		Nov. 1776	Apr. 1777		*Jan. 1782*	
Campbell, Robert	Pa.	Miles's Pa.		Apr. 1777	Feb. 1778	Trans. Invalid	Oct. 1779	*1779*
Chambers, Benjamin	Pa.	1st Cont. Infantry			Nov. 1776		Feb. 1778	1813
Chambers, William	Pa.	2nd Pa. Battalion			Dec. 1776		Jan. 1778	
Craig, Robert	Pa.			Nov. 1776			Feb. 1778	1838
Duncan, James	Pa.			Nov. 1776	Mar. 1778		**Jun. 1783**	1844
Lee, Andrew	Pa.		Nov. 1776	Sep. 1779			*Jun. 1783*	1821
Manning, Lawrence	Pa.	Sgt./Sgt. Maj.	Sep. 1778	Jul. 1779		Trans.	Mar. 1780	
McConnell, Matthew	Pa.	1st Cont. Infantry			Nov. 1776	Trans. Invalid 1781	*Oct. 1783*	1816
McMichael, William	Pa.	Sgt.		Feb. 1777			May 1777	
O'Hara, Henry	Pa.	Wynkoop's 4th N.Y.			Nov. 1776		Sep. 1777	
Pry, Thomas	Pa.			Nov. 1776	Feb. 1778		**Nov. 1783**	1789
Reid, James R.	Pa.	4th Pa. Battalion			Nov. 1776	Maj. 1777	**Jun. 1783**	1789
Selin, Anthony	*Pa.*	Ottendorf's			*Jan. 1781*		**Jun. 1783**	1792
Thompson, John	Pa.	Miles's Pa.			Nov. 1776		Oct. 1777	1834

Name	Place	Previous Service[a]	Ensign	2nd /1st Lt.[b]	Captain	Other Rank/Info.	End	Death
Stuart (Stewart), William	Pa./N.Y.			Nov. 1776		Adj. 1777	**Jun. 1783**	1831
Thompson, Thomas	Pa./N.Y.	Pvt.	May 1782			QM 1782	**Jun. 1783**	
Sanford (Sandford), Samuel	R.I.	*R.I. militia*	Dec. 1776	Mar. 1780			Apr. 1780	1804
Bugbee, Edward	R.I./Mass.	Baldwin's	Jan. 1781			QM 1781	Jan. 1783	1804
Montgomery, Michael	Va.			Nov. 1776			Jan. 1781	
Taylor, John	Va.	1st Va.				Maj. 1776	Feb. 1779	1824
Taylor, Reuben	Va.			Nov. 1776	Feb. 1778		Oct. 1781	
Walden, Ambrose	Va.	Va. minute co.	May 1777	Feb. 1778			Oct. 1778	1840
Woodson, Tarlton	Va.	1st and 10th Va.				Maj. 1777	*Jan. 1782*	*1818*

Mentioned in one or more sources, but questionable association in terms of rank, time, or name:

Name	Place	Previous Service[a]	Ensign	2nd /1st Lt.[b]	Captain	Other Rank/Info.	End	Death
Brindamour, Jean Ménard dit	Canada	Ind. co. of Canadian volunteers				Cpt. 76		
de Colerus, Christian	France			Bvt Maj. 1776		Maj. May 77		
DeKelley, Theodore		*Pvt. Decale or De Calla?*				*Surg. mate?*		
Delazenne, Joseph C.	Canada					*C. H. Delagard?*		

(continued)

Congress's Own Officers (*continued*)

Name	Place	Previous Service[a]	Ensign	2nd /1st Lt.[b]	Captain	Other Rank/Info.	End	Death
Hamtramck, John Francis	Canada	Duggan's		*Lt. 1776*		Cpt. 76		
Markle, Charles (Carl Marckle)	Md.	Ottendorf/Armand		*Nov. 1776*				
Monty, François	Canada	1st Canadian to 1780				Vol. Jan. 1781		
Glenny, James?	*Canada?*	*Lt. William Glenny, NY line?*						

Source: Drawn from COR Roll, CSR, RWPBF, and, for a few deaths, newspaper accounts.

Key:

ADC = Aide-de-camp	FC = Flying Camp	QM = Quartermaster	
Adj. = Adjutant	Ind. = Independent	Surg. = Surgeon	
Bde. = Brigade	Invalid = Corps of Invalids	Trans. = Transfer	
Bvt. = Brevet	PM = Paymaster	Vol. = Volunteer	

Bold = End of service by death or with discharge of regiment.

Italics = Uncertain or unconfirmed information.

? = Speculation.

[a]Previous service in other units or as an enlisted member in Hazen's before commission.

[b]Earliest commission as a lieutenant, whether as second or first lieutenant.

ABBREVIATIONS

AA4	Force, Peter, ed. *American Archives, Fourth Series.* 6 vols. Washington, D.C.: M. St. Clair Clarke and Peter Force, 1837–1846.
AA5	Force, Peter, ed. *American Archives, Fifth Series.* 3 vols. Washington, D.C.: M. St. Clair Clarke and Peter Force, 1848–1853.
AHN	America's Historical Newspapers databases (including Early American Newspapers, 1690–1922).
BMC	Bailey-Moore [Mooers] Collection, no. 74.7. Feinberg Library, Special Collections, State University of New York (SUNY) College at Plattsburgh, Plattsburgh, N.Y.
BAC/LAC	Bibliothèque et Archives/Library and Archives Canada, Ottawa, Ont., Canada.
COR Roll	Congress's Own Regimental Roll. Compilation includes: "Names of Persons in the Congress own Regiment Commanded by Colonel Moses Hazen Brigadier General by Brevet, in the service of the United States 1782," with "Copy of a Caption . . . made out in 1783 by Benjamin Mooers Lieut. And adjutant thereof—Copied for the use of the Secretary of Treasury of the United States," Plattsburgh, 15 June 1830, RWR M246, film 4, reel 132; with additions from fall 1782 roll by Sergeant Major John H. Hawkins (JHJ); and information from CSR, RWPBF, and RWR files.
CSR	Compiled Service Records of Soldiers Who Served in the American Army during the Revolutionary War, 1775–1783. Record Group 93, microfilm M881. War Department Collection of Revolutionary War Records. Washington, D.C.: National Archives and Records Administration.
DLAR	David Library of the American Revolution, Washington Crossing, Pa.
Founders Online	Founders Online digital archives. National Historical Publications and Records Commission (NHPRC), National Archives, Washington, D.C. (EA indicates early access document.)
GLC	Gilder Lehrman Collection, Gilder Lehrman Institute of American History, New York, N.Y.
GW	George Washington

GWP   George Washington Papers. 9 series. Manuscript Division. Washington, D.C.: Library of Congress.

HSP   Historical Society of Pennsylvania, Philadelphia, Pa.

JCC   Ford, Worthington C. et al., eds. *Journals of the Continental Congress, 1774–1789.* 34 vols. Washington, D.C.: Library of Congress, 1904–37.

JHJ   Hawkins, John H. "Journal of Sergeant Major John H. Hawkins, 1779–1782." Collection Am.0765, HSP.

JSS   Jack and Shirley Silver Special Collections Library, University of Vermont, Burlington, Vt.

LOC   Library of Congress, Manuscripts Division, Washington, D.C

LDC   Smith, Paul H., ed. *Letters of Delegates to Congress, 1774–1789.* 26 vols. Washington, D.C.: Library of Congress, 1976–2000.

MH   Moses Hazen

MHOB   Moses Hazen [John H. Hawkins] Orderly Books. 2 vols. Collection Am.649, HSP.

NYHS   New-York Historical Society, New York, New York.

NYSL   New York State Library, Special Collections, New York, N.Y.

PCC   Papers of the Continental Congress, 1774–89. Records of Continental and Confederation Congresses and Constitutional Convention. Record Group 360, microfilm M247. Washington, D.C.: National Archives and Records Administration.

PGW   Abbot, W. W. et al., eds. *The Papers of George Washington.* Multiple series. Charlottesville: University of Virginia Press, 1985–2019 (ongoing).

PGW:RWS   Chase, Philander D. et al., eds. *The Papers of George Washington: Revolutionary War Series.* 26 volumes and continuing. Charlottesville: University of Virginia Press, 1985–2019 (ongoing).

PHMC   Pennsylvania Historical and Museum Commission, Harrisburg, Pa.

RWPBF   Revolutionary War Pension and Bounty-Land-Warrant Application Files. Records of the Veterans Administration. Record Group 15, microfilm M804. Washington, D.C.: National Archives and Records Administration.

RWR   Revolutionary War Rolls, 1775–1783. Record Group 93, microfilm M246. War Department Collection of Revolutionary War Records. Washington, D.C.: National Archives and Records Administration.

2CROB   Second Canadian Regiment, Continental Army, Orderly Books. 2 vols. Collection Am.632, HSP.

SOC   Society of the Cincinnati, Washington, D.C.

WGW   Fitzpatrick, John C., ed. *The Writings of George Washington from the Original Manuscript Sources, 1745–1799.* 39 vols. Washington, D.C.: United States Government Printing Office, 1931–44.

Notes

Preface

1. William Shakespeare, *Romeo and Juliet,* act II, scene II, in *William Shakespeare: The Complete Works,* ed. Alfred Harbage (Baltimore, Md.: Penguin Books, 1969), p. 869; Paine, *Common Sense,* in *Writings,* ed. Conway, 84–85, 86–88; Mooers to John J. DeGraff, Plattsburgh, N.Y., 16 April 1830, in Daniel O'Keiff (Keath) file, RWPBF, S.43101, reel 1840.
2. Ebenezer Griswold, RWPBF, S.37025, reel 1137.

Introduction

1. Regimental Formation, 20 January 1776, and Army Discharge, 29 October and 4 November 1783, *JCC,* 4:75, 25:753, 806; Proclamation, 4 November 1783, *WGW,* 27:229–30.
2. Drake, "Appropriating a Continent," 323–25.
3. Washington, General Orders, Cambridge, 4 July 1775, *PGW:RWS,* 1:54; Samuel Ward to Henry Ward, Philadelphia, 21 November and 27 December 1775, *LDC,* 2:370, 530. A true continental establishment was a hotly debated concept. See John Adams's Notes of Debates, 10 October 1775, *LDC,* 2:155–56.
4. Congress authorized twenty-six infantry regiments for the 1776 establishment, but designating the Pennsylvania Rifle Regiment with associated Virginia and Maryland companies on the day the army was born, 14 June 1775, as the 1st Continental Regiment made the total twenty-seven. R. K. Wright, *Continental Army,* 47, 54; 14 June 1775, *JCC,* 2:89; Council of War, [Cambridge, 2 November 1775], *PGW:RWS,* 2:279–80.
5. 23 October and 11 November 1776, *JCC,* 6:900, 940.
6. John Manning recorded that he had served in Livingston's "Congress" Regiment. See RWPBF, S.34422, reel 1624. Julian Belanger said that Hazen's regiment was "called one of the congress regiments." See RWPBF, S.21654, reel 203.
7. 3 October 1780, *JCC,* 18:894, 896.
8. 15 April 1777 and 24 November 1778, *JCC,* 7:270, 12:1159; Moses Hazen (hereafter MH), "The Case with Colonel Hazen's Regiment," White Plains, 3 September 1778, JSS; R. K. Wright, *Continental Army,* 125–28.
9. Congress's Own Regimental Roll (hereafter COR Roll) of 1,452 soldiers' names compiled from rosters by Benjamin Mooers and John H. Hawkins, with extra data

from CSR, RWPBF, and RWR files. Additional names are in CSR and on officer lists.

10. This relates to Paul Kennedy's "*mid-level* History" in "History from the Middle," 38. See also Ruddiman, "'A record in the hands of thousands,'" 748, 754–57, 763.

11. B. Anderson, *Imagined Communities*, 6, 53–54; on "military pilgrimages," see ibid., 57n35. John Adams showed his northern bias when he said that the characters of people in the different colonies differed as if they were almost from different nations, but "an Alteration of the Southern Constitutions, which must certainly take Place if this War continues will gradually bring all the Continent nearer and nearer to each other in all Respects." See letter to Joseph Hawley, Philadelphia, 25 November 1775, *LDC*, 2:385–86.

12. The editors of the Franklin papers used "impromptu" in the headnote to "Minutes of the Conference between a Committee of Congress, Washington, and Representatives of the New England Colonies." See Franklin, *Papers of Benjamin Franklin*, 22:224.

13. R. Smith, *Stories of Peoplehood*, 4–8, 12–13, 20–21.

14. On "internal frontiers," see Black, "Frontiers and Military History," 1048. My definition owes much to the preface in S. Evans, *Borderlands of the American and Canadian Wests*, and in particular to Victor Konrad's definition on p. xxi: borderlands "exist when shared characteristics set a region apart from the countries that contain it, and residents share more with each other than with members of their respective national cultures."

15. This is a nod to Oscar Handlin's *The Uprooted*. He studied nineteenth-century immigrants and their alienation in the United States and "continued connectedness" (260) to their old homes as they created new communities, ghettos, within other rapidly growing communities (144–45). Paul Vitello wrote that Handlin made a case that "immigration—more than the frontier experience . . . was the continuing, defining event of U.S. History." (Paul Vitello, "Oscar Handlin, Historian Who Chronicled U.S. Immigration, Dies at 95," 23 September 2011, *New York Times*.)

16. Writ large and small in institutional and human bodies, this study offers aspects of the "spatial mobility, situational identity, local contingency, and the ambiguities of power" that Pekka Hämäläinen and Samuel Truett say identify "the brave new world of borderlands history." See Hämäläinen and Truett, "On Borderlands," 338.

17. This connection picks up on María de la Luz Ibarra's "narratives of disillusionment" and "narratives of crossing" in "Buscando La Vida: Mexican Immigrant Women's Memories of Home, Yearning, and Border Crossings," in Castañeda et al., *Gender on the Borderlands*, 262–63.

18. Jeremy Adelman and Stephen Aron have argued that frontiers be seen as "*borderless* lands" of intercultural mixing and accommodation and that the term borderlands be used "for the contested boundaries between colonial domains" that ultimately became "*bordered* lands" between nations. They called for studying borderlands and frontiers as interrelated but separate issues. See Adelman and Aron, "From Borderlands to Borders," 814–16. In response, Evan Haefeli argued that a borderland "as a place where autonomous peoples of different cultures are bound together by a greater, multi-imperial context" should be more clearly differentiated from frontier. See Haefeli, "A Note on the Use of North American Borderlands," 1224.

Christopher Ebert Schmidt-Nowara applauded Adelman and Aron's "conceptual tools" but questioned the narrow, Anglo focus. See Schmidt-Nowara, "Borders and Borderlands of Interpretation," 1228. John R. Wunder and Pekka Hämäläinen criticized the proposed model as "'old' western history" and simplistic in using colonial-imperial relations as the major determinant rather than incorporating more economic, environmental, and Native American factors. See Wunder and Hämäläinen, "Of Lethal Places and Lethal Essays," 1230–31. Adelman and Aron responded that although they limited their case studies (as historians must), they welcomed expanding the approach, but challenged the challengers for dismissing other aspects of their proposal about how and why there should be a demarcation between frontier and borderlands in interpretations. See Adelman and Aron, "Of Lively Exchanges and Larger Perspectives," 1237–38.

19. Kathleen DuVal said "two entities," but there could be more. She noted the move away from "European-centered definitions of cores and peripheries," and "that a borderland can also refer to the contested space between an American Indian power and a non-Indian one, or two American Indian powers." See DuVal, *Borderlands*, introduction. One might thus consider other contesting groups and spaces. Furthermore, as Andrew K. Frank and A. Glenn Crothers noted, the "explosion" of borderlands scholarship has shattered its definition—or definitions—as place or process. See Frank and Crothers, *Borderland Narratives*, 1.

20. Time or timing helps explain the diversity in encounters and anglicization in the expanding English empire. See Bailyn and Morgan, *Strangers within the Realm*, 20–21.

21. Gregory H. Nobles argued that while Turner's "frontier thesis" is an anachronism, the basic issue at its foundation is not. See Nobles, "Breaking into the Backcountry," 641–43, esp. 642. For Bernard Bailyn's idea of periphery, with the interpretative limitation being European centers, see Bailyn, *Peopling of British North America*, esp. 112–14.

22. Nobles, *American Frontiers*, xii–xiii; Spero, *Frontier Country*, 106, 195–96, 260–76.

23. For example, see Matthew Ward's *Breaking the Backcountry* and Warren Hofstra's definition and summary in "Backcountry Frontier of Colonial Virginia." Richard White provided a paradigm shift with *The Middle Ground*, and Daniel K. Richter reverses the usual east-west focus in *Facing East from Indian Country*.

24. Usner, "Borderlands," and Countryman, "Postscript," in Vickers, *Companion to Colonial America*, 416–19, 533.

25. In the January 2006 issue of the *William and Mary Quarterly*, Richard White stated that "the middle ground as a process is replicable in other places and other times," but every place or instance where it may be found is not the equivalent of the Upper Country of French Canada that he studied in *The Middle Ground*. In the same issue, Philip J. Deloria addressed "cross-social" contexts and the general application of White's argument. R. White, "Creative Misunderstandings and New Understandings," 9–14, esp. 10; Deloria, "What Is the Middle Ground, Anyway?" 15–22, esp. 16.

26. Gitlin, *Bourgeois Frontier*; Smith and Hilton, *Nexus of Empire*.

27. François Furstenberg, with a focus on the Native American struggle for control in the trans-Appalachian West, notes how older frontier studies concentrated on imperial centers, whereas current attention is on local actors (soldiers not listed),

and he posits combining the two in an Atlantic perspective. See Furstenberg, "Significance of the Trans-Appalachian Frontier," 647–77, esp. 650–53. Samuel Watson provides a good annotated bibliography with an antebellum military and national frontier analysis. See Watson, "Continuity in Civil-Military Relations," 221–50, esp. 221–32.

28. A. Taylor, *Divided Ground*, 7.

29. The expansion and development of forts, posts, cantonments, arsenals, depots, and stations into what became known as military reservations may be gleaned from discussions about property at West Point, 25 January and 4 February 1780, 31 July 1786, *JCC*, 16:86–87, 124, 30:447–8; and via *U.S. Senate Journal*, 1st Cong., 2nd sess., 18 and 25 June 1790, 1:163, 165, and 12th Cong., 2nd sess., 17 December 1812, 5:218. The use of the term "reservation" for a military post evolved through the early nineteenth century, but by the 1840s and 1850s, "military reservation" was apparently coming into common usage.

30. Colonel Henry Bouquet suggested that Light-Troops be established for frontier service, and that after they served fifteen or more years, they should be given plantations within districts reserved for that purpose; this would induce enlistment and secure the frontier where they settled. See W. Smith, *Bouquet's Expedition Against the Ohio Indians*, 259. General Thomas Gage suggested forming a "Military Settlement round Fort-Pitt, by granting the Lands Gratis, in Lots, not exceeding two Hundred Acres each, on Military Tenures ... We may by such means, become formidable on the Ohio, at no Expence and in a short Time; And the Fort may be supplied at an easy Rate." See Gage to the Earl of Halifax, 14 April 1764, in *Correspondence of General Thomas Gage*, 1:24–25.

31. For an introduction to the "New England town studies," see J. P. Greene, "Autonomy and Stability," 171–94. For a modern review comparing such community and other studies for attention to land as place within a transatlantic rather than protonational framework, see Halttunen, "Grounded Histories," 513–32.

32. Greven, *Four Generations*; Lockridge, *New England Town*.

33. Gross, *The Minutemen and Their World*, 18–21, 59–60, 143–51.

34. Lockridge, *New England Town*, xiii.

35. Michael N. McConnell presents British regiments as mobile communities that both reflected and were separate from British civilian society. See McConnell, *Army and Empire*, 53–72, esp. 53–55.

36. Mayer, *Belonging to the Army*. Others include Cox, *A Proper Sense of Honor* and *Boy Soldiers of the American Revolution*; Ruddiman, *Becoming Men of Some Consequence*; Neimeyer, *America Goes to War*; and Resch, *Suffering Soldiers*.

37. Higginbotham, "The Early American Way of War," 230–73, quotation on 237.

38. Royster, *Revolutionary People at War*, prologue, esp. 3–8, 23.

39. F. Anderson, *A People's Army*.

40. Lee, "Early American Ways of War," 272–73, 279, 283.

Chapter 1

1. Continental Congress, *Observations on the American Revolution*, 12, 28.

2. Continental Congress, *Observations on the American Revolution*, 71–72. This is an example of people-making as analyzed in R. Smith, *Stories of Peoplehood*, in particular, 32, 34–37.

3. 11, 15, 16, 18, and 25 May 1775, *JCC*, 2:24–25, 51–53, 55–56, 59–60.

4. 26 May and 12 June 1775, *JCC*, 2:64–65, 87.

5. Delegates from New Hampshire to South Carolina comprised the 17 June commission. The follow-up resolution about assistance said, "the delegates of all the colonies, from Nova-Scotia to Georgia, in Congress assembled, have unanimously chosen George Washington, Esq. to be General and commander in chief." Delegates from Georgia did finally arrive, but the inclusion of Nova Scotia was wishful thinking. Congress followed the process of appointment first, then commission, with the other general officers. See 13–17 June 1775, *JCC*, 2:89–97.

6. R. K. Wright, *Continental Army*, 23–29.

7. Don Higginbotham noted that Congress retained control of the army in accordance with Whig ideas, adding that "as the civil government" (a questionable designation for 1775), it determined policy but only occasionally strategy (as with the invasion of Canada). Higginbotham, *War of American Independence*, 91–93. Pauline Maier argued that the responsibilities Congress assumed made it "for all practical purposes a national government," but the authority for tackling those responsibilities was limited, except in creating and directing the army. Maier, *American Scripture*, 14. Congress made the army and, arguably, the army made Congress a government.

8. Eliphalet Dyer to Jonathan Trumbull Sr., Philadelphia, 16 June 1775, *LDC*, 1:495–96.

9. One could argue that the French Canadians became subjects in 1759 with the British conquest of Quebec, but confirmation came with the Treaty of Paris in 1763.

10. See Higginbotham's summary of one of Carleton's observations in *War of American Independence*, 107.

11. The term *"Canadien"* is used interchangeably with French Canadian to specify the francophone subjects of French descent within Canada and to differentiate them from the anglophone newcomers, but "Canadian" encompasses both groups.

12. The "melting pot" metaphor, popularized later, was already implied in the eighteenth century: J. Hector St. John de Crèvecoeur wrote in 1782, "*He* is an American, who, leaving behind him all his ancient prejudices and manners, receives new ones from the new mode of life he has embraced, the new government he obeys, and the new rank he holds. . . . Here individuals of all nations are melted into a new race of men, whose labours and posterity will one day cause great changes in the world." Crèvecoeur, *Letters from an American Farmer*, 70. Alberto Lena offered another take on the melting pot, arguing that Franklin "did not believe that a multicultural population could consolidate American national identity in the post-revolutionary era," based on analysis of Franklin's 1760 *The Interests of Great Britain with Regard to her Colonies*. Lena did not connect the Franklin of 1760 to Franklin the commissioner in 1776, except to conclude that Franklin gave up the idea of a British Canada for one of a Canada integrated into the United States, which included the assimilation of the one into the manners and language of the other. Lena, "Benjamin Franklin's 'Canada Pamphlet,'" 36–49, 47–48. As Lena interpreted the 1760 pamphlet, Franklin wanted peace and security via "a world," meaning America, "without neighbors" who were different culturally and politically and who competed for space and power. Crèvecoeur offered a benign, bottom-up version of the melting pot, whereas Franklin's was an imperial, top-down view.

13. Anderson and Cayton, *Dominion of War*, 168–69.
14. M. Anderson, *Battle for the Fourteenth Colony*, 58–64.
15. Edmund Pendleton to Joseph Chew, Philadelphia, 15 June 1775, *LDC*, 1:489.
16. 1 June 1775, *JCC*, 2:75.
17. After ordering the printing of a memorial to inhabitants of the British colonies, the First Continental Congress resolved to send letters to the colonies of St. John's, Nova Scotia, Georgia, and East and West Florida "who have not deputies to represent them in this Congress." At the same time, it resolved that "an address be prepared to the people of Quebec." 21 October 1774, *JCC*, 1:101.
18. Nova Scotia was seen as a distinct province rather than within the "Canada" of Quebec province. The responses of its inhabitants to the American Revolution offer interesting comparisons with those of francophone and anglophone Canadians elsewhere. One starting point to such a comparison might be two essays, published fifty years apart: Armstrong, "Neutrality and Religion in Revolutionary Nova Scotia," 50–62; and Plank, "The Two Majors Cope," 18–40. The first serves as a reminder that struggles over religious accommodations or tolerance encompassed Protestant sectarian issues, not just Protestant versus Catholic ones. The second examines "ethnic or national group-consciousness" in the heterogeneous (i.e., Native American, Acadian, French, British, and Anglo-American) province and debates over whether national identity was to be narrowly or broadly construed.
19. See for example Colley, *Britons*; Calloway, *White People, Indians, and Highlanders*; and Brown, "The Impact of the Colonial Anti-Catholic Tradition on the Canadian Campaign," 559–75.
20. Similar ideas were addressed in Daunton and Halpern, eds., *Empire and Others*, in particular Morgan, "Encounters between British and 'Indigenous' Peoples," 44–45. See also Colley, *Britons*, 3–6, 132–37; and Hanson, *Necessary Virtue*, 7–14.
21. C. A. Bayly notes how the concept of "indigenous" was contested and changing. Bayly, "The British and Indigenous Peoples," 20–21.
22. George F. G. Stanley indicated that the 1784 census recorded 113,012 provincials in Canada (Quebec, Montreal, and Trois-Rivières areas), which must have included thousands of newly arrived loyalists, whereas during debates over the Quebec Act, Carleton said there were probably only about 360 Protestants—besides women and children—in the area. Stanley, *Canada Invaded*, 3–5, 165n4. Justin H. Smith referred to General Frederick Haldimand's 1780 estimate of 60,000 French Canadians against 2,000 Anglo-Canadians, but noted that Haldimand's estimate must have been low given the 1784 census. J. Smith, *Our Struggle for the Fourteenth Colony*, 48n4. By comparison, when Anglo-Canadians protested the Quebec Act, they said that the French population was no more than 75,000 and overstated the British settlers as numbering 3,000 and rising. See Lanctot, *Canada and the American Revolution*, 31.
23. Gustave Lanctot argues that the seeds of the Quebec Act were planted as early as 1764, but changes in the ministry in England and the Anglo minority's opposition in Canada delayed the bill's presentation till May 1774, with it finally implemented in May 1775. See Lanctot, *Canada and the American Revolution*, 25–26. Besides illuminating contemporary reactions on both sides of the Atlantic, Philip Lawson notes how British imperial historians tend to assess the Quebec Act as "benign statesmanship," whereas American scholars tend to accept contemporary colonial

views that it "threatened the very bedrock of civil society." Lawson, "'Sapped by Corruption,'" 301–2. Lawson does well in trying to bury the old Whig interpretation of the act in *The Imperial Challenge*, especially on pp. 123–24 and 141, but in arguing against the myth of the Quebec Act as one of Britain's Coercive Acts, he downplays the American reception of it as one of the "Intolerable Acts."

24. Anburey, *Travels Through the Interior Parts of America*, 66.

25. As Paul David Nelson notes, escalating tensions in Massachusetts and elsewhere "galvanized officials in London to pay attention to Quebec." Nelson, *General Sir Guy Carleton*, 54.

26. Elizabeth Mancke makes an argument for Parliament's putting institutional concerns above ideological and cultural ones in the interest of empire. Mancke, "Early Modern Imperial Governance," 3–20, esp. 7–11.

27. A copy of the Quebec Act is published with original emphases in Lanctot, *Canada and the American Revolution*, 229–37.

28. For a dramatization about French Canadian perceptions, see [Maseres], *The Canadian Freeholder* (1777), SOC. Lawrence Levine noted how such an assumption about groups has challenged historians: "What looked like a group becomes an amalgam of groups; what looked like a culture becomes a series of cultures." Levine, *Opening of the American Mind*, 155.

29. Stanley, *Canada Invaded*, 10–11, 19. Ainslie, "Journal of the most remarkable occurrences in the Province of Quebec," HSP.

30. Vachon, "Briand, Jean-Olivier," in *Dictionary of Canadian Biography*.

31. Hanson, *Necessary Virtue*, 36, 52.

32. This implies another facet to the argument that the American Revolution may have been "a crisis of integration rather than disintegration," which Stephen Conway explored from another angle in "From Fellow-Nationals to Foreigners." Conway, as others have, noted how demands for British rights dovetailed with assertions of Britishness, of being Britons; but he also argued that while many Britons accepted "Americans" as British through the beginning of the war, that changed with the Franco-American alliance. That association "convinced a wide spectrum of Britons that the Americans were no longer part of the same nation. The French alliance flew in the face of the Gallophobia that had united Britons and Americans for generations." Conway, "From Fellow-Nationals to Foreigners," 65–100, esp. 68.

33. Codignola, "Roman Catholic Conservatism in a New North Atlantic World," 720–23; Carleton to Dartmouth, Montreal, 7 June 1775, in *History of the Organization, Development and Services of the Military and Naval Forces of Canada*, 2:52 (hereafter cited as *History of the Military of Canada*).

34. Carleton to Dartmouth, Montreal, 7 June 1775, and Carleton, *A Proclamation* (enacting martial law and ordering the raising of militia), 9 June 1775, *History of the Military of Canada*, 2:51–53, 53–54. Hazen, with divided sentiments and Canadian property, had been a captain in the provincial Rogers' Rangers and then a lieutenant in the British army's 44th Regiment of Foot. Everest, *Moses Hazen and the Canadian Refugees*, 5–14, 29.

35. Gabriel, *Quebec during the American Invasion*, xxxii, xli–xlii, xxxvii, 4, 27–28, 128n31. Examiners Baby, Taschereau, and Williams did not always record full names.

36. Gabriel, *Quebec during the American Invasion*, 30, 43, 49, 57.
37. Gabriel, *Quebec during the American Invasion*, 107. Brief biographical sketches of Germain Dionne and Clément Gosselin are found in Fr. Owen Taggart's "Québécois Combatants in the Continental Army."
38. Carleton to General James Murray, 15 June 1776, *History of the Military of Canada*, 2:167. Also, echoing prejudices against provincials—if not ethnocentrism—from the last war, Canadian "officers were to rank below the youngest grade in the regular army." J. Smith, *Our Struggle for the Fourteenth Colony*, 338.
39. Rodrigue, "An Album in the Attic," 45–73. Although Ethan Allen boasted to Montgomery on 20 September 1775 that he had 250 Canadians and would soon have 500, he apparently had only about 80 following him to St. Johns. That November, Livingston reported having 1,000 Canadians with him, but by the following April 1776 he had perhaps 200, and Moses Hazen could report only 250 Canadians on his rolls. See J. Smith, *Our Struggle for the Fourteenth Colony*, 1:380–81, 384, 469; 2:201.
40. On Whig use of anti-popery to gain support for revolution, see Cogliano, *No King, No Popery*; 17 September 1774, *JCC*, 1:31–40.
41. Cogliano, *No King, No Popery*, 49; 14 and 20 October 1774, *JCC*, 1:70–71, 76.
42. "To the people of Great Britain . . .," in Lanctot, *Canada and the American Revolution*, 237–47.
43. Cogliano, *No King, No Popery*, 60–64; Metzger, *Catholics and the American Revolution*, 31; Johnson, "The Patriot," *Works of Samuel Johnson*, 14: 81–93. Greater toleration of Catholic persons and practices was part of the Revolution, but there was not a revolutionary sweeping away of all prejudice, as noted in Hanson, *Necessary Virtue*, 219–20.
44. M. Lawson, "Canada and the Articles of Confederation," 40–41; "To the Inhabitants of the Province of Quebec," 26 October 1774, *JCC*, 1:105–13. Gustave Lanctot notes that Thomas Cushing, John Dickinson, and, primarily, Richard Henry Lee wrote the "Letter Addressed to the Inhabitants of the Province of Quebec." Lanctot, *Canada and the American Revolution*, 27.
45. Shklar, *Montesquieu*, esp. 21, 68–69. Bernard Bailyn argued that the leading Enlightenment thinkers, including Locke and Montesquieu, "were quoted everywhere in the colonies, by everyone who claimed a broad awareness." Bailyn, *Ideological Origins of the American Revolution*, 26–27. Questions remain, however, about how widely read revolutionary pamphlets were in all of the colonies, and how deeply understood were the references to the philosophers. See Preudhome (or Prudent) La Jeunesse of Montreal to the Committee of Secret Correspondence, on or before 14 February 1776, in Franklin, *Papers of Benjamin Franklin*, 352. Michel Tétu posited that the *Canadiens* were not ensnared by American rhetoric because they maintained some independence under the British government, they did not want another war, "they were monarchists rather than republicans," and the church encouraged loyalty to Britain. See Tétu, "Quebec and the French Revolution," 2–6, esp. 3. Although the *Canadiens* first supported the French Revolution—especially after the publication of the *Declaration of the Rights of Man* in 1789—by the end of 1792, as reports circulated of the vicious bloodletting in France, some *Canadiens* shelved (at least temporarily) sentiments of the Enlightenment in favor of order touted by the British government and by the immigrant,

refugee French priests who laid "the second foundation of the Church in Canada." Tétu, "Quebec and the French Revolution," 5.

46. See "To the Inhabitants of the Province of Quebec," 26 October 1774, *JCC*, 1:104–13; "To the oppressed Inhabitants of Canada," 29 May 1775, *JCC*, 2:68–70; and "The letter to the Inhabitants of the Province of Canada," 24 January 1776, *JCC*, 4:85–86. Put another way: "God and nature" gave Catholics "a right to the enjoyment of their religion." *AA4*, III, 1749, in "Congress and George III Agree on 'Popery,'" Griffin, *Catholics and the American Revolution*, 3:221. Related excerpts include "For Religious Liberty" and "Hated Popes and Bishops" (3:220, 221). This was seen in Britain too, for as Philip Lawson noted, Advocate-General James Marriott proposed toleration for "the Catholics' practice of their religion but not the doctrine, organization, or government of the Roman church." Lawson, *The Imperial Challenge*, 118.

47. England imposed religious toleration on the Puritan dissenters of the Massachusetts Bay Colony in the 1690s, at which time Increase Mather argued that accepting the new charter's dictates rebounded on the dissenters in securing their religion. Accommodation could benefit both sides. See B. Tucker, "Reinvention of New England," 318–19.

48. Livingston to Schuyler, Ste. Therese, 8 September 1775, PCC, roll 172, item 153, vol. 1, p. 148; Allen to Schuyler, 6 [14] September 1775 transcript, PCC, roll 189, item 170, vol. 1, pp. 107–9; Schuyler, "To the Inhabitants of Canada," 5 September 1775, transcript, PCC, roll 189, item 170, vol. 1, pp. 90–91.

49. GW, "Address to the inhabitants of Canada," Cambridge, 7 September 1775, PCC, roll 186, item 169, vol. 1, p. 52.

50. General Orders, Cambridge, 5 November 1775, *WGW*, 4:65.

51. Metzger, *Catholics and the American Revolution*, 50–51; Lanctot, *Canada and the American Revolution*, 98; Montgomery's answer to Montreal's offer of a treaty of capitulation, 12 November 1775, in Trudel, *La Tentation Américaine*, 95; Committee of Congress to Montgomery, Ticonderoga, 30 November 1775, PCC, roll 183, item 166, p. 13.

52. Stanley, *Canada Invaded*, 110–12; Lanctot, *Canada and the American Revolution*, 104. Mark Anderson provided a laudatory account of Goforth's civil-military relations based primarily on the journal of Jean-Baptiste Badeaux, a local notary fluent in English. Anderson also challenged the prevailing negative assessment of Wooster's actions in Montreal to argue, among other things, that what the general did to clamp down on loyalist opposition was not much different than what other patriot leaders did in their communities. In Wooster's case, however, he did it as a military (not civilian) leader, and that—plus his unflattering comments to Seth Warner that ended up in enemy hands—led to attacks on his reputation then and later. On Goforth, see M. Anderson, *Battle for the Fourteenth Colony*, 246–57; for Anderson's evaluation of Wooster, see 208–9, 212–19, 241–42, 273, and 359–60.

53. Paine, *Common Sense*, 82, 84, 85, 97, 109.

54. Gregory Knouff made that point in discussing what motivated Pennsylvanians to serve. Knouff, *The Soldiers' Revolution*, xiii, 38.

55. "'Ethnic'" nations espouse "senses of national identity that have rested on notions of shared kinship and ancestry that are broadly ethnic or racial. . . . In 'civic' nations members are bound together by voluntary, shared allegiance to political

principles and procedures. . . . '[C]ivic' nations have most often been identified with systems of democracy or popular government, in which, in theory, the nation is comprised of free and equal self-governing citizens." R. Smith, *Stories of Peoplehood*, 74.

56. Rogers Smith presented "ethically constitutive stories" as similar to stories of economic benefits and those of personal and collective political power, but often more "quasi-religious, kinship-like." R. Smith, *Stories of Peoplehood*, 69. Mónica Judith Sánchez-Flores pointed out problems with Smith's typology, and also used it to promote the "construction of an ethically constitutive story that encompasses humanity" rather than "peoples" that are almost synonyms for nations. She acknowledged that "even liberal political authorities use shared symbols, myths, and memories to tap into the emotional life of the group" so as to create belonging, and that a sense of such belonging is "an ongoing process of negotiation." Sánchez-Flores, *Cosmopolitan Liberalism*, 7–8, 42–47.

57. "The weaving and tailoring of stories of peoplehood must also take into account the more specific established interests and identities of core constituents and the particular economic, military, and political contexts in which the people-building is occurring." R. Smith, *Stories of Peoplehood*, 69–70.

58. Franklin's committee work is noted in Introduction and Chronology and Article XIII in "Proposed Articles of Confederation," July 1775, Franklin, *Papers of Benjamin Franklin*, 22:xli–lii, 125.

59. Congress to Franklin, Charles Carroll, and Samuel Chase, Instructions and Commission for the Canadian Mission, 20 March 1776, Franklin, *Papers of Benjamin Franklin*, 22:381–86; Lanctot, *Canada and the American Revolution*, 127–28.

60. Lanctot, *Canada and the American Revolution*, 135–36; Wade, *The French Canadians*, 71–72; Richard Smith's Diary, "popish Priest," Wednesday, 14 February 1776, *LDC*, 3:257; 15 February 1776, *JCC*, 4:151–52.

61. Carroll, *Journal of Charles Carroll*, 30–31.

62. C. O'Donnell, "John Carroll and the Origins of an American Catholic Church," 101–26, esp. 105, 121.

63. General Wooster to Colonel Warner, Montreal, 6 January 1776, *AA4*, 588–89; *Quebec Gazette*, 14 March 1776, in *History of the Military of Canada*, 2:138–39.

64. Commissioners to Canada to [John Hancock], Montreal, 6 and 8 May 1776, and Goforth to Benjamin Franklin, Three Rivers, 22[–23] February 1776, Franklin, *Papers of Benjamin Franklin*, 22:360, 418, 424–25; M. Anderson, *Battle for the Fourteenth Colony*, 235, 252–54, 299–300.

65. French Canadians used the term *"Les Bostonnais"* (or *"Bostonais"*) to refer not only to Bostonians but also at times to New Englanders and Americans in general. See Gabriel, *Quebec during the American Invasion*, 127n14. Commenting on the possibility of U.S. annexation of Canada in response to British actions during the American Civil War, an Australian paper noted that French Canadians used the term "Bostonais" interchangeably with Yankee. See "Canada and the Canadians," 11 January 1865, *The Mercury* (Hobart, Tasmania); Coleman, "How 'Continental' Was the Continental Congress?," 541. "Congréganistes," referring to Canadians who supported the American cause, appears in Everest, *Moses Hazen and the Canadian Refugees* (38) and Lanctot, *Canada and the American Revolution* (117), perhaps pulled from Garneau, *History of Canada from its Discovery to our Days*.

Chapter 2

1. John Hancock, by order of Congress, "Address to the inhabitants of Canada," 24 January 1776, PCC, roll 23, item 12A, vol. 1, p. 50. Slightly different version with memorial by Canadian refugees in PCC, roll 49, item 41, p. 136.

2. Melvin, *Journal of the Expedition to Quebec*. Melvin, taken prisoner at Quebec, kept a record of conditions. See the 9 and 18 January and 7, 21, and 26 February entries.

3. Reed, *Memoirs of Antoine Paulint*, 25. Likely reflecting oral family history (her grandmother was Paulint's youngest daughter), Reed said that the regiment was sometimes called "Hazen's Infernals" due to the men's fighting "qualities." Samuel H. Parsons construed it otherwise when he wrote in March 1778 that he did not want "'Congress' Own' regiment of infernals," in C. Hall, *Life and Letters of Samuel Holden Parsons*, 150.

4. Greven, *Four Generations*, 170–71. Hazen's move to Canada, land speculation, and later settlement attempts in New York and New Hampshire dovetail with Greven's analysis of third- and fourth-generation migration out of Andover (156–58, 226–28).

5. Among numerous online sources tracing the Hazen genealogy is J. Hazen, *Genealogy of the Hazen Family*, 9, 16, which says that Moses Hazen the elder was born 17 May 1701, and that his daughter Abigail Hazen married Moses Mooers. (Her son said that his father's name was Benjamin. See Benjamin Mooers, "Recollections," BMC, series 4, box 14, folder 226.) For more information on Hazen and his relations, see Genealogy.com, "Descendants of Edward Hazen."

6. Everest, *Moses Hazen and the Canadian Refugees*, 2–4, 13–14; Everest, "Moses Hazen," in *Dictionary of Canadian Biography*. Hazen did not mention the 1755 enlistment, when he listed his lieutenancy in the provincial service in 1756 and then in "the Ranging Service" in 1757–58 and company command in 1759–60, including at the Louisburg stronghold on Cape Breton, Quebec (Sainte-Foy). See "Reduction of Canada," in MH to GW, Camp Near Morristown, 12 February 1780, *PGW:RWS*, 24:453–54.

7. Everest, "Moses Hazen"; MH to Colonel Theodore Atkinson, Secretary of New Hampshire, Montreal, 30 May and 11 October 1764, Peter Force Papers and Collection, series 9, reel 100, box 10, LOC; Calloway, *Western Abenakis of Vermont*, 194.

8. Joseph Kelley to the Printers of the *Quebec Gazette*, Montreal, 15 October 1766, AHN; *Newport Mercury* [Newport, R.I.], 5–12 January 1767 issue, AHN. The soldiers took Kelley at "the house of Mr. James Robertson, inn-holder at St. John's," who was probably the same man who sold five farms to Hazen and Christie. Everest, *Moses Hazen and the Canadian Refugees*, 16–17.

9. Everest, *Moses Hazen and the Canadian Refugees*, 16; Noël, *The Christie Seigneuries*, 12–13, 8–9.

10. Noël, *The Christie Seigneuries*, 12, 15–18; Indenture between Moses Hazen of Saint-John's and William Hazen and Leonard Jarvis, merchants in New England, Saint-John's, Quebec, 13 February 1769, BAC/LAC, MG8-F99, R12039-791-3-E, microfilm H-2941.

11. Munro, *Seigniorial System in Canada*, 65–66, 132. For issues with the system, see Pritchard, *In Search of Empire*, 80–83.

12. "Extract of a letter from Quebec, 9 November 1775," *History of the Military of Canada*, 2:122.

13. Everest, *Moses Hazen and the Canadian Refugees*, 29, 32; M. Anderson, *Battle for the Fourteenth Colony*, 63, 65, 106.

14. Schuyler to GW, Ticonderoga, 20 September 1775, *PGW:RWS*, 2:18, 22n4.

15. Hazen to Hancock, Montreal, 18 February 1776, PCC, roll 96, item 78, vol. 11, p. 17; M. Anderson, *Battle for the Fourteenth Colony*, 112, 115. "Narrative of the Seige [*sic*] of St Johns Canada" (attributed to John André) noted: "Mr. Hazen and Mr. Tucker who were found with the rebels (tho' indeed without Arms) were kept prisoners in the Forts. In this Affair, as there has since been throughout the Campaign in Canada There were Englishmen fighting against Englishmen, French against French and Indians of the same Tribe against each other." JSS, 18 October 1775. Timing and peas in "Hazen," Commissioners' report about Hazen's losses, Montreal, 14–17 February 1776, *AA4*, 4:1189.

16. MH to Hancock, "Inventory of Stock, &c. at St. John's [certified by Samuel Elmer, Marinus Willett, James Jeffry]," Montreal, 14–17 February 1776, *AA4*, 4:1187–90.

17. "Narrative of the Seige [*sic*]," 23 October 1775, JSS; M. Anderson, *Battle for the Fourteenth Colony*, 108, 115, 161; MH Memorial to GW, Camp near Morristown, 12 February 1780, *PGW:RWS*, 24:454; Lanctot, *Canada and the American Revolution*, 91.

18. Sypher, *New York State Society of the Cincinnati Biographies*, 6–7; W. Nelson, *Edward Antill*, 19–22; Antill to Benjamin Lincoln, 4 March 1782, PCC, roll 48, item 41, vol. 1, p. 81; Edward Antill Barrister and Attorney at Law and Public Notary appointments, Quebec, 2 June 1766, Canadiana Héritage, collection C-3921, BAC/LAC, images 218–21. There is also Audet's sketch, "Edward Antill," in *Le Bulletin des Recherches Historiques*, 548.

19. Antill's "Oath for the Office of Deputy Commissary of the Court of Vice Admiralty," Quebec, 9 November 1768, Canadiana Héritage, collection C-3921, BAC/LAC, image 845. See also Petition of Thomas Valentine and Edward Antill, 14 November 1772, BAC/LAC, RG1-L3L, vol. 198, reel C-2567, no. 93505-07; Petition of Edward Antill, 6 August 1773, BAC/LAC, RG1-L3L, vol. 32, reel C-2505, no. 16751-6; Petition of Edward Antill, 18 August 1774, BAC/LAC, RG1-L3L, vol. 32, reel C-2505, no. 16757-8; and the birth record for Charlotte Riverain Antill, in *New England Historical & Genealogical Register and Antiquarian Journal*, 19:165–66.

20. Stanley, *Canada Invaded*, 10; M. Anderson, *Battle for the Fourteenth Colony*, 46; Petition to Lt. Governor for an Assembly, Quebec and Montreal, 29 November 1773, and Petition to the King, Quebec, 31 December 1773, and Montreal 10 January 1774, Shortt and Doughty, *Canadian Archives*, 345–49. Chinn signed both, whereas Torrey's name was only on the first. Chinn and Torrey—but not Antill—signed the Petitions to King, Lords, and Commons for the Repeal of the Quebec Act, 12 November 1774, with signers from both Quebec and Montreal. See Shortt and Doughty, *Canadian Archives*, 414–16. The *Quebec Gazette* on 23 July 1772 reported that Montreal merchants, including Antill, had signed a resolution about "light" gold coinage, and on 15 September 1774, the *Gazette* printed Antill's ad offering a reward for securing a runaway servant. See "*Quebec Gazette* de Quebec Index from 1764–1824." In 1767, Chinn and other merchants protested against being prohibited from trading with the Indians at Tadousac and Chegotimi. On the petition and the King's decision to uphold the prohibition, see the *Quebec Gazette*, 20 October 1768.

21. Lanctot, *Canada and the American Revolution*, 102.
22. Carleton, Proclamation, 22 November 1775, *History of the Military of Canada*, 2:134–35; Stanley, *Canada Invaded*, 86–87.
23. Montgomery to Schuyler, Holland House near Heights of Abraham, 5 December 1775, *AA4*, 4:189.
24. Stanley, *Canada Invaded*, 92; M. Anderson, *Battle for the Fourteenth Colony*, 46, 194, 213.
25. Campbell to Wooster, Holland-House, 31 December 1775, *AA4*, 4:480–81; Colonel Ritzema to Peter V. B. Livingston, Montreal, 3 January 1776, noting Antill's arrival that morning, *AA4*, 4:1113; Wooster to Schuyler, and James Price to Schuyler, Montreal, 5 January 1776, *AA4*, 4:668–69.
26. At 6:00 P.M., within a "half hour" of Antill's arrival at Albany on 13 January 1776, Schuyler wrote to the president of Congress about the critical situation requiring more troops, for the Canadians were "not to be depended upon"—only 160 were at Quebec with Livingston "and those behaved ill, as Mr Antill will inform you." See *AA4*, 4:666; M. Anderson, *Battle for the Fourteenth Colony*, 196–98.
27. Morrison, ed. "Colonel James Livingston"; M. Anderson, *Battle for the Fourteenth Colony*, 96, 100–101.
28. M. Anderson, *Battle for the Fourteenth Colony*, 106–8, 122; Stanley, *Canada Invaded*, 39–41; Philip Schuyler to John Hancock, Ile Aux Noix, and James Livingston to Schuyler, Ste. Therese, 8 September 1775, PCC, roll 172, item 153, vol. 1, pp. 125, 148.
29. Livingston to Colonel Bedel, [from] Mr. Hazen's, opposite St. Johns, 5 October 1775, in Saffell, *Records of the Revolutionary War*, 24.
30. John Hancock to Schuyler, 11 October 1775, *LDC*, 2:161–62. GW to Richard Henry Lee (Cambridge, 27 November 1775), and Lee responded (Philadelphia, 6 December 1775) that a congressional committee had already been sent with directions to raise a regiment in Canada, among other things. See *PGW:RWS*, 2:436, 501.
31. "Instructions to R. R. Livingston, Robert Treat Paine, and John Langdon, Esquires," 8 November 1775, *JCC*, 3:339–41.
32. Schuyler to GW, Ticonderoga, 28 November 1775, *PGW:RWS*, 2:453.
33. R. K. Wright, *Continental Army*, 59, 317; "Instructions to R. R. Livingston, Robert Treat Paine, and John Langdon, Esquires," 8 November 1775, *JCC*, 3:340–41; "Report of the Committee directed to repair to Ticonderoga," 23 December 1775, *JCC*, 3:448.
34. 24 January 1776, *JCC*, 4:82–84.
35. 24 January 1776, *JCC*, 4:85–87. The draft in the congressional journal differed slightly from the final version.
36. 2 January 1776, *JCC*, 4:18–21.
37. New Jersey delegate Richard Smith noted that Edward Rutledge made a motion for a War Office and that "much was said about Independency and the Mode and Propriety of stating our Dependence on the King." Congress formed committees to address those among other tasks on 24 January 1776. See R. Smith, "Diary of Richard Smith," 495. For examples of committees and minutiae, see 9 and 10 January 1776, *JCC*, 4:41–48.
38. 8 and 17 January 1776 (including note 2.2), *JCC*, 4:39–40, 64. According to Richard Smith's diary, Congress ordered that James Livingston and other officers

"of the new Canadian Regiment" be commissioned on 21 December 1775. See *LDC*, 2:504.

39. Wooster to Schuyler, Montreal, 5 January 1776, noted why he was sending Antill, and then Schuyler wrote to the president of Congress on 13 January that Antill had just arrived that evening with the accounts of Quebec and would pass on the news to Congress. Schuyler also mentioned that Hazen "has stood our friend in the contest," but not what Hazen did—just what he had lost, and that he had referred him to Congress for recompense. See *AA4*, 4:666–67, 669.

40. R. Smith, "Diary of Richard Smith," 493–94.

41. 19 January 1776, *JCC*, 4:70. Congress read Antill's "Opinion" about raising another battalion in Canada and submitted the option for committee review. See R. Smith, "Diary of Richard Smith," 494. That day, Congress also voted against enlisting troops for three years or the duration of the war.

42. M. Anderson, *Battle for the Fourteenth Colony*, 214, 222–23; 20 January 1776, *JCC*, 4:73–76. The Secret Committee, which became the Commercial Committee, was different from the Committee of Secret Correspondence, which became the Committee for Foreign Affairs.

43. 22, 23, and 25 January 1776, *JCC*, 4:78, 79–80, 92. Price's appointment was noted on 29 March 1776 (*JCC*, 4:240–41). Hazen's 18 February letter with an estimate of losses was read in Congress on 8 March 1776 (*JCC*, 4:192). Hazen's executors continued to press claims in the 1820s. See M. White, *Statement of Facts*. Smith on 25 January 1776 reported that the committee had conversed with Hazen "about his Parole of not serving agt. the King, this from the Circumstances of it, was thot. Void." See R. Smith, "Diary of Richard Smith," 496; MH Memorial to GW, Camp near Morristown, 12 February 1780, *PGW:RWS*, 24:454.

44. Thomas McKean presented Hazen's request on 27 January 1776, which Congress opposed. See *JCC*, 4:95. Hazen's acceptance is noted in R. Smith, "Diary of Richard Smith," 497. (Hazen later said he had been offered the rank of brigadier, which he refused. See 28 November 1780, Defense Proceedings of Hazen Court Martial, Peter Force Papers and Collection, series 7E, reel 14, box 20, p. 76, LOC.) Hazen and Antill may have traveled together, stopping first at Albany on 1 February, where Antill delivered letters and resolutions to Schuyler. They were at Point au Fer on Lake Champlain by 7 February, when Antill wrote to Schuyler of their alarm about the "confusion and irregularity" at Montreal. Schuyler to President of Congress, Albany, 1 February 1776, *AA4*, 4:906; Antill to Schuyler, Point-aux-Fer, 7 February 1776, *AA4*, 4:1132.

45. M. Anderson, *Battle for the Fourteenth Colony*, 111, 223, 260–61; 9 and 17 February 1776, *JCC*, 4:123, 158.

46. 27 February 1776, *JCC*, 4:174.

47. Robert Gross notes the ideal in old Concord. See Gross, *Minutemen and Their World*, 14.

48. 9 and 13 February 1776, *JCC*, 4:122, 134–39.

49. 13 February 1776, *JCC*, 4:140–41.

50. 13 February 1776, *JCC*, 4:141. For the entire address and comments, see *JCC* 4:134–46.

51. 16 and 23 March 1776, *JCC*, 4:208–9, 229–32.

52. 14 and 15 February 1776, *JCC*, 4:148–49, 151–52.

53. From drafts to vote on final instructions, see 9, 11, 12, and 20 March 1776, *JCC*, 4:192–93, 196, 198, 215–18.

54. 20 March, and earlier resolves of 12 March 1776, *JCC*, 4:217–19, 198–99. Carroll recorded staying at Hazen's wrecked house on 27 April in Carroll, *Journal of Charles Carroll*, 90.

55. 20 January 1776, *JCC*, 4:73–76. In "Recollections of Benjamin Mooers," the former adjutant recalled the regiment's different organization. BMC, series 4, box 14. In a letter to Washington on 2 January 1777, Antill noted the rifle companies and added an adjutant, quarter master, paymaster, surgeon, and surgeon's mates to the complement. GWP, series 4, LOC.

56. 4 November 1775, *JCC*, 3:321–22; R. K. Wright, *Continental Army*, 46–47.

57. 24 September 1776, *JCC*, 5:811–12; 23 October 1776, *JCC*, 6:900.

58. 27 May 1778, *JCC*, 11:539; R. K. Wright, *Continental Army*, 126–27.

59. Curtis, *Organization of the British Army in the American Revolution*, chap. 1. The number goes up to 809 when counting the two recruiting companies, contingent men, and all of the officers. See R. K. Wright, *Continental Army*, 48.

60. R. K. Wright, *Continental Army*, 59. See also Hazen to Lincoln, Lancaster, 8 June 1782, PCC, roll 54, item 42, vol. 3, p. 528: "That my Regiment is not, nor has it ever been in the Line of the Army; and that my remaining at the Head of a respectable Corps, raised and kept up at my own Expence is the only Reason that can possibly be urged against my enjoying the Pay and Emoluments of a Brigadier-General."

61. R. K. Wright, *Continental Army*, 133–34, 320, 349–50. Although Schott's men were transferred, "no provision was made" for their captain. See Schott to Congress, Philadelphia, 25 September 1781, PCC, roll 56, item 42, vol. 7, p. 127.

62. On postulating a French model, see R. K. Wright, *Continental Army*, 59; and Barker and Huey, *The 1776–1777 Northern Campaigns*, 115 n4. Likelier precedents are noted in F. Anderson, *Crucible of War*, 320; 29 June 1756, 23 July 1756, in *Documents Relating to the Colonial History State of New Jersey*, 17:5:35–36, 41–42; and Brumwell, *Redcoats*, 18n19.

63. Brumwell, *Redcoats*, 264–66, and 315, 318–19, tables 1, 5, and 6; Campbell, *Royal American Regiment*, 73–75; Abstract of Royal Orders to Reduce the Army, [London, 18 May 1763], in Bouquet, *Papers of Henry Bouquet*, 6:186–89. The orders included disbandment of the 3rd and 4th and reduction of the 1st and 2nd Battalions of Royal American Regiment, and established two battalions of nine (one grenadier) companies, each with fifty-five officers and men for a total of 1,001. The 3rd and 4th Battalions reformed in 1775.

64. Loescher, *History of Rogers' Rangers*, 2:114–22. Everest, *Moses Hazen and the Canadian Refugees*, 24; Campbell, *Royal American Regiment*, 195–97; Noël, *The Christie Seigneuries*, 18, 28–29; Rogers, *Genealogical Memoirs of the Scottish House of Christie*, 22–23.

65. Antill's father, also named Edward, was present at discussions on 4–5 September 1757. See *Documents Relating to the Colonial History State of New Jersey*, 17:5:128, 121–22.

66. Campbell, *Royal American Regiment*, 20–25.

67. Wallace, *Regimental Chronicle*, 1–2.

68. Marston, "Swift and Bold," 26–28; Wallace, *Regimental Chronicle*, 21.

69. St. Clair, *St. Clair Papers*, 1:2–3, 6–7.

70. This is a major strand in Mark Anderson's argument in *Battle for the Fourteenth Colony.*
71. 22 January 1776, *JCC,* 4:78; R. K. Wright, *Continental Army,* 60–61. Congress initially appointed Charles Lee to command in Canada, but then sent him to the Southern Department and promoted Thomas to the Canadian command. See 17 February, 1 March, and 6 March 1776, *JCC,* 4:157, 180–81, 186.
72. 20 January 1776, *JCC,* 4:74–76. In designating such powers, each body authenticated the other's authority. There was a precedent for sending out blank commissions signed by the president of Congress, but those went to conventions or councils of safety; Congress preferred that state bodies appoint officers and it commission them. See 4 November 1775, *JCC,* 3:325–26.
73. Hancock to Schuyler, 20 January 1776, *LDC,* 3:122–23. Congress had asked that directions and commissions be sent by express to Schuyler, but that "express" was Antill, who apparently did not leave until after the election of the 2nd Canadian's colonel was settled.
74. Schuyler to President of Congress, Albany, 1 February 1776, *AA4,* 4:906.
75. MH to Congress, "The Case with Colonel Hazen's Regiment," White Plains, 3 September 1778, JSS.
76. 20 March 1776, *JCC,* 4:218–19.
77. 19 June 1776, *JCC,* 5:465.
78. MH to Schuyler, Montreal, 16 February 1776, Schuyler Papers, reel 13, RWR, roll 134, folder 231 (thanks to Mark Anderson for reference and "Capt. Minard of Genl. Hazen's Regt." account); Commissioners' Report, Montreal, 14–17 February 1776, *AA4,* 4:1189–90; M. Anderson, *Battle for the Fourteenth Colony,* 114, 237; Hazen to Antill, Montreal, 26 March and 3 April 1776, *History of the Military of Canada,* 2:150–51. At West Point, on 25 August 1784, Antoine Paulint certified that Montgomery employed Jean Bernard (or Brindamour) on the Chamblee River in 1775 but said nothing of his being connected to Hazen's regiment. See Antoine Paulint records, CSR, roll 89.
79. Duval as an ensign for Liébert's company is mentioned in Hazen to Antill, Montreal, 3 April 1776, *History of the Military of Canada,* 2:151. No reference to Duval appears in the regimental records, but there was a Lieutenant Antoine Duprie/ Dupuir.
80. Basic information appears in Heitman, *Historical Register,* but there are deviations in spellings and commissioning dates compared with Hazen's "Return of the Names, Rank, and Dates of Commissions of the Officers in the Regiment of Foot commanded by Col. Moses Hazen," Camp near West Point, 2 November 1780, additional miscellaneous records, no. 18–42, RWR, film 4, reel 132; and Mooers, "Names of Persons in the Congress own Regiment Commanded by Colonel Moses Hazen Brigadier General by Brevet, in the service of the United States 1782," RWR, film 4, reel 132. For brief biographies on Dionne, Ferriole, McPherson, and Olivie, see Sypher, *New York State Society of the Cincinnati Biographies,* 129–30, 152–53, 319, 354–55. On Gosselin and Liébert, see Kilbourne, *Virtutis Praemium,* 1:424–27, 538–40. Neither "Ayotte" nor "Ayott" appears in Heitman, *Historical Register,* or Mooers's master roll (the basis of the COR Roll), but Antill and others testified to his early service when as a refugee he applied for recompense. See *Reports from the Court of Claims . . . Thirty-fifth Congress,* vol. 1, nos. 92–93. Hay is not on the

regiment's rolls, but is in correspondence: see MH to GW, West Point, 12 November 1780, Founders Online, EA. Also see the editorial note in Hay to GW, New York, 16 December 1784, *PGW, Confederation Series*, 2:190–92.

81. General Orders, Cambridge, 12 November 1775, *PGW:RWS*, 2:353–55; 17 January 1776, *JCC*, 4:63.

82. 14 June 1775, *JCC*, 2:90.

83. "Names of People who engaged for the Congress," in MH to Antill, [20?] April 1776, BAC/LAC, MG21-Add Mss21687, vol. B27, folio 397, pp. 260–61, microfilm A-616 (thanks to Jotham Parsons for translation help); 23 February 1776, *JCC*, 4:168.

84. MH, 10 February 1776, Recruiting Warrant, Montreal, in BAC/LAC, MG21-Add Mss21687, vol. B27, folios 385–86, p. 248, microfilm A-616; translated in *History of the Military of Canada*, 2:144. Gustave Lanctot wrote, "On February 10, the public crier in Montreal read Hazen's proclamation inviting Canadians to enlist for one year or the duration of the war. Volunteers would receive a bonus of forty *livres* or eight dollars and be paid forty *livres* a month." Lanctot, *Canada and the American Revolution*, 115. The warrant confirmed the forty livres, which worked out to what Congress had authorized at six and two-thirds dollars. See also M. Anderson, *Battle for the Fourteenth Colony*, 399n39.

85. MH to Hancock, Montreal, 18 February 1776, PCC, roll 96, item 78, vol. 11, p. 17. On 12 March, a committee reported that Hazen had not estimated his losses with sufficient accuracy. See PCC, roll 27, item 19, vol. 3, p. 93. On the escalating costs of Hazen's service (for that February, Hazen had given Antill money for recruiting, which he asked Congress to reimburse), see 25 August 1777, *JCC*, 8:671.

86. MH to Antill, Montreal, 10 March 1776, *History of the Military of Canada*, 2:145–46. Hazen's advice to "lay off the gentleman" contrasts with what Joseph Jones in Philadelphia wrote to Washington on 11 August 1777: Jones said Captain Monroe had been diligent but met with poor recruiting results with Virginians because Monroe or anyone "preserving the Character a Gent. Ought to support" could not be effective except by methods Jones could not recommend. *PGW:RWS*, 10:586.

87. Gershom Mott to Samuel Adams, Headquarters Holland-House before Quebec, 21 February 1776, Samuel Adams Papers, New York Public Library (courtesy of Mark Anderson); R. Smith, "Diary of Richard Smith," 515; 28 March 1776, *JCC*, 4:238–39. Duggan was to enlist three hundred men for three companies. The unit was short-lived, as was Ritzema's dedication to the American cause.

88. Stanley, *Canada Invaded* (107) and Lanctot, *Canada and the American Revolution* (115–16) mention the 150 and that Gosselin and Pierre Ayotte were busy recruiting.

89. Ferriole's "Return of men recruited . . . in the Months of February and March 1776," certified by Antill on 26 July 1785, RWR, roll 132, item 36, p. 213; "Rolle de La Comp.nie du Cap. [ollivie], le Février 1776," RWR, roll 132, folder 213. Olivie spelled them "Dupres" and "Guillmat"; Dupres may have been Hazen's Duval, and is likely the ensign recorded on other rosters as "Duprie" or "Dupuir." RWR, roll 132 (folder 213-1), p. 145.

90. "Return of the Troops Before Quebeck," 30 March 1776, *AA4*, 5:550; MH to Schuyler, Montreal, 1 April 1776, in PCC, roll 172, item 153, vol. 2, p. 105; *AA4*, 5:869–70. In comparison, Arnold estimated "Colo. Livingston's Regiment of 200 Canadians, and some scattered Canadian Forces amounting to 200 more" on 2 January, in Schuyler to GW message, 22 January 1776, *PGW:RWS*, 3:168n3.

91. Wooster to MH, Montreal, 23 March 1776, PCC, roll 71, item 58, p. 389; MH to Schuyler, Montreal, 1 April 1776, PCC, roll 172, item 153, vol. 2, p. 105. Washington wrote to Hancock that Congress should note Hazen's comments about the Indians; the general thought they would soon take an active role, and thus Congress should send forces to take Niagara and Detroit and a committee to treat with the Indians in Canada. See 19 April 1776, JCC, 4:87.

92. Hancock to Hazen, 24 April 1776, PCC, roll 23, item 12A, vol. 1, p. 109.

93. Adams to James Warren, 18 February 1776, LDC, 3:275.

94. MH to Antill, Montreal, 20 April 1776, History of the Military of Canada, 2:146. Hazen wrote that he had made Floquet his chaplain, but there is no official record. Lanctot writes of Arnold commissioning Lotbinière as chaplain to Livingston's regiment on 26 January 1776, in Canada and the American Revolution, 113. Lotbinière, "priest of Canada and Chaplain of united States," to President of Congress, for increased wages, August 1779, PCC, roll 98, item 78, vol. 14, p. 279. He reminded Congress that he had lost his estates and pensions, as well as incurred the hatred of his family, the clergy, and nobility in Canada by espousing liberty. In Lotbinière to President of Congress, August 1780, PCC, roll 98, item 78, vol. 14, p. 367, he asked Congress to remember that he had countered the despair of Canadians about the bishop's orders and made them more zealous for the cause. M. Anderson, Battle for the Fourteenth Colony, 261, 298.

95. Commissioners to Canada to John Hancock, Montreal, 1, 8, and 17 May 1776, PCC, roll 183, item 166, pp. 21, 33, 49.

96. MH to Antill, Montreal, 20 April 1776, and Hazen to Antill about sending Brindamour to Quebec, Montreal, 3 April 1776, History of the Military of Canada, 2:146, 151.

97. Commissioners to Canada to Philip Schuyler, Montreal, 6 May 1776, Franklin, Papers of Benjamin Franklin, 22:420; Commissioners to Hazen, Montreal, [16] May 1776, Samuel Chase letters, MS 2958.1775, NYHS.

98. John Thomas to the Commissioners to Canada, Point Deschambault, 7 May 1776, Franklin, Papers of Benjamin Franklin, 22:421–23; Council of War, Point Deschambault, 7 May 1776, AA4, 6:454–55. At the council of war, Thomas asked whether it was "prudent for the Army in its present situation to attempt to make a stand at this place?" Twelve, including Wooster, Livingston, and Buel, said no, and three—including Antill and Allen—said yes.

99. Cubbison, American Northern Theater Army in 1776, 92–97.

100. Ibid., 97–99.

101. Everest, Moses Hazen and the Canadian Refugees, 41–42. The commissioners in Canada reported to Hancock on 27 May that "council of war, notwithstanding," Arnold was determined to attack until Forster sent word that "the savages were determined to kill their prisoners if attacked." Commissioners in Canada to President of Congress, 27 May 1776, AA4, 6:591. James Wilkinson noted "reproachful language" between Arnold and Hazen in Memoirs of My Own Times, 1:46. See also Report and Resolutions about cartel between Arnold and [Forster], 10 July 1776, JCC, 5:533–39; and MH to Congress, "Case with Colonel Hazen's Regiment," JSS. Angry British officials rebutted the American and congressional accounts about the Battle of the Cedars as they denounced American ingratitude and injustice and urged "ye intoxicated Dupes of Faction and Sedition" to return to the imperial fold. See Quebec Gazette, 29 August 1776, in History of the Military of Canada, 2:182–83.

102. MH to Congress, "Case with Colonel Hazen's Regiment," JSS.
103. Major Butterfield's testimony, Montreal, June 1776, *AA5*, 1:166. Butterfield also noted that the Native Americans took "several young lads, and all the blacks, also one young child from one of the women."
104. "Lieutenant David Dill Fellows," in "Tribute," Friends of the Fishkill Supply Depot; Heitman, *Historical Register*, 224.
105. 10 August, *JCC*, 5:646; Hamtramck Petition to Congress, Philadelphia, 11 July 1776, PCC, roll 96, item 78, vol. 11, pp. 71–73 (thanks to Mark Anderson, and to Jotham Parsons for translation aid). Brindamour did not appear as Jean Ménard either. Anderson, in *Battle for the Fourteenth Colony* (237), lists Jean-François Hamtramck, Pierre du Calvet, and Pierre Boileau among the early officers in Hazen's regiment. Neither Hamtramck nor Calvet appear on the regiment's master rolls, but Boileau appears as of 1778. Heitman's *Historical Register* (140, 271) has Calvet as Calvert in Hazen's regiment as of 10 December 1776 and Hamtramck as a captain in the 5th New York in November 1776. Hamtramck and Hazen contended over whether the former had ever been in Hazen's regiment through April 1777. See William L. Otten Jr., *Colonel J. F. Hamtramck*, 26–27, 34, 37–38, 48–49, 55, 62, 72–73. Also showing the 1776 disarray, former Montreal merchant Pierre du Calvet (a relative of the ensign) had to later petition Congress for payment on the vouchers Montgomery, Wooster, Arnold, and Hazen gave him for goods in 1775–76. See 21 April 1784, *JCC*, 26:260–61.
106. MH to Congress, "Case with Colonel Hazen's Regiment," JSS. Although distance and direction were skewed, Hazen was probably referring to Wooster sending Antill and some men to fortify Deschambault in April. See M. Anderson, *Battle for the Fourteenth Colony*, 305.
107. Commissioners to President of Congress, Montreal, 27 May 1776, *AA4*, 6:590–91.
108. Arnold to Sullivan, Chambly, 13 June 1776, and Antill to Sullivan, Chambly, 13 June 1776, *AA4*, 6:1104, 1106.
109. Porter, "Diary: Colonel Elisha Porter," 25–30 May 1776; 29–30 May, 2 June 1776, Carroll, *Journal of Charles Carroll*, 100–101 (Franklin and Father Carroll left in mid-May); Council of War at Chambly, 30 May 1776, *AA4*, 6:628.
110. "Diary: Colonel Elisha Porter," 2–3 June 1776; Sullivan to GW, Sorrell, 5–6 June 1776, *PGW:RWS*, 4:441.
111. "Diary: Colonel Elisha Porter," 8–17 June 1776; Wilkinson, *Memoirs of My Own Times*, 1:51–54.
112. "Diary: Colonel Elisha Porter," 17–19 June 1776.
113. Sullivan to Schuyler, Isle-aux-Noix, 19 June 1776, *AA4*, 6:1103–4; Schuyler to GW, Albany, 25 June 1776, *AA4*, 6:1102–3.
114. Cubbison, *American Northern Theater Army in 1776*, 126–28. The island is approximately ten miles to the current U.S. border and twelve miles to where Lake Champlain flows into the Richelieu River.
115. MH to Congress, "Case with Colonel Hazen's Regiment," JSS. Hazen's antagonist, Duggan, passed on hearsay to Sullivan that men were "daily deserting from Col. Hazen." See St. Tours, 5 June 1776, GWP, series 4, MSS 44693, reel 036, LOC.
116. M. White, *Statement of Facts* (9) affirmed that Charlotte Hazen had followed her husband during the war and mentioned her losses before and after her husband's death. MH to Antill, Montreal, 26 March 1776, *History of the Military of Canada* (2:150) confirmed that Charlotte Antill had room and board at Château Ramezay.

117. Antoine (Theotist) Paulin[t] Pension Application, W.16671, specifically Theotist Paulin[t] declaration, 17 January 1837, and translated extract from marriage register, RWPBF, reel 1891.
118. Hughes, "Captain Antoine Paulin of Hazen's Canadian Regiment," 17–18, 23–26. Hughes wrote that Paulin[t] was born in 1734, but the 1767 marriage register noted him as thirty, and his company could not have been attached to Hazen's regiment in January if it was not mustered until February.

Chapter 3

1. "Diary: Colonel Elisha Porter," 1 July 1776; Cubbison, *American Northern Theater Army in 1776*, 129.
2. John Hancock to Certain Colonies, Philadelphia, 25 June 1776, *LDC*, 4:318. Some delegates saw retreat as a positive, but John Adams did not. See Adams to Joseph Ward, Philadelphia, 5 July 1776, *LDC*, 4:391.
3. Peter (and Polly) Chartier Pension Applications, and John (and Sally) Chartier Pension Applications, RWPBF, W.23786 and W.17598, reel 524. Robinson, like some others who disappeared early, was not on Mooers's later regimental roster.
4. Wilkinson, *Memoirs of My Own Times*, 1:62; "Diary: Colonel Elisha Porter," 3–5 July 1776; Beebe, "Journal of a Physician on the Expedition against Canada," 3–4 July 1776, 339; Gates to Trumbull, Ticonderoga, 11 August 1776, *AA4*, 1:899.
5. Schuyler to GW, Albany, 1 July 1776, *PGW:RWS*, 5:173–75.
6. 17 June 1776, *JCC*, 5:448; Samuel Adams to Richard Henry Lee, 15 July 1776, *LDC*, 4:457. Jonathan Gregory Rossie suggests that congressional subversion of the army's chain of command for the Northern Department was a continuing issue, but one that Washington used in 1777 to avoid an appointment fight. See Rossie, *Politics of Command in the American Revolution*, 37, 164.
7. Schuyler to GW, Albany, 1 July 1776, *PGW:RWS*, 5:175.
8. Sullivan to GW, Crown Point, 2 July 1776, *PGW:RWS*, 5:187.
9. "Minutes of a Council of War," Crown Point, 7 July 1776, *AA5*, 1:233.
10. "Remonstrance of Field-Officers at Crown-Point," 8 July 1776, *AA5*, 1:233–34.
11. MH to Hancock, Albany, 25 November 1776, *AA5*, 3:843.
12. Sullivan (mistitled Moses Morse) to Schuyler, Crown Point, 6 July 1776, *AA5*, 1:235.
13. "Address to General Sullivan by the Field Officers lately under his command," Crown Point, 8 July 1776, *AA5*, 1:127. Porter jotted in his diary that the officers signed the address on 9 July, the day that Sullivan left.
14. J. K. Martin, *Benedict Arnold, Revolutionary Hero*, 227.
15. Beebe, "Journal of a Physician," 7 July 1776, 341.
16. "Minutes of Council of General Officers," Crown Point, 8 July 1776. Woedtke was not at this council.
17. Trumbull to GW, Lebanon, Connecticut, 4 July 1776, *PGW:RWS*, 5:208–9. The concerns also weighed on officers from Timothy Bedel's regiment who petitioned Gates to take post on the frontier to protect their homes and families. Ticonderoga, 17 July 1776, *AA5*, 1:398.
18. Trumbull to GW, Lebanon, CT, 6 July 1776, *PGW:RWS*, 5:226–27.
19. GW to Trumbull, New York, 7 July 1776, *PGW:RWS*, 5:234–35; GW to Gates, New York, 19 July 1776, *AA5*, 1:650.
20. Hancock to Woedtke, Philadelphia, 19 March 1776, *AA4*, 5:410; Carroll letter extract, Montreal, 1 May 1776, *AA4*, 5:1167; Woedtke to Franklin, [Crown Point],

3 and 4 July 1776, Franklin, *Papers of Benjamin Franklin*, 22:498, 500; Cubbison, *American Northern Theater Army in 1776*, 137–39; Gates to Hancock, Ticonderoga, 6 August 1776, *AA5*, 1:796.

21. Beebe, "Journal of a Physician," 1 September 1776, 346

22. MH to Sullivan, Chambly, 13 June 1776, *AA4*, 6:1105.

23. J. K. Martin, *Benedict Arnold, Revolutionary Hero*, 218–19, 230, 235; Beebe, "Journal of a Physician," 9 July 1776, 341–42.

24. Gates to Arnold, Ticonderoga, 15 July 1776, *AA5*, 1:357–58.

25. James Kirby Martin provides a good account of the trial in *Benedict Arnold, Revolutionary Hero*, 237–43. Among the associated letters, see "General Arnold's Protest against the Proceedings," n.d., *AA5*, 1:1272; Poor to Gates, Ticonderoga, 6 August 1776, *AA5*, 1:802; and Arnold to Gates, Ticonderoga, 7 August 1776, *AA5*, 1:1274.

26. Field Officers [of Court] at Ticonderoga to Hancock, 19 August 1776, *AA5*, 1:1072. Congress had a memorial from Hazen that likely referred to this affair and his sacrifices, but the content appears lost. 3 September 1776, *JCC*, 5:720.

27. Gates to Hancock, Ticonderoga, 2 September 1776, *AA5*, 1:1268. Excerpt of this letter and others noted above appear in Wilkinson, *Memoirs of My Own Times*, 1:70–75.

28. 18 September 1776, *JCC*, 5:780. The decision may have been affected by an earlier report by the committee looking into "the Miscariages [sic] in Canada," submitted 30 July 1776, PCC, roll 71, item 58, p. 383. The report mentioned Hazen's refusal to take goods that Arnold claimed as private property but that appeared to have been goods the commissioners impressed to supply troops.

29. Court of Inquiry on General Arnold, Albany, 2 December 1776, *AA5*, 3:1042–43. J. K. Martin, *Benedict Arnold, Revolutionary Hero*, 291, 309. Martin noted Hazen among the "artists of calumny." Another was Lieutenant Colonel John Brown; see his letter to Gates, Albany, 1 December 1776, *AA5*, 3:1158. Among those supporting Brown's petitions for greater rank and recompense was William Satterlee, who had served in Samuel Elmore's regiment and had just accepted appointment in Hazen's. 12 November 1776, *JCC*, 6:942.

30. This echoes Alan C. Cate about Arnold and John Paul Jones as extremely ambitious fighters. See Cate, *Founding Fighters*, 98.

31. Report of Committee, 12 March 1776, PCC, roll 27, item 19, vol. 3, p. 93.

32. Duggan to Sullivan, 5 June 1776, GWP, series 4, MSS 44693, reel 036, LOC; Duggan's complaints of Sullivan to GW, Sorrell, 5–6 June 1776, *PGW:RWS*, 4:444–45n7; "Notes of Witnesses' Testimony concerning the Canadian Campaign," [1–27 July 1776], *Papers of Thomas Jefferson*, 1:433–54; Abuse complaint, 30 July 1776, *JCC*, 5:619.

33. Gates to Hancock, 2 September 1776, *AA5*, 1:1268.

34. Schuyler to Hancock, Albany, 16 August 1776, *AA5*, 1:983.

35. Woedtke to Franklin, 3 July 1776, *Papers of Benjamin Franklin*, 22:498.

36. Lee to GW, Charlestown, 1 July 1776, *PGW:RWS*, 5:168–71.

37. This is an adaptation of Bernard Bailyn and Philip D. Morgan's contention, in *Strangers within the Realm* (1), that the British Empire linked many systems indirectly "through a common center of power and an extraordinarily pervasive language/culture."

38. "Declaration of Independence proclaimed at New-York," 11 July 1776, *AA5*, 1:144; "Extract of a letter from Albany," two versions, 12 and 19 August 1776, *AA5*, 1:923,

1070; "Diary: Colonel Elisha Porter," 16 July 1776 [Crown Point]; Schuyler to Gates, German Flats (west of Albany), 18 July 1776, enclosing copy of Declaration, *AA5*, 1:423; "Declaration of Independence Proclaimed at Ticonderoga, 28 July 1776, *AA5*, 1:630. Some may have thought, like the Ticonderoga recorder, "now we are a people," but it is doubtful that the Canadian Continentals did.

39. Inhabitants of Shelburne to Gates, Lake Champlain, 6 August 1776, *AA5*, 1:803.

40. Gates to Arnold, Ticonderoga, 7 August 1776, *AA5*, 1:826.

41. Schuyler to Gates, Albany, 17, 20, and 25 August 1776, *AA5*, 1:999–1000, 1083, 1153.

42. The two Canadian regiments were ghosts. The "Return of the Continental Forces in Canada, June 12, 1776" (*AA4*, 6:915) recorded "near Two Hundred Canadian volunteers," but Livingston's regiment was not mentioned, and there was no return from Hazen. Neither was mentioned in "General Return of the Army of the Forces of the United States of America, serving in the Northern Department, under the command of the Honorable Major-General Gates," Ticonderoga, 24 August and 22 September 1776, *AA5*, 1:1199, 2:479. Both returns listed regiments at Albany, German Flats, Mohawk River, and Oneida Carrying Place, but not Ticonderoga. The Canadian regiments were also not listed in "Return of the Sick in the General Hospital at Fort George," 12–26 July 1776, *AA5*, 1:857.

43. S. Metcalf to Colonel Jacob Bayley, Prattsburgh, 21 July 1776, *AA5*, 1:488; "Examination of Two Canadian Captains," [2 August 1776], *AA5*, 1:798–99; "Examination of Captain Mesnard," 7 August 1776, *AA5*, 1:828. Carleton practiced leniency, so his threats did not always result in such punishments.

44. Lanctot, *Canada and the American Revolution*, chap. 11. Bishop Briand demanded more penance than the governor.

45. 12 September 1785, *JCC*, 29:692. Ayotte left Canada after the war and petitioned Congress for aid, as he feared being imprisoned for debts incurred helping the American invasion.

46. Kilbourne, *Virtutis Praemium*, 1:424–27, 538–40.

47. Antill to Benjamin Lincoln, Minister of War, 4 March 1782, PCC, roll 48, item 41, vol. 1, p. 81.

48. MH to GW, Camp near West Point, 12 November 1780, Founders Online, EA. Hazen noted 250 men in a letter to Schuyler, Montreal, 1 April 1776, PCC, roll 172, item 153, vol. 2, p. 105. In that letter and in one to Benjamin Lincoln on 8 June 1782 (PCC, roll 54, item 42, vol. 3, p. 528), he said he raised 477 in Canada (in about fourteen days), chiefly at his own expense, before Congress proved it could not protect the "unfortunate Volunteers," and he had to leave connections and property behind as the army retreated. It is possible that he conflated his and Livingston's (and possibly Duggan's) numbers. Antill said that he and Hazen had enrolled "near 500 men" and that by the time they arrived in Albany after the retreat, they had "between 80 & 100 men." Antill to GW, Baltimore, 2 January 1777, GWP, series 4, MSS 44693, reel 039, LOC. Congress finally resolved to send Hazen the pay for the field officers and four companies "of which his battalion then consisted" from 18 June to 1 November 1776. See 30 July 1777, *JCC*, 8:588–89. Gilbrand (or Galbrun/Guilbrand), Lewis Lavoix (or Louis/Lavois), Monty, and others beyond those noted appear in Ferriole's February–March 1776 recruiting roll, certified 26 July 1785, and Mooer's "Names of Persons in the Congress own Regiment," RWR, roll 132. Mooers's roster listed soldiers by earlier to later enlistments. The earliest

ones, predominantly with French names, show late 1776 enlistments under the new establishment, but it may be inferred that many had been previously enlisted.

49. Woedtke to Gates, Fort George, 20 July 1776, *AA5*, 1:475; After Orders (with emphases), Ticonderoga, 21 July 1776, *AA5*, 1:656. Woedtke died at the end of July. Gates to Hancock, Ticonderoga, 6 August 1776, *AA5*, 1:795.

50. Antill to Lieutenant Colonel Peter Gansevoort, 3 August 1776, Gansevoort Military Papers, 1:125, New York Public Library.

51. Schuyler to Hancock, Albany, 18 August 1776, *AA5*, 1:1030. On Antill's orders, Paymaster Trumbull provided funds to the wife of soldier/refugee François (Francis) Monty on 7 July. See J. Trumbull to Richard Peters, Albany, 29 August 1776, Peters Papers, vol. 8, HSP.

52. "Landscape of refugees" adopted from Sleeper-Smith, "The Middle Ground Revisited," 5.

53. Such foreign officers were promised the following: colonel, 1,000 acres; lieutenant colonel, 800; major, 600; captain, 400; lieutenant, 300; ensign, 200; and every noncommissioned officer, 100. 27 August 1776, *JCC*, 5:707–8. By comparison, in September, Congress promised the following to the officers and soldiers serving until the end of the war or discharge by Congress: colonel, 500 acres; lieutenant colonel, 450; major, 400; captain, 300; lieutenant, 200; ensign, 150; and each noncommissioned officer and soldier, 100. 16 September 1776, *JCC* 5:763.

54. 10 February 1784, *JCC*, 26:75–76 (including notes).

55. 26 August 1776, *JCC*, 5:700–701.

56. 10 August 1776, *JCC*, 5:645–47. Lotbinière acted more refugee than priest throughout the war as he petitioned Congress for pay rather than attending to the Canadian regiments.

57. Besides the report on 10 August, the committee(s) made recommendations on 29 and 30 August 1776, *JCC*, 5:716, 728.

58. 15 August 1776, *JCC*, 5:657. James Livingston had "orders to raise a regiment out of the people who are friendly to the United States in Canada." See Philip Livingston to the New-York Convention, Philadelphia, 16 August 1776, *AA5*, 1:977.

59. Deposition of Thomas Day re. British forces in Canada, 12 September 1776, PCC, roll 189, item 170, vol. 2, p. 5.

60. Francis Monty, Statement re. Canada, June 1777, PCC, roll 189, item 170, vol. 2, p. 191.

61. He sent "a German, who was a mate of the Revenge, and a New-England man, who speaks French well," and one of whom had been a "Ranger with Rogers" in the last war, to spy and recruit in Canada. See Arnold to Gates, Isle Valcour, 28 September 1776, *AA5*, 2:591. "Frontiers not only shifted across space and over time but moved according to the status of the people on either side of the divide. . . . A. G. Roeber finds much value in the concept of cultural brokers, often merchants and clergy, who acted as bilingual patrons bridging two cultures." Bailyn and Morgan, *Strangers within the Realm*, 21.

62. 24 and 30 September 1776, *JCC*, 5:811–12, 838.

63. 12 June 1776, *JCC*, 5:433–34. Resolutions for independence and preparing a plan of confederation were presented on 7 June, followed by the appointment of a committee to prepare a declaration on 10 June. *JCC*, 5:425–26, 428–29.

64. Adams to Heath, Philadelphia, 3 August 1776, *AA5*, 1:739.

65. 28 August 1776, *JCC*, 5:713–14.

66. 19 and 20 September 1776, *JCC*, 5:784, 788–807. The resolution drafted by the Committee on Spies was actually approved before the new articles on 21 August 1776 (*JCC*, 5:693), and it simply referred to the resolution of 24 June (*JCC*, 5:475) about noncitizens abiding by the laws. Congress approved an oath for officers on 21 October 1776 that specifically acknowledged the independence of each state and abjured allegiance to the King (*JCC*, 6:893–94).

67. "List of Letters brought up by a flag with Rev. Mr. Inglis and Mr. Moore," 3:368–69; Moore to Pierre Van Cortlandt, Verplanck's Point, 9 December 1776, 3:1155–56; Livingston to James Duane, Verplanck's Point, 9 December, 3:1156; Inglis to Heath, Verplanck's Point, 11 December 1776, 3:1167–69; all in *AA5*.

68. "Report on the application of John Moore, Charles Inglis, and Others," Fishkill, 13 December 1776, *AA5*, 3:1204–07. Also see Heath, *Memoirs of Major-General Heath*, 89–90, and his letter to GW, Haverstraw, 11 December 1776, *PGW:RWS*, 7:298–300 (with footnotes). Lady Johnson was a hostage for her husband's behavior. See Schuyler to GW, Albany, 15 June 1776, *PGW:RWS*, 4:536–37. By comparison, the Board of War advised Washington to facilitate an exchange of ladies in and out of New York on 8 November 1776, whereas Governor William Livingston of New Jersey wanted officers to end permissions to women, those "Mistresses of infinite craft & Subtlety." *PGW:RWS*, 7:114–15, 126.

69. 16 September 1776, *JCC*, 5:762–63.

70. 27 December 1776, *JCC*, 6:1045–46. If Schuyler had disbanded Livingston's regiment on 20 December as Roussi said in his February 1777 petition, this provision would have allowed Washington to overrule that act and continue the regiment. See Heath to GW, 18 November 1776, *PGW:RWS*, 7:178n2 (with reference to PCC, no. 41, VIII, folio 260). Whether or not that happened, Livingston's regiment continued. Samuel Adams confirmed the distribution and total to his cousin John (Baltimore, 9 January 1777, *LDC*, 6:65). John Battin (Batten) said that he enlisted in Hazen's regiment, "one of the sixteen additional regiments on the Continental Establishment," in his 1819 deposition (RWPBF, W.4413, reel 177).

71. 28 December 1776, *JCC*, 6:1047; Circular from President of Congress, Baltimore, 30 December 1776, *AA5*, 3:1478–79.

72. 27 December 1776, *JCC*, 6:1045. Washington supported the use of local connections to recruit and retain men, but he also wanted men to join for love of liberty and good of country, as inferred in General Orders, Cambridge, 12 November and 28 December 1775, and letter to Lieutenant Colonial Joseph Reed, Cambridge, 25 December 1775, *PGW:RWS*, 2:354–55, 614–15, 607. See also R. K. Wright, *Continental Army*, 50, 57. Another indication of Schuyler's approbation is found in MH to Hancock, Albany, 25 November 1776, PCC, roll 96, item 78, vol. 11, p. 105.

73. Congress authorized twenty-six infantry regiments for the 1776 establishment, but the designation of the Pennsylvania Rifle Regiment, with its associated Virginia and Maryland companies, as the 1st Continental Regiment made the total twenty-seven. R. K. Wright, *Continental Army*, 47, 54; Council of War, [Cambridge, 2 November 1775], *PGW:RWS*, 2:279–80; *JCC*, 2:89.

74. GW to Hancock, Morristown, 20 January 1777, *PGW:RWS*, 8:115.

75. 23 October 1776, *JCC*, 6:900. Hazen indicates that he and Antill were in Philadelphia when he received orders and money to recruit to the original establishment. MH to Hancock, Albany, 25 November 1776, PCC, roll 96, item 78, vol. 11, p. 105.

76. 11 November 1776, *JCC*, 6:940; 7 November 1776, *JCC*, 6:932.

77. Heath to GW, Peeks-kill, 18 November 1776, *PGW:RWS*, 7:178n2. Schuyler did not disband the 1st Canadian as Roussi indicated; instead, he gave Congress Livingston's recommendations for officers on 30 December 1776 (*AA5*, 3:1496). That spring Congress again empowered Schuyler to fill commissions "agreeable to the ranks the officers respectively hold in the said regiment." 27 May 1777, *JCC*, 7:392. Colonel Henry Beekman Livingston wrote to Washington asking for Roussi rather than the "two Shoe makers" that the New York convention had proposed. One of those he derided was William Goforth, who had served well at Trois-Rivières in early 1776 (see chapter 1). Washington supported Livingston, and Roussi was transferred to the 4th New York by that March. See H. B. Livingston to GW, Fish Kill, GW to John Jay, Morristown, and GW to Livingston, 15 and 20 February 1777, *PGW:RWS*, 8:343, 383–84.

78. 13 November 1776, Ticonderoga, in *Orderly Book of the Northern Army* [Wayne's 5th Pennsylvania Regiment], 76.

79. Beebe, "Journal of a Physician," November 1776 (esp. 12–23 November), 357–59.

80. Schuyler to GW, Albany, 11 November 1776, *PGW:RWS*, 7:145. A visiting congressional committee substantiated Schuyler's appraisal by noting that the Northern Army needed 2,500 officers and soldiers at Ticonderoga and Mt. Independence and another 2,500 "cantoned upon the Mohawk and Hudson's Rivers, Albany therein included." See "List of Wants of the Northern Army," *Orderly Book of Northern Army*, 164.

81. Heath to GW, Peekskill, 18 November and 8 December 1776, *PGW:RWS*, 7:176–77, 275; Jacques Pyon of Livingston's regiment remembered doing bateaux service, road duty, and guarding Albany in 1776–77. RWPBF, W.18786, reel 1988.

82. Gates to Schuyler, Ticonderoga, 30 September 1776, *AA5*, 2:619; Schuyler to Gates, Albany, 3 October 1776, *AA5*, 2:859.

83. Schuyler to Congress, Albany, 6 November 1776, *AA5*, 3:1585.

84. Duggan and his wife petitioned for compensation in 1777 and then Mrs. Duggan wrote to Washington for information and aid. The general responded that Duggan had gone to St. Eustatius and that he did not know if his accounts were settled. West Point, 4 September 1779, *PGW:RWS*, 22:350.

85. MH to GW, Camp near West Point, 12 November 1780, Founders Online, EA; MH to Hancock, Albany, 25 November 1776, PCC, roll 96, item 78, vol. 11, p. 105; Antill to GW, Baltimore, 2 January 1777, GWP, series 4, MSS 44693, reel 039 LOC.

86. General Orders, Cambridge, 31 October 1775, *PGW:RWS*, 2:269.

87. On Hay, see MH to GW, West Point, 12 November 1780, Founders Online, EA; General Orders of Gates, 30 and 31 July 1776, *AA5*, 1:800–801; Losses sustained by Hay, *AA5*, 3:744–45; 9 January 1777, *JCC*, 7:23; and Risch, *Supplying Washington's Army*, 30–31. Ranks and service dates gleaned from Mooers's COR Roll, other regimental rolls, Heitman's *Historical Register*, and Society of the Cincinnati publications. Calvert's pay and brevet rank noted on 10 August 1776, *JCC*, 5:646.

88. Numbers gleaned from above sources. Analysis of the rage militaire in Royster, *Revolutionary People at War*, 25.

89. See Officer Roster in Appendix. See also Schuyler to Gates, Albany, 20 and 25 August 1776, *AA5*, 1:1083, 2:1296; Hancock to Schuyler, Philadelphia, 9 November 1776, *AA5*, 3:614; Schuyler to Hancock, Albany, 30 December 1776, *AA5*, 1495; and R. K. Wright, *Continental Army*, 57–58.

90. MH to Hancock, Albany, 25 November 1776, PCC, roll 96, item 78, vol. 11, p. 105. See also Officer Roster in Appendix.

91. Heitman's register has Charles Markle, along with John Conrad Latour, Lawrence Myers, and John Sharp, commissioned in the regiment as of November 1776, but Mooers did not record them on the master roll. They were with Selin's company in the Ottendorf/Armand corps and appear to have left before Selin's company was attached to Hazen's regiment in 1781.

92. Ambrose Walden, RWPBF, S.38453, roll 2471 (see "1850 Petition of Heirs").

93. Antill to Colonel Benjamin Harrison, Lancaster, 20 January 1777, PCC, roll 53, item 42, vol. 1, p. 25; 24 January 1777, JCC, 7:60; 8 April 1777, JCC, 7:243–44.

94. MH to GW, Camp West Point, 12 November 1780, Founders Online, EA.

95. MH to Hancock, Albany, 25 November 1776, AA5, 3:843.

96. Antill to Congress, 30 December 1776, PCC, roll 48, item 41, vol. 1, p. 5.

97. GW to Antill, Morristown, 8 January 1777, PGW:RWS, 8:12–13.

98. Mayer, Belonging to the Army, 162.

99. Hamilton to William Duer, Morristown, 6 May 1777, in Papers of Alexander Hamilton, 1:246–47; Spall, "Foreigners in the Highest Trust," 344–44, 349, 352–53.

100. 2–3 July 1777, 8:525–26, 528; 5 July, 8:531; 7 July, 8:537; 15 July, 8:552–53; 21 July, 8:569; and 15 September 1777, 8:745, all in JCC. See also the following in LDC: James Lovell to Benjamin Franklin, 4 July 1777, 7:292–93; William Williams to Jonathan Trumbull Sr., 5 July 1777, 7:301–3; John Adams to Nathanael Greene, 7 July 1777, 7:305–7; Hancock to GW, 8 July 1777, 7:324; John Hancock to Dorothy Hancock, and to GW, 17 September 1777, 7:686–87; and James Lovell to William Whipple, 17 September 1777, 7:688.

101. James Lovell to Benjamin Franklin, Philadelphia, 4 July 1777, LDC, 7:292–93; Spall, "Foreigners in the Highest Trust," 351–52, 354, 357, 363.

102. Colerus to GW, Philadelphia, 1 May 1777, PGW:RWS, 9:320; GW to Colerus, Morristown, 19 May 1777, PGW:RWS, 9:470.

103. GW to MH, Middlebrook, 4 June 1777, PGW:RWS, 9:604; Everest, Moses Hazen and the Canadian Refugees, 51.

104. MH to GW, Camp West Point, 12 November 1780, Founders Online, EA.

105. Ibid. In the midst of this dispute, Lewis Morris Jr. (actually IV) refused a majority in "Hazens and Antills regit." See Lewis Morris to John Jay, Philadelphia, 11 March 1777, LDC, 6:434. Morris of Morrisania, N.Y., was Antill's cousin. Antill had written to Washington: "Lewis Morris Junr now with General Sullivan has by Some means been Left Out in the Appointments of New York State if he is not yet provided for, and Merits your Approbation I would be happy he had a Majority in Our Corps ... his Father a Near Relation of Mine first Mentioned it to me & would be happy in the Appointment." Antill to GW, Philadelphia, 13 February 1777, PGW:RWS, 8:322.

Chapter 4

1. 10 December 1776, JCC, 6:1018–19; "The Crisis I," in Writings of Thomas Paine, 170.

2. Jonathan Trumbull Sr. to GW, Middletown, 14 January 1777, PGW:RWS, 8:70.

3. GW to Samuel Washington, Morristown, 5 April 1777, PGW:RWS, 9:72; GW to Joseph Ward, Morristown, 21 April 1777, PGW:RWS, 9:233.

4. Martin and Lender, "*A Respectable Army*," 3:90–92.

5. James (and Mercy) Wakeland (Wakelee), RWPBF, W.25845, reel 2470. Waterbury's 5th Regiment and Elmore's Regiment, in Johnston, *Record of Connecticut Men in the Military*, 70, 115.

6. MH to GW, Camp West Point, 12 November 1780, Founders Online, EA.

7. Everest, *Moses Hazen and the Canadian Refugees*, 35–36; R. K. Wright, *Continental Army*, 59; Stanley, *Canada Invaded*, 86–87; List of Hazen's Officers, 3 September 1778, typescript in Hazen accounts and petitions, JSS. Overall figure calculated by adding the 1,452 names on the COR Roll and an additional 374 found in the CSR. There were possibly others and likely repetitions due to spelling or other issues.

8. R. K. Wright, *Continental Army*, 317–18; MH to Hancock, Albany, 25 November 1776, AA5, 3:842–43.

9. William Hooper to Joseph Hewes, Philadelphia, 5 November 1776, LDC, 5:439.

10. Ibid.

11. 4 November 1776, JCC, 6:920–21.

12. Hancock to Schuyler, Philadelphia, 9 November 1776, AA5, 3:614.

13. R. K. Wright, *Continental Army*, 50.

14. 22 November 1776, JCC, 6:972–73.

15. 27 December 1776, JCC, 6:1045–46.

16. $3,000 was advanced to Hazen on 2 November 1776, and the same to Pennsylvania delegates on 27 February 1777 (*JCC*, 6:918, 7:164).

17. 14 April 1777, JCC, 7:261–63.

18. 23 July 1777, JCC, 8:576.

19. 31 July 1777, JCC, 8:593–95; Scudieri, "The Continentals," 61–68.

20. 14 October and 7 November 1776, JCC, 6:874, 932; Hancock to GW and Hancock to Schuyler, 9 November 1776, LDC, 5:460, 461.

21. Captain Liébert's Recruiting Account, and "Return of Men, recruited for the Service of the United States of America, by Lieut. Alexander Ferriole of Colonel Moses Hazen's Regiment of Canadians," November 1776–January 1777, RWR, roll 132, items 44, 32.

22. Examples of allowances include 17 January 1776, JCC, 4:63; 14 October 1776, JCC 6:874; and 22 January 1777, JCC, 7:55.

23. Stedman, "Return of Men, recruited for the Service of the United States," n.d., RWR, roll 132, item 34.

24. Satterlee, "Return of Men, recruited for the Service of the United States," [1777], RWR, roll 132, item 35. The two who joined late were James Squires, who died in December 1777, and William Willis, who deserted in March 1779.

25. Robert Morris, George Clymer, and George Walton to Hancock, Philadelphia, 10 January 1777, PCC, roll 150, item 137, vol. 4, p. 81.

26. On funding, see 2 November 1776, JCC, 6:918; 3 December 1776, JCC, 6:1002; Antill to Hancock, Wilmington, 6 February 1777, PCC, roll 90, item 78, vol. 1, p. 55.

27. Congress approved payment of $10,000 to claimants from whom Antill "borrowed" to cover regimental expenses, on 5 April 1777, JCC, 7:228; see also a list of February to August 1777 articles and expenses in "United States To Lt. Col. E. Antill in Acct.," 1 July 1783, RWR, roll 132, item 51. Other memos and accounts, including one about vouchers, the earliest dated 2 November 1776 and the latest 12 July 1777 for a total of $13,792, in Antill file, CSR, roll 78. Hazen and Antill

were already behind in settling accounts by August 1776, according to Paymaster Trumbull to Richard Peters, Albany 29 August 1776, Peters Papers, vol. 8, HSP.

28. 16 September 1776, *JCC*, 5:762–63.

29. 8 October 1776, *JCC*, 5:854–56.

30. Headquarters, Ticonderoga, 24 October 1776, in *Orderly Book of the Northern Army*, 24–25.

31. John (Jean Marie) Chartier, Antoine Chartier, Michael Harbaur, Francis James Harper, Pierre Hubert, Thomas Hughes, the drummer Francis Martin (possibly enlisting in 1778 and then 1782), Charles Rata (Rate), Joseph Smith (Shmit), and Piere Suba (Sube) in CSR, rolls 80, 84, 87, 89, and 90.

32. 13 February 1779, *JCC*, 13:180–81; 15 March 1779, *JCC*, 13:316–17.

33. John Ryan, 21 and 22 February 1820, RWPBF, S.40378, reel 2106.

34. Jeremiah Parmelee, 7 April 1818, RWPBF, S.41048, reel 1878; Henry Young, 16 June 1818, RWPBF, S.35165, reel 2663; John Carter, 25 August 1818, RWPBF, S.35817, reel 485.

35. GW to Henry Knox, Morristown, 11 February 1777, *PGW:RWS*, 8:307. Washington inadvertently doubled Hazen's authorized number to 2,000.

36. Schuyler to Hancock, Saratoga, 19 November 1776, *AA5*, 3:770.

37. MH to Hancock, Albany, 25 November 1776, PCC, roll 96, item 78, vol. 11, p. 105.

38. Headquarters, 12 November 1776, in *Orderly Book of the Northern Army*, 72.

39. John Ryan, 24 April 1818 and 21 February 1820, RWPBF, S.40378, reel 2106; Stephen Collins, 7 April 1818 and 21 July 1820, RWPBF, S.34221, reel 615.

40. Jacob Doddridge, 28 December 1818, RWPBF, S.42180, reel 825.

41. Regimental Orders, Ticonderoga, 30 October 1776, in *Orderly Book of the Northern Army*, 46.

42. Headquarters, Saratoga, 11 December 1776, in *Orderly Book of the Northern Army*, 123–24.

43. Resolution of a Council of War held at Saratoga, 21 November 1776, *AA5*, 3:797; Schuyler to Trumbull, Albany, 19 December 1776, *AA5*, 3:1301.

44. Schuyler to the President of Congress, Albany, 30 December 1776, *AA5*, 3:1496.

45. Cf. Satterlee, "Return of Men, recruited for the Service of the United States," [1777], RWR, roll 132, item 35; Elmore's Regimental Roll, in Johnston, *Record of Connecticut Men in the Military*, 113–19. Comparison with the later regimental roster shows that more than those noted as reengaged on the Elmore roll enlisted in Hazen's regiment.

46. Amos Ames, 16 April 1818, RWPBF, S.45505, reel 51.

47. Heath to GW, Peekskill, 8 December 1776, *AA5*, 3:1124; GW to Heath, Headquarters near Trenton Falls, 12 December 1776, *AA5*, 3:1185–86.

48. General Orders, Morristown, 1 February 1777, *PGW:RWS*, 8:209.

49. Henry Hilger at Lancaster, RWPBF, S.39688, reel 1273; John Gregory at Cumberland County, RWPBF, S.39624, reel 1127.

50. James Livingston, New York Committee of Safety, to GW, Fishkill, 22 January 1777, *PGW:RWS*, 8:131.

51. In RWPBF: Colin McLachlan, W.25687, reel 1692; John Barr, S.45244, reel 156; Henry Young, S.35165, reel 2663; James Dixon, S.42165, reel 822; William Liggins, S.41769, reel 1562; Hugh McCleland, S.41834, reel 1668; Angus O'Near, S.40217, reel 1845; John Battin, W.4413, reel 177; Charles Badger, S.34632, reel 106; and Edward Quigley and William Sharp, in CSR, rolls 394, 89, and 90.

52. Deposition of John Walden in heirs of Ambrose Walden pension file, RWPBF, S.38453, reel 2471; Ambrose Walden, CSR, roll 91.
53. Antill to Congress, 30 December 1776, PCC, roll 48, item 41, vol. 1, p. 5. Among many requests, Antill asked that Colonel Samuel Patterson be authorized to muster the regiment's companies from Virginia, Maryland, and Delaware that were to pass through Christiana Bridge.
54. Hancock to GW, Philadelphia, 9 November 1776, *LDC*, 5:461; 12 and 21 November 1776, *JCC*, 6:944–45, 971.
55. William Calder, 1818, and 1820, including witness account, RWPBF, S.44725, reel 448.
56. Royster, *Revolutionary People at War*, 195–96, 211, 230.
57. Alexander McDougall (about Gansevoort's detachments) to GW, Peekskill, 12 April 1777, *PGW:RWS*, 9:134.
58. Arnold to Washington, Camp before Quebec, 27 February 1776, *PGW:RWS*, 3:382.
59. *Congréganistes* in Everest, *Moses Hazen and the Canadian Refugees*, 38; Lanctot, *Canada and the American Revolution*, 117; and Garneau, *History of Canada from its Discovery to our Days*, vol. 3, book 12, chap. 1. Mason Wade referred to them as *congressistes* in *The French Canadians* (69–72).
60. R. Smith, *Stories of Peoplehood*, 65. Some ethically constitutive stories are historical "in that they present the communities . . . as the contingent products of past human actions" that may shape identities.
61. "The United States of America to Captain [Lié]bert," with entries for 22 December 1776 to 9 January, in New York currency, RWR, roll 132, item 2. "Congress's Own Regiment" appears in a 16 December 1788 review of what appear to be November and December 1776 receipts (RWR, roll 132, item 29), but the heading may be a postwar reversion to the COR title.
62. Antill to Congress, 30 December 1776, PCC, roll 48, item 41, vol. 1, p. 5.
63. Antill to GW, Baltimore, 2 January 1777, GWP, series 4, MSS 44693, reel 039, LOC.
64. Francis Lester, 8 April 1818, Greenfield, Mass., RWPBF, S.32972, reel 1552.
65. In RWPBF: Peter Chartier, 14 June 1820, W.23786, reel 524; Charles Tessie, 3 October 1820, S.42465, reel 2355; Abijah Stowe, 1 April 1818 and 17 June 1820, W.19404, reel 2310.
66. With reference to Rogers Smith on how "stories of peoplehood do not merely serve interests, they also help to constitute them;" see R. Smith, *Stories of Peoplehood*, 43–48, 53, 58, 90.
67. Noah Lee, CSR, roll 86.
68. March and April 1777 Returns, RWR, roll 132, item 37; James Livingston to GW, Albany, 3 April 1777, *PGW:RWS*, 9:54–55.
69. Putnam's Division Returns, Princeton, 3 and 10 May 1777, in Sullivan, *Letters and Papers of Major-General John Sullivan* (hereafter *Sullivan Papers*), 1:335, 338; Lesser, *Sinews of Independence*, 46; GW to Hancock, Morristown, 21 May 1777, *PGW:RWS*, 9:492; Sullivan's Division Return, Princeton, 1 June 1777, *Sullivan Papers*, 354; MH to Congress, "The Case with Colonel Hazen's Regiment," White Plains, 3 September 1778, JSS. Hazen repeated the 720 figure: Memorial, Camp, Peekskill, 20 November 1779, *PGW:RWS*, 23:367; Camp Near Morris Town, 12 February 1780, *PGW:RWS*, 24:455; and Hazen to Lincoln, 8 June 1782, PCC, roll 54, item 42, vol. 3, p. 528.
70. GW to McDougall, Morristown, 6 March 1777, *PGW:RWS*, 8:523–24.

71. Benjamin Mooers listed Dill as John on the regimental roll, but Heitman's *Historical Register* recorded him as Robert, echoing Congress's appointment of 2 January 1777 (*JCC*, 7:10). Mooers did not include Delagard on the roll. Delagard is listed in Heitman's *Historical Register*, with Delezeume listed as an assistant engineer, but CSR, roll 81 has records for both a Delagard and a Delezenne or Delageme belonging to Hazen's regiment. The same roll has records for both John and Robert Dill as paymaster.

72. The lower numbers are based on the COR Roll and the higher ones account for additional members found in the CSR. In RWPBF: Edward Wall, S.46346, reel 2478; Abijah Stowe, W.19404, reel 2310; Alexander Ferriol (spelling distinguishes him from his father Alexandre Ferriole), S.43551, reel 0868; and Henry Young, S.35165, reel 2663. Not all pension applications note ages, which limits evaluations. The 114 with them that I found do not indicate a major shift to younger ages at enlistment from the beginning of the war to the end.

73. COR Roll and a comparison to Ferriole's "Return of Men," November 1776–January 1777, RWR, roll 132, item 32; "Congregation of the dead" (John Adams to Abigail Adams, 13 April 1777, *LDC*, 6:574) refers to the thousands of soldiers buried in Philadelphia. Besides being an inoculation site for smallpox, Philadelphia housed sick soldiers in numerous "hospitals" in late 1776 through mid-1777, including at least nine from one or both of the Chambers' companies in Hazen's regiment ("Sick Soldiers—[Dec.] 1776," *Pennsylvania Archives*, series 2, 1:535–36.)

74. McConnell desertion notice, Philadelphia, 25 January 1777, *Pennsylvania Evening Post* [Philadelphia], AHN. The January/February 1777 desertion of William Cockran (or Cochran) was recorded in the rolls, but Patrick Ferrel (Farril) had an August 1782 desertion recorded, which indicates that he likely deserted, returned, and deserted again.

75. William Cochran/Cockran, CSR, roll 80; Patrick Farril/Ferrel, CSR, roll 82.

76. Chambers desertion notice, Philadelphia, 8 March 1777, *Pennsylvania Evening Post*, AHN. Isaac Baker, John Grimes (Grahams), and James Reid, CSR, rolls 78, 83, and 89.

77. Thomas Spice, John Taylor, Joseph McCurree, Joseph Michael, CSR, rolls 90, 91, 87, and 88. Popham recorded that McCurree and Michael "desd same day [they] enlisted."

78. Antill notice, Philadelphia, 29 March 1777, *Pennsylvania Evening Post*, AHN.

79. On Congress's criticism of Maryland's resolution, see 30 October 1776, *JCC*, 6:912–13. See also Rush's contention that "the salvation of this continent depends upon the Authority of this congress being held as sacred as the cause of liberty itself," in Rush's Notes of Debates, 14 February 1777, *LDC*, 6:274. On the congressional resolution about taking up deserters, see 25 February 1777, *JCC*, 7:154–55; and Thomas Burke's Notes of Debates, 25 February 1777, *LDC*, 6:356–63.

80. General Orders, Morristown, 6 February 1777, *PGW:RWS*, 8:256–57; Robert Morris to GW, Philadelphia, 6 March 1777, *LDC*, 6:402–3; GW to Hancock, Morristown, 3 May, *PGW:RWS*, 9:334–35; Hancock to GW, Philadelphia, 10 May, *PGW:RWS*, 9:375; GW to Hancock, Morristown, 12 May 1777, *PGW:RWS*, 9:395; Proclamation of Pardon to Deserters, [Morristown, 6 April 1777], *PGW:RWS*, 9:74; GW to George Clinton, Morristown, 5 May 1777, *PGW:RWS*, 9:348.

81. Michael Jmeel "Goaler," receipt, RWR, roll 132. For an additional receipt dated 11 August 1777, see James Johnson file, CSR, roll 85.

82. Hugh Wallace, Richard Burrows, CSR, rolls 91 and 79. See also Neagles, *Summer Soldiers*, 265, 95 (Burrows spelled Burrest [*sic*]).
83. Mayer, *Belonging to the Army*, 248–50; Rees, "'Sospecting the prisoner to be a tory,'" 45–46. Wood was not on the regiment's master roll, but Popham recorded that Games Ward enlisted 13 February 1777 and deserted 30 July; the master roll said Pendergrass deserted in July, but Popham noted him as omitted in September. See Ward and Pendergrass, CSR, rolls 91, 89; GW to de Borre, Philadelphia, 3 August 1777, *PGW:RWS*, 10:495.
84. McMullen's sentence in General Orders, 13 July 1777, *PGW:RWS*, 10:265.
85. In the same May return that recorded the 2nd Canadian at 460, which was an incomplete count, only two regiments exceeded that number: the 7th Virginia with 577 and the 9th Virginia with 468. The low was 25 for the 2nd Pennsylvania. The total for Washington's infantry was 10,003 among 41 regiments or battalions, which works out to an average of 244. Lesser, *Sinews of Independence*, 46–47.
86. MH to Congress, "The Case with Colonel Hazen's Regiment," JSS.
87. In RWPBF: Charles (Baptiste) Amlin, W.20604, reel 52; James Hole, S.45371, reel 1307; Deadluff Sloughter (Shadow), S.40404, reel 2155; Charles Tessie, S.42465, reel 2360. In CSR: Henderson (Hendrickson), roll 84; Rose, roll 89; White, roll 91; Hicks, roll 84; Dunevan (Donnavan), roll 81. Hicks was not recorded in Mooers's master roll but the others were.
88. March and April 1777 Returns, RWR, roll 132, item 37, p. 213. Deserters included John Howel on 20 March, Daniel Madson and Samuel McCloud on 7 February, James Price on 16 March, Daniel Reid on 20 March, James Weyman on 11 April, and John Ryley (Reily) as prisoner; CSR, rolls 84, 87, 89, 91, and 89. The names of these deserters did not appear on Mooers's master roll, which recorded Ryley as killed rather than prisoner in 1777.
89. Board of War's directive to commanding officers of regiments recruiting in Pennsylvania, Delaware, Maryland, and Virginia, 24 February 1777, *JCC*, 7:149–50.
90. Krebs, *Generous and Merciful Enemy*, 133–36; Miller, *Dangerous Guests*, 149–50.
91. Committee for Lancaster County to Pennsylvania Delegates in the Continental Congress, 20 March 1777, and Lancaster County Committee, "Examination into the death of Jacob Gross," 18 March 1777, PCC, roll 83, item 69, vol. 1, pp. 335, 339. Antill said Minyier was French, not French Canadian (though undoubtedly commanding French Canadian soldiers), in his representation to Congress, n.d. [March/April 1777], PCC, roll 57, item 43, p. 5.
92. Committee for Lancaster County to Pennsylvania Delegates, 20 March 1777.
93. Minyier (or Minyer/Minyear) deposition to Lancaster County Committee, "Examination," 18 March 1777; Committee to Pennsylvania Delegates, 20 March 1777.
94. Lancaster County Committee, "Examination," 18 March 1777.
95. Committee for Lancaster County to Pennsylvania Delegates, 20 March 1777.
96. Ibid.
97. 29 March 1777, *JCC*, 7:208; Hancock to Antill, Philadelphia, 31 March 1777, *Pennsylvania Archives*, series 1, 5:269.
98. Antill to Congress, n.d. [March/April 1777], PCC, roll 57, item 43, p. 5. This is numbered "2," which may, perhaps, indicate that Antill had provided an earlier address.
99. 7 and 8 April 1777, *JCC*, 7:229–30, 238–46.

100. 15 April 1777, *JCC*, 7:270; Colonel Thomas Hartley to GW, York Town, Pa., 12 Feb 1777, *PGW:RWS*, 8:317–18. Hartley wrote, "I have generally understood that the 16 Regements were called Guards—some here said Washingtons Guards, this Name if agreeable to your Excellency would be pleasing to all." Davidson, "Disapprobation," 321–24.

101. GW to Congress, 19 April addition to 8 April 1777 letter, Morristown, GWP, Series 3a, Varick Transcripts 1775–1785, Letterbook 2, p. 241, MSS 44693, reel 002, LOC; General Orders, Morristown, 1 February 1777, *PGW:RWS*, 8:209; GW to Knox, 11 February 1777, *PGW:RWS*, 8:307–8.

102. Gara, "Loyal Subjects of the Crown," 30–42.

103. Headings for the June through August 1778 returns of Anthony Selin's independent company noted Washington's command "of the Armies of the Independent States of America." See Antony (Anthony) Selin file, CSR, roll 90.

104. Stuart, "'Engines of Tyranny,'" 185–86.

105. Resolution, 27 December 1776, *JCC*, 6:1045–46; Circular to the States, Baltimore, 30 December 1776, *JCC*, 6:1053.

106. 27 December 1776, *JCC*, 6:1045–46. See also 23 April 1778, *JCC*, 10:384 for the resolution extending to 10 August 1778 the powers vested in Washington in September and October 1777.

107. Abraham Clark to John Hart, Baltimore, 8 February 1777, *LDC*, 6:240–41; John Adams to Abigail Adams, Philadelphia, 6 April 1777, *LDC*, 6:540–41.

108. James Sykes to George Read, Philadelphia, 10 April 1777, *LDC*, 6:569–70; Thomas Burke to Richard Caswell, Philadelphia, 29 April 1777, *LDC*, 6:671–73.

109. For honorary and commandant ranks, see J. Wright, "Some Notes on the Continental Army," 96–97.

110. The army was supposed to be composed of "yeomen and artisans . . . rather than a conglomeration of flotsam and jetsam." Higginbotham, *War of American Independence*, 93.

111. Captain Pry's Company Payrolls, June 1778–July 1779, RWR, roll 132, p. 209. Pry added a little "COR" in June and then an even tinier one in July 1778, but not thereafter. Captain Carlile's Company Payrolls, June 1778–July 1779, RWR, roll 131, p. 197. COR appears on the March, April, May 1779 return but not on the earlier or later rolls.

112. Antill, Certificate and Receipt, 23 August 1782, Quartermaster General Timothy Pickering, MS 2958.247, NYHS. COR for "Canadian Old" or "Congress's Own" Regiment.

Chapter 5

1. Morris to William Bingham, Philadelphia, 26 February 1777, *LDC*, 6:376–77.

2. GW to McDougall, Morristown, 17[–18] April and General Orders, 18 April 1777, *PGW:RWS*, 9:187, 198. For other signs and ceremonies of service and status, and controversies thereof, see Irvin, *Clothed in Robes of Sovereignty*, esp. chap. 7.

3. Hurt, *Love of Our Country*, 6–9, 18. For sermons and public prayers as rituals for unity and patriotism, see Engel, "Connecting Protestants," 38–42.

4. General Orders, Morristown, 12 April 1777, *PGW:RWS*, 9:126; Middlebrook, 28 June and 31 May 1777, *PGW:RWS*, 10:135, 9:567–68.

5. 27 May 1777, *JCC*, 8:390–91. See also Metzger, "Chaplains in the American Revolution," 31–79.

6. GW to Hancock, Middlebrook, 8 June 1777, *PGW:RWS*, 9:644–45.

7. 5 August 1777, *JCC*, 8:609; 10 January 1778, *JCC*, 10:40; 14 June 1781, *JCC*, 20:643–44.

8. GW to Reformed Protestant Dutch Church, Kingston, New York, 16 November 1782, *WGW*, 25:346–47.

9. One of many Lotbinière's examples appears in 9 June 1777, *JCC*, 8:430.

10. 18 May 1778, *JCC*, 11:507.

11. Some records note Armstrong as regimental chaplain on 3 November 1776, resigning 12 February 1778, but others do not mention Hazen's regiment, nor does his widow's pension application. Armstrong, CSR, roll 78; Susanna Armstrong, RWPBF, W.5638, roll 75. The May/June 1777 roll at Princeton shows no chaplain with the regiment. Armstrong mentioned service with Smallwood, not Hazen's regiment, when he testified in September 1777 about Sullivan's conduct at the Battle of Staten Island. See *Provincial and State Papers*, 17:176–77.

12. JHJ, [near Danbury, Ct.] 18 October [1778], and Redding, 16 February [1779], HSP.

13. 23 March 1779, *JCC*, 13:356–57; General Orders, [West Point], 2 October 1779, *PGW:RWS*, 22:581–82.

14. Exceptions included the 1st Rhode Island's white uniforms and the green facings of Thompson's Pennsylvania riflemen. Drums and "Colours" in Board of War to GW, War Office [Philadelphia], 10 May 1779, *PGW:RWS*, 20:410, 411n2.

15. See Katcher, *Uniforms of the Continental Army*; Troiani, *Military Buttons of the American Revolution*; Troiani, *Soldiers of the American Revolution*.

16. List of February to August 1777 articles and expenses in "United States to Lt. Col. E. Antill in Acct.," 1 July 1783, RWR, roll 132, 213–14, item 51; Copeland and Zlatich, "2nd Canadian Regiment," 40–41; Katcher, *Uniforms of the Continental Army*, 67–69. Some caps also displayed *"Pro Aris et Focis,"* meaning for home and hearth. Thanks to Marko Zlatich (2013), Matthew Keagle (Fort Ticonderoga, 2014), and Erik Goldstein (Colonial Williamsburg, 2014) for uniform information.

17. George Measam, Fishkill, Return of clothing needed for various regiments, 2 June 1778, PCC, roll 91, item 78, vol. 3, p. 149.

18. MH to GW, 8 January 1781, Founders Online, EA; From General Orders, Totowa, 15 November 1780, on 18 November in [Lloyd], Orderly Book, 2nd Canadian, SOC.

19. Troiani, *Military Buttons of the American Revolution*, 97. O'Hara's notice, 20 July 1779, *Pennsylvania Packet* [Philadelphia], listed that among goods stolen from his house were "a blue broadcloath coat with a red velvet cape, silver buttons marked in cypher C.O.R."

20. MH to GW, Camp Near Danbury, 24 December 1778, 7 and 13 March 1779, *PGW:RWS*, 18:499–500, 19:468–69; GW to MH, Middlebrook, 21 March 1779, *PGW:RWS*, 19:556–57.

21. Regimental Orders, Fishkill, 5 and 10 January 1781, [Lloyd], Orderly Book, 2nd Canadian, SOC.

22. Ethnicity was noted in desertion notices but not regimental rosters. McConnell's 25 January 1777 notice in the *Pennsylvania Evening Post* [Philadelphia], AHN, mentioned that Cockran was born in Ireland. An ad for Hazen's Camp Reading of 23 January 1779 in the 4 February *Independent Chronicle and the Universal Advertiser* [Boston], AHN, listed Germans William Bude (Beder), Christain Creamer, Francis Dabuch (Dubrach), Tobias Feller (Fuller), Jacob Hawn (Horn), John Hope, and John Ryling (Railing). Francis Mallet was a Frenchman, Patrick Madden was Irish, Thomas Larkins (alias Kidman/Kedman) and Richard Osman (alias Barry)

were English, Barnabas Potter was "this Country born," and there was no designation for Dennis Kellatham (Kellyhan).

23. Hazen's ad from 16 August at Camp Haverhill noted eight deserters, six Irish and two French, in "hunting shirts and overhalls," in *Connecticut Courant and Weekly Intelligencer* [Hartford, Conn.], 24 August 1779, AHN. From Charlestown, dated 26 April 1779, Hazen advertised a reward for three French sailors—Jacque Beetan (Beeton), Peter Darbucks (Jean Piere Darboux), and Roney Shippell (Remee Shekell)—in the *Independent Chronicle and the Universal Advertiser* [Boston], 20 May 1779, and the *Connecticut Courant and Weekly Intelligencer*, 4 May, AHN. The latter paper published other notices, on 4 and 18 May and 24 August, for desertions between March and August as the regiment moved from Connecticut through New Hampshire. See also the 21 December notice for Connecticut-born, dark-complexioned Josiah Freeman, who deserted on 27 November 1779 when the regiment was in Hartford, *Connecticut Courant and Weekly Intelligencer*, 21 December 1779, AHN.

24. John Saratoga, CSR, roll 90; Edward Chinn, CSR, roll 80; Chinn to John Pierce, 8 June 1786, "Records in a letter to the commissioner of Army Accounts," Papers of the War Department, record group 93, miscellaneous numbered records RG93, M859. Questions about whether Saratoga was properly enlisted in the regiment appear in Hughes Deposition and Hazen Response, 14 and 28 November 1780, Proceedings of Hazen Court Martial, Peter Force Papers and Collection, series 7E, reel 14, box 20, pp. 25–26, 49, LOC.

25. Captain Michael Gilbert deposition, 16 November 1780, Proceedings of Hazen Court Martial, pp. 31–32. There was discussion about whether Hailstock, the "Property" of Taylor, was properly mustered as a soldier and whether he remained on the roll after Taylor left the regiment. Mooers did not list him on his compiled roll, but Hailstock was on Gilbert's company roll.

26. Prime Petty Bone, CSR, roll 89; Cato Mumford, CSR, roll 88; Prince Pettibone, in "Free Colored Persons" column, Whitehall, Washington County, N.Y., "United States Census, 1830," NARA M19, roll 111, FamilySearch; Cats Mumford, in "Other Free Persons" column, Providence, R.I., NARA M32, roll 45, FamilySearch.

27. Van Buskirk, *Standing in Their Own Light*, 11–12.

28. Alexander Scammell, "Report on the Negroes in the Continental Army," 24 August 1778, GWP, series 4, MSS 44693, reel 051, LOC.

29. COR Roll; *Muster Rolls and Other Records of Service of Maryland Troops*, 597–98. Hawkins did not specify states for more than half of the 495 soldiers he named, but noted more than 100 with a U.S. designation, more than 90 Pennsylvania soldiers, 34 for Maryland and Connecticut, 16 for New York, with fewer for others. See JHJ, "List of the Non-commissioned Officers and Privates of the Canadian Old Regiment," 6 September 1782, HSP. See also Return of Moses Hazen's Regiment, 1781, series SDEA1004, box 1, file no. 67, New Jersey State Archives; *Pennsylvania Archives*, series 5, 3:765–81; and Roberts, *New York in the Revolution*, 63.

30. JHJ, Memo, Albany, 9 March 1778 and 28 April and 6 May 1779 entries about printing in Dresden, HSP.

31. JHJ, 31 August, 25 and 29 [March 1781], and Memo [possibly 1782], HSP.

32. "Genealogical Data Regarding the Allied Families of Breintnall, Fawcett, and Harper of Philadelphia," HSP. See also Philadelphia County, Pennsylvania, Will

Books, nos. I–K (1748–1757, file 161, for Oliver Williams, 1750), L–M (1757–1762, file 80, for Jane Williams, 1758), and P–Q (1770–1778, file 279, for Jane Hawkins, 19 July 1776), HSP. Additionally, see Philadelphia Monthly Meeting records for marriage of Hannah's sister Mary to Jacob Townsend [d. 1740?] in 1739 and Hannah's reading out in 1742 in HSP. Jane Hawkins married Oliver Williams at Christ Church in Philadelphia on 8 July 1735. See Christ Church online archives.

33. *Pennsylvania Gazette* [Philadelphia], 18 February 1768, Accessible Archives CD-ROM, folio 3: 1766–1783, item 4728; Thomas, *History of Printing in America*, 379–80, 390.

34. John Hawkins, CSR, rolls 799 and 84; Hawkins, "Memoranda, 1780," HSP, Am.6071; JHJ, 17 October 1777, HSP; Albany, 25 February 1778, in 2CROB, vol. 1, HSP.

35. Lawrence Manning, CSR, rolls 87 and 93. Manning enlisted as a sergeant in McConnell's company in December 1776 and was sergeant major in March 1777.

36. GW to Hancock, Morristown, 21 May 1777, *PGW:RWS*, 9:492; General Orders, Morristown, 22 May 1777, *PGW:RWS*, 9:495; Greene to GW, Bound Brook [24 May 1777], *PGW:RWS*, 9:516; Greene to Sullivan, [Bound Brook, 24 May 1777], and d'Arendt to Greene, [Quibbletown, 24 May 1777], in N. Greene, *Papers of General Nathanael Greene*, 2:90–92.

37. De Borre to GW, Camp Hanover, 17 August 1777, *PGW:RWS*, 10:653; GW to de Borre, 19 August, *PGW:RWS*, 11:6–7.

38. Putnam to GW, Peekskill, 25 June 1777, *PGW:RWS*, 10:127.

39. Colin McLachlan, RWPBF, W.25687, reel 1692. See declaration, 5 July 1820.

40. William Deacons, RWPBF, S.13009, reel 776.

41. Thomas Smith, John Brooks, and Edward Chinn, CSR, rolls 90, 79, and 80. Heitman's *Historical Register* notes Chinn as a prisoner, but other accounts indicate that he was with the regiment in July and August.

42. Examples of letters and orders relevant to Sullivan's division and by extension Hazen's regiment, all in *PGW:RWS*, include After-Orders, Morristown, 4 July 1777, 10:179; Sullivan to GW, Pompton, 5 July 1777, 10:202; GW to Sullivan, Morristown, 7 July 1777, 10:223–24; GW to Continental Congress Committee to Inquire into the State of the Army, Camp at the Clove, 19 July 1777, 10:332–36; James Mease, Philadelphia, 22 July 1777, 10:357–59; GW to Hancock and GW to Putnam, Ramapough, 25 July 1777, 10:410–11, 414–15; GW to Sullivan, Pompton Plains, 25 July 1777, 10:420; GW to Sullivan, "Coryels" Ferry, 31 July 1777, 10:471; General Orders, at Col. Hills, Roxborough, 4 August 1777, 10:496; and Sullivan to GW, Hanover, 7 August 1777, 10:547–49.

43. General Orders, Cross Roads [Pa.], 11 August 1777, *PGW:RWS*, 10:581–82; GW to Hancock, Neshaminy Camp, 16 August 1777, *PGW:RWS*, 10:637.

44. A. Lee, "Sullivan's Expedition to Staten Island," 169–70; Major John Taylor to MH, Hanover, 24 August 1777, PCC, roll 103, item 78, vol. 22, p. 525.

45. Congress was reviewing his memorial and accounts. 21, 25, 26 August 1777, *JCC*, 8:663, 671, 678.

46. Taylor to MH, Hanover, 24 August 1777, PCC, roll 103, item 78, vol. 22, p. 525. Court-martial materials about Sullivan's actions at Staten Island and Brandywine appear in *Provincial and State Papers*, 17:154–210; and *Sullivan Papers*, 1:482–532. See also Abbott, "Sullivan's Staten Island Raid."

47. Taylor's list of "unfortunate" actions appears in Taylor to MH, Hanover, 24 August 1777, PCC, roll 103, item 78, vol. 22, p. 525. See also 11 October 1777, *Provincial and State Papers*, 17:162–63.

48. Reid's testimony, Camp, 11 October 1777, *Provincial and State Papers*, 17:164–65; Major Eustace in Testimony H, no. 11, Camp near Newport, 6 September 1777, *Provincial and State Papers*, 17:181.

49. Chambers Evidence, 11 October 1777, *Provincial and State Papers*, 17:163–64.

50. Reid's testimony, *Provincial and State Papers*, 17:164–65. Smallwood said that if Heron had obeyed orders and marched with the brigade, Heron and other officers would not have been killed or taken at Decker's Ferry. Testimony E, no. 8, *Provincial and State Papers*, 17:165–66, 174.

51. Taylor to MH, Hanover, 24 August 1777, PCC, roll 103, item 78, vol. 22, p. 525.

52. A. Lee, "Sullivan's Expedition to Staten Island," 170. Sullivan wrote to Washington on 24 August 1777 that Heron was wounded and captured while defending a Dutch church near Decker's Ferry (*PGW:RWS*, 11:57–60), but Enoch Anderson of the 1st Delaware implied in a later account that Heron was focused on plunder. See Abbott, "Sullivan's Staten Island Raid," part VI.

53. Heitman's *Historical Register* (140) notes du Calvet or Calvert as taken prisoner. Company and regimental rolls noted the same.

54. Taylor to MH, Hanover, 24 August 1777, PCC, roll 103, item 78, vol. 22, p. 525; Sullivan to GW, Hanover, 24 August 1777, *PGW:RWS*, 11:57–60.

55. McBurney, *Abductions in the American Revolution*, 4–5.

56. Sullivan to Antill, Hanover, 16 August 1777, in *Sullivan Papers*, 1:431–32.

57. A. Lee, "Sullivan's Expedition to Staten Island," 172–73.

58. Charlotte Antill to President of Congress, received 22 November 1777, PCC, roll 90, item 78, vol. 1, p. 131.

59. Prisoners of War, American, Long Island, to Congress, May 1778, PCC, roll 51, item 41, vol. 7, p. 181. Edward Antill to Elias Boudinot, Long Island, 5 May 1778, "Continental Officers in the American Revolution," Elias Boudinot Papers, HSP, Am.0068, case 4, box 17.

60. Worthington et al., "British and American Prisoners of War," 159–74; "Copy of a Letter from Mr. Edward Antill," *Royal Gazette* [New York], 28 October 1778, AHN. Rivington appeared a rabid loyalist but was in fact a spy for the Americans.

61. Antill, "Principles of Geography and Astronomy," 1780, Antill Papers, Am.0077, HSP. In Irving-Newbold Family Papers, collection 1890, Series 8, box 77, HSP: James Irvine and Edward Antill to Colonel Beatty, 22 November 1778; Captain Adye for Major General Pattison to Lieutenant Colonels Antill and Ramsey, &c, 7 August 1779 and Response, Flatbush, 11 August 1779; General James Irvine to Colonels Magaw, Swoope, Marborry, Eli, and Antill, Flatbush, 25 October 1779.

62. United States in acct. with Edwd. Antill, 24 December 1788, Antill file, CSR, roll 78; 18 August 1777, *JCC*, 8:651.

63. CSR files and regimental rolls. On Lee's parole controversy, see Van Buskirk, *Generous Enemies*, 80.

64. MH to Congress, "The Case with Colonel Hazen's Regiment," White Plains, 3 September 1778, JSS; Taylor to MH, Hanover, 24 August 1777, PCC, roll 103, item 78, vol. 22, p. 525; A. Lee, "Sullivan's Expedition to Staten Island," 172; Sullivan to

Hancock, Camp on [Perkiomen Creek], 27 September 1777, PCC, roll 178, item 160, p. 57.

65. COR and 1778 company rolls have additional names. Mooers listed Patterson as dead in August 1777, but company rolls show later payment and death in April 1778. It is possible that some listed as deserted were taken prisoner but not accounted for on prisoner lists and never returned.

66. Cox, *Proper Sense of Honor*, 201–2.

67. Antill to Elias Boudinot, Long Island, 5 May 1778, in "Continental Officers in the American Revolution," Elias Boudinot Papers, HSP, Am.0068, case 4, box 17.

68. Sullivan to Hancock, Camp on [Perkiomen Creek], 27 September 1777, PCC, roll 178, item 160, p. 57; Major Lewis Morris Testimony, *Provincial and State Papers*, 17:179.

69. Summary of the Evidence by General Stirling, and Opinion of the Court of Inquiry, Camp at Foamensing, 12 October 1777, *Provincial and State Papers*, 17:186–88. As Taylor continued to dispute Sullivan, John Penn asked Brigadier General William Woodford to talk to Taylor (19 November 1777, *LDC*, 8:286).

70. Sullivan to Congress, Camp on [Metuchen] Hills, 17 October 1777; Certificate of Lieut. Erskine; Address from Officers in Colo. Hazen's Regt., *Provincial and State Papers*, 17:190–92, 203–4. The court acquitted Erskine but found a Lieutenant Lee guilty of disobeying Major Taylor's orders. That Lee (likely Noah, for Andrew was a prisoner) may not have thought much of Taylor. See Court decisions in Orders, Pompton, 8 July 1777, *Sullivan Papers*, 410.

71. General Orders, Towamensing [now Towamencin], 14 October 1777, *WGW*, 9:369; Lyman Hitchcock, RWPBF, S.43687, reel 1290; Cady, Erskine, and Munson, CSR, rolls 80, 82, and 88. John Erskine, resignation, 7 October 1777, *Sullivan Papers*, 1:480. Heitman's *Historical Register* lists a Lieutenant William Erskine from April 1777 until omitted in November, but he does not appear on the regiment's master roll or in the CSR. There is the possibility that this "William" was John.

72. O'Hara to Sullivan, Camp Hanover, 12 August 1777, *Sullivan Papers*, 1:428. O'Hara said that he and his company had received no pay since January, and that when they were on detached duties, he had borrowed money to pay the men. Joseph Howell to Chinn, New York, 21 September 1785, asked for an accounting of $9,000 received by Chinn in July 1777. See Papers of the War Department, record group 93, miscellaneous numbered records RG93, M859.

73. 22, 23, and 26 August 1777, *JCC*, 8:665–68, 677–78.

74. John to Abigail Adams, Philadelphia, 29 August and 2 September 1777, *LDC*, 7:568, 589–90.

75. Hancock to William Livingston, Philadelphia, 30 August 1777, *LDC*, 7:573–76; Henry Laurens to Lachlin McIntosh, 1 September 1777, *LDC*, 7:587–88; Congress, 3 September 1777, *JCC*, 8:707–8; Paine, "The Crisis, III," with Address to Council of Safety, Philadelphia, 19 April 1777, in *Writings of Thomas Paine*, 1:202–8, 216–29; Taaffe, *Philadelphia Campaign*, 228.

76. John to Abigail Adams, Philadelphia, 29 August and 8 September 1777, *LDC*, 7:568–69, 627–29.

77. Harris, *Brandywine*, 128, 139–40; General Orders, Wilmington, 4, 5, and 6 September 1777, in *Valley Forge Orderly Book of General George Weedon*, 31–32, 34–36.

78. McGuire, *Philadelphia Campaign*, 169, 172.

79. McGuire, *Philadelphia Campaign*, 171; Harris, *Brandywine*, 207–8.
80. De Borre to Congress, Trenton, 18 September 1777, PCC, roll 91, item 78, vol. 2, p. 257. The speculative number is derived from adding enlistments but subtracting deaths and desertions noted for June through August in regimental records. There appear to have been about nineteen or twenty desertions of men not listed on the roll, and thirty-three listed deserters (fewer than the forty Hazen reported). During that period, a few officers resigned and at least eight were taken at Staten Island. Even depleted as it was, the regiment made Borre's brigade bigger than Smallwood's, and when Smallwood complained of the inequity, Washington explained that Hazen's regiment had "increased considerably" after he made the assignments for the campaign season. Camp in Bucks County, 20 August 1777, *WGW*, 9:103.
81. Privates Samuel Johnson (Johnston), John Pool (Poole), Ambrose Willson (Wilson), and James Willden had enlisted in Carlile's company. See CSR, rolls 85, 89, and 91.
82. MH to Sullivan, Jones Ford, 11 September 1777, *Provincial and State Papers*, 17:197.
83. McGuire, *Philadelphia Campaign*, 173, 183–84; Harris, *Brandywine*, 236–38, 247–49.
84. Sullivan to Hancock, Camp at [Perkiomen], 6 October 1777, *Sullivan Papers*, 1:475–77; Sullivan to GW, Brinton's Ford, 11 September 1777, *Sullivan Papers*, 1:451; Harris, *Brandywine*, 247–49. Criticized for not taking the initiative to gather more intelligence, Sullivan countered by saying that he did not have the light troops or horsemen to do it. Sullivan to Hancock, Camp near White Marsh, 25 October 1777, *Sullivan Papers*, 1:549.
85. Sullivan to Hancock, Camp at [Perkiomen], 6 October 1777, *Sullivan Papers*, 1:476; Sullivan to GW, 2:00 P.M. [11 September 1777], *Sullivan Papers*, 1:453; Harris, *Brandywine*, 260–62.
86. JHJ, 11 September 1777, HSP.
87. Sullivan to Hancock, Camp on [Perkiomen], 27 September 1777, *Sullivan Papers*, 1:463–64 (and PCC, roll 178, item 160, p. 57); Taaffe, *Philadelphia Campaign*, 70–71.
88. De Borre to Congress, Trenton, 18 September 1777, PCC, roll 91, item 78, vol. 2, p. 257.
89. Sullivan to Hancock, Camp on [Perkiomen], 27 September 1777, *Sullivan Papers*, 1:464; JHJ, 11 September 1777, HSP; Taaffe, *Philadelphia Campaign*, 72, 74.
90. Sullivan to Hancock, Camp on [Perkiomen], 27 September 1777, *Sullivan Papers*, 1:465; JHJ, 11 September 1777, HSP.
91. JHJ, 11 September 1777, HSP; Peebles, *John Peebles' American War*, 133. Depending on where and when the regiment was hopping fences, it is possible that the Highlanders were of Fraser's 71st.
92. JHJ, 11, 13, 14 September 1777, HSP.
93. JHJ, 11 September 1777, HSP. In "The Case with Colonel Hazen's Regiment" (JSS), Hazen reiterated almost word for word Hawkins's contentions that the regiment was the first attacked and among the last on field, as well as the praise he supposedly delivered at the time and the numbers lost.
94. On Mazuzen, McConnell, Parmelee, and Teas, see CSR, rolls 88, 87, 89, and 91. Heitman's *Historical Register* (427) noted Parmelee as wounded. On McConnell, see Kilbourne, *Virtutis Praemium*, 1:555–57. See also Furguson (Ferguson), RWPBF, S.35924, reel 966; Thompson (Thomson), CSR, roll 91.

95. JHJ, 24 September 1777, HSP.
96. General Orders, Germantown, 13 September, and Pennypackers Mills, 27 and 28 September 1777, in *Valley Forge Orderly Book*, 47–48, 59, 60–61; Paine, "The Crisis IV," in *Writings of Thomas Paine*, 1:229; McGuire, *Philadelphia Campaign*, 271–72.
97. Samuel Adams to James Warren, Philadelphia, 17 September 1777, *LDC*, 7:678.
98. 18 September 1777, *JCC*, 8:754.
99. 17 September 1777, *JCC*, 8:752; Hancock to GW, York, 9 October 1777, *LDC*, 8:92.
100. GW to Colonel John Siegfried [Pennsylvania militia], Philadelphia County, and to Brigadier General William Woodford, Headquarters, 6 October 1777, and to President of Congress, Camp, 26 miles from Philadelphia, 10 October 1777, *WGW*, 9:318–19, 352.
101. McGuire, *Philadelphia Campaign*, 308–18.
102. JHJ, 6 October 1777, HSP. Washington approved Craig's acquittal in General Orders, Skippack, 1 October 1777, *WGW*, 9:296. Washington's thanks in General Orders, Perkiomy, 5 October 1777, *WGW*, 9:312.
103. John to Abigail Adams, York, 7 October 1777, *LDC*, 8:71.
104. General Orders, at Wentz's, Worcester Township, 3 October 1777, *WGW*, 9:303–8; McGuire, *Surprise of Germantown*, 30–34.
105. Sullivan to Meshech Weare, Camp at White Marsh, 25 October 1777, *Sullivan Papers*, 1:542–47.
106. Howard, "Col. John Eager Howard's Account of the Battle of Germantown," 314–20; Lambdin, "Battle of Germantown," 375–90.
107. Lambdin, "Battle of Germantown," 393.
108. JHJ, 6 October 1777, HSP; MH to Congress, "The Case with Colonel Hazen's Regiment," JSS.
109. On Thompson, Garnet, Harris, McClure, Bass, and Jordan, see CSR, rolls 91, 83, 84, 87, 78, and 85. A few of the casualties might be inferred from those omitted from regimental records in late 1777.
110. JHJ, 8, 9, and 10 October 1777, HSP. Farndon of Hartley's regiment was sentenced on 7 October, but his execution was postponed due to other events. General Orders, Perkiomy, 7 and 8 October 1777, *WGW*, 9:329; Towamensing, 9 October 1777, *WGW*, 9:341–42.
111. GW to Pres. of Congress, near White Marsh, 1 November 1777, *WGW*, 9:476–83.
112. GW to Baron D'Arendt and Lieutenant Colonel Samuel Smith, 18 October 1777, *WGW*, 9:394, 396; to Lieutenant Colonel John Green, 28 October 1777, *WGW*, 9:458; and to Brigadier General David Forman, 1 November 1777, *WGW*, 9:489–90. As Smith's detachment "must be much distressed for Cloathing," Smith was to call upon Forman for what he needed; that likely led to receipts for clothing delivered by Smith at Mifflin to "Soldiers of the Congress Regiment under his Command." Receipt examples in John Carlile file, CSR, roll 80.
113. GW to President of Congress, 13 October 1777, *WGW*, 9:366–67.
114. GW to President of Congress, near White Marsh, 21 October, and Proclamation, 24 October 1777, *WGW*, 9:406–7, 426–27.
115. GW to President of Congress [Henry Laurens], and to Board of War, near White Marsh, 11 November 1777, and to Board of War, Gulf [Gulph] Creek, 14 December 1777, *WGW*, 10:36–39, 152.

116. General Orders, White Marsh, 18 and 24 November 1777, *WGW*, 10:79, 102.

117. 8 and 10 December 1777, *JCC*, 9:1010–11, 1013–15; GW to the "Officers Ordered to Remove Provisions from the Country Near the Enemy," [15? December 1777], *WGW*, 10:162–63.

118. 16 December 1777, *JCC*, 9:1029–31.

119. Sullivan, Maxwell, and Wayne to GW, White Marsh, 23 November 1777, and Protest of General Officers to Congress, Valley Forge, 31 December 1777, *Sullivan Papers*, 1:580–83.

120. Remarks on Plan of Field Officers for Remodeling the Army, November 1777, *WGW*, 10:125–26.

121. A number of general accounts use the label without reference to a primary source. Compare Adela Peltier Reed's construction in *Memoirs of Antoine Paulint*, 25, to Parsons's disparagement of "'Congress' Own' regiment of infernals" in C. Hall, *Life and Letters of Samuel Holden Parsons*, 150.

122. McMichael, "Diary of Lieut. James McMichael," 216.

123. General Orders, at the Gulph, 17 December 1777, *WGW*, 10:167–68.

124. JHJ, 20 December 1777, HSP.

Chapter 6

1. 15 and 17 November 1777, *JCC*, 9:907–28, 932–35.

2. 25 and 26 June 1778, *JCC*, 11:648–58.

3. 29 November and 2 December 1777, *JCC*, 9:981, 985–87.

4. 19 and 22 December 1777, *JCC*, 9:1037, 1049; Henry Laurens to James Duane, York, 24 December 1777, *LDC*, 8:470–71; 27 December 1777, *JCC*, 9:1059–63.

5. Lafayette to GW, [Valley Forge], 5 January 1778, *PGW:RWS*, 13:145.

6. 25 June 1778, *JCC*, 11:642–44.

7. Higginbotham, *War of American Independence*, 216–22; Ferling, *Almost a Miracle*, 282–84, 290–93; and Lender, *Cabal!*, 227–30.

8. Lafayette to GW, 20 January 1778, *PGW:RWS*, 13:291–92.

9. Resolution for "irruption" into Canada, 22 January 1778, *JCC*, 10:84–85; Gates to GW, War Office [York], 24 January, and GW to Gates, Valley Forge, 27 January 1778, *PGW:RWS*, 13:329–30, 361. Also see Lender, *Cabal!*, 161–64.

10. Taylor to GW, Wilmington, 26 January 1778, *PGW:RWS*, 13:358–59.

11. Records indicate about fifteen desertions and a dozen deaths from December 1777 to February 1778. Other absences are noted between the 21 December 1777 and 13 August 1778 entries in JHJ, HSP.

12. GW to Smallwood and to Taylor, Valley Forge, 28 January 1778, *PGW:RWS*, 13:371, 373–74.

13. Return of provisions and stores issued to the army in camp under GW for February 1778, Commissaries Office, 11 March 1778, PCC, Quartermaster Department Letters, roll 199, item 192, p. 425.

14. Noah Lee certificate to Col. [Stourd], Deputy Quartermaster General, White Horse, 14 February 1778, MS 2958.5709, NYHS; Carriage resolution, 22 February 1777, *JCC*, 7:144–47.

15. Bedel to MH, Haverhill, 7 February 1778, and Vermont Committee of Safety to MH, Bennington, 9 February 1778, PCC, roll 183, item 166, pp. 63, 85; Heath to GW, Boston, 7–10 February 1778, *PGW:RWS*, 13:469–70.

16. Albany, 24 and 25 February 1778, in 2CROB, vol. 1, HSP; Observations with General Return of Troops under Lafayette's Command, Albany, 20 February 1778, PCC, roll 183, item 166, p. 77b.

17. General Return of Troops under Lafayette's Command, Albany, 20 February 1778, PCC, roll 183, item 166, p. 77a.

18. Albany, 24 February 1778, in 2CROB, vol. 1, HSP; Heitman, *Historical Register*, 247, 248.

19. Albany, 24 February 1778, in 2CROB, vol. 1, HSP; captains and commands list in additional miscellaneous records, RWR, roll 132, items 43–63; and Chambers Genealogical Files, including Lenore E. Flower to R. E. Morton, 5 August 1931, Cumberland County Historical Society, Carlisle, Pa.

20. JHJ, "Memo. (Albany)," 9 March 1778, HSP.

21. Officers' promotions and commands, additional miscellaneous records, RWR, roll 132, items 43–63.

22. Lesser, *Sinews of Independence*, 65.

23. GW to Brigadier General Thomas Nelson Jr., Valley Forge, 8 February 1778, *PGW:RWS*, 13:481.

24. MH to Conway, Albany, 17 February; Conway to MH, Albany 18 February 1778, and Conway to Gates, Albany 19 February 1778, PCC, roll 183, item 166, pp. 103, 65, and 111–13.

25. Lafayette to MH and MH to Lafayette, Albany, 18 February 1778, PCC, roll 183, item 166, pp. 59–60, 67–69.

26. Lafayette to GW, Albany, 19 and 23 February, *PGW:RWS*, 13:594–95, 648–49.

27. General Return, and MH to Gates, Albany, 20 February 1778, PCC, roll 183, item 166, pp. 78, 117–19.

28. Example in Ambrose Walden file, RWPBF, S.38453, reel 2471. Congress had passed a resolution requiring oaths of allegiance on 3 February.

29. James Duane to George Clinton, Livingston Manor, and Henry Laurens to Lafayette, 13 March 1778, *LDC*, 9:287–89, 292–93; 13 March 1778, *JCC*, 10:253–54; [Albany], 26 March 1778, in 2CROB, vol. 1, HSP.

30. MH, "The Case with Colonel Hazen's Regiment," White Plains, 3 September 1778, JSS.

31. Everest, *Moses Hazen and the Canadian Refugees*, 38.

32. MH to Bedel, Albany 29 January; Conway to Bedel, Albany, 15 February; Bedel to Gates, Albany, 14 March; Lafayette to Bedel, Albany 16 March 1778, *Provincial and State Papers*, 17:212–13, 218–19, 222–23.

33. Baldwin, "The Hazen Military Road," 297–323; Everest, *Moses Hazen and the Canadian Refugees*, 71.

34. Bedel to Gates, [undated 1778]; Bayley to Gates, Newbury, 13 July; Bedel to Gates, Haverhill, 15 July; MH to Bedel, Camp at White Plains, 25 July 1778, *Provincial and State Papers*, 17:210, 240–41, 248.

35. Gates, Bayley, and MH to GW, [White Plains, 10 September 1778], *PGW:RWS*, 16:550–51.

36. GW to Bayley [White Plains, 11 September 1778] and GW to Henry Laurens, White Plains, 12 September 1778, *PGW:RWS*, 16:565–66, 586–88. Bayley copied them to Bedel, Newbury, 13 October 1778, *Provincial and State Papers*, 17:276.

37. Bayley to GW, Newbury, 23 November 1778, *PGW:RWS*, 18:258–62; Gosselin to Madame Clément Gosselin, de Lobinier [*sic*], 29 October 1778, *History of the*

Military of Canada, 3:78–79. Traversie (no first name) and Hall in CSR, rolls 536, 535, and 894.

38. 22 October 1778, *JCC*, 12:1042–48.

39. Lanctot, *Canada and the American Revolution*, 178–79. See also d'Estaing, "A Declaration Addressed in the Name of the King to all the Former French Subjects in North America," 28 October, and LaFayette, Letter to the Indians of Canada, 18 December 1778, *History of the Military of Canada*, 3:75–78, 82–85.

40. GW to Henry Laurens, [Fredericksburg, N.Y.], 11 November 1778, *PGW:RWS*, 18:94–95.

41. GW to Philip Schuyler, Fredericksburg [N.Y.], 20 November 1778, *PGW:RWS*, 18:237–42.

42. 5 December 1778, and 1 January 1779 *JCC*, 12:1190–91, 13:11–14.

43. Gates to GW, Boston, 27 December 1778, *PGW:RWS*, 18:511; Lanctot, *Canada and the American Revolution*, 180–88.

44. On Haldimand's worries, see *History of the Military of Canada*, vol. 3, chaps. 6–7, particularly pp. 13–14, 29–31; on Washington's advice to Congress, see Lawson, "Canada and the Articles of Confederation," 49–50; and on Washington's use of Hazen, see Everest, *Moses Hazen and the Canadian Refugees*, 68–71.

45. Williams, *Year of the Hangman*, 189–90; GW to Continental Congress, Committee of Conference, Philadelphia, 13 January 1779, *PGW:RWS*, 18:624–29.

46. GW to John Jay, Middlebrook, 14 April 1779, *PGW:RWS*, 20:57–64 (esp. 58).

47. Ibid., esp. 59.

48. GW to Clinton, and to Schuyler, Philadelphia, 25 January 1779, *PGW:RWS*, 19:69–70, 72–74; GW to Schuyler, Middlebrook, 11 February 1779, *PGW:RWS*, 19:176–79; GW to Committee of Conference, Philadelphia, 13 January 1779, *PGW:RWS*, 19:624–29.

49. Lanctot, *Canada and the American Revolution*, 181.

50. GW to Gates, to Putnam, and to Sullivan, Middlebrook, 6 March 1779, *PGW:RWS*, 19:377–78, 387, 388–89.

51. GW to MH, [6 March] & Middlebrook, 14 March 1779, *PGW:RWS*, 19:379–80, 476–77.

52. MH to GW, Camp Near Danbury, 13 March 1779, *PGW:RWS*, 19:468–69.

53. MH to GW, Camp Near Danbury, 8 March 1779, *PGW:RWS*, 19:400.

54. JHJ, [11 February] 1779, HSP.

55. JHJ, 23–30 March 1779, HSP. Perhaps 303 officers and soldiers were fit and present (not on command or furlough) for the march out of 476 total, as recorded in Lesser, *Sinews of Independence*, 109. Crowley's detachment is also noted in GW to Major General Robert Howe, West Point, 24 October 1779, *PGW:RWS*, 23:21–23n6. For Edward Hinman's complaint against Hazen's threats and actions to procure teams, see GW to Edward Hinman, Middlebrook, 12 April 1779, *PGW:RWS*, 20:40–41n1.

56. JHJ, 31 March–2 April 1779, HSP.

57. JHJ, 3–5, 9 April 1779, HSP.

58. MH to Bedel, Springfield, 12 April; Bedel to MH, Haverhill, 8 February 1779, *Provincial and State Papers*, 17:329, 316–17. Hazen informed Washington of misrepresenting mission goals to residents on 26 April 1779. *PGW:RWS*, 20:221–24.

59. Peaslee (Peasley), Zacheus, CSR, roll 89.

60. JHJ, 10–16 April 1779, HSP.

61. JHJ, 17–21 April 1779, HSP.

62. JHJ, 22–24 April 1779, HSP.

63. MH to GW, Camp near Danbury, 8 March 1779, *PGW:RWS*, 19:399; MH to Bedel, Camp Peekskill, 14 November 1779, *Provincial and State Papers*, 17:350. Gregory Nobles argued that in the western borderlands, "different frontier groups took different sides in order to promote their own immediate interests. The intensity of these local conflicts seems all the more striking because they had so little apparent connection to the larger ideological or imperial issues." Nobles, *American Frontiers*, 87–88. In the northern borderlands, ideological and imperial issues were very much in play with individual interests.

64. Bennett, *A Few Lawless Vagabonds*, 21–25.

65. Ibid., 42–43, 139–42.

66. MH to officials, Charlestown, 22 April, and MH to Major Childs [Jonathan Child], Charlestown, 25 April 1779, *Provincial and State Papers*, 17:331–33.

67. MH to GW, Charlestown or No. 4, 26 April 1779, *PGW:RWS*, 20:221–24.

68. JHJ, 25 April 1779, HSP.

69. JHJ, 26–28 April 1779, HSP.

70. John Adams to Abigail Adams, Baltimore, 3 February 1777, *LDC*, 6:199–200.

71. JHJ, 29–30 April 1779, HSP.

72. Ibid., 1–3 May 1779.

73. Ibid., 4–7 May 1779.

74. Ibid., 8–10 May 1779.

75. MH to Bedel, Camp Haverhill, 24 May 1779, *Provincial and State Papers*, 17:330.

76. MH to Major General Horatio Gates, Camp Haverhill [Coos, N.H.], 22 September 1779, in Bayley to GW, Newbury [Vt.], 11 November 1779, *PGW:RWS*, 23:238–39n1; Calloway, *Western Abenakis of Vermont*, 160, 162–63, 182–83, 188.

77. Calloway, *Western Abenakis of Vermont*, 214–15.

78. GW to Samuel Huntington, West Point, 3 November, and GW to MH, West Point, 6 November 1779, *PGW:RWS*, 23:144–45, 172–73, including footnotes; Charland, "Gill, Joseph-Louis."

79. JHJ, 4, 8, 10 May 1779, HSP.

80. JHJ, 16 May 1779, HSP. See also the 1837 pension abstract of Lydia Sanborn, widow of Ebenezer, in Draper, *N. H. Revolutionary Pension Papers*.

81. JHJ, 16 May 1779, HSP.

82. Ezra Gates, RWPBF, S.15129, reel 1055

83. John (Sarah) Shepherd, RWPBF, W.11452, reel 2169.

84. Thomas (Ruth) Hazleton recorded as Hazeltine, RWPBF, W.19677, reel 1238.

85. Josiah (Mary) Pratt, RWPBF, W.27466, reel 1968.

86. Jonathan (Polly) Pratt, RWPBF, B.L. Rej. 304209–55, reel 1967. The account says he may have enlisted in 1777 or 1779, but regimental roster records enlistment on 1 June 1779, the same day as Josiah Pratt.

87. Michael Salter and Joel Ried (Reid), CSR, rolls 90, 89.

88. Eden Burroughs to GW, Hanover, N. Hampshire, 24 December 1779, *PGW:RWS*, 23:705–6. Stephen Burrows enlisted 28 September and deserted in December 1779. See CSR, roll 79.

89. William (Abigail) Gledin, RWPBF, W.16588, reel 1081.

90. Benjamin (Dolly) Heath, RWPBF, W.23273, reel 1243.
91. Merifield (Anny) Victor (or Vickory), RWPBF, W.6365, reel 2459; CSR, roll 91.
92. GW to John Jay, Middle Brook, 3 May 1779, *PGW:RWS*, 20:306–7.
93. GW to MH, Middle Brook, 5 May 1779, *PGW:RWS*, 20:336–37.
94. JHJ, 28 May and 7 June 1779, HSP.
95. GW to Governor George Clinton, New Windsor, 28 June 1779, *PGW:RWS*, 21:290.
96. GW to Colonel Goose Van Schaick, West Point, 3 August 1779, *PGW:RWS*, 22:27–28.
97. GW to MH, New Windsor, 20 July 1779, *PGW:RWS*, 21:577.
98. JHJ, 1 and 6 June 1779, HSP.
99. JHJ, 7 June 1779, HSP; on Bedel and Duncan supporting each other, see MH to Bedel, Camp, Davises Lake, and 20 August, Camp at the end of the Road, 24 August, and Camp, Hazens Rout, 31 August 1779, *Provincial and State Papers*, 17:344–45, 347.
100. "Extract of a Letter from an Officer on the Northern Expedition," Co'os, 28 June 1779, *Virginia Gazette* [Williamsburg], 11 September 1779, AHN. See also *New Jersey Gazette* [Burlington, N.J.], 15 September, and *American Journal* [Providence, R.I.], 7 October 1779, AHN.
101. Theodore (Naomi) DeKalla or De Calla (DeKelley), RWPBF, R.5832, reel 788; COR Roll. The widow and her advocates said Theodore (d. 1789) had been a surgeon's mate. The regiment, however, had recorded him as a private, and the commissioner of pensions noted that a Theodore DeCalla had received a land warrant in 1795 for services as a private. That aside, the deponents confirmed DeKelley's presence with Hazen's regiment at Haverhill in 1779.
102. Baldwin, "The Hazen Military Road"; Northeastern Vermont Development Association, "In Search of Bayley-Hazen," 21.
103. Baldwin, "The Hazen Military Road"; MH to Bedel, Camp at the end of the Road, 50 miles, 24 August 1779, *Provincial and State Papers*, 17:345.
104. GW to MH, West Point, 28 August 1779, *PGW:RWS*, 22:278.
105. MH to Bedel, Camp, Hazens Rout, 31 August, and Haverhill, 8 September 1779, *Provincial and State Papers*, 17:347. Mooers mentioned the eleven-man expedition in "[Auto-]Biography of Major-General Benjamin Mooers," 92–94.
106. GW to Jeremiah Wadsworth, [West Point, 9 September 1779], *PGW:RWS*, 22:392–93.
107. Substance of a Conference with La Luzerne, West Point, 16 September 1779, *PGW:RWS*, 22:438–42.
108. GW to MH, West Point, 17 September 1779, *PGW:RWS*, 22:448–49.
109. GW to Jeremiah Wadsworth, [West Point], 25 September 1779, *PGW:RWS*, 22:508.
110. GW to MH, West Point, 3 October 1779, *PGW:RWS*, 22:624.
111. MH to Bedel, Camp Peekskill, 14 November 1779, *Provincial and State Papers*, 17:350. Hazen wrote to Friedrich Wilhelm von Steuben that he hoped the time was "Drawing near when Canada will be a fourteenth state in the union," and asked Steuben to support the regiment in its requests for support from Board of War and Congress. MH to Steuben, Camp near Morristown, 11 Feb. 1780, Steuben Papers, DLAR, reel 2, item 198.
112. Massachusetts Council letter, 22 October 1777, in Huntington to GW, Philadelphia, 11 November 1779, *PGW:RWS*, 23:243–45n6; and GW to Samuel Huntington, West Point, 20 November 1779, *PGW:RWS*, 23:378.

Chapter 7

1. GW to Congress Conference Committee, [Valley Forge, 29 January 1778], *PGW:RWS*, 13:382.
2. GW, General Orders, Cambridge, 4 July 1775, *PGW:RWS*, 1:54.
3. GW to John Banister, Valley Forge, 21 April 1778, *PGW:RWS*, 14:577.
4. Carp, "Origins of the Nationalist Movement of 1780–1783," 365–70.
5. R. K. Wright, *Continental Army*, 318.
6. Nathanael Greene to GW, [January 1778], *PGW:RWS*, 13:424–25, 427; R. K. Wright, *Continental Army*, 125–27.
7. R. K. Wright, *Continental Army*, 124–27, 146; "Establishment of the American Army," 27 May 1778, *JCC*, 11:538–43.
8. 26 February and 28 May 1778, *JCC*, 10:199–203, 11:545.
9. Parsons to GW, Camp West Point, 7 March 1778, *PGW:RWS*, 14:90–92; Parsons to Clinton, [Robinson's House], 10 March 1778, in C. Hall, *Life and Letters of Samuel Holden Parsons*, 149–50.
10. Lafayette to GW, Albany, 19 and 23 February, *PGW:RWS*, 13:594–95, 648–49. See also chapter 6.
11. Parsons to Clinton, 5 March 1778, in C. Hall, *Life and Letters of Samuel Holden Parsons*, 149.
12. John Welles's Statement, Case of Capt. Allin, Albany, 10 October 1778, in *Sullivan Papers*, 2:383–86; John Baptist Allen and James Robichaux, CSR, rolls 94 and 97; Headquarters, 14 June 1778, in 2CROB, vol. 1, HSP. *Sullivan Papers* (2:372–73) and CSR records reveal that in September 1778, Allen was charged with theft, convicted, and dismissed.
13. Chapter 3, endnote 77; Roussi to GW, Valley Forge, 24 March 1778, *PGW:RWS*, 14:297; General Orders, Valley Forge, 28 May 1778, *PGW:RWS*, 15:242–43n2.
14. GW to Henry Laurens, Valley Forge, 17 March 1778, *PGW:RWS*, 14:210–11
15. GW to Lafayette, Headquarters, 20 March 1778, *PGW:RWS*, 14:238–39; GW to Henry Laurens, Valley Forge, 21 March 1778, *PGW:RWS*, 14:251–52; Lafayette to GW, Albany, 25 March 1778, *PGW:RWS*, 14:306–7; GW to McDougall, Valley Forge, 25 March 1778, *PGW:RWS*, 14:311.
16. GW to McDougall, Valley Forge, 31 March 1778, *PGW:RWS*, 14:369–70; McDougall to GW, Fishkill, 3 April 1778, *PGW:RWS*, 14:392; McDougall to GW, Fishkill, 13 April 1778, *PGW:RWS*, 14:496–97.
17. McDougall to GW, Fishkill, 13 April 1778, *PGW:RWS*, 14:497; Brigadier John Nixon to GW, Camp White Plains, [24] July 1778, *PGW:RWS*, 14:16:155–56; Picket and forage excursion in 24 July report by Parsons, enclosed in Nixon to GW, White Plains, [24] July 1778, *PGW:RWS*, 16:156n5.
18. JHJ, White Plains, 13 August 1778, HSP.
19. Campbell and Carlile (Carlisle), CSR, roll 80. Campbell's records suggest that he may have broken parole at some point.
20. Payrolls in RWR, rolls 131–32; JHJ, 3 September 1778 list, HSP.
21. JHJ, 3 September, HSP; MH, "The Case with Colonel Hazen's Regiment," White Plains, 3 September 1778, JSS.
22. "Petition of Colonel Moses Hazen," Philadelphia, 20 September 1778, JSS.
23. MH to GW, Charlestown, 26 April 1779, *PGW:RWS*, 20:222.
24. MH Memorial to GW, Peekskill, 20 November 1779, *PGW:RWS*, 23:367–71.

25. MH to GW, Peekskill, 20 November 1779, *PGW:RWS*, 23:371n (letter with emphasis).
26. Lesser, *Sinews of Independence*, 81, 85, 133, 180.
27. 24 November 1778, *JCC*, 12:1159.
28. Mooers, "[Auto-]Biography."
29. American Prisoners of War (including Antill and Woodson) to Congress, Long Island, May 1778, PCC, roll 51, item 41, vol. 7, p. 181; Commissioners for the Army reporting on Memorial of William Stewart, 4 October 1786, Papers of Paymaster Pierce, PCC, roll 76, p. 194. The report incorrectly states that Woodson was on furlough until 1782 after his October 1780 release. See CSR and "Heirs of Maj. Tarleton Woodson, Deceased," 29 March 1898, report 870, 55th Congress, MSSIW868792, Virginia Historical Society. Manning's appointment as ensign in Regimental Orders, 6 October, in 2CROB, vol. 2, HSP; Hawkins's promotion to sergeant major in his Memoranda, 1780, HSP.
30. MH to John Sullivan (in Congress), West Point, 15 October 1780, JSS. MH to Steuben, Camp Near Morristown, 11 and 24 February 1780, Steuben Papers, DLAR, reel 2, items 198, 214; Steuben's "Proposals for the formation of our Army for the next Campaign," 15 March 1780, and Stirling's comments to GW, Baskingridge, 19 March 1780, *PGW:RWS*, 24:212–15, 25:57–59, 94–96.
31. 3 and 21 October 1780, *JCC*, 18:893–98, 958–61; R. K. Wright, *Continental Army*, 156–59.
32. MH to GW, Lancaster, 26 March 1782, Founders Online, EA.
33. Fishkill, 15 March 1781, Moore [*sic*], Orderly Book, NYSL.
34. Lesser, *Sinews of Independence*, 189; COR Roll; MH to GW, Fishkill, 8 January 1781, Founders Online, EA.
35. Schott to Congress, Philadelphia, 25 September 1781, PCC, roll 56, item 42, vol. 7, p. 127; and Schott and Selin entries, CSR, roll 838. Schott to GW, Wyoming, 10 July 1780, and 18 July 1781; and Adjutant General Edward Hand to Antill, New Windsor, 3 April 1781, about incorporating Selin's troops, Founders Online, EA. See also Sullivan to GW, Philadelphia, 29 July 1781, *LDC*, 17:457–58; and 14 April 1781 Fishkill Regimental Orders, which placed two sergeants from Selin's company into Popham's, another with Gilbert's, and two sergeants and remaining men into Munson's company. See Moore [*sic*], Orderly Book, NYSL.
36. MH to GW, Camp [Yorktown], 4 November 1781, enclosing Antill's letter of same date, Founders Online, EA. Antill asked for promotions of Olivie, Satterlee, Dionne, and McPherson, and appointments to ensign for Peaslee, T. Thompson, and Dixon. The following were appointed or promoted between 1779 and 1782: Bell, Bugbee (quartermaster), Chinn (as paymaster made second lieutenant), Guilmat, Hoops, Lee, Manning, Mooers, Olivie, Peaslee, Sanford, and T. Thompson. Noncommissioned officer transfers and promotions are noted 13 January 1781, Fishkill, [Lloyd], Orderly Book, 2nd Canadian, SOC. Sergeants MGlockland (McClennan?) and Peren (Jean Baptiste Peron from Livingston's) had company transfers, and corporals T. Donaldson, M. Maison (Moison), and W. Woodward made sergeant, while privates D. Norget, C. Tessie, and E. Trusdall became corporals. Hazen promoted Reed (Peter Reid) to sergeant, and I. White and J. Pierce to corporal. See Regimental Orders, Fishkill, 18 February 1781, Moore [*sic*], Orderly Book, NYSL.
37. "Strength of General Hazens Regimt. at different Periods," 1786, PCC, roll 52, item 41, vol. 9, pp. 395–401.

38. Hazen ordered that the Canadians in Gilbert's company be transferred to the companies of Olivie, Liébert, and Gosselin on 24 December 1780, at Fishkill ([Lloyd], Orderly Book, SOC); forerunner in Regiment Orders, Preakness, 15 July 1780, in MHOB, vol. 2, HSP.

39. Sherrill E. Grace discusses the concept of borderlands as relational and tied to identity narratives. See Grace, "Comparing Mythologies."

40. Lynn, *Women, Armies, and Warfare*, 18, 33.

41. A few men listed with the regiment on CSR cards were contractors—their papers were receipts, not musters. For soldier as temporary "sutler," see 21 May 1781, Fishkill, Antill's orders permitting James King "to sell Cyder to the Regiment till further Orders," Moore [*sic*], Orderly Book, NYSL.

42. M. White (MH's cousin once removed), *Statement of Facts*, 9; MH to Antill, Montreal, 26 March 1776, *History of the Military of Canada*, 2:150; J[onathan] Trumbull to Richard Peters, Albany, 29 August 1776, Peters Papers, vol. 8, HSP.

43. For more on women's roles and actions, see Mayer, "Bearing Arms, Bearing Burdens," 169–87, and *Belonging to the Army*, 145–51.

44. Hay to Greene, Fishkill, 24 November 1779, in *Papers of General Nathanael Greene*, 5:115; 29 January and 1 February 1782, Mooers, Travel Accounts and Daybooks, BMC, file 184, box 12, series 3; Greene to Catharine Greene, Camp Tappan [N.Y.], 7 October 1780, in *Papers of Nathanael Greene*, 6:350–51. (The meeting did not happen as Greene was ordered South.) About cholic, see MH to William A. Atlee, Pompton, 23 February 1783, Atlee Papers, Peter Force Papers and Collection, series 9, reel 100, box 32, LOC. About "Ague," see MH to Colonel Jeremiah Wadsworth, Camp West Point, 24 October 1780, GLC02499.08. See also MH to Henry Knox, Lancaster, 20 May 1782, GLC02437.01423; MH to Henry Knox, Pompton, 22 November 1782, GLC02437.01723; and Charlotte Hazen to Knox, New York, 23 April 1789, GLC02437.04187.

45. Charlotte Antill, who bore ten children over seventeen years, died in September 1785 at age thirty-two. See *New England Historical & Genealogical Register and Antiquarian Journal*, 19:165–66; Antill to GW, Flatt Bush [N.Y.], 27 March 1780, *PGW:RWS*, 25:185; Heath to GW, West Point, 18 November 1780, *WGW*, 20:500–501; General Orders, New Windsor, 20 December 1780 and 1 January 1781, *WGW*, 21:45–46.

46. George Woodson to brother Tarlton, 29 September 1777, Woodson Family Papers, Library of Virginia; Tarlton to sister Sally, Long Island, 9 November 1777, Woodson Family Papers; Frederick Woodson to brother Tarlton, "Kacaah," 12 October 1779, Woodson Family Papers. (All spelled "Tarlton," not "Tarleton.") The October 1779 letter does not indicate impending marriage, but a year earlier, in addition to asking for money, Tarlton noted a desire for more conversation with "Madam" and "the Young Ladies." See also Woodson to Madam [no name], Long Island, 30 June 1778, MSSIW8687a1, Virginia Historical Society; "Woodson Family," *William and Mary Quarterly* 10, no. 3 (January 1902): 185; and Woodson, *Historical Genealogy of the Woodsons*, 1:81.

47. Some wives are noted in Sypher, *New York State Society of the Cincinnati Biographies, passim*. Lieutenant Lewis deposed on 13 November 1780 that in February 1779, he was at Munson's New Haven home and saw a five- or six-year-old boy in uniform, whom Munson said was his son, and that he mustered and drew

pay for him (19). Hazen dismissed the concern about the Munson recorded as a volunteer on furlough and said that Captain Munson merited an "indulgence" (61). In Proceedings of Hazen Court Martial, Peter Force Papers and Collection, series 7E, reel 14, box 20, LOC. See also William Munson, private/volunteer, on Munson's company payrolls between November 1778 and July 1779, RWR, roll 0131; Weithaed-Pry 26 August marriage, in Baptismal and Marriage Records of the Rev. John Waldschmidt, in *Pennsylvania Archives*, series 6, 6:260. On the Simon-Schuyler marriage (by Lutheran pastor Gotthilf Heinrich Ernst Mühlenberg), see Brener, *Jews of Lancaster*, 22.

48. Alexander Ferriole, RWPBF, S.43551, reel 967; Antoine and Theotist Paulint, RWPBF, W.16671, reel 1891.

49. Theotist Blow, affidavit for Sally Chartier application, 6 November 1837, John Mary Chartier file, RWPBF, W.17598, reel 524.

50. Theotist Blow, 6 November 1837, Ibid. John Chartier is Jean Marie Chartie in "Pay Roll of an Independent Company Command. by Captain Antoine Paulint ... August 1778," and "Roll of Captn. Antoine Paulint Independent Company ... annexed to Colo. Moses Hazens Regiment, Septr. 13th 1778—Engaged until the Conquest of Canada," RWR, film 4, roll 131. For more on this case and some of the others summarized herein, see Mayer, "Wives, Concubines, and Community," 248–56.

51. Alexander Fernial (Ferriol), statement, 9 June 1837, and Basil Nadeau, 18 October 1837, in John Chartier file, RWPBF, W.17598, reel 524.

52. Polly Chartier, statements, 22 February 1837 and 2 May 1837, in Peter Chartier file, RWPBF, W.23786, reel 524.

53. Alexander Ferriol, statement, 1 May 1837, and Sally Chartier, 20 February 1837, in Peter Chartier file, RWPBF, W.23786, reel 524.

54. Sally Chartier, deposition, 22 February 1837, Alexander Fernial (Ferriol), 9 June 1837, and Basil Nadeau, 18 October 1837, John Chartier file, RWPBF, W.17598, reel 524.

55. E. D. Woodbridge to William Slade, Vergennes, [illegible] 22, 1837, John Chartier file, RWPBF, W.17598, reel 524.

56. "Father Defarm" named in Peter Chartier file, RWPBF, W.23786, reel 524. On Ferdinand Steinmeyer as Father Farmer, see Schuyler, "Ferdinand Steinmeyer." See also Griffin, *Catholics and the American Revolution*, 1:125–26.

57. "Chaplains of the French Army," *American Catholic Historical Researches* (1911), 67–75; "Father Peter Huet de La Valiniere," *American Catholic Historical Researches* (1906): 209–10, 217–18, 237–38. See also Metzger, "Chaplains in the American Revolution," 52.

58. E. D. and F. E. Woodbridge to James L. Edwards, Commissioner of Pensions, Vergennes, 12 June 1849 for Peter and James Chartier; Polly Chartier, deposition, [1849], Peter Chartier file, RWPBF, W.23786, reel 524.

59. COR Roll; John Monty pension application, S.43006, Joseph (Mary) Monty, W.5384, and Alexander Ferriol, S.43,551, RWPBF, reels 1750 and 967; Francis Monty to GW, Camp Mendham [N.J.], 29 April 1780, *PGW:RWS*, 25:518–19. For context, see Cox, *Boy Soldiers of the American Revolution*. Sidenote: Mary (Polly) Monty (b. ~1764), daughter of Lieutenant Monty, married veteran Lewis Lisote in 1784. RWPBF, W.24533, reel 1570.

60. Alexander "Ferrial," deposition, 20 March 1846, Nicholas (and Charlotte) Constantine pension file, RWPBF, R.2239, reel 631. Also in Constantine pension file: Mary Louisa La Fond of Point Au Meule Canada East, 6 October 1846; Charlotte Constantine, 5 October 1841; Mary Cayeaux (widow of Joseph Cayeaux in Livingston's regiment), 4 September 1841. Ferriol declared that he had been with the refugees constantly from Canada to discharge at Newburgh, and that Gen. Mooers and David B Mc.Nicl (of the pension department) had asked him to help them determine who was a refugee and who had served in the war. He had learned to read and write and believed that his recollections were accurate. Ferriol to Henry C. Dickinson, Judge of Clinton County courts, 15 December 1842, Constantine file, RWPBF.

61. Alexander "Fernioll," depositions, 6 October 1841 and 8 December 1841, Nicholas (and Charlotte) Constantine file, RWPBF, R.2239, reel 631. Ferriol's contention that he did not recall a priest visiting except in 1781 challenged his statements supporting other applications.

62. Peter Blanchard, depositions, 31 March 1818 and 3 October 1820, and Benjamin Mooers, April 1818, Peter (and Martha) Blanchard file, RWPBF, W.16506, reel 264. See also COR Roll.

63. Martha Blanchard, statement, 14 September 1836, and Basil Nadeau, 4 March 1837, Blanchard file, RWPBF, W.16506, reel 264.

64. Elizabeth Heaton, application, 4 August 1836, James (and Elizabeth) Heaton file, RWPBF, W.7.716, reel 1245; [Henry Augustus Philip] Muhlenberg to J. L. Edwards, Commissioner of Pensions, Reading, 25 August 1836, Heaton file, RWPBF.

65. Mary Dick, declaration, 24 January 1840, Jacob (and Mary) Dick file, RWPBF, W.9407, reel 809; also in Dick file: declarations before Orphans Court of Baltimore County, 25 March 1840 and 12 May 1841; Stephen Freeland, statement, Baltimore County, 3 February 1840.

66. Abigail Roberts, declaration, 28 November 1838, William (and Abigail) Roberts file, RWPBF, W.20033, reel 2060.

67. MH to Governor George Clinton, Fishkill, 10 January 1781, M1182, NYSL, asking for relief for Captain Olivie's wife and family at Albany while Olivie served with the regiment at Fishkill.

68. Rees, "'The Multitude of Women'"; Estimate of the Number and Cost of the Rations necessary for an Army of 25000 Rank and file and its appendages, undated but in 1782 file of Estimates & Statements of Expenditures, 1780–88, PCC, roll 154, item 141, vol. 1, p. 25. (5–6 percent: 1,536 women for a proposed army of 25,000 rank and file, or of 28,227 with noncommissioned officers, and 31,963 including officers). See also General Orders, Newburgh, 28 December 1782, WGW, 25:478, 480; and JCC, 23 October 1783, 25:725–35.

69. "Provision Return for a Detachment from the Canadian Old Regiment and a Quartermaster from the York County Militia for Four Days Commencing the First and Ending the fourth of June 1782," and other returns for June and July, Revolutionary War—Provision Returns, 1782 June–August, BMC, file 102, box 7, series 2B.

70. Headquarters, Stenrapie, 19 September 1780, [Mooers], Orderly Book, Papers of Benjamin Mooers, 1780, LOC; and in Moore [sic] Orderly Book, NYSL: Headquarters, New Windsor, 19 June 1781; "embarrassed," Regimental Orders, On board the

Tryon, 9 July 1781; Regimental Orders, Albany, 17 June 1781; Regimental Orders, Cognawaga, 29 June 1781; milk in Regimental Orders, West Point, 28 July 1781; and "good order" in Regimental Orders, Fishkill, 15 March 1781.

71. Garrison Orders, West Point, 6 May 1781, Moore [sic] Orderly Book, NYSL; Doctor's Report on Charles McCormick, West Point, 1 September 1782, GLC02437.01557.

72. Kwasny, *Washington's Partisan War*, 230; JHJ, 11 February 1779, HSP.

73. Regimental Orders, 5 July, and Proceedings, 7 July 1780, in MHOB, vol. 2, HSP.

74. Headquarters, 8 [9] July 1780, Ibid. McLachlan was recorded as sergeant and sergeant major in the account, but payrolls and rosters show him as sergeant.

75. Headquarters, "Proceedings," 8 [9] July 1780, Ibid.

76. Ibid.

77. Court-martial proceedings "on board the sloop *Liberty*," 8 June 1781, Moore [sic], Orderly Book, NYSL.

78. Court-martial proceedings "aboard the *Tryon*," 7 July 1781, Moore [sic], Orderly Book, NYSL.

79. GW to Stirling, Morristown, 13 January 1780, explanatory note, *PGW:RWS*, 24:110; Mooers, "[Auto-]Biography"; Battin file, RWPBF, W.4413, reel 177.

80. Correspondence in *PGW:RWS*: MH to GW, Cranes Mills near Connecticut Farms, 19 January 1780, 24:110–11; GW to MH, Morristown, 21 January 1780, 24:182–84; MH to GW, Cranes Mills, 23 January 1780, 24:200–202; MH to GW, Morristown, 24 January 1780, 24:226–27; MH to GW, Cranes Mills, 25 January 1780, 24:241–42; GW to MH, Morristown, 25 January 1780, 24:243–44; MH to GW, Cranes Mills, 26 January 1780 (proposing the 27th), 24:245–46; MH to GW, Elizabethtown, 26 January 1780 at 3:00 A.M., 24:256–57; then 6 A.M. announcing enemy attack, 24:257–59; MH to GW, Cranes Mills, 26[–27] January 1780, 24:260–63. For orders to the parade detachment on 25 January, see Headquarters, 24 January 1780, in MHOB, vol. 1, HSP.

81. Correspondence in *PGW:RWS*: GW to MH, Morristown, 27 January 1780, 24:284–85; St. Clair to GW, Cranes Mills, 28 January 1780, 24:307–9; MH to GW, Cranes Mills, 29 January 1780, 24:314–15; St. Clair to GW, Cranes Mills, 2 February 1780, 11:00 A.M., 24:360–61; St. Clair to GW, Springfield, 4 February 1780, 24:376–77.

82. St. Clair to GW, Springfield, 31 January 1780, *PGW:RWS*, 24:338; General Orders, Morristown, 22 March [1780], *PGW:RWS*, 25:112–14.

83. MH to GW, Morristown, 8 February 1780, *PGW:RWS*, 24:410–11; MH's charges against Tichenor, Morristown, 8 February 1780, *Provincial and State Papers*, 17:356; MH to Bedel, Camp Near Morristown, 7 March, 1780, *Provincial and State Papers*, 17:358; MH to Bedel, Camp West Point, 16 October 1780, *Provincial and State Papers*, 17:381; General Orders, Totowa, 16 October 1780, *WGW*, 20:199–201.

84. MH Memorial to GW, Camp near Morristown, 12 February 1780, *PGW:RWS*, 24:453–56.

85. Correspondence in *Provincial and State Papers*: MH to Bedel, Camp near Morristown, 7 March 1780, 17:358; MH to Bedel, Waltham, 6 June 178017:363; MH to Bedel, Camp near Morristown, 15 June 1780, 17:365–67; MH to Bedel, Camp West Point, 12 October 1780, 17:379.

86. James R. Reid, &c. to Joseph Reed, Camp near Morristown, 14 December 1779, and Hazen to Reed, Camp near Morristown, 11 February 1780, *Pennsylvania Archives*, series 1, 8:44–45, 105. Andrew Lee added his own promotion issues. See Lee to GW,

14 June 1780, Founders Online, EA; and GW to Edward Hand, Springfield, 17 June 1780, *WGW*, 19:20.

87. Reed (In Council) to GW, Philadelphia, 16 February 1780, *PGW:RWS*, 24:490–91; GW to Reed, Morristown, 23 February 1780, *PGW:RWS*, 24:557.

88. MH to Steuben, Camp Near Morris Town, 11 February 1780, Steuben Papers, DLAR, reel 2, item 198.

89. MH Memorial to GW, Memorial, Peekskill, 20 November 1779, *PGW:RWS*, 23:368–70.

90. Carlile [et al.] to GW, Camp, and GW to Carlile, Headquarters, 16 September 1780, Founders, Online, EA.

91. Regiment Orders, Preakness, 15 July 1780, in MHOB, vol. 2, HSP. Hazen folded smaller companies into larger ones for deployment, discipline, and provisioning, but said it was not a dissolution of companies (which would reduce captains), for they would be continued on separate muster and pay rolls. Hazen rescinded the incorporation at Fishkill, 3 January 1781, after moving the Canadians in Gilbert's company on 24 December 1780 to those of Olivie, Liébert, and Gosselin so that Gilbert could take command of Taylor's company. See [Lloyd], Orderly Book, 2nd Canadian, SOC.

92. [Reid et al.] to GW, Camp, 20 September 1780, Founders Online, EA.

93. Patrick Lacroix puts more emphasis on ethnicity issues in looking at power relationships in Lacroix, "Promises to Keep," 69.

94. GW to MH, Preakness, 6 November 1780, *WGW*, 20:306–7; MH to GW, West Point, 12 November 1780, Founders Online, EA.

95. Charges, West Point, 9 November 1780, Proceedings of Hazen Court Martial, Peter Force Papers and Collection, series 7E, reel 14, box 20, p. 2, LOC; Reid to GW, Fishkill, 7 December 1780, Founders Online, EA.

96. Prosecution, 9–17 November 1780, Proceedings of Hazen Court Martial, pp. 3–37. On the controversy over mustering Munson's son, see footnote 47.

97. Defense, 28–29 November 1780, Proceedings of Hazen Court Martial, pp. 38–80.

98. Reid to GW, Fishkill, 7 December 1780, Founders Online, EA. Although 126 is higher than the master roll indicates, the latter is incomplete.

99. After Orders, Ramapough, 27 June 1780, and Brigade Orders, Preakness, 6 July 1780, in MHOB, vol. 2, HSP.

100. MH to GW, Preakness, 21 July 1780, and MH to GW, Camp, 17 July 1780, Founders Online, EA.

101. GW to MH, Bergen County, 20 July 1780, and MH to GW, Preakness, 21 July 1780, Founders Online, EA.

102. General Orders, Steenrapia, 17 September 1780, *WGW*, 20:65–66.

103. MH to Bayley, Camp State of New Jersey, 13 September 1780, *Provincial and State Papers*, 17:376; MH to Bedel, Camp State of New Jersey, 13 October 1780, *Provincial and State Papers*, 17:379; MH to Bedel, Camp West Point, 15 October 1780, *Provincial and State Papers*, 17:380; Steuben, Apology in Court-martial of Moses Hazen, [13 September 1780], Steuben Papers, DLAR, reel 2, item 487.

104. Regimental Orders, 16 and 22 July 1780, in MHOB, vol. 2, HSP. Morris Casey was not on the master roll, but Morris Kessey is noted as enlisted on 7 May 1777 and discharged on 1 August 1780, in CSR, roll 85.

Chapter 8

1. Headquarters, Orangetown, 26 September, and Regimental Orders, Tappan, 29 September 1780, [Mooers], Orderly Book, Papers of Benjamin Mooers, 1780, LOC. Avery was likely Ebenezer Averill.

2. General, After, and Evening Orders, Orangetown, 1 October 1780, *WGW*, 20:109–11; letter from Major Benjamin Russell in Thacher, *Observations Relative to the Execution of Major André*, 12–13; Mooers, "[Auto-]Biography"; William Baird letter, 20 September 1890, in William Torrey, RWPBF, W.16446, reel 2401. Samuel Bowman is generally noted as the lieutenant with André.

3. Regimental Orders, Tappan, 4 October 1780, [Mooers], Orderly Book, Papers of Benjamin Mooers, LOC. See also Headquarters, West Point, 13 and 20 October 1780, Evening Orders, 24 October 1780, and Headquarters, West Point, 29 October, 27 and 29 November 1780, [Lloyd], Orderly Book, 2nd Canadian, SOC.

4. [Garrison orders] and extract from General Orders, Fishkill, 1 January 1781, [Lloyd], Orderly Book, 2nd Canadian, SOC.

5. Cornell to Nathanael Greene, Philadelphia, 19 September 1780, *LDC*, 16:85.

6. Wolcott to Andrew Adams, Philadelphia, 27 December 1780, *LDC*, 16:508.

7. Wolcott to Adams, Philadelphia, 27 December 1780, *LDC*, 16:509.

8. Virginia Delegates to Jefferson, Philadelphia, 1 January 1781, *LDC*, 16:528–29.

9. John Sullivan to Meshech Weare, Philadelphia, 21 January, *LDC*, 16:617; Virginia Delegates to Jefferson, Philadelphia, 23 January 1781, *LDC*, 16:622.

10. See Carp, "Origins of the Nationalist Movement of 1780–1783," 363–92.

11. GW to President of Congress [Samuel Huntington], New Windsor, 1 March 1781, *WGW*, 21:326–27; Scammell to GW, Williamsburg, 25 September 1781, Founders Online, EA.

12. James M. Varnum to William Greene, Philadelphia, 8 January 1781, *LDC*, 16:575.

13. John Sullivan for Congressional Committee, Barclays House near Trenton, 10 January 1781, *LDC*, 16:588.

14. Heath to GW, West Point, 11, 13, 24 January and 4 February (with 1 and 3 February enclosures from Scammell) 1781, Founders Online, EA; GW to President of Congress, New Windsor, 23 January 1781, *WGW*, 21:135–36; General Orders, New Windsor, 30 January 1781, *WGW*, 21:158–60.

15. John Mathews to William Livingston, Philadelphia, 29 January 1781, *LDC*, 16:637–38; 3 and 7 February 1781, *JCC*, 19:110–13, 124–25.

16. Huntington to the States, Philadelphia, 2 March 1781, *LDC*, 17:5.

17. Thomas Rodney's Diary, 5 March 1781, *LDC*, 17:17–19; Varnum to William Greene, Philadelphia, 2 April 1781, *LDC*, 17:115–17.

18. Noted and quoted in Kranish, *Flight from Monticello*, 314; E. Evans, *Thomas Nelson of Yorktown*, 122–23.

19. Jefferson, *Notes on the State of Virginia*, query XIII, section 5, 122–25.

20. Meacham, *Thomas Jefferson*, 131.

21. "Extract of a letter from a gentleman in Virginia," 22 January 1781, *Pennsylvania Gazette* [Philadelphia], 31 January 1781. Mark Edward Lender and James Kirby Martin argue that Arnold attempted to protect private property. See Lender and Martin, "A Traitor's Epiphany," 314–57.

22. Sullivan to Meshech Weare, Philadelphia, 21 January 1781, *LDC*, 6:616–17.

23. McDonnell, *Politics of War*, esp. 5–7, 376–79, 384–88, 398–410.

24. Kranish, *Flight from Monticello*, 196.

25. R. K. Wright, *Continental Army*, 167; GW to Heath, New Windsor, 17 February 1781, *WGW*, 21:234–35; GW to Lafayette, 22 February 1781, *WGW*, 21:274; Regimental Orders, Fishkill, 18 February 1781, Moore [*sic*], Orderly Book, NYSL.

26. Lafayette to GW, Elk, 12 April 1781, and Susquehanna Ferry, 14 April 1781, Founders Online, EA; GW to William Heath, New Windsor, 21 March, *WGW*, 21:343; GW to Steuben, New Windsor, 30 April 1781, *WGW*, 22:8–9; William Galvan to GW, Philadelphia, 4 August 1781, Founders Online, EA; Barber to Colonel [Elias] Dayton, Trenton, 28 February 1781, Gerlach, *New Jersey in the American Revolution*, 351. Apparently rebuffed in love (as in promotion), Galvan committed suicide in July 1782. See Rolph, "The Service and Tragic Death of French Officer Major William Galvan."

27. Lafayette to GW, New Kent Mountain, 11 August 1781, Founders Online, EA.

28. Jefferson to Lafayette, Richmond, 10 March 1781, Jefferson, *The Papers of Thomas Jefferson*, 5:113–14; Lafayette to Jefferson, Williamsburg, 16 and 17 March 1781, *Papers of Thomas Jefferson*, 5: 159–60, 166–67; Jefferson to Lafayette, Richmond, 19 March 1781, *Papers of Thomas Jefferson*, 5:179–82.

29. Jefferson to Greene, Richmond, 1 April 1781, *Papers of Thomas Jefferson*, 5:313–14; Greene to Jefferson, [28 April 1781], *Papers of Thomas Jefferson*, 5:567–69.

30. Jefferson to Penn, Richmond, 4 May 1781, *Papers of Thomas Jefferson*, 5:598–99.

31. Jefferson to Speaker of the House of Delegates, Charlottesville, 28 May 1781, *Papers of Thomas Jefferson*, 6:28–29; Jefferson, *Autobiography*, 79.

32. On the martial law bill, see 2, 8, 9, 12 (includes Nelson appointment), 13, 15, 18, 23 June 1781, *Journal of the House of Delegates of the Commonwealth of Virginia*, 9–10, 11, 12, 14–16, 18–19, 21, 32.

33. Nelson to Lafayette, Richmond, 3 August 1781, McIlwaine, *Official Letters of the Governors of the State of Virginia*, 3:20; David Jameson to Nelson, Council Chamber, 18 September 1781, *Official Letters of the Governors*, 3:57. See also McDonnell, *Politics of War*, 460–69, for a summation of mobilization problems in 1781 and the election of almost-"dictator" Nelson.

34. General Orders, New Windsor, 18 February 1781, [Lloyd] Orderly Book, 2nd Canadian, SOC.

35. Ibid.; Heath to GW, West Point, 20 February 1781, Founders Online, EA.

36. Heath to GW, West Point, 5 April 1781, Founders Online, EA; Declaration by Clément Gosselin, Joseph Torrey, et al., Fishkill, 3 March 1781, Founders Online, EA.

37. [Garrison orders], Fishkill, 1 January 1781, and Regimental orders, 5 and 10 January 1781, [Lloyd], Orderly Book, 2nd Canadian, SOC.

38. Regimental orders, 10 January 1781, [Lloyd], Orderly Book, 2nd Canadian, SOC.

39. Pickering to GW, Newburgh, 14 January 1781, with 20 December 1780, 13 January 1781 Garrison orders, Founders Online, EA; Heath to GW, West Point, 16 January 1781, with 4 January 1781 enclosure, Founders Online, EA; GW to Heath, New Windsor, 20 January and 5 February 1781, *WGW*, 21:118–19, 187–89.

40. Parsons to GW, Camp in Highlands, 10 January 1781, C. Hall, *Life and Letters of Samuel Holden Parsons*, 326–27.

41. C. Hall, *Life and Letters of Samuel Holden Parsons*, 327–35, including letters from Parsons, 25 and 31 January 1781, account from Major Alden, and excerpts from Washington letters; Scammell to Heath, Pompton, 1 February 1781, and

Verplanck's Point, 3 February 1781, enclosed in Heath to GW, 4 February 1781, Founders Online, EA.

42. Regimental Orders, Fishkill, 28 January 1781, and General Orders, New Windsor, 30 January 1781, Moore [sic], Orderly Book, NYSL; 13 February 1781, *Pennsylvania Packet* [Philadelphia], AHN.

43. Closen, *Revolutionary Journal*, 15, 61; 5, 11, 15 March 1781, Moore [sic], Orderly Book, NYSL; William Stuart to GW, Camp, 2 October 1781, Founders Online, EA.

44. JHJ, 15–21, 25, 29 March 1781, HSP. The script on the 2 April and 31 May petitions mirrors the script in Hawkins's journal and orderly books.

45. MH to Congress, Philadelphia, 2 April 1781, PCC, roll 54, item 42, vol. 3, p. 405; 26 April 1781, *JCC*, 20:448.

46. 20 April 1781, *JCC*, 19:427–28; MH to Congress, Philadelphia, 31 May 1781, PCC, roll 54, item 42, vol. 3, p. 409; 7 July 1781, *JCC*, 20:728–29; Francis Hopkinson to Board of Treasury, Philadelphia, 18 July 1781, PCC, roll 96, item 78, vol. 12, p. 45.

47. 20 April 1781, *JCC*, 19:428–29; MH to Sullivan, Philadelphia, 30 April 1781, JSS; 29 June 1781, *JCC*, 20:711–12; MH to Huntington, Philadelphia, 3 July 1781, PCC, roll 96, item 78, vol. 12, p. 155; Thomas McKean to MH, 12 July 1781, PCC, roll 24, item 16, p. 42.

48. Corbett, *No Turning Point*, 312; 18 and 25 May, 1 and 20 June 1781, *Diaries of George Washington*, 3:367, 371, 376, 381.

49. Clinton to GW, Albany, 15–18 June 1781, Founders Online, EA; General Orders, [West Point], 2 May 1781, about McPherson, *WGW*, 22:26–27; Clinton to Antill, Albany, 27 June 1781, James Clinton letters, MS 2958.1983, NYHS; 14–17 June 1781, Albany, Moore [sic], Orderly Book, NYSL; 27 June–3 July 1781, "Cognawaga," in Moore [sic], Orderly Book, NYSL; 10 July 1781, West Point, Moore [sic], Orderly Book, NYSL.

50. Corbett, *No Turning Point*, 313–15.

51. 22 and 28 May 1781, *Diaries of George Washington*, 3:369–70, 373.

52. 18 and 25 June 1781, *Diaries of George Washington*, 3:381, 382–85.

53. 28 June, 2, 4, 6 July 1781, *Diaries of George Washington*, 3:385–86, 388–90; Johnston, *Yorktown Campaign*, 70–83.

54. 10 July 1781, *Diaries of George Washington*, 3:392.

55. 20 July and 1 August 1781, *Diaries of George Washington*, 3:397, 404–5.

56. JHJ, 28 July–4 August 1781, HSP.

57. 3 August 1781, Moore [sic], Orderly Book, NYSL.

58. 4 August 1781, Moore [sic], Orderly Book, NYSL.

59. JHJ, 6 August 1781, HSP.

60. 8 July 1781, Dobbs Ferry, observation by Jean François Louis, comte de Clermont-Crèvecoeur, *Diaries of George Washington*, 3:390n1.

61. 8 and 10 August 1781, *Diaries of George Washington*, 3:407, 408.

62. After Garrison Orders, 11 August 1781, Moore [sic], Orderly Book, NYSL; JHJ, 10–12 August 1781, HSP.

63. JHJ, 13 August 1781, HSP.

64. JHJ, 14–15 August 1781, HSP.

65. 14, 15, 16 August 1781, *Diaries of George Washington*, 3:409–11.

66. JHJ, 17–19 August 1781, HSP. Most accounts say that Washington's army commenced crossing on the 20th, but if one counts the advance party, then it started on the night of the 18th.

67. JHJ, 20 and 21 August 1781, HSP.
68. 19–29 August 1781, *Diaries of George Washington*, 3:411–14; Johnston, *Yorktown Campaign*, 87–90.
69. JHJ, 27 and 28 August 1781, and insertion beside them, HSP.
70. [29 rather than 30] August 1781, *Diaries of George Washington*, 3:414–16; Johnston, *Yorktown Campaign*, 90–91.
71. JHJ, 29 August 1781, HSP.
72. JHJ, 30 August 1781, HSP.
73. JHJ, 31 August 1781, HSP.
74. 31 August 1781, *Diaries of George Washington*, 3:416; Johnston, *Yorktown Campaign*, 91–93.
75. JHJ, 1 September 1781, HSP.
76. JHJ, 2 and 3 September 1781, HSP (parts of the 1–3 September entries were inserted out of order when the journal was bound).
77. Johnston, *Yorktown Campaign*, 94–95, 101.
78. GW to MH, Philadelphia, 2 September, *WGW*, 23:78; MH to GW, Head of Elk, 10 September 1781, Founders Online, EA.
79. Lincoln to GW, Head of Elk, 11 September 1781, Founders Online, EA; Duncan, "Diary," 745.
80. J. Greene, *Allies at Yorktown*, 9–11; Grainger, *Battle of Yorktown*, 96.
81. Approximations based on Jerome Greene's figures in *Allies at Yorktown*, 78–79.
82. Williamsburg, 11 September 1781, M. J. Lafayette, *Lafayette in Virginia*, 59; Tyree's Plantation, 1 July 1781, *Lafayette in Virginia*, 19–20; Camp on Pamunkey, 7 August 1781, *Lafayette in Virginia*, 44; Camp, 26 August 1781, *Lafayette in Virginia*, 54.
83. Selig, *March to Victory*, 43; J. Greene, *Allies at Yorktown*, 109–10.
84. Thomas McKean to Nathanael Greene, Philadelphia, 21 September, *LDC*, 18:66; James M. Varnum to Greene, Philadelphia, 17 September 1781, *LDC*, 18:52–53.
85. 4–23 September 1781, Feltman, *Journal of Lt. William Feltman*, 12–14.
86. General Orders, Williamsburg, 24 September 1781, *WGW*, 23:134–35; Lafayette to GW, Williamsburg, 8 September 1781, Founders Online, EA.
87. Duncan, "Diary," 746; 30 [September], S. Tucker, "Journal of the Siege of Yorktown." Both sources appear to recount the same event, but Duncan's dating is vague, and only Tucker names Reid.
88. 2–7 October 1781, Duncan, "Diary," 748–49. Tucker notes only three men taken by the shot on the 3rd. See 2–4 October, S. Tucker, "Journal of the Siege of Yorktown."
89. Morning Orders, 29 September, and Headquarters before York, 2, 4, 5, 13 October 1781, *Orderly Book of the Siege of Yorktown*.
90. Regulations, Camp before York, 6 October 1781, *Orderly Book of the Siege of Yorktown*.
91. 7 October 1781, Duncan, "Diary," 749; J. Greene, *Allies at Yorktown*, 140.
92. J. Greene, *Allies at Yorktown*, 264–74; George Lamb, RWPBF, S.35514, reel 1514; 13–14 October 1781, Duncan, "Diary," 751.
93. Duncan, "Diary" (752) notes the casualties in "Captain Fry's camp," which should have been transcribed as Pry. Duncan would have taken more notice of a fellow regimental captain, and it appears that neither of the captains Frye with the 1st New Hampshire were with detached companies at Yorktown. William Liggins was at Yorktown and noted Davis's death, and that he later married Davis's widow. See RWPBF, S.41769, reel 1562; Mooers, "Recollections of Benjamin Mooers," BMC.

94. 14 October 1781, Duncan, "Diary," 751–52; Smallwood to GW, Annapolis, 9 August, and GW to Smallwood, King's Ferry, 24 August 1781, Founders Online, EA.

95. 14–15 October 1781, Duncan, "Diary," 752; J. Greene, *Allies at Yorktown*, 277–83.

96. Hamilton to Lafayette, Camp before Yorktown, 15 October 1781, Hamilton, *Papers of Alexander Hamilton*, 2:679–81; Lafayette to GW, Camp before York, 16 October 1781, PCC, roll 171, item 152, vol. 10, pp. 277–78; 15 October 1781, Duncan, "Diary," 752.

97. In RWPBF: William Calder, S.44725, reel 448; Isaac Chace, S.37849, reel 526; James Heaton, W.7,716, reel 1245; Jonathan Pratt, R.304209–55, reel 1967; Adam Sybert, Invalid Pension Applicant List, 1794, reel 2333; Merifield Victor (Vicory), W.6365, reel 2459; Colin McLachlan, W.25687, reel 1692; Zachariah Sherwood, S.36313, reel 2174; Edward Clark, invalid pension, New Hampshire, Clark, *Pension Lists of 1792–1795*, 83.

98. "Return of the Killed and Wounded of the American Army from the 28th of September ... to the Storm of the Enemy's Redoubts on the Night of the 14th of October," PCC, roll 72, item 59, vol. 2, p. 203. The siege tally included sixteen Continentals killed and forty wounded, and four militia members killed and sixteen wounded; of that total, eight Continentals were killed and twenty-eight wounded at the storming of the redoubt.

99. J. Greene, *Allies at Yorktown*, 287–322.

100. General and After Orders, Headquarters before York, 20 October 1781, *WGW*, 23:244–47; General Orders, Headquarters near York, 27, 28, 31 October and 3 November 1781, *WGW*, 23:275–76, 283, 304–6, 320–23.

101. McHenry to Lee, 27 October 1781, McHenry, *A Sidelight on History*, 76; Gottschalk, *Lafayette and the Close of the American Revolution*, 336, 342, 345.

102. GW to Lincoln, [29 October 1781], *WGW*, 23:293–94; Lincoln to GW and Division Orders, Head of Elk, 22 November 1781, Founders Online, EA; Pry to Secretary at War Lincoln, [Philadelphia], 26 December 1781, PCC, roll 162, item 149, pp. 67–71.

103. Heath to GW, Highlands, 18 December 1781, Founders Online, EA; GW to Hazen, Philadelphia, 6 December 1781, *WGW*, 23:374.

104. GW to Reid, Philadelphia, 27 December 1781, *WGW*, 23:409; John Hughes, CSR, roll 84; Dubé as Duba, RWPBF, S.45349, reel 857.

Chapter 9

1. See Charles Thomson's Notes of Debates, 30 and 31 July 1782, *LDC*, 18:687–89, 693–97.

2. GW, Farewell to the Army, Rock Hill near Princeton, 2 November 1783, *WGW*, 27:226.

3. GW to MH, Philadelphia, 18 March 1782, *WGW*, 24:74. Constabulary actions included dealing with civil resistance and fugitives. See Watson, "Continuity in Civil-Military Relations," 222–23, 226.

4. MH to GW, Lancaster, 26 March and 22 April 1782, Founders Online, EA; GW to MH, Newburgh, 10 April 1782, *WGW*, 24:107–10.

5. MH to GW, 26 March 1782; Miller, *Dangerous Guests*, 156–63.

6. Proclamation mentioned in GW to William Heath, Philadelphia, 29 January 1782, *WGW*, 23:469; Jacob Horn (with Blakeslee 1819 affidavit), RWPBF, S.44940, reel 1327; Frederick (and Mary) Horn, RWPBF, W.4994, reel 1327; the three Horns in

COR Roll. The Convention of Saratoga allowed the return of the surrendered troops, but problems led to Congress revoking returns and marching the enemy troops into long-term confinement.

7. MH to Knox, Lancaster, 20 May 1782, GLC02437.01423; MH to Knox, Pompton, 22 November 1782, GLC02437.01723; Board of War, Report, 21 November, in Congress, 23 November 1781, *JCC*, 21:1132–33. On German loyalty and labor as prisoners, see Krebs, *A Generous and Merciful Enemy*, esp. 225–32, 249–55. On the choice of indenture or enlistment, see Jones, *Captives of Liberty*, 235.

8. Data derived from COR Roll; additional names found in CSR. About eight to ten men with French names joined between 15 October and mid-December 1781, which added to the regiment's diversity.

9. GW to Lincoln, Headquarters, 3 October 1782, *WGW*, 25:234–35; Lincoln to GW, War Office, 9 October 1782 (title and office changed to Secretary of War in 1789); British officer complaints about subsequent restrictions in John Hathorn to GW, and John de Beckh to GW, Dobbs Ferry, 29 October 1782, Founders Online, EA. Hawkins named forty-nine men "taken up by the Parties sent into the Country by Brigr. Genl. M. Hazen in the Years 1782 and 1783." See List of Canadian Old Regiment Deserters, Pompton, 1 May 1783, Hazen accounts and petitions, JSS.

10. Miller, *Dangerous Guests*, 161–63; 30 March 1782, *JCC*, 22:154–55; Captain Noah Lee or Lieutenant Andrew Lee (differing family/popular accounts) in "Extract of a letter from a gentleman in Lancaster to his friend in this city [23 September]," 26 September 1782, *Pennsylvania Packet* [Philadelphia], AHN.

11. Boudinot, *Journal or Historical Recollections*, 60–61; GW to MH, Headquarters, 3 May 1782, *WGW*, 24:217–18; 29 April 1782, *JCC*, 22:217–18. Recent analyses of the Huddy-Asgill crises include Jones, *Captives of Liberty*, 231–34, and, with emphasis on ethics and partisan and civil war, Hoock, *Scars of Independence*, 336–37, 340–57.

12. Duane to GW, 12 October 1782, *LDC*, 19:248–50; Hamilton to Knox, [Albany, 7 June], and Knox to Hamilton, New Windsor, 24 July 1782, Founders Online, EA. Legitimate retaliation, as they defined it, appears distinct from current definitions of retaliation versus retribution.

13. GW to MH, Headquarters, 18 May 1782, *WGW*, 24:263–64; MH to GW, Lancaster, 27 May 1782, Founders Online, EA; GW to MH, Headquarters, 4 June 1782, *WGW*, 24:305–6.

14. James Madison to Edmund Randolph, Philadelphia, 29 October 1782, *LDC*, 19:322; Boudinot, *Journal or Historical Recollections*, 61–65; 7 and 8 November 1782, *JCC*, 23:715–20.

15. GW to James Tilghman, Mount Vernon, 5 June 1786, Founders Online; Asgill Letter, London, 20 December 1786, in Ammundsen and Abel, "Saving Captain Asgill," 135–41; Mooers to the Editor of the *Plattsburg[h] Whig* [Plattsburgh, N.Y.], 17 January 1835, in *Essex Gazette* [Haverhill, Mass.], 31 January 1835. Mooers was rebutting a November 1834 account in the *United Service Journal* (London).

16. MH to GW, Lancaster, 27 May 1782, Founders Online, EA.

17. Reid to GW, Lancaster, 30 May 1782, and "At Major Barbers quarters," 2 December 1782, Founders Online, EA.

18. General Orders, Newburgh, 21 February 1783, *WGW*, 26:149–52.

19. Reid to GW, "at the Maryland Hutts," 22 February 1783, Founders Online, EA.

20. Reid to GW, "at Major Lansdales," 18 May 1782, Founders Online, EA; MH to GW, Pompton, 31 March 1783, Founders Online, EA; Jedediah Huntington to GW, West Point, 1783, Founders Online, EA. (The aggrieved officers also wanted Judge-Advocate Thomas Edwards court-martialed for lack of abilities and neglect of duty in the 1780 court-martial of Reid. See MH to GW, Pompton, 29 January 1783.)

21. MH to GW, Pompton, 29 May and 6 June 1783 (with enclosures, including Reid's note), Founders Online, EA; GW to MH, Newburgh, 1 June 1783, WGW, 26:460–61.

22. GW to MH, Headquarters, 9 June 1783, WGW, 26:489–90; Proceedings in case of Moses Hazen vs. James Reid, Board of General Officers, [Newburgh], 24 June 1783, Steuben Papers, DLAR, reel 6, item 178; GW to MH, Headquarters, 24 June 1783, WGW, 27:30–31.

23. Antill to GW, Pompton, 29 May 1783, Founders Online, EA.

24. See endnotes 16 and 21. See also Antill to Lincoln, 4 March 1782, PCC, roll 48, item 41, vol. 1, p. 81; Antill to [Congress], Pompton, 25 April 1783, PCC, roll 163, item 149, vol. 3, p. 387; MH to GW, West Point, 17 May 1783, with enclosure from Stuart, and Pompton, 24 November 1782, with enclosure from Duncan, Founders Online, EA; GW to MH, Newburgh, 9 December 1782, WGW, 25:409; and MH to GW, Pompton, 26–29 December 1782, Founders Online, EA. For the September 1780 petition, see chapter 7, endnote 92.

25. Paine, "The Crisis, XIII," in Writings of Thomas Paine, 370–76.

26. GW, Farewell to the Army, Rock Hill near Princeton, 2 November 1783, WGW, 27:222–27.

27. Webster, "Sketches," 183–85.

28. GW to Lincoln, Headquarters, 2 October 1782, WGW, 25:226–27; MH to Lincoln, 8 June 1782, PCC, roll 54, item 42, vol. 3, p. 528; MH to Hand, New Windsor, 3 July 1783, and Hand to GW, Orderly Office, 4 July 1783, PCC, roll 171, item 152, vol. 11, pp. 403, 405; GW to Hand, Newburgh, Headquarters, 3 and 4 July 1783, and GW to President of Congress, Newburgh, 5[–8] July 1783, WGW, 27:42–46; Elias Boudinot to GW, Princeton, 17 July 1783, explaining why there was a hold on promotions, Founders Online, EA.

29. GW to Lincoln, Headquarters, 2 October 1782, WGW, 25:227–29.

30. Newburgh Address, GW to John Augustine Washington, Newburgh, 15 June 1783, GW letter to the Marquis de Lafayette of the same day, WGW, 27:11–14.

31. RWPBF pamphlet, 1; Documentary History of the First Federal Congress, 129.

32. Pierce's Register, 3.

33. Pierce's Register, 4

34. White to John Pierce, Boston, 27 July 1787; Joseph Howell to White, New York, 8 August 1787; White to Howell, Boston, [1] October 1787; Pierce to White, 1 October 1787, denying White interest on the certificate he returned; Howell to Oliver Wolcott Jr., 29 April 1794, all in Papers of the War Department. On the resolution about invalid pensions, see 7 June 1785, JCC, 28:435–37.

35. William Torrey, RWPBF, W.16446, reel 2401; Mooers, RWPBF, S.23815, reel 1751; Noah Lee, RWPBF, S.18939, reel 1542.

36. General Orders, 2 June 1783, WGW, 26:463–65; MH to GW, Pompton, 7 and 12 June 1783, and Lincoln to GW, Headquarters, 7 June 1783, Founders Online, EA; General Orders, 6 June 1783, WGW, 26:471–72.

37. There were discrepancies between Mooers's 2 July and Hazen's 3 July counts. See "Return of Brigadier General Hazens Regt.," 2 July 1783, BMC, series 2B, box 7, file 101. See also "Return of the Canadian Old Regiment of Foot Commanded by Brig. Genl. Hazen," 3 July 1783, PCC, roll 171, item 152, vol. 11, p. 404; COR Roll with additional data from CSR, RWPBF, and RWR files; Hand to GW, Orderly Office, 4 July 1783, PCC, roll 171, item 152, vol. 11, p. 405; GW to MH, Headquarters, 24 and 30 June 1783, WGW, 27:30–31, 38–39; and Satterlee, Report of Detachment, 29 June 1783, RWR, roll 132, item 41. Congress approved brevet promotions for officers under the rank of major general and who had held their rank since 1777 on 30 September 1783 (JCC, 25:632).

38. "List of the Non-commissioned Officers and Privates of the Canadian Old Regiment—Taken this 6th Day of September 1782," in JHJ, HSP; "Regimental List or Roll made out in 1783 by Benjamin Mooers Lieut. and Adjutant . . . Names of Persons in the Congress own Regiment Commanded by Colonel Moses Hazen Brigadier General by Brevet, in the service of the United States 1782," RWR, roll 132.

39. Headnote and Petition of Richard Lloyd, New York, 15 August 1785/2 August 1790, and Report of the Secretary of War, 22 February 1791, Bowling et al., Documentary History of the First Federal Congress, 174–76. Distribution examples include that of soldier Andrew Boetger authorizing Lloyd to deliver his certificates to Christian Frederick, and Frederick acknowledging receipt of the certificates at Albany on 21 September 1784, in "Certifies accounts of Major Lloyd," 25 September 1795, William Simmons, War Accountant's Office, and of Thomas Hazeltine, Newbury, Coos, 25 August 1785, authorizing the release of his certificates to his old commander, in "Receipts for certificates," Hazen to Pierce, 18 April 1786, Papers of the War Department.

40. Bowling et al., Documentary History of the First Federal Congress, 165.

41. R. E. Wright, One Nation Under Debt, 49–50, 52–53, 58. In present terms, depreciation amounted to inflation, for the circulation of more money or bills of credit connected to rising prices. See Colonial Fiscal Documents, Massachusetts: Treasury Certificates—January 1, 1780," Colonial Currency Collection, University of Notre Dame; State Revolutionary War Debt Certificates, 1775–1789, Massachusetts Historical Society.

42. White [Boston] to Benjamin Mooers, Haverhill, 27 February 1783, BMC, series 1, box 1, file 1. White and Mooers at least had a treasurer with whom to argue. Those of Hazen's regiment, "not of the quota of any state," had to establish recompense with the Treasury Board so as to have their depreciation "made up by the United-states." See Report of the committee re. depreciation of pay for Hazen's Regiment, 7 July 1781, PCC, roll 27, item 19, vol. 3, p. 97.

43. White to Mooers, 4 December 1783, and White, Boston, to Mooers, Haverhill, 26 December 1783, BMC, series 1, box 1 file 1. For a summary about Robert Morris and his notes, see R. E. Wright, One Nation Under Debt, 61–67.

44. 31 July 1781, JCC, 21:817; 23 April 1783, JCC, 24:268–69; 9 August 1783, JCC, 24:496–98.

45. Everest, Moses Hazen and the Canadian Refugees, 115–17; 31 July 1781, JCC, 21:816–17.

46. MH wrote to McPherson that Congress ordered the provisioning in 1782, but it is likely he was referring to the August 1783 resolution. See MH to Murdock

McPherson, Albany, 21 August 1784, BMC, series 1, box 1, file 2; and "Genl. Hazens List of Canadians" and "Memorandum of Persons drew Provisions from Commissary at Albany," BMC, series 2B, box 7, file 103.

47. "Genl. Hazens List of Canadians," [August 1784], and "List of Names returned to the Land Office by Hazen & Levingston [sic]," [c. 1782], BMC, series 2B, box 7, file 103.

48. MH to McPherson, Albany, 24 September 1785, BMC, series 1, box 1, file 3. On how they were still trying to settle accounts, and adding names to the earlier 1784 list, see "Memorandum of Persons drew Provisions from Commissary at Albany," [September 1788], BMC, series 2B, box 7, file 103; Everest, *Moses Hazen and the Canadian Refugees*, 128–29.

49. Receipt of four refugees for sums from Hazen via Mooers, 16 June 1785, Point Auroch, and McPherson Certificate, Plattsburgh, 19 April 1792, BMC, series 3, box 13, files 197, 200. Duer had been an interwar land speculator and developer in the Albany region. See Corbett, *No Turning Point*, 23. Another form of a "due bill" may be "The Address and Petition of the Officers of the Army of the United States," December 1782. Among other things, the officers noted that portions of their and the soldiers' rations had often been retained, and that although there had been some compensation, still much was due. See 29 April 1783, *JCC*, 24:291–93.

50. These receipts and others in BMC, series 3, box 13, file 197; MH to McPherson, New York, 20 July 1785, BMC, series 1, box 1, file 3.

51. 30 June 1786, *JCC*, 30:381.

52. O'Callaghan, *Calendar of New York Colonial Manuscripts*, 301, 653; *The Balloting Book*, 5–10. Hazen and Beekman came to terms over the settlement within the 1769 Beekman Patent in 1786. See Everest, *Moses Hazen and the Canadian Refugees*, 127, 142–44.

53. "Memorandum Book Lt. Benjamin Mooers, July 25th, 1783, No. 1," BMC, series 2B, box 7, file 101. Also see Mooers, "[Auto-]Biography."

54. "Memorandum Book Belonging to Benjamin Mooers, No. 2, 1783" and "A Journal from the 11th Oct to [4 Nov 1783]," in Mooers-Travel Acc'ts and Daybooks 1782–1794, BMC, series 3/3A, box 12, file 184. On settling financial affairs, see M[oses] White to Mooers, Boston, 13 November and 26 December 1783, 22 January and 26 February 1784, BMC, series 1, box 1, files 1 and 2.

55. Lloyd to Mooers, Fishkill, 7 January 1784, and White to Mooers, Boston, 26 February 1784, BMC, series 1, box 1, file 2; "Lieutenant William Stuart," in Kilbourne, *Virtutis Praemium*, 2:936–38. See also Mooers, "Recollections," BMC, series 4, box 14, file 226.

56. This can be seen on other frontiers at other times. For the Gulf of Mexico region, see Smith and Hilton, *Nexus of Empire*, 5–6.

57. Smith, "Method of Forming such Settlements upon the Frontiers," in *Bouquet's Expedition Against the Ohio Indians*, 259; Gage to the Earl of Halifax, 14 April 1764, in Gage, *Correspondence of General Thomas Gage*, 1:24–25.

58. GW to President of Congress, Headquarters, 16 July 1783, *WGW*, 27:69–70; 9 August 1783, *JCC*, 24:496–98.

59. MH to Steuben, Camp near Morristown, 11 February 1780, Steuben Papers, DLAR, reel 2, item 198. One of the infirm officers may have been Lieutenant Francis Monty of Livingston's regiment, who had been hit in the thigh by a musket ball in Rhode Island in 1778. See Clark, *Pension Lists of 1792–1795*, 26.

60. "List of Names returned to the Land Office by Hazen + Levingston [*sic*]," BMC. There were 187 listed, but some men were named twice.

61. "Return of the Number of Non-commissioned Officers and Private Men now actually serving the United States, in the Canadian Old Regiment," Lancaster, 31 August 1782, listed fifteen members from New Hampshire, sixteen from Massachusetts, one from Rhode Island, thirty-three from Connecticut, fourteen from New York, seven from New Jersey, ninety-two from Pennsylvania, seven from Delaware, thirty-one from Maryland, and one from Virginia, plus others without states. See RWR, film 4, reel 132.

62. Among the COR veterans living on other frontiers were the following in RWPBF: Benjamin (and Dolly) Heath (W.23273, reel 1243) in Maine; John Barr (S.45244, reel 156), William Liggins (S.41769, reel 1562), Hugh McClellend (S.41834, reel 1668), and Merrifield (and Anny) Vickory (W.6365, reel 2459) in Ohio; Abijah (and Lucinda) Stowe (W.19404, reel 2310), who moved from Clinton County after 1818 and was in Ohio by 1820; and John Carter (S.35817, reel 485), George Lamb (S.35514, reel 1514), and Nicholas Miller (S.36137, reel 1729) in Kentucky. Jonathan (Polly) Pratt (B.L.Rej.304209–55, reel 1967) died in Indiana.

63. See *The Balloting Book* (7) on the New York "Act for granting certain Lands promised to be given as Bounty Lands," passed 11 May 1784; "An act for raising two regiments for the defence of this state, on bounties of unappropriated lands," passed 20 March 1781; and "An Act for raising troops to complete the line of this state in the service of the United States; and the two regiments to be raised on bounties of unappropriated lands, and for the further defence of the frontiers of this state," passed 23 March 1782.

64. In 1796, Congress established the United States Military District in Ohio to reward veterans, and in 1798 it provided Ohio land for Canadian refugees who had assisted in the Revolution. See "Land Grants and Sales" and "Refugee Tract," Ohio History Central online encyclopedia.

65. Vecsey and Starna, *Iroquois Land Claims*, 8–9, 50–56.

66. Ibid., 8, 55–59; "Records Relating to the Revolutionary War—Land Bounties," New York State Archives. See also in RWPBF: Samuel Johnson, S.45420, reel 1428; John (and Sarah) Shepherd, W.11452, reel 2169; David Murray, R.7525, reel 1795; and Patrick (and Zadia) McGee, W.9184, reel 1683. *The Balloting Book* (75–77, 115–41) listed at least a dozen soldiers and three officers (William Popham, Palmer Cady, and surgeon Nicholas Schuyler) and a few others with questionable ties to Hazen's regiment, with warrants or patents for the New Military Tract. Warrants noted eligibility; patents specified which lands.

67. Acts of 20 March 1781, 23 March 1782, and 11 May 1784, in *The Balloting Book*, 7, 10.

68. *The Balloting Book*, 6. The state clarified limits to its generosity in the 28 February 1789 resolution that established the New Military Tract: brevet promotions conferred by Congress on 30 September and 1 November 1783 did not entitle such officers to more land based on those ranks (*The Balloting Book*, 11–12). Another caveat was that a veteran who relinquished his claim to Congress's designated one hundred acres in Ohio was entitled to draw six hundred acres in New York, but failure to relinquish meant the one hundred over the original New York grant would revert back to the state. See G. Pierce, "Military Tract of New York State," 17.

69. On the 1776 act, see *The Balloting Book*, 5. Congress allocated 850 acres to brigadier generals and 1,100 to major generals in its resolution of 12 August 1780 (*JCC*, 17:726–7). For comparison with offers to foreign officers in 1776, see chap. 4, fn53.

70. Alan Taylor described the War of 1812 as "a civil war between kindred peoples, recently and incompletely divided by the revolution." A. Taylor, *Civil War of 1812*, 6. French-Canadian veterans demonstrated the incomplete division as they traversed both sides of the Canadian-American border.

71. A few of the Canadians who went back to Canada and submitted their later pension requests from there were John Gauley, RWPBF, S.46358, reel 1057; Paul Hubert, RWPBF, B.L.13170, reel 1354; and Charles Racine, RWPBF, R.7162, reel 1993.

72. Distance by way of Google Maps. See Allen, *Mapping of New York State*, chap. 8, p. 8.

73. MH to Mooers, New York, 27 March 1786, 10 and 16 April 1786, BMC, series 1, box 1, file 4

74. White to Mooers, Boston, 22 August 1786, BMC, series 1, box 1, file 4.

75. Mooers was Hazen's chief agent until 1790, then William Torrey, and finally Moses White, who served until the general's death in 1803. See Everest, *Moses Hazen and the Canadian Refugees*, 145–47. This calculation is based on a check of the pension rolls, but many of the bounty warrant cards show no assignee.

76. Moses McDavis of Vermont in 1853 wrote on behalf of Ruth Burnham, Amos Ames's daughter, saying that she had received $16.25 in "bounty land Mony" but had no recollection of her father ever having received a pension or actual bounty land. Amos Ames, RWPBF, S.45505, reel 51.

77. Spelling complicates comparisons between "Canadian and Nova-Scotia Refugees," in *The Balloting Book*, 185–88, and "List of Names returned to the Land Office by Hazen & Levingston [*sic*]," BMC. See also Everest, *Moses Hazen and the Canadian Refugees*, 127–31, 136–37.

78. D. K. Martin, "1798 Tax Assessment for northern New York." All were refugees except for Mooers. Massachusetts-born William Torrey was in Canada when the war began, which apparently made him a refugee. Hazen, in Everest, *Moses Hazen and the Canadian Refugees*, 146.

79. Deed transfer notes in Mooers-Deed, Contracts, Agreements, Certificates 1784–1789, BMC, series 3, box 9, file 125. See also Everest, *Moses Hazen and the Canadian Refugees*, 134–35.

80. McPherson to Mooers, promissory note, Plattsburgh, 30 November 1789, BMC, series 3, box 13, file 197.

81. In April 1776, Charles Carroll remarked that "the lands bordering on Lake Champlain will be very valuable in a short time, and that great trade will be carried on over Lake Champlain, between Canada and New York" should America succeed. See *Journal of Charles Carroll*, 88–89. The activities of the francophone merchants in the republic's "new Creole Corridor" from New Orleans through St. Louis to Detroit offer a comparison with what Mooers and others wanted in New York. Mooers, however, was Anglo, so he represented what was already an Anglo-American settlement frontier, albeit with francophone settlers. Furthermore, his endeavors were more land-based than mercantile-based, and so seemed more attuned to earlier colonial speculation than nineteenth-century land commoditization. See Gitlin, *Bourgeois Frontier*, 14–16, 27, 121.

82. "Memorandum of my travels on the west side of Lake Champlain, Sept. 1785," BMC, series 3, box 12, file 184.

83. *Revolutionary War Pension and Bounty-Land-Warrant Application Files* (RWPBF) pamphlet, 2–3.

84. Reflecting on Appleby, *Inheriting the Revolution*, esp. 5–7, 248–50; Tang, "Writing the American Revolution," 64–66; and Resch, *Suffering Soldiers*. Appleby defined personal independence more in terms of modern individualism than the older concept of competency, yet it was not new to her "first generation." Tang and Appleby argue that Americans of the early republic celebrated change, which meant that the Continentals were a conundrum as they connected past and present.

85. Benjamin Davidson (Davison) and Thomas Donaldson, CSR, roll 81; Boston, 25 September 1783, in 2 October 1783 *Massachusetts Spy, or Worcester Gazette* [Worcester, Mass.], XIII, issue 649, and 9 October 1783 *Pennsylvania Evening Post* [Philadelphia], AHN.

86. John (and Sarah) Shepherd, RWPBF, W.11452, reel 2169.

87. MH to GW, [Philadelphia], 24 April 1789, *PGW, Presidential Series*, 2:126–27; Knox to John Maunsell, 31 December 1789, GLC02437.04456; Knox to John Maunsell, 25 May 1790, GLC02437.04617. See also Charlotte de La Saussaye Hazen to GW, New York, 3 August 1795; MH to GW, New York, 9 September 1793; and Moses White to GW, Rutland, Mass., 8 February 1791, *PGW, Presidential Series*, 18:500–501, 14:51, 7:323–25. Also see Everest, *Moses Hazen and the Canadian Refugees*, 142–70.

88. Antill to David Humphreys, Coldenham, 25 January 1783, Founders Online, EA; Knox to Antill, 14 September 1783, GLC02437.10137; Antill to Knox, Coldenham, 14 September 1783, GLC02437.02509; "To Be Let" ad, 8 March 1784, *New-York Packet* supplement, AHN; Antill to Congress, 20 January 1784, PCC, roll 53, item 42, vol. 1, p. 75; Antill to John Jay, Golden Hills, 16 December 1785, PCC, roll 90, item 78, vol. 1, p. 473; Angelica Church to Hamilton, [London, 2 October 1787], including footnote 4, Founders Online; W. Nelson, *Edward Antill*, 21–22.

89. Parsons stopped at Reid's farm on the way to Carlisle. See C. Hall, *Life and Letters of Samuel Holden Parsons*, 473; "Major James R. Reid," in Kilbourne, *Virtutis Praemium*, 2:837; Shalhope, *John Taylor of Caroline*, 20–34.

90. Cauchon, "Liébert, Philippe"; Dufour and Goyer, "Gosselin, Clement," both in *Dictionary of Canadian Biography*; Hughes, "Captain Antoine Paulin," 38–41. Louis Gosselin's house is mentioned in Lt. Col. Commandant Mooers, Militia Regimental Orders, Plattsburgh, 19 October 1798, BMC, series 2, box 6, file 78. See also the C. Gosselin and Liébert entries in Kilbourne, *Virtutis Praemium*, 1:424–27, 538–40; and Ferriole, L. Gosselin, Olivie(r) and Paulint in Sypher, *New York State Society of the Cincinnati Biographies*, 152–53, 183–84, 354, 372–73.

91. "Captain James Duncan," in Kilbourne, *Virtutis Praemium*, 1:370–73; "General Hazen's Regiment," Munson has certificates, 25 August 1784, *Connecticut Journal* [New Haven, Conn.], AHN; Munson to GW, New Haven, 21 April 1789, *PGW, Presidential Series*, 2:102–5 (including footnotes).

92. William Popham, RWPBF, S.9989, reel 1952; Boulden, "Correcting Accounts about the Life of 'Major' William Popham," 56–59.

93. William (and Margaret) Torrey, RWPBF, W.16446, reel 2401; "William Torrey," Sypher, *New York State Society of the Cincinnati Biographies*, 499–500.

94. Mooers, "Recollections," BMC; Mooers, "[Auto-]Biography."

95. "A Patriot and Soldier Dead," *New-York Spectator,* 8 March 1838, Nineteenth-Century U.S. Newspapers database, New York Public Library; *Salem Gazette* [Salem, Mass.], 6 April 1838, AHN.

96. Baptist or Charles (and Agathe) Amlin, RWPBF, W.20604, reel 50. Recorded as Amlan by Hawkins in COR Roll.

97. Claud Monty, RWPBF, S.41017, reel 1750; John (Jean B.) Vinet, RWPBF, S.43211, reel 2460.

98. Louis Marney, RWPBF, S.42924, reel 1631. Mooers's support is also seen in other RWPBF: Julian (and Margaret) Belanger, W.21654, reel 203; Peter (Pierre and Martha) Blanchard, W.16506, reel 264; Michael Dufaut, S.46380, reel 859; Alexander Ferriol, S.43551, reel 967; John Gauley, S.46358, reel 1057; Theotist Paulin[t] (widow of Antoine), W.16671, reel 1891; and Abijah (Lucinda) Stowe, W.19404, reel 2310. For Mooers's support of others outside Clinton County, see John Ken[n]elly, S.42778, reel 1471, and John Shottler, BLWt 904–100, reel 2179, elsewhere in New York; and John McNamara, S.40982, reel 1698, and Peter (Pierre) and John Chartier, W.23786 and W.17598, reel 524, in Vermont.

99. John Gauley, RWPBF, S.46358, reel 1057. Unfortunately, Ferriol's offense was not named.

100. James Hole (Hale on COR Roll), RWPBF, S.45371, reel 1307.

101. Abraham (and Jennett Barclay) Lufberry, RWPBF, W.12235, reel 1599; occupations extracted from RWPBF, including William (and Lydia) Woodward, W.26089, reel 2640.

102. Francis (and Mary) Turcot (Tearcot), RWPBF, W.22390, reel 2354; Jacob Doddridge, RWPBF, S.42180, reel 825; Joseph (Mary) Martin, RWPBF, W.27971, reel 1640; report from Hartford, 9 June, in *Litchfield Monitor* [Litchfield, Conn.], 16 June 1788, AHN.

103. Abraham (Hannah) Shelley, RWPBF, W.26463, reel 2168.

104. JHJ [November 1782], "Old Mr. Arent Schuyler's House, Pompton, HSP.

105. JHJ, passim, HSP; Lieutenant Zacheus Peaslee and Captain Matthew McConnell, in Kilbourne, *Virtutis Praemium,* 2:769–71, 1:555–57; McConnell dry goods and exchange office ads, *Pennsylvania Packet,* 30 March 1784, and *Independent Gazetteer* [Philadelphia], 9 February 1787, AHN; Mester, "From Philadelphia Country House to City Recreation Center," 22–26.

106. "Hawkins," in *Philadelphia Directory* (1785 and 1791); "Hopkins" marriage, 4 August 1784, Christ Church, Marriage Records; land indenture between Hawkins and Murray, 10 February 1787, PHMC; Hawkins, no. 13198 warrant, *U.S. Revolutionary War Bounty Land Warrants . . . Ohio,* M829, roll 11, 687–88.

107. GW, Farewell to the Army, Rock Hill near Princeton, 2 November 1783, *WGW,* 27:224.

Bibliography

This bibliography lists sources cited rather than all of the works and collections consulted. Yet as some of the published secondary as well as primary materials recorded below were accessed at these special libraries, the following should also be noted for providing sources: the Fred W. Smith National Library for the Study of George Washington at Mount Vernon; the Jefferson Library in Monticello; the John D. Rockefeller Jr. Library at the Colonial Williamsburg Foundation; the Library Company of Philadelphia; and the Maryland State Archives in Annapolis.

ARCHIVES AND MANUSCRIPT COLLECTIONS

American Philosophical Society, Philadelphia, Pennsylvania
 Hall, David. Papers, 1745-1822. MSS B.H142.1-3.
Bibliothèque et Archives/Library and Archives Canada (cited as BAC/LAC), Ottawa, Ont., Canada.
 Executive Council Office of the Province of Lower Canada. Fonds, land petitions and related records of the Executive Council, vols. 1, 32, and 198. RG1-L3L.
 Haldimand, Frederick. Papers, Miscellaneous Papers, Orders and Returns. Collection MG21, Add. MSS 21687, microfilm A-616.
 Hazen, Moses. Collection MG23-B4, vol. 1.
 Indenture between Moses Hazen and William Hazen and L. Jarvis. MG8-F99, R12039-791-3-E, microfilm H-2941.
Cumberland County Historical Society, Carlisle, Pa.
 Chambers Genealogical files.
David Library of the American Revolution (cited as DLAR), Washington Crossing, Pa.
 Compiled Service Records of Soldiers Who Served in the American Army During the Revolutionary War (cited as CSR). Record group 93, microfilm M881. War Department Collection of Revolutionary War Records. Washington, D.C.: National Archives and Records Administration. Also accessible at www.fold3.com.
 Papers of the Continental Congress, 1774–89 (cited as PCC). Records of Continental and Confederation Congresses and Constitutional Convention. Record group 360, microfilm M247. Washington D.C.: National Archives and Records Administration. Also accessible at www.fold3.com.

Revolutionary War Pension and Bounty-Land-Warrant Application Files (cited as RWPBF). Record group 15, microfilm M804. Records of the Veterans Administration. Washington, D.C.: National Archives and Records Administration. Also accessible at www.fold3.com.

Revolutionary War Rolls, 1775–1783 (cited as RWR). Record group 93, microfilm M246. War Department Collection of Revolutionary War Records. Washington, D.C.: National Archives and Records Administration. Also accessible at www.fold3.com.

Steuben, Friedrich Wilhelm Augustus, Baron von. Papers, 1777–1794 (cited as Steuben Papers). Microfilm 229, reels 2, 6.

Historical Society of Pennsylvania (cited as HSP), Philadelphia, Pa.

Ainslie, Thomas. "Journal of the most remarkable occurrences in the Province of Quebec From the Appearance of the Rebels in September 1775 Untill their Retreat of the Sixth of May" 1776. With copy of "Journal of the Siege of Quebec 1775," 74–237. HSP, collection Am.610.

Antill, Edward Papers. Collection Am.0077.

Boudinot, Elias Papers. Collection Am.0068.

Continental Army. Second Canadian Regiment Orderly Books (cited as 2CROB). 2 vols. Collection Am.632 (formerly 2nd Canadian Regiment Orderly Books, Am.632, 633.)

Genealogical Data Regarding the Allied Families of Breintnall, Fawcett, and Harper of Philadelphia. Call no. FC Br.

Hawkins, John H. "Journal of Sergeant Major John H. Hawkins, 1779–1782" (cited as JHJ). Collection Am.0765.

Hawkins, John H. Memoranda. Collection Am.6071.

Hazen, Moses. Moses Hazen Orderly Books (cited as MHOB). 2 vols. Collection Am.649 (formerly Hawkins, John H. Orderly Books, 1 and 2, Am.649, 6491.)

Irving-Newbold Family Papers. Collection 1890, series 8: General James Irvine, 1775–1786, box 77.

Philadelphia, Philadelphia County, Pennsylvania, Will Books, XW-PA-PH. Richard Peters Papers. Volume 8. Collection 498.

Jack and Shirley Silver Special Collections Library (cited as JSS), University of Vermont, Burlington, Vt.

[André, John]. "Narrative of the Seige [sic] of St Johns Canada." Copy from BAC/LAC.

Hazen, Moses. Canadian Regiment, account of, petitions, 1778–1783. Vermont Manuscript files. Includes copied transcripts from Moses Hazen's Papers, MG.23-B4, BAC/LAC.

Library of Congress (cited as LOC), Manuscript Division, Washington, D.C.

Peter Force Papers and Collection. 1492–1977.

Series 7E: Transcripts.

Series 8D: Manuscript Collection, Other.

Series 9: Miscellaneous Manuscripts.

Mooers, Benjamin, Papers of, 1780. MSS 96156.

Orderly Book, 16 September–19 November 1780, microfilm 16819.

Washington, George, Papers (GWP).

Series 3: Varick Transcripts, 1775–1785.

Series 4: General Correspondence, 1697–1799.

Library of Virginia, Richmond, Va.
  Woodson Family Papers. Personal Papers Collection, 1740–1945. Collection 0005624808, folder 1, 1775–178[?], letters concerning the Revolutionary War service of Tarleton Woodson.
New Jersey State Archives, Trenton, N.J.
  Department of Defense, Adjutant General's Office (Revolutionary War), Copies of Miscellaneous Records, 1774–1837, series SDEA1004.
New-York Historical Society (cited as NYHS), New York, New York.
  American Historical Manuscript Collection, Patricia D. Klingenstein Library.
New York Public Library, Manuscripts and Archives Division, New York, N.Y.
  Gansevoort Military Papers, vol. 1. MSS collection 23873.
  Samuel Adams Papers. MSS collection 20.
New York State Library (cited as NYSL), Manuscripts and Special Collections, Albany, N.Y.
  Hazen, Moses to Governor George Clinton, Fishkill, 10 January 1781. Collection M1182.
  Moore [Mooers], Benjamin. Orderly Book, 22 June [28 January]–16 August 1781. Collection BD8175.
Society of the Cincinnati (cited as SOC), Washington, D.C.
  [Maseres, Francis.] *The Canadian Freeholder: In Two Dialogues between an English-man and a Frenchman, Settled in Canada.* Vol. 1. London: Sold by B. White, 1777.
  [Lloyd, Richard], Orderly Book, 2nd Canadian Regiment [New Hampshire Brigade], 11 October 1780–5 March 1781. MSS L1176.
Special Collections, Feinberg Library, SUNY, College at Plattsburgh, Plattsburgh, N.Y.
  Bailey-Moore [Mooers] Collection. No. 74.7 (BMC).
  Series 1: Correspondence.
  Series 2: Military Affairs.
    Series 2A: Military Correspondence and Orders.
    Series 2B: Military Papers.
  Series 3: Business and Legal Affairs.
    Series 3A: Benjamin Mooers Papers.
  Series 4: Miscellaneous.
Virginia Historical Society, Richmond, Va.
  "Heirs of Maj. Tarleton Woodson, Deceased." Adverse Report, Report 870, 29 March 1898, by 55th Congress House of Representatives. MSSI W868792.
  Woodson, T[arlton]. Letter to Madam [no name], Long Island, 30 June 1778. MSSI W8687a1.

DIGITIZED PRIMARY SOURCES AND DATABASES

America's Historical Newspapers (cited as AHN). Accessed through Readex Early American Newspapers. Accessed 28 July 2020. www.readex.com/content/early-american-newspapers-1690-1922. Also accessible through NewsBank. Accessed 30 July 2020. https://www.newsbank.com/libraries/public/solutions/historical/america.
Canadiana Héritage. Commissions from Quebec, Upper and Lower Canada, Province of Canada and Canada. C-3921. BAC/LAC Accessed 31 May 2020. http://heritage.canadiana.ca/view/oocihm.lac_reel_c3921.

Christ Church, Philadelphia, Pa. Online archives. Accessed 10 June 2020. www
.christchurchphila.org/collections-genealogy.

FamilySearch. United States Census databases with images. Accessed 2 June 2020.
https://familysearch.org.

Fold3 by Ancestry. Accessed 10 June 2020. www.fold3.com.

Force, Peter, ed. *American Archives, Fourth Series* (cited as *AA4*). 6 vols. Washington,
DC: M. St. Clair Clarke and Peter Force, 1837–1846. University Libraries, Digital
Collections and Collaborative Projects, Northern Illinois University, DeKalb, Ill.
Accessed 10 June 2020. http://amarch.lib.niu.edu.

Force, Peter, ed. *American Archives, Fifth Series* (cited as *AA5*). 3 vols. Washington, DC:
M. St. Clair Clarke and Peter Force, 1848–53. Ibid.

Founders Online. Digital archives. National Historical Publications and Records Commission (NHPRC). National Archives. Washington, D.C. Accessed 30 May 2020.
http://founders.archives.gov. (EA indicates early access document.)

Genealogy.com. "Genealogy Report: Descendants of Edward Hazen." Accessed 16 June
2020. www.genealogy.com/ftm/h/a/z/Walter-Eugene-Hazen/GENE1-0011.html .

Gilder Lehrman Institute of American History (cited as GLC), New York, N.Y. American History, 1493–1945. Via Adam Matthew Digital, Marlborough, Wiltshire, UK.
Accessed 5 June 2020. www.americanhistory.amdigital.co.uk.

Massachusetts Historical Society, Boston, Mass.
   State Revolutionary War Debt Certificates, 1775–1789. Special Collections: Cur-
      rency. Accessed 6 June 2020. www.masshist.org/collection-guides/view/fa00004
      ?terms=state%20revolutionary%20war%20debt%20certificates.

New York Public Library. Nineteenth-Century U.S. Newspapers database. Accessed 6
June 2020. www.nypl.org/collections/articles-databases/nineteenth-century-news
papers.

Ohio History Central. Online encyclopedia.
   "Land Grants and Sales." Accessed 6 June 2020. https://ohiohistorycentral.org/w
      /Land_Grants_and_Sales.
   "Refugee Tract." Accessed 6 June 2020. https://ohiohistorycentral.org/w/Refugee
      _Tract.

Papers of the War Department, 1784–1800. Roy Rosenzweig Center for History and
New Media. George Mason University, Fairfax, Va. Accessed 2 June 2020. http://
wardepartmentpapers.org. Many documents are from the U.S. National Archives
and Records Administration (NARA) War Department Collection of Revolutionary
War Records, record group 93. Accessed 2 June 2020. www.archives.gov/research
/guide-fed-records/groups/093.html.

The Pennsylvania Gazette [Philadelphia]. Accessible Archives CD-ROM.

Pennsylvania Historical and Museum Commission (cited as PHMC). "Indenture
John H. Hawkins to Francis Murray," 10 February 1787. In Donation Claimant
Papers and Miscellaneous Patents. RG-17. Records of the Land Office, Surnames
beginning with "H," pp. 82–83. Accessed 27 July 2020. www.phmc.state.pa.us/bah
/dam/rg/di/r17DonationLandSeries/r17-168DonationClaimantPapers/r17
-168DonationClaimantB%20114.pdf.

The Quebec Gazette. Accessed 29 July 2020. https://bac-lac.on.worldcat.org/oclc
/1007008626. See also "*Quebec Gazette* de Quebec Index from 1764–1824." Accessed
31 May 2020. http://data2.archives.ca/pdf/pdf001/p000002153.pdf.

PUBLISHED PRIMARY SOURCES

Anburey, Thomas. *Travels through the Interior Parts of America in a Series of Letters.* Vol. 1. London, 1789. Reprint, New York: New York Times & Arno Press, 1969.

The Balloting Book, and Other Documents Relating to Military Bounty Lands, in the State of New-York. Albany: Packard & Van Benthusen, 1825.

Beebe, Lewis. "Journal of a Physician on the Expedition against Canada, 1776." Edited by Frederic R. Kirkland. *Pennsylvania Magazine of History and Biography* 59, no. 4 (October 1935): 321–61.

Biddle, Clement. *The Philadelphia Directory.* Philadelphia: James & Johnson, No. 147, High-Street, 1791. Library Company of Philadelphia, Philadelphia, Pa.

Boudinot, Elias. *Journal or Historical Recollections of American Events during the Revolutionary War.* Philadelphia: Frederick Bourquin, 1894. Reprinted as *Journal of Events in the Revolution.* New York: New York Times & Arno Press, 1968.

Bouquet, Henry. *The Papers of Henry Bouquet.* Vol. 6. Edited by Louis M. Waddell. Harrisburg, Pa.: Pennsylvania Historical and Museum Commission, 1994.

Bowling, Kenneth R., William Charles DiGiacomantonio, and Charlene Bangs Bickford, eds. *Documentary History of the First Federal Congress of the United States of America, 4 March 1789–3 March 1791.* Vol. VII. In *Petition Histories: Revolutionary War-Related Claims.* Baltimore: The Johns Hopkins University Press, 1997.

Carroll, Charles. *Journal of Charles Carroll of Carrollton, During his Visit to Canada in 1776.* Memoir and notes by Brantz Mayer. Baltimore, 1876. Reprint, New York: New York Times & Arno Press, 1969.

Closen, Ludwig von. *The Revolutionary Journal of Baron Ludwig Von Closen, 1780–1783.* Translated and edited by Evelyn M. Acomb. Chapel Hill: University of North Carolina Press, 1958.

Continental Congress. *Observations on the American Revolution.* Philadelphia: Styner and Cist, 1779. Library Company of Philadelphia, Philadelphia, Pa.

Crèvecoeur, J. Hector St. John de. *Letters from an American Farmer and Sketches of Eighteenth-Century America.* Edited by Albert E. Stone. New York: Penguin Classics, 1986.

Documents Relating to the Colonial, Revolutionary and Post-Revolutionary History of the State of New Jersey. 1st and 2nd series. 47 vols. Newark: Archives of the State of New Jersey, 1880–1949.

Documents Relating to the Colonial History State of New Jersey. 1st series, vol. XVII. Edited by Frederick W. Ricord. Vol. 5, 1756–1768. *Journal of the Governor and Council,* Trenton, N.J.: John L. Murphy Publishing Co., 1892.

Duncan, James. "Diary of Captain James Duncan of Colonel Moses Hazen's Regiment: In the Yorktown Campaign, 1781." In *Pennsylvania Archives,* series 2, vol. 15, edited by William H. Egle, 744–52. Harrisburg, Pa.: E. K. Meyers, 1890.

Feltman, William. *The Journal of Lt. William Feltman of the First Pennsylvania Regiment, 1781–82.* Philadelphia, 1853. Reprint, New York: Arno Press, 1969.

Franklin, Benjamin. *The Papers of Benjamin Franklin.* Vol. 22, *March 23, 1775 through October 27, 1776.* Edited by William B. Willcox. New Haven, Conn.: Yale University Press, 1982.

Gabriel, Michael P., ed. *Quebec during the American Invasion, 1775–1776: The Journal of François Baby, Gabriel Taschereau, and Jenkin Williams.* Translated by S. Pascale Vergereau-Dewey. East Lansing: Michigan State University Press, 2005.

Gage, Thomas. *The Correspondence of General Thomas Gage with the Secretaries of State, 1763–1775.* Vol. 1. Edited by Clarence Edwin Carter. New Haven, Conn.: Yale University Press, 1931.

Gerlach, Larry R. *New Jersey in the American Revolution, 1763–1783: A Documentary History.* Trenton: New Jersey Historical Commission, 1975.

Greene, Nathanael. *The Papers of General Nathanael Greene.* Vol. II: 1 January 1777–16 October 1778. Vol. V: 1 November 1779–31 May 1780. Vol. VI: 1 June 1780–25 December 1780. Edited by Richard K. Showman. Chapel Hill: University of North Carolina Press, 1980, 1989, 1991.

Hall, Charles S. *Life and Letters of Samuel Holden Parsons, Major General in the Continental Army and Chief Judge of the Northwestern Territory, 1737–1789.* Binghamton, N.Y.: Otseningo Publishing Co., 1905.

Hamilton, Alexander. *Papers of Alexander Hamilton.* Vol. I: 1768–1778. Vol. II: 1779–1781. Edited by Harold C. Syrett et al. New York: Columbia University Press, 1961.

Hazard, Samuel, ed. *Pennsylvania Archives.* Series 1, vols. 5, 8. Philadelphia: Joseph Severns & Co., 1853, 1855.

Heath, William. *Memoirs of Major-General Heath.* Boston, 1798. Reprint, New York: William Abbatt, 1901.

A History of the Organization, Development and Services of the Military and Naval Forces of Canada From the Peace of Paris in 1763, to the Present Time (cited as *History of the Military of Canada*). 3 vols. Edited by Historical Section of the General Staff. Ottawa, Canada: Department of Militia and Defence, 1919–1920.

Howard, John Eager. "Col. John Eager Howard's Account of the Battle of Germantown." *Maryland Historical Magazine* IV (December 1909): 314–20.

Hurt, John. *The Love of Our Country, A Sermon Preached Before the Virginia Troops in New-Jersey.* Philadelphia: Styner and Cist, 1777. Library Company of Philadelphia, Philadelphia, Pa.

Jefferson, Thomas. *Autobiography of Thomas Jefferson, 1743-1790: Together with a Summary of the Chief Events in Jefferson's Life.* New York and London: G. P. Putnam's Sons, 1914.

Jefferson, Thomas. *Notes on the State of Virginia.* Edited by William Peden. Chapel Hill: University of North Carolina Press, 1955. Reprint, 1982.

Jefferson, Thomas. *The Papers of Thomas Jefferson.* Vols. 1 (1760–76) and 5 (25 February—20 May 1781). Edited by Julian P. Boyd. Princeton, N.J.: Princeton University Press, 1950, 1952.

Johnson, Samuel. "The Patriot" (1774). In *The Works of Samuel Johnson*, Vol. 14, 81–93. Troy, N.Y.: Pafraets & Co., 1913. Accessed 31 May 2020. www.samueljohnson.com /thepatriot.html.

Journals of the Continental Congress, 1774–1789 (cited as *JCC*). 34 vols. Edited by Worthington C. Ford et al. Washington, D.C.: Library of Congress, 1904–1937. Accessible at http://memory.loc.gov/ammem/amlaw/lwjc.html.

Journal of the House of Delegates of the Commonwealth of Virginia [7 May–23 June 1781]. In *Journal of the House of Delegates of the State of Virginia.* Richmond, Va.: Thomas W. White, 1828.

Lafayette, Marie Joseph. *Lafayette in Virginia: Unpublished Letters from the Original Manuscripts in the Virginia State Library and the Library of Congress.* Edited by Gilbert Chinard. Baltimore: The Johns Hopkins Press, 1928.

Lee, Andrew. "Sullivan's Expedition to Staten Island in 1777." *Pennsylvania Magazine of History and Biography* 3, no. 2 (1879): 167–73.

Linn, John B. and William Henry Egle, ed. *Pennsylvania Archives*. Series 2, vols. 3, 8, 9. Harrisburg, Pa.: E. K. Meyers, 1876–1890, 1896.

McHenry, James. *A Sidelight on History: Being the Letters of James McHenry, Aide-de-Camp of the Marquis de Lafayette, to Thomas Sim Lee, Governor, of Maryland, Written During the Yorktown Campaign, 1781*. Privately printed, 1931.

McIlwaine, H. R., ed. *Official Letters of the Governors of the State of Virginia. Vol. III: The Letters of Thomas Nelson and Benjamin Harrison*. Richmond: Virginia State Library, 1929.

McMichael, James. "Diary of Lieut. James McMichael, of the Pennsylvania Line, 1776–1778." *Journals and Diaries of the War of the Revolution with Lists of Officers and Soldiers, 1775–1783*. In *Pennsylvania Archives*, series 2, vol. 15, edited by William H. Egle. Harrisburg, Pa.: E. K. Meyers, 1893.

Melvin, James. *A Journal of the Expedition to Quebec, in the Year 1775*. Philadelphia: Franklin Club, 1864.

Montgomery, Thomas Lynch, ed. *Pennsylvania Archives*. Series 5, vol. 3. Harrisburg, Pa.: Harrisburg Publishing Co., 1906.

Montgomery, Thomas Lynch, ed. *Pennsylvania Archives*. Series 6, vols. 1, 6. Harrisburg, Pa.: Harrisburg Publishing Co., 1906–1907.

Mooers, Benjamin. "[Auto-]Biography of Major-General Benjamin Mooers of Plattsburg, Clinton-County, N.Y., Written in 1833, By Request of His Son, Benjamin B. Mooers." *The Historical Magazine and Notes and Queries Concerning the Antiquities, History, and Biography of America*. Series 3, vol. 1, no. 2 (February 1872): 92–94.

Muster Rolls and Other Records of Service of Maryland Troops in the American Revolution, 1775–1783. Baltimore: Maryland Historical Society and the Lord Baltimore Press, Friedenwald Co., 1900. Vol. 18 of Archives of Maryland Online series. Accessed 2 June 2020. http://aomol.msa.maryland.gov/000001/000018/html.

O'Callaghan, E. B., compiler. *Calendar of New York Colonial Manuscripts, Indorsed Land Papers: In the Office of the Secretary of State of New York, 1643–1803*. Albany, N.Y.: Weed, Parsons & Co., 1864. Revised reprint, Harrison, N.Y.: Harbor Hill Books, 1987.

Orderly Book of the Northern Army, at Ticonderoga and Mt. Independence, from October 17th, 1776, to January 8th, 1777. Albany, N.Y.: J. Munsell, 1859.

Orderly Book of the Siege of Yorktown, from September 26th, 1781, to November 2nd, 1781. Philadelphia: Horace W. Smith, 1865.

Paine, Thomas. *Common Sense*. Edited by Isaac Kramnick. 1976. Reprint, New York: Penguin Classics, 1986.

Paine, Thomas. *The Writings of Thomas Paine*. Vol. I. Edited by Moncure Daniel Conway. New York, AMS Press, Inc., 1967.

Peebles, John. *John Peebles' American War: The Diary of a Scottish Grenadier, 1776–1782*. Edited by Ira D. Gruber. Mechanicsburg, Pa: Stackpole Books, 1998.

Porter, Elisha. "Diary: Colonel Elisha Porter, 1776—The Invasion of Canada." The Patriot Files, Library of Congress Veterans History Project Founding Partner website. Accessed 24 July 2020. www.patriotfiles.com/index.php?name=News&file=article&sid=80.

Poulson, Charles A. "Philadelphia Directory for 1767–68 compiled from advertisements &c, in old newspapers, and other authentic materials." Philadelphia, (1862) 1900. Library Company of Philadelphia, Philadelphia, Pa.

Provincial and State Papers. The State of New Hampshire (cited as *Provincial and State Papers*). Vol 17. Pt. 1: *Rolls and Documents Relating to Soldiers in the Revolutionary War.* Edited by Isaac W. Hammond. Manchester: John B. Clarke, 1889. Accessed 2 June 2020. https://archive.org/stream/provincialstatepv17newh/provincialstatepv 17newh_djvu.txt.

Reports from the Court of Claims . . . Thirty-fifth Congress. 3 vols. Washington, D.C.: James B. Steedman, 1858.

Saffell, William T. R., ed. *Records of the Revolutionary War: Containing the Military and Financial Correspondence of Distinguished Officers.* Philadelphia: G. G. Evans, 1860.

Shortt, Adam, and Arthur Doughty, eds. *Canadian Archives: Documents Relating to the Constitutional History of Canada, 1759–1791.* Ottawa, Canada: S. E. Dawson, 1907.

Smith, Paul H., ed. *Letters of Delegates to Congress, 1774 1789* (cited as *LDC*). 25 vols. Washington, D.C.: Library of Congress, 1976–2000. Accessible at http://memory.loc .gov/ammem/amlaw/lwdg.html.

Gawalt, Gerard W., Rosemary Fry Plakas, and Eugene R. Sheridan, asst. eds. Vol. 6: 1 January–30 April 1777 (1980).

Gawalt, Gerard W. and Ronald M. Gephart, assoc. eds. Vol. 16: 1 September 1780–28 February 1781 (1989).

Gawalt, Gerard W. and Ronald M. Gephart, assoc. eds. Vol. 17: 1 March–31 August 1781 (1990).

Gawalt, Gerard W. and Ronald M. Gephart, assoc. eds. Vol. 18: 1 September 1781–31 July 1782 (1991).

Gawalt, Gerard W. and Ronald M. Gephart, assoc. eds. Vol. 19: 1 August 1782–11 March 1783 (1992).

Smith, Richard. "Diary of Richard Smith in the Continental Congress, 1775–1776. II." *American Historical Review* 1, no. 3 (April 1896): 493–516.

Smith, William. *Bouquet's Expedition Against the Ohio Indians in 1764 by William Smith.* Edited by Martin West. Kent, Ohio: Kent State University Press, 2017.

St. Clair, Arthur. *The St. Clair Papers: The Life and Public Services of Arthur St. Clair.* Vol. 1. Edited by William Henry Smith. Cincinnati, Ohio: Robert Clarke & Co., 1882.

Sullivan, John. *Letters and Papers of Major-General John Sullivan, Continental Army* (cited as *Sullivan Papers*). Vol. 1, 1771–1777. Edited by Otis G. Hammond. Concord: New Hampshire Historical Society, 1930.

Thacher, James. *Observations Relative to the Execution of Major André as a Spy in 1780: Correcting Errors and Refuting False Imputations.* Boston: 1834. Accessible via Sabin Americana, 1500–1926, Gale Digital Collections. Accessed 29 July 2020. www.gale .com/c/sabin-americana-history-of-the-americas-1500-1926.

Trudel, Marcel. *La Tentation Américaine, 1774–1783. La Révolution américaine et le Canada, textes commentés.* Sillery, Québec: Septentrion, 2006.

Tucker, St. George. "Journal of the Siege of Yorktown and Surrender of Cornwallis." Special collection PH 0231. Photostat copy. John D. Rockefeller, Jr. Library, Colonial Williamsburg Foundation, Williamsburg, Va.

United States Senate Journal. 1st Cong., 2nd sess., January 1790–August 1790; and 12th Cong., 2nd sess., November 1812–March 1813. Accessible at http://memory.loc.gov /ammem/amlaw/lawhome.html.

Valley Forge Orderly Book of General George Weedon of the Continental Army under Command of Gen. George Washington, in the Campaign of 1777–8. New York: Dodd, Mean & Co., 1902.

Waldschmidt, John. "Baptismal and Marriage Records. Lancaster County, Penna. 1752–1786." In *Pennsylvania Archives,* series 6, vol. 6, edited by Thomas Lynch Montgomery. Harrisburg, Pa.: Harrisburg Publishing Co., 1907.

Washington, George. *The Diaries of George Washington. Volume 3: 1771–75, 1780–81.* Edited by Donald Jackson et al. Charlottesville: University of Virginia Press, 1978.

Washington, George. *The Papers of George Washington* (cited as *PGW*). Edited by W. W. Abbot et. al. 1983–2019 (ongoing).

> *Revolutionary War Series* (1775–1783) (cited as *PGW:RWS*). Vols. 1–26. Edited by Philander D. Chase et al. 1985–2019 (ongoing).

> *Confederation Series* (1784–1788). Vol. 2 (July 1784–May 1785). Edited by W. W. Abbot. 1992, 1995.

> *Presidential Series* (1788–1797). Vol. 2: April–June 1789; vol. 7: December 1790–March 1791; vol. 14: September–December 1793; and vol. 18: April–September 1795. Edited by Dorothy Twohig, Jack D. Warren, David R. Hoth, and Carol S. Ebel, respectively. 1987, 1998, 2008, 2015.

Washington, George. *The Writings of George Washington from the Original Manuscript Sources, 1745–1799* (cited as *WGW*). Edited by John C. Fitzpatrick. 39 vols. Washington, D.C.: Government Printing Office, 1931–1944.

Webster, Noah. "Sketches of the Rise, Progress and Consequences of the late Revolution." No. XV. In *A Collection of Essays and Fugitive Writings in Moral, Historical, Political and Literary Subjects.* Boston, 1790. Reprint, Delmar, N.Y.: Scholars' Facsimiles and Reprints, 1977.

White, Francis. *The Philadelphia Directory.* Philadelphia: Young, Stewart, & McCulloch in Chesnut-St. [*sic*], 1785. Library Company of Philadelphia, Philadelphia, Pa.

White, Moses. *Statement of Facts: Relating to the Claim of Major Moses White.* Salem, Mass., 28 February 1820 (published 1827). Boston Public Library, Internet Archive, Open Library. Accessed 10 June 2020. https://archive.org/details/statementoffactsoowhit/page/n7/mode/2up.

Wilkinson, James. *Memoirs of My Own Times.* 3 vols. Philadelphia: Abraham Small, 1816.

SECONDARY LITERATURE

Abbott, Tim. "Sullivan's Staten Island Raid (1777)." 12-part series, 15 February–8 April 2011. *Walking the Berkshires* (blog). Accessed 2 June 2020. http://greensleeves.typepad.com/berkshires/sullivans-staten-island-raid-1777.

Adelman, Jeremy and Stephen Aron. "From Borderlands to Borders: Empires, Nation-States, and the Peoples in Between in North American History." *American Historical Review* 104, no. 3 (June 1999): 814–41.

Adelman, Jeremy and Stephen Aron. "Of Lively Exchanges and Larger Perspectives." *American Historical Review* 104, no. 4 (October 1999): 1235–39.

Allen, David Yehling. *The Mapping of New York State: A Study in the History of Cartography.* 2011. www.dyasites.com/maps/nysbook/Preface.htm.

Ammundsen, Anne, and Martha Abel. "Saving Captain Asgill" [with primary documents]. *Journal of the Lancaster County's Historical Society* 120, no. 3 (Winter 2019): 83–181.

Anderson, Benedict. *Imagined Communities: Reflections on the Origin and Spread of Nationalism*. New York: Verso, 1983.

Anderson, Fred. *Crucible of War: The Seven Years' War and the Fate of Empire in British North America, 1754–1766*. New York: Alfred A. Knopf, 2000.

Anderson, Fred. *A People's Army: Massachusetts Soldiers and Society in the Seven Years' War*. Chapel Hill: University of North Carolina Press, 1984.

Anderson, Fred and Andrew Cayton. *The Dominion of War: Empire and Liberty in North America, 1500–2000*. New York: Penguin Books, 2005.

Anderson, Mark R. *The Battle for the Fourteenth Colony: America's War of Liberation in Canada, 1774–1776*. Hanover, N.H.: University Press of New England, 2013.

Appleby, Joyce. *Inheriting the Revolution: The First Generation of Americans*. Cambridge, Mass.: Belknap Press of Harvard University Press, 2000.

Armstrong, Maurice W. "Neutrality and Religion in Revolutionary Nova Scotia." *The New England Quarterly* 19, no. 1 (March 1946): 50–62.

Audet, Francis-J. "Edward Antill." In *Le Bulletin des Recherches Historiques*. Québec : Pierre-George Roy–Lévis, 1932, 548.

Baldwin, Frederick W. "The Hazen Military Road." *The Vermonter* XI, no. 16 (November 1906): 297–323.

Bailyn, Bernard. *The Ideological Origins of the American Revolution*. Cambridge, Mass.: Belknap Press of Harvard University Press, 1967.

Bailyn, Bernard. *The Peopling of British North America: An Introduction*. New York: Alfred A. Knopf, 1986.

Bailyn, Bernard and Philip D. Morgan, eds. *Strangers within the Realm: Cultural Margins of the First British Empire*. Chapel Hill: University of North Carolina Press, 1991.

Barker, Thomas M. and Paul R. Huey. *The 1776–1777 Northern Campaigns of the American War for Independence and Their Sequel: Contemporary Maps of Mainly Germany Origin*. Fleishmanns, N.Y.: Purple Mountain Press, 2010.

Bayly, C. A. "The British and Indigenous Peoples, 1760–1860: Power, Perception and Identity." In *Empire and Others: British Encounters with Indigenous Peoples, 1600–1850*, edited by Martin Daunton and Rick Halpern, 19–41. Philadelphia: University of Pennsylvania Press, 1999.

Bennett, David. *A Few Lawless Vagabonds: Ethan Allen, the Republic of Vermont, and the American Revolution*. Philadelphia: Casemate, 2014.

Black, Jeremy. "Frontiers and Military History." *Journal of Military History* 72, no. 4 (October 2008): 1047–59.

Boulden, Jim. "Correcting Accounts about the Life of 'Major' William Popham of Scarsdale, New York." *Westchester Connections* 3 (1997–98), 56–59.

Brener, David A. *The Jews of Lancaster, Pennsylvania: A Story with Two Beginnings*. Lancaster, Pa.: Congregation Shaarai Shomayim, 1979.

Brown, Gayle K. "The Impact of the Colonial Anti-Catholic Tradition on the Canadian Campaign, 1775–1776." *Journal of Church & State* 35, no. 3 (Summer 1993): 559–75.

Brumwell, Stephen. *Redcoats: The British Soldier and War in the Americas, 1755–1763*. Cambridge, UK: Cambridge University Press, 2002.

Calloway, Colin G. *The Western Abenakis of Vermont, 1660–1800: War, Migration, and the Survival of an Indian People*. Norman: University of Oklahoma Press, 1990.

Calloway, Colin G. *White People, Indians, and Highlanders: Tribal Peoples and Colonial Encounters in Scotland and America*. New York: Oxford University Press, 2008.

Campbell, Alexander V. *The Royal American Regiment: An Atlantic Microcosm, 1755–1772.* Norman: University of Oklahoma Press, 2010.

Carp, E. Wayne. "The Origins of the Nationalist Movement of 1780–1783: Congressional Administration and the Continental Army." *Pennsylvania Magazine of History and Biography* 107, no. 3 (July 1983): 363–92.

Cate, Alan C. *Founding Fighters: The Battlefield Leaders Who Made American Independence.* Westport, Conn.: Praeger Security International, 2006.

Cauchon, Michel. " Liébert, Philippe." In *Dictionary of Canadian Biography.* Vol. 5. University of Toronto/Université Laval, 2003–. Accessed 29 July 2020. http://www.biographi.ca/en/bio/liebert_philippe_5E.html. (Original citation: "Philippe Liébert [1733–1804]." Religious Heritage/Patrimoine Religieux. http://collections.ic.gc.ca/relig/liebert.htm [accessed July 2005; no longer accessible]).

"Chaplains of the French Army in the American Revolution." *American Catholic Historical Researches* 7, no. 1 (January 1911): 67–75.

Charland, Thomas-M. "Gill, Joseph-Louis, Magouaouidombaouit." In *Dictionary of Canadian Biography.* Vol. 4. University of Toronto/Université Laval, 2003–. Accessed 31 May 2020. www.biographi.ca/en/bio/gill_joseph_louis_4E.html.

Clark, Murtie June, compiler. *The Pension Lists of 1792–1795, with Other Revolutionary War Pension Records.* Baltimore: Genealogical Publishing Co., 1991.

Codignola, Luca. "Roman Catholic Conservatism in a New North Atlantic World, 1760–1829." *William and Mary Quarterly* 64, no. 4 (October 2007): 720–23.

Cogliano, Francis D. *No King, No Popery: Anti-Catholicism in Revolutionary New England.* Westport, Conn.: Greenwood Press, 1995.

Coleman, John M. "How 'Continental' Was the Continental Congress? The Thirteen Colonies and the Rest of North America." *History Today,* 18, no. 8 (August 1968): 540–50.

Colley, Linda. *Britons: Forging the Nation, 1707–1837.* New Haven, Conn.: Yale University Press, 1992.

"Colonial Fiscal Documents, Massachusetts: Treasury Certificates—January 1, 1780." Colonial Currency Collection, University of Notre Dame Libraries Department of Special Collections, Notre Dame, Ind. Accessed 6 June 2020. https://coins.nd.edu/ColCurrency/CurrencyText/FiscalDocsMA-22.intro.html.

Conway, Stephen. "From Fellow-Nationals to Foreigners: British Perceptions of the Americans, circa 1739–1783." *William and Mary Quarterly* 59, no. 1 (January 2002): 65–100.

Copeland, Peter F. (art) and Marko Zlatich (text). "2d Canadian Regiment ('Congress's Own'), 1777–1779." *Military Collector & Historian* 53, no. 1 (Spring 2001): 40–41.

Corbett, Theodore. *No Turning Point: The Saratoga Campaign in Perspective.* Norman: University of Oklahoma Press, 2012.

Cossette, Joseph. "Floquet, Pierre-René." In *Dictionary of Canadian Biography.* Vol. 4. University of Toronto/Université Laval, 2003–. Accessed 31 May 2020. www.biographi.ca/en/bio/floquet_pierre_rene_4E.html.

Countryman, Edward. "Postscript: Large Questions in a Very Large Place." In *A Companion to Colonial America,* edited by Daniel Vickers, 530–40. Malden, Mass.: Blackwell, 2003.

Cox, Caroline. *Boy Soldiers of the American Revolution.* Chapel Hill: University of North Carolina Press, 2016.

Cox, Caroline. *A Proper Sense of Honor: Service and Sacrifice in George Washington's Army.* Chapel Hill: University of North Carolina Press, 2004.

Cubbison, Douglas. *The American Northern Theater Army in 1776: The Ruin and Reconstruction of the Continental Force.* Jefferson, N.C.: McFarland & Co., 2010.

Curtis, Edward E. *The Organization of the British Army in the American Revolution.* New Haven, Conn.: Yale University Press, 1926. Accessed 30 July 2020. www .americanrevolution.org/britisharmy.php.

Daunton, Martin and Rick Halpern, eds. *Empire and Others: British Encounters with Indigenous Peoples, 1600–1850.* Philadelphia: University of Pennsylvania Press, 1999.

Davidson, William Evans. "Disapprobation: Congress' Own Regiment and General Washington's Life Guards." *Military Collector & Historian* 59, no. 4 (December 2007): 321–24.

Deloria, Philip J. "What Is the Middle Ground, Anyway?" *William and Mary Quarterly* 63, no. 1 (January 2006): 15–22.

Drake, James D. "Appropriating a Continent: Geographical Categories, Scientific Metaphors, and the Construction of Nationalism in British North America and Mexico." *Journal of World History* 15, no. 3 (September 2004): 323–57.

Draper, Mrs. Amos G., preparer. *N. H. Revolutionary Pension Papers.* Concord, N.H.: New Hampshire Historical Society, 1917–22. Accessed 30 July 2020. http://files .usgwarchives.net/nh/grafton/military/revwar/pensions/sanbornl.txt.

Dufour, Pierre and Gerárd Goyer. "Gosselin, Clément." In *Dictionary of Canadian Biography.* Vol. 5. University of Toronto/Université Laval, 2003–. Accessed 31 May 2020. www.biographi.ca/en/bio/gosselin_clement_5E.html.

DuVal, Kathleen. *Borderlands: Oxford Bibliographies Online Research Guide.* New York: Oxford University Press, 2011.

Engel, Katherine Carté. "Connecting Protestants in Britain's Eighteenth-Century Atlantic Empire." *William and Mary Quarterly* 75, no. 1 (January 2018): 37–70.

Evans, Emory G. *Thomas Nelson of Yorktown: Revolutionary Virginian.* Charlottesville: University of Virginia Press, 1975.

Evans, Sterling, ed. *The Borderlands of the American and Canadian Wests: Essays on Regional History of the Forty-ninth Parallel.* Lincoln: University of Nebraska Press, 2006.

Everest, Allan S. *Moses Hazen and the Canadian Refugees in the American Revolution.* Syracuse, N.Y.: Syracuse University Press, 1976.

Everest, Allan S. "Moses Hazen." In *Dictionary of Canadian Biography.* Vol. 5. University of Toronto/Université Laval, 2003–. Accessed 31 May 2020. www.biographi.ca /009004-119.01-e.php?&id_nbr=2455.

"Father Peter Huet de La Valiniere, The 'Fiery, Factious and Turbulent' 'Rebel' Canadian Priest." *American Catholic Historical Researches* 2, no. 3 (July 1906): 203–39.

Ferling, John. *Almost a Miracle: The American Victory in the War of Independence.* New York: Oxford University Press, 2007.

Frank, Andrew K. and A. Glenn Crothers, eds. *Borderland Narratives: Negotiation and Accommodation in North America's Contested Spaces, 1500–1850.* Gainesville: University Press of Florida, 2017.

Friends of the Fishkill Supply Depot (website). Accessed 1 June 2020. www.fishkill supplydepot.org/tribute.html#CA.

Furstenberg, François. "Significance of the Trans-Appalachian Frontier in Atlantic History, c. 1754–1815." *American Historical Review* 113, no. 2 (June 2008): 647–77.

Gabriel, Michael P. *Major General Richard Montgomery: The Making of an American Hero*. Madison, N.J.: Fairleigh Dickinson University Press, 2002.

Gara, Donald J. "Loyal Subjects of the Crown: The Queen's Own Loyal Virginia Regiment and Dunmore's Ethiopian Regiment, 1775–76." *Journal of the Society for Army Historical Research* 83, no. 333 (Spring 2005): 30–42.

Garneau, F. X. *History of Canada from Its Discovery to Our Days*. Vol. 3, book 12, chap. 1. Quebec: Imprimerie de Frechétte et Frère, 1848. Accessed 31 May 2020. http://history.furman.edu/benson/hst121/GarneauHistoireCanada1775.htm.

Gitlin, Jay. *The Bourgeois Frontier: French Towns, French Traders, and American Expansion*. New Haven, Conn.: Yale University Press, 2010.

Gottschalk, Louis. *Lafayette and the Close of the American Revolution*. Chicago: University of Chicago Press, 1942.

Grace, Sherrill E. "Comparing Mythologies: Ideas of West and North." In *Borderlands: Essays in Canadian-American Relations*, edited by Robert Lecker, 243–62. Toronto: ECW Press, 1991.

Grainger, John D. *The Battle of Yorktown, 1781: A Reassessment*. Woodbridge, Suffolk, UK: Boydell Press, 2005.

Greene, Jack P. "Autonomy and Stability: New England and the British Colonial Experience in Early Modern America." *Journal of Social History* 7, no. 2 (Winter 1974): 171–94.

Greene, Jerome. *The Allies at Yorktown: A Bicentennial History of the Siege of 1781*. Washington, D.C.: National Park Service, 1976.

Greven, Philip J. Jr. *Four Generations: Population, Land, and Family in Colonial Andover, Massachusetts*. Ithaca, N.Y.: Cornell University Press, 1970.

Griffin, Martin I. J. *Catholics and the American Revolution*. Vols. 2 and 3. Philadelphia, 1909, 1911.

Gross, Robert A. *The Minutemen and Their World*. New York: Hill and Wang, 1976.

Haefeli, Evan. "A Note on the Use of North American Borderlands." *American Historical Review* 104, no. 4 (October 1999): 1222–25.

Halttunen, Karen. "Grounded Histories: Land and Landscape in Early America." *William and Mary Quarterly* 68, no. 4 (October 2011): 513–32.

Hämäläinen, Pekka and Samuel Truett. "On Borderlands." *Journal of American History* 98, no. 2 (September 2011): 338–61.

Handlin, Oscar. *The Uprooted: The Epic Story of the Great Migrations that Made the American People*. Boston: Little, Brown and Co., 1951.

Hanson, Charles P. *Necessary Virtue: The Pragmatic Origins of Religious Liberty in New England*. Charlottesville: University of Virginia Press, 1998.

Harris, Michael C. *Brandywine: A Military History of the Battle that Lost Philadelphia but Saved America, September 11, 1777*. El Dorado Hills, Calif.: Savas Beatie, 2014.

Hazen, James King. *Genealogy of the Hazen Family: Eight American Generations*. Richmond, Va.: Whittet & Shepperson, 1892. Bangor Public Library, Maine. Accessed 31 May 2020. http://digicom.bpl.lib.me.us/books_pubs/63.

Heitman, Francis B. *Historical Register of Officers of the Continental Army during the War of the Revolution, April, 1775, to December, 1783*. Washington, D.C.: Rare Book

Shop Publishing Company, 1914. Reprint, revised edition, with addenda by Robert H. Kelby, 1932. Reprint, Baltimore: Genealogical Publishing Co. 1982.

Higginbotham, Don. "The Early American Way of War: Reconnaissance and Appraisal." *William and Mary Quarterly* 44, no. 2 (April 1987): 230-73.

Higginbotham, Don. *The War of American Independence: Military Attitudes, Policies, and Practice, 1763-1789.* New York: Macmillan, 1971. Reprint, Boston: Northeastern University Press, 1983.

Hofstra, Warren. "Backcountry Frontier of Colonial Virginia." In *Encyclopedia Virginia.* 31 January 2012. Accessed 5 June 2020. www.EncyclopediaVirginia.org /Backcountry_Frontier_of_Colonial_Virginia.

Hoock, Holger. *Scars of Independence: America's Violent Birth.* New York: Crown, 2017.

Hughes, Dorothy C. "Captain Antoine Paulin of Hazen's Canadian Regiment 'Congress' Own' and the American Revolution." *French Canadian and Acadian Genealogical Review* 6, no. 1. (Spring 1978): 17-51.

Ibarra, María de la Luz. "Buscando La Vida: Mexican Immigrant Women's Memories of Home, Yearning, and Border Crossings." In *Gender on the Borderlands: The Frontiers Reader,* edited by Antonia Castañeda et al., 261-81. Lincoln: University of Nebraska Press, 2007.

Irvin, Benjamin H. *Clothed in Robes of Sovereignty: The Continental Congress and the People Out of Doors.* New York: Oxford University Press, 2011.

Johnston, Henry P. *The Yorktown Campaign and the Surrender of Cornwallis, 1781.* New York: Harper & Brothers, 1881. Reprint, New York: Eastern Acorn Press, 1981.

Johnston, Henry Phelps, ed. *The Record of Connecticut Men in the Military and Naval Service During the War of the Revolution, 1775-1783.* Hartford, Conn., 1889.

Jones, T. Cole. *Captives of Liberty: Prisoners of War and the Politics of Vengeance in the American Revolution.* Philadelphia: University of Pennsylvania Press, 2020.

Katcher, Philip. *Uniforms of the Continental Army.* York, Pa.: George Shumway, 1981.

Kennedy, Paul. "History from the Middle: The Case of the Second World War." *Journal of Military History* 74 (January 2010): 35-51.

Kilbourne, John Dwight. *Virtutis Praemium: The Men Who Founded the State Society of the Cincinnati of Pennsylvania.* Vols. 1 and 2. Rockport, Maine: Picton Press, 1998.

Knouff, Gregory T. *The Soldiers' Revolution: Pennsylvanians in Arms and the Forging of Early American Identity.* University Park: Pennsylvania State University Press, 2004.

Kranish, Michael. *Flight from Monticello: Thomas Jefferson at War.* New York: Oxford University Press, 2010.

Krebs, Daniel. *A Generous and Merciful Enemy: Life for German Prisoners of War during the American Revolution.* Norman: University of Oklahoma Press, 2013.

Kwasny, Mark V. *Washington's Partisan War, 1775-1783.* Kent, Ohio: Kent State University Press, 1996.

Lacroix, Patrick. "Promises to Keep: French Canadians as Revolutionaries and Refugees, 1775-1800." *Journal of Early American History* 9, no. 1 (April 2019): 59-82.

Lambdin, Alfred C. "Battle of Germantown." *Pennsylvania Magazine of History and Biography* 1, no. 4 (1877): 368-403.

Lanctot, Gustave. *Canada and the American Revolution, 1774-1783.* Translated by Margaret M. Cameron. Cambridge, Mass.: Harvard University Press, 1967.

Lawson, Murray G. "Canada and the Articles of Confederation." *American Historical Review* 58, no. 1 (October 1952): 40-41.

Lawson, Philip. *The Imperial Challenge: Quebec and Britain in the Age of the American Revolution*. Buffalo, N.Y.: McGill-Queen's University Press, 1989.

Lawson, Philip. "'Sapped by Corruption': British Governance of Quebec and the Breakdown of Anglo-American Relations on the Eve of the Revolution." *Canadian Review of American Studies* 22, no. 3 (December 1991): 301–23.

Lee, Wayne E. "Early American Ways of War: A Reconnaissance, 1600–1815." *The Historical Journal* 44, no. 1 (March 2001): 269–89.

Lefferts, Charles M. *Uniforms of the Armies in the War of the American Revolution, 1775–1783*. New York: New-York Historical Society, 1926.

Lena, Alberto. "Benjamin Franklin's 'Canada Pamphlet' or 'The Ravings of a Mad Prophet': Nationalism, Ethnicity and Imperialism." *European Journal of American Culture* 20, no. 1 (April 2001): 36–49.

Lender, Mark Edward. *Cabal! The Plot Against General Washington*. Yardley, Pa.: Westholme Publishing, 2019.

Lender, Mark Edward and James Kirby Martin. "A Traitor's Epiphany: Benedict Arnold in Virginia and His Quest for Reconciliation." *Virginia Magazine of History and Biography* 125, no. 4 (2017): 314–57.

Lesser, Charles H., ed. *The Sinews of Independence: Monthly Strength Reports of the Continental Army*. Chicago: University of Chicago Press, 1976.

Levine, Lawrence. *The Opening of the American Mind: Canons, Culture, and History*. Boston: Beacon Press, 1996.

Lockridge, Kenneth A. *A New England Town: The First Hundred Years*. Enlarged edition. New York: W. W. Norton, 1985.

Loescher, Burt Garfield. *The History of Rogers' Rangers*, Vol. II: *Rogers Rangers, The First Green Berets*. San Mateo, Calif., 1969.

Lynn, John A. II. *Women, Armies, and Warfare in Early Modern Europe*. New York: Cambridge University Press, 2008.

Maier, Pauline. *American Scripture: Making the Declaration of Independence*. New York: Vintage Books, 1998.

Mancke, Elizabeth. "Early Modern Imperial Governance and the Origins of Canadian Political Culture." *Canadian Journal of Political Science* 32, no. 1 (March 1999): 3–20.

Marston, Daniel P. "Swift and Bold: The 60th Regiment and Warfare in North America, 1755–1765." Master's thesis, McGill University, 1997.

Martin, David Kendall. "1798 Tax Assessment for northern New York." NYGenWeb Project (website). Accessed 6 June 2020. www.rootsweb.ancestry.com/~nyclinto /1798tax.html.

Martin, James Kirby. *Benedict Arnold, Revolutionary Hero: An American Warrior Reconsidered*. New York: New York University Press, 1997.

Martin, James Kirby and Mark Edward Lender. *"A Respectable Army": The Military Origins of the Republic, 1763–1789*. 1st ed., 1982. 3rd ed., Hoboken, N.J.: John Wiley & Sons (Wiley-Blackwell), 2015.

Mayer, Holly A. "Bearing Arms, Bearing Burdens: Women Warriors, Camp Followers and Home-Front Heroines of the American Revolution." In *Gender, War and Politics: Transatlantic Perspectives, 1775–1830*, edited by Karen Hagemann, Gisela Mettele, and Jane Rendall, 169–87. Basingstoke, England: Palgrave Macmillan, 2010.

Mayer, Holly A. *Belonging to the Army: Camp Followers and Community during the American Revolution*. Columbia: University of South Carolina Press, 1996.

Mayer, Holly A. "Canada, Congress, and the Continental Army: Strategic Accommodations, 1774–1776." *Journal of Military History* 78, no. 2 (April 2014): 503–35.

Mayer, Holly A. "Wives, Concubines, and Community: Following the Army." In *War and Society in the American Revolution,* edited by John Resch and Walter Sargent, 235–62. DeKalb: Northern Illinois University Press, 2007.

McBurney, Christian. *Abductions in the American Revolution: Attempts to Kidnap George Washington, Benedict Arnold and Other Military and Civilian Leaders.* Jefferson, N.C.: McFarland & Co., 2016.

McConnell, Michael N. *Army and Empire: British Soldiers on the American Frontier, 1758–1775.* Lincoln: University of Nebraska Press, 2004.

McDonnell, Michael. "National Identity and the American War for Independence: A Reappraisal." *Australasian Journal of American Studies* 20, no. 1 (July 2001): 3–17.

McDonnell, Michael A. *The Politics of War: Race, Class, and Conflict in Revolutionary Virginia.* Chapel Hill: University of North Carolina Press, 2007.

McGuire, Thomas J. *The Philadelphia Campaign: Volume I, Brandywine and the Fall of Philadelphia.* Mechanicsburg, Pa.: Stackpole Books, 2006.

McGuire, Thomas J. *The Surprise of Germantown, October 4th, 1777.* Gettysburg, Pa.: Cliveden of the National Trust for Historic Preservation & Thomas Publications, 1994.

Meacham, Jon. *Thomas Jefferson: The Art of Power.* New York: Random House, 2012.

Mester, Joseph C. "From Philadelphia Country House to City Recreation Center: Uncovering the Architectural History of the Building Known Successively as Blockley Retreat, Kirkbride Mansion, and Lee Cultural Center through Building Archaeology." Master's thesis, University of Pennsylvania, 2016.

Metzger, Charles H. *Catholics and the American Revolution: A Study in Religious Climate.* Chicago: Loyola University Press, 1962.

Metzger, Charles H. "Chaplains in the American Revolution." *Catholic Historical Review* 31 (April 1945): 31–79.

Miller, Ken. *Dangerous Guests: Enemy Captives and Revolutionary Communities during the War for Independence.* Ithaca, N.Y.: Cornell University Press, 2014.

Morgan, Philip D. "Encounters between British and 'Indigenous' Peoples, c. 1500–c. 1800." In *Empire and Others: British Encounters with Indigenous Peoples, 1600–1850,* edited by Martin Daunton and Rick Halpern, 44–45. Philadelphia: University of Pennsylvania Press, 1999.

Morrison, James F., ed. "Colonel James Livingston: The Forgotten Livingston Patriot of the War of Independence." Fulton County (N.Y.) Bicentennial of the U.S. Constitution Committee, 1988. Accessed 30 July 2020. http://fulton.nygenweb.net/military/livingston.html.

Munro, William Bennett. *The Seignorial System in Canada: A Study in French Colonial Policy.* New York: Longman's, Green and Co., 1907.

Neagles, James C. *Summer Soldiers: A Survey & Index of Revolutionary War Courts-Martial.* Salt Lake City, Utah: Ancestry Incorporated, 1986.

Neimeyer, Charles. *America Goes to War: A Social History of the Continental Army.* New York: New York University Press, 1997.

Nelson, Paul David. *General Sir Guy Carleton, Lord Dorchester: Soldier-Statesman of Early British Canada.* Madison, N.J.: Fairleigh Dickinson University Press, 2000.

Nelson, William. *Edward Antill: A New York Merchant of the Seventeenth Century, and His Descendants*. Patterson, N.J.: Press Printing & Publishing Co., 1899.

The New England Historical & Genealogical Register and Antiquarian Journal. Vol. 19. Boston: David Clapp & Son, 1865. Accessed 31 May 2020. https://books.google.com /books?id=Grs-AAAAYAAJ&pg=PR1#v=onepage&q&f=false.

Nobles, Gregory H. *American Frontiers: Cultural Encounters and Continental Conquest*. New York: Hill and Wang, 1997.

Nobles, Gregory H. "Breaking into the Backcountry: New Approaches to the Early American Frontier." *William and Mary Quarterly* 46, no. 4 (October 1989): 641–70.

Northeastern Vermont Development Association. "In Search of Bayley-Hazen." *The Bayley Hazen Military Road Field Guide: Resources, Events and History of the Road from Wells River to Hazen's Notch* (n.d.), 21–22. Accessed 24 July 2020. www.nvda .net/Transp/documents/bk_rd_bk_pln_final.pdf.

Noël, Françoise. *The Christie Seigneuries: Estate Management and Settlement in the Upper Richelieu Valley, 1760–1854*. Montréal: McGill-Queen's University Press, 1992.

O'Donnell, Catherine. "John Carroll and the Origins of an American Catholic Church, 1783–1815." *William and Mary Quarterly* 68, no. 1 (January 2011): 101–26.

Otten, William L. Jr. *Colonel J. F. Hamtramck: His Life and Times*. Vol. 1, 1756–1783. Port Aransas, Tex.: W. L. Otten Jr., 1997.

Pierce, Grace M. "The Military Tract of New York State." *New York Genealogical and Biographical Record* 40, no. 1 (January 1909): 15–22.

Pierce's Register: Register of the Certificates Issued by John Pierce, Esquire, Paymaster General and Commissioner of Army Accounts for the United States, to Officers and Soldiers of the Continental Army Under Act of July 4, 1783. Baltimore: Genealogical Publishing Co., 1984.

Plank, Geoffrey. "The Two Majors Cope: The Boundaries of Nationality in Mid-18th Century Nova Scotia." *Acadiensis* 25, no. 2 (Spring 1996): 18–40.

Pritchard, James. *In Search of Empire: The French in the Americas, 1670–1730*. Cambridge, UK: Cambridge University Press, 2004.

Provost, Honorius. "Chartier de Lotbinière, Eustache (baptized François-Louis)." In *Dictionary of Canadian Biography*. Vol. 4. University of Toronto/Université Laval, 2003–. Accessed 31 May 2020. www.biographi.ca/en/bio/chartier_de_lotbiniere _eustache_1716_1785_4E.html.

Reed, Adela Peltier. *Memoirs of Antoine Paulint, Veteran of the Old French War, 1755 to 1760*. Los Angeles: D. M. Peltier–San Encino Press, 1940.

Rees, John U. "'The Multitude of Women...': An Examination of the Numbers of Female Camp Followers with the Continental Army." In *The Brigade Dispatch (Journal of the Brigade of the American Revolution)* 23, no. 4 (Autumn 1992), 5–17; 24, no. 1 (Winter 1993), 6–16; and 24, no. 2 (Spring 1993), 2–6. Accessed 5 June 2020. www.revwar75.com/library/rees/wnumb1.htm.

Rees, John U. "'Sospecting the prisoner to be a tory ...': A Continental Army Court Martial, July 1777" [*sic*]. *The Continental Soldier*, IX, no. 1 (Winter/Spring 1997): 45–46. Accessed 30 May 2020. http://revwar75.com/library/rees/tory.htm.

Resch, John. *Suffering Soldiers: Revolutionary War Veterans, Moral Sentiment, and Political Culture in the Early Republic*. Amherst: University of Massachusetts Press, 1999.

Richter, Daniel K. *Facing East from Indian Country: A Native History of Early America.* Cambridge, Mass.: Harvard University Press, 2001.

Risch, Erna. *Supplying Washington's Army.* Washington, D.C.: Government Printing Office, 1981.

Roberts, James A. *New York in the Revolution as Colony and State.* 2nd ed. Albany, N.Y.: Brandon Printing Co., 1898.

Rodrigue, Barry Hadfield. "An Album in the Attic: The Forgotten Frontier of the Quebec-Maine Borderlands During the Revolutionary War." *Journal of the Historical Society* 3, no. 1 (Winter 2003): 45–73.

Rogers, Charles. *Genealogical Memoirs of the Scottish House of Christie.* London: Royal Historical Society, 1878. Accessed 1 June 2020. https://archive.org/details /genealogicalmem06rogegoog.

Rolph, Daniel. "The Service and Tragic Death of French Officer Major William Galvan of the Revolutionary War." *History Hits* (blog), Historical Society of Pennsylvania (HSP). 26 August 2015. Accessed 30 July 2020. https://hsp.org/blogs/history -hits/the-service-tragic-death-of-french-officer-major-william-galvan-of-the -revolutionary-war.

Rossie, Jonathan Gregory. *The Politics of Command in the American Revolution.* Syracuse, N.Y.: Syracuse University Press, 1975.

Royster, Charles. *A Revolutionary People at War: The Continental Army and American Character, 1775–1783.* New York: W. W. Norton, 1979.

Ruddiman, John A. *Becoming Men of Some Consequence: Youth and Military Service in the Revolutionary War.* Charlottesville: University of Virginia Press, 2014.

Ruddiman, John A. "'A Record in the Hands of Thousands': Power and Negotiation in the Orderly Books of the Continental Army." *William and Mary Quarterly* 67, no. 4 (October 2010): 747–74.

Sánchez-Flores, Mónica Judith. *Cosmopolitan Liberalism: Expanding the Boundaries of the Individual.* New York: Palgrave Macmillan, 2010.

Schmidt-Nowara, Christopher Ebert. "Borders and Borderlands of Interpretation." *American Historical Review* 104, no. 4 (October 1999): 1226–28.

Schuyler, Henry. "Ferdinand Steinmeyer." In *The Catholic Encyclopedia.* Vol. 14. New York: Robert Appleton Company, 1912. Accessed 5 June 2020. www.newadvent.org /cathen/14285b.htm.

Scudieri, James D. "The Continentals: A Comparative Analysis of a Late Eighteenth-Century Standing Army, 1775–83." Ph.D. diss., City University of New York, 1993.

Selig, Robert A. *March to Victory: Washington, Rochambeau, and the Yorktown Campaign of 1781.* Pub. 70–104–1. Washington, D.C.: U.S. Army Center of Military History, 2005.

Shalhope, Robert E. *John Taylor of Caroline: Pastoral Republican.* Columbia: University of South Carolina Press, 1980.

Shklar, Judith N. *Montesquieu.* Oxford, UK: Oxford University Press, 1987.

Sleeper-Smith, Susan. "The Middle Ground Revisited, Introduction." *William and Mary Quarterly* 63, no. 1 (January 2006): 3–8.

Smith, Gene Allen and Sylvia L. Hilton, eds. *Nexus of Empire: Negotiating Loyalty and Identity in the Revolutionary Borderlands, 1760s–1820s.* Gainesville: University Press of Florida, 2010.

Smith, Justin H. *Our Struggle for the Fourteenth Colony: Canada and the American Revolution.* 2 vols. New York and London: G. P. Putnam's Sons, 1907. Reprint, New York: Da Capo Press, 1974.

Smith, Rogers M. *Stories of Peoplehood: The Politics and Morals of Political Membership.* Cambridge, UK: Cambridge University Press, 2003.

Spall, Eric. "Foreigners in the Highest Trust: American Perceptions of European Mercenary Officers in the Continental Army." *Early American Studies* 12, no. 2 (Spring 2014): 338–65.

Spero, Patrick. *Frontier Country: The Politics of War in Early Pennsylvania.* Philadelphia: University of Pennsylvania Press, 2016.

Stanley, George F. G. *Canada Invaded, 1775–1776.* Toronto, Canada: A. M. Hakkert Ltd., 1973.

Stuart, Reginald C. "'Engines of Tyranny': Recent Historiography on Standing Armies during the Era of the American Revolution." *Canadian Journal of History/Annales canadiennes d'histoire* 19, no. 2 (August 1984): 183–99.

Sypher, Francis J. Jr. *New York State Society of the Cincinnati Biographies of Original Members & Other Continental Officers.* Fishkill, N.Y.: New York State Society of the Cincinnati, 2004.

Taaffe, Stephen R. *The Philadelphia Campaign, 1777–1778.* Lawrence: University Press of Kansas, 2003.

Taggart, Fr. Owen. "Québécois Combatants in the Continental Army." *Késsinnimek-Roots-Racines,* 1 February 2003. Accessed January 2005 (no longer available). www .leveillee.net/roots/frowen4-5.htm.

Tang, Edward. "Writing the American Revolution: War Veterans in the Nineteenth-Century Cultural Memory. *Journal of American Studies* 32, no. 1 (April 1998): 63–80.

Taylor, Alan. *The Civil War of 1812: American Citizens, British Subjects, Irish Rebels, and Indian Allies.* New York: Vintage Books, 2011.

Taylor, Alan. *The Divided Ground: Indians, Settlers, and the Northern Borderland of the American Revolution.* New York: Alfred A. Knopf, 2006.

Tétu, Michel. "Quebec and the French Revolution." *Canadian Parliamentary Review* 12, no. 3 (Autumn 1989): 2–6.

Thomas, Isaiah. *The History of Printing in America: With a Biography of Printers & an Account of Newspapers.* 2nd ed. Edited by Marcus A. McCorison. New York: Weathervane Books, 1970.

Troiani, Don. *Military Buttons of the American Revolution.* Gettysburg, Pa.: Thomas Publications, 2001.

Troiani, Don. *Soldiers of the American Revolution.* Mechanicsburg, Pa.: Stackpole Books, 2007.

Tucker, Bruce. "The Reinvention of New England, 1691–1770." *The New England Quarterly* 59, no. 3 (September 1986): 318–19

Usner, Daniel H. Jr. "Borderlands." In *A Companion to Colonial America,* edited by Daniel Vickers, 408–24. Malden, Mass.: Blackwell, 2003.

Vachon, André. "Briand, Jean-Olivier." In *Dictionary of Canadian Biography.* Vol. 4. University of Toronto/Université Laval, 2003–. Accessed 31 May 2020. www .biographi.ca/en/bio/briand_jean_olivier_4E.html.

Van Buskirk, Judith L. *Generous Enemies: Patriots and Loyalists in Revolutionary New York*. Philadelphia: University of Pennsylvania Press, 2002.

Van Buskirk, Judith L. *Standing in Their Own Light: African American Patriots in the American Revolution*. Norman: University of Oklahoma Press, 2017.

Vecsey, Christopher and William A. Starna, eds. *Iroquois Land Claims*. Syracuse, N.Y.: Syracuse University Press, 1988.

Vickers, Daniel, ed. *A Companion to Colonial America*. Malden, Mass.: Blackwell, 2003.

Wade, Mason. *The French Canadians, 1760–1967*. Revised ed. Toronto: Macmillan of Canada, (1955) 1968.

Wallace, Nesbit Willoughby. *A Regimental Chronicle and List of Officers of the 60th, or the King's Royal Rifle Corps, Formerly the 62nd, or the Royal American Regiment of Foot*. London: Harrison, 1879. Accessed 1 June 2020. https://archive.org/details/aregimentalchrooowallgoog.

Ward, Matthew. *Breaking the Backcountry: The Seven Years' War in Virginia and Pennsylvania, 1754–1765*. Pittsburgh, Pa.: University of Pittsburgh Press, 2003.

Watson, Samuel. "Continuity in Civil-Military Relations and Expertise: The U.S. Army during the Decade before the Civil War." *Journal of Military History* 75 (January 2011): 221–50.

White, Richard. "Creative Misunderstandings and New Understandings." *William and Mary Quarterly* 63, no. 1 (January 2006): 9–14.

White, Richard. *The Middle Ground: Indians, Empires, and Republics in the Great Lakes Region, 1650–1815*. New York: Cambridge University Press, 1991.

Williams, Glenn F. *Year of the Hangman: George Washington's Campaign Against the Iroquois*. Yardley, Pa.: Westholme, 2005.

"Woodson Family." *William and Mary Quarterly* 10, no. 3 (January 1902): 185–91.

Woodson, Henry Morton. *Historical Genealogy of the Woodsons and Their Connections*. Part 1. Memphis, Tenn.: H. M. Woodson, 1915.

Worthington, C. Ford et al. "British and American Prisoners of War, 1778." *Pennsylvania Magazine of History and Biography* 17, no. 2 (1893): 159–74.

Wright, John W. "Some Notes on the Continental Army." *William and Mary Quarterly*, 2nd series, 11, no. 2 (April 1931): 81–105.

Wright, Robert E. *One Nation Under Debt: Hamilton, Jefferson, and the History of What We Owe*. New York: McGraw Hill, 2008.

Wright, Robert K. Jr. *The Continental Army*. Washington, D.C.: United States Army Center of Military History, 1983.

Wunder, John R. and Pekka Hämäläinen. "Of Lethal Places and Lethal Essays." *American Historical Review* 104, no. 4 (October 1999): 1229–34.

INDEX